A MENNONITE IN RUSSIA:
The Diaries of Jacob D. Epp
1851–1880

Translated and edited, with an Introduction and Analysis, by Harvey L. Dyck

In the lives of ordinar … truths abound
in the diaries of Jacob … er, lay minister,
farmer, and village sec … d translation of
his diaries offers a rem … munity life in
Imperial Russia during … itings reveal a
skilled and honest diari … y that no con-
ventional historical acco…

The diaries overflow … details of his workaday world. Family, village, church, and community routines are broken by trips to market, visits to other Mennonite settlements, and a memorable steamer voyage to boomtown Odessa on the Black Sea. He chronicles his long-time involvement in an unusual Imperial experiment in which Mennonites were "model farmers" in Jewish villages.

Harvey L. Dyck places the diaries in their historical, ethnocultural, social, religious, economic, and political settings. Based on archival research, interviews, travels, and consultations with other scholars, his detailed and perceptive introduction and analysis trace Jacob Epp's life and present a sketch and interpretation of his larger family, community, and Imperial world.

With striking clarity the diaries and introduction together re-create a time and way of life marked by controversy and flux. They reflect significant facets of the experience of ethno-religious minorities in Imperial Russia and of the development of the southern Ukrainian frontier. Above all, they fill significant missing pages of the great community-centred story of Russian Mennonite life.

This book is richly illustrated with maps, black-and-white photographs, and watercolour paintings by Cornelius Hildebrand, Jacob Epp's former village school pupil and later brother-in-law.

HARVEY L. DYCK is Professor of History at the University of Toronto and Chairman of the University of Toronto/Conrad Grebel College Research Program in Russian Mennonite Studies. He is also the author of *Weimar Germany and Soviet Russia, 1926-1934: A Study in Diplomatic Instability.*

Jacob and Judith Epp and their children Elisabeth and Johann, circa 1880

A MENNONITE IN RUSSIA: The Diaries of Jacob D. Epp 1851–1880

Translated and edited,
with an Introduction and Analysis,
by Harvey L. Dyck

UNIVERSITY OF TORONTO PRESS
Toronto Buffalo London

Toronto Buffalo London
Printed in the U.S.A.

Reprinted in paperback 2013

ISBN 978-0-8020-2788-7 (cloth)
ISBN 978-1-4426-1541-0 (paper)

Printed on acid-free paper

Canadian Cataloguing in Publication Data

Epp, Jacob D. (Jacob Davidovich), 1820-1890
A Mennonite in Russia:
the diaries of Jacob D. Epp, 1851-1880

Includes bibliographical references and index.
ISBN 978-0-8020-2788-7 (bound). – ISBN 978-1-4426-1541-0 (pbk.)

1. Epp, Jacob D. (Jacob Davidovich), 1820-1890 - Diaries.
2. Mennonites - Ukraine - Khortitsa (District) - Social life and customs.
3. Judenplan (Ukraine) - Social life and customs.
4. Khortitsa (Ukraine: District) - Social life and customs.
5. Mennonites - Ukraine - Khortitsa (District) -Diaries.
6. Farmers - Ukraine - Khortitsa (District) - Biography
7. Farmers - Ukraine - Judenplan - Biography
I. Dyck, Harvey L. (Harvey Leonard).
II. Title.

BX8143.E66A3 1991 289.7'092 C91-093146-1

This book has been published
with the help of a grant from the
Canadian Federation for the Humanities,
using funds provided by the
Social Sciences and Humanities
Research Council of Canada.

For Anne

Contents

Acknowledgments

I am grateful to Lawrence Klippenstein, archivist of the Mennonite Heritage Centre, Winnipeg, Manitoba, for first drawing the existence of the Jacob Epp diaries to my attention, making them available to me in photocopy, and commenting on drafts of the introduction and translation. For help in research I also thank Ken Reddig, archivist of the Centre for Mennonite Brethren Studies, Winnipeg, Manitoba, and the staff of the Bethel College Historical Library, North Newton, Kansas, the Conrad Grebel College Library, Waterloo, Ontario, the John Robarts Library, University of Toronto, and the Rosthern (Saskatchewan) Museum.

The Office of Research Administration and the Centre for Russian and East European Studies, both of the University of Toronto, generously provided funds for research and travel. The maps were prepared by William Schroeder, Winnipeg.

Over the last eight years I have met and corresponded with many descendants of the Jacob D. Epp family, whose help I warmly acknowledge. They shared memories and sat with me over kitchen tables poring over family copybooks, Bibles, and photo albums. Scouring attics and phoning or writing to one another, they tracked down sources I could use. They lent me precious family records and photographs, took me to the Eigenheim, Saskatchewan, Museum and cemetery and provided introductions. I would mention in particular: Otto Andres (Toronto, Ontario), Anna Dyck (Leamington, Ontario), David C. Epp (St Catharines, Ontario), the late Mr and Mrs David G. Epp (Eigenheim, Saskatchewan), Dick H. Epp (Saskatoon, Saskatchewan), Ewald Epp (Rosthern), the Murray D. Epp family (Waldheim, Saskatchewan), Justina and Heinz Heese (Steinbach, Manitoba), Mary Heinrichs (Toronto), Aaron Klassen (Kitchener, Ontario), Bernard and Henry Pauls (Leamington), and Mr and Mrs Wilmer H. Roth (Rosthern).

Katherine Penner (St Catharines) and Peter Rempel (Toronto) lent me valuable photographs.

The following offspring and relations of the Epp family also graciously contributed to the costs of including in this volume the rustical, bright, and evocative water-colour paintings of Jacob Epp's one-time pupil and later brother-in-law, Cornelius Hildebrand: Otto Andres, Clarence Epp (Saskatoon), D.H. Epp (Saskatoon), Ewald Epp, Leona E. Epp (Saskatoon), Oscar Epp (Rosthern, Saskatchewan), Paul W. Epp (Saskatoon), Peter A.F. Epp (Regina), William H. Epp (Saskatoon), Cornelius Goerzen (Saskatoon), Martha Grams (Calgary, Alberta), Victor Heinrichs (Toronto), Robert D. Jantzen (Rosthern), Peter P. Janzen (Saskatoon), William Janzen (Rosthern), Jacob W. Klassen (Rosthern), Carl Krause (Saskatoon), Eldon Krause (Rosthern), Helena Krause (Rosthern), Adella Regier (Rosthern), George Riekman (Saskatoon), Henry Riekman (Rosthern), Robert Riekman (Hague, Saskatchewan), Ed Roth (Rosthern), Elsie Roth (Rosthern), and Wilmer H. Roth.

I am much indebted to the following colleagues and friends who commented on drafts of the volume and gave encouragement and advice: Peter Brock, Leonard Friesen, Herman Konrad, Jacques Kornberg, David G. Rempel, and John Thomas.

Members of my own family know Jacob Epp almost as well as I do, referring to him on occasion, perhaps too familiarly but warmly, as 'Jake baby.' They have shared in diary discoveries, told me to cut when I grew too attached to particular entries and phrases, read drafts, and made suggestions. I thank Maria, Toozie and Alexander for their interest and encouragement and Toozie also for her skill in keeping my style 'correct and consistent.'

Loving thanks go to my wife, Anne Konrad, for repeatedly urging me to 'let Jacob Epp tell it himself' and for her sharp, and helpful, editorial eye. Walking together in Sherwood Park, or through the meadows and woods of Purple Valley, we talked and tested ideas. We also took trips together, in Ontario and Western Canada, to 'meet the Epps,' and, in the Soviet Union, to visit the former Mennonite Old Colony and the former Judenplan. These shared experiences have given to years of hard work moments of great satisfaction and delight.

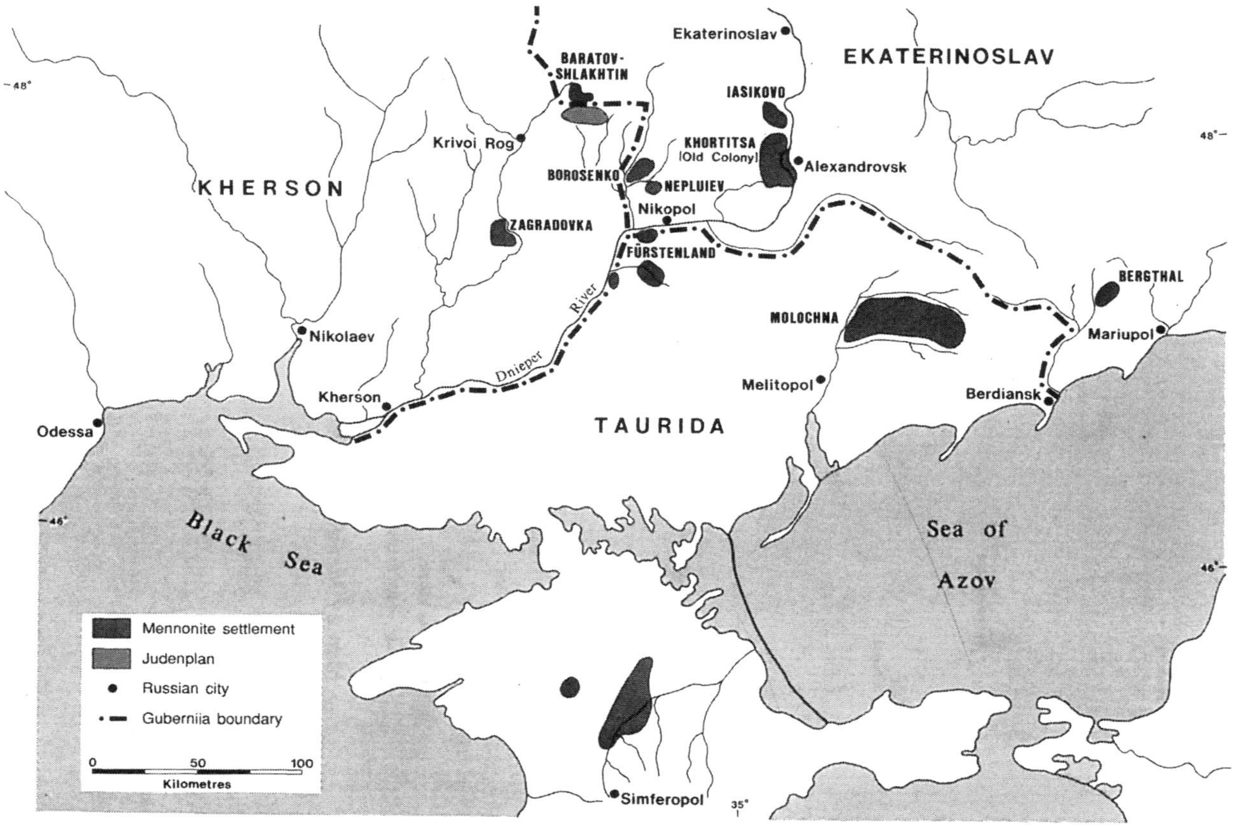

Map 1 / Mennonite settlements in New Russia, 1875

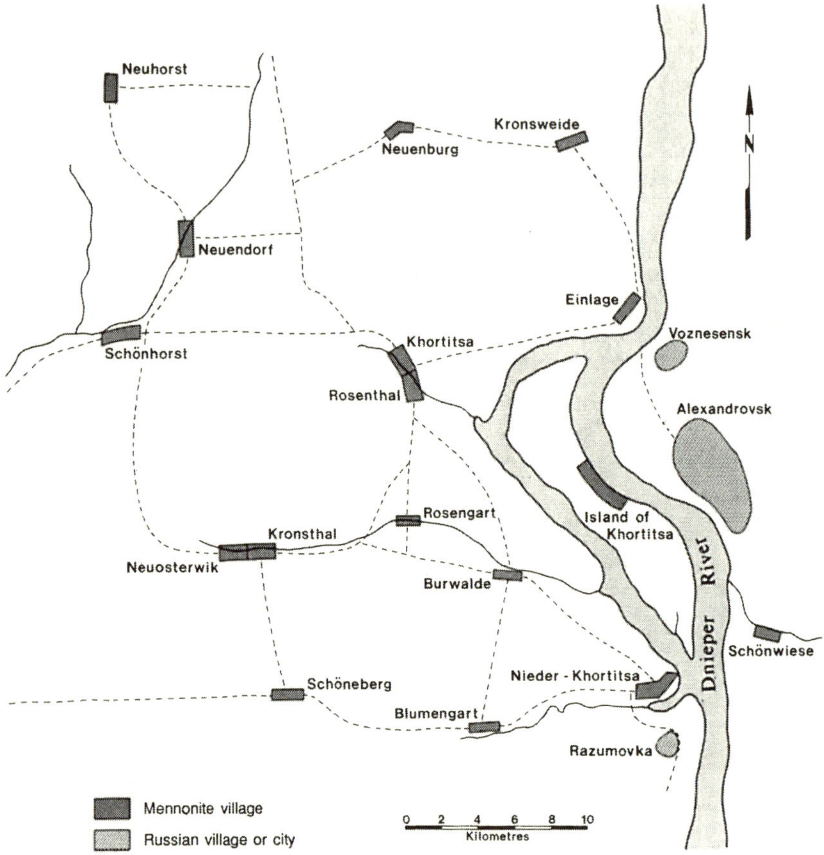

Map 2 / Mennonite 'Old Colony' (Khortitsa), 1850

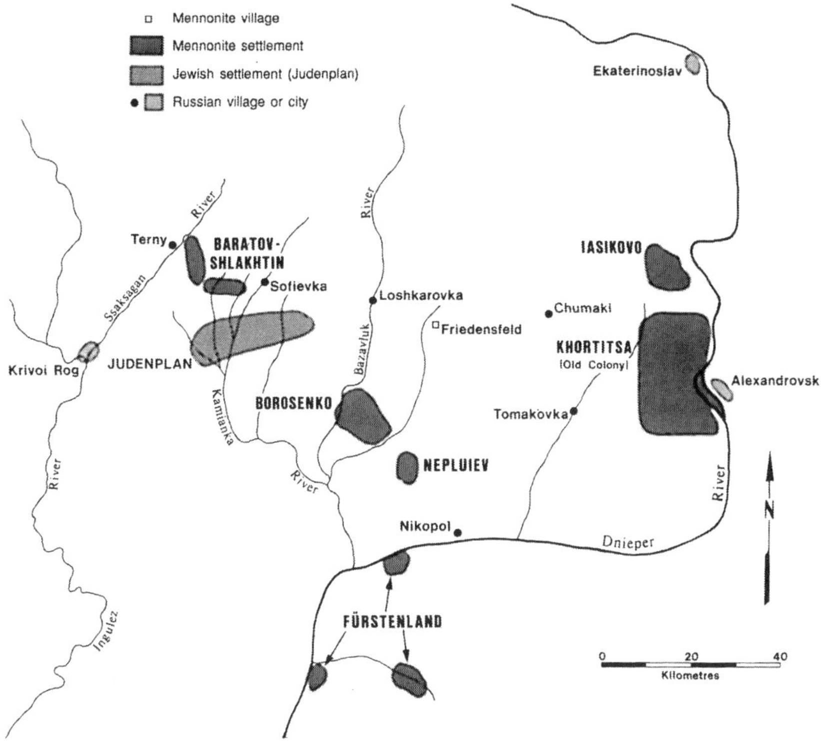

Map 3 / The world of Jacob D. Epp, 1875

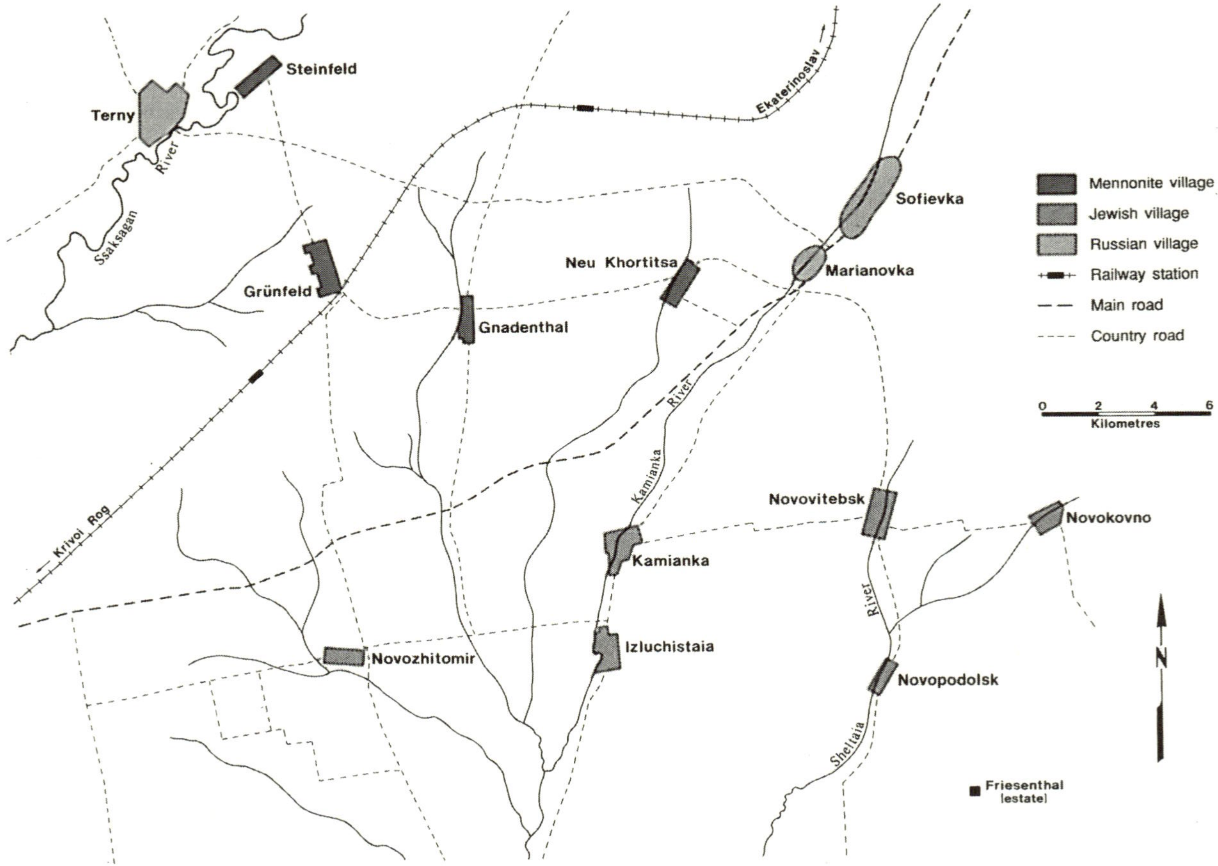

Map 4 / The Judenplan and Baratov-Shlakhtin settlements, 1880

A MENNONITE IN RUSSIA

Introduction and Analysis

'Out there you'll find only God's blue sky and Epps.' 'Out there' is Eigenheim, a crossroads on a flat prairie six miles west of Rosthern, Saskatchewan, Canada. Established in the 1890s as a pioneering Mennonite community in what was then the Northwest Territories, Eigenheim is today not even on the local travel pamphlet maps.[1] But its church, the 'pearl' of Eigenheim, is there. Despite renovations one can still recognize its 1902 shape.[2] Off to one side of the white, clapboard church, separated from grain fields by a mature windbreak of trees, lies the graveyard.

I have come here with Wilmer Roth, retired Rosthern farmer, entrepreneur, civic leader and amateur historian. 'They're all here,' he says. 'I mapped the cemetery, and found every one.' He is talking about the Eigenheim Epps. An Epp offspring himself, he points out several polished granite markers, and we dig among the dry prairie grasses looking for small steel medallions with names. Eventually we identify the graves of all of the Epps, of matriarch Judith Epp and ten of her children and their spouses (one married son, Heinrich, and his family remained in Russia). At the centre of the churchyard stands the pillared marker for the mother Judith (born 11 March 1832, died 15 July 1906). It is engraved in German with a verse from Isaiah, 'Lo, I was in dire want of consolation, but thou hast heeded the distress of my soul.'[3]

Wilmer Roth and I trade anecdotes. He tells me about the pioneering Epps in Canada, who as farmers, tradesmen, entrepreneurs, churchmen, and teachers were community builders. I relate stories about their community roots and life in imperial Russia. The stories come from the diaries printed in this volume. They were written by Jacob Davidovich Epp (1820–90), the paterfamilias of the Eigenheim Epps. A Mennonite agriculturalist, lay minister, and sometime teacher, he lived in the vast frontier steppe region of New Russia north of the Black and Azov seas, the southern Ukraine today. In 1851, as a young, thirty-year-old, village schoolteacher on the Island of

Khortitsa (who had some time earlier lost his left eye), he started keeping a diary that he apparently continued until his death four decades later.[4]

Jacob Epp came from a family of prominent church and civic leaders. Indeed, the Epps of the Khortitsa settlement were one of the most important Mennonite families in Russia, wide-ranging in the scope of their involvements and influence. Jacob Epp's grandfather and father were both influential churchmen. One brother was employed as a government administrator in a Jewish agricultural settlement, another became chief administrator of a Mennonite district administration, and a third served as head teacher of a prominent Mennonite secondary school before being elected Elder of the Khortitsa Flemish Mennonite church. A sister married the first medical doctor in the Khortitsa district and another was married to a man who helped pioneer the development of the farm-implements industry in the southern Ukraine. Providing Epp with a link to urban Russia was an uncle, a wealthy miller in the provincial capital of Ekaterinoslav.

While his illustrious family provided numerous, influential links to the Mennonite community, and thus became a mine of information for his diaries, Epp was himself the quintessential insider/outsider. Bonded tightly to his community through family and friends, he also shared the poverty and uncertainties of the poorer and less secure strata of his society. This bifocal slant gave him an unusual perspective on his society. In 1852, landless and in need of a living for his growing family, he left the Khortitsa Mennonite 'mother' settlement, where his family had lived since coming to Russia, to settle with about fifty other landless Mennonite families as 'model agriculturalists' in the Judenplan. The latter was a poor, state-sponsored Jewish agricultural settlement of six villages about 130 kilometres west of Khortitsa.

In this unusual mixed Jewish and Mennonite settlement he farmed for twenty-two years, supposedly teaching agriculturally inexperienced Jews farming by example. In that time he buried his first wife and several infant children and remarried. Elected a lay minister, he also devotedly pastored his community of five hundred to one thousand landed and landless Mennonites through difficult times. In the 1860s and 1870s, as a way of alleviating the land shortage among

Mennonites in the Khortitsa district, the district administration established daughter settlements close to the Judenplan. Jacob Epp helped several of his now married, landless children to acquire properties in these settlements and to establish separate households. As an experienced and trusted lay minister, he assisted in organizing the church life of these communities. In 1874 he and his family left the Judenplan, taking up a virgin homestead in one such Mennonite daughter settlement, Baratov-Shlakhtin. The family lived there until Jacob Epp's death in his seventieth year, in 1890.

Following his burial in the village cemetery, his diaries were sold at auction to members of the immediate family. As treasured keepsakes, stuffed in crates and wicker trunks of his immigrant widow and ten of her eleven children and their families, they travelled overseas and reached Eigenheim, Saskatchewan, in the 1890s as settlers' belongings. Of the seven diary volumes likely authored by Jacob Epp, only three seem to have survived.[5] The rest were presumably lost in family clean-ups and moves. There exists, in addition, an informative, detailed family and ministerial journal kept by Jacob Epp, containing crop, genealogical, and church-related information and occasional poems.[6] Penned in a neat, uniform Gothic script in the colloquial Russian Mennonite High German of the time, the extant diaries cover the years 1851 to 1853 and 1859 to 1880. This was a quarter century period of troubled change in the Russian Empire and in Russian Mennonite life.

Jacob Epp's surviving diaries capture intensely personal, first-hand impressions of many sides of his afflicted world with an immediacy no third-person history can match. Unlike other important records of Russian Mennonite life, the diaries reflect the routine and heartbeat of the family and of the village community and the rhythm of field-work and of worship. Documenting also the dilemmas confronting the larger Russian Mennonite brotherhood, the diaries, which revolve largely around the theme of community, fill in significant missing pages of the great communitarian story of Russian Mennonite life. This is a dominant theme in the history of the Mennonites of Russia.

Moreover, since agriculturalists in Eastern Europe have rarely kept detailed accounts of their personal, family, and community life, the diaries and journal constitute a unique record of the changing world of a largely agrarian religious and ethnic minority in imperial Russia. Their value as a major historical source is enhanced by the fact that important records of Russian Mennonite life have been lost in the twentieth century through revolution, war, and the upheavals of the Stalin era. In addition to their value as a chronicle of Mennonite history, the diaries illuminate the development of the important frontier region of the southern Ukraine, and thus constitute a valuable record of its broader history.

The diaries appear here in a much shortened edition of about one-third their original length. The diary entries have been chosen for translation and edited with several goals in mind: to establish the story-line and essential facets of the life of Jacob Epp, his immediate family, and his village community; to illustrate the relations of Mennonites with their neighbours; and to chronicle the principal subjects and themes in the history of the larger Mennonite society. Entries reflecting the recurring crop-year cycles help sketch in the larger frame of Jacob Epp's world and that of Russian Mennonitism. They also document changes in the agricultural practices of the time and provide examples of economic experiences ranging from bumper harvests to crop failures. Numerous entries have been deleted and individual diary entries abridged to avoid repitition. The translation is a relatively free rendition that seeks to remain faithful to the content, style, and spirit of the original.

In the eighteenth and nineteenth centuries, the broad prairie grasslands north of the Black Sea were populated by large numbers of Ukrainians, Russians, Tartars, and Jews. Also to be found there were smaller numbers of Germans, Greeks, Armenians, Bulgarians, Gypsies, and others. Religiously, the dominant Orthodox church shared this prairie stage with Moslems, Jews, Molokans, Doukhobors, Catholics, Lutherans, and Old Believers, as well as Mennonites and newer religious groups such as Shtundists and Baptists.[7] Mennonite immigrants from Danzig and the West Prussian lands of the Vistula estuary were first drawn to this region as a frontier with free land where they could establish their conservative religious communities in relative isolation from the larger world.[8]

The original settlement of the Vistula Mennonites, Khortitsa, popularly known as the Old Colony, was founded in 1789 on rolling, unploughed state-owned lands at the great bend on the Lower Dnieper River.[9] About 140 kilometres to the southeast, close to the Sea of Azov, on a largely flat, treeless but fertile and well-drained virgin prairie, a second, larger and more prosperous community, the Molochna Mennonite settlement, was established in 1804 (see map 1, 'Mennonite Settlements in New Russia, 1875').[10]

When Jacob Epp began keeping his daily diary in the 1850s, Russian Mennonite life already evidenced solidity and promise. From 1789 to 1825, during the reigns of Catherine the Great, Paul I, and Alexander I, the first generation of Mennonite pioneers, including Jacob Epp's grandparents, braving frontier hardships, adapted with considerable difficulty to the unaccustomed natural setting, the imperial system, and village life. With hard work and state encouragement and support, they nevertheless succeeded in establishing clusters of neat, usually single-street, tree-lined villages with substantial farmyards, gardens, orchards, churches and schools, set among common pastures and open fields. 'Oases of the steppe' was a phrase commonly used to describe them.

During the authoritarian rule of Nicholas I (1825–55), the second generation of Mennonites, including Jacob Epp's parents, consolidated mixed sheep-raising and grain-growing economies with autonomous village and district institutions to achieve a degree of modest prosperity. It was during these decades that Mennonites like the Epps solidified their pattern of village and church life and gained the reputation of being the best agriculturalists in New Russia. These achievements also attracted the attention of prominent foreign travellers whose popular writing about them brought them to the notice of a larger European public.[11] Jacob Epp, belonging to a third generation of Russian Mennonites, and the first that was Russian-born, might well have anticipated a life of relative stability lived in accordance with the traditions of his immediate communitarian forbears.

Yet the end of the Crimean War in 1856 marked the start of a dynamic age of sweeping economic and social changes in New Russia that continued until 1914. In 1861 serfdom was abolished, removing one of the main obstacles to change. High birth rates and internal migration led to a rapid increase in population throughout the area. The steppe grasslands, where cattle and sheep had grazed, were now ploughed up for grain growing, and new villages sprang up. Rail and steamship lines were developed to knit together the region, linking it to imperial centres in the north and to export markets in the south. Furthermore, rich seams of coal and iron ore running east–west along hilly ridges through the centre of the region enabled New Russia to play a leading role in Russia's industrialization.

As the prairie soil was turned, rails laid down, mines dug, and foundries built, new hamlets, railway towns, river and sea ports, and mining, manufacturing and administrative cities came to dot the landscape. By the end of the century, this development, coupled with fundamental administrative, social, and educational changes, made New Russia into one of the most rapidly modernizing regions of the Empire.[12] Change, however, was also cyclical, uneven, even wrenching, and brought in its wake much instability and tension.

From the 1850s onwards, Mennonite life was inevitably influenced by these multi-faceted developments. Much that had become familiar suddenly was made strangely new. Spurred by a buoyant market for grains, wheat growing became king in New Russia, bringing a measure of affluence and dynamism to many of the Mennonite villages as well. Modern agricultural technologies and education combined with new religious currents, changes to the political environment, and demands for reform, to provoke widespread questioning and uncertainty.

The outcome among Mennonites in the decades of the 1860s and 1870s was economic development, but also bitter conflict and a generation-long crisis. At mass public meetings and in petitions to the courts and to the government, disputes raged over the questions of authority in the community, widespread landlessness, the use of community pastures, and access to the franchise in village and district elections. At the same time, newer, more personal forms of religious experience shattered confessional unity. Filling the cup of uncertainty to the brim in the 1870s were military and other reforms along with assimilative policies of the imperial government. These developments, interpreted by the Mennonites as an attack on their autonomy and pacifism, triggered a mass emigration to Canada and the United States in the 1870s of from one-quarter to a third of their numbers living in the Empire at the time.

At the start of this era of troubled change, the world of Jacob Epp was still bounded by the religious community, the Mennonite church. With its customs and practices, Mennonitism in imperial Russia had by the 1850s evolved out of its sixteenth-century Netherlands Anabaptist beginnings and more recent Vistula lowlands Mennonite background into both a way of life and a set of beliefs.[13] A common pattern of worship, village life, and agricultural labour helped unify the community and buttressed the dominant Mennonite view of the time that life was essentially religious in all its dimensions. Salvation was deemed to be life's purpose. Devotion and brotherhood, as evidenced in a simple piety, community-mindedness, charity, and mutual aid, were regarded as the chief means to this goal.

What distinguished Mennonite community life was adherence to essentially a single set of social norms. Conformity followed logically from the community-minded tenets of Mennonite theology, from a mixture of bitter and prideful memories of a common martyr past, dating back to the Reformation, and from the obvious need for solidarity if the community was to survive as a small ethnic and religious minority in Russia. Compliance with one code of behaviour growing out of a common life was enforced through sometimes strict church rules and discipline. Moreover, through an elected lay leadership of elders, preachers and deacons, the Mennonite church asserted its dominance in community life. It was compass, helmsman, and guardian combined. In practice this broad claim was often challenged by imperial authorities and members of the Mennonite laity, and became a source of considerable friction. Yet in the day-to-day running of community life in the Old Colony, the elected religious leadership tended to work closely with the elected Mennonite civil leadership of district and village mayors and subordinate officials, often meeting as a diarchy to resolve common issues.

Mennonites called themselves a Christian 'Brotherhood,' and Jacob Epp took this self-definition seriously as a yardstick for measuring his own conduct and that of his community. Demanding of himself, he was also inclined to judge disputes among his fellow Mennonites sternly as 'unbrotherly' lapses and moral failures. As the narrow path to personal reconciliation, he urged confession and moral betterment. Since there was often great tension between his exacting standards and day-to-day village life, and since causes other than moral failure were responsible for many of the problems encountered daily, he experienced deep disappointments as well. For

Mennonites like Jacob Epp, the term 'Brotherhood' also implied that Mennonite communities should be homogeneous in character, in practice religiously and ethnically separate agricultural village settlements.

A religious moralist in his basic outlook, Jacob Epp was nevertheless often uncertain about the changes flooding his world. His response was thus multifaceted, accommodating here, retrenching there, sometimes welcoming change, yet as often worried about it. On many of the great questions facing his Brotherhood, he became in practice a man of compromise, frequently choosing a middle ground in order to avoid abrupt changes and sharp breaks within his community. By generally skirting extreme positions while defending traditional values and practices, he in fact fostered gradual change. Thus he came to support a more modern, machine-oriented agriculture, a dynamic administration, and up-to-date schools with trained teachers, defined curricula, and ready supplies of teaching aids and books. At the same time, he championed a personal, deeper piety, an elevated moral tone in family and village life, and also greater freedom of choice in expressing these goals. Above all else, doggedly – and also very movingly – he sought permanence in an era of change through the power and efficacy of his self-segregating Mennonite subculture.

In his diaries and other writings one can discern the indelible traits of Jacob Epp as a figure of transition. As a man with one foot in the world of his community-minded immigrant forbears of the early nineteenth century and another in that of his more individualistic Eigenheim grandchildren of the early twentieth, he appears to the attentive reader as a symptomatic figure. Like the pendulum of a 'Kröger Uhr,' a Russian Mennonite wall clock, the moods of this personally modest, kindly, deeply religious, yet vulnerable and often depressive, man swung back and forth between hope and disappointment. Self-doubts, cares of office, and the frictions of daily life even aroused in him on occasion a wish for death. Yet, by adapting selectively to change, this seemingly ambivalent man could become an example to his fellows, demonstrating how one might go about preserving some of the essential facets of a religious and community-minded way of life while adjusting to the opportunities and dangers of the larger imperial Russian and modern world.

The diaries served several major purposes for Jacob Epp. Recording daily events each evening, or in moments snatched from field and pastoral work, was a conscious act of filial identification with his revered father, the late David D. Epp, also a lay minister who had also kept a diary. Symbolic of Jacob Epp's yearning for continuance was his decision to fill the empty pages of his late father's last diary volume (which he received from his mother's estate as part of his inheritance) with a volume of his own diary entries.[14] On the level of his household, the diaries constitute an invaluable though incomplete annal of the cycle of family life. Since the roles of men and women tended to be separate and distinct, Jacob Epp records larger family events and watersheds, but includes relatively few homely details about food, dress and the myriad of interactions of daily family living. The diaries are richer and more complete in regard to the uncertainties of agriculture in a still largely pre-modern era: the variable and often mercurial weather, with its uncertain rainfall; the ups and downs in the lambing, shearing, and marketing of sheep; the recurring rounds of soaring hope and equally bottomless despair in the plowing, seeding, and harvesting of the grain fields; and the sheer misery of frequent pest infestations, crop failures, and epidemics of cattle, sheep and horse disease.

As a lay minister, Jacob Epp also records the details of his religious office: sermons, weddings, deaths, and the great celebrations of the church calendar, together with the sorrows and triumphs, as well as peccadillos and moral transgressions, of his parishioners. Furthermore, Jacob Epp was acutely aware of fundamental modifications occurring around him, and expressly noted that his diaries were to be preserved as a family remembrance of this changing world.[15] In this respect they are indeed a quarry of information. Conversely, as a man of unfeigned devotion, subject periodically to bouts of depression, his diaries revolve around the central motif of God's often mysterious ways, yet unflagging constancy, in an unpredictable world.

What gives particular force to the diaries is their unalloyed humanity. They appear to the observant reader as Jacob Epp's vital private outlet to vent his otherwise often repressed feelings and to digest the experiences of his cramped ministerial profession. He felt the need to write, to express his innermost sentiments, and to interpret and give meaning to the seemingly random events of his daily life.

Also, he felt compelled simply, as a writer, to record and to craft stories out of his experiences and those of his community. In his diary, a veritable confessional, Jacob Epp seems to have found the intimate expression of his life's personal pilgrimage, which he craved, and which was often denied him in his public persona and office.

Jacob Epp is a writer of honesty, deep feeling, and considerable skill. With little formal schooling but with a craftsman's sharp eye for the unique or typical detail, he often composes lengthy entries that overflow with workaday, naïve minutiae. He records a number of poignant and haunting dreams, including one of a tender reunion with his recently deceased first wife. Some of his sketches revolve around horse-drawn cart or carriage trips to Mennonite settlements, market towns, ports on the Dnieper River, and provincial capitals. A memorable entry is about a river and lake steamer voyage down the Dnieper into the Black Sea and to the boom town metropolis of Odessa.

Jacob Epp was born on 26 December 1820 in the Mennonite village of Khortitsa. With a population of 350 to 400 at the time, the village was the hub of the Old Colony, containing the mother church of the largest Mennonite congregation, the seat of the district administration and several artisanal, milling, commercial, and trading enterprises. In the 1820s Khortitsa village was one of eighteen villages of the Khortitsa Mennonite District, popularly known as the Old Colony. (Khortitsa was confusingly the name of the village, of the district, and of a large island in the Dnieper River belonging to the Mennonites.)[16] From 1820 to 1850, the Old Colony roughly doubled in population, increasing from around 4000 to 8000 people, and population growth continued as a dynamic force among Mennonites to the end of the Russian Empire.

In the period of Jacob Epp's childhood and youth, during the 1820s and 1830s, the Old Colony was still part of a rugged frontier of colonization, cattle and sheep raising, and slowly expanding grain marketing.[17] Sixteen of the eighteen villages of the Old Colony occupied an area about twenty kilometres square, mainly hilly terrain, the bulk of it on the high west bank of the Dnieper River at its great bend. This area, directly south of a series of turbulent and historically important rapids, was known as Zaporozhe (literally 'beyond the rapids'). Later treated as a crown grant, the land at the time of its settlement had been carved out of an undeveloped estate belonging to

Russia's greatest colonizing statesman, Catherine's favourite and Vice-Regent of New Russia, Count Grigori Potemkin. A well-connected benefactor and Catherine's sometime lover, Potemkin had been keenly involved in the Mennonites' original migration and had shown solicitude for its success.[18]

Traversing the lands of the Old Colony Mennonite District were a number of wooded steppe stream valleys and deep ravines, and along these many of the Mennonite villages, including Khortitsa, were picturesquely situated. Several villages were also located along the steep and wooded bank of the Dnieper River, and one small village was on the large (twelve kilometres long and three kilometres wide) Dnieper Island of Khortitsa (see map 2, 'Mennonite "Old Colony" [Khortitsa], 1850').

With its heroic Ukrainian Cossack past, plough-lands, meadows, mixed forests, valleys, sandbanks, steep granite cliffs, and small Mennonite village, the island exuded an aura of mystery, beauty, and romance.[19] Here Jacob Epp would teach village school from 1844 to 1852. Eastward, directly across the Dnieper River from the main settlement and the Island of Khortitsa, was the Old Colony village of Schönwiese, on the southern edge of the still-primitive county capital of Alexandrovsk (today the large industrial city of Zaporozhe). The last of the Old Colony villages, Kronsgarten, was to the north, quite distant from the rest, close to the city of Ekaterinoslav.

During Epp's childhood and youth the area around the Old Colony seemed vast and thinly populated. Much of it consisted of huge, uncultivated, grassland gentry estates averaging more than 5000 desiatinas (5500 hectares) each.[20] Starting in the 1860s, Old Colony Mennonites would push out from their over-populated village settlements, buying or leasing such gentry estates to develop as privately owned estates or as the sites of daughter settlements for their landless. But in the first half of the century, development was still slow and communications poor. The sparse, mainly Ukrainian, peasant population consisted of gentry-owned serfs in tiny hamlets or small villages and of government-administered state peasants (in effect wards of the state) in a few elephantine settlements whose populations numbered in the thousands. Across the Dnieper River from the main Old Colony settlement was one such large village, Voznesensk. Another, west of the Old Colony, was Tomakovka.

The Old Colony district was situated in the province of Ekaterinoslav, one of three provinces in New Russia (the other two being Taurida and Kherson). Its capital, also called Ekaterinoslav (now Dnepropetrovsk), lay some seventy kilometres north of Khortitsa, reachable only over rutted, muddy, or dusty roads. The chief administrative market and productive centre of the area and a hub of regional development, it was the object of frequent trips by local Mennonites, including the Epp family. Transportation, still poor until mid-century, mainly by horse-drawn wagon or buggy along dirt roads, developed rapidly thereafter. In the 1860s a regularly scheduled Dnieper River steamship line, on which Jacob Epp once travelled, opened service south to the Black Sea, and in the 1870s rail-lines appeared.[21] For Mennonites, this developing region of New Russia, with its opportunities and insecurities, encouraged personal traits of frugality, hard work, patience, and co-operation. It also rewarded highly self-conscious, clearly planned, goal-directed activities.

The Old Colony was the focus of Jacob Epp's entire life. He spent the first three decades of his life there and returned frequently in later life on family visits, for shopping, to sell produce, and on church business. Cementing his ties to the Old Colony was the leadership that members of his family had given the community since its beginnings. His grandfather, David Epp (1750–1802), 'Ohm Doaft' in the Mennonite Low German vernacular, was an Elder of the fledgling church in the 1790s. Embroiled in frequent controversy, he was best remembered as one of the fathers of the Charter of Privileges granted the Mennonites by Paul I in 1800. This ten-point document confirmed, and somewhat expanded, the terms of the Mennonites' original settlement in the Empire. (Of great controversy during Jacob Epp's adult life was article six of the charter, which promised that no one would 'at any time be forced to serve in the military or civil service.') During a celebrated two-year stay in St Petersburg, from 1798 to 1800, David Epp had helped negotiate the terms of the agreement with imperial officials, meeting Emperor Paul I personally. He returned to Khortitsa in triumph with the 'Eternal Charter,' a parchment with gold lettering, signed by the Monarch himself.[22]

Later housed in a specially constructed building in Khortitsa, the charter grew in the eyes of Mennonite leaders until it had achieved a mythic stature. In truth, as one tsar after another extended it to succeeding generations, it came to be widely seen as the foundation stone of an intimate, God-willed connection between the Mennonite community and the Russian monarchy. This view was reinforced by the successive monarchs Catherine II, Paul I, Alexander I, and Nicholas I, who, personally receiving leaders of the Mennonite communities at court or paying visits to their settlements, showered them with fulsome compliments. Jacob Epp took great pride in his grandfather's legacy. The supposition of imperial solicitude for his Brotherhood, anchored in an 'eternal Charter,' became the basis of his problematical adult political theology.

We know few details of Jacob Epp's early life. He likely grew up helping his father on their standard 65-desiatina (71-hectare) family farm (Wirtschaft) in the village of Khortitsa. Their house-and-garden plot with its customary house, barn, and implement shed under a single roof (an architectural style dating back to sixteenth-century Netherlands Anabaptism) was located centrally on the Alte Reihe, the main street, and their plough, hay, and pasture lands lay scattered in the common fields surrounding the village.[23] At the age of seven, he was probably enrolled in the one-room, six-year village school where he was taught the rudiments of the three Rs, some prayers and hymns, as well as Bible stories and the Mennonite catechism.

Schooling, beyond the basic literacy needed to acquire essential religious knowledge, was not accorded great value among Mennonites in the Old Colony at the time. According to contemporary stereotypes, teaching had lower status than herding the village cattle. The school year was short, attendance irregular (classes were interrupted for seed-time and sheep-herding), and Jacob's teacher was almost certainly untrained for the job. In all likelihood he had no more than village schooling himself (since there was as yet no secondary school in Khortitsa), spoke a stilted High German, and little or no Russian, and conducted most classes in the vernacular Low German. It is highly probable that his teacher was a landless villager, perhaps an artisan marking time while waiting either to take up a trade or to establish a regular household with a dwelling, yard, and garden plot and full 65-desiatina allotment of land.

The first fleeting glimpses of Jacob Epp date from the years 1837 to 1843. They are contained in laconic entries, in a crabbed hand, in the rare surviving diary volume of his father, David Epp (1781–1843), a prominent, though poor, Old Colony churchman. In mid-May 1837 we see Jacob for the first time as a seventeen-year-old, on a five-day, fifty-kilometre wagon trip with his father and a brother, travelling to their rented sheep farm to pay a salt tax.[24] We meet him again a half-year later, accompanying his father, who was part of an official delegation of the religious and secular leadership of the Old Colony. This time it is the grander occasion of a visit of the empress and her daughter the Grand Duchess Maria Nicolaevna. To meet these royal personages, they travel to Ekaterinoslav in three horse-drawn carriages and on their way home visit his uncle Heinrich Thiessen, a prosperous Ekaterinoslav miller and head of one of the first prominent urban Mennonite families in Russia.[25] A month later, he and his father again visit the uncle in Ekaterinoslav.[26]

In January 1839 eighteen-year-old Jacob again accompanied his father on a similarly memorable three-week trip to the larger and more prosperous sister settlement of the Molochna, two days' distance by wagon to the southeast.[27] Unlike many of their co-religionists, the Epps valued education, and the purpose of this trip was to drop off Jacob's younger and later more distinguished brother Heinrich to study German and Russian at a privately run, pioneering secondary school on the Steinbach estate. The Molochna settlement had about double the Old Colony's population, three times its number of villages and landholdings, heavier and more fertile soils, and a socially and culturally more diverse population. In the government's view it was also the most successful foreign settlement in Russia and a prime example of agricultural and cultural progress.[28]

At the time, however, the settlement was embroiled in controversy. The main dispute was over the question of leadership and authority: should the direction for the Molochna settlement be charted by churchmen following religious principles or by a state-backed, somewhat secularized Mennonite hierarchy headed by the brilliant and imperious reformer Johann Cornies (1789–1848), the favourite of the government?[29] As an influential Old Colony minister, David Epp made the rounds of the Molochna's religious and civic leaders, including Johann Cornies. Epp, reputed to be Cornies's friend, while sharing the latter's vision of a modern agriculture and education, excoriated his anticlericalism and 'tyrannical' methods.[30] Young

Jacob must certainly have overheard his father's worried conversations. This intensely provocative interlude ended half-way through the trip when Jacob came down with the measles and was left to recuperate at the home of a relative in a Molochna village. Such visits with his father nevertheless broadened young Jacob's understanding of the wider Mennonite and imperial Russian world, which was gradually being beset by change, familiarized him with the patterns and rules of in-group discourse, and sensitized him to the acute dangers of community fissures.

Also in 1839, in spring, still as an eighteen-year-old, Jacob Epp was baptized, with eighty-six other young people in the Khortitsa Flemish Mennonite church by Jacob Dyck, the Elder. This event took place on Pentecost Sunday, as was the custom. The ritual had been preceded by a lengthy period of instruction in the catechism by the Lehrdienst, the Ministerial Committee, consisting of the Elder, lay ministers (which included his father), and the deacons. Likely assisting as well was the 'Church Mother,' a woman appointed to oversee the baptismal maidens to ensure they were suitably garbed, had their hair parted in the centre, and behaved appropriately during the question-and-answer sessions.[31]

Baptism was a significant rite of passage that marked Jacob Epp's entry into full membership in the Mennonite religious and civil community and his assumption of the responsibilities of adulthood. 'Baptize him, my Saviour, with thy Spirit and with fire,' his father wrote in his diary.[32] Two weeks later, Jacob took his first communion with 477 fellow communicants in the large, spartan, recently built clay mother church in Khortitsa.[33] At a transition point in his life, and in the presence of the entire adult community, this solemn ceremony further bonded Jacob Epp securely to his religious community.

In the months following his baptism, Jacob went to make hay and to shear sheep on the family's leased sheep farm. There were also excursions to Ekaterinoslav and local fairs. By this time several Old Colony families were moving from the villages onto privately owned or leased landholdings called khutors, an early signal of a trend to greater occupational and social differentiation. Marriages between such families and children of ministers were not uncommon. After the harvest in late August 1839, we find Jacob, a brother, a sister, and his parents present at the marriage of their older brother Diedrich to the daughter of a leaseholder, Peter Siemens, on the khutor of Dalbich.[34]

Among Russian Mennonites, virtually everyone married (this was also true of Russian and Ukrainian peasants). Women, on average, entered into wedlock between the ages of 18 and 22 and men between 19 and 23. The practice was for a young man to pick out a prospective bride. Then his father, or an adult male family friend, would act as a go-between and make the first official contacts with the bride's parents. In his diary entries for September 1840, Jacob's father notes the bare-bone particulars of a bride-search for his nineteen-year-old son.

Jacob was first deposited with the Thiessen relations in Ekaterinoslav to cool his heels while his father drove to Kronsgarten, the most distant village of the Old Colony District. There, father David Epp writes, on the afternoon of 6 September 1840, in the company of a local villager H. Gertz, 'We went to see Mrs Fr[anz] Peters to ask for the hand of her daughter Susanna for our son Jacob. At 4 o'clock he came himself to hear the daughter give her joyous "yes."'[35].

The engagement festivities, which would normally have followed almost immediately, were put off until the return of Susanna's father who was away in the Molochna settlement at the time. A month later Jacob left for his appointed wedding day but returned, embarrassed, with, as his father wrote, the 'matter unaccomplished.'[36] The reasons for this are unclear. At this date, Jacob Epp had likely already lost his left eye. He was perhaps thought a physical oddity, even ugly, and Susanna Peters, on reflection, may have rejected him as a poor catch. On the other hand, the problem may also have been confessional. At the time, Old Colony Mennonites were still divided into two wings, whose origins went back to the sixteenth-century Netherlands. The Epps were of the majority Flemish church, while the village of Kronsgarten belonged to the smaller, more austere Frisian church. This once-bitter confessional divide was of little significance to the Epps, but marriage across it was still difficult and infrequent at the time. It may have been thought an insuperable obstacle by the family of Jacob Epp's desired bride.[37]

The year 1841, Jacob Epp's twentieth year and his father's sixtieth, brought success. In August he was again in the Molochna settlement, this time with several siblings 'to visit friends' and perhaps in search of a bride.[38] The year's high-point was his engagement on 2 November and marriage two weeks later to Maria Klassen, the nineteen-year-old daughter of a next-door neighbour in Khortitsa village. The simple rites were performed in the home of the bride by the Old Colony Elder.[39] The marriage was a tender love match lasting twenty-two years, until Maria's death of tuberculosis in 1863.

From the marriage also dates the earliest surviving writing by Jacob Epp, a nineteen-line love verse, given as a 'bridal gift' to his fiancée, Maria, and presumably recited at the engagement festivities. Affectionately preserved by family members for later generations, it reads in part:

Take this little gift, my child,
And think about its meaning:
You are *mine*, and I *thine*.
To thee I give in love
More than this gift of mine.
My entire heart is thine,
And offered thee in love.
This is by God designed
And through His will defined
That we are now but one.[40]

Endearing and naïve, this verse for his fiancée Maria affirms traditional Mennonite patriarchy. The husband is head and sustainer and the wife, as dependent, a 'child.' Yet the verse also verbalizes inklings of something novel – lively sensibility, romantic love, and strong feelings clothed in simple yet heartfelt verse. Here is nascent individualism. In later life, Jacob Epp's desire for self-expression, for his own clear and authentic voice, would become for him a source of frustration, and even bitter pain, as it collided with his community's demand for conformity and ritualized expression. For the rest of his life, Jacob Epp nevertheless tried to place his inimitable mark on what he did, preserving in his journal the verses, prayers, and songs he wrote privately and for family, school, and community occasions.

The 1840s were the golden years of imperial solicitude for the Mennonites as pace-setters of a modern agriculture in New Russia, and important personages visited the settlements regularly. In August 1841 Russia's most influential reforming minister, General Count P.D. Kiselev, minister of state domains, was received by the Old Colony civil and religious leaders, including Jacob's father. The leaders spoke only German, Kiselev only Russian, and the salaried secretary of the District administration interpreted.[41] Since all foreign colonists came under his ministry's jurisdiction, Kiselev knew the Mennonites well, valued their accomplishments highly, and looked for ways of adapting their widely praised administrative and land-tenure practices to his monumental administrative reform of Russia's state peasantry (in effect peasants under direct state administration, who constituted about half the peasant population of Russia, the other half being serfs).[42]

In October 1841, the German-born Grand Duchess Elena Pavlovna and her daughter Maria Michaelovna, important reforming allies of Kiselev, were fêted at a brief stopover at the Dnieper village of Einlage. The grand duchess praised the exemplary character of Mennonite accomplishments. Jacob Epp was almost certainly there, and his father recorded the brief encounter:

> These important visitors arrived at the Dnieper at 3:15 in the afternoon. The Grand Duchess was very friendly, graciously received Elder Jacob Dyck's thanks and offered several words of congratulation. She also spoke to the private schoolteacher Hausknecht.[43] He and his pupils sang several verses of a song in French as the Grand Duchess stepped from the ferry onto the shore. She conversed with the teacher, H[einrich] Heese, about the [proposed] Zentralschule, accepted a copy of drawings for the school from him and a picture from his daughter Agata. Then, without stopping in to see anyone else, these distinguished travellers continued on their journey accompanied by a retinue of eight Cossacks.[44]

At the behest of Kiselev's Ministry of State Domains, plans were made in 1841 for the establishment of the already mentioned Zentralschule (secondary school) in Khortitsa. The Zentralschule was to train young Mennonites as village schoolteachers and local administrators and spread knowledge of the Russian language. In time it would become a vehicle for the percolation of modern influences from Germany and urban Russia down through the village schools to the entire Old Colony. Many conservative Mennonites, vaguely concerned about such possibilities, were hostile to the initiative. Jacob's father, however, championed the establishment of the secondary school as a way of raising the skills, morals, and piety of his community, and as an influential lay cleric plunged ahead in the role of facilitator. He helped to draft statutes for the school, arrange finances, locate quarters for its classes, and hire its first teacher, Heinrich Heese.[45] Talk at the Epp dinner table doubtless turned on the fortunes of the school whose establishment would become a major watershed in the educational history of the Old Colony. To be sure, the Zentralschule opened its doors too late for Jacob to benefit from it directly for his own education. Several of his siblings and children would, however, attend the school and his brother Heinrich later had a distinguished career as its head teacher.

The Epp household of the later 1830s and early 1840s was thus obviously quite open to the wider world. Indeed Jacob Epp's parental home seemed constantly abuzz with the comings and goings of Mennonite and non-Mennonite guests passing through for counsel, a visit, or an overnight stay with his father, the respected and experienced Old Colony churchman. During the years 1841 and 1842, for instance, David Epp's surviving diary makes note of visitors from the troubled Molochna, indigents from the struggling settlement of Bergthal, and guests from the Mennonite mother churches in Prussia. Also stopping in were Russian state officials and Bible and mission society envoys, colporteurs, and evangelists from Germany and England.[46]

The latter supplied David Epp with Bibles, as well as new devotional and expository literature and song-books that he added to his reputedly substantial library, or sold in his community. The guests also brought journals and newspapers and talked about broader issues. Many of these travellers were steeped in the resurgent pietism of the 1820s and 1830s, with its centre in Germany and its stress on a more personal and inward faith, on foreign missions, abstinence, and moral rectitude.[47] Much of the imported literature also strongly reflected this emphasis. David Epp's own marked religious bent in this direction, including the glimmerings of an apocalyptical expectation, was thereby strengthened and given much sharper definition within his household and circle of close friends.

Growing up in a churchman's household also, it bears noting, became for Jacob a kind of apprenticeship for his later work as a lay minister, whose twofold roles were defined by the words 'watchman' and 'shepherd.' Through daily observation he absorbed pointers on how to perform one of these prime pastoral functions of a Mennonite Lehrer, or minister, that of watchdog over community morals. Mennonite behavioural standards of the time were based on interpretations of the Scriptures and of the Mennonite catechism. These were translated into a set of guidelines at congregational meetings (known as Brotherhood meetings), often on the advice of the Ministerial Committee. These guidelines were, in turn, propagated from the pulpit and in the village schools and enforced through counselling, reprimands, and, failing all else, court-like proceedings of the Ministerial Committee and Brotherhood Meeting.

The Ministerial Committee often met on Thursdays to discuss difficult cases. It heard witnesses, allowing only corroborated testimony, and following rough-and-ready rules of evidence tried to establish the facts of a situation. Confession, contrition, and reconciliation were the goals. In extreme cases, discipline was imposed that included the ban, a not overly severe form of disfellowshipping or public shaming, usually of two weeks' duration. Following public repentance before the Brotherhood, wrongdoers were readmitted to full church membership. In cases also involving civil wrongdoing, members of the Ministerial Committee met jointly with the members of the District Mayor's Office (Oberschulz) to resolve matters.

The cases of discipline noted in David Epp's diary related to the gamut of behaviour found in an agrarian society. Patterns, moreover, changed very little in later decades, and appear once again in Jacob Epp's own diaries. The less serious cases were mediated by the Ministerial Committee, ending usually in apologies, reconciliation, and, where appropriate, restitution. These involved gossiping, quarrels, and fisticuffs among church members, maintaining overly close relations with someone in the ban, marital discord, blasphemy, cursing, refusal to pay church dues, indiscretions or immoral goings-on at local markets such as carousing, petty thievery (for example, of a sheep or a sack of flour), violations of the Sabbath (ploughing, carting or smithing) and disputes over inheritance. In the case of a broken engagement, the Ministerial Committee negotiated monetary compensation for the aggrieved party.[48]

Drunkenness was a thornier issue of growing concern, which explains David Epp's advocacy of abstinence as a norm. Yet in their West Prussian homeland, Mennonites had brewed and consumed beer and spirits, and they had no tradition of teetotalism. In the 1830s and 1840s, however, the drinking of hard liquor seemed to be on the rise, presumably as Mennonites succumbed to local quaffing habits on visits to Ukrainian markets and fairs. But problem drinking and alcoholism probably also reflected deeper community problems, including growing social uncertainty among an increasing class of Mennonite landless households.

First offenders appearing before the Ministerial Committee or Brotherhood who apologized and promised 'betterment' were given a warning and allowed to 'go in peace.' But habitual drunkards were placed in the ban. When after repeated apologies there was no improvement, the Ministerial Committee was in a quandary as to what to do next, often floundering in its response.

Jacob Epp further witnessed the strict treatment meted out to miscreants for breaches of church rules that, by affecting non-Mennonites or coming under the authority of the government, threatened wider complications with the outside world. For instance, six youthful church members caught stealing watermelons from a 'Russian melon patch' were, as David Epp recorded, ordered to pay twenty rubles compensation and do six days of community work, and were placed in the ban.[49] Murder was almost non-existent, and only one case appears in his father's diary. It concerned the illegitimate birth in the Old Colony daughter settlement of Bergthal of a baby girl who was found dead in a manure pile, and had presumably been murdered.[50]

Sexual infractions naturally existed but seem to have been relatively infrequent. Old Colony society in the 1830s and 1840s appears not to have been strongly repressive sexually, or obsessively puritanical. Almost everyone wed at a relatively early age and marriage partners were usually a personal choice, as had been true for Jacob Epp. Only one instance of homosexual conduct appears in David Epp's diary. Cases of bestiality, dalliances, and sexual relations outside of marriage were usually punished with a two-week ban, and the homosexual offence will have been included here.[51] Simple survival for a religious and agrarian society like the Old Colony demanded no less. Standing together as a minority against an uncertain and variable climate, surrounded by an alien host society, and ruled by an authoritarian government, the Old Colony had no tolerance for random or unlicensed sexual encounters that would have inevitably weakened or divided the community.

Jacob Epp thus observed a relatively effective enforcement of community norms through ritualized purging under the ultimate threat of social and religious ostracism. The successive stages in the process – confession, repentance and, in more serious cases, separation through the ban, followed by reconciliation and reintegration of the wrongdoer into the religious and civil community – allowed for discipline and coherence without provoking division. The system worked for those who ultimately bent.

But what of individuals who kicked over the traces and refused to yield? What were their choices? Cases of this sort were quite rare. In the three that appear in David Epp's diary, individuals simply fled the discipline of the Mennonite community and church by breaking all ties with them. Such persons either moved to a nearby town, city, or Russian estate, or took up residence in a nearby Ukrainian village and there formally sought membership in the Orthodox church.[52]

After their marriage in the fall of 1841, Jacob Epp and his young bride Maria moved into the so-called summer-room (Sommerstube) of his parents' home in Khortitsa, as was the custom. The next spring he took over from his father the operation of the rented family sheep farm some fifty kilometres away, and there followed for the newly married couple, as he later recalled, a year of 'tranquil happiness.'[53] Adversity struck suddenly in May 1843, however, with the unexpected death of his father. Although a prominent minister, David Epp had been poor and was probably deeply in debt. Within half a year the rented sheep farm on the Kromida Estate had been dissolved and even the 65-desiatina family property in the village of Khortitsa sold at a three-day public auction.[54] Jacob's widowed and impoverished mother and five under-aged brothers and sisters were forced to move into a small cottage on the Neue Reihe, a side-street, in Khortitsa.[55] Young, recently married, landless, and with few immediate prospects himself, Jacob Epp and his wife moved into a room in Khortitsa as modest, landless Einwohner (renters).

Although David Epp died poor in material possessions, he left a legacy that significantly shaped his son Jacob's adult impulses and spiritual and intellectual outlook. As the most eminent Old Colony churchman of his day, and a man of deep piety, David Epp stood for a highly personal Christian faith of regeneration, inwardness, and holiness evidenced through missionizing, mutual aid, and charity. He advocated considerable openness of his community to the changing imperial Russian and European world. Moreover, he was zealous in defending the unity of his community and condemned internal splits of the kind that had pitted religious and civil leaders against one another in the Molochna settlement. To his mind, conflict invited day-to-day imperial intervention in community affairs and paved the way for outside control and creeping secularization.[56]

Yet while championing the primacy of religious leadership and the need for intimate co-operation between civil and church leaders in the Old Colony, David Epp was sharply critical of his own society and its leadership. This was no doubt due in part to his pietist sensibility and in part perhaps to his injured feelings at having been passed over for the position of Elder of the church himself. In any case, in his diary he repeatedly decried what was to him the Old Colony's weak leadership, shallow spirituality, deteriorating morality, and legalistic ethics. 'Everything was pro forma,' he wrote, 'dead moralism, lacking both spirit and life.'[57] Overcasting his world was the threat of divine retribution and vague prospects of the apocalypse.[58] As almost a panacea for the ills of his community, he advocated a better school system under the supervision of the Ministerial Committee which would be attuned to economic progress (that is, a modern agriculture), while dispelling religious ignorance and nurturing in its pupils a spiritual attitude of childlike piety.

Jacob Epp embraced much of his kindly, visionary but strong-willed father's outlook, later mentioning him frequently in his diary and in a long narrative poem. But of more immediate importance to him in the year after his father's death was a job. As already mentioned, the Zentralschule had been founded during the last years of his father's life, High German (instead of Low German) was made the language of instruction in the village schools, and a system of compulsory school inspection by the Ministerial Committee was introduced. These were the beginnings of a coherent and modern system of education that evolved over the following generations.

Buoyed up perhaps by these early changes and inspired by the educational dreams of his late revered father, but also unquestionably in need of a livelihood (as his wife was pregnant with their first child), Jacob Epp in April 1844 took a job as village schoolteacher on the lovely nearby Dnieper Island of Khortitsa.[59]

Epp arrived on the Island of Khortitsa as a twenty-three-year-old novice, with little formal schooling and largely self-taught. In this respect he was no different from most other village schoolteachers, but he came from a family that valued learning, discussed issues, and had ready access to traditional Mennonite and current pietist literature. He seems to have established himself quickly as one of a small group of devoted teachers in the Old Colony to whom teaching mattered because it served important, even ultimate, purposes. In his severely plain and cramped teacherage-and-schoolhouse, we see him first, in a rare unpublished reminiscence, through the eyes of a pupil, Cornelius Hildebrand. Hildebrand, who lived on the Island, was the son of the Elder of the Old Colony Frisian church. Later he married Jacob Epp's sister and became an important farm-implements industrialist in New Russia.[60]

About his school years, Hildebrand writes:

At that time we did not yet follow a timetable, but proceeded about in this way. First we sang a morning song and then prayed together. We then had reading, writing, and arithmetic and practised looking up hymns by number in our song-books. Whoever found the hymn first was the best pupil. The pages of our song-books suffered but we learned dexterity.

In 1844 Jacob Epp came to us from Khortitsa. He and his wife were still very young and had one child. He had only one eye but could see well enough to spot the mistakes we made. School now became a livelier place. In addition to the already mentioned subjects, we now did calligraphy, memory work, Bible stories, and some penmanship.

Russian was also taught. What an afternoon that was when our teacher made Jacob Janzen, Abraham Hoeppner and me (we three sat in a row) recite the Russian alphabet out loud for the first time. What a confusion of hiss and sish, of the *tverdyi znak* and *miagii znak*. It was as though the whole class was laughing. Yet we had to take the greatest efforts to get all of the sounds right. Later I noticed that our teacher was also, as one might say, not exactly fluent in Russian. And yet I am grateful to the teacher and my father, who so strongly desired this, because even the little I learned has been of great benefit to me.

This teacher also allowed me to draw and to paint, which I was very interested in doing. I did landscapes, for instance. Hunters, foxes, rabbits and birds were my subjects. I painted the real and the fantastical, green fields and stones and trees or a winter landscape when the willows or poplars were thickly covered with frost. But on white paper I somehow had difficulty with a winter landscape as God had made it.

I always enjoyed going to school, first alone and then with my sisters and brother. And we had so many lovely recesses, especially in the summertime when we played mainly on the rocky hill. We ran uphill and downhill, as fast as we could go, and when we had found a really good hiding place, we would hear the call, 'schooltime.' Oh, how we hated to leave our hiding places, and yet we had to obey. Our heads were hot and our hair soaked, as though we had been pulled from the water, and it took a while for us to cool down.

This teacher was always very good to us. He never scolded me, but he scolded very little in general. Somehow he knew how to treat us so that we obeyed without being scolded. How he could pray. To my dying day I will never forget how before a holiday, for instance, at the close of the day, he created a solemn atmosphere with all kinds of explanations and exhortations to obey our parents. Then came the prayer, which consisted in him commending us to the dear Saviour Jesus that he might make us his own, as little lambs, as recompense for his suffering and death. And who would thus not be moved to tears?[61]

Handicapped by the loss of his left eye at an indeterminate earlier age (a source of recurring infection, embarassment, and excruciating pain), and shaky in his Russian, but personally warm, open to innovations, and interested in the needs of his pupils, Jacob Epp taught village school on the Island from 1844 to 1852. During two of these years, from 1846 to 1848, Johann Cornies, the Mennonite 'autocrat' from the Molochna settlement, who had received broad governmental authority over the Old Colony, began laying the basis of better schooling. Jacob Epp saw this as a sign of 'new life' and when, after Cornies's sudden death in 1848, the 'old indifference' slowly returned, he was discouraged.[62]

Yet he recalled the years of teaching on the Island as a relatively satisfying time. The Island village of that day had eighteen landowning and perhaps again as many landless cottager families. With its social intimacy and close friendships, unusual mix of confessionally Frisian and Flemish church-goers, and great natural contrasts, it seemed to brim with memories and life. Mennonite ploughmen still regularly turned up rusted pieces of rifles, cannon, sabres, and shot, relics of the Island's historically significant Ukrainian Cossack past.[63] While vagabonds and thieves were a problem from time to time, the children of the Island enjoyed great freedom, to judge by Cornelius Hildebrand's reminiscences. They played among its ravines and cliffs, hunted wildlife including wolves (some of them rabid), swam and fished in the Dnieper River, and exuberantly clambered over rock faces and old and crumbling Cossack defence ramparts. From time to time, the boys also raided Ukrainian village melon patches across the Dnieper, provoking an occasional fist-fight with their 'Kochol' neighbours.[64]

The Island's village looked away from the main Old Colony settlement, eastward toward the fishing and traffic on the Dnieper River and across to the slowly developing county seat of Alexandrovsk. With unique occupations like fishing, rafting, and ferrying, the Island allowed for a degree of spontaneity and a tolerance for differences unusual for the Old Colony. Here, among novelties, Jacob Epp witnessed extemporaneous preaching by the Frisian Elder Jakob Hildebrand (father of Epp's pupil, Cornelius, noted earlier). This stood in sharp contrast to the starched reading of sermons by a seated minister in his own Flemish church.[65] Such 'free preaching' would become a painful symbolic issue for him later in life.

Jacob Epp's family life on the Island of Khortitsa followed a conventional cycle. He fathered five children (one of whom suffered a crib death) and regularly attended divine services conducted by Frisian ministers in the Island's teacherage-schoolhouse or by Flemish ministers in the mother church in Khortitsa. Crossing the Dnieper's narrow western arm by ferry, he witnessed the marriages of three siblings and often dropped in on friends, relatives, and his widowed mother and his mother-in-law in the village of Khortitsa. His social status as teacher, however, continued to be low and his remuneration in money, goods, and services very meagre. With a growing family it was also inadequate. He earned a little extra as record-keeper at the occasional auction and then as part-time, and minimally recompensed, secretary to the Island's village assembly.[66]

The job of appointed and salaried Village secretary was an eye-opener for Jacob Epp, bringing him into direct touch with village and district administration, and controversy as well. In the late 1840s and early 1850s, nothing was more divisive in the Old Colony than a recurring contest over civil authority between two institutions that were pitted against one another: the Old Colony District Administration of locally elected Mennonites and the Old Colony Agricultural Commission composed of government-appointed Mennonites. The Mennonite church leadership supported the elected District officials, while imperial officials stood four-square behind the Agricultural Commission, enforcing its will on matters of local governance through reprimands, fines, and even dismissals of local elected officials for 'wilful disobedience.' Jacob Epp describes numerous instances of this kind and laments the animosity that they engendered.[67]

Like the unholy controversy that Jacob Epp and his father had witnessed a decade earlier in the Molochna settlement, this conflict over authority had deep roots in the discipline and autocratic desire for control of the regime of Nicholas I (1825–55).[68] These inevitably threatened local autonomy. Indeed, the potential for friction between the Mennonite settlements and the imperial government had been present from the time of the first Mennonite immigration. It arose from a basic conflict between the clergy's claim to primacy and leadership in Mennonite community affairs and the government's ultimate monopoly on all decision making.

In actual fact, however, this reality had long been masked. Since the early nineteenth century the imperial government, recognizing the weakness of its bureaucracy in the countryside, had granted foreign colonist settlements wide-ranging local authority. At the village level, authority was vested in assemblies of landowners that elected village mayors and assistant mayors and, in often spirited, even acrimonious, sessions, resolved important village matters relating to tax distribution, crop rotations, fire insurance, inheritances, and the hiring of village secretaries, herdsmen, watchmen, and schoolteachers.

The eighteen villages of the Old Colony constituted an administrative District (later known as volost), with comparable powers of self-administration. Here, legislative authority lay with an assembly of delegates representing the villages, which included village mayors. Executive authority was vested in a District mayor and two assistants, who employed a secretary and other staff. As a court for minor cases, the executive could impose punishments on members of the settlement, including monetary fines, community labour, corporal punishment, and expulsion from the settlement.[69] This two-tiered system of local village and district self-administration, with its elective character, well-defined jurisdiction, clear lines of authority, and diffusion of power, fitted well with Mennonite congregational traditions and enjoyed popular legitimacy. Politics seemed to revolve largely within the Mennonite community. There was strong local control, and the life-tenured clergy could call many of the shots in regard to policy while working co-operatively with elected civic leaders. These circumstances, moreover, enhanced the Old Colony's own identity as a religious community.

But this situation changed radically in the 1830s and 1840s when the imperial government began to assert more direct control over the colonists' affairs. In 1837, government jurisdiction over foreign settlements, including the Old Colony District, was transferred from the Ministry of the Interior to Kiselev's new, reforming Ministry of State Domains (responsible, as noted, for about half of Russia's peasantry known as the 'state peasants'). Kiselev exercised his authority in regard to the settlements of foreign origin through an already existing subordinate office in Odessa, the 'Guardianship Committee of Foreign Colonists in Southern Russia,' popularly known as the 'Guardianship Committee.' The Committee, which communicated with the settlements in German, had a president, bureaucracy, and subordinate regional inspectorates whose staff regularly visited the settlements, often incognito. It confirmed in office, and could dismiss, all local elected Mennonite officials.[70] For men like Jacob Epp, the Guardianship Committee was *the* Government.

With Kiselev's encouragement, the Guardianship Committee in the 1830s became a gathering place for agrarian reformers with ambitious plans. Impressed with the Mennonites' well-publicized social cohesion and agrarian accomplishments, it singled them out as models of progress for the development of New Russian agriculture. To ensure that they played this role to the hilt, the Guardianship

Committee then created new centrally appointed institutions of initiative and control at the district level – the previously mentioned agricultural commissions. Through these commissions (which were also established in other German colonist settlements) Mennonite society could be subjected to massive, paternal state intervention. In 1830, the first such commission was established in the Molochna settlement and placed under the lifetime command of its Chairman, the often-mentioned visionary and authoritarian Mennonite reformer Johann Cornies (1789–1848).[71]

Cornies, a paternalistic disciplinarian in the mould of Emperor Nicholas I, whose command approach to public issues he faithfully duplicated, gradually concentrated governmental authority at the village and district levels in his hands. Using these powers, he carried through a sweeping program of agrarian and educational reforms in the Molochna settlement. In the process he co-opted and cowed his local clerical and lay opponents, enforcing his will through the heavy use of penalties such as community labour, corporal punishment, and even banishment from the settlement.[72] Acting on behalf of the Guardianship Committee, he, in effect, usurped the authority both of the church leadership and of locally elected civic district and village Mennonite officials. The Guardianship Committee established a second Agricultural Commission in the Old Colony in the 1830s, and in 1846 appointed Cornies chairman of it as well. In this role, and true to form, he enforced a program of equally ambitious, and hotly contested, secular changes in the Old Colony. Following Cornies's death in 1848, these reforms were continued by his successor into the early 1850s.

Jacob Epp's diary in the early 1850s echoes with the noise of controversy that Cornies's regime provoked between appointed Agricultural Commission members, on the one side, and the clergy and elected civic leaders, on the other. Epp championed the Agricultural Commission's reforms in the Old Colony, lamenting the 'insubordination' they aroused and the state-inflicted discipline that followed. Ever the moralist, he failed to see that the root of the conflict within the Old Colony lay chiefly in the extreme centralization and penchant for control of the autocratic system. Mistakenly, he traced it to a lack of 'brotherhood,' a cancerous sin, among his fellows and expressed sympathy for the state-backed Agricultural

Commission. With the death of Nicholas I and Russia's mortifying loss of the Crimean War in the mid-1850s, this era of autocratic-engendered control and controversy in the Old Colony tailed off. Gradually the Agricultural Commission's state-enforced primacy in Mennonite affairs came to an end and authority gravitated to local, elective institutions at the Village and District levels. During its dominance, however, the institution of the Agricultural Commission had opened the floodgates to a host of external religious and secular influences and sparked heated controversy.

In 1852 Jacob Epp moved out of the Old Colony, an event that marked the start of an important new chapter in his life. As a child of his times, he seems never to have considered the low station and poorly paid job of teaching a lifetime profession. (This view seems to have been part of a broader pattern in pre-industrial agrarian societies, where the village schoolteacher tended to be marked as someone less than fully complete because of his inability to join fully in the agricultural cycle.)[73] For years Epp had been on the look-out for something better – land and the status to go with it that would give him a better livelihood and raise him to equality with his land-holding fellows. Above all he cherished the hope that the government would endow the Old Colony with a further crown grant of land for its landless population.

Repeatedly frustrated in this expectation, however, he and about fifty other landless Mennonite families, in the early 1850s, reluctantly accepted a government offer to settle in a new state-sponsored Jewish agricultural settlement as 'model settlers.' Thus began one of the most unusual colonization ventures in Russian Mennonite history. Called the Judenplan, the six-village settlement was located more than a hundred kilometres west of the Mennonite Old Colony, in the neighbouring guberniia of Kherson, on an attractive, fertile, virgin steppe-land. The Judenplan was part of a government program eventually embracing several settlements and thirty-nine villages (twenty-two villages in Kherson guberniia and seventeen in Ekaterinoslav guberniia; see map 3, 'The World of Jacob D. Epp, 1875').[74]

Like their Mennonite counterparts, these Jewish settlements were under the administrative jurisdiction of the Ministry of State Domains and its Guardianship Committee in Odessa. The Judenplan, with eventually some four to six hundred people in each village, came in time to have a population of around three thousand. Two of the villages, Kamianka and Izluchistaia, traced their beginnings to the early nineteenth century, while four were created in the late 1840s and early 1850s. With prefixes 'novo' ('new'), these latter were named Novokovno, Novopodolsk, Novovitebsk, and Novozhitomir, after the provinces from which their Jewish crafts and tradesmen settlers had come. In each of these villages some eight or nine Old Colony Mennonite families were settled as 'model settlers.'[75]

Yoking Jews and Mennonites together in the Judenplan was a characteristic experiment of Russian autocratic paternalism in the first half of the nineteenth century. Direction, superintendence, and control were its watchwords – unencumbered 'guardianship' in the fullest sense of that term. The program started in the early 1800s with the government's establishment of several Jewish agricultural villages in New Russia with two aims in mind: to relieve pressures among impoverished Jews in the northwestern provinces; and to engineer a 'more normal' social structure among Jews by turning some of them into peasants.[76] But in the mid-1840s a major government review concluded from the continuing misery of these early villages that before the program could be expanded it needed to be basically reformed. The review attributed the poverty to tangled ministerial lines of planning and control and to graft and oppression in local village and district administration. Most important perhaps, the review attributed the program's failure to the negligence of the state in not teaching the agriculturally inexperienced Jews methods of good farming.

As remedies, it proposed that the Ministry of State Domains be given exclusive administrative control over the Jewish villages and that competent German-speaking colonists from New Russia be recruited as salaried state overseers at the village and settlement levels. To flesh out the system of tutelary guidance, the government review recommended the appointment of 'model settlers' to live in each village. The review finally singled out Mennonites as persons ideally suited to serve both as 'overseers' and as 'model settlers.' The review concluded:

> In every Jewish colony a certain number of qualified Christian farmers should be settled. They would teach the Jewish colonists agriculture and be present at all times with advice and help and so prevent wilful or unintended

negligence in respect of any aspect of Jewish agriculture. Undoubtedly the German Christian colonists are well suited to be such teachers and instructors ... Among these the Mennonites would be by far the best, for when all is said and done, they are genuinely outstanding models of virtuous and industrious people both physically and spiritually. Cornies, the leader of the Mennonites, who exercises superintendence over all of their colonies, should be contacted to see if there is any possibility that members of his community would be willing to settle in the Jewish colonies and take on the task of instructors. This is quite unlikely, however, for the Mennonite treasures his communal existence and his brotherhood highly and would not easily agree to exchange these for material benefits.[77]

There is no evidence that the Old Colony religious and lay leadership debated the potential merits and pitfalls of Mennonites taking up the recommended places in the Judenplan. But Johann Cornies, who, from 1846 until his death in 1848, did indeed exercise wide-ranging governmental authority over all Mennonite settlements, embraced the program as one way of relieving population pressures in the Old Colony and gave it his hearty endorsement.[78] It was rapidly implemented. Kiselev's Ministry of State Domains took control of the program. And in 1848 a notice appeared in the Guardianship Committee's monthly German-language journal, *Unterhaltungsblatt für deutsche Ansiedler im Südlichen Russland*, inviting German colonists and Mennonites to apply for positions as village overseers and as model settlers. Promised the retention of their legal status as colonists, prospective model-settler families were offered 40-desiatina grants of good land, long-term tax exemptions, and the right to maintain their own schools.[79]

By 1850 the landlessness that Jacob Epp experienced was already widespread in all Mennonite settlements.[80] About 60 per cent of all Old Colony households were by now without landed property, and the situation was deteriorating from year to year. Population was increasing at 3 per cent annually, two times the imperial Russian average, doubling every twenty-five years. Also, the amount of allotment land in the Old Colony was fixed, with state-sanctioned Mennonite land-tenure practices expressly prohibiting the fragmentation of the normal Mennonite 65-desiatina household village landholdings to create new farmsteads.

The landless were themselves differentiated. A tiny handful of the better-off and more enterprising bought landed estates and began to prosper. About a third of the landless, those who owned their own modest home-and-garden plots with a house and a barn in the villages (the so-called Anwohner, or cottagers), dabbled in sidelines like peddling, bee-keeping, silk-worm culture, and linen-weaving, while leasing land on nearby gentry estates for sheep and cattle raising and a little grain growing. A further third, mostly cottagers as well, while doing a little farming on the side, took up teaching or engaged in crafts as smiths, cabinet builders, watch-makers, and wheelwrights. From these crafts and trades, within three decades, would spring a modern farm-implements industry.

Many of the last third of the landless, at the bottom of Old Colony society, heads often of younger families, occupied rented quarters as Einwohner and worked as day-labourers on the fields of their landed neighbours.[81] As this was the repressive age of Nicholas I and of Johann Cornies, they quietly chafed at their lot. Yet, since land-holding, status, and identity were vitally interlocked at the time, the Anwohner and Einwohner, however employed, yearned for a regular land allotment of their own that would give them the rights and station of their more fortunate landed brethren in village and settlement life.

Though Old Colony officials of the day seem to have done little to alleviate the problem, landlessness was already widely recognized as an explosive charge that needed to be defused. In 1851, the first official Old Colony history, written by the well-informed long-time Khortitsa secondary-school teacher Heinrich Heese, and published in the *Unterhaltungsblatt*, summarized the dilemma, predicting grave problems if remedies were not found:

The Mennonite is not especially quick, but he can reason and is able and persevering. He is religious according to the practices of his forbears, quiet, sober and agreeable. In general he has the quality to reach his goal under the careful guidance of his superiors. While he is short of land himself, his diligence prompts him to lease and work the steppe land of nearby estate owners, to sell agricultural products brought from near and far, and to seek a living through the sale of his smithing and woodworking outside of the settlement. But once the estate owners decide to work all of their own land, then our community will find itself in a precarious situation because of its rapid natural increase in population. The [landless] cottagers, who now earn a living in the surrounding area, will then be reduced to menial day labourers and the balance between them and the landowners will be destroyed.[82]

As a village schoolteacher, Jacob Epp presumably learned of the Judenplan project from the *Unterhaltungsblatt*, which was sent free to each school.[83] But as the architects of the scheme had foreseen, the strongly community-minded Old Colony Mennonites were at first reluctant to commit themselves to settling anywhere other than in a homogeneous Mennonite village. In 1851, however, Jacob Epp's older brother Diedrich, one of the Old Colony's best-known cabinet-makers, and three other Old Colony Mennonites were appointed state overseers in the Judenplan villages.[84] At his brother's urging, Jacob and his wife, who still felt, as he wrote, a 'deep personal aversion' to such a mixed Jewish/Mennonite settlement,[85] twice visited the Judenplan to assess prospects first-hand.

The developing settlement, surrounded by a few serf hamlets and a larger number of sizable but undeveloped landed-gentry estates, was favourably located on land well-drained by several tributary rivers and streams of the Dnieper River. Their melodious Turkic and Slavic-sounding names, Ssaksagan, Kamianka, Sheltaia, and Basavluk, appear frequently in Epp's diary. The Old Colony was only a long day's journey east by horse-drawn wagon. The provincial capital of Ekaterinoslav was about the same distance northeast. And nearby were the market towns of Sofievka and Krivoi Rog (the latter a booming industrial and iron-ore mining town from the 1880s onwards). Seventy kilometres to the southeast, lay the Dnieper port of Nikopol, slowly evolving as the main entrepôt for grain exports from the region via the Black Sea to world markets. In the 1860s and 1870s, at times of the year when the earthen roads were dry or frozen, this commercial magnet attracted a steady stream of grain-laden carts from the Judenplan and the rest of the region (see map 4, 'The Judenplan and Baratov-Shlakhtin Settlements, 1880').

Eight to nine Mennonite model-settler families lived in each of the six Jewish villages. In time, they were joined by about an equal number of poor landless Mennonite families, the bulk of whom leased agricultural land and dwellings from the Jews, and lived scattered throughout the villages. Several Mennonites were also merchants, traders, and artisans. Over the years, the Mennonite population of the Judenplan probably ranged between 100 and 160 families, from 500 to 800 people, with a total Jewish population roughly five or six times this number.[86] The possibility that such a fairly numerous Mennonite population mass would settle in the Judenplan and allow for the re-creation there of normal Old Colony Mennonite community and church life probably clinched Jacob Epp's decision to risk the move. In the spring of 1852, after negotiating a teaching position with his fellow Mennonites in the village of Novovitebsk, the Epp family settled in the Judenplan, where they were to remain for twenty-two years.[87]

Unlike conventional Old Colony–planned one-street villages, Novovitebsk had an unfamiliar configuration as a cluster village. About half a mile square, it was surrounded by pastures and fields, and running along either side of a low marshy area were two main village roads that had several side-streets branching off. Along one of these the Mennonite model settlers, including the Epps, lived clumped together as neighbours.[88] Their houses, barns, and orchards, Old Colony–style to the last detail, were on one side of the street and their gardens (the so-called upper garden) on the other.

Laboriously the Epp family dismantled and moved an implement and storage shed from the Old Colony and converted it into a dwelling. They marked off their house-and-garden plot, planted an orchard and garden, helped organize the common pastures and open fields around the newly founded village, and hand-sowed the first crops.[89] Soon, as Jacob Epp's historian nephew D.H. Epp later wrote, in each of the six Judenplan villages, to the sound of hammers and saws, the 'high, pointed gables' of the traditional Mennonite homes and barns could be seen 'towering' above the squat, two-family sod Jewish dwellings of the village.[90]

Soon also, under the guidance of Gerhard Dyck, the Khortitsa Elder, the Judenplan Mennonites organized themselves as an affiliate congregation of the Old Colony (Khortitsa) Flemish Mennonite church. Jacob Epp was elected as the first minister of the new congregation, a position he held until his death.[91] The surviving diaries cover the Epps' last two years on the Island of Khortitsa and their first year on the new settlement. There is then a regrettable six-and-a-half-year gap, until the end of 1859, when the extant diaries resume, continuing for two decades to 1880. During this undocumented period, from 1853 to 1859, presumably with his brother's assistance, Jacob Epp achieved recognition as one of the model settlers in Novovitebsk, a status later challenged by the Jewish community. He also abandoned teaching and, following in the footsteps of his illustrious father and grandfather, devoted the rest of his life to steppe agriculture and the ministry.

Mennonite life on the Judenplan deliberately followed well-trodden paths, faithfully reproducing basic Old Colony religious and community institutions and mores. Life revolved around the patriarchal family, Mennonite village schools, the church, and mutual institutions such as the Khortitsa Fire Insurance Office (Brandordnung) and the Orphans' Administration (Waisenamt). On church policy and discipline, inheritances, landlessness, relations with the state, and much else, Judenplan Mennonites invariably followed inherited practice and the lead of Old Colony religious and secular leaders. Also cementing ties to the mother settlement, notably during the early years, were close trade and business relations and frequent visits back and forth among relatives and friends.

Mirroring the ethnic and religious exclusiveness of the Mennonites was the equally isolated world of the Jews. At least during the first decades of their coexistence on the Judenplan, Jews and Mennonites, both products of East European communitarian separateness, related to one another with considerable incomprehension and only grudging tolerance. To be sure, the languages of the Yiddish-speaking Jews and Low German–speaking Mennonites were close enough to allow for relatively easy communication. Yet their separate systems of schools, religion, and inheritances, contrasting occupational orientations and dress, and pre-modern beliefs, which emphasized the need for strictly segregated living, limited their contacts considerably. Although to this day 'I-think-there-was-a-Jewish-great-grandmother-in-my-family' talk persists among a few Mennonites, Jacob Epp does not record a single close friendship or romantic or sexual liaison between a Jew and a Mennonite on the Judenplan.

Jewish and Mennonite solitudes did of necessity, however, intersect in several areas. Some Judenplan Jewish petty craftsmen and merchants leased out their dwellings and land (many to landless

Mennonites from the Old Colony), and moved to urban centres. Not surprisingly, many of the Jews remaining in the villages seem to have poured their main energies less into unfamiliar field-work than into their traditional occupations of the wool and grain trade, money-lending, shopkeeping, innkeeping (Jacob Epp's fiercest ire was reserved for Jewish liquor vendors), and crafts such as tailoring, smithing, shoemaking, saddlery, tanning, and tin-smithing. Mennonite model settlers and Old Colony landless leased some of the Jewish land thus made available and took advantage of the Jewish crafts and trades. In at least one case a Mennonite and a Jew teamed up as partners in the ownership of a mill, to the displeasure of the Mennonite villagers (and probably of the Jewish as well).

Jews and Mennonites interacted more strongly in areas where administration and landholding were intertwined. Each of the six villages constituted separate administrative and land-regulating entities. Around the villages the plough-lands of Jews and Mennonites lay intermingled in communal fields and cattle and sheep grazed on common pastures, requiring a single system of crop and fallow rotation and rules respecting the use of pastures and hay-lands. The village Jews understandably bristled at the humiliation implicit in the tutelary role assigned to Mennonite 'model farmers' as mentors. They looked for opportunities to put them in their place. Mennonites, for their part, were resentful when uncultivated or weed-choked Jewish field strips adjoined their own, or cattle of Ukrainian herdsmen on rented Jewish lands were permitted to roam over their grain and fallowed fields.

On occasion, simmering resentments erupted in conflict. Quarrels over trampled grain fields, the ownership of runaway cattle, insults made on the street, or injured cattle were routinely resolved through discussions among the parties, intervention by the religious leadership or by elected Jewish and Mennonite village officials, or de facto arbitration by the appointed overseers. As a man of probity and deep personal piety, Jacob Epp pastored his sometimes fractious parishioners as best he could, enjoining them to be honest in their dealings, respectful of differences, observant of Sunday as a day of rest, and helpful to their neighbours. This behaviour befitted them as chosen 'models' of enterprise and deportment. Otherwise, as he once reproached a Mennonite smith repairing a ploughshare on Sunday, they risked becoming a 'mockery to the Jews.'[92]

More tangled disputes involving the virtually separate Jewish and Mennonite village administrations, each with its own landowner assemblies and village leadership, were, however, less amenable to resolution. The parallel Jewish and Mennonite administrations operated tolerably well where functions were separate, as with inheritances and schools. But where a single administrative system was required, as in the regulation of plough- and pasture-lands, lines of authority easily became knotted, leading to mutual charges of capricious, even vengeful, behaviour. There were then complaints and counter-complaints on both sides, many addressed to the Guardianship Committee in Odessa. Matters reached their nadir in the early 1870s. The model settlers of the Judenplan accused the majority Jewish administration of staging confrontations and imposing harsh limitations on the number of their cattle permitted on the common grazing lands as a way of provoking their departure from the settlement.

Among several counter-measures, a two-man Judenplan Mennonite delegation, including Jacob Epp, on the longest, most exotic trip of his life, elicited from the Guardianship Committee in Odessa verbal and written guarantees of the security of tenure of their landholdings and residence. In the paternalistic bureaucratic idiom of the day, the Committee president assured the Mennonites that they 'could stay where they were forever' and urged them to 'return home and, in God's name, work diligently.'[93] Such recurring, enervating disputes over administration and land use ended finally only in the early 1880s, after the Epps had already left the Judenplan. At that time, the government ordered that the Jewish and Mennonite plough- and pasture-lands be separated physically and administratively, removing the main bone of Jewish/Mennonite contention on the Judenplan. A decade later a Mennonite observer noted that, after decades of 'maladministration,' this separation had 'released creative energies [among the Mennonites] and resulted in increased productivity.'[94] An added benefit was apparently improved relations between Jews and Mennonites.

On a personal level, the Jewish administration in the 1860s repeatedly challenged Jacob Epp's status as a model settler, saying he was the ninth in Novovitebsk, while the norm allowed only eight. The issue dragged on for years, arousing in him feelings of anger and anxiety. Finally in 1868 (his sixteenth year on the Judenplan), on the urging of his administrator brother Diedrich, he resettled in the neighbouring village of Novopodolsk where his position as model settler was uncontested.[95] There, secure in his juridical status and 40-desiatina (44-ha.) landholding, he and his family resided next door to his brother Diedrich until 1874, when they moved to the nearby, recently founded Mennonite Old Colony daughter settlement of Baratov.

Troublesome encounters between Jews and Mennonites, coupled with vague feelings of being boxed in by a different, alien world, bred inward-looking attitudes among Judenplan Mennonites. Most Mennonites also seem never to have accepted living on the Judenplan as more than a tolerable necessity. Not surprisingly, Epp and his family made plans more than once to move to an exclusively Mennonite settlement. Thus prior to settling in the Judenplan he had applied for land in the Bergthal settlement where the founding of a new village was rumoured.[96] In 1860, Russia's seizure of the Amur River basin led to the dispatch of a Mennonite delegation to explore whether a settlement for landless Mennonites could be founded in the area. Jacob and his brother Diedrich immediately declared their interest in the venture, prompting 'all' Judenplan Mennonites to do likewise.[97] Several years later, Epp came close to returning to the Old Colony to take over the 65-desiatina Wirtschaft of his second wife's aged parents.[98] And in the early 1870s, he and many other Judenplan Mennonites came within a hair of joining the large-scale Old Colony emigration to Manitoba, Canada.[99] Yet, repeatedly, resettlement proved impossible or was rejected by Jacob Epp out of a deeply felt sense of duty to his church and his community.

Contemporary assessments of the efficacy of the imperial Russian experiment of establishing Judenplan-like settlements in New Russia varied greatly. For Russian Mennonites, however, there was no ambivalence: the Judenplan became a negative example, something to be avoided. Until modernity had sunk deeper roots in their communities, Mennonites were ill-equipped to function comfortably in a pluralist multiethnic and multireligious society. Proud of their agrarian accomplishments, strongly isolationist theologically, and in consequence of their tragic martyr past, they unquestionably preferred what was still within their grasp: familiar, homogeneous, largely self-administered Mennonite settlements.

In the 1860s, Jacob Epp's insular Mennonite world was nevertheless gradually breached by powerful market forces in the region. In the early part of that decade, there was suddenly a rapid increase in export wheat prices, which remained high throughout the 1860s and 1870s. A simultaneous downturn in the international wool market led agriculturalists to cut their sheep and cattle stocks to a minimum. In fact, in Jacob Epp's village of Novopodolsk, all villagers, Jews and Mennonites alike, sold off their entire, now unremunerative, sheep flocks in 1871.[100] This definitive action lopped off a branch of the village economy that had given Mennonites productive diversity and a ready source of cash income since the earliest settlement. Gone, too, was a slower-paced way of life and a vivid imagery, the pastoral biblical good shepherd protecting his sheep from a fractured landscape and the ravaging wolf.

High grain prices triggered a ploughing spree, a veritable revolution in tillage practices that transformed the face of New Russia in two decades.[101] For example, in 1852 Jacob Epp seeded only about five desiatinas to crops (one-eighth of his 40-desiatina allotment), the rest being in pasture- and hay-land.[102] Over the following decade, he tripled the area under cultivation, doubling it once again during the decade thereafter. By the early 1870s, he was cultivating and fallowing well over thirty desiatinas (33 ha.), around 75 per cent of his total land allotment,[103] a proportion that would remain relatively constant thereafter. From time to time, he also rented or share-cropped Jewish land in the Judenplan, and for several years ploughed around forty desiatinas, a huge area given the labour-intensive technology used.

Yet this dramatic expansion of plough-land, under favourable market conditions, had surprisingly contradictory results. Family work-loads rose steeply and life became more harried without apparently providing commensurate financial rewards. Seemingly better off than the bulk of Ukrainian and Jewish villagers in the area, the Epps nevertheless remained poor, often close to the subsistence margin and desperate for the cash needed for taxes and basic household necessities. Thus, on more than one occasion, cattle diseases, which periodically cut deeply into the Epps' stock of horses, milk cows, and beef cattle, threatened to plunge the household into crisis.

More efficient ploughs, mechanical reapers and threshers, fanning mills, and oil presses were already available from developing farm-implement enterprises in Khortitsa. But, with little capital and still at an early stage of farm mechanization, Judenplan Mennonites only slowly changed their labour-intensive techniques of ploughing, seeding, and harvesting, which remained family-centred. To be sure, the one-shared plough gave place to the three-shared plough, but seed was still cast by hand. At harvest-time, family groups of hand-mowers swinging cradle scythes could be seen cutting, hand-tying, and stooking sheaves of grain in ever expanding fields, often to the point of exhaustion.

Spacious Mennonite ladder wagons were used to cart the dried sheaves to the village. There they were either stored in outbuildings for fall threshing or laid out on the reaping floor in the yard and immediately threshed by threshing stone. This horse-drawn, drum-shaped, seven-ridged stone contrivance, revolving around a central axle, was rolled over the grain stalks. Thumping on flattened ridge after flattened ridge, it freed kernel from husk, and though slow and laborious, it represented a great advance over the flail or horses' hoofs, its recent predecessors. To separate grain and chaff, the Epps used a modern, hand-turned fanning mill. During several better crop years, Jacob Epp hired Ukrainian day-labourers at season's peak, but remained confused about both the intricacies and the potential advantages and pitfalls of an unfamiliar and volatile labour market. To conserve precious moisture, fallowing became more general and the Epps even resorted to the novelty of compressing newly seeded fields with rollers.

Throughout the 1860s and 1870s there were low average yields, with one year in three a crop failure. Rainfall and snow on the south Ukrainian steppe, averaging from 28 to 45 centimetres, was normally variable and uncertain, but during these decades problems were compounded by a streak of abnormally poor weather. Like Job himself no stranger to adversity, Jacob Epp repeatedly notes how germination was impeded by early drought, how tender grain stalks were damaged by late frosts, and how spring hopes dissipated in summer's scorching heat. Further contributing to weak outputs were the already mentioned problems of Jewish agriculture such as weeds and trampled crops and accompanying uncertainties. Finally, the frantic drive to maximize plough-land with largely fixed resources of draught power and family labour led to corner cutting, poor

Mennonite tillage practices including hasty and shallow ploughing, and inadequate harrowing and weed control,[104] practices ended only in the 1880s.

It should be remembered, however, that despite the much-accelerated workday tempo in the 1860s and 1870s, and the need to adapt to change, rhythms of life clung largely to inherited patterns. Little in Jacob Epp's everyday experience, other than its accelerated pace, was novel or unfamiliar. The year still followed the crop cycle, the reassuring succession of seasons, and the church calendar.[105] The hard but relatively short New Russian winters usually allowed storm-windows, emblems of season's change, to be removed in late February or early March. At that time, sheep and cattle were let out to graze on village pastures and ploughing and seeding of grain fields began. To optimize germination, plough-lands for the spring grains were prepared at breakneck speed, compressed into a period of two or three weeks. This difficult, and increasingly hurried, field-work coincided with lambing time. Until sheep breeding ended in the early 1870s, the Epps kept from forty to sixty sheep. They monitored their birthing closely, careful to avoid losses from sudden temperature drops. As days grew longer and warmer in late May, the sheep were shorn and the wool sold to a local Jew or to a Mennonite merchant in Khortitsa.

In the agricultural cycle, between the fever-paced phases of seed-time and harvest, May and June were a less hurried interval. In that time, the Epps joined in communal tasks like repairing the dam enclosing the watering pond, smoothing roads rutted by the spring breakup, or digging a village well. They also planted and weeded their kitchen garden, pruned their fruit and berry orchard, and planted potato and melon patches, the latter often in communal fields. For winter fuel, sheep dung was cured and barn manure mixed with old straw, spread out, cut into briquette squares, laid out in the yard to dry, and then stacked and stored. In the last weeks of June, pre-harvest preparations often concluded with haying, repairs to buildings and implements, and the purchase in Ukrainian villages of young pigs for fattening. Also in late June, in their free time, Jacob Epp, his wife, and younger children anxiously toured the grain fields on horse-drawn wagon to gauge harvest prospects.

Between the busy periods of seed-time and harvest, the slower-paced May/June hiatus was also a time of more active church, community, and family life. As the diaries show, Jacob Epp had to fit his time-consuming and unpaid ministerial duties around farm work schedules. Until the Judenplan church was built in Novovitebsk in 1862, weekly Sunday services were held in homes in two or three villages on a rotating basis. From 1862 onwards, the new, unheated church was closed for winter and multiple house services resumed. The church reopened in spring. In the weeks leading up to Easter Sunday and Pentecost, it throbbed with activity as Jacob Epp and his associates taught the eighteen- and nineteen-year-old baptismal candidates the question-and-answer Mennonite catechism. In the first decade of the settlement, Mennonite youth had travelled to the Old Colony for baptism. Thereafter, preparations culminated in the solemn observances of baptism and communion in the Novovitebsk church, the focal point of social interaction. They were conducted by the Khortitsa Elder (with the help of the local ministers) around Eastertime or Pentecost (that is, from late April to the end of May). Marking the climax of the church calendar, these observances solemnly affirmed the historical legacy and spiritual unity of the community and its collective identity.

The May/June interval also witnessed longer, annual family trips to the Old Colony, lasting up to a week. There the Epps made the rounds of their relatives and friends, looked up kinfolk enrolled in the Zentralschule, sold or bartered wool and butter, shopped for household essentials, and occasionally took a side-trip to Ekaterinoslav (see map 3). From time to time, Jacob Epp was invited to preach a Sunday sermon in the Khortitsa mother church. Catching up on Old Colony news, directives, and gossip, he not infrequently consulted the Elder and his ministerial colleagues about new or disputed church policies and difficult cases of Judenplan discipline. For him there was also important business to conduct on behalf of parishioners with the Waisenamt or with the Khortitsa Fire Insurance Office.

In the early years of the daughter-colony movement, in the late 1860s and early 1870s, during the May/June pause and then again in fall, Jacob Epp visited recently founded Molochna and Old Colony daughter colonies within a fifty-kilometre radius of the Judenplan. These included the Molochna Kleine Gemeinde settlement of Borosenko and the Khortitsa settlements of Nepluiev, Baratov, and Shlakhtin. In the Khortitsa settlements he helped organize regular church life, adjudicated cases of church discipline, and assisted the Elder and other church officials in conducting the rituals of baptism and communion.

Harvest-time, the most hectic season of the agricultural year, began at the end of June, when the threshing floor was smoothed and hardened. Depending on the luck of weather and yield, the harvest usually took a few weeks, but it could also stretch into September. With all Epps on deck, the fields of rye, wheat, barley, oats, and millet were scythed in turn. Stone-threshing on the outdoor threshing floor usually proceeded simultaneously, though in bumper years wagon-loads of sheaves were also stored for barn-threshing in fall. In years when roofs were in need of repairs, the rye was harvested by flail to save the straw for thatch. On rainy days, Jacob Epp had the mowers turn the fanning mill, separating grain from chaff in the barn or driving shed, measure out and sack the cleaned grain, and carry it up the stairs on to the roomy storehouse attic of the house (where the grain served also as insulation). During harvest-time, Epp's wife and younger children also weeded the vegetable garden and picked and dried apples, plums, and cherries. In late July or early August, as field crops matured, the Jacob Epps joined other villagers in hiring a Ukrainian watchman to guard their melon and potato patches.

Carting the grain to market – in the 1850s, east to Khortitsa, and thereafter, south to export markets via the Dnieper River port of Nikopol – was basically a fall activity. It started with summer's passage in late August, continued briskly in September and October on days when roads were dry enough to permit travel, and finished off in winter-time after the onset of frost. Most Judenplan Mennonites, including Jacob Epp and his older sons, carted their own sacked grain to Nikopol in five-chetvert (30-bushel) wagon or sled loads. Smaller quantities were sold locally, and grain needed at home for flour or fodder was ground in local Judenplan grist and flour treadmills.

In September the Epps ploughed and seeded two or three desiatinas to winter rye and cultivated the fallow field for the last time. Potatoes, melons, and fruits were now harvested and stored and the storm doors and windows put in. Thanksgiving was celebrated in church in early October. Communal pasturing usually ended early in November, when the sheep of the individual villagers were separated out and stabled in their pens. Pig butchering, a co-operative and sociable endeavour among relatives and neighbours, was done with the onset of cold weather in late October or early November.

Fall and then early spring were tax-paying times, and habitually cash-poor Jacob Epp often had no choice but to supplement his husbandman's income. His sons hired out occasionally for field-work and did odd jobs and some cartage, while he himself earned a little extra as a local glazier, by keeping the books at village auction sales, and by doing some record-keeping for his administrator brother Diedrich. The sale of a little butter in Sofievka, Krivoi Rog, and Khortitsa provided pin money. From time to time, during a second major family trip to Khortitsa in fall, usually in September, he also received small gifts from kinfolk in Ekaterinoslav and the Old Colony to help him over a subsistence crisis or to pay his taxes and local communal dues. There were then also other trips to the Old Colony and nearby settlements for business and family visits.

The first frosts followed by snow heralded the end of heavy field-work for horses and men and the start of the social season. A less-strenuous farm routine and good sledding tracks between the villages fostered visiting back and forth. The Eigenheim Epps have preserved memories of matriarch Judith Epp, Jacob's second wife, after the morning service on a wintry Sunday, standing at the front window, counting approaching guests before setting the table for the noontime meal.[106] Christmas was still a simple church celebration, without lavish feasting and the exchange of gifts. Only towards the end of the 1870s does the local school introduce the novelty of a Christmas program – a village sensation – replete with sweets for the children and a decorated tree. Toward winter's close, in early February, Jacob Epp and his ministerial colleagues completed their yearly round of public duties by half-day, usually rather perfunctory, inspections of each of the Judenplan Mennonite village schools. Despite the quickening pace of daily life and the appearance of secular trends, the church and its leadership continued to assert their central role in daily family and community life.

While the annual rhythms of agrarian life continued to be set by the agricultural year, the succession of the generations – the life cycle –

from the nuptials of the parents through the founding of new households by their adult married children and on into old age, helped mould broader community patterns. The family remained the primary economic, social, and welfare unit of Mennonite society. Its development was fundamentally shaped by demographic patterns and marriage practices. In the Mennonite world of the 1860s and 1870s marriage was still for most persons early and virtually universal, making for an extended period of parental fertility. Annual birth rates of 5 to 6 per cent and death rates of 2 to 3 per cent, both high (as was infant mortality), resulted in a yearly population growth of around 3 per cent.

Jacob Epp provides an illuminating demographic profile of his community, his diaries for the 1860s and 1870s including birth and death data for 230 members of his community, family, and circle of friends, recorded at the time of their funerals. Analysis shows that around a third of this number were infants who died during the first three years of life. The average age at death of the entire sample group was nineteen years. For the two-thirds who survived infancy, life expectancy was still only thirty-four years. Within this latter group, persons from age three to age ten and then again those in their forties, fifties and sixties died in large and about equal numbers. This chilling fact of frequent deaths across many of these age categories (with substantially lower rates for persons in their teens, twenties, and thirties) was background to Jacob Epp's often-expressed distress over the likelihood of his own early demise.

The demographic experience of Jacob Epp's parental family and of his own family mirrors that of his community. His father David, who had been widowed and remarried, fathered a total of nineteen children, thirteen of whom survived infancy.[107] Of these, eleven reached adulthood. A half-brother remained a bachelor, an extremely rare exception in Mennonite society, to judge by the diaries of both father David and son Jacob. The remaining ten wed (three of these who lost their spouses remarried) and, on average, sired families of ten children each, six of whom survived their third birthday. Jacob Epp, like his father, lost his first wife and remarried, the second time to a woman a decade his junior. Over a period of thirty years he fathered fifteen children, eleven of whom reached adulthood.[108]

The growth and development of Jacob Epp's family was the main goad to his relentless, often valiant, struggle to earn a simple living. A first child, a daughter, was born shortly after Jacob and Maria Epp moved to Khortitsa Island in 1844. Eight years later, when the Epps moved from their crowded Island teacherage and schoolhouse to their 40-desiatina virgin allotment on the Judenplan, it was to provide for their growing family of now four young children, aged one to eight years. A fifth child, who suffered a crib death, lay buried in the Khortitsa Island village cemetery. Over the next eleven years, from 1852 until the death of Maria from tuberculosis in March 1863, the Epps had a further five children. The last, an hour-old infant Margaretha, predeceased her mother by less than two weeks.

Thus in 1863, at the age of forty-two, Jacob Epp found himself a widower, poor, burdened with the cares of his ministerial office and responsible for his eight motherless children, aged two to eighteen. (The eighteen-year-old was a bride of only half a year.) In his diary, in moving detail, he grieved and lamented his loss.[109] At the same time, following Mennonite inheritance practices, he chose guardians to represent the interests of his children. They, together with village and church officials, under the authority of the Khortitsa Orphans' Administration (Waisenamt), met to draw up an inventory of the pitifully modest Epp property and to help in the division of half of the estate, his wife's share (according to unique Mennonite inheritance practices that were enforceable through the courts), equally among the eight children. During the weeks of his wife's grave illness and then during his bereavement, one witnesses the clearly articulated roles of family and community intertwining in myriad ways.

Within three months of his wife's death, on 25 June 1863, Jacob Epp entered into a second marriage with Judith Dyck, a thirty-year-old devout spinster from an Old Colony ministerial family in the village of Neuosterwick. In cases of this kind, where the death of a parent left behind a large family with infant children, early remarriages were not uncommon. Yet the decision to marry, in this case, for both parties, must have been a difficult one. Judith Dyck's mother had a long history of mental illness, and it is likely that the daughter had put off marriage for so long herself in order to care for her. One can, in any case, only regret that the six detailed pages of Epp's diary chronicling the period of his courtship and remarriage, from 12 May to 2 July 1863, are missing. According to family lore, they were neatly scissored out in later life by wife Judith, sensitive to the delicacy of their contents.

Surviving in the family records, however, is a letter from Jacob Epp to Judith Dyck offering a rare glimpse of the moment of betrothal. Dated 11 June 1863, and written in his Novovitebsk home, it was, as befitted the circumstances, matter-of-fact in tone. 'I am pleased,' Jacob writes, 'that you have decided to become my companion.' It is God's will 'that a person should not be alone.' With a clear but worried eye to the imminent harvest and the needs of his young children, he urged haste in the engagement and marriage: 'Now is an opportune moment. I would therefore ask you to keep our matter as short as possible since I cannot be away from home for long, as you yourself can see.' He proposed an absence from home of no more than a week, planning to arrive on a Thursday, to celebrate their engagement on Saturday ('But try to keep it simple, to avoid needless expenses.'), to be wed on Tuesday, and to arrive back at the Judenplan the following Thursday. If possible, he suggested, some of their siblings should be present from the time of his arrival, to act, so to speak, as chaperons. In that way, he and his bride would be able to see one another before the nuptials, 'which otherwise we would have to forego.' He concluded on a softer, more intimate, note: 'Give your parents my kindest regards, and I greet you in heartfelt love.'[110] The small wedding, on the eve of the harvest, conducted by Elder Gerhard Dyck, took place in the bride's parents' home. Jacob Epp seemed well satisfied to have found a devoted mother for his bereaved young children and a deeply religious, kindly, and hard-working partner for himself.

After abandoning their initial intention to move and take possession of her parents' 65-desiatina Wirtschaft in the Old Colony village of Neuosterwick[111] (which was probably intended to permit Judith to continue caring for her sick mother), the newly married couple settled into Judenplan life. Within a little more than a year, their first child was born, and over the following decade four more followed, two of whom died in childhood. At the time of the birth of their last child Johann in December 1874, Judith Epp was forty-three years old. Jacob Epp was fifty-four. Thirty years had passed since the birth of his first child. By the mid-1870s the completed family numbered eleven children, consisting of five daughters and six sons. Three sons and two daughters from his first marriage were already married and at various stages in the development of their own families. Jacob Epp thus had children who were younger than some of his grandchildren, a not uncommon situation of complex relationships in his largely pre-modern society marked by many early deaths.

The marriage and formation of new families by his children was one of the chief dynamics in Jacob Epp's later life. As his children came of age, their decisions regarding wedlock were shaped by the courtship and marriage practices of their larger Mennonite community. These seemed to have changed relatively little over two generations. For his own generation, the average age at first marriage of Jacob Epp, his siblings, and their spouses was 20.3 years for women and 23.2 for men.[112] Comparable figures for his parishioners, a generation later, are only slightly higher, 21.6 years for brides and 23.65 for grooms at the time of first marriage.[113] Jacob Epp's own eleven children and their spouses married, on average, at 21.7 years of age for women and 24.2 for men.[114] These specific averages, over two generations, approximate one another and are also remarkably close to the mean age at first marriage for the Orthodox population of the central regions of the Empire in the mid-1880s.[115] This correlation suggests, perhaps, a broader East European pattern.[116] In all cases, family and community controls over courtship and marriage remained strong.

Despite close ties with the Old Colony, the preponderance of Judenplan Mennonites married within their immediate community, accenting a growing insularity. Only one of the Epp children, for instance, a teacher, Peter, found his bride in a Khortitsa village.[117] Marriages into the more distant Molochna settlement were very rare, although one of Jacob Epp's half-sisters had done so.[118] Marriage proposals, delivered personally or through an intermediary, reflecting a freedom of personal choice, were not infrequently rejected. When successful, they were followed within a week by the engagement festivities. These, too, were becoming more varied in form. The nuptials were usually a few days later.

During his thirty-eight-year ministry, Jacob Epp officiated at 191 weddings. About 70 per cent of these were first marriages for bride and groom alike. Timing followed the agricultural year and was highly patterned. Over 60 per cent of first-time marriages were held during the slower-paced winter months of October, November, December, and January, when farm work was less demanding and the roads passable. Another 10 per cent took place in June, in the interval between the intensive periods of spring field-work and summer harvest. There were almost no first weddings during the rasputitsa, the spring and fall 'seasons of bad roads,' and in times of heavy agricultural work. Around two-thirds of the weddings were held on Sundays in the Novovitebsk church, immediately following the service or in the afternoons. The remaining third, following long-time traditions, took place on Tuesday or Thursday afternoons, usually in the home of the bride.

The timing for marriages in which at least one of the partners was a widow or widower was more random throughout the year, however. Three out of every ten marriages conducted by Jacob Epp were of this kind. They were often deemed emergencies, especially where motherless children were involved, and followed their own rules. Moreover, in the Epp sampling, one and a half times as many widowers remarried as did widows, and almost half the widowers who remarried wed previously unwed brides. Wedlock between a widow and a bachelor, by contrast, while not unheard of, was fairly unusual.[119] Marriages between widows and widowers seem to have been most common in periods immediately following a major epidemic, such as cholera or other rampant disease in the Judenplan.[120] The end result was often quite complicated 'step' and 'foster' relationships throughout Mennonite society. These generated their share of heartbreak, tension, conflicts, and abuse, causing Jacob Epp, in his pastoral calling, no end of trouble. Through kinship ties, neighbourly networks, and the formal Mennonite church and civic village and district institutions, the community played a supportive, mediatory, and disciplinary role in all such family relationships.

As his large family came of age, Jacob Epp, like other Mennonites in the Old Colony and the Judenplan, was also forced to grapple with the problem of livelihoods for his children. Landlessness among Russian Mennonites, including Judenplan families, was, after all, a recurring phenomenon. This was the logical result of the patterns just described: early first marriages, high birth rates, presumably slowly falling death rates, and a ban on property divisions. Growing out of Mennonite land tenure and inheritance practices, there was also a pattern of the nuclear family. Newlyweds, after gaining a six-month-to-a-year start in the parental Sommerstube, founded new households. Complex, multigenerational households were very rare.[121]

To prepare his numerous progeny for an uncertain future, which until the late 1860s and early 1870s one assumed would be as landless individuals, Jacob Epp had several of them attend secondary school in the Old Colony[122] and try their hand at village schoolteaching.[123] For other of his children he arranged apprenticeships in carpentry, cabinet-making, and wagon construction, or encouraged his sons-in-law in such trades. Except for one son who took up teaching as a lifetime occupation, all his children came to depend for their subsistence principally on agriculture. The building trades, however, were an important subsidiary occupation for many members of his family.[124]

By the late 1860s and early 1870s, a number of his children were married and had started their own families or were reaching marriageable age. At first Jacob Epp helped them pursue their trades and rent land and accommodations from Jews in the Judenplan. He also shared his implements and draught animals with them and, on occasion, negotiated share-crop arrangements with Jewish villagers on their behalf.[125] Then, however, came the great watershed in the history of Mennonite colonization in Russia as the Molochna and Old Colony administrations launched their daughter-colony movement. Starting in the late 1860s, the Old Colony administration established several multi-village settlements on leased or purchased gentry estates within a 40-kilometre radius of the Judenplan. These included the settlements of Nepluiev, Baratov, and Shlakhtin.[126] A number of private Mennonite khutors and estates were also established in the area.

Under these altered circumstances, Jacob Epp assisted several of his married children to acquire land, construct dwellings and barns, and otherwise pioneer new villages. These were, first of all, in the lease-land Nepluiev settlement[127] and then, later, in the nearby four-village Baratov-Shlakhtin settlement purchased by the Old Colony for its landless. The landless included the Anwohner of the Judenplan.[128] Many migrants from the Molochna settlement to its recently founded, large daughter settlement of Zagradovka[129] also passed through the Judenplan. Thus, within a few years of the start of the daughter-colony movement, numerous landless Mennonite families from the Judenplan, Khortitsa, and Molochna settlements could be seen travelling the rutted, dusty roads around the Judenplan on their way to their new abodes. Herding caravans of livestock, they had their long dust-encrusted ladder wagons heaped high with implements, household belongings, and children.

In 1872, observing this phenomenon and with the gift of accurate observation and prophecy, Jacob Epp wrote: 'Members of our Mennonite community seem to be scattering themselves to all parts of Russia.'[130] Two years later, Epp and his family moved from the Judenplan themselves, joining his married children on a virgin farmstead in the nearby Baratov settlement village of Gnadenthal. In his fifty-fourth year he thus faced the difficulties of a new pioneer start. But it was his own place in a new Mennonite settlement – the fulfilment of a lifetime dream.

The recurring rhythms of the agrarian year and of the generational cycle, given direction by his Mennonite community and church, thus filled Jacob Epp's life with familiar markers and themes. These, however, stood in sharp contrast to a series of already mentioned major changes, sharp discontinuities, which he and his co-religionists experienced at the same time. Among these none were more significant than the problems of landlessness and religious dissent. Long ignored and held in check, these flared into crisis in the 1860s. Then, during the 1870s, government-initiated administrative and military reforms triggered a mass migration to North America of a quarter to a third of all Russian Mennonites. The words 'confusion,' 'troubles,' 'divisions,' and 'disorders' have been applied to this era of Russian Mennonite history. It has also been called an age of 'innovation' and 'reform,' a bracing era of fundamental adjustment that set Mennonite society on a course of development that persisted until the end of the Empire. This adaptation arguably permitted Russian Mennonites to accommodate themselves to important challenges of modernity without having to jettison essential facets of their religious and temporal community life.

Powerful forces, of varied provenance, were at work throughout the 1860s and 1870s. Mennonite society, which was slowly undergoing social and economic differentiation, was itself riven with latent social and ideological conflicts. Economically, the previously described quickening of market forces stimulated a frenzy of land ploughing and the enthronement of grain growing and marketing for an international clientele as the dominant productive activity of

Mennonite villagers. Penetrating Mennonite society from the German-speaking world were dynamic pietistical and evangelical influences of a highly personal and activist religious bent. But in the 1860s and 1870s, the state itself, through Empire-wide reforms of landholding relations, local administration, and the judicial and military systems, was the most direct and significant stimulus to change.

Known collectively as the Great Reforms, these pivotal state initiatives marked the single greatest watershed in imperial Russian history.[131] The regime of Alexander II, its self-confidence and sense of legitimacy corroded by the Crimean War defeat of 1856, and fearing peasant unrest, set out to recover its poise and great-power status through the establishment of a new conservative domestic stability. Spearheading the program of renovation, which began with the serf emancipation in 1861, were a small group of reform-minded bureaucrats from various ministries,[132] including several individuals who knew the Mennonites well. Moreover, during the first decade of Alexander's reign, from 1855 to 1865, a relaxation of censorship, a period of veritable 'glasnost' (a term then broadly used), fostered wide-ranging discussion of controversial public issues in the press and journals.[133]

A handful of Mennonites were awakened to new prospects of reform by this probing atmosphere, which was mediated through the monthly *Unterhaltungsblatt*, visitors, and daily developments. The direction that reform might take was, moreover, suggested by principles that, at least initially, underlay the Great Reforms. Imperial reformers of the time tagged landlessness as a social evil productive of a revolutionary proletariat. They trumpeted local authority, resting on broad participation, as the solution to maladministration. Equal justice was demanded for all. The Russian reformers' agendas included demands for better schooling, recognition of public opinion as a legitimate social force, and greater receptivity to ideas from abroad, including Germany.[134]

The authoritarian style of governance, first questioned and then modified in St Petersburg, had difficulty maintaining itself in the Mennonite world. There it had sunk deep roots as well, especially in the Molochna settlement, under Johann Cornies and his successors. But reformist stirrings in the Mennonite world seemed to point in various directions. Hesitantly and then with greater confidence, individual Mennonites and groups began to point to irregularities in administration and chided the clergy for presiding over what they called a religion of dead formalism. The poor and voiceless, reform-minded Mennonites averred, were being beggared by the landholding cream of society. Challenged in specific areas, Mennonite religious and administrative élites adopted a defensive posture and dug in, asserting their traditional authority with considerable harshness.[135] Yet once unleashed, the reform wave alerted persons like Jacob Epp to basic issues of social justice, spiritual identity, religious pluralism, and Mennonite relations with the larger imperial Russian world.

Within a short time, it became clear that simple traditional religious practices and sensibilities were incapable of meeting the needs of a more dynamic political, economic, and educational environment. Initially, the main Mennonite carriers of religious innovation were teachers, merchants, proto-industrialists, and estate owners – products of the Mennonite Zentralschulen, Cornies-styled administration and an expanding economy. More educated and experienced in dealing with the non-Mennonite world, they were strongly attuned to stirrings beyond their settlement boundaries. Within their own communities they became critical of what they saw as a declining morality marked by unseemly behaviour and excessive feasting and imbibing at wedding and holiday celebrations, drunkenness and sexual laxity at local and regional fairs, strict formalism in worship, and an indifferent, or purely formalistic, church discipline. A number joined in circles, or conventicles, for mutual edification, religious growth, and moral betterment through Bible study and prayer.[136]

The reform-minded stratum, by and large, seemed to share a desire to recover something of the evangelical vision of their founder, Menno Simons, as well as to realize the activist goals of contemporary German pietism in its north German Baptist and south German Württembergian manifestations. Mediated to Russian Mennonites through tracts, books, volumes of sermons, missionary journals, mission festivals, and visiting revivalist ministers, pietism was outward looking. It stood for a more thoroughgoing personal renewal and an openness to the external world religiously. At the movement's centre was also an unbending moral puritanism.[137]

Mennonites sharing a broad orientation to religious and moral change eventually found themselves in three broadly defined camps. First, a small minority, almost exclusively in the Molochna settlement, in an exotic deviation, embraced the rationalistic outlook of the socially reformist Christian Templer movement of south Germany. Finally breaking away almost entirely from their Mennonite community theologically and physically, Templer adherents resettled to the Caucasus foothills region or emigrated to Palestine. They thus largely disappeared as a factor from Russian Mennonite history.[138] Second were the majority of the reformers, many of them teachers and even ministers, often with kinship or other ties to Mennonite leadership circles. Many in this group were exponents of an earlier, seemingly more dated, quietist variant of pietism. They tended to remain in the established Mennonite Frisian and Flemish churches as a 'ginger' group, a leaven, working organically for basic changes. Jacob Epp and his siblings may be seen as belonging to this second group.

A third group, more alienated from the dominant leadership and perhaps more individualized, comprised more zealous religious reformers. As activists they demanded a new and purified church consisting only of the 'personally redeemed.' As breakaways from the established churches, they founded the separatist Mennonite Brethren church, which required an individual, emotional conversion, a spiritual 'rebirth,' as a condition to membership. Rebaptism or baptism by immersion, a Baptist borrowing, became its abiding symbol. The Brethren, committed to abstinence from the use of tobacco and alcohol under pain of church discipline, restricted communion to the like-hearted, 'since believers can have no communion with unbelievers.' Conventionally Mennonite in their basic theology, however, the Brethren embraced the main tenets of Menno Simons, adhering, for instance, to the principles of pacifism and to the making of a simple affirmation in court in place of an oath.[139]

The storm surrounding the Brethren movement broke in January 1860, when eighteen pietistically minded Molochna Mennonite teachers and merchants issued a detailed indictment of the established churches.[140] An act of sectarian withdrawal, the document triggered a decade of tumult. Like-minded Mennonites in the Old Colony, under German Baptist influence, quickly joined the Brethren movement.[141] Early on, the small group divided over the issue of charismatic exuberance (shouted exclamations and the beating of drums and tambourines were common at services), before settling into more conventional habits of ritual expression.

In an attempt to reimpose ecclesiastical unity, church and civic officials in the Molochna and Old Colony settlements resorted to the religious ban, corporal punishment, imprisonment, and the threat of exile from the settlements. Through appeals to sympathizers among the Mennonite leadership and to reforming state officials in St Petersburg, the Brethren ultimately succeeded in having their group legally recognized as a bona fide Mennonite church.[142]

Jacob Epp observed the troubled Brethren movement closely through family and church contacts in the Old Colony and was at first equivocal in his attitude towards them. As a devout Christian moralist himself, he found much of their critique of Mennonite society echoing serious reservations of his own. He also pointedly rejected persecution of the Brethren by church and settlement leaders as a violation of the principles of Christian tolerance and love.[143] Yet after a difficult inner personal struggle, he concluded that the Brethren were deluded for breaking away. Theirs was, he said, the sin of pride.

Strengthening his negative judgment were adverse personal encounters with the Brethren church, which he records. During its early existence, the movement grew slowly. Not until 1888 was an affiliate of the Brethren church established in the Judenplan.[144] But already in the early 1860s, Brethren tried to missionize among his parishioners, under the forceful leadership of Aron Lepp, a state-employed Judenplan Mennonite village overseer. Lepp had joined the Brethren soon after its formation and later served as a prominent Old Colony Mennonite Brethren Elder.[145] In several run-ins with new proselytes and encounters with Lepp, Jacob Epp found himself being harshly typecast as a faithless shepherd leading his charges astray. Such allegations, often delivered in a bumptious tone, Epp experienced as deeply perplexing and wounding.[146] In the mid-1860s, the Guardianship Committee in Odessa relieved Lepp of his job because of his proselytizing activities, in all likelihood at the prompting of the Old Colony leadership. Thereafter sectarian controversy in the Judenplan area seemed gradually to subside.

At a deeper level, however, Epp's early ambivalence and later opposition to the Brethren seem also to have been rooted in his intense discomfort with aspects of the tone and content of Brethren piety. A man of resolute sobriety and decorum himself, Epp was offended by the assertiveness and emotionalism of much of the early Brethren movement. Equally, he felt out of step with the self-confident triumphalism of the Brethren neo-pietism of his day, with its tendency to believe that man could personally achieve ultimate certainty about his eternal salvation, and should exult in that knowledge.

Epp's contrary views reflected a mixture of traditional Mennonite theological understandings and earlier, more quietist, modes of pietist perception, based on the views of his father during the 1820s and 1830s. To his mind, Brethren triumphalism was the fruit of egregious pride. It violated God's ultimate sovereignty, belied one's own experiences of imperfection and failure, and undercut the very basis of a muscular Christian ethic – the need to struggle and to strive in order finally to enter heaven's narrow portals. Indeed, although not always consistent in his views, he was inclined to see the labour of faith, attended by lingering apprehensions, continuing until one's own death. This conviction was movingly reflected in his description of his first wife's death struggle and in the record of his own last days.[147]

The provocatively bold dissent of the Brethren undoubtedly encouraged the ventilation of other grievances in Mennonite society, including those of the landless majority. The Brethren and landless movements were not identical, to be sure, but they interacted in various, complex ways that await more nuanced study. What is clear, however, is that authority, questioned in the area of religious thought and experience, gradually came under attack more broadly and that at least part of the Brethren leadership, in its early years, supported the movement of the landless (as was also the case of the Mennonite leadership of the Templer movement). What is also true is that years of conflict in the Molochna settlement, which coincided with the Brethren tempest, eventually led to a resolution of the landless issue.

In the Molochna settlement in the early 1860s, general hopes for land reform combined with a series of crop failures and the abrupt loss of extensive rental lands in the surrounding area to transform the issue of widespread landlessness into a crisis of sheer economic survival for numerous households.[148] In the early 1860s, spokesmen for the landless pleaded with local officials to distribute existing unallocated public lands in the settlement to landless cottagers. This land totalled about a quarter of the entire Molochna area.

Rebuffed, the cottagers and renters then flooded the Guardianship Committee in Odessa and the St Petersburg Ministry of State Domains with petitions in a tightening spiral of social and political protest. Appealing equally to the principles of Mennonite religious brotherhood and of the Great Reforms, the landless leadership drafted proposals, organized mass meetings, and mobilized the support of some influential Mennonite merchants and landholders (including Johann Cornies's influential son-in-law Philip Wiebe) with government contacts in St Petersburg.[149]

Crown land in New Russia was in short supply at the time, and the government, under sharp nationalist attack for favouring its German-speaking population, insisted the issue be resolved without additional state land grants. Thrown back upon their own resources, and deeply divided, the Mennonite landed minority and landless majority fought over approaches. At one extreme was the notion of directing part of the landless stratum permanently into the crafts and trades while reducing the others to a rural quasi-proletariat working the fields of their landed co-religionists. At the other extreme was the socially radical idea of redistributing all allotment and reserve lands – perhaps even periodically – in the Mennonite settlements equally among all landed and landless families, both Anwohner and Einwohner households. Periodic repartition of allotment land was a common practice in Russian and Ukrainian villages.[150]

In the late 1860s and early 1870s, state mediation and arbitration of the dispute led finally to a strategic compromise of great historic significance. To remedy the political imbalance between the landed and landless populations, a limited franchise in village and settlement affairs was extended to Molochna householders without land. The key problem, landlessness, was addressed through decisive measures. Full landholders were granted permission to retain their 65-desiatina holdings, but also allowed to divide them in two, creating a small category of half-holders. Additionally, well over half of the unallocated land was distributed equally in 12-desiatina allotments among the large mass of landless cottagers. This brought into being a numerous class of energetic smallholders, whose livelihoods from the crafts and trades could now be supplemented by part-time agriculture on their own fields.

Until the reforms of the 1860s, the traditional Mennonite system of indivisible 65-desiatina household allotments had maintained a strong class of agriculturalists as the backbone of the Mennonite economy. Moreover, Mennonite inheritance practices (where husbands and wives co-owned their landed property as peers and inheritances were divided equally among all surviving sons and daughters) tempered the polarizing tendencies of this system. Upon the death of a landholder, a child or outsider purchased the undivided property at a family or village auction. The proceeds of such sale were merged with the other assets of an inheritance and distributed equally among the heirs.

This combination of indivisible landholdings and equal division of monetized inheritances had the effect of preserving viable agrarian household economies while diffusing wealth broadly within families. The result was the release of great capital-backed entrepreneurial energy, channelled into agriculture, the crafts, and trades. This partly accounted for the striking success of the Mennonite economy from the 1830s to 1850s. The grievous long-term flaw in this system, however, was its insensitivity to population increases under premodern conditions where the economy remained essentially agrarian. This led ultimately to the already noted sizable population of landless families, their gradual impoverishment and social polarization culminating in class warfare.

To remedy this serious deficiency, the crowning piece of the agrarian reform of the 1860s, an imperial decree, ruled that the Molochna Mennonite community would henceforward be corporately responsible for providing existing and new generations of landless households with access to land. This was to be accomplished through the establishment of daughter settlements on purchased land. To help fund the heavy outlays required by this ruling, the imperial government permitted about 10 per cent of the total area of the Molochna settlement (the unallocated Molochna settlement lands remaining after the land distribution to the cottagers) to be set aside as a perpetual community-owned lease-land. Income from this rental area was designated solely for the purchase of additional land for new daughter settlements.[151]

Demands for fundamental reform by the Old Colony landless were only slightly less strident than those in the Molochna settlement.[152] In his numerous visits to the Old Colony, Jacob Epp heard echoes of this strife and was sharply critical of the leaders of the landless for fomenting conflict. Yet he also strongly favoured the outcome of the state-mediated settlement. In 1867, the government directed that the principles of the Molochna reform be applied to all remaining Mennonite and colonist settlements in New Russia, including the Old Colony.[153] The result was a definitive land reform, a veritable revolution in village landholding and social relations. Although the implementation of the reforms, as noted by Epp, was often contentious and attended by confusion, and strife over pasture use continued to dog relations among landholding groups, the land reform succeeded in breaking the back of Russian Mennonitism's gravest social problem.

The upshot, within two decades, was a Mennonite society significantly less polarized. Settlements split between contending strata of landholders and landless gave way to ones more differentiated among full-holders (65-desiatina allotment holders), half-holders, and smallholders as well as a much smaller number of landless households numbering no more than 10 per cent of the total.[154] Moreover, new generations of landless families were periodically given the opportunity of pioneering daughter settlements.[155] Supported by the profits of the grain trade and weaned of their dependence on crown-land grants, Mennonites evolved organizations and means to push out from their centres, buying or leasing undeveloped gentry estates as daughter settlements for their landless.

From 1865 to 1914, Mennonites established an average of about six new villages each year, including the daughter settlements close to the Judenplan. The 'daughter colony' phenomenon had palpable long-term consequences. Being corporately responsible for the needs of the landless gave Mennonite settlements a new and inescapable common purpose that Mennonite ideas of religious peoplehood helped validate. In time, the reform somewhat bridged differences created by religious divisions, reduced social tensions, and breathed fresh life into flagging Mennonite practices of mutual aid. Above all, this development created substantial communitarian counterweights to the individualizing pressures increasingly at work in Mennonite economics, education, and religion.

But the energetic development of daughter settlements also had an external under-side. As Mennonite individuals and communities appeared on the real-estate market throughout New Russia, aggressively buying up neglected gentry estates, they aroused resentment among poor Ukrainian and Russian peasant communities mired in backward economies and repartitional land-tenure practices. In some instances, Ukrainian peasant communities had previously been leasing the very estates purchased by the Mennonites, and found their 'land hunger' thus worsened. (Resulting resentments exploded violently against Mennonite settlements in the revolutions of 1917 to 1921.) The new daughter colonies also drew the attention of extreme Russian nationalists who sought to tar Mennonites and other German-speaking agriculturalists as territorial agents of a conquering imperial German nationalism.[156] These far-fetched charges, which undergirt demands for a discriminatory curb on the freedom of German colonists and Mennonites to buy land, emerged during the last years of Jacob Epp's life and caused him and his community deep and continuing worry.

Although the state, throughout the tempestuous 1860s, demanded greater local initiative in the resolution of community problems, it continued otherwise to play its accustomed, somewhat paternalistic role in Mennonite life. In both the Mennonite Brethren and landless controversies it acted, so to speak, as a court of final appeal to which quarrelling Mennonite groups looked for decisions. In the early 1870s, however, the imperial government suddenly appeared to cast off this historic middleman role and emerge in a new, more threatening guise. Withdrawing from its previous role of adjudicator of community differences, it authored a set of homogenizing changes that many Mennonites interpreted as a frontal assault on the essence of their life: their autonomous district and village administrations, separate schools, and blanket exemption from military service.

The Great Reforms were intended to integrate the disparate regions and groups within the Empire into a more uniform and coherent social and economic system. Thus, in the early 1870s, Mennonites were pressed to teach more Russian in their schools and adopt national educational guidelines. Administratively, the Guardianship Committee, the Ministry of State Domains' separate administrative organ for the foreign colonies in New Russia, was abolished and colonist and Mennonite settlements placed under regular county, provincial, and central administrative networks. Although local self-administration was retained at the village and settlement levels, here, too, the names of administrative units, offices, and office-holders were Russianized, and Russian was required as the official language of local administration.[157]

Despite their limited immediate impact, these changes caused serious anxieties among Mennonites about possible cultural and religious assimilation and longer-term government intentions. This was the background to a crisis that soon followed. Anxieties stemming from the disputes over land and pietism were much inflated by the government's announcement of a fundamental military reform. Geared to recovering imperial Russia's great-power position, the reform was first publicly broached in 1870, given legislative form in secret deliberations during the following years, and implemented in 1874.[158]

Since universal military service was the basic feature of the reform, first news of it had the effect of a bombshell upon Mennonite settlements. Interpreted as an assault on their faith and breach of the Mennonite Charter of Privileges, it prompted emergency conclaves of Mennonite ministers and lay officials in the main settlements. The long-standing guarantee of exemption from military service seemed to have vanished almost overnight.

After broad consultations in an atmosphere at fever pitch, the Mennonite settlements dispatched delegations to lobby in the imperial capital. One group began to explore emigration prospects in North America. Under threat of a mass emigration, and desirous of retaining the Mennonites as exemplary agriculturalists, the state finally agreed to a system of alternative service that allowed young Mennonite military inductees to discharge their service in military-style afforestation camps, mainly under Mennonite direction and superintendence.[159] As a minister, Jacob Epp attended several crisis sessions in the Old Colony and Molochna settlements and was privy to information from his brother Heinrich, one of the delegates to St Petersburg. Strongly tempted himself to join the stream of emigrants to North America (it would total up to a third of all Russian Mennonites), he drew back under pressure from his influential

Khortitsa siblings. In 1881–2, he served as chaplain in one of the newly established alternative afforestation service camps.

In the 1860s and 1870s, Jacob Epp, scrutinizing his deepest thoughts and emotions and peering into an unsure future, had difficulty seeing precisely the direction of the changes pervading his Mennonite world. Could one strike a balanced view? Was the world, and was his community, getting better, spiritually and morally, or was it in decline? Believing the universe to have significance and design, and his own life purpose, he strained to see the larger picture. He scanned the horizon, but the signs and symbols pressing in from the external world, his community, and his kinfolk were often perplexing and contradictory. Progressive members of his larger family, technological advances, and his own cravings for a personal, unique public voice encouraged hope. Yet natural misfortunes, seemingly unbridgeable community divisions, threatening state policies, and the traditionalist bias of his local community nurtured a darker view of what might lie ahead.

In visits described in the diaries, Epp often met his prominent relatives in the Old Colony. This closely knit, strongly supportive clan included leading members of the Old Colony's small modernizing stratum. Better off and self-confident, they exuded optimism, and overwhelmed Jacob Epp with their accomplishments and generosity. While providing broader vistas and serving as a rich source of information, such visits also, on occasion, gave Epp feelings of self-doubt and even worthlessness.

There was, as noted, his brother-in-law Cornelius Hildebrand, a captain of Mennonite industry.[160] A second brother-in-law, 'Dr' Bernhard Schellenberg (1840–88), who had trained as a feldsher (a kind of paramedic), pioneered modern health care in the Old Colony as its first medical professional.[161] A brother Johann (1830–88), nicknamed *Fuchtel*-Epp (gesticulator) for the expressive use of his hands, was the influential secretary, or chief administrator, of the Old Colony. This powerful senior post involved him in all manner of community affairs including key efforts to defuse the landless crisis.[162] In addition to these illustrious kinfolk, Jacob Epp would meet successful relatives in the milling industry on his travels to the developing Dnieper centres of Ekaterinoslav, Nikopol, and Kherson.

The person who may have affected Jacob most deeply, however, was his brother Heinrich (1827–96). Seven years his junior, fluent in Russian, well-educated for the time, and deeply religious, he was one of the most significant Mennonites of his day. He had served briefly himself in the 1850s as overseer in a Jewish settlement before becoming head teacher of the Khortitsa Zentralschule. There he presided over a 'new bright era' in the reform of education throughout the Old Colony. Elected a lay minister of the Khortitsa church in 1864, he became a forceful preacher with an avuncular, pietistic style, known for his tolerance towards the Brethren church. A trusted leader, he was repeatedly chosen to represent the Old Colony in negotiations in St Petersburg regarding military service.[163] A second marriage to the moneyed widow of Peter Lepp (one of the 'fathers' of New Russia's farm machinery industry) allowed him to stop teaching in the early 1870s and devote the rest of his life to the ministry. During the last decade of his life he served as the active Elder of the Khortitsa mother church.[164]

Modern technology seemed likewise to encourage a sanguine view of the future. In 1872 the Epp family acquired their first petroleum lamp, a symbol of modernity, prompting the diary entry: 'Everything is changing save only the Word of God, with its enduring power through all eternity.'[165] Jacob Epp acknowledged that the lamp would provide cheaper light than the tallow candles it replaced, and he was also generally enamoured of other modern contrivances with their potential for secular betterment. On a trip down the Dnieper River and along the Black Sea coast to booming Odessa he rhapsodized over taps spouting water and steam-engines, almost magically, driving boats, trains, flour and lumber mills, and printing presses.[166]

Well-heeled industrialist Thiessen family relatives of his in Ekaterinoslav and Kherson had already installed such engines in their own flour mills, and Cornelius Hildebrand (1833–1920), his brother-in-law and former pupil, was in the throes of developing a modern farm-implements industry in Khortitsa. One ambitious relative even had his own steamboat that he used for outings through the hazardous Dnieper rapids north of Khortitsa.

Closer to home, the Epp family also achieved a modest degree of progress. Among fellow village farm families the already noted multi-shared ploughs, fanning mills, and improved seed helped expand tillage-agriculture, as did a stricter regimen of fallowing and field rolling. Some Ukrainian wage labour, employed at season's height in years of good harvest, and better record-keeping, contributed to a more rational husbandry. At the same time, Jacob Epp's married children, in contrast to his own bleak prospects at a similar age, had realistic hopes of owning land in Mennonite daughter colonies, with commensurate security and status.

Schooling, pulling at his heart-strings, showed modest progress as better-prepared graduates of the Khortitsa Zentralschule (including several of his children) took up positions as village schoolteachers. Simultaneously, the well-informed, politically moderate German-language newspaper, the *Odessaer Zeitung* (which he borrowed to read from his neighbour brother Diedrich), employed the latest telegraph and rotary-printing-press technology to put him in contact with headline developments at home and abroad and with news from Mennonite sister settlements.[167]

Yet these intimations of spiritual and material progress suggested by his siblings, community politics, and modern technology were offset by less positive experiences, much closer to the bone. The period still offered little technological respite from the age-old scourges of sickness, epidemics, early death, and natural disasters, and much of Jacob Epp's pastoral ministry revolved around such difficult problems.

Moreover, two other sets of particularly wearing community controversies in the 1860s and 1870s left him despondent. The first was a decade-long rancorous quarrel over the introduction of four-part singing in church services, using a system of number notation. The sonorities of the 'new way' of singing, inspired from abroad and diffused to Mennonite communities through new teacher graduates of the Khortitsa Zentralschule, challenged the harsher-toned, even haunting, chant-like unison singing of the 'old way.' Known as the 'cipher music' controversy, it pitted innovators of the 'new way' against traditionalists of the 'old way' in a highly symbolic fight over modernity.[168] The second controversy, equally symbolic, was over 'free,' extemporaneous preaching, which Epp avidly favoured, rather than a read sermon. He was severely humiliated over this issue, which he chronicles trenchantly in his diaries.

The wounds of such conflicts seem to have reinforced Jacob Epp's growing doubts about the future. Throughout the 1860s he entertained the idea that his Mennonite community was in a state of moral decay. Interpreting volatile, many-layered change as a sign of decline, he came to see the great confrontations over the Brethren and landless questions as the bitter fruits of egoism. They were in direct conflict with the command of Christian love. Buttressing his increasingly gloomy prognosis was, ironically, an avalanche of confessions by adult parishioners about misbehaviour they had engaged in earlier in their lives. Such admissions he erroneously construed as symptoms of growing wickedness in his own day. It would seem that the perfectionist demands implicit in the religious pietism flooding the established and Brethren churches in the 1850s and 1860s precipitated a penitential mood among Mennonites, giving rise to the phenomenon of the stricken conscience. Social and political uncertainties of the time, coupled with sermon calls by Epp and other ministers for repentance and conversion, not infrequently precipitated emotional disclosures of failings. Often they took the form of deathbed repentances of acts of deceit, spiritual unfaithfulness, drunkenness, sinful merry-making, pre-marital and extra-marital sexual exploits with both Mennonite and Ukrainian partners (the latter invariably called 'Russian' rather than the more correct 'Little Russian'), and youthful bestiality ('defilement with cattle,' a vice seemingly not uncommon in agrarian communities).

Chronicling his purportedly wicked times, Jacob Epp pondered whether his community was perhaps destined to 'pass through the valley of desolation.'[169] This was no idle query for a Christian moralist, nor was his answer long in coming. Epp was not credulous about eclipses, blood red sunsets, northern lights, mock suns, and earthquakes, comprehending their natural explanation. But he also queried their higher, extra-natural logic. Did they perhaps also portend the last judgment and the 'early return of Christ'? In the early 1870s, faced by imperial changes to Mennonite and colonist education and administration, culminating in the military reforms of 1874, he occasionally preached about 'end times' and the 'final judgment.'[170]

Jacob Epp was not an original or systematic thinker, but his ideas, which reflected the outlook of part of his Mennonite community, had an inner logic that he reflectively pieced together from his late father's views, along with his own readings and personal experiences. His thinking tended to revolve around the Mennonite Charter of

Privileges, negotiated by his grandfather in 1800. Many Mennonites, including Jacob Epp, concluded that changes to the Mennonites' administration and abrogation of their blanket exemption from military service in the 1870s had rendered the charter null and void. This, it was thought, could have grave implications for the future. Basic to Jacob Epp's analysis was his view of the charter as a kind of social contract between the imperial monarchy and the Mennonite community concluded under the protection of the Almighty.

According to this view, the monarchy in 1789 had undertaken to provide Mennonites with refuge, land, protection and succour on the condition that they would serve as models of moral deportment and agrarian progress. Through their internal divisions, trumpeted by their many petitions to the government in the conflicts over land and religious orientation, they had failed, however, to hold up their end of the bargain. This had freed monarchy of its reciprocal responsibilities. The result was an abrupt change in state policy, a withdrawal of protection, culminating in grave damage to the central tenet of their confession of faith – non-resistance. The ensuing travail, he thought, was neither trifling nor chance, but had profound meaning as God's cleansing wrath.[171]

There were, in his view, two possible outcomes. If suffering induced individual and community contrition, repentance, and confession, leading to reconciliation within the community, with God and one's fellow man, the threat of divine retribution might well pass and the personal, mutually advantageous link between the monarchy and Mennonite community be restored. Basically, as he once wrote, he believed that the government was 'favourably disposed towards us, caring for us as a father.'[172]

Given the sharp inter-state tensions of the Franco-Prussian war of 1870–1 and the Balkan crisis of 1875–8, however, Jacob Epp inferred that if intra-community conflict persisted and remorse was weak, feigned, or even absent, human history might well end. At the peak of the crisis over military service and emigration in the early and mid 1870s, he briefly expected the millenarian resolution, an imminent apocalypse. Such catastrophic glimmerings seem, however, to have been part of his outlook throughout much of his adult life and were rooted also in the clearly articulated views of his revered late father.

Following the assassination of Alexander II by social revolutionaries in 1881, a shocked Jacob Epp gave definitive form to his budding apocalytical interpretation of the times in a twenty-three-verse poem composed on the centennial of his father's birth. It was entitled, 'On the Occasion of the 13th of September 1881: Composed by Me in Honour of the Memory of My Late Blessed Father.' As he admitted, the intimations of tumult arising from the convulsions of his time had led him to seek instruction in his father's theology of ultimate things. According to Jacob Epp, his father, through the eye of faith, had glimpsed the 'Kingdom of Jesus,' a thousand-year earthly paradise ending with the Final Judgment and the creation of a New Heaven and a New Earth. But pre-dating that post-historical age 'would be evil days and a sombre night,' the 'Kingdom of the Anti-Christ,' a time of rigorous testing for the devout. His father had said that he himself would likely not live to see that day, but his children might and should prepare accordingly. The poem concluded:

> Let us then watch and pray,
> Through thine own truth and grace,
> As we move toward the day,
> Arising now apace.
>
> When faith and love will vanish,
> The truth made crystal clear,
> That now the child of evil,
> Will hastily appear.
>
> Grant us in this dark hour,
> The guidance of thy light,
> That we with all thine power,
> Continue in thy sight.
>
> Then grant us a safe haven,
> From our betrayer's wiles,
> That freed of every torment,
> We rest in Jesus' arms.[173]

In the mid-1870s Jacob Epp's diaries began to lose much of their previous vitality. They turned more laconic and humdrum as diary entries were now confined largely to details of weather, crops, and family visits. (Relatively few diary entries are included in this volume for the period 1876 to 1880.) Village or settlement episodes, on the rare occasions when they were still recorded, lacked enlivening detail. For Epp, such a palpable falling-off of energy in his mid and late fifties was typical of a generation deeply etched by hard work and early deaths. A man like Epp was already regarded as being quite elderly, and viewed himself accordingly. In the mid-1870s, Jacob Epp, as mentioned, moved to a virgin homestead in the Baratov-Shlakhtin settlement village of Gnadenthal, near several of his married children. Slowly his public involvement decreased as other lay preachers assumed part of his ministerial load. He was also freed of the duty of having to accompany the Elder on his toilsome visits to other settlements. In the villages lay officials took over the inspection of local schools, sparing him that onerous duty as well.[174]

In 1881, however, he plunged back briefly into community life as administrator-chaplain in one of the recently opened alternative-service afforestation camps for young Mennonite conscripts (the Forstei). The surviving diaries break off just as Jacob Epp left for the Old Colony to negotiate the terms of his appointment, offered him through his brother Heinrich.[175]

Few details survive of Jacob Epp's truncated one-year service in the Forstei. Family memories preserve only captivating impressions of the old, gentle minister, the former lenient village schoolmaster, frustrated in his every effort to give military-style order and religious direction to the eighteen-year-old homesick village recruits in his care. Freed for the first time of parental and village controls, the youths gleefully turned his life into purest torment at every chance.[176]

What further survive are several Forstei-related verses recorded in his journal. They were composed for special occasions and sung to popular hymn tunes.[177] Several songs commemorated his personal leave-taking from his village as well as tearful farewells of anxious young recruits from their homes and congregations. At the Forstei itself, he wrote song-verses to greet and bid adieu to Mennonite servicemen, to mark the dedication of a barracks assembly hall, as mealtime songs of thanks, and so on.

As an imperial loyalist and social conservative, Jacob Epp tried also to inculcate patriotic emotions in his charges. Thus in 1882, a year after Alexander II's violent death, Jacob Epp wrote a paean to monarchy and social order on the occasion of the birthday of the reactionary Tsar Alexander III. One of the three verses reads as follows:

> Shelter him with thy protection,
> That those who wish to do him ill,
> Using their contempt and cunning,
> Might never, ever, injure him!
> And grant that every worthy deed,
> Of which in spirit he's taken heed,
> May prosper with thy blessing.[178]

In 1882, following his dispiriting year-long Forstei service, Jacob Epp returned to his village of Gnadenthal where he resumed his farming and ministry. His detailed crop records show low grain yields and continuing poverty throughout the first decade of the new settlement, with larger yields only in the late 1880s.[179] In his sixties, he was older now than his father at the time of his death. Seemingly less involved in agricultural work, he had time also to recopy parts of his journal, make genealogical entries, and reflect on his life. In periodic journal inventories he quantified his labours as a minister. His last reckoning in 1890 recorded that during thirty-eight years of unpaid pastoral service he had preached 1610 sermons, officiated at 390 funerals and performed 191 marriages.[180] Still active as a minister in his last full year of life, he preached thirty-five times and presided at twelve burials. This activity amounted to more than half the number of yearly services performed by him at the height of his ministry.

His inventory extended also to his rapidly growing family, for whom he had more time now too. By 1890 ten of his eleven children were married, and with a three-decade age spread between his oldest and youngest children, their families were at various stages of development. A loving Opa, he played a lot with his grandchildren, seeming to have a special fondness for several named Judith and Jacob. He also wrote verses to mark their birthdays. In several, which to the modern ear ring almost macabre, he held out to his grandchildren the hope of a blissful death if they obeyed their parents, did not quarrel with one another, and prayed earnestly to God.

Summaries of family births and deaths, also contained in Epp's journal, reflect the grim well-spring of his sombre reveries and jottings. By 1890, Jacob Epp had become grandfather to sixty-eight children, forty-four of whom, that is, fewer than two-thirds, had survived.[181] Even during the last five years of his life, a total of twenty-two grandchildren were born to members of his family, and nine died. This was an average of almost two deaths a year.

In September 1890, the Epps sold their property in Gnadenthal to two of their recently married children for five thousand rubles.[182] Jacob, by now in his seventieth year, and Judith Epp probably intended to build a granny-cottage in the yard as a retirement home, a common Mennonite practice. But whatever their plans, in mid-October he took sick with an unidentified illness. Its duration and outcome, including a final struggle of faith, are described by his son Gerhard, in diaries carrying on a three-generation family tradition.

November 5, 1890. Today our beloved father died. Sickly for some period, his final time of suffering lasted for eighteen days. His last struggle was not an easy one. The Lord let him drain the cup of bitterness to its very bottom. Before taking his faithful servant to himself, he purged him in the fire of suffering, thus fulfilling what he himself had prayed on his deathbed.[183]

The funeral took place three days later in the Gnadenthal schoolhouse, crowded with members of his immediate family, other relatives and friends, and parishioners from the surrounding villages. His brother-in-law Cornelius Hildebrand, the industrialist, and brother Heinrich, the Elder, travelling by train on a rail-line newly constructed across a corner of the Baratov-Shlakhtin settlement, arrived from the Old Colony after Jacob Epp's death, but in time for the interment.[184]

The funeral followed the reassuring pattern of countless others that had been conducted by Epp himself. The generational cycle had completed another full round. His brother Heinrich gave the funeral sermon. After a prayer and the singing of a hymn, his body was carried by horse-drawn wagon to the Gnadenthal cemetery. After another hymn and a prayer, the simple coffin was lowered into the grave and the grave closed.

Soon thereafter, the Epp family decided to leave Russia for

Canada. Freed of the contraints of Jacob Epp's abiding sense of obligation to his local church community, the family made this decision under the spur of very strong urging by mother Judith. She pressed for an early emigration lest her youngest son, Johann, the last child still at home, be drafted into the Forstei service. But a mass famine in Russia in 1891, followed by an epidemic outbreak of cholera, delayed matters.[185] Anxious to leave, members of the Epp family watched restlessly as white-painted hospital trains with cholera victims passed within sight of their villages and fields. The appearance of the last such train in the winter of 1891–2 heralded the end of the cholera outbreak.[186] Finally, two and a half years after the death of Jacob Epp, his family left Russia by rail and ocean steamer, settling on homesteads of the Canadian crossroads pioneer community of Eigenheim in the Northwest Territories.

Accompanying them to this new grassland frontier were Jacob Epp's diaries, which, as mentioned, had been sold at auction to members of the immediate family before leaving Russia. During the following years, on many a cold winter's evening, the diaries were brought out in Eigenheim. By the light of a kerosene lamp, favourite selections were read to family members and friends around the kitchen table. A grandson of Epp, one of the last survivors of that generation, remembered that as time passed some entries took on an air of remoteness, especially for younger listeners. Yet many entries touching on local and church affairs, on the great issues of land, piety and emigration, and especially on the personal struggles of Jacob Epp, retained their power to evoke the yearning for intimacy and oneness of the Russian Mennonite community during its great age of tumult and adaptation.

BOOK I,[1] 1851–1853

Old Colony Teacher and Judenplan Settler

'Most of the children told me
they would have to tend their sheep and
would be stopping school tomorrow.'

March 26, 1851

'We can hardly have too many arrangements
which serve the common good.'

June 6, 1851

'It was our bounden duty to live blameless
Christian lives, especially for the Jews,
to whom we were to be an example.'

February 2, 1853

Background

'I stretch forth my hands unto thee: my soul *thirsteth* after thee, as thirsty land ... Hear me speedily, O Lord: my spirit faileth: hide not thy face from me, lest I be like unto them that go down into the pit. Cause me to hear thy loving kindness in the morning; for in thee do I trust: cause me to know the way wherein I should walk; for I lift up my soul unto thee.' Psalm 143:6–8

I was born on December 26, 1820, at 5:30 in the morning, and received holy baptism from the Reverend Elder Jacob Dyck in 1838. On November 18, 1841, I was joined in marriage with Maria Klassen, who was born on August 29, 1822. We lived in my parents' home until the spring of 1842 when we moved to my father's rented sheep-fold, which belonged to the estate owner Kromida. Here we spent a year in tranquil happiness. After the sheep-fold was dissolved in 1843, we returned to Khortitsa and rented the back room of Jacob Töws's house.

On May 15 of that year, my beloved father David Epp, after an illness of 18 days, passed away in the Lord at the age of 61 years, 8 months, and 2 days. He had served as a minister for 37 years. After the funeral, at my mother's request, we moved in with her to manage my father's household until it could be sold at public auction. This took place in the fall of 1843 when his establishment was taken over by Jacob Päthkau of Blumengart. After the harvest that winter, we returned to Khortitsa and again rented the back room of Jacob Töws's house.

I became village schoolteacher on the Island of Khortitsa in mid-April 1844. Our daughter Helena was born there on June 3, 1844. The Dnieper River overflowed its banks in the spring of 1845, and the schoolhouse in which we lived was flooded to the windows. During that time we lived in Johann Peters's implement shed (Scheune). Our daughter Katharina was born during the night from July 24 to 25. My father-in-law Peter Klassen died on Friday, October 10, 1847, in his 60th year. A daughter Maria was born on February 28, 1848, and the Lord took her from us ten weeks and a day later. She had seemed fine earlier that morning when we got up, but we found her dead and already cold in her bed at 9 a.m. A son David was born to us on January 28, 1849 and a daughter Maria on December 15, 1850.[2]

A Review of the Past Year, 1850

'I have smitten you with blasting and mildew: when your gardens and vineyards and your fig trees and your olive trees increased, the palmerworm devoured *them*: yet have ye not returned unto me, saith the Lord.' Amos 4:9

The grain harvest was very poor. On average we got little more than the seed. The drought continued for so long that small grasshoppers appeared in large numbers and caused much damage. We harvested very little fodder as well. The orchard did reasonably well, but even the apples were full of caterpillars and vermin, and rotted. We have had three crop failures in a row now, and food is scarce and dear. Grain prices on average were: rye, 13 to 14 bank R. a chetvert, wheat, 20 to 21 R., barley, 11 to 12 R., and oats, 10 R.

The situation in the church is very bleak. People are quite satisfied to be known as church members, and parade an external Christianity, but they lack love. Matters have reached the point where our leaders are not in agreement, and the church has become quarrelsome and full of discord. People refuse to be reconciled to one another and arouse suspicions of their neighbours with the authorities, blaming others and shrugging off any personal responsibility for what occurs. Lord, we are deaf to thy punishments and unwilling to humble ourselves before thee. Have mercy on us, whom thou has purchased so dearly with thy blood, and grant us thy peace. Extinguish the fire of discord, which Satan has ignited, and keep it from consuming us. May thy grace be with us always. Amen.

1851

I have hired on as teacher for another year and will receive a salary of 90 bank R. in cash, 11½ chetvert of grain, and 18½ funt of lighting oil. As Village secretary, I will receive an additional 50 bank R. and 18 funt of lighting oil. This totals 140 bank R., 11½ chetvert of grain, 36 funt of lighting oil, free pasture for my cattle, hay for fodder, a day's labour in haymaking from each of the 18 landowners, one desiatina of plough-land, which the community has agreed to plough and harrow, and cartage for the hay and grain. Each landowner is further obliged to winter one of my sheep. Lord Jesus, give me the talent and skill to teach the children, and may thy blessing rest on our school always. Lord, grant me the grace to lead the children to thee. Take them to thy bosom, Lord, and bless them.

February 3 I travelled to Alexandrovsk and Schönwiese by sled and bought two chetverik of potatoes from the widow Janzen in Schönwiese. I met my brother Johann in town and drove home with him. My brothers Diedrich and Heinrich dropped in for a visit with their wives in the afternoon and left again at four o'clock.

February 15 I and my wife attended a funeral for the youngest daughter of the local landowner Abraham Pätkau, and Elder Jakob Hildebrand delivered the funeral sermon. At home we found our little son David ill. Trienchen [Katharina] has just recovered from a serious illness, my wife has been suffering from earaches and toothaches off and on, and now another illness! Lord, we come to thee in times of tribulation, knowing that thou wilt answer our prayers.

February 24 Our little son's illness is becoming more serious, and our little Maria is also very sick. [Later in the day:] The Lord has answered our prayers. Our sick children are on the way to recovery.

I have put in my name to settle in a new village which is to be established in the spring of 1852 in the existing Mariupol Mennonite settlement [of Bergthal] after a notice appeared inviting interested persons to register.[3] Lord, show me thy will in this matter.

March 2 My brother Heinrich Epp was our guest this afternoon. He had some business to do with Peters, a member of the [Agricultural] Commission.

March 4 Winter hangs on, the ground is snow-covered and there is heavy frost. Several days of beautiful spring weather gave us the hope that we might soon be able to pasture our cattle, but then the wind shifted to the east, and rain, some snow, and frost formed a crust of ice. The cold and frost has continued now for a week, many have had to buy more feed and my own supplies are getting low. Yet our faithful Lord lives, and we should not despair. He will bring spring weather in his good time and meet our needs. Last night my brother Johann arrived from Khortitsa, and this morning I took him out to see the community woods.

March 8 Thursday my wife and I and the children drove to Khortitsa to visit our two mothers. The road was terribly muddy, and we had to proceed slowly for most of the way. In Khortitsa we heard of a tragic accident involving Peter Wilms Jr who had tried to cross the Dnieper ice at Nieder Khortitsa. The ice had given way, his wife had drowned in the frigid waters, and the wagon had also disappeared. When we got home, we heard that the story was indeed true, and that the local fishermen Jakob Hoeppner and Abraham Klassen had been instructed to recover the wagon and its load. This is a sad event, yet we know that 'all things work together for good to them that love God.' Romans 8:28. May God comfort poor Mr Wilms.

March 10 The accident has led to an outpouring of sympathy for Wilms. The load on the wagon has been recovered and its back half, but the front part of the wagon and the horses as well as the body are still missing. Today I visited Khortitsa and brought back my brother-in-law Johann. Because of the spring run-off, we had to make our way over the embankment in the sand flats. The mud in Rosenthal and Khortitsa was knee-deep and the run-off very strong. I had planned to drop in at the brick plant on our way home but could not because of the deep water at the bridge. Peter Hildebrand Jr helped me out with two of his horses, driving me to the Einlage hill from where I walked home safely across the thin Dnieper ice. The Lord be praised.

I asked the District Office about the planned settlement on the Mariupol steppe and learned that nothing was likely to come of it as I was the only one who had signed up. My brother Diedrich, who was to have been appointed an overseer in the Jewish colonies, has not yet been told anything definite in this regard by the Guardianship Committee [for Foreign Settlers in Southern Russia].

March 17 'He causeth the grass to grow for the cattle, and herb for the service of man.' Psalm 104:14. We have now had beautiful spring weather for a week, and the landowners have been out ploughing and seeding. The horses not needed for field-work have been put out to pasture, which is already quite green. The ice opposite our village broke up and drifted past on the 12th, and the ice at the rapids, which usually collects there and towers up in great piles, started to drift by in a dense pack during the night from the 16th to 17th of March. Lord, bless this year and grant us an abundant harvest.

March 18 Sunday. Towards evening we asked Aron Peters's wife for advice about my wife's gums and upper lip, which have been sore for over a week. Peters gave us something to brush on the sores, and by Monday morning an abscess had formed which my wife opened with a needle and drained. The Lord be thanked.

March 19 Monday. I taught Bible stories today, specifically about David's persecutions. May the Lord bless our school abundantly and grant me, in my weakness, the gift and understanding to guide our children along the path of salvation. May thy Spirit lead them in truth and keep them from becoming enslaved to sensual pleasures.

March 25 I and my family drove to Khortitsa, where the Lord had called Johann Wiebe's infant son Heinrich to himself at the age of a little more than 11 weeks. After being confirmed as Village overseer, my brother Diedrich plans to move to the Jewish colonies tomorrow. Lord Jesus, be thou his guide and counsel.

March 26 Monday. I taught the Bible story of David becoming king as briefly as possible today so that I would still have time before the holidays to talk about Christ's passion. This afternoon, most of the children told me they would have to tend their sheep and would be stopping school tomorrow, and several were already absent. I therefore told them the main parts of the Passion story and exhorted them to follow the Lamb of God.

March 28 This evening I attended the Village assembly as secretary. The District Office had submitted the draft of a resolution to a recent meeting of village mayors that committed the village communities to assume a guarantee for lease payments on 6515 desiatinas of crown land close to the village of Krasnogrigorievka (usually called Chernyshev).[4] The lease by the District Office had been made on behalf of all [landless] cottagers in the [Khortitsa] District, and was to be presented to the government as such. Yet only half of the landowners were willing to sign. People too often seem to have reservations when it comes to doing something for their fellow man, and in the hearts of many people *love* has been extinguished.

The [Village] assembly was further asked to resolve a dispute involving Klas Wiebe, a landowner and assistant Village mayor, who had quarrelled bitterly with his brother-in-law Johann Wienz over the planting of trees on a plot belonging to the latter. The assembly decided the matter in favour of Wienz. The mayor (who is Wiebe's brother and Wienz's brother-in-law) exhorted the two men to settle their differences and be reconciled, but they refused. Ye children of the Lord, what has happened to our love? 'Behold, how good and how pleasant *it is* for brethern to dwell together in unity!' Psalm 133:1.

March 30 I observed the examinations in the Khortitsa Zentralschule conducted by the teacher [Heinrich] Franz.[5] My brother Abraham was among those being examined, and his performance gave me great pleasure, especially his singing (an aptitude his brothers lack totally). The examination subjects were Bible stories, grammar, mental and blackboard arithmetic, German and Russian reading, orthography, geography, science, and geometry.[6] Quite a large number of observers were present.

April 3 Today I finished teaching school until after the holidays. In the morning I asked the children to recite chapter 53 of the prophet Isaiah and the song from our hymn-book entitled 'Farewell to Vain Pleasures.' In the afternoon I related the story of Jesus' suffering and resurrection and tried to impress upon the children the true meaning of Palm Sunday, Good Friday, and Easter Sunday, and how they should be celebrated. Lord, bless the seed which thy humble servant has sown, and let it bear rich fruit.

April 9 Easter, the third holiday. I attended a general Brotherhood Meeting in the Khortitsa church where the landowner Jacob Pätkau of Khortitsa was elected minister by majority vote. Speaking on behalf of the Ministerial Committee (Lehrdienst), the Elder proposed that the rye grain which the landowners were providing to needy Jewish colonies at the government's request be turned into a donation. The landowners, at their own expense, had each carted two chetvert of rye from the communal granaries to the Mariupol [Jewish] colonies. If we were now to donate that grain, the Elder said, it would become an expression of Christian compassion and charity and also win the government's favour. God, thou knowest the true mainspring of this measure, whether it is honour-seeking or charity. About a month ago, after the rye had been shipped, a letter of commendation was received [from the government]. If the rye were now to be donated, it would produce double praise. Yet our Lord and Master (in Matthew 6:1) has taught us, 'Take heed that ye do not your alms before men, to be seen of them. But when thou doest alms, let not thy left hand know what thy right hand doeth that thine alms may be in secret: and thy father which seeth in secret himself, shall reward thee openly.'

The question was also raised as to whether the Ministerial Committee should call brethren to account who scorned Christian charity by refusing to pay the poor tax. I would have thought that this question really answered itself. A proposal to build a hospital for the poor was unanimously accepted. The Elder received Abraham Blatz of Rosenthal, who had been placed in the ban, back into the church as a brother. Lord Jesus, grant him genuine remorse and atonement. After the Brotherhood Meeting I visited my mother for supper, and looked in on my mother-in-law.

I and my young daughter, Helena, and my brother Heinrich then visited Carl Jäger, where a small group had gathered. We talked about miracles in the Scriptures and several obscure passages regarding them. Christian Hamm was of the view that there must be a misprint in Isaiah 53:9, where it reads, 'And he made his grave with the wicked, and died with the rich.' He thought it should have the opposite reading, namely, 'died with the wicked and buried with the rich,' for he had indeed died as a criminal and a godless one on the cross and been buried in the manner of a rich Jew. I was of the same opinion since I had often thought about this passage myself but could not hit on its true meaning. But we soon agreed that it could not be a misprint, as all Bibles contained the very same reading, and must therefore have been correctly translated from the original.

Heinrich Franz, teacher in the Zentralschule, explained the passage in approximately this way. Jesus had been buried as a godless one, in that many were always present at the funeral of a rich man. In Jesus' case, his body had been laid in the grave by Joseph and Nicodemus in the presence of three women, who had looked on. And the beloved Saviour had truly died as a rich man, for even as many gather at the death of a rich man so many were present at the Saviour's death, which had caused a great sensation. Also, even as a rich man leaves a legacy, or inheritance, at the time of his death, Jesus had done so also in that his death had given us eternal salvation, the greatest riches of all. After about an hour, Lehnchen [Helena] and I left for home.[7]

April 11 I gave religious instruction in school today, witnessing to the need for prayer, and tried to kindle a love for the Saviour in the children's hearts. I am unworthy for this work, for I am desperately in need of learning myself and yet am called upon to teach others. Lord, help me in my incompetence, lead me along the path of eternal life, work a rebirth in me, and let me live a new life. It often seems to me that my entire divine service is in vain, and does not come genuinely from the heart.

April 20 In the afternoon I accompanied [Agricultural] Commission member Peters to the natural woods on the Island to conduct some experiments with the trees. The Guardianship Committee for Foreign Settlers has instructed the Agricultural Commission [in the Khortitsa District] to undertake a number of scientific experiments and to report their results.[8]

The pasture lands on the Island are truly magnificent. The buckthorn trees in the woods, the free-standing trees on the heights of hills and in the ravines are in full blossom. The pasture is lush and plentiful, and there is enough hay to cut by scythe even where the cattle have trod. The fields seeded to rye and wheat look very promising, and we have high hopes for a rich harvest. Lord, who makest rain to fall on the righteous and unrighteous and sun to shine on the blessed and the wicked, reveal thy grace and mercy to us, and bless our fields of grain.

April 22 Sunday morning, after the cottager Peter Braun of Rosenthal had driven his cattle out [to pasture], his barn burned down. The fire broke out in the attic before he had lit his stove.

April 24 My brother [Heinrich] was here for the night, and we discussed our planned trip to the Jewish settlements where our brother Diedrich now lives.

April 27 *Trip to the Jewish Colonies in Kherson Province.* We started out for the Jewish colonies with my brother Heinrich, his wife, and [brother] Johann, and spent the night with the Abraham Wiebes on the Khutor Friedensfeld. We arrived safely at Diedrich Epp's place the following noon. Only eight Jewish houses have been finished here to date. The Mennonite settlers were cheerful and in good spirits and busily at work completing the foundations of their houses. The places we passed through were Khortitsa, Neuendorf, Petrikovka, the so-called cabbage khutor, the state-peasant village of Chumaki, the German khutor of Friedensfeld (which is on the land of the estate owner Prince Kudashev), the village of this same man, called Kudashev Kromida, Loshkarovka on the Basavluk [River], and several other khutors.

On the 29th, my brother Diedrich accompanied us to the Jewish colonies of Kamianka and Izluchistaia. Lüttner, the assistant to the Guardianship Committee, lives here, and Mennonites are supposed to be settled in these villages as well. Only the Lord knows whether I will join them. It is certainly true that German settlers in the Jewish colonies could earn a good living, but I feel a deep personal dislike for such a settlement. On the morning of May 1, we drove to Novovitebsk to see Peter v Kampen, who is overseer of that colony, and then in God's name started for home. We drove through the night and reached Schönhorst before sun-up, and by ten in the morning I was with my family again. The Lord be praised. Although the grass is everywhere lush and it looks like a bountiful harvest, it is still too early to tell how the grain will do. We still hope for the best, but the heat wave gives us real concern. Open thy heavens, dear Lord, send us rain, give us a living and bless our fields.

May 3 The corpse of Peter Wilms's wife, who drowned in the Dnieper [River] in winter, has been found and buried. The landowners on the Island are busily making hay, and a heaping wagon-load just went by. People have taken part of the pasture land and divided it up for hay. I must say, I have never before seen such an early harvest.

May 4 A lightning strike in Einlage around five in the afternoon destroyed the treadmill of the private tutor Johann Friesen.

May 9 With my students, I opened the missions box and counted the money, which came to 5 bank R. Lord, bless these humble gifts. I closed school today until after the holidays.

At six this evening the Village assembly met in the mayor's office, where all of the landowners now signed the draft of the communal resolution designating as a gift the rye grain sent last year from our communal granaries to the Jewish colonists. After an appeal from the mayor it was also decided that each homestead should provide me with one haymaker for next Saturday.

May 11 I visited my family in Khortitsa. I was at my mother-in-law's for dinner (where all of her children were gathered) and visited Isaak Dyck in Rosenthal in the afternoon. We had hardly reached home, however, when a violent hail and thunder storm broke, which threatened to fill our cellar with water. It continued through the night and washed out deep gullies in the garden.

May 12 Saturday. I and my wife attended the engagement in Kronsgarten of the widow Rempel and Heinrich Bartel. Last night's hailstorm is said to have seriously damaged grain fields in Alexandrovsk and Schönwiese [across the Dnieper River]. The bridge in Khortitsa could not be used until it had been repaired, and the Johann Dycks had to spend the night in their wagon on the street in Khortitsa, where hail had punched a number of holes in its covering. They say that the hail reached as high as a man's waist on the Voznesensk steppe and destroyed all of the grain. May God grant that this is not true.

May 13 The hail did indeed cause great damage on the east side of the Dnieper, but it reached to a man's waist only in the gullies. Where the storm struck with full force the crops have been destroyed. Yesterday, the day after the storm, Heinrich Janzen, the mayor of Schönwiese, surveyed the fields and found some hailstones in the ditches of the post road as large as chicken eggs, at least six in number, and several dead birds on the ground. Janzen related this to me himself.

May 14 Today I started raking hay in Deer Valley.

May 18 At a [Village] assembly meeting in the mayor's office we were told of a directive from the District Office ordering the election of new candidates for the Agricultural Commission. The alleged reason was that the government had refused to confirm the three chosen late in 1850 – the landowners Martin Klassen of Kronsthal,

Martin Klassen of Neuhorst, and Aron Lehn of Rosenthal. In the words of the directive, 'The two Klassens had said that they would not serve in office with the present chairman of the Commission.' Our [Village] assembly refused, however, to hold a new election, and the mayor's office has therefore decided to submit a formal report in this regard to the District Office. In such ways people are everywhere causing discord.

May 22 Community affairs continue in a bad way. The discord between the District Office and the Agricultural Commission has now reached the stage of open hatred. The District Office, for its part, in co-operation with the Khortitsa church Convent [that is, the Council of Ministers], is doing its best to drive Chairman Siemens from office.[9] His removal is being pursued with such bitterness and zeal that there seems little chance of a reconciliation. The mood in the community is very bleak. Initiatives by the District Office are received favourably, while those by the Agricultural Commission are interpreted in the most negative fashion. We know that the situation in a Christian community should be quite otherwise. Our leaders are also in conflict over the dismissal of the shepherd Schmidt. Last fall the Guardianship Committee of Foreign Settlers issued instructions clearly stating that the old Agricultural Commission was reponsible for the improvement of the sheep-folds, but the District Office maintains that the hiring and firing of the shepherd is purely an administrative matter. On the basis of this view, and without first consulting the Agricultural Commission, the District Office has fired the shepherd Schmidt and hired Bernd Bärgen. The Guardianship Committee opposes this action and has ordered the District Office not to proceed with this appointment until it has secured the agreement of the [Agricultural] Commission.

Today Commission member Peters showed me a directive from the Guardianship Committee in which the authorities express their displeasure [with the District Office]. The directive orders that the matter be taken up with the Commission and that appropriate action follow. In the meantime, however, an experienced man has been let go and an inexperienced one hired. Actions of this kind taken in defiance of the authorities can have only unhappy consequences. An evil matter like this cannot end well, for the government, which seeks only our welfare, will inevitably regard us as being ungrateful.

May 23 The storm of May 11 caused terrible destruction in Schönhorst, where more than 30 houses were badly damaged or destroyed, a windmill was overturned, a second had its roof blown off, a third was badly damaged, and a number of grain fields were flattened. It was so bad that the storm even carried the brick top of a chimney for some distance in one piece. The *poor* people have suffered a terrible loss.

May 24 At a two-day public auction, the estate of the late Jakob Rempel of the Island [of Khortitsa] was sold. The property was knocked down to Johann Wienz, of our village, for 4270 bank R. The implement shed is very run down. I purchased a plough for 30 bank R.

May 27 The first holiday of Pentecost. At the service in our local school, the Elder Jakob Hildebrand delivered a sermon based on John 14:23.[10] Lord Jesus, thou hast promised thy Spirit to those who ask for it. I am unworthy, Lord, but fill me with thy power, and pour out thy Spirit over me and over thy beloved church. Lead me in all truth. Be thou my guide, and do not let me wander from thy path or grow weary of seeking thy face day and night.

May 29 On the third day of Pentecost an elder was elected from among the ministers in the Khortitsa church. The minister, Franz Wienz, received 150 votes. Also receiving votes were the minister Peter Dyck, from Nieder Khortitsa, and a few others. Elder Jacob Dyck[11] preached on Paul's words to Timothy, the Second Epistle 2:2. Lord, bless this choice and equip thy servant with the gifts needed for his office. 'Take heed therefore unto yourselves, and to all the flock, over the which the Holy Ghost hath made you overseers, to feed the church of God, which he hath purchased with his own blood.' Acts 20:28. In 1 Timothy 31:1 we read: 'This is a true saying, If a man desire the office of a bishop, he desireth a good work.' Such an office is important and so let us read and take Paul's words to the Hebrews 13:17 to heart. 'You watchmen who have been set on the walls of Zion, cry out loudly and preach courageously, exhort and punish without timidity, and be not like the blind watchmen, who are called dumb dogs and are incapable of punishing.' Isaiah 56:10. Such faithful shepherds and teachers are doubly necessary because of the present turmoil in our church.

June 3 Sunday. 'As for man, his days are as grass: as a flower of the field, so he flourisheth. For the wind passeth over it, and it is gone; and the place thereof shall know it no more.' Psalm 103:15–16. People who go through life so self-confidently are really as nothing for they live their lives heedlessly day in and day out, and go to their graves without thinking about eternity, scarcely heeding the commandments of Christ. They are baptized, take communion, and attend church regularly, yet ignore the commandment of love without which all is in vain, as the Scriptures say. Lord Jesus, thou hast said that the heart speaks whereof it is full and that one's heart will be found where one's treasure is. It is quite clear where the hearts of such nominal Christians are.

June 15 Elder Jakob Hildebrand let me read the copy of a letter from a Prussian minister addressed to his fellow ministers in the Molochna. It is about the quarrels that divide the Mennonite communities of southern Russia. The letter is well worth copying, and so I include it here.

Schönsee near Tiegenhoff
January 27, 1851

To my dear friends and colleagues
in the Molochna

My brethren, several of you have asked me to give you my views regarding the circumstances, or, better said, the problems, existing among you. This I do gladly. Yet I must acknowledge that my stay with you was too fleeting to make a definitive judgment. I would therefore ask you to show me the truth where I have seen matters wrongly.

I was pleased to find so many good arrangements generally in the colonies and in the churches, but also deeply grieved to find so much division and discord among you. Indeed, I left you with tear-filled eyes over the decay of our people. Many of you have grown up with prejudices, and it seems to me that quite a few of you are not familiar with the Charter of Privileges, under which you live, and do not sufficiently value the goodwill of His Imperial Majesty, which you enjoy. I think that if you were willing to consider matters without prejudice, you would undo many a thing that has occurred, were that possible. To address these matters in greater detail, let me, as a basis, quote the introductory words of the Charter of Privileges:

'Graciously condescending to the petition of the Mennonites who are settled in the New Russian province and whose superior industry and seemly conduct, according to the testimony of their overseers, may serve as an example to the other colonists settled there, we have, with this Imperial Charter, not only graciously confirmed all of the rights and privileges contained in the preliminary agreement concluded with them, but, in order further to enliven their diligence and attention to agriculture, graciously granted them the additional benefits contained in the following, etc.'

From the above it is clear that our fellow-believers in Russia have assumed the obligation of being a model not only to their immediate neighbours *but also to the other colonists* in their *diligence* as well as in their *conduct* generally. And to ensure that they might be even more zealous in these matters, further benefits were graciously granted them. This signifies that they should pursue these goals by establishing villages, roads, gardens, wood lots, by constructing buildings and by tilling the soil. All this was to be done in a way conforming to our faith, in order that the government appointed over them might always be able to point to them as examples for the other colonists.

Clearly if all of this is to be achieved the matter requires leadership. And who is to assume leadership in external developments? The Ministerial Council certainly should not. When the number of disciples grew, the apostle, according to Acts 6, said, 'It is not reason that we should leave the word of God, and serve tables,' and so they choose men for this service. Equally, our Ministerial Council should be happy when men can be found from among the brethren who are able to give such leadership by example and prudent directives. The duty of the Council of Ministers remains, as before, to instil the word of God in both young and old through instruction and exhortation. 'Let every soul be subject unto the higher powers. For there is no power but of God: that powers that be are ordained of God.' Romans 13:1. 'Submit yourselves to every ordinance of man for the Lord's sake' (1 Peter 2:11), so that also in this regard conduct may be manifest that is in keeping with our confession. If you had worked towards this goal over the past 30 years or so, I believe that much of the discord that presently exists would not have arisen.

It pains me to say that on occasion efforts are still made to work in opposition to *that* which is spelled out in the Charter of Privileges and which the crown desires. We wish to be the peaceable, obedient people whose 'yes,' in lieu of an oath, remains a 'yes.' Whoever works in opposition to the directives of the higher authorities resists God's ordinances and denies that very 'yes,' spoken in lieu of an oath.

I wish that those of you who complain about the difficulty of carrying out these directives (whose proceeds flow into your own coffers) had been here before I left when the militia was mobilized. You would have seen wives and mothers piteously weeping, not knowing whether their bread-winners would ever return. If you were put on an equal footing with your neighbours and the glorious Charter of Privileges were taken from you, you would be happy and grateful for the duties given you as Mennonite-Russian subjects. Great privileges demand great accomplishments. I am not familiar with any other people with a Charter of Privileges like the one given our fellow believers in southern Russia.

As regards the disorders in the congregation, or between the congregations, it would seem to me that many put greater stress on outward forms than upon the life hidden with Christ in God. The result of that is a dead orthodoxy rather than a living awareness of being a member of the body of Christ. Differences within the congregation may of course exist but these should not be of such a magnitude as to preclude sincere and brotherly co-operation. Christ says: 'By this all men will know that you are my disciples, if you have love for one another.' Yet when these differences provoke anger and lead to quarrelling, the words of Paul about his colleagues after the flesh are applicable: 'For I bear them record that they have a zeal of God, but not according to knowledge. For they being ignorant of God's righteousness, and going about to establish their own righteousness, have not submitted themselves unto the righteousness of God.' Romans 10:2–3.

Many a person believes himself to be a Mennonite when he observes strictly one side of the article of non-resistance. At the same time, however, he ignores the fact that he is in other respects resisting and opposing divine as well as human ordinances. People deny that they are seeking revenge, yet their hearts are full of vengeance and malice against their brothers who do not fully agree with them. *This bad blood is the source of all quarrels and disputes.* I have met men whose faces turned red when matters involving other congregations were discussed. If we are to become disciples of Christ, His words must take root in our hearts: "Love your enemies, bless them that curse you, do good to them that hate you, pray for those who offend and persecute you, that ye may be children of your father in heaven.' We are genuine members of our congregations, not when we give appearances by adhering to outward forms, but when we evidence the fruits of the spirit, which are: love, joy, peace, long-suffering, gentleness, goodness, faith, meekness, and purity. Galatians 5:22.

Instead, however, works of the flesh are revealed, which are, among many others: hatred, variance, envy, anger, quarrelling, enmity, etc. Galatians 5:19–21. Where the fruits of the spirit prevail, the fruits of the flesh are suppressed. But when our members no longer let themselves be guided and set right by God and his word and no longer wish to follow after the Saviour of the Gospel, we should not be surprised when the government intervenes, indeed is forced to intervene, in the affairs of our congregations. For when one comes to the government with grievances, it must decide. That our congregations are in this way maintained through external force is not the fault of government, nor of those who execute its commands, but only of ourselves. Thank God that one need not fear those in power in Russia because of our good deeds, but only for our evil deeds. Whoever does not wish to live in fear of government can win its praises simply by doing good.

I was deeply grieved to learn that differences and divisions had arisen even where efforts were made for a time on behalf of the spiritual welfare of mankind. Were the apostle Paul to write to these parties he would probably write as to the Galatians: 'O foolish people of G[nadenfeld], who hath bewitched you, that ye should not obey the truth, before whose eyes Jesus Christ hath been evidently set forth, cruficied among you? Are ye so foolish? Having begun in the Spirit, are ye now made perfect by the flesh?'

Is this overstating the matter? The apostle says: 'For whereas there is among you envying, and strife, and divisions, are ye not carnal, and walk as men.' 1 Corinthians 3:3. Were the heathen, to whom you have sent the word of God, or have helped in this regard, to see your discord, would they not be astonished and ask: How can this be the soul-saving fruit of the Gospel? Because in blindly opposing our joining in bringing the word of God to the non-Christian peoples, you blaspheme the name of God. I am not opposed to missionary activity, for I am a member of such a society myself, without giving up anything of my confession. Those who have experienced the vastness of God's love in Christ Jesus in sending his only son into the world to redeem us damnable sinners from eternal perdition should happily contribute something to bring this great truth to those who know nothing of it.

Nor am I opposed to the temperance societies, for I am also a member of such a society: first of all, because we have been encouraged to do so by the local police; and, secondly, because I know of no better way to discourage drunkenness in general than if the moderate drinker makes this small sacrifice. Yet when matters arise among members of such societies that bring shame upon Christianity, and such conduct is defended, then preaching and exhorting people to participate in this otherwise desirable activity does not help but hinders, and instead of arousing an interest in the cause subjects it to ridicule.

These are, in brief, the impressions I have gained of your problems, and which have caused me sorrow. But I do not mean to suggest that the decay in your congregations is greater than in ours. This is not the case. Nor do I mean to criticize those who mean well. Indeed, the longing for peace which I found almost generally among you justifies great hopes for the future. I wish this longing were genuinely heart-felt, and that many of you would seek rest and peace where it can alone be found. Then you could not only forgive but forget what has happened, and reach out fraternally to one another. Surely spiritual and physical well-being would then be your lot. Let us pray that this might happen and that the Lord might empower all of us according to the richness of his glory, to become strong in the inner man, and that Christ might dwell in our hearts in faith and become rooted in love. With all of the saints, let us fathom the depth and breadth and height of God's love and come to recognize that *to love Christ is better than all knowledge*, that we might be filled with God's grace. But to him who can accomplish more than we can ask or understand, according to the power that worketh in us, to him be honour among those of all times who believe in Christ Jesus. With this fervent wish I greet you and commend myself to you. Your loving brother, Johann Wall.

Postscript of a Molochna Minister: May this precious letter be read widely and achieve its purpose. As the author hopes, might it find ready acceptance in congregations and in every home. May the Lord accompany you with his blessing and fashion a new and lasting peace within a people that has been grievously divided by groundless dislikes and prejudices.

I would hope that we might all reflect on these matters and recognize what brother Wall hopes to achieve through his letter.[12]

June 17 Although the foregoing letter is addressed to the Molochna churches, the author has also, I think, hit the nail on the head respecting our own church. The events described [earlier] in this diary are pretty clear evidence that these very circumstances exist in our District and that we have more than our share of zeal and divisions. Lord, grant us thy peace!

June 18 Yesterday's hailstorm caused great damage to the grain fields of the Neuendorf colony and of the noble estate of Lukashev.

June 20 Jakob Klassen of Nieder Khortitsa, who is 60, has been arrested for theft. He had stolen a horse from the Burwalde steppe at night and sold it to a Jew on the other side of Besborodka. In his statement he says that he has been involved in such evil matters since the age of 14 and has committed other disreputable acts. He has the reputation of being a terrible drunkard, had been suspected earlier of stealing, and served time in the Ekaterinoslav jail for robbery some time ago. He is said to show no remorse, but only fear of civil punishment. When the Mayor's Office came to arrest him, he tried to drown himself in the Dnieper and was revived only with the greatest effort. In this case one can see clearly the consequences of sin.

June 21 My wife and I and the children visited our mothers in Khortitsa. Kleinmichel, the [imperial] minister, drove through Neuenburg today, on his way from the Dnieper rapids.[13]

June 26 I visited Khortitsa today on business. It has been raining almost daily for some time now and one becomes impatient with all the moisture. First we had too little rain and now we have too much. The human heart is really a strange thing, so restless and full of despair. I have made a resolve to end my servitude to sin and have begged my Saviour for the strength needed to do this. I must confess with Paul: 'For I know that in me (that is, in my flesh) dwelleth no good thing: for to will the good is present with me; but how to perform that which is good I find not. For the good that I would I do not; but the evil which I would not, that I do.' Romans 7:18–19. This is my experience daily. Lord, I am weak; become mighty in me. I want to serve Christ and to crucify my flesh with its lusts and desires and to walk in the Spirit, according to Galatians. Let me quake in the face of sin and look to Jesus, until I have found the grace to prevail. My Saviour, do not judge me, a miserable sinner, but arm me with thy Spirit to work my salvation.

June 29 With several other Islanders, I and my daughter Helena attended the annual fair in Alexandrovsk, going by boat to the fortress village and the rest of the way on foot. We heard that the body of a Russian child, who had drowned while swimming in a tributary of the Dnieper, had been found and buried.

July 2 Today my wife and I and the children as well as my brother

Johann left for the Jewish colonies. We were anxious to be on our way, and because it was raining I borrowed a covered wagon from Mrs Abr. Klassen, the widow of my wife's late uncle. We spent the night on the Kudashev land at Abr. Wiebe's place, and arrived at my brother Diedrich's place the following day at noon. We and the Epps drove to the home of the Peter v Kampens in Novovitebsk where the German settlers [of that village] had gathered to hire me on as the teacher for their children. We finally reached an agreement that I would build a house, furnish one room in it for the school, and teach the children in winter, receiving in return 8 desiatinas of plough-land, enough pasture and hay-land for 12 head of mature cattle, one load of fuel straw from each of the 8 landholders, and 20 silver R. in cash. We will move a year from now in spring, when the construction will also be done. Lord, give me thy blessing.

We arrived home safely at my mother's place in Khortitsa at midnight on July 5 and were home by noon on the 6th. Lord, I thank thee for thy gracious protection.

July 6 Landholders at a [Village] assembly meeting in the mayor's office [on the Island of Khortitsa] were asked to provide a subsidy for the victims of the recent storm in Schönhorst and to consider a fire-insurance arrangement like that of the Khortitsa District for the future. Both proposals were agreed to. This is only right, for we can hardly have too many arrangements that serve the common good. Lord, grant us unity and peace, and may all discord, division, and hatred be removed from thy church.

July 8 On Sunday in the Khortitsa church, Elder Jacob Dyck confirmed in office the recently elected Elder Franz Wienz through the laying on of hands. In his opening words, Elder Dyck spoke of our congregation's emigration from Prussia some 63 years ago, during Empress Catherine II's reign. The first Elder elected [in Russia] was Bernhard Penner, who was followed by David Epp (my grandfather, who died in 1802), Johann Wiebe, Bernhard von Bärgen, and Jacob Dyck, the present Elder. After a prayer, the Elder listed the duties of an elder to his congregation and those of the congregation to its elder. The newly chosen Elder replied affirmatively to several questions addressed to him, and the congregation gave its assent to the questions asked of it by remaining silent. As Franz Wienz fell to his knees, Elder Dyck blessed him by placing his hand on his head and consecrated him to his service with solemn words. He then raised him to his feet, kissed him, and wished him the Lord's blessing. All of the ministers and deacons now assembled in order, kissing the newly confirmed Elder, blessing him and wishing him grace, each in his own way. Finally, the new Elder gave a short and moving address, followed by a closing statement by Elder Dyck. After a hymn of praise, the congregation was dismissed.

The church was so crowded that one could see and hear very little. I found a seat myself downstairs among the women, while others entered through the windows. The church's entrance, two adjoining rooms, doorways, aisle, and stairs were full to overflowing. May the Lord, who has appointed this man as a watchman on the walls of Zion, be with him and grant him strength and wisdom to repair the ramparts, restore peace, and pasture his flock as a true shepherd. Unfortunately, often the shepherds and watchmen become tired and sleepy and abandon their flocks. Lord, be merciful to us and constrain the destroyer, who works mightily among thy people.

July 9 The authorities intend to introduce bee-keeping into the Khortitsa District and have sent us a master bee-keeper, a Russian. The District Office and Agricultural Commission have taken steps to experiment with bee-keeping. Although several people in our colonies have kept bees for years, bee-keeping remains a minor activity. It is more highly developed only in the colony of Kronsgarten where quite a lot of honey and wax is produced annually and sent to market. One hopes that bee-keeping will develop and flourish and help to increase our income.

July 14 Sunday I drove to Petrikovka, near Lugovoi, with my brother Heinrich and brother-in-law Dyck to buy pigs (which are very dear given the high demand arising from the excellent harvest), and I paid 22 R. 25 C. for two boars. I drove them home in the stifling heat, which was very difficult, and did not arrive there until the morning of the 16th.

July 16 Monday. Late this morning there was an eclipse of the sun, its disc becoming completely obscured except for a glimmer around the edge. It was very dark and the stars in the heaven became crystal clear. Lord, thy creation is marvellous. Who can fathom the multitude of thy wonders.

July 18 I and the three Dycks threshed the wheat, which was grown from their seed-grain, and divided it in half. My half came to nine chetverik, and the yield was nine-fold.

July 23 and 24 I winnowed the rye, which had been trodden out by horse in Driediger's barn, and brought home the grain and chaff. The yield from one desiatina was four chetvert of clean grain, an eight-fold increase, and this year's harvest is even better.

July 28 Saturday. We went to Khortitsa on business where we met my brother Johann and his fiancée Helena Siemens, who were just back from celebrating their engagement at my brother Diedrich's place in the Jewish colony of Novo-Odessa. The newly engaged couple and my brother Abraham visited us on the 31st.

August 1 The dangers involved in leaving children unattended were brought home to us again today by a tragic accident – a stern warning to everyone. The wife of Peter Kasper, a cottager from the Island [of Khortitsa], put her almost year-old infant son into a wheelbarrow at the door and went about her work. Suddenly, without warning, the child screamed pitifully. The horrified mother rushed to the scene only to discover her child with its hand almost bitten off by one of the pigs that had been left free to wander about. Lord, the child has now become a cripple because of his parents' negligence. Looking after children is a job for angels, and whoever takes it on must also take on the responsibility that goes with it. Yet who among us can really guard a child from every possible danger. Thou, Lord and Saviour, art the protector and shield of the little ones, and into thy care do I entrust my children. I ask thee to help me to raise them in the fear of thee.

August 3 I have heard that Bartsch, the mayor of the Khortitsa District, and Wilhelm Penner, District secretary, have gone to see the Guardianship Committee in Odessa regarding the dispute with the Agricultural Commission. Although the Committee has ordered that Schmidt be reinstated in his former job as [chief] shepherd, the District Office refuses to comply. This dispute continues on, seemingly without end.

August 7 Following coffee in the afternoon, my wife and I and the children went to Khortitsa on business and found two of our relatives quite ill at my mother-in-law's place: Agatha is again in bed with sores, and Johann, who had fallen from a tree, had been brought home unconscious, with serious injuries.

August 9 I bought a load of brushwood fuel for my mother-in-law and carted it to her place in Khortitsa. Agatha is getting better but Johann is still sick in bed.

August 12 Sunday. Today I started teaching school again. Lord, be thou present, and may thy blessing and grace rest upon the school.

August 15 In the afternoon my family and I drove to Khortitsa to settle the accounts with Jacob Dyck in regard to the wool we had sold and the debts that remain from our various purchases. I sold 1 pud 39 funt and received 27 bank R. per pud of wool. Wound silk is now fetching 14 bank R. 50 C. per funt, wheat 13 bank R. and rye 5 bank R. per chetvert.

August 19 Sunday. My wife and I and the children attended a funeral at the home of Elder Jakob Hildebrand for his stepmother-in-law, the widow P. Hildebrand.[14] Peter Unrau of Kronsweide delivered the funeral sermon. The first verse of the hymn 'Christ Is My Life' was sung as the coffin was placed on the wagon, the second as the wagon departed, and the remaining verses at the cemetery during the burial. Reverend Unrau read a prayer as the grave was being closed, and the whole gathering said the Lord's Prayer in silence together at the end.

August 21 Thursday afternoon, after school, I went to Khortitsa to see my brother-in-law, Johann, who is out of bed but still a little mixed up, but no one was home. I learned that my mother-in-law had gone with him to get help at Diet. Hildebrand's place in Burwalde. There is, however, a physician who can help, and helps gladly, if we turn to him in trust, namely Jesus, our Lord and Saviour. However intelligent and wise we may think we are, we can accomplish nothing without his help. My brother Abraham, who has been attending the Khortitsa Zentralschule as a bursary student, has been let go by the District Office, supposedly because of bad eyes. But he will be allowed to attend classes in winter-time as a private student, without having to pay tuition.

August 24 Friday. A strong wind has been blowing since last Monday, spreading dust and sand in all directions. We have had no rain for a long time, and it is terribly dry. If the Lord does not take pity on us soon, we will have to start feeding the cattle.

August 28 My family and I were in Khortitsa on a visit. My brother Heinrich, who is secretary to the Agricultural Commission, showed me a directive from His Excellency Baron von Rosen, president of the

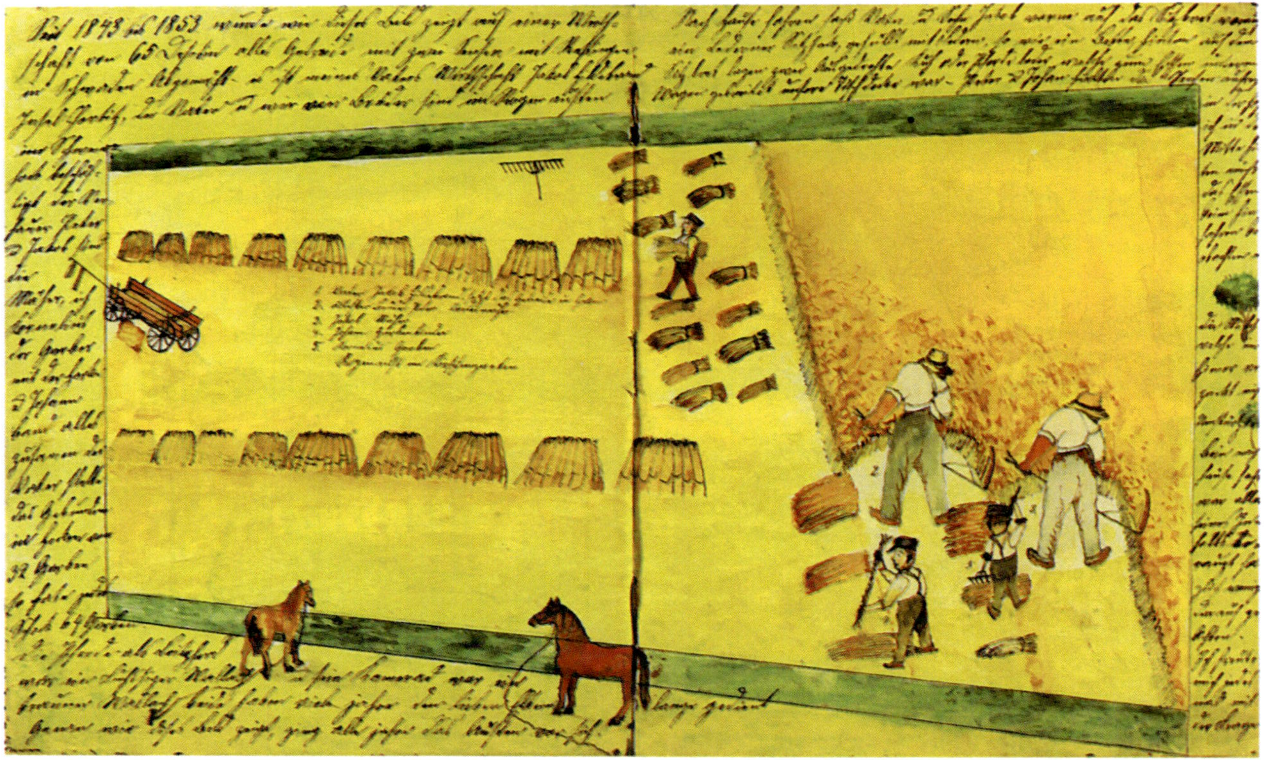

Harvest scene involving Jakob Hildebrand and sons, Island of Khortitsa, 1840s
(From Cornelius Hildebrand's *Lebenserinnerung*)

Jakob Hildebrand's *Wirtschaft* overlooking the Dnieper River, 1830s
(From Cornelius Hildebrand's *Lebenserinnerung*)

Jakob Hildebrand's *Wirtschaft* (enlargement), Island of Khortitsa, with brisker and more modern river traffic, 1850s
(From Cornelius Hildebrand's *Lebenserinnerung*)

Sketch and layout of Jakob Hildebrand's home, 1850s
(From Cornelius Hildebrand's *Lebenserinnerung*)

Guardianship Committee,[15] which instructs the District Office to inform the [Village] communities through the Village mayors that responsibility for supervising the Village schools lies with the [Agricultural] Commission. The directive states further that instructions and regulations issued previously in this regard remain in force.

The Village mayors met today in the District Office. The District Office is determined that persons who have not yet agreed to make a donation of the rye grain to the Jews should do so now in order to win the government's praise. This effort to trumpet our good deeds is meant to cover up a lot that is not very uplifting. We should give our alms in Christian charity, freely, yet this seems not to be the case in this instance. Many donate their rye but complain. If only the leaders in the District Office and members of the [Agricultural] Commission could be reconciled. But this is unlikely to happen, and meanwhile the community continues to decay.

August 29 *Incidents.* One night last week some of the best horses in Khortitsa were stolen. In Alexandrovsk two infants were found on the street, swaddled and alive. The town police are trying to find their mother or mothers, but the chances of this happening are rather slim.

August 30 At a general Brotherhood Meeting in Khortitsa, Gerhard Enz, the deacon from Neuendorf, was relieved of his office because of a moral transgression. The congregation was also given notice that a poor tax would be collected of 1 bank R. 75 C. from each household, 50 bank C. from each male, and 25 bank C. from each female communicant. Money is also to be collected for the construction of a church for the evangelical congregation in the Caucasus. I was absent because I did not want to miss school.

Today God blessed us with a cool shower, which started at night and continued through the day. We had feared that the grass would dry up completely, but all of nature is now fresh and new again: 'Every good gift and every perfect gift is from above, and cometh down from the Father of lights, with whom is no variableness, neither shadow of turning.' James 1:17. God is the Lord over all nature, and his governance is meant to lead mankind to him.

September 1 My wife and I and the children attended the funeral of Helena, the infant daughter of my brother Heinrich, who had died at birth. We could not find my horses and so we hired Peter Kasper to take us there and back.

September 3 About 900 Cossacks on horseback passed through Khortitsa and Einlage, and were billeted for the night in Khortitsa and Rosenthal.[16] They were on their way home from the Hungarian campaign.

September 7 I feel vulnerable to Satan's arrows, which strike and wound me daily. Lord, be at my side and protect me from my adversary.

September 15 Sunday. My wife and I and the children drove to Khortitsa for a visit. At my mother-in-law's we hired my sister-in-law Agatha as our maid-servant for 1852. We will pay her 30 bank R., 2 shirts, a blue apron, a pair of shoes, and 2 funt of wool for stockings. I gave her 3 R. as earnest money.

September 21 Our guests for dinner (a little late) were my brother Diedrich, his wife and children (Peter, Diedrich, and Helena), my brother Heinrich and his wife, and my mother and my sister Katharina. They drove to Nieder Khortitsa for the night.

September 22 At 4:30 Saturday morning, my wife and I and the two children, David and Maria, left for Ekaterinoslav. We arrived at the home of my uncle, Heinrich Thiessen, at sundown, started for home Monday after breakfast, and got to Khortitsa shortly before midnight. We spent the night with my mother and arrived home safely Tuesday morning. The entire trip was terribly dusty. My mother-in-law looked after our household while we were gone. Since my last visit the city of Ekaterinoslav has been embellished with large new palaces and plantings of trees along the main avenues, which are now also paved. I asked my uncle for a loan to build my house, but got an evasive answer. It is naturally preferable to lend money to people who are sure to repay the capital and interest than to poor people who are having difficulties. I had hoped that he might help in some way, even perhaps by lending me money for a few years at no interest. Yet it is better to count on the Lord than on people, for blessed is the man who depends on the Lord and has his trust in him.

September 26 The two elders of the Khortitsa church, Jacob Dyck and Franz Wienz, were here on the Island to get Jakob Hildebrand, the Elder of the Kronsweide [Frisian] church, to sign a document affirming that the schools in the Khortitsa District were under the exclusive jurisdiction of the Church Convent and not of the Agricultural Commission. The document was to be forwarded to the

Guardianship Committee for [its] confirmation and as a response to the directive mentioned earlier in this diary. Since Elder Hildebrand had not been involved in the drafting of the document, he asked for several days in which to consider it, but this was denied him. Imagine if a document like this had been drafted two decades ago or even a decade ago. What a difference that would have made to [the quality] of our schools. It used to be that the Council of Church Ministers [Convent] was largely indifferent to education, and [village] assemblies put more care into hiring a reliable herdsman than a competent teacher who had the desire and ability to teach their children. The cheapest was also the best. Matters in this regard began to improve only when the [Khortitsa] District was placed under the jurisdiction of the late Johann Cornies, then chairman of the Molochna Agricultural Commission.[17] Through his efforts leadership of the school system was transferred to the Khortitsa Agricultural Commission, and only then did a new and more vital life begin in our schools. But after Cornies's death [in 1848], the old quarrels between the Agricultural Commission and District Office flared up again and the old indifference returned. The wall primers, which had just made their appearance, were removed from the schools, and proper instruction and attendance came to an end. Regular teaching of the Bible, for instance, takes place in only a few village schools today. Lord, what will be the end result of this?

September 30 Sunday. I went to the market in Alexandrovsk with my brother Heinrich, who had come to the Kamp [the Island of Khortitsa] with his wife yesterday. Prices: 7 bank R. per hundred head of cabbage (I bought 40 head); salt, 1 R. 60 C. per pud (I bought 1 pud); and soap, 26 C. for 10 funt (I bought 10 funt).

October 1 Last Saturday night a thief broke into the home of Jacob Penner, the cottager, at the ferry landing. He got into the entranceway through a hole in the wall, and in the morning two new shirts were missing and a basin of milk had been spilled. Johann Schellenberg had a similar experience the following night, but only lost a loaf of bread and several other provisions. The landowners Johann Peters and David Penner also reported chasing pesky guests of this kind away [from their places]. In Khortitsa horses have again been stolen.

October 3 Wednesday morning, Abraham Klassen seized a tramp from among the willow bushes along the sandbank. He is a Russian who claims to come from Bereslav. The stolen goods mentioned earlier were found among his posssessions: Jacob Penner's shirts as well as a pair of scissors, a fire chair, a Dutch book, a tie, and an old piece of cloth belonging to Johann Schellenberg. The vagabond had probably been hiding out on the Island for some time. The [Village] Mayor's Office confiscated the stolen goods and returned them to their owners, and the thief was sent off to the Khortitsa District Office.

October 10 I composed the following evening prayer for the children in school.

> Be with us now, Lord Jesus,
> For night is drawing near;
> Be close when dangers threaten,
> A shield against our fear.
> Be gracious Lord, be kindly,
> Count not our sins too dear.
> Judge not our world too harshly,
> With countenance severe.
> For thou dost love the children,
> And would their voices hear.
> Rule over us and guide us,
> We pledge ourselves to thee. Amen

Another prayer, which I wrote last week, reads:

Loving Saviour, Lord Jesus, we come to thee and praise thee for the many benefits which thou hast granted us undeservedly. We have food and clothing and have been able to do our school work this day. We praise thy goodness and glorify thy mercy. Compassionate Jesus, who gladly receiveth transgressors, forgive us our sins. Do not reject us. Cleanse us through thy blood, which thou hast shed for us. Grant us the courage and the strength to turn our backs on sin and to walk henceforward in thy light. Protect us from dangers this night, and when our last hour is come, Lord, receive us into thy kingdom. Amen.

I usually recite prayers from memory, and the children follow me in their thoughts, but sometimes I ask the class to recite a prayer as well. At the beginning of my teaching career I composed the following prayer.

A Morning Prayer

Holy Father, graciously accept our childlike thanks for thy protection, which has been ours this night, and for the good things which we receive from thy merciful hand hourly. We bring thee praise, honour and glory and ask thee to bless our labours this day in order that all that we do might bring honour to thy name. Amen.

At the end of the morning class the children recite the Lord's Prayer, as Jesus taught us in Matthew 6. It seems better and more heartfelt for the children to recite a prayer that they have learned by heart than for the teacher to read a prayer.[18] Which is more pleasing to the Lord? Lord Jesus, teach us to pray, each according to thy will, for prayer protects us from the snares of sin. Yet so many people, even those who call themselves by thy name, neglect to do this.

October 11 I bought a sheep barn from Johann Wienz on the Island of Khortitsa for 100 silver R. and plan to transfer the debt to my account with the Orphans' Administration [Waisenamt]. At his expense, Wienz has undertaken to remodel and reassemble the barn as a dwelling in the Jewish colony of Novovitebsk. I will have to go into debt to pay for the resettlement, but Lord, thou hast abundant riches. Bless my labours that I may be able to pay off these debts that I have incurred for my family's sake: 'Grant me neither riches nor poverty, but only my modest share.'

October 12 Johann Wienz and I went by boat to Einlage and bought six beams from Heinrichs for 4 R. 20 C. apiece. Heinrichs refused to sell me the timber on credit, however, saying he did not know me, even though I promised to repay him by fall. Since the Lord supports those in need, I asked him for his help and his counsel, and he heard my prayer. My wife suggested that we sell our small flock of sheep and use the money to pay the outstanding building costs. Meanwhile Johann Peters has offered to buy the sheep, and so our greatest problem has been solved for the time being. We praise and thank thee, O Lord.

October 13 Saturday. I went to Alexandrovsk for supplies and bought 10 funt of lard and Russian sheep tails at 25 bank C. per funt.

October 14 My family and I visited my mother on Sunday. In the afternoon I asked Jacob Dyck whether he, together with Johann Peters, would guarantee my loan at the Orphans' Administration [Waisenamt].[19] He was happy to give his consent and gave me the needed attestation.
October 18 Thursday. Around noon, a wolf ran along the street through the village, pursued by Kasdorf's son, Isaak, who, with several others, had chased him from the steppe. The wolf then disappeared in the bushes along the sand dunes. (Two weeks later this same wolf was killed on the street.)
October 20 Saturday. I took a load of brushwood fuel to my mother-in-law's in Khortitsa and then drove on to Kronsweide where I bought three planks for window heads from Kruse at 1 R. 90 C. apiece.
October 23 Today I assumed Johann Wienz's debt of 100 silver R. at the Orphans' Administration, with interest starting on May 1. Jacob Dyck of Khortitsa and Johann Peters of the Island were my guarantors.
October 28 Sunday. Their Lordships His Excellency Baron von Rosen, privy councillor and president of the Guardianship Committee, and Baron von Stempel, the supervisor, were in Khortitsa today to see the chairman of the Agricultural Commission and to hold court regarding the many disputes that have arisen in the community. His Excellency was extremely dissatisfied with the District Office and with Elder Jacob Dyck, who was ordered to appear before him together with Elder Hildebrand. The new school regulations, which had been distributed by the District Office without the prior confirmation of the authorities, were withdrawn. Today, the Village Mayor's Office received a directive from the District Office affirming that the [Village] schools would henceforward be under the jurisdiction of the Agricultural Commission, as they had been earlier.[20]

Martens, mayor of Einlage, and Johann Epp, mayor of Khortitsa, were relieved of their duties because of their insubordination to the Agricultural Commission. Johann Penner, mayor of Rosenthal, was similarly punished, and this morning all of the village mayors were summoned to the District Office, where the baron made public the dismissals and counselled all officials to be obedient and orderly. He promised to return in spring. In the late afternoon, these high-ranking persons left for the Jewish colonies in a carriage with Siemens, chairman [of the Agricultural Commission].

Postscript. The transgression of the mayor of Einlage was that he had followed the orders of the District Office, but not those of the Agricultural Commission, in regard to the care of the local woods. Last summer, moreover, the mayor of Khortitsa had refused to provide transportation for officials on government business who had come to see Chairman Siemens. He had told Siemens that he would provide horses only upon the written authorization of the District Office. These important persons had then written to Baron von Rosen recommending that the heavy-handed mayor be punished. The mayor of Rosenthal had similarly refused to provide a conveyance without the District Office's authorization. Such behaviour hardly accords with our responsibilities to the authorities as spelled out in Romans 13 and 1 Peter 2:13–14. What will the conclusion of this matter be?

November 1 *Continuation of the Foregoing.* Peters, a member of the [Agricultural] Commission, told me that the Lord Supervisor, Baron von Stempel, had also dismissed the deputy district mayors Johann Siemens of Rosenthal and Heinrich Dyck of Khortitsa. Johann Epp of Khortitsa, a member of the [Agricultural] Commission, has been relieved of his office for repeatedly petitioning the Guardianship Committee, and Martin Klassen, the candidate member of the Commission, has been appointed in his place. Schmidt, the head shepherd, is to be employed again, starting on Monday. His Lordship, von Stempel, left for home yesterday. I wonder whether we will finally now have peace and whether brotherly love will guide the hearts and minds of our civil and religious leaders? This I very much hope.

November 3 Saturday. On instructions of the District Office, the Village Mayor's Office [on the Island] proceeded with the election of the two new deputy District mayors and the candidates for these offices. We also elected a candidate for the previously elected deputy Village mayor. This happened quite peacefully in the local [Island of Khortitsa] mayor's office, and I was surprised that no one expressed any opposition to the government's orders. The directive from the District Office reads as follows: 'His Excellency, Privy Councillor Baron von Rosen, president of the Guardianship Committee for

Foreign Settlers, has informed the District Office by means of Directive 255 of October 30 that close relatives may not serve in office together since this is contrary to the interests of public service. Since they are closely related to the District mayor, His Excellency has found it necessary to relieve the two deputy District mayors, Dyck and Siemens, of their duties and ordered that others be elected in their place and that the candidate positions be filled by election as well.' We can be happy that such an insignificant pretext has been found for this action for otherwise it might have ruffled a lot of feathers. These people are no more closely related than they were before and yet they have served together for many years. People have difficulty acknowledging their faults and are always looking for excuses.

November 8 This morning, Johann Siemens, chairman of the Agricultural Commission, and Johann Peters, another member, visited the school together with Jakob Wiebe, the Village mayor. They first examined the penmanship exercise books, then I dictated a short sentence for the better students, which they wrote out on their slate boards. After they had exchanged slate boards and corrected one another's errors, I wrote out another sentence on the board with mistakes, and the pupils were asked to find and correct the errors. Finally, I gave the class short tests in Bible stories and grammar. The chairman examined the class register, noted that attendance was irregular, and ordered that pupils could be absent only with the permission of the teacher (an absence of several days would require the permission of the Village mayor). Lord, grant that the schools might soon blossom, and give them thy blessing. Endow the teachers with the skills needed to instruct the children in the fear of thee.

November 11 Sunday. My wife and I and the children visited our mother in Khortitsa where my brother Diedrich, Peter van Kampen, and their wives arrived by wagon in the afternoon. My wife's sister Agatha has agreed to stay with us now already.

November 17 'Let not sin therefore reign in your mortal body, that ye should obey it in the lusts thereof.' Romans 6:12. Grant that I might keep this verse constantly in mind and watch and pray earnestly, for often I am inclined to yield to the temptations of sin. Be with me, merciful Saviour, and help me in my struggle against the lusts of the flesh. Grant me thy strength that I might be able to vanquish the foe who often threatens to overwhelm me. Thou art the

Lion of Judah who hast conquered wondrously and destroyed the Kingdom of Darkness. Grant me courage and strength to fight on to victory. Hear my prayer, dearest Jesus, forgive me my transgressions for the sake of thy bitter suffering and death. *Thy blood cleanseth us from all sin.* Grant me thy Holy Spirit that it might reign in me and lead me in the path of salvation. Carry out thy promise of Luke 11:13. Thou art my shepherd; I shall not want. And though I walk through the valley of the shadow of death, I will fear no evil; for thou art with me; thy rod and thy staff they comfort me. Thou, O Lord, wilt guide the afflicted and teach them thy way. The Lord is my salvation, my glory, the rock of my strength. My hope, too, is in God.

November 21 A missionary report from an apostle to the heathens on the Island of Rarotonga appearing in the *Magazin für die neuste Geschichte der Missions und Bibel Gesellschaften* (Journal of the Modern History of Missions and Bible Societies) witnesses to the blessings that accompany the distribution of Holy Scriptures among all nations.

November 26 In response to my petition of November 17, I received a directive from the Agricultural Commission (no. 365, dated November 17) granting me permission to settle in the Jewish colony[21] of Novovitebsk.

November 30 I have heard a reliable report about a serious accident at the Dnieper rapids. On November 17, some workers sought shelter from the rain in an old abandoned shack that had presumably been used as an overnight shelter before. But the old dilapidated building could not withstand the strong wind and collapsed. Of the 20 people there, all from Voznesensk, two were killed instantly, and the rest injured in various ways.

December 1 I went by wagon to Khortitsa. The ice at the landing had broken through, and we made the crossing by ferry.

December 6 I am told that the government will not permit the founding or settlement of a [new] colony in the Mariupol Mennonite District [also called Bergthal]. A directive from the District Office announces that the land is to be leased out for another year. Settlers had already seeded rye in fall, dug wells, and now all of this work and expense is for nought. They had also sold their immovable property, gotten themselves ready for settlement, and these arrangements will probably now have to be cancelled. The District Office had simply gone ahead with this project without first consulting the [Agricultural] Commission or getting the government's approval. This is another consequence of our divisions.

December 8 There was a fire at night in Neuenburg that destroyed the buildings of the landowner Sudermann. The lives of the people and cattle were spared, except for a heifer cow, but only a clock and a few other possessions were saved.

December 9 At the service in the local school, Elder Hildebrand preached a sermon about the return of our Lord Jesus based on Luke 21:25–36.

The Village Mayor's Office received a notice from the Agricultural Commission saying that Johann Epp of Khortitsa had asked for permission to stand down as a member of the Commission. In accordance with the instructions of His Excellency, the chairman of the Guardianship Committee, Martin Klassen of Kronsthal, had been appointed in his place.

December 14 At a meeting of representatives of the village mayors in the District Office several subjects were raised for discussion. One, the victims of the May 11 storm in the village of Schönhorst are to receive compensation. Two, it was proposed that an insurance scheme be developed to cover such instances in future, but while some supported the idea and others opposed it nothing concrete was decided. Three, Julius Janzen, leaseholder of the liquor distillery and of the sale of spirits in the Khortitsa colonies, demands compensation of 3000 silver R., which he claims as the loss incurred as a result of his inability to brew spirits because of certain developments. He was granted part of this sum. Four, the supplying of [obligatory] cartage was discussed at length. The village community of Khortitsa had complained [about its unequal responsibilities] in this regard, and asked the other villages for relief. The issue remained undecided.

December 15 Saturday. I drove to Khortitsa by sled with my wife and two youngest children and took the ferry, which is still making the crossing. Yesterday in Khortitsa a rabid dog bit a cow and several pigs, but no people were harmed, thank God.

December 17 The Village assembly met in the Village Mayor's Office to hear an application for compensation from the liquor leaseholder, Julius Janzen, which was forwarded from the District Office. He claimed a personal loss of 3000 R., stemming from a prohibition on distilling, which the District Office, after consulting with the mayors, had reduced to 2000 silver R. The District Office, for its part, had petitioned the Guardianship Committee in this matter and been advised that "the community was at liberty to offer its leaseholder a fair measure of relief." In its directive, the District Office, in a document for their approval, therefore instructed [the Village assemblies] that a compensation award of 2000 silver R. be made. The Village assembly, however, refused to sign the document and would agree to underwrite a sum of 100 silver R., a decision that the Village Mayor's Office will report to the District Office. Has Janzen really suffered such a large loss? I am inclined to think that he might have been able to earn an extra 3000 R., but I am ignorant of these matters: 'Gather treasures in heaven and not on earth, where neither moth nor rust can consume them.' Whoever belongs to the Lord Jesus is far richer, even if he appears poor by worldly standards, than a man who possesses millions, or even more. 'Have pity on the rich, who can recompense you.'

December 20 During the night from the 20th to the 21st a strong wind tore the rafters from Peter Kasper's barn and smashed them. In the evening it was still thawing, but by morning there was a lot of frost and a strong driving wind so that travelling with unshod horses has become very difficult.

December 21 Friday. I closed school today until after New Year's. Merciful Saviour, thou holdest the hearts of these children in thy hand and canst guide them as thou dost a water stream. Draw these children, whom I have taught thy Word, to thee, and bless what has been learned that it may bear rich fruit. Lord, I am at a loss for words, I am unworthy and feel that I have not lived up to my obligations in school. Lord, forgive me.

Saturday I walked to Khortitsa where W. Töws inoculated our daughter Maria against smallpox.

December 25 Tuesday. Our Christmas day service was held in school, where we live. Elder Hildebrand delivered the sermon, which was based on Luke 2:10 and 14. Lord, bless this celebration to my heart, and grant me the comfort of knowing that thou wast born also for me. Towards evening I drove my brother-in-law Johann to the ferry crossing over a muddy road. In the evening I and my wife visited at the home of Abraham Janzen Sr.

December 26 The second holiday. The moon began its eclipse at daybreak, and its disc was completely covered as it set. I drove to fetch my sister-in-law, Margaretha, at the ferry crossing in the morning.

'What shall I render unto the Lord for all his benefits toward me?' Psalm 116:12. Today is my 31st birthday, and over the years I have sinned often and feel grieved and despondent. God, how will things end with me? Be gracious, merciful Saviour, who art come to save sinners and not the righteous. Cleanse my heart of all impurity, and grant that I might strive more and more to renounce my slavery to sin.

December 27 My sister-in-law Margaretha went home today, and I drove her to the ferry crossing.

December 28 My brother Abraham visited us and returned home on the 30th.

December 29 I picked up my brother Johann, his wife, and my brother Diedrich's daughter Helena from the Dnieper at Nieder Khortitsa and drove them back on the 31st. On the evening of the 30th we and our wives dropped in to see Elder Hildebrand and participated in an interesting conversation. There is circulating in our village a copy of a letter from Prussia in which the author, who identifies himself as a Mecklenburger, creates quite a sensation. Some visionaries had come to the author's place of residence, and in a trancelike state had foretold the early return of Christ. The author, and others, regard these people as prophets of the highest. Yet neither in the Old nor the New Testament do we read that people who are to proclaim God's will to mankind had first to fall into such a state. The Day of the Lord is surely near, but one can test the times simply by searching the Scriptures and comparing what is found there with the signs that have already been revealed. Lord, teach us to be watchful and to pray, that the day of wrath may find us ready. Let us be on our guard.[22]

Review of the Year 1851

'By this shall all men know that ye are my disciples, if ye have love one for another.' John 13:35. Yet in searching the paths of the church for those with true love as disciples of Christ one finds very few despite much talk about love and about doing good. For the moment the government has suppressed the divisions among our leaders, and there is a certain external peace, but there has not yet been a genuine reconciliation. Mission work among the heathen is flourishing, and heralds of peace proclaim the Gospel throughout the world. At the behest of our Lord Jesus Christ, the kingdom is being extended, and the young church that has arisen among the heathen reminds us of the devout life led by the first Christians, who were of one heart and mind. Yet how are matters among us? Lord have mercy.

The harvest in the Khortitsa District was very good, but God has also sent us stern warnings in nature to arouse us from our sleep and to draw us to himself. Hail caused serious damage in Schönwiese, Schönhorst, Neuendorf, and a number of other places. The people of Schönhorst were again reminded of the Creator's great power by a violent storm that overturned and wrecked many houses. At the end of the harvest grain prices in bank R. were as follows: wheat, 12–14 R. per chetvert; rye, 4½–7½ R.; oats, 5 R.; and barley, 4–5 R.

1852

January 1 Tuesday, New Year's Day. At the service held in the school, Elder Hildebrand preached a sermon based on Ephesians 4:22–5. Lord, renew my heart and mind and let me shed the old Adam. Work a new birth in me that I might become a new being through the riches of thy grace. Be near me, thou King of Glory, as I struggle with sin, which rules in my flesh. Embolden me in my feebleness, that I might walk uprightly and devoutly before thee. Bless my work, let thy peace rest on my family, and protect us from all evil. Strengthen me in my teaching, and endow me with the gift to instruct and to lead our young people to thee.

January 5 Saturday. My sheepskins from the tanner in Alexandrovsk were not ready.

January 6 The Epiphany of Christ. Reveal thyself to me, Jesus, my light and my salvation, for darkness surrounds my heart and leads my mind astray. Dawn in me, brightness of majesty, break the chains that bind me, and speak to my spirit thus: 'Thou art free and shalt from this hour on walk in my light, for I am thy Saviour who hath freed thee from these bonds.' Grant this, dear Lord and Saviour for I plea: 'Amen, let it be done.'

January 7 Monday. I had to miss school today because of the so-called [year-end] reckoning. As is the custom, beer was consumed to excess, but fortunately it does not cloud the mind or hurt one's health. I have been to these kinds of festivities before where brandy was drunk and matters really got out of hand.

January 9 Wednesday. My wife was sick today with what people here call the drepp. The pains in her chest, head, and back were so severe that I went for advice to Aron Peters. He suggested boiling a tea of lilac blossoms and Loestak,[23] which we did and which brought relief. Two days later we went to Khortitsa by sled. At the present time my wife has very sore nipples, and they have been painful for some time.

January 12 On Saturday I drove to Einlage and bought ground millet for 2 R. a pud and a quart of linseed oil for 1 bank R. The children Helena and Katharina, as well as Agatha, came along till Khortitsa.

January 13–16 My wife has been bedridden most of this time, and our infant Maria has had teething fever. We praise and thank thee, Lord, for thy help.

January 20 Sunday. I drove to Khortitsa with my wife and youngest child Maria. We had 20 degrees of frost in the morning and the sledding was excellent. We reached my mother-in-law's place by noon and continued on to Martin Dyck's place in the afternoon where we met my brother Diedrich, who drove on to Schönhorst at night with his foster child, Jakob Neufeld. May the guardian angels protect them. My brother Heinrich and his wife were also at the Dycks.

January 23 An accident in Halbstadt on the Molochna. A maid found a rifle in the bed of one of the hired hands in the home of the District mayor Friesen. A boy who worked there picked up the gun and put a tinder in it to frighten the girl. But when he pressed the trigger it fired and a shell passed through the girl's cheek and nose. With God's help, it is hoped that the girl can be saved. The frightened boy ran away, and his tracks on the Molochna River showed that he had tried to break through the ice and drown himself. He was finally discovered in the snow where he had tried to hide himself.

January 24 Our daughter Maria was today inoculated for the fourth time against smallpox, this time by the inoculator from Voznesensk. The time before last only one small pox formed and there were none the other times. May the Lord give his blessing. (This fourth attempt also failed.) The inoculator told us that the government had ordered the Russian clergy to ring the church bells every night in winter-time to help travellers who have lost their way.

January 25 Friday. This morning Elder Jakob Hildebrand did me the unexpected honour of visiting the school. I gave the children a short test on the Bible, had them do some reading, dictated a sentence, which they wrote on their slate boards as a spelling test, and wrote another sentence on the board full of spelling errors, which I had them correct. After the Elder had looked at the penmanship exercise books, I closed the lesson with a prayer. The Elder then spoke briefly, urging the children to study conscientiously and to be obedient.

January 26 Today I and eight other Islanders carted loads of lumber from my [dismantled] barn at J. Wienz's place to my brother-in-law Martin Dyck's place in Khortitsa. It is thawing and the sledding was good.

January 27 Sunday. There was a general Brotherhood Meeting following the church service concerning a complaint made to the Elder against the minister Jakob Janzen. The latter's preaching was allegedly neither clear nor true and went about as follows. 'Since everything proceeds from God the Lord, that is, both what is good and what is evil, those who commit a sin have really no choice since this too comes from God. Since man must therefore sin, he is not at fault.' This teaching clearly denies any need for man to strive or to struggle. It is a great pity about Janzen as he is known as a first-class speaker. False teachings are beginning to arise in our midst. Jakob Bark, a highly intelligent and skilled man in mill construction and other trades, has been led astray by a false spirit and is infecting others with his wild ideas. Janzen probably got his views from him.

January 28 Monday morning several Islanders again carted lumber to Khortitsa for me. The Village assembly met at the Village mayor's office in the evening where a directive was read from the District Office asking for contributions of grain or money for victims of the storm in the colony of Schönhorst. I conducted the appeal, which produced some five chetvert of grain.
January 30 The turn-out at the auction sale at my mother-in- law's in Khortitsa was small. Only 315 bank R. was bid on the house and barn, and they were not sold. A cow went for 51 R. 50 C., and the total proceeds came only to 70 bank R.
February 16 Saturday. Today I asked the District Office in Khortitsa for a list of my outstanding debts and other obligations and for written permission to settle in the Jewish colonies. Since last March my wife has been suffering from swollen nipples (which some people here call the 'Schwemme'), but none of the treatments have worked. At times the nipples seem to have healed and then they are worse than ever. Today the weaver Peter Penner suggested a remedy, which we tried out. First, I bought the ingredients at Dyck's store: a funt of honey, a measure of cloves, two measures of bay leaves, two measures of mace, a nutmeg, a handful of resinous pine shavings, a handful of houseleek, and a quart of beer. These were to be tightly sealed and boiled for an hour and a half. The sediment was then to be re-boiled in a half quart of beer, for drinking later. A small cupful was to be taken twice in the morning and twice in the afternoon, and after each treatment the patient was to perspire strongly for two hours. During this time the patient was to abstain from eating pork or strongly salted and acidic foods, keep warm, and stay indoors. I proceeded as prescribed, except for the houseleek. Lord, thou hast put healing into nature itself, and we ask thy blessing. Thou art the source of health and of life, of sickness and of death, and hast sent sickness for the salvation of our souls. Thou leadest us in marvellous ways. Let thy name be praised. *Postscript*: The treatment was not successful.
February 24 Sunday morning our daughter Helena became very sick, and I think her condition may be serious. Lord, I commend her to thy care. Be thou her comfort and joy.
February 25 It is two in the morning. I have spent the night keeping vigil at Helena's bedside, and it will soon be dawn. The dear child is suffering with a violent cough, which gives her great pain, and she

complains of a stomach-ache. Only God knows if she will die. I would miss her terribly. She is ready to die and happy at the thought of being in heaven with a kindly Saviour, who loves children. Last night I asked her if she had prayed, and she said that she had prayed all night long. I asked her what she had been praying for, and she said, 'That Jesus might make me well.' I took the opportunity to talk to her about the Saviour and his suffering and death, and was delighted at her childish response, which showed her love of the Lord Jesus. Yesterday I asked her how she expected to find salvation, and she said, 'Because Jesus has died on the cross.' At her bedside today she said, 'Helena Penner (who is a fellow pupil of the same age) says that heaven is not as beautiful as this world, since people cry over someone who has died. But I don't believe this.' Jesus, merciful Saviour, be with her and comfort her.

February 28 At three o'clock this afternoon my pupil Klas Wiebe, son of the landowner Klas Wiebe, died at the age of 14 years. He had been in school all day yesterday and then died after an illness of less than 23 hours. I used the opportunity to remind my pupils that they should be ready to die at any time. This had the desired effect for I saw tears in many an eye.

It is ten in the evening. Our sick daughter seemed much better during the day, but towards evening became worse again. She asked me in a weak voice to pray with her, and this I did three times.

March 1 Our child is recovering, with God's help.

March 3 The Village Mayor's Office today received a statement from the District Office respecting my debts, obligations, and my settlement in the Jewish colony.

News regarding the communal disputes. The Village mayor today received a directive from the District Office (no. 606, dated March 1 that reads: 'His Lordship, Baron von Stempel, Supervisor of the Jewish Settlements, has been instructed to inform the District Office (no. 156, dated February 16) that the Lord President of the Guardianship Committee has confirmed the appointments of the following individuals as deputy mayors of the Khortitsa District: the Mennonite Johann Stäsz of Rosenthal and Jacob Dyck of Khortitsa.'

This week a certain Dietrich Pauls of Neuosterwick hanged himself tragically. May God have mercy on him. Helena has been out of bed all day today, and we thank the Lord Jesus for restoring her health.

March 4 Our beloved mother-in-law was here today.
March 9 My brother Johann and his wife from Nieder Khortitsa visited us. I picked them up in the morning at the Dnieper and drove them back in the evening.
March 12 Winter still has us in its powerful grip, although it is a little less cold than it was. This puts me under great strain because our fodder is running out. But he who feedeth the cattle will help us again in his own time.
March 13 God be praised. The frost is over, the air is mild and the snow is melting. The ice on the Dnieper opposite the village [to the east] has gone out, but we can still cross the ice to Khortitsa [on the western side of the Island].
March 15 The prospects of a string of warm days are gone again. The ground is frozen hard again, and the north wind is blowing cold and raw. Nevertheless we had to drive out our cattle with the herdsman, including our cows and young stock, because we are very low on feed.

I had to help in the Village mayor's office to calculate deductions for crown revenues: (a) land tax and fees of 5 silver R. 21$\frac{1}{3}$ C. per landowner; and (b) a head tax of 1 R. 2$\frac{1}{2}$ silver C. from each able-bodied person. We made the appropriate deductions for each person.
March 21 I took leave of my students today, and most cried as we shook hands. I myself was overcome with sadness and could not contain my deep feelings. This was, after all, the last time I would have all of my pets together. I pray that the Lord Jesus might bless the seed that I have sown in weakness, that it might sprout in their hearts.
March 23 Sunday. We left today, in God's name. My brother Diedrich loaded his wagon with seed-grain and took my wife and children along while I carted only the most essential household belongings on my ladder wagon. The road was hard and dry. The schoolboys drove my horned cattle to Martin Dyck's place in Khortitsa, and we spent the first night at my brother-in-law Peter Rempel's in Schönhorst. Here Isaak Siemens, who is also moving to the Jewish colonies, teamed up his horse with mine, and loaded a few of his belongings on to my wagon. He and my sister-in-law Agatha drove the cattle. My brother Diedrich drove on ahead with a lighter load and I followed, meeting five other wagons in Neuhorst. We had

planned to spend the night with the Mennonites on Kudashev's land, but nightfall overtook us before we could reach our destination and we had to stop over [along the road] beyond the state peasant village of Chumaki. Tuesday at daybreak we started out again but got stuck in the slough of a small valley where my wagon sank down in the mud to over its axle. After digging out the wheels it took six horses to pull us out. My brother and my wife had gotten stuck in the same slough the previous evening, and we did not meet them until we reached the already mentioned German settlement. From there they continued on and reached my brother Diedrich's place in the evening. We were delayed at Kudashev's sheep-farm while the swing tree of my wagon was repaired, spent the night at Loshkarovka on the Basavluk [Stream], and did not reach Novovitebsk until noon on the 26th. The peasants along the way were out ploughing and seeding, enjoying the warm spring weather, which God had given us. No one dreamt for a moment that winter might yet return in its full fury.

March 27 I left for Khortitsa Maundy Thursday, reaching the Island of Khortitsa on Sunday, a bright and warm day, where I loaded as many essentials as I could. I spent the night with my brother Heinrich and attended church service in Khortitsa Easter Sunday. There was a thunderstorm in the afternoon.

I left Khortitsa Easter Monday morning under overcast skies. It rained hard, the road was muddy, and I had great difficulty getting up the hill in Neuendorf. I stopped to unhitch and feed the horses at the school in Neuhorst where the mayor Abraham Enz asked me in and told me to put the horses in the barn. After two hours of rest, I started out again in the rain on a muddy road and reached Abraham Wiebe's place by nightfall. Toward evening, however, the wind had veered to the north and brought bitterly cold weather. I was soaked and shivering from walking beside the wagon in the cold, but Wiebe's friendly reception filled me with the kindliest feelings. I was in a warm room and the exhausted horses were at a crib full of hay in the barn. I uttered a prayer of thanks to God, my guide and sustainer. Since I was determined to reach my loved ones the following night, I planned to make an early start, but a miserable sight greeted us in the morning. The windows were frost-covered, a howling blizzard outside obscured even the neighbour's house, and there were huge drifts of snow everywhere. This pretty well meant that I would not be seeing my wife that day. What I needed was patience, and I thanked God that the storm had not caught me out on the steppe. But my gratitude was a little premature.

The following morning, Wednesday April 2, the storm had died down somewhat, but the ground was covered in deep snow. I lightened my load a little and, trusting to God's guidance, started out again. The day was quite mild, the sky overcast, the wind was from the south, and the snow fell in large flakes on the already deeply covered ground. Yet as I inched my way along and it became darker, I had difficulty seeing the road, and was sorry that I had even started out. Fortunately, I was able to reach the next village, owned by the nobleman Kudashev, which was about 15 verstas distance. There a kindly Russian invited me in to his yard and took me into his house. The house was very cold, however, because of his lack of fuel. My feet, legs, and body were soaked to the midriff, and while the wind howled from the north and the blizzard was worse than the day before, the horses stood shivering uncontrollably beside the wagon. I tried to protect them with my coat and a blanket, but they would not eat. I was in a room but so stiff with the cold that I could only think with longing of my family. I worried about my wife and cattle – they were without fodder and food – and as it became colder I was almost overcome with anxiety. Remaining here overnight seemed quite unthinkable. Yet as the raging wind reached a crescendo, I could see nothing beyond a few steps from the house, and so I commended myself and my family to God and tried to get a little rest.

Around three in the afternoon the wind died down a little, it started to clear, and I was anxious to be on my way again. The stream in the Ssolonne valley, however, was impassable with huge drifts and so in this dangerous situation I offered my Russian host a half silver R. to take me to the main road. Putting a shovel over his shoulder to dig us out, if that should become necessary, we again started out, in God's name. He took a roundabout way to avoid getting stuck, and even then the snow reached to the middle of the wheels. Then the guide left me. As the wind rose and it started to get dark, I was again alone. The direction of the road was so hard to make out that I became frightened and called on the Lord, who answered my prayers by sending his holy angels to watch faithfully over me and to keep me from losing my way. Through his great mercy I was able to reach Loshkarovka, where the gardener and administrator, a German by the name of Peter Zieger, asked me in and let me shelter and feed my horses in his barn. He offered me hot tea and a night's lodging, and I was very happy and grateful. The sky had cleared by the following morning, and although there was still a cold north wind, I resumed my hard journey in God's name. In the deep snow, I lost my way but then found it again within half an hour. I also became stuck in a snow-drift and pulled myself out by hitching the horses to the back of the wagon. Finally at noon I reached home, and what a joyous meeting that was with my loved ones.

April 4 Friday. My wife and I took the sled to visit my brother Diedrich in Novopodolsk. The blizzard has taken a terrible toll in people and livestock. The estate owner Sharif had flocks of sheep numbering 1700, and now has only 200 left, the storm having driven the others into a cattle-watering pond. Another 500 dead sheep were found under snow-drifts in the Sheltaia valley, between Novovitebsk and Novopodolsk. Frozen horned cattle have also been uncovered in our area, and I am certain that there is much more that has taken place.

April 5 Saturday. I and the owner of the [rented] house where we are living bought a load of hay for 4 bank R. 68 C. in the state peasant village of Sofievka. Winter hangs on, the cattle need to be fed, and fuel is very scarce and dear.

April 6 Sunday. The snow is gradually disappearing, although there is still frost in the shade. We have started to pasture the cattle in the snow-free areas and long for warmer weather.

April 8 This afternoon Peter v Kampen and I teamed up our horses and started to plough his garden.

April 9 Ploughed the garden and planted potatoes in the morning and started ploughing the field in the afternoon.

April 13 We visited my brother Diedrich in Novopodolsk.

April 20 Sunday. The cold, rainy, raw weather continued through the week, and one morning there was even frost on the windows. We have finished ploughing, but we still have the millet to sow.

April 27 Sunday. My wife and I attended service at Peter Rempel's home in Novopodolsk, where my brother Diedrich read a sermon from Kröker's book of sermons.[24] We had dinner at my brother's. My wife had a toothache and shooting pains in her arm, so we left early in the afternoon.

April 28 I finished the sowing today: wheat, 1 chetvert on 2 desiatinas; barley, 7 chetvert on 1 desiatina; oats, 7 chetvert on 1 desiatina; and millet, ½ chetvert on ⅓ of a desiatina. I borrowed the grain for seed and for our own use: 2 merka wheat from both my mother-in-law and my brother Johann, i.e., a total of ½ chetvert; and 1 chetvert 5 merka barley from the same brother.

April 29 v Kampen and I planted the melon field and finished the sowing.

April 30 I left to cart another load from Khortitsa. We started back on the 5th with five other wagons loaded with my lumber, including one belonging to Johann Wienz, the builder. It rained hard, and the going was difficult. My mare became so tired that we had to stop and pasture the horses on Loshkarovka's land. I had just gotten the mare out of the traces when the nobleman on whose hayfield we had stopped rode up, and forced me to pay two silver R. [damages] and then to move on.

Lightning struck and destroyed the home of Johann Epp, the former member of the Agricultural Commission. In Einlage lightning killed a certain Abraham Isaak.

May 8 At the service in our village, my brother Diedrich read a sermon from Kröker's book regarding true faith in Jesus Christ.

May 9 My [new] house was put up this afternoon, and Johann Wienz [the builder] returned to his home on the 11th.

May 11 Sunday. We visited my brother Diedrich.

May 18 Pentecost Sunday. We attended service in the home of Johann Friesen in Novokovno where Daniel Wiebe read Kröker's Pentecost sermon. In the afternoon we had a visit from my brothers Heinrich and Diedrich and their wives, and the Heinrich Epps stayed over for the night. On the second holiday, we attended the service in Novopodolsk with the H. Epps where Reverend Jak. Wienz of Kronsthal preached a sermon about Jesus' words, 'For God so loved the world,' etc.

May 21 Before sunrise D. Wiebe and I left for Khortitsa. We arrived there at 5 p.m., loaded our wagon, started back at two o'clock Thursday morning, and were home safely before sunrise on Friday. We had been away only 48 hours.

May 28 We went to Khortitsa for more lumber and returned home on the morning of the 31st.

June 1 Sunday. Believers gathered for service at the home of Daniel Wiebe, where my brother Diedrich read from Kröker's sermons. We moved into our far-from-finished new house after Vesper.

July 1 Haying is finished, and I think we have enough to feed the cattle. The harvest began on June 9, and I did the mowing myself, like the other Germans. As there was no rain the first week, I managed to gather up all of the cut hay. But during the second week I had such terrible chest pains that I had to give up scything entirely. For three days and nights I could not even sleep and this was difficult for me because I needed mowers, but there were none for hire, and it was hard for me to borrow money. Finally, on Saturday, June 21, I hired five Russian men to mow, at $1\frac{1}{2}$ bank R. per day, and on the 25th and 27th three more at the same rate. That came to 16 R. 50 C., 2 quarts of brandy at 60 C. each (or 1 R. 20 C.), and 25 C. for fish (a total of 17 bank R. 95 C. for bringing in the hay). Then it rained, and I had such great trouble getting in the hay that some of it was mouldy. Thus while others were starting to harvest their rye, I was still busy haying. Yet I was grateful to God that my chest was better. Some local Jews offered me their [uncut] grain for a one-third share and I agreed to harvest a large desiatina of rye and one of wheat. This morning I cut rye, and in the afternoon attended the funeral for Kornelius Harder who had died at the age of $15\frac{1}{4}$ years. At his father's request, I read a funeral sermon that I wrote yesterday. God gave me the necessary strength, but it was done imperfectly.

August 5 I have been so busy with the harvest that I have not had time for my diary. God is now blessing us with a marvellous shower, so I have time to catch up. Before this shower we had a fierce thunder and lightning storm that caught me under way on the road with a load of barley and almost toppled it over. I finished cutting grain this morning.

August 9 It rained until yesterday. The grain is still in the fields in stooks. It is starting to germinate and could spoil. God only knows what our real needs are. During the storm at night some horses broke out of the paddock and disappeared, and even though none were mine, I rode out for a day and a half looking for them. We found the last of them penned up in Loshkarovka on the Basavluk. They had caused some damage, and we had to pay compensation to have them released.

August 18 I finished bringing the grain home today, and for this we thank God. The Guardianship Committee has sent two surveyors to survey and allocate the lands and fields in the colonies of Novovitebsk, Novopodolsk, and Novokovno. I and my wife attended the funeral in Kamianka for 15-year-old Katharina Wiebe where I read the funeral sermon.

August 19 Friday. My family and I left early in the morning for Khortitsa on a business and pleasure trip, carting grain there and bringing back a load of lumber. We spent the first night in Schönhorst at my brother-in-law Peter Rempel's, had dinner on the 23rd at the Heinrich Epps, and stayed for the night with my mother. We visited my brother-in-law Martin Dycks on Sunday, had Vesper at my mother-in-law's, and spent the night with the Isaak Dycks. On the 25th we accompanied my brother Heinrich and my mother-in-law to the Island of Khortitsa. On the 26th we drove to Kronsweide for lumber, and spent the night with the M. Dycks. We had dinner on the 27th with my mother-in-law in Rosenthal, Vesper at my mother's in Khortitsa, and spent that night with my brother Heinrich. We started for home at 8 a.m. Thursday morning, spent the night on the Friedensfeld khutor, and reached our place safely on the 29th.

September 20 Saturday. Johann and I left at 5 in the afternoon for Khortitsa with a load of grain, which we sold for 13 bank R. 50 C. per chetvert. We loaded my wagon with lumber on Monday, started back on Tuesday, and arrived home safely on Wednesday.

September 24 Wednesday. Today the ministerial group consisting of Elder J. Dyck, the ministers Peter Dyck, Jakob Dyck, and Jakob Pätkau, and the deacon, Jakob Klassen, arrived in our village.

September 26 Friday morning Jakob Dyck, the minister, gave the preparatory sermon [for communion] in Gerhard Koslowski's home in Novovitebsk. We celebrated communion on the 28th with 90 persons in attendance. Following the service there was an election of ministers in which Heinrich Penner was chosen as minister and I as deacon (with 27 votes). Lord, strengthen me in this calling.

September 30 Thursday. There was a Brotherhood Meeting this morning at Klas Heide's. Because of a moral failing (he having slept prematurely with his wife), Heinrich Penner had declined to accept the office of minister, and so another election was held. Daniel Wiebe was first chosen as deacon with 25 votes, and then I (unworthy as I am) was elected minister by majority vote. Of a total of 35 ballots cast, 18 were for me and 17 for Daniel Wiebe. Lord, how am I to preach and to teach when I am desolate and weak myself. Grant both of us thy Holy Spirit that it might illumine our understanding, and make me worthy of proclaiming thy Word with joy. Do this, Lord Jesus, I pray. Amen. The [visiting] ministers left in the afternoon. May the guardian angels watch over them.

October 19 Sunday. With God's help, I gave my inaugural sermon today on the responsibilities of a spiritual householder. Text, 1 Corinthians 4:1–2. The service was in the home of Dietrich Thiessen in Kamianka.

October 21 I went to Khortitsa on business with my neighbour K. Martens and Jakob Wieler. There was a steady rainfall. I fetched my yearlings from the Island and sold the oldest to my brother Heinrich for 133 bank R. 17 C. In the evening, I discussed church matters with Elder J. Dyck. We arrived home on the 26th. I also brought home my sheep from the khutor.

November 2 I preached a sermon in Novovitebsk in the home of J. Krause based on Psalm 119:32. There was a Brotherhood Meeting following the service. First of all, since local church members had expressed the hope that Jakob Dyck, the minister from Neuosterwick, would move here, we talked about how this might be accomplished, but reached no definite conclusion. Secondly, we set the order of church services, which will be held on alternate Sundays in the colonies of Novovitebsk, Novopodolsk, Kamianka, and Izluchistaia, with the last two [villages] counting as one. Finally, I informed the brethren that the Holy Scriptures could be purchased from me.

November 16 The brethren Aron Lepp, Dietrich Thiessen, Heinrich Dyck the short one, and Gerhard Braun from Kamianka and Izluchistaia asked me to draft a petition to Siemens, chairman of the Agricultural Commission, requesting his help in getting the government to protect us from our neighbour, the estate owner Maevski. Maevski treats the Germans with great brutality whenever he can. Since the beginnings of this settlement he has wilfully allowed large numbers of his cattle, including oxen and pigs, to stray on to their lands. The latter have tried to live peaceably with him and have only penned up his cattle (some 35 oxen) once.

At harvest-time, for no apparent reason, he seized Cornelius Harms on the road like a common criminal and only let him go after giving him a dressing down. Some time later, Jacob Wiebe's son Johann did a foolish thing. While chasing Maevski's oxen from their garden, he cut off their tails with his pocket-knife. Maevski lodged a complaint and the matter was resolved, but the incident enraged this wrathful man and gave him a pretext for wreaking vengeance on all Germans. He had a horse stolen from Heinrich Dyck (the small one) on a Sunday morning. Dyck was in bed at the time with a fever, but rushed over to Maevski's place and demanded his horse back. Maevski insisted that Dyck first summon Wieler, for whom he had a particular hatred, and when Dyck refused, he abused him and chased him away. Dyck then sent his wife to try her luck, but the brute had one of his hired hands chase her and beat her with his fists. She was bedridden for two full weeks, and it took Dyck five days to get his badly battered horse back. Maevski's anger knew no bounds so he had nine horses belonging to Gerhard Braun and David Penner seized in broad daylight from the Jewish pasture. When they came to complain he greeted them in his usual way, denouncing them as robbers and cheats, and so on, and condemned all Germans in similar terms. Braun was very angry and told Maevski that he would be held fully accountable for his actions. The madman then ordered that Braun be seized, but he took flight and called to Penner that he should also escape (both were on horseback). Penner did not understand Russian, however, and being a kindly person hesitated until he was torn from his horse by Maevski's people, two of whom held him firmly while Maevski beat him with a big stick himself. Finally, Maevski gave orders to have Penner shot, but Büttner [his assistant] prevented this from happening. Of the horses, eight were finally released, but one ran into Braun's barn, from where Maevski had it forcibly removed. It is still being held.

November 30 I preached a sermon in Izluchistaia based on Romans 13:11–12. In the afternoon the residents of Izluchistaia and Kamianka met at Aron Lepp's to sign a petition addressed to Chairman Siemens requesting the government's protection against Maevski.

December 2 Daniel Wiebe and I dropped in to see Jakob Wieler in Kamianka who lives together with Heinrich Dyck in the house of a Jew, which is unbelievably filthy and presents a desolate appearance.

Wieler's wife, who has been sick all summer, lay in bed and pleaded with us to have her taken to Khortitsa, which we arranged. I also talked to Wieler about his heavy drinking, and he promised to stop. Jacob Redekopp complained about his nephew David Redekopp, with whom he has had a quarrel. We asked two of the brethren to seek a reconciliation between them, and if that failed, to order them both to appear [before the Ministerial Committee] in Novovitebsk on Thursday. (The Redekopps, God be praised, have been reconciled.)

December 14 Third Advent. I preached a sermon in Novovitebsk on the subject of the hope that genuine and nominal Christians have of a future life. We left for Khortitsa in the afternoon to get medical help for my daughter Katharina, whose mouth is sore from an infected tooth. We reached the German settlement on the Kudashev land (which is called Friedensfeld) at 7:30 p.m. the first day and were at my brother Heinrich's place at 4 p.m. the second. Tuesday afternoon I took Trienchen to Töws, the colonial doctor, and then to Jacob Wiebe, who extracted her tooth.

Problems are again growing in the community. A general Brotherhood Meeting was held regarding Aron Thiessen's refusal to pay the poor tax on the grounds that the ministers were using it improperly. The Ministerial Committee had [already] reported him to the government, and now the brethren failed to act in a spirit of true love and simply denied him spiritual communion. Also, the District Office, for quite trivial reasons, has removed members of the Einlage village administration from their posts and appointed others in their place. Some say the District mayor was seeking vengeance against certain members of the Village Office. The community is rapidly sinking into decay, and we have a cancer here that cannot be healed with bandages applied from the outside by civil authority. Unless we undergo the painful surgery of deeply felt and genuine pardon and reconciliation, the decline will continue. This is the end result of every cancer that is not removed. Woe to those Christians who would destroy the peace of the community and to those who refuse to be reconciled and only seek revenge. Woe to those who would undermine others simply for their own ends, for a terrible judgment awaits those who defy the teachings of our Lord Jesus.

December 25 Thursday, the first Christmas holiday. I preached a sermon to a large congregation on the joy of a true Christian at the

birth of Christ. Text, Luke 2:10–11. The congregation was large. May God bless the seed of his word.
December 26 On the second holiday I preached a sermon in the home of Dietrich Thiessen in Kamianka on the reason for Jesus' birth. Text, Luke 2:1–14. Before the service, Isaak Wölk, Heinrich Dyck, and their wives appeared before the Ministerial Committee in regard to their quarrels and were reconciled. Blessed are the peaceable.
December 30 I delivered a sermon in Izluchistaia at the funeral of Mrs Johann Bärgen, who is the first adult to have died in our settlement.

Close of the Year

Another year has passed, with its dangers, sufferings, and joys. We praise the Lord whose grace we have experienced each morning in new ways.

I harvested the following grain: wheat, 17 chetvert 3 merka from 1 chetvert seed; barley, 25 chetvert from 7 merka seed; the other grains have not yet been cleaned.

1853

Please Lord Jesus, let us prosper,
Help in this thy year of grace.
Grant thy power to assist us,
As we seek to run the race.
True salvation and true light,
With thy grace will make it right.

January 1 New Year's Day. I preached a sermon in Novovitebsk on the words of Jeremiah 4:3–4. Grant us thy blessing, dear Lord.

January 4 I delivered a sermon at the funeral of Johann Hiebert's 14-day-old son Heinrich, who is the first to have died in the New Year.

January 11 I preached a sermon in the home of Dietrich Thiessen. I feel deeply unworthy, Lord. How can my soul be edified by what I say?

January 20 I delivered a funeral sermon in Kamianka for Heinr. Dyck's child.

News from the Khortitsa Community. In the colony of Einlage, Abraham Dyck and his bachelor brother Peter beat and seriously injured Gerhard Friesen, Jacob Braun, and Johann Wiebe. Braun is reported to be close to death and will, in any case, be crippled. Whoever hates his brother is a murderer.

January 25 Sunday. In the afternoon, my wife and I attended the funeral for Johann Hiebert's wife, who after an illness of five weeks died in her 29th year. She had been married one year less five weeks. I delivered the funeral sermon.

February 3 Tuesday. I officiated at the marriage of Abraham Klassen's widow to the widower Johann Bärgen, which was held in the latter's home in Izluchistaia. The road was muddy from the rain, and we had to drive slowly. I wonder if we will have any snow this winter.

February 8 I preached a sermon in the home of D. Wiebe in Novovitebsk on the subject of the true peace of a believing soul. Text, Romans 5:1. Before the service I told my colleague Wiebe about the stories circulating regarding his wife. It is rumoured that after he left the [Bärgen] wedding, his wife stayed over for the night and wallowed in carnal pleasures, drinking brandy and doing what she should not have done. She is said to have sat on Johann Bärgen's lap and exchanged kisses with Jakob Dyck of Nieder Khortitsa (he was visiting his brother Isaac Dyck in Izluchistaia, and so was present at the wedding). She is also supposed to have spent time with Dyck in a separate room and probably committed adultery.

This morning I talked to the Johann Kruses to see if they could shed any light on the story. They had attended the wedding and confirmed seeing the second of these follies. I told Wiebe all of this, as was my duty, and he was distressed and angry. In the evening, he called his wife to account, and she tried to deny everything. She had to admit having kissed Dyck, but denied sitting on Bärgen's lap. She had meant no harm, she said, and if this was her only sin, and there were no others, she would be able to die in peace, etc. I reproached her for speaking in this way and asked her for an honest confession. This she had already done, she replied, and as God was her witness, she was innocent in regard to Dyck. On the morning of the 9th, the Kruse couple and Wiebe's wife met at my invitation, but she repeated what she had said. As she admitted only to a bit of indiscretion, we concluded the matter for now. May God have mercy on her and grant her the grace to repent. Yet she sees no need for this.

February 11 At two o'clock this morning my wife woke up with labour pains, and at 2:30 I roused [my sister-in-law] Agatha to light a fire. I then awoke the children, helped them to dress, and drove them away. The midwife, Mrs Cornelius Martens, arrived at three o'clock, and during the following hours we lived through terrible anxiety. We prayed fervently to the true obstetrician, who helped us as he had promised he would, at the right time. At 9:30 a.m. my wife gave birth to a healthy son, whom we have named Jacob. I cried tears of thanks, particularly since my wife was feeling well after the delivery.

A letter from the Reverend Jacob Pätkau reports that eight people from Einlage, the innocent as well as the guilty, have been placed in the ban (see entry for January 20).

February 12 Thursday. Wiebe's wife appeared before the Ministerial Committee together with the Kruse couple, Peter Görzen, Cornelius Andres, and Johann Bärgen. They had been summoned by the brethren Wilhelm Martens and Jacob Neudorf of Novovitebsk and Diet. Thiessen and Isaac Friesen of Kamianka. Since I did not want to deal with this serious matter on my own, I asked these brethren to join the hearing. They took the side of Wiebe's wife, however, and seem to have intimidated the witnesses into saying as little as possible. Nothing could be proved beyond what she had already admitted, namely that she had unwillingly sat on Bärgen's lap, which the witnesses confirmed. No one said it in so many words, but it was implied that a matter such as this which caused conflict within a marriage should not have been raised in the first place. Contrary to my intention, Wiebe was hurt and angry. I gave him my hand, saying there should be no discord between us. His wife had given offence by what she had been seen doing, even though nothing unchaste had happened. The others, however, were of a quite opposite view. Since I had no wish to be both prosecutor and judge, and since nothing deserving of punishment could be proved, I suggested reconciliation all around. This also took place, and so the matter was settled. 'But the Lord will bring to light what is concealed in darkness, and reveal the secrets of the heart.'

February 19 Thursday. Peter v Kampen and Daniel Wiebe's wife appeared before the Ministerial Committee. [Meanwhile], v Kampen had admitted to having acted improperly with Wiebe's wife at the wedding (but not adultery), after she had enticed him by holding his hand and kissing him. He wept, apologized for his behaviour, and asked our forgiveness. Wiebe's wife was at first rude, and I was stern in order to strengthen my authority. She then ran away, saying she had not come to be insulted. Wiebe asked for permission to look for his wife and reason with her, and this was granted him. She returned with tear-filled eyes and finally owned up to what v Kampen had confessed. She also admitted to carrying on with Johann Bärgen as reported above. She apologized for her rude behaviour, and her tears were proof of the genuineness of her remorse. In this way, a matter that had been concealed last Thursday was revealed, and she had been found guilty of the charges against her. We sent for v Kampen's wife, to whom Mrs Wiebe apologized for the wrong she had done her. We hoped that their contrition would make good the deed and so pardoned both v Kampen and Mrs Wiebe. Towards evening Bärgen and several others stopped by on their way to Khortitsa, and Bärgen finally admitted his own guilt. He too asked for forgiveness.

February 22 I preached a sermon at Isaac Wiebe's in Novopodolsk based on 2 Timothy 4:2. At a Brotherhood Meeting after the service I raised the above matter and asked the brethren if they were willing to forgive v Kampen, Bärgen, and Mrs Wiebe, to which they agreed. I then asked them what they thought of Neudorf's opinion that I had no business concerning myself with a matter of this kind in the first place. This the entire congregation rejected. Neudorf was present and asked our forgiveness for having spoken out of turn. Finally, I exhorted the congregation to keep weddings and other celebrations from degenerating into brandy drinking as they had in Izluchistaia. It was our bounden duty to live blameless Christian lives, especially for the Jews, to whom we were to be an example.

March 19 I ended classes today because of the field-work.

March 22 Three baptismal candidates responded to my invitation. I announced the engagement of Aganeta Tilitzki and Johann Hiebert. In the afternoon, however, the bachelor Johann Koslowski came by and told me that he and Aganeta had earlier promised marriage to one another, and that she should now be summoned to appear before the Ministerial Committee on this account. If she were to retract her promise to him he would let the matter rest. Monday morning Koslowski and the engaged couple appeared before the Ministerial Committee, but now the bride said that she wished to marry Koslowski. Only God knows the meaning of this. *Postscript.* Hiebert is now demanding 60 bank R. as compensation for the injury he has suffered (to be paid by the bride or by Koslowski on her behalf). I cannot find Christ's teaching in any of this.

March 24 Tuesday. I and my wife attended the engagement of Koslowski to Aganeta Tilitzki, which took place in the home of Gerhard Koslowski, his brother.

March 28 We ploughed the garden and planted potatoes.

April 5 I preached a sermon in Novopodolsk on the subject of the suffering and death of our Saviour.

April 7 This morning we had seven degrees of frost.

April 17 Good Friday. Crucified Saviour, Lord Jesus, I am a poor sinner. Heal me through thy wounds.

There were two funerals this afternoon, one for Isaac, the infant son of the Johann Bärgens, and the other in Novokovno for the two-year old son of the Abraham Ungers, Abraham. The Unger's invitation to conduct the service had arrived earlier than the Bärgens', and so after the service we drove to their place, where I delivered the funeral sermon.

April 18 Peter Wienz, his wife, and several children (from the Island of Khortitsa) spent the night with us.

April 19 Easter Sunday. At today's service in Novovitebsk, I preached a sermon based on Mark 16:1–8. Risen Saviour, grant that I might awaken from the sleep of sin.

April 20 Second Holiday. The service at Peter Rempel's in Novopodolsk attracted a large congregation, and I preached a sermon based on Luke 24: 13–35. My wife and I and the Isaac Klassens from Repetten had dinner at the Diedrich Epps'. In the afternoon we attended the funeral service in Novokovno for Margaretha, the three-year-old daughter of the Jacob Günthers, where I delivered the sermon.

BOOK II, 1860–1866

Family and Village Life on the Judenplan

'Cipher music ... was not a cause for worry
because it came from olden times,
as could be seen from the notations
in the very old song books.'

February 8, 1860

'I have a heavy heart and feel no Sunday today.'

March 17, 1863

'Dear God, thou hast tormented us so long.
Have mercy. Turn again thy countenance toward us
and show us thy kindly face.'

July 8, 1866

1860

January 3 At the service in Novopodolsk, I preached that salvation can be found only through Jesus Christ. Text, Acts 4:12. Merciful Saviour, grant that my own heart might be certain of thy wondrous grace.
January 4 We visited my brother Diedrich, who was back from Khortitsa with the information regarding births and deaths [in the Khortitsa church] in 1859. Of those born during the last century, who are therefore 60 years of age or older, 7 men and 5 women died and 139 men and 130 women are living. Of those born this century, and joined to the church through Holy Baptism, 8 males and 23 females died, and 1654 males and 1674 females are still living. A total of 43 [church members] died and 3587 are living.

[Figures for the entire community:]

Births	232 males	220 females	452 total
Deaths	80 males	92 females	172 total
Increase	152 males	128 females	280 total

Of the 172 people who died, 43 were Church members and 129 were minors.
January 6 Wednesday, the Epiphany of Christ. I preached a sermon in the home of Isaac Friesen based on Matthew 2:1–12. Lord, reveal thyself as my Saviour, and let me find peace in thy wounds. At the close of today's service I made public the figures regarding births and deaths [in the Khortitsa District].
January 7 Peter Friesen is seeking new guardians for the children of his first marriage, and my cousin David Klassen and Johann Friesen complained about this. [David] Klassen and Peter Teichröw had been chosen [as guardians] earlier, but had not as yet been confirmed by the Orphans' Administration [in Khortitsa]. The children's step-mother had neglected the children so seriously that they had gotten

lice, and people had talked about this. She had then started giving them better care to stop the rumours. The guardians had confirmed this information. Friesen's son-in-law, Michael Hamm, had then volunteered to become one of the [new] guardians and had told Klassen and Teichröw that they lacked [official] confirmation. Since the Orphans' Administration had entrusted such matters [in the Judenplan] partly to me, the parties sought me out. Since I will be in Khortitsa shortly, I agreed to pursue the matter, sending a letter in this regard to Isaac Bärgmann, head of the Orphans' Administration in Neuendorf.

January 8 I received a letter from Isaac Klassen, my [ministerial] colleague, complaining that the divine service on the Day of Epiphany in Novozhitomir had been disturbed by the singing of a cipher song.[1] But the story told by Peter Banmann's wife, who was present at the service with her husband, and who brought me the letter, was that 'the preaching had been disturbed by the laughter of several mischievous girls,' prominent among whom had been Reverend Isaac [Klassen's] own daughter. May the Lord have mercy on us.

January 9 Our guests this evening were Heinrich Olfert, the school-teacher from Novozhitomir, Abraham Günther from our village, and their wives. In the service mentioned above, Olfert, the precentor, had announced a song with a cipher melody. He now criticized Ohm[2] Isaac Klassen for comparing this kind of singing to a drinking song and for speaking such nonsense about it. Olfert went on to say that Klassen had been the cause of the disturbance by rising in the middle of the singing and giving the congregation his blessing. Thereupon his brother Franz Klassen and Peter Neufeld had left the service while the rest of the congregation had finished singing three stanzas of the song, as announced. There would have been no disruption if Ohm Klassen had remained seated. Olfert justified his selection of the music by saying that he knew only one tune for the song, and if it was wrong to sing a cipher melody, and if he had sinned, he demanded that such singing of [four-part harmony by numbers] also stop in the schools. 'Salt is good: but if the salt have lost its saltness, wherewith will ye season it? Have salt in yourselves and have peace one with another.' Mark 9:50 and Luke 14:34.

January 10 Sunday afternoon, I and my wife attended the wedding at the Johann Hieberts of Johann Thiessen and Helena Hiebert. In the evening we visited the Peter v Kampens, where Peter Löwen from Novozhitomir and his wife were also present. Ohm Peter [Löwen] disagrees with Ohm Isaac [Klassen] about the matter [of the cipher music] and thinks the commotion was caused more by the latter's behaviour than by the singing.

January 11 In the morning, my wife and I attended the wedding festivities at the home of the Johann Hieberts, where we also had dinner. We drove to my brother Diedrich's place in the afternoon where Peter v Kampen and Reverend Peter Löwen and their wives were also present. The road was drifted over.

January 14 Franz Dyck of Novokovno complained to me that his neighbour Isaac Friesen had accused him of beating his old mare to death. I asked him about the dispute, and he told me that during harvest-time last fall, Friesen's horses, led by the mare, had caused damage on his threshing floor several nights in a row. He had chased them away and informed Friesen of the matter, who had tethered them. During the night in question, the wayward horses had again been driven home and Friesen had again tied them up. Around midnight, however, he had found a horse lying on his threshed barley and beaten it with a stick. But when he had recognized that it was his neighbour's mare he had chased it away. I asked the church members Peter Teichröw and Heinrich Penner to order the two men to appear before the Ministerial Committee on Sunday.

January 15 In regard to the question of guardianship (mentioned under January 7), I today received confirmation from the Khortitsa Orphans' Administration of the appointments of David Klassen and Peter Teichröw as guardians, which I passed on to Teichröw. This ends the dispute. Martin Harder and I also received a document from the Orphans' Administration confirming us as guardians of the motherless orphans and children of Bernhard Giesbrecht of Kamianka.

January 17 Isaac Friesen and Franz Dyck appeared before the Ministerial Committee in my home (I was the only minister in attendance). My exhortations seem to have had little effect on Friesen, for the reconciliation from his side appeared half-hearted. Yet it did take place, and the two were allowed to go in peace.

Reverend Isaac Klassen caught up to us on the way to the service and preached the sermon. He and his wife then had dinner with us, stayed for coffee, visited with us at the David Klassens', and remained here for the night.

January 18 After breakfast, our guests picked up their wagon at the Wilhelm Martens' and left for home. Reverend Is. Kl. was quite angry about the cipher singing (see entry for January 9), comparing it to the anti-Christian goings-on of the end times. His brother, Franz Klassen, had told him that such songs were military songs, to which I took strong exception.

He also told me about some heavy drinking that had gone on among Germans gathered at the Jägers' place where his sons-in-law had also overindulged. He explained that his brother Franz had to provide the brandy in exchange for some straw, etc., etc. I responded with a loud lament: Dear, merciful God, a melody to thy glory sung to numbers in a divine service causes an outcry, but a large drinking party can be so simply explained away. What is all of this leading to? As Klassen left, he insisted that we should reprimand the precentors. I replied that he and Löwen should have done this at the time [of the singing incident] rather than aggravating the issue at this time, as they were now doing. I suggested we continue the discussion when I came to the service, when we should also take up the matter of the drinking. But Klassen did not want to hear anything about the latter subject, looking for every possible excuse to avoid having it raised. He had only related the incident, he said, in order that I might know about it, etc., etc. Merciful Lord and Saviour, what are things coming to? Keep us from slipping down into the pit of darkness. Strengthen me, for I am weak, that I might guide the flock which thou hast entrusted to me, onto green pastures. Let those who have gone astray recognize that true worship does not consist in the externals of singing, but takes place when we strive to enter into eternal life through the narrow gate. It also means driving out from our congregations the vices of drunkenness, unchasteness, and quarrelling so that we might truly become the people that is called by thy name. Amen!

Earlier, Klassen had told me how much he valued the teaching of my brother Abraham, but now he said that Abraham's pupils were not learning anything. He also denied that the girls, including his two daughters, had giggled and laughed during the above-mentioned service. Peter Braun's wife and Reverend Peter Löwen had, he said, lied when they had told me this. Dear Lord, the situation in this regard looks bleak.

January 20 Wednesday. My wife and I and daughter Trienchen visited the Isaac Wiebes in Novopodolsk. Trienchen has been learning to knit women's woollen caps at Abraham Epp's place and had another knitting lesson from her aunt.

January 21 Thursday at Vesper Reverend Peter Löwen and Anton Günther from Novozhitomir asked me to come with them to my brother Diedrich's place in Novopodolsk, where Carl Jäger, their Village overseer, was also present. They wanted me to draft an appeal to the Khortitsa District Office requesting its intercession with the Guardianship Committee on behalf of the German settlers in Novozhitomir. The Jews [in that village] had purchased their own Russian bull for breeding and hired a herdsman for their own cattle. Jäger had reported this matter to the supervisor, but had not yet received a reply. The German model landowners now wanted to pursue the issue, in part by means of a written submission to the District Office, as I suggested. I therefore went with them to see my brother who told us that his secretary had just returned from seeing the Supervisor and informed him of the latter's decision. I suggested that Epp and Jäger question the secretary about this in detail, which they did, concluding that a decision [in support of the action of the Jews] had been taken and that we could do nothing more until further inquiries had been made. We drove home by moonlight.

January 24 Sunday. The service was held in the home of old Peter Rempel in Novopodolsk, where I preached a sermon on the subject of the excuses that people usually offer for evading an earnest repentance. Acts 24:25.

January 25 My neighbour Mrs Wilhelm Martens had a miscarriage, and her condition took a bad turn today. I was called in to visit her in the afternoon, and when she saw me coming from a distance she cried out that she desperately wanted to hear the sweet Word of the Lord. I read a chapter to her from the Gospels and a prayer from Fried. Starck,[3] and we then sang several hymns. At night, the terrible pains let up a little and she had a somewhat easier time of it.

Towards evening, my brother-in-law Wilhelm Krause from Kronsweide arrived in Novovitebsk with a load of belongings for his brother Abraham, who has rented a place from a Jew.

January 26 Two wolves got into my flock this afternoon and attacked two sheep, an old one and a young one. The old one was barely alive, and I slaughtered it.

January 27 Old Heinrich Banmann from Novozhitomir complained that his married son Heinrich was treating him badly, refusing to esteem his fatherly love or listen to his admonitions, and demanding too much money for a joint business deal. I advised the old man to be patient and promised him that if matters between them had not improved by the time I came to his place, I would try to mediate. Honour father and mother.

January 28 Thursday morning, my brother-in-law Abraham Hiebert and I set out for the Khortitsa colonies on my wagon, to which we had harnessed two of his horses and one of mine. We spent the night with old Jacob Wiebe on the Kudashev khutor.

January 29 We resumed our trip in the morning and stopped to feed the horses in Neuendorf, at the Orphans' Administration. I spent the night with my brother Heinrich in the Zentralschule in Khortitsa, while Hiebert visited his relatives.

January 30 I did my business with the District Mayor and shopkeeper Dyck and had dinner at my brother-in-law Jacob Pätkau's place. In the afternoon I accompanied him to see Elder Gerhard Dyck[4] and informed the latter of the incident regarding the cipher music (see Jan. 8, 9, 10, 18) and the conduct of Reverend Is[aac] Kl[assen] in this regard. He had already heard about the matter and strongly disapproved of my colleague's behaviour. The decision has been made to start building the church.

February 2 We arrived home safely toward evening. God be praised. There is considerable unrest in the Khortitsa community arising in the first place from strong opposition to the methods of instruction used by the new schoolteachers in the Khortitsa Zentralschule. There is also great uneasiness regarding the [proposed] emigration to the Amur River, and many lies are making the rounds about this matter. Just before leaving [Khortitsa], a reply was received from the imperial government to a petition from the District mayor and the elders asking for land in Ekaterinoslav guberniia on which 200 [landless] Mennonite families could be settled. If this were granted, it would mean that the migration to the Amur [River area] could be put off for now. It is reported that the three deputies [to the Amur] are already on their way home.

February 7 I preached a sermon in the school in Izluchistaia, driving there alone on my wagon, and had dinner with the teacher. Is. Klassen joined us, and I informed him that we wanted to start the school visitations tomorrow morning, to which he agreed, asking me to call for him with my wagon. I told him I would be leaving at one o'clock and would drop by his home. Otherwise, [if he was not at home,] I would spend the night elsewhere. Yet when I arrived, Ohm Isaac was not home and so I dropped in on the Peter Janzens and spent the evening with Reverend Peter Löwen.

February 8 When I dropped in at Ohm Isaac's this morning, he and his wife reproached me for not dropping by yesterday, but I reminded them of our understanding. They again raised the subject of the cipher music, and I told them what the Elder had said in this regard, namely that such music was not a cause for worry because it came from olden times, as could be seen from the notations in the very old song-books. In this way I tried to bring the matter to a close, but his wife talked herself into such a rage that her face turned beet red and her features became distorted. Ohm Isaac, on the other hand, agreed with me and did not agree with me, which is his way.

Löwen caught up to me, and we agreed on the order in which we would visit the schools. Together with Carl Jäger, the local overseer, we visited the local school where the teacher Heinr. Olfert began the lesson with singing. The children knew the Bible stories well. May our dear Lord inscribe these stories in their hearts that they may learn to love and honour him as their deliverer and saviour. The most advanced pupils read well, the others were only average, and the youngest seemed to suffer from neglect. The teaching of arithmetic was on only a low level. The register showed that the children had been attending school very irregularly, and I asked the local overseer to send around a circular letter reminding the parents of their duties in this respect.

In the afternoon, we visited the schools in Izluchistaia and Kamianka. The teacher in Izluchistaia is Johann Schellenberg. Penmanship was good, reading average, arithmetic in its infancy, and there was no religious instruction of any kind. Singing here was by ear, and Ohm Isaac said that he preferred this to singing by numbers. I asked the children to sing on their own, but they could not. Joh. Klassen is the teacher in Kamianka, and his school was on an even lower level, without any instruction about the life and sufferings of Christ. I reminded both teachers of the injunction contained in 2 Timothy 3:15–16, and they promised to do what they could to improve the situation. Aron Lepp, the local overseer, was present at both schools.

As we left the school, Klassen said mockingly to me that he had no desire to participate in any further visitations since he did not approve of the cipher music I replied that he should have told me this earlier, for he had an obligation to stick to our previous agreement and continue our visitation at eight o'clock tomorrow morning. Of course, when it comes right down to it, he can do as he pleases. Yet what will such disunity lead to? I had a cup of coffee at Herman Peter's place and drove home.

February 9 After waiting for Klassen until nine o'clock, Löwen and I proceeded to the local school [in Novovitebsk]. The local overseer, v Kampen, was away on a trip to the Khortitsa colonies, and present were Aron Lepp and the teacher P. Klassen. Aron Neusteter is the local teacher, and his instruction was very inadequate because he has little knowledge himself. The teaching of religion was good, but not understandable to the younger children. We had dinner at my brother Diedrich Epp's place.

In the afternoon, my brother, who is the overseer, accompanied us to the school, where Reverend Isaac Klassen again joined us. He was evasive about why he had not showed up in Novovitebsk. The teacher here is my brother Abraham, who started off with singing. The Bible story from the New Testament was well taught, and the children showed understanding of the road leading to salvation. They had also made significant progress in writing, reading, and arithmetic, and in the other subjects, and only one child could not read. Songs were sung from our hymn-book, and at the close a few chorales in parts. The singing was very good. If only such schools existed everywhere.

February 10 On a trip to the Khortitsa District, Gerhard Andres of Izluchistaia dropped by to discuss a matter involving the Orphans' Administration. One night, his son Johann, David Redekopp's son Peter, and several friends had played boyish pranks at the Jacob Hamms' and Heinrich Dycks' places, removing the wheels of Hamm's wagon, smearing the axles with human excrement, and then

exchanging the wheels of the two men's wagons. The boys had already apologized to the aggrieved parties and promised to clean the wheels to everyone's satisfaction. Dyck was willing to forgive the boys but Hamm was not, and so the overseer Epp had ordered the boys to cancel their planned trip to Khortitsa until the matter had been settled. But the boys were reluctant to do this and so had come to see me in the hope that I might intercede on their behalf. I spoke earnestly to Redekopp, who had been baptized only last year, and he began to cry, saying that the liquor had led him astray. Since the boys would be returning in any case, I suggested they get on with their trip. My dear young people, if you would only recognize your own interests and see how much the Lord loves you and how bitterly you have disappointed him. Why do you drink so greedily from the cup of sin which will turn into the bitterest bile? Joy and pleasure would be yours if you were to dedicate these best years of your lives to the Lord Jesus. Lord, remember not the sins of my youth. When I think of the time that has been so thoughtlessly wasted. Lord, forgive me.
February 12 Yesterday we experienced an incident that can only give Germans a distaste for living among Jews. A cow belonging to a Jew was found in Martin Harder's yard with a broken foot. Harder and his family had no idea how it had gotten there or how it had been injured. The Jews, however, flocked together and started to shriek that the foot had been cut with a sharp object. I would guess, and so it appears, that the cow's leg had been broken while jumping across a ditch onto hard frozen ground. Yet since no one had seen it, nothing could be proved.

The Jews expressed their hatred of us by threatening legal action with the government to force our departure. Several Jews said as much to me this morning. I replied that if the authorities were ever to ask us to move, I would be the first to leave. Nor would I shed a tear, I said. A Jew responded, 'Oh, no, we'll ask for permission to move ourselves.' And if that were to happen, I said, no German here would have the slightest regrets. Several Jews laughed at this point and suggested that if matters continued like this, our separation would be a happy one. Towards noon, the German model settlers met regarding this incident in the home of v Kampen, the local overseer. The Jews had sold the injured cow for 10 silver R., and we agreed to collect a further 10 silver R. as compensation for the owner. The Jews are still determined to continue their action, however, and are using every means to put us in the wrong.

February 21 Tuesday. An auction sale was held today at Koslowsky's place and various items were sold with the proceeds coming to 179 silver R. 79 C. Earlier Koslowsky had sold his place to Jacob Dyck of Khortitsa for 2975 bank R. I conducted the auction and received a fee of 1 per cent of the proceeds. I noted with great sorrow that brandy was again being consumed to excess, sold by a Jew without my foreknowledge. Diedrich Rempel of Novopodolsk was the most drunk and behaved like a swine. Oh, that help might come from Zion, and the Lord deliver his people.

February 25 My wife and I visited my brother Abraham in Novopodolsk, and on our return home, David Penner, Jacob de Veer, and Gerhard Braun from Izluchistaia dropped by and were soon joined by Jacob Görzen and his son Gerhard. The visit was in connection with an inheritance matter involving the sale of a windmill. The Görzens felt wronged that the windmill had not been sold to them at auction. This is a love of money, greediness. Since the Orphans' Administration is alone competent to resolve the dispute, I told them to raise the matter there. I gave Gerhard Braun, the guardian, the auction account as well as the auction proceeds.

Later young Peter and Heinrich Redekopp (who are already church members) came by and asked to be forgiven for their prank (see entry for Feb. 10). After I had exhorted them to repentance, and since I did not want to conclude the matter on my own, I told them to appear Sunday morning at the home of Ohm Isaac Klassen. The two, who had already made their peace with the wronged parties, accepted the proposed arrangements for Sunday and left.

February 28 I preached a sermon in the school in Novozhitomir on the subject of Christ's spiritual suffering in Gethsemane. Text, Matthew 26:36–46. Before the service, Peter and Heinrich Redekopp appeared before the Ministerial Committee in the home of Isaac Klassen (see Feb. 25), again asked forgiveness, promised betterment, and were allowed to go in peace. I had driven down the preceding day, spent the night with the Carl Jägers, and left my wagon at the Peter Janzens' place. The trip there over frozen ground went well, but there was a heavy rain at night, and on the way home, with water flowing in all of the valleys, the road was bottomless.

The Orphans' Administration has validated the previously mentioned agreement regarding the windmill and inheritance.
March 5 My brother Abraham was here for several hours, and we talked about the impending emigration to the Amur River. The three deputies are back from there and have good things to say about the land. We are still unsure, however, about the Crown's willingness to support the settlers [financially], and only such support would make the move possible. God, resolve the matter to our benefit.
March 6 I preached a sermon in the home of Isaac Friesen in Novokovno on the subject of Pilate's assertion, 'Behold the man!' John 19:1–5. Lord, grant us thy blessing. On a good sledding track, my wife and I visited the Heinrich Penners, where several neighbours were gathered, and the entire conversation revolved around the trip to the Amur. When I mentioned that I was thinking of moving myself, everyone was enthusiastic about venturing the settlement, in God's name. Lord, Lord, if it is thy doing let it succeed, but if it is man's work then stop the deed, and let us consider other possibilities. Show me what I should do. Amen.
March 9 My brother Diedrich and his wife were here today. He had been to Khortitsa to find out more about the prospective emigration to the Amur. He and his family and we have both decided to join the move, if it is God's will.
March 14 I bought a sazhen of fuel dung from a peasant in the nobleman's village of Petrovka for 3 silver R. and carted a load of it home. Water from the melting snow is flowing [in the valleys], and the weather is very springlike.
March 17 Heinrich Banmann Jr from Novozhitomir, came to see me. His father had complained about him (see Jan. 27) some time ago, and I had turned the matter over to the local overseer for investigation. Recently the two had reached an agreement on the money matters in dispute, without, however, achieving a personal reconciliation. Now his father informed me that that too had finally been achieved, but that peace had not yet been made between the young Heinrich Banmann, his brother Peter Banmann and their uncle Martin Harder. Reverend Peter Löwen informed Reverend Isaac Klassen (who is the young Heinr. Banmann's father-in-law) that they were now prepared to be reconciled as well. Yet Heinrich Banmann dropped by today and tried to absolve himself of any blame

[for the alienation] while laying the responsibility upon his brother and uncle. I finally persuaded Heinrich Banmann to talk to the Harders. But Harder's wife insisted to me that the [financial] arrangements made by Jäger, the local overseer, were unsatisfactory. These could no longer be changed, I told her. Finally at the Harders' place, and with my encouragement, a reconciliation was achieved. May God grant that it is genuine. Amen.

March 18 With tear-filled eyes, Gerhard Koslowski came to see me this morning about his misfortunes with the Jews. Three years ago he had broken the leg of a heifer belonging to the tailor Jankel, a Jew, after the animal had caused much damage. After his neighbour Abr. Günther had divulged the matter to the Jews, Koslowski had reached an agreement with Jankel to pay 3 silver R. Now, however, the Jew was demanding compensation of two cows and had submitted his claim to the Village Office. This episode is in the same spirit as that of February 12.

April 10 Before today's service the Ministerial Committee met in my home. Also present were Isbrand Friesen of Novokovno, the mill owner David Klassen from our village, and, towards the end of the meeting, Reverend Isaac Klassen. The meeting was to discuss a dispute about a sack, but since several other people were to have appeared, the issue could not be clarified and all present were finally allowed to go in peace.

April 13 A cold drizzly rain from the east this morning, which caused the horses to refuse to move, forced us to stop ploughing. Since we had no fodder at home, I put the horses out to pasture in the hope the rain would stop, but it turned into a downpour, and the horses shivered from the cold and rain and would not work. At noon we finally hitched them to the wagon [and left for home]. Rain continued all day and through the night, the wind shifting to the north, and now it looks as though winter will continue. The cold is especially hard on the sheep and lambs.

April 19 I had just gotten home from the field and sat down to dinner when we learned of the disappearance of Margaretha, my nephew Peter Rempel's infant daughter, and our appetites vanished. As the children and I got ourselves ready to join the hunt, the overjoyed mother with her lost child returned to the village with the other searchers. A Russian ploughman had found the crying child, picked her up, and tried to calm her. The guardian angel had protected her from all harm.

April 24 *Brotherhood Meeting.* A list of baptismal candidates was presented, containing the names of eight young women.

April 28 I finished sowing today: wheat, 2 chet. 4 merka on $5\frac{1}{2}$ desiatinas; barley, $2\frac{1}{2}$ chet. on 4 des.; oats, 3 chet. on 3 des.; millet, $\frac{1}{2}$ merka on $\frac{1}{2}$ des. I have planted a total of 13 desiatinas of summer grain. God, bless what we have sown that it might sprout in the earth's womb and become our daily bread. We scatter it simply, it returns manyfold, and gratitude sings thy praises. Amen.

May 2 Early Monday morning, my mother, my wife, and I drove to Novopodolsk to say goodbye to my brother Abraham, who has taken a teaching position in Einlage. The wagons carrying his belongings started out at eight o'clock in the morning, and he and his small family followed at 10:30. May the Lord go with him. Bless his school that the children might go forth from there as true Christians and useful members of the community.

May 5 We had a visit this afternoon from Isaac Wiebe of Novopodolsk and members of his family from the Island of Khortitsa, David and Anna Janzen, and Bernd Penner's wife from Neuosterwick, who seem not to have forgotten their old teacher. Lord, grant that my imperfect teaching might remain in their memories.

May 8 Before today's service, the Isbrand Friesens lodged a complaint against their neighbour Abraham Unger. While ploughing one day, Unger's nine-year-old daughter had thrown Friesen's son (who is a little older) from a teeter-totter. The boy had called her a mad dog, and other names, and she had struck him with a whip. The boy had then fled out onto the field, at which point Unger had jumped on his horse, run the boy down, and struck him with his whip. The parents showed me the boy's back, which had four welts across it, two of them quite large. I presented the incident to my colleagues, and we decided to summon the parties to appear before us at my home. Towards evening, Unger asked permission to drive to Ekaterinoslav since he had undertaken to cart eight loads to the city and had already received 10 silver R. as an advance. Since he promised to visit the Isbrand Friesens and apologize, I finally agreed.

May 10 Heinrich Penner of Novokovno told me this morning that Unger had apologized to the Friesens, and that they had made their peace. The Ministerial Committee regarded the matter as closed. May the Lord grant us his peace.

Accidents. Recently, Jacob Wall of Neuendorf was killed almost instantly when the wagon he was using to cart home wood from Kronsweide ran over his chest. A few days ago a certain Unrau drowned in the Dnieper at Kronsweide, and when we were there his body had not yet been recovered. In Einlage, a Prussian carpenter working for Julius Heinrichs died accidentally when a cupboard he was lifting and balancing on a threshold tipped over and crushed his head. In the Molochna, a young boy running after his father who was haying was accidentally cut in the stomach with a scythe and died a pitiful death.

During the night from the second to the third day of Pentecost, a Jewish woman and her seven-year-old daughter were found murdered in their house in Novozhitomir. They were discovered in the morning, the woman lying in a pool of blood in the centre of the room. She had been stabbed in the stomach with a pitchfork, beaten about the head, and had her throat cut. The girl was discovered in bed with her throat slit. The authorities have taken several suspects (Russians) into custody, including Reverend Peter Löwen's hired man. The Saviour says, 'What I have said I say to all of you: watch!'

June 3 I asked that my nephew Peter Rempel appear in my home after it was reported that on a trip to Khortitsa he had bought a cap from a Jew in Tomakovka for 80 silver C., passed himself off as a certain Jacob Wienz from the Kudashev khutor, taken the cap on credit, and signed a note for the sum in the name of this Wienz. At first, Rempel stubbornly denied everything, but then he broke down and confessed, promising to write to his stepfather Johann Sawatzki to ask him to pay for the cap. I failed to detect genuine remorse, although he did say that he regretted what he had done. Last fall Rempel had taken a silver R. from David Klassen to pay the latter's debt of 60 silver C. to a certain Esau in Schönhorst. He gave Klassen the 40 silver C. change on his return and said that he had paid the debt. Sometime later, Dav. Klassen, hearing that Esau knew nothing about the payment, had settled the debt himself. Rempel made various excuses for his behaviour, but finally promised to repay the 60 C. and to ask Klassen's forgiveness. Thus the matter rests for now.

June 4 Saturday. I took my wool to Khortitsa (some 5 puds 2 funt), and left it with Jacob Dyck on consignment. Judith Wiebe, Anna Klassen, Helena Redekopp, and my son David came along for the communion service in Khortitsa.

June 5 I attended holy communion service with the congregation of 708 people in the Khortitsa church.

June 6 On our way home we were overtaken by a violent thunderstorm on Prince Kudashev's land. The rain came down in buckets, accompanied by thunder and lightning, as well as hail, and we had a hard time controlling the horses.

June 12 I preached a sermon in the home of Peter Rempel in Novopodolsk on the text, Acts 21:28–9. *Brotherhood Meeting.* The previously noted matter involving Peter Rempel was presented to the congregation. To the very last moment he continued to tell lies, but he asked our forgiveness and was allowed to go in peace. May God grant him true repentance.

June 19 As I was getting ready to leave for the service early Sunday morning, I received an invitation to the funeral of my brother Abraham.[5] Who would have thought that death would overtake you so soon, my brother. I grieve for you with all my heart. You have endured your suffering, and the Lord will reward you graciously for your great faithfulness as a teacher. We decided to go to the funeral, and my wife and I and son Jacob set out at once. My brother Diedrich and his wife caught up with us in Loshkarovka on the Basavluk, where we had stopped to feed the horses, and we continued the journey together, reaching Khortitsa at ten in the evening. We took our quarters at the Pätkau's, while Diedrich stayed with my brother Heinrich.

June 20 Day of the funeral. This afternoon, we accompanied the body of our beloved brother to his final rest. May the Lord Jesus comfort our poor sister-in-law. The funeral sermon was delivered by Elder Gerhard Dyck. Last Friday, the 17th, at seven in the evening, my beloved brother had entered into the peace of Christ, as we hope, at the age of 24 years, 2 months, and 3 days. He had been married 3 years, 9 months, and 15 days and fathered 2 daughters. Helena, the oldest, had predeceased him, and only Anna, the baby, and the grieving widow survive him. Despite his great talents as a teacher, our dear brother was not destined to become the glory of Einlage.

June 21 Tuesday, the second funeral day. Since our grieving sister-in-law is determined to drive back with Diedrich Epp we had to make an inventory of my brother's estate. This the Village mayor of Einlage did after we had finished breakfast and sung a hymn. The widow asked me and my brother Diedrich to be her trustees and chose my brother Heinrich Epp and her brother Heinrich Friesen as guardians of the poor orphan Anna. In the afternoon, we loaded her essential household effects on to a wagon and took the remaining belongings next door to the Diedrich Hildebrands.

June 22 We left for home Wednesday morning with the wagon of the deceased, which was loaded down with belongings. The Lord's ways are not man's ways.

July 13 Wednesday at sundown, my son David, our neighbours the Wilh. Martens and Heinrich Sawatzki, David Klassen, and I left for Ekaterinoslav to buy wood for fencing. We arrived at sundown on Thursday, and spent the night at my uncle Johann Thiessen's place, where I borrowed 10 silver R. from my aged aunt. Next morning we tended to our business and loaded our wagon. I had bought 30 boards and 5 rafters, the former at 12 C. and the latter at 40 silver C. apiece. Leaving Ekaterinoslav at noon, we were overtaken by a heavy, soaking rainfall, some nine verstas from the city.

August 6 A swarm of grasshoppers passed along the borders of our land in the direction of the Kudashev land.

August 20 I left for Khortitsa with a load of barley and spent the night with the Gerh. Giesbrechts on the Kudashev khutor, where I conducted a service Sunday morning. In Khortitsa we found a funeral service in progress at the Jacob Pätkau's, whose stepdaughter Margaretha Dyck had just been buried. A week ago, my brother Heinrich's son Heinrich had also died.

August 23 My sons Jacob and David accompanied me to Khortitsa where the latter is to attend the Zentralschule. He is being boarded with the Cornelius Hildebrands for 1 chetvert wheat, 1 chetvert rye, and 4 chetvert barley.

August 28 At 7:45 p.m., with God's help, my wife was delivered of a son, whom we have named Heinrich.[6] Her labour started last night, and in the morning I called my neighbour Mrs Gerhard Wiebe to come and help. The contractions let up enough for me to attend service, and we had a number of visitors for dinner. They became more intense again in the afternoon, but without result. Around six o'clock, the midwife told us that she *now realized* that she could *accomplish nothing*. I sent the wagon to fetch Mrs Isaac Friesen, who arrived at 7:15. She said that the child was not properly placed. In our fear we called on the Lord, and by the hands of this second midwife he answered our prayers. Within half an hour the new-born proclaimed his arrival with a loud cry. Note: the injured womb was also a great hindrance.

September 1 The Heinrich Penners and Peter Teichröws appeared as requested. Penner had permitted a young cow to wander about loose. The cow had been seized, pawned, and brought to the Jewish Village mayor. Penner had become so enraged that he had sold the cow to Teichröw, who had redeemed it with his own money. Penner's wife, who had refused to accept the sale, had tried quietly to spirit the cow out of Teichröw's barn. Teichröw had resisted, and Penner's wife had struck him on the arm with the handle of a whip. He had lodged a complaint. They were reconciled and allowed to depart in peace, and the agreement was confirmed.

September 12 This morning my small children and I went to my brother's place in Novopodolsk. Here we met Reverend Heinrich Bärgen of Neuendorf who asked me to summon his son-in-law Bernd Bärgen and Pet. v Niessen to appear before me in his presence to resolve a dispute over an account on which the two men could not agree. v Niessen claimed that he had worked for Bärgen six weeks, and the latter insisted it was only two weeks. v Niessen could account for only 18 days, however, and so we mediated the time at 15 days, which both accepted. They then were reconciled and were allowed to go in peace.

September 14 My son Jacob and I carted a wagon-load of barley to Khortitsa and returned on the 18th.

October 8 This morning we left for Khortitsa to pick up a load of meal that Joska, a local Jew, had purchased. My brother-in-law Jacob Pätkau's son Jacob, who will be learning the carpentry trade with my brother Diedrich, drove back with us.

October 15 Sunday evening. The Lord is punishing us with the cattle plague. Of the four milk cows, one heifer due to calf this winter, one steer, and three calves we had, the cows and the heifer are dead, the steer has recovered, and the three calves are still sick. We have no milk, which is very difficult for a large family like ours. May the Lord's rod serve to make us better.

October 16 I preached to only a small congregation in the home of

Corn. Giesbrecht in Kamianka, while many more were present at the market on the land of our neighbouring nobleman Maevski. Many have now found a favourite place to gather, idly desecrating the day of the Lord in drinking and useless amusements, and this is leading to the perdition of our fellow believers. Look down upon us in thy mercy, Lord, and remove this evil, which is drawing so many under its influence.

My wife and I went to visit the Julius Janzens, and when we came home the largest of our three calves was dead.

October 17 Our last two calves died today, and so we have lost all of our livestock, with the exception of the steer, which has recovered. The Lord hath given and the Lord hath taken away, blessed be the name of the Lord.

October 25 Today I preached a sermon in the home of Abr. Günther in Novovitebsk on the broad and narrow ways and their respective ends. Text Matthew 7:13–14.

October 26 I left at 4 a.m. for the annual fair in Nikopol, and my neighbour Gerhard Wiebe's son David came along as company. We reached the home of my brother-in-law Abraham Friesen at three in the afternoon. Friesen bought our 2 chetvert of wheat for 6 silver R. 50 C. The price at the market was 7 R. per chetvert.

October 30 I gave the preparatory sermon for the Holy Communion service at Peter Rempel's place in Novopodolsk. Text, Jeremiah 31:1. On the way home there was a great storm from the east, and we had to travel against wind.

November 6 The Elder is not here yet and growing numbers of communion guests are arriving. The Elder failed to show up, and I do not know why. I finally had no choice but to go to the service and deliver the sermon.

In the evening greetings and a message arrived from Elder Gerhard Dyck saying he might come next Sunday. This is regrettable since the sick and frail, who had gotten themselves ready for holy communion, had been misled. It would be better henceforward to postpone the preparatory sermon until the Elder's arrival.

November 10 The model landholders were asked to meet at v Kampen's place in the presence of two overseers from the Jewish colonies closer to Kherson. They had brought along a petition addressed to the Guardianship Committee (already signed by their model landholders), asking for provisions regarding lease rates to ensure that we would not be treated on the same basis as leaseholders whose rents are set by bidding at auction. The petition, which was well-formulated, had already been signed by the landholders in Novo-podolsk and we followed their lead. May the Lord bless this matter.

November 12 The Isaac Wiebes from Novopodolsk were our guests. 'Brauchscheidtism' is a method of treatment recently discovered by a certain Karl Brauchscheidt from the Prussian Rhineland.[7] [The over-seer] v Kampen had sent away for one of these 'life awakeners' and had successfully used it a number of times. The apparatus was fastened twice on our infant son for infected eyes, and with good results. Today we tried it on my wife, who has a fungal ulcer. May God bless the treatment.

November 13 This afternoon we went to fetch my sister-in-law, Mrs Abr. Epp, who wanted to help my wife with her sewing.

November 16 I accompanied Peter v Kampen to Loshkarovka to see Peter Zöger the gardener who is, according to his doctor, going blind with cataracts and can see only poorly with glasses. v Kampen attached the life awakener behind each of his ears once and repeatedly on his back (for rheumatism). He then rubbed these places with oil. I am very curious to see what happens since the life awakener has certainly had positive results with my wife.

November 18 I bought a cow for 20 silver R. from my sister-in- law Mrs Abr. Epp, and brought it home.

November 29 Tuesday. I officiated at the marriage of Jacob v Kampen, Peter v Kampen's son, and Anna Klassen, the daughter of my cousin David Klassen, in the home of the local overseer.

December 19 My wife and I took our infant son Heinrich to the home of the Peter Peters to have him vaccinated against smallpox. In the afternoon we attended the funeral for Bernhard Rempel's six-week-and-two-day-old infant son Bernhard, who was found dead in his cradle yesterday morning. I gave the funeral sermon.

December 22 Last night my brother-in-law Abr. Hiebert ran to our place to ask me to help restore peace at the Peter Rempels' (my sister's son). Rempel was drunk and raging about the house. I sent for my neighbour Wilh. Martens, and then the three of us went over together and found the situation as Hiebert had described it. Rempel was very drunk, and had given his wife a hard box on the ears and broken the lantern. As we entered, he become frightened and spoke as only a drunken person can. I told him to come along and spend the night at our place to protect his wife from further abuse. He did as I said and lay down on the bed to sleep off his stupor.

December 23 Rempel slept through the night, got up at the usual time in the morning, and went home. Later he returned and asked my forgiveness. He is ashamed of himself and fears the consequences of his behaviour.

December 25 Christmas Day. I preached a sermon in the home of Johann Hildebrand in Novopodolsk, based on Luke 2:1–14. My wife and I and Peter v Kampen and his wife visited my brother Diedrich and discussed the recent wedding at the v Kampen's place where v Kampen and my cousin David Klassen had gotten quite drunk. The two tried to make light of the matter by saying that this was the custom and could not so easily be changed. They were also a bit rough with one another, and my brother said, 'The world too must be given its rightful due.' To this I replied, 'It most surely would when the Lord appeared at the final judgment and had his reckoning with them.' That ended the dispute.

December 31 Another year has passed with its sufferings and joys. Dear Lord, grant that the sins I have committed this past year might be covered up by thy mercy. I thank thee for the benefits we have received, for thou art our sustainer. Thou hast granted us a rich harvest, and we have plenty to eat. But thou hast also chastened us with a cattle plague, and of the nine head of cattle I owned only one remains. Thou hast also encouraged my beloved Islanders (where I taught school for eight years) to send me a gift of 22 silver R. The Lord has provided for me marvellously. I will trust him, knowing that he will help further.

1861

January 1 I preached a sermon in the home of Abraham Günther in Novovitebsk based on Jeremiah 4:3–4. The congregation was large and the building crowded.

January 2 I took the students, who were home for the holidays, back to the Zentralschule in Khortitsa. We were seven on the sled: brother Diedrich's boys Peter and Diedrich, v Kampen's son Johann, my son David, Peter v Kampen, and my sister Katharina, who had been visiting [from Khortitsa].

January 11 Wednesday. The Elder celebrated Holy Communion with 97 persons in attendance at the home of the Abr. Günthers.

January 24 We had dinner in Kamianka at the Julius Janzens, and then drove to Izluchistaia to visit the David Redekopps, where we spent the night. The next day we had dinner and Vesper at the Gerhard Andres and returned home for the night.

February 1 Wednesday. At an auction sale in Neuendorf of the estate of the late Jacob Wall, conducted on behalf of the Orphans' Administration, Peter Wiebe bought a workbench for 20 silver R. On reaching home, he examined it and discovered a secret drawer that opened by means of a concealed spring. You can picture his surprise when he found 145 gold pieces hidden in the drawer, each coin a half imperial crown worth 5 silver R. 15 C. He returned the coins to the Orphans' Administration and received a reward of 10 per cent of their value. Neither the widow nor the other heirs had known of the treasure. In the meantime, the widow Wall has married the widower Wilhelm Redekopp of Neuendorf. ([Marginal entry opposite this date] Correction: Many years later I learned from a relative of the late Wall that Wiebe had given Redekopp's wife only 40 gold pieces and received a reward of 2 gold pieces. The remainder had been lawfully distributed [to the other heirs].)

The aged Franz Dyck, long-time head of the Orphans' Administration, and his wife died in Neuendorf and were buried in a single grave.

February 6 My wife and I dropped by to discuss our prospective church building with Johann Friesen, who is negotiating with a nobleman to buy a manor-house that we might be able to use.

February 14 At a general communal meeting in the home of the overseer Peter v Kampen we decided that several brethren should visit the estate, which is about 30 verstas from here, to see if the above-mentioned building could be used as a church. After Wilh. Martens had excused himself from going because of his wife's illness, Johann Friesen of Novokovno was chosen as the second building foreman. We agreed that if the building was found to be suitable, the two foremen and the overseer should discuss its purchase with the nobleman in Verchnedneprovsk.

At 9 p.m. one evening in Rosenthal a wolf attacked and seriously injured the night-watchman Ewert. It also attacked the teacher Wallmann, who was less seriously hurt. Three wolves broke into the pen at the fire house, ravaged some cattle, and seriously injured a Russian worker on his head. This same wolf was beaten to death the following morning in the village of Rosengart, where it had attacked several people.

February 16 My neighbour Martin Harder, several others, and I (see Feb. 14) drove to inspect the building mentioned above. We liked what we saw and decided that the chosen individuals should negotiate its purchase with the estate owner. In our presence, my brother Diedrich gave the overseer v Kampen 200 silver R. God grant that we manage to buy the building.[8]

February 17 We visited the Isaac Wiebes in Novopodolsk, who had recently returned from the Khortitsa colonies. They told us of the tragic suicide of the youngster Heinrich Dyck, son of the late Isaac Dyck (my wife's half-brother), who had hanged himself for reasons that are still unknown. May the gracious Lord have mercy on him.

March 6 My brother Diedrich, Aron Lepp, the two foremen, and I met at Peter v Kampen's place to discuss the church building. We decided to build the church of wood, and prepared the design and cost estimates. The building is to be 47 feet long, 24 feet wide, and 10 feet high from floor to ceiling. It will cost roughly 600 silver R. *Lepp was opposed to building.*[9] We will prepare a communal declaration in this regard, and the overseers Epp and v Kampen will have it signed in the [six Judenplan] colonies. If the signatures are not forthcoming construction will not proceed.

I drafted the declaration, which my brother Diedrich took along: 'March 6, 1861. We, the undersigned Mennonites from the Khortitsa District settled in Jewish colonies in Kherson Province, mindful of our need for a house of prayer in which to conduct our church services and of the willingness of fellow believers from the Khortitsa and other communities to make donations to this end, pledge to make payments of 5 silver R. for each of the model agriculturalists settled in the six colonies as well as provide labour needed for this purpose. The sum thus raised, together with the monies collected, will cover the costs of 600 silver R., as specified in the estimates.'

March 9 Thursday evening. The landholders gathered at the home of the overseer v Kampen, and signed the declaration in the presence of my brother Diedrich.

March 13 Monday. All of the model landholders have now signed the declaration, except Jacob Hamm, who is still opposed.

March 15 Around 5 p.m. we heard a cry from my neighbour's son, 'There is fire at the Banmanns'.' I took one horrified look and saw the fire was spreading from the already fiercely burning house towards the village threshing floor, which was surrounded with stacks of hay, straw, and grain. Peter Banmann and Johann Quiring, who lease their land from Jews, live in a Jewish house built for two families. Soon Quiring's barn, hay, and grain stacks and Banmann's hay, grain and straw were on fire. The flames spared only the household belongings, Banmann's barn, and the large haystack and stack of barley belonging to each of the men. The fire burned the night through, and many people stood watch.

March 16 The fire was still burning this morning. Water was then brought to the site, the fire put out, and the scene cleaned up. Mennonites from Novopodolsk came to help. The Fire Insurance Office asked for an appraisal of the loss, which the overseer and I estimated to be about 530 R.

March 29 Wednesday, 9 p.m. We had just gone to bed when we were awakened by the cry 'fire.' I rushed out and saw the hay and rye stacks of a Jew going up in flames. We took every precaution to contain the fire, which did not spread.

April 2 The incident involving the wolves ended tragically (see Feb. 14). The wolf was rabid, Ewert has died a horrible death, but the others have recovered, through God's mercy.

One night in Kronsweide, a rich, elderly couple by the name of Nickel were robbed. The husband had noticed a light in the porch of the small house where they live, and gone to check. There he was struck on the head, fell to the ground, was grabbed and thrown into the cellar. His still sleeping wife was then dragged from her bed, and before she knew what was happening to her she too was forced into the basement. A few blankets were thrown down to the Nickels and the trapdoor closed and weighted down with chests. The couple remained in this situation until the following afternoon at two, when they were freed by neighbours. The robbery is said to have involved thousands of rubles, including 94 gold pieces. The aged Nickel, who is childless and has the reputation of being miserly, had gathered treasure for himself that thieves could find and steal. Grant, Lord, that we might amass treasure in heaven which neither moth nor rust can corrupt and where thieves do not break through. Matthew 6:20.

April 29 Carl Jäger, the overseer in Novozhitomir, died Friday evening at nine o'clock. Since he had various papers and objects in his possession, another overseer, v Kampen, was called, and he asked me to accompany him. But Jäger's affairs had already been looked after and there was little for v Kampen to do.

May 2 Carl Jäger was buried today at the age of 43 years, 10 months, and 10 days.

May 6 Saturday. At 5:45 this morning, Anna, the wife of my neighbour Gerhard Wiebe, died after a long illness. I arrived at the beginning of her death struggle and was there to close her eyes. May the Lord receive this woman's sorely tested spirit.

May 9 We were present today at a triple funeral in the home of our neighbour Gerhard Wiebe. His wife had reached the age of 46 years, 9 months, and 10 days, been married for 29 years, and given birth to 15 children, of whom 7 sons and 6 daughters are alive. She was grandmother to 9 children, of whom 3 died. We also buried Aron Neusteter's infant daughter Elisabeth, who was one year, two months, and six days old, and Franz Isaac's infant daughter Miriam, who was two weeks younger than the Neusteter child, all three bodies in a single grave, and I gave the funeral sermon.

Funeral guests from the Khortitsa colonies told us that Franz Siemens of Rosengart had cut his throat. May God have mercy on his troubled soul.

May 14 Gerhard Wiebe, whose soul is being sorely tried, asked that we include him in our intercessory prayers. Lord, hear the prayers of thy church and have mercy on his pitiable soul.

May 17 Wednesday. My sons Jacob and Peter and I carted a load of grain to Khortitsa over muddy roads. I returned with a steer, which Jacob Wiebe of the Island of Khortitsa gave me. David came home with us from school.

May 30 Today I catechized the youth, asking them to answer the first half of the questions, which they did to my great satisfaction. In the afternoon we attended the funeral of Bernhard Abram, infant son of Jacob Abram, who died at the age of 1 year, 6 months, and 24 days.

June 1 Day of Ascension. After a short sermon I asked our [baptismal] youth to answer the questions in the second half of the catechism, which all recited well. In the afternoon, we attended a funeral in the home of Heinrich Sawatzki in Novovitebsk for his daughter Maria, who had died of the measles at the age of 1 year, 5 weeks, and 2 days. An epidemic of the measles is rampant here.
June 4 The articles [of faith] were read for the sixth time, in their entirety. The baptismal candidates responded to the three customary questions by saying 'Yes.' Lord Jesus, make them worthy, at the time of their baptism, of also receiving the inner baptism of thy spirit. Do this, we pray, out of thy great love.

This afternoon we were present at the funeral of Gerhard Braun's daughter Maria, who died at the age of 1 year, 3 months, and 13 days.
June 5 I and my son David took 2 puds and 14 funt of wool to Khortitsa, which we left on consignment with Jacob Dyck. Dyck, who is the District mayor, told me that Dietrich Neufeld of Schönhorst (earlier of Novokovno) had hanged himself while under house arrest for insubordination.

The extermination of grasshoppers [in the Khortitsa colonies] is causing a great stir.
June 6 This morning we left for Ekaterinoslav to pick up lumber for our church, and the next morning we started back with several other wagons also loaded with lumber for the church.
June 10 This morning I carted a load of stones from Izluchistaia for our church, which I bought from David Redekopp.
June 13 The government ordered the entire village community of Jews and Germans to go out looking for grasshoppers, but we found none. May God save us from this plague. Tonight Jews and Germans [from Novovitebsk] gathered in Izluchistaia to be ready at dawn to help kill the grasshoppers.
June 20 On my way to the Jewish treadmill with grain, Jakob Friesen stopped by and asked me to talk to his father-in-law Johann Hiebert, who had complained about him to the District mayor and the Elder in Khortitsa. During a visit by his parents-in-law to his home, Friesen had abused them in the foulest language. Racing after them as they drove away, he tried to wedge a pole in among the legs of the horses. The Hieberts had feared he was trying to kill them and would then kill himself. I explained the seriousness of his offence to

Friesen, but his remorse seemed superficial – mainly out of fear of punishment. I promised to report the disposition of the matter to the Elder.

June 22 A rainy day. The Germans from here went to Izluchistaia to kill grasshoppers, but many are still alive. May the Lord protect us from this plague.

July 11 From time to time we are still called upon to help exterminate grasshoppers. Today I was again along, but most of the grasshoppers can now fly and the work has become rather useless. Also helping were Jacob Görzen, his son Gerhard, and Hein. Siemens, but in such a drunken state that they seemed to be only looking for a fight to settle scores with their neighbours. My presence kept them from laying a hand on anyone, but they were quite abusive. The situation, dear Lord, is sad.

July 23 The overseers called a general communal meeting regarding the lumber bought for the church. Members of the community had examined the lumber, for which the building foremen Johann Friesen and Martin Harder had paid high prices, and found it unsuitable. The two said they were innocent of any wrongdoing, but the gathering concluded that the foremen had acted unfaithfully in this serious matter. We asked the overseers Epp and v Kampen to accompany the foreman on a visit to the lumber dealer to remedy the situation as best possible.

August 13 Before today's service, Heinrich Siemens and the young woman Agatha Görzen appeared before the Ministerial Committee. Mrs Joh. Schellenberg, Mrs Gerh. Görzen, and the Gerh. Redekopps had accused them of committing fornication. Their behaviour had aroused suspicion, but they denied any wrongdoing. Agatha's mother was present, even though she had not been invited, and supported her daughter. Peter Löwen reminded her that her presence was not desired, and this made her very angry. The matter was put over until later on.

September 3 An accident this evening in Novovitebsk reminds us again to 'be watchful.' A local Jew by the name of Borvinski was carting a load of flour past Jacob Dyck's place when a dog jumped over the fence and barked. The Jew did not have the reins firmly in hand, and the skittish horses veered sideways towards the ditch. To keep the wagon on the road, Borvinski ran around behind it but ended up in the ditch with the wagon. The axle struck his chest, and when they reached him he was already dead. What I say I say to all, 'Be watchful.'

September 27 Suddenly while working on the threshing floor this afternoon, we noticed a huge cloud of smoke rising over Novopodolsk. After harnessing the horses, we raced over and were met by a terrifying sight: the houses, barns, hay, and grain stacks of the Jew Grabinovich, Peter Rempel, Heinrich Friesen, and the Prussian Fischbotter were all burning fiercely. Strict measures were taken to contain the blaze.

September 30 On Saturday I and several others carted grain to Nikopol. I sold the wheat for 6½ silver R. and the oats for 2 silver R. per chetvert.

October 1 I had the bad luck in Nikopol of losing my valise, which contained 11 silver R. and valuable documents. 'Be watchful for ye know not the hour when the Lord will appear.'

Johann Neufeld of Einlage was found stone-dead, sitting on the edge of his wagon, after visiting the inn of the estate owner Sakharov. His death was totally unexpected.

October 16 We celebrated Holy Communion with 81 people in the home of C. Krause.

October 21 At three this morning, my brother Abraham's surviving child Anna died at the age of two years less five days. She followed her father quickly into eternity, and my poor sister-in-law is now forsaken and alone. May the Lord comfort her.

October 25 Wednesday. In a double funeral, Anna [Epp] was buried in one grave with the infant daughter of the schoolteacher Franz Niccel.

November 10 On behalf of the Orphans' Administration, I organized the auction at the home of my neighbour Gerhard Wiebe. His property was sold to Heinrich Olfert, the Novozhitomir teacher, for 755 silver R. Sales totalled 1144 silver R. Wiebe's under-aged children have been placed with good people, and only the youngest son will stay with him for the time being.

November 26 Serious discord has arisen between my colleagues Isaac Klassen and Peter Löwen over an old, outdated, and discarded herdsman's list found among the papers of the late Carl Jäger. Klassen is using it to create conflict, but I would guess from what he has said that he is at fault. God have mercy on us.

November 30 Abraham Unger and Isaac Wiebe appeared before the Ministerial Committee in the presence of my colleagues Klassen and Löwen. They are accused of acting falsely in the purchase and carting of lumber from Ekaterinoslav. At the lumber market, Unger had loaded 23 planks for the church, as confirmed by a merchant's receipt, but had dropped off one plank at his place and delivered only 21. Wiebe had carted rafters for the church, one of which he had exchanged at his place for a shorter one. Unger insisted that he had paid the merchant for the plank himself, and this question was left on his conscience. Wiebe, however, confessed, promised to exchange the rafters, and asked our forgiveness. They were allowed to go in peace.

December 31 I preached a sermon in the home of Johann Hildebrand on Matthew 23:37–9, the last sermon on the last day of the old year.

During the past year there have been changes in the lives of many people in our [Old Colony Flemish] church. Of those born during the last century, who are therefore 62 years of age and older, 6 men and 13 women died and 118 men and 112 women, a total of 230 are living. Of those born this century, and joined to the church through Holy Baptism, 19 males and 13 females died, and 1654 males and 1825 females are still living. A total of 51 church members died and 3859 are still living.

[Figures for the entire Khortitsa community]:

Births	243 males	216 females	459 total
Deaths	114 males	119 females	233 total
Increase	129 males	97 females	226 total
Couples married	93		

Births and deaths in the Judenplan in 1861 (included in the above figures):

Births	24 males	18 females	42 total
Deaths	13 males	16 females	29 total
Increase	11 males	2 females	13 total
Couples married	6		

Of the 29 people who died, 6 were Church members and the others were minors.

At the close of this year, I must record another unusual event. Over the holidays, Martin Wiebe, an old dear friend of mine from Neuosterwick, went home to do chores while visiting in his village, saying he would return in the evening. But as he stepped out of his barn, he cried out in a loud voice, 'Children, I have pain in my chest.' He lit his pipe, set it down again, and saying, 'It hurts terribly,' fell from his chair, and when his hurriedly summoned neighbours arrived, he was already a corpse. His sudden death is a warning to us that we should always be ready for the day of our death. Grant me the grace to remember that I must die in order that I might become wise. Forgive me my sins, and let me find salvation in thee.

The harvest was quite good, and, in the end, the grasshoppers caused only a little damage. Our merciful Lord has faithfully stood guard over our crops and commanded our enemies to pass us by. To him be honour and praise. Amen.

1862

January 17 God protected us from a great fire today. This morning, our neighbour Gerhard Wiebe lit his stove, which is in rather poor shape, and flames shot up the chimney, setting fire to the wooden flue and burning a spot through next to the ridge of the straw roof. The fire was fortunately extinguished before it could spread. There was a strong wind at the time, and had Wiebe's house caught fire, my house and our entire row of houses would probably have burned to the ground. The danger was serious because the yards are full of hay and straw stacks. We thank God from the depths of our hearts for protecting us.

January 18 Thursday. I gave the sermon at the funeral for Mrs Cornelius Giesbrecht of Kamianka, who died of a miscarriage. She was 33 years and 26 days old, had been married 13 years, 2 months, and 12 weeks and given birth to 9 children, 3 sons and 6 daughters, of whom 2 sons and a daughter are still living.

January 23 Tuesday. We attended the funeral for Peter Teichröw's son who died of the measles at the age of 7 years, 5 months, and 6 days.

January 25 My neighbour Gerhard Wiebe and his youngest son Bernhard dropped by around Vesper-time. Wiebe continues to be tormented by doubts and believes that he is lost. He had been illumined at *one time*, he said, but then he had rejected salvation and was now totally without hope. He seemed a little comforted when he left. His son had in the meantime fallen asleep at our place and remained here, but around midnight I got an urgent call to come over and found Wiebe in his bed whimpering. He was confused and missed his son. Wiebe's son-in-law Letkemann fetched the boy from our place, undressed him, and placed him in bed next to his father. Then Wiebe calmed down a little. May the Lord be his consolation.

January 26 On his last trip from the Khortitsa colonies, Isbrand Friesen, a leaseholder of Jewish property in Novopodolsk, got quite drunk and insulted my brother Diedrich, the overseer, calling him a good-for-nothing, etc. Friesen admitted that the reports were true, but excused himself on the grounds that he had been drunk. He promised to apologize to my brother, and I replied that once this was done the matter would be of no further concern to the Ministerial Committee. I warned him [about the drink], and he promised betterment.

February 1 Thursday. I gave the sermon at the funeral for Abraham Unger's two children, Cornelius (40 weeks and 4 days old) and Katarina (6 years, 8 months, and 3 weeks old), who had died of the measles.

February 5 Monday. At night, Johann Rempel and I took turns watching over our mentally ill neighbour Gerhard Wiebe (we are all taking turns this week), who tried to kill himself on Sunday. He took straw from the beds, stuffed the straw into the stove-pipes, opened the draught so that the straw caught fire, and then stuck his head into the stove. We have been watching over him constantly ever since. Tonight he again threatened to commit suicide and begged us to take his life. He is full of despair, applies Paul's words to the Hebrews (Hebrews 6:4–6) to himself, and refuses consolation of any kind for his cold and lifeless soul. He rejects the hope of salvation, has a deranged mind, is restless, and can never stay in bed for any length of time. Those who watch over him have to be very careful not to fall asleep. There is really nothing that we can do but to appeal to the merciful heart of Jesus, and this we have done without ceasing. Lord, we beseech thee, harken unto our supplications. Here we can see, as in a looking glass, the entire issue of repentance.

Sectarianism is spreading rapidly in the Khortitsa colonies. I recorded earlier in my diaries how the movement had been kept somewhat in check by the District Office and the church leadership.[10] From this [earlier] seed a healthy new growth has sprouted in [the village] of Einlage.[11] Yet the devil never rests, and while others slumbered he sowed weeds among the seed, which have now come up. In the Molochna colony of Liebenau a fanatical sect has emerged that practises a second baptism by immersion, and has principles quite contrary to the Scriptures. Gerhard Wieler, a former teacher in Liebenau, was dismissed from that post, went to Einlage, where the 'believers' hired him on as their private teacher.[12] But your glorying is not good. Know ye not that a little leaven leaveneth the whole lump? 1 Corinthians 5:6. God, it is eternally sad that where the Holy Spirit awakens new life, the spirit of delusion appears more strongly, and it is the false spirit. Watch and pray!

February 7 Wednesday. We visited Julius Janzen in Kamianka. As we left home, the weather was mild and the sleighing quite good, but before we started back it turned bitterly cold, the road drifted over, and we had to proceed at a walk. There are many stories this winter about travellers losing their way and tragedies that follow. In the Khortitsa colonies, a married couple got lost and have not been seen since. Another couple, from Rosenthal, one day drove to Einlage and on the way home became lost in a fierce blizzard with heavy drifting. They finally stopped, tipped over the sled, and the wife and two children took refuge under it for the night. Meanwhile the husband looked after the horses. The night was presumably very long, but they were saved. As morning dawned they realized they were close to home, on the hill overlooking the firehouse of Rosenthal. Not far from Nikopol a coachman and two noblemen with a sled and horses were found in a hollow under a snow-drift, the horses and people frozen stiff. When I hear stories like this, I remember my own trip in the spring of 1852, when I was caught underways by a huge winter storm. There were many accidents at that time too, yet God protected me and led me home in a marvellous way. May the Lord lead us further through life's storms to that blessed eternity and keep us safe and secure on the path of righteousness.

February 13 Today we took our deranged neighbour Gerhard Wiebe to Khortitsa. Wilhelm Martens drove him on his sled, and I took his children Judith and Bernhard, as well as Abr. Günther, along with me. We stopped for the night at the Gerh. Giesbrechts on the Kudashev khutor, where they watched closely over our patient the whole time. There was a fierce storm.

February 15 We brought Wiebe to the H. Martens in Khortitsa.

February 24 Saturday. On behalf of the Orphans' Administration, I conducted an auction sale of Gerh. Wiebe's remaining effects.

March 14 We began seeding.

April 9 Easter Monday. While visiting at the David Klassens' place, we heard a wagon approaching at great speed and hurried to the window to look. Coming around the corner at Klassen's garden, the wagon rolled over, and the horses bolted with the front end of the wagon. Klassen and I ran out to help. The occupants of the wagon, Abraham Unger, Franz Redekopp of Novokovno, and their wives and children, made a frightful racket, and you could hear Unger's wife wailing, 'That's what you get for drinking.' Unger lay on the ground in pain, and his wife scolded him for not listening to her. The Klassens took in Unger, his wife and children. As Redekopp entered the house he said to his wife, 'Well, Mumchi, that's what comes of the brandy.' They were all seriously injured, but the worst off were Redekopp and Unger's wife. Klassen and Heinrich Sawatzki set out to fetch Doctor Hildebrand from the Khortitsa colonies, and while I tended to Mrs Unger, Mrs Thiessen carried on about the heavy drinking. They had all been at Cornelius Thiessen's place, but he declared that no one had been drinking to excess at his home. I put a halt to his denials by saying that he had already desecrated the morning through excessive drinking with another group, and this set off another explosion against me and those who had confided in me. He was obviously still quite drunk. I suggested we continue the discussion some other time, but he would not stop, carrying on about a torn rein having caused the accident. Our neighbours took the victims into their homes. While driving on the wagon later, Thiessen took Hiebert to task for mentioning the morning's drinking (this my wife heard from Hiebert's wife). Heavy drinking can incite terrible sins, and this is true of every addiction that comes to rule over our hearts. Dear God, have mercy on us.

April 15 Sunday. There are troubling reports from the Khortitsa colonies that the sectarian cause is gaining ground. They baptize a second time by immersion, and have other practices of this kind.

This afternoon David Redekopp of Voronzovka (previously of Izluchistaia) came to see me. He started by telling me he belonged to the [new] group, but had come to talk to me about his son Jacob, who wanted to be baptized. He wanted me to know that he had no objections to this. His son, he said sarcastically, would want to marry in time, etc. I asked him why he did not have his son baptized among his [new] associates, to which he replied, 'Baptism there is based on faith and among you only on an empty verbal confession.' I will not record everything that he said, only that no one in our church would find salvation without leaving it. He admitted, finally, that there might be a few. He also talked a great deal about the robberies and murders that we ministers had committed. I did not argue with him very much, but I asked him again whether he was serious in his request for his son. He replied that his son had no faith, or at best one that was dead, but he nevertheless wished to join the church. Redekopp also told me in so many words that I had not been converted myself. I asked him not to judge, and he replied, 'I make no judgments,' and then continued in this same vein. Examine me as to my true motives, Lord, and give me the strength and power to act in accordance with my office. Help me to bear the burden which thou hast laid on me.

April 23 We started building our new church. The foreman is Jacob Dyck, currently of Chernoglas, who has eleven people working under him. The foreman is paid 2 R. per day, Gerhard Andres is to work for 1 R. and the others for 90 or 70 silver C. per day. For board they are making the rounds of the landholders, which is calculated as [a cost of] 20 C. per man.

April 29 Today we announced the names of the 14 baptismal candidates, 4 young men and 10 young women, including my daughter Helena. May the Lord Jesus make their hearts worthy of this great act.

I and my wife had dinner at the Peter v Kampens', where I

officiated at the marriage of their son Martin to Judith Nickel. Before the ceremony we had quite a scare when the straw-roofed smithy house next door caught fire and a strong wind threatened the v Kampens' house. But there was no further damage.

May 12 Sunday. We returned from our visit to the Khortitsa colonies. The sectarian movement there continues to grow and the dispute seems to be taking a serious turn. As we reached Khortitsa, the District police officer was investigating the matter, and on his orders the leaders Heinrich Neufeld, Abraham Unger, and Johann Isaac had been arrested and taken to the police station in Chernyshev. Elder Gerhard Dyck and the District mayor Jacob Dyck have raised the subject with the Guardianship Committee in Odessa, and God only knows what will happen next. [Comment in margin:] These people are deluded, but it seems to me unfair and unjust to persecute them in this way. One hopes that the movement might become a powerful voice rousing our church from its present drowsy stupor.

May 20 The articles of faith were read for the sixth time in their entirety. Our young people then answered the three usual questions by saying 'Yes.' After a short compelling exhortation, the service ended. Dear Lord Jesus, work in the hearts of these dear young people that they might be found worthy also of being baptized with fire and with thy spirit.

May 28 Elder Gerhard Dyck today baptized the candidates including our young people from the Jewish colonies (among them my daughter).

May 29 The situation in the Khortitsa colonies in regard to the sectarian movement looks very bleak. These people refuse to admit that they are misguided. Neufeld, Unger, and Isaac are still under arrest by the District police. May the Lord have mercy on them.

June 9 Saturday. We attended the engagement of my sister Katharina to Bernhard Schellenberg in the Zentralschule in Khortitsa.

June 10 Sunday. My wife, daughter Helena, and I celebrated Holy Communion [in Khortitsa] in the presence of 694 members.

June 11 The Lord Inspector Biller has had the fanatics Johann Töws and Peter Nikkel of Nieder Khortitsa arrested and taken under guard to the police station. How I pity these poor people.

June 17 Today was the first service in our new church, and I delivered the dedicatory sermon based on 1 Corinthians 3:16–17.

The congregation was very large. Lord Jesus, make thy presence evident among us.

June 24 Before the service, the three ministers gathered in the home of H. Dyck to hear our fellow believers from Kamianka respond to a complaint made against them by their former teacher Peter Klassen. Klassen told me on several occasions that he had been cheated in the [final] settlement [of his salary]. Since the matter had been previously resolved by the overseer Lepp, Isaac Klassen and I had decided that we would not mediate but try to arbitrate the dispute and restore peace. Things today, however, developed quite otherwise. Isaac Klassen now took a strongly partisan stand in support of Peter Klassen, who became coarse and insulting towards me. Forgive us, Lord, that we as ministers cannot agree among ourselves.

July 2 Monday. I preached a funeral sermon in the home of Wilhelm Fischbotter in Novopodolsk (Prussian subject, Lutheran church) for his son who had died in his first year of life.

August 14 Tuesday morning. My wife and I and our son Jacob left for the annual market in Nikopol with 4 chetvert of oats, which I sold for 4 silver R. per chetvert. We spent the night with the Abraham Friesens, made our purchases Wednesday afternoon, and then left for home. In Nikopol we were witnesses to a swindle when a Jewish merchant by the name of Westermann (I do not know from where) bought a pair of oxen from a Russian for 47 silver R. and paid him with counterfeit 25- and 10-R. notes. When the Russian realized what had happened he made quite a fuss. The Jew, who had also been lodging with Abraham Friesen, asked the latter to witness in court to his *good character*, telling him that he had given the Russian a 50-R. note and gotten back 3 R. in change. He promised that this would be confirmed by a Russian witness. But the Russian in question could only say that he had seen the transaction but not the denomination of the notes that had been passed. The man who had sold the oxen produced 12 witnesses who testified they had observed him receiving the bills from the Jew, as reported. We left Nikopol at this stage and I do not know how the matter was resolved.

We got caught in a huge dust storm on our way to Nikopol and shortly before arriving there were overtaken by a downpour, accompanied by violent thunder, lightning, and hail. As we reached Nikopol the horses stood in swirling waters that reached over their knees.

August 18 Saturday. Our daughter [Katharina] celebrated her engagement to Johann Andres, son of Gerhard Andres of Izluchistaia.
August 19 My wife and I drove to the service in Kamianka with our engaged couple, where I preached the sermon. We had dinner at the home of the bridegroom's parents, the Gerh. Andres.
August 27 Early Monday morning my son David and I drove to Khortitsa and also paid a visit to the Island of Khortitsa where we were showered with gifts of Kruschtje [plums], which are plentiful this year. The new sect is causing a great stir. Gerhard Wieler's petition to Our Lord and Emperor has been returned to him by the Guardianship Committee with the demand that he answer to the complaints contained therein.
September 16 I preached a sermon in our church on how we might appropriate our salvation. Text, Romans 13:11–12. Lord Jesus, grant that we might all truly experience thee. Be merciful to me. Before the sermon Peter Teichröw and Franz Dyck appeared before us in the ministers' room. Johann Friesen had informed me that Abraham Unger had told him how he and his Russian servant had butchered a sheep belonging to someone else in his barn at night. Since Abraham Unger was not at home, consideration of the matter was postponed. How I wish all of the tares could be rooted out.
September 19 Wednesday. The Reverend Isaac Klassen and his brother Franz Klassen dropped by on their way home from the Khortitsa colonies. I had reported to the Elder the dispute with Klassen in Kamianka (see entry for June 24). Klassen now asked my forgiveness and promised to work more co-operatively with me in the future. The dear Elder and his colleagues arrived today.
September 20 Thursday. The following appeared in church before the Ministerial Committee: Abraham Unger of Novokovno and Johann Friesen. Also present were Heinrich Penner and Franz Dyck, who had been summoned to appear by the witnesses Isaac Friesen and Peter Teichröw. Dyck and Penner related that Unger had told them he had taken a sheep bought from the herdsman (and thus stolen) and slaughtered it at night in his barn. He had taken great care to cover every window crack to ensure that the neighbours could not see the light. Unger admitted saying this, but claimed that the story was incorrect insofar as the herdsman and his Russian servant had done the slaughtering. They had awakened him only after it was

almost finished. He admitted that he had stored the meat in his cellar, but had not used any himself. The matter was put over until after the communion service.

Finally, after the others had left, the Elder asked Reverend Klassen to say truthfully whether he was innocent of the charge that he had twice taken payment for the bread baked in Kronsthal for Carl Jäger, the overseer. He affirmed his innocence. The beloved Elder then exhorted him (as well as the rest of us) to live in peace with one another. Klassen again asked my forgiveness, and I gave him my hand.

September 21 The congregational election was held Friday morning. First, my cousin [David Klassen] was chosen deacon with 19 votes. Other votes: Diedr. Thiessen 9, Bernh. Wiebe 5, Aron Neusteter 4, Johann Penner 3, Diet. Friesen 2, and Isbrand Friesen 1. Then, in the election for minister, my cousin again received the most votes, 44.[13]

September 23 Sunday, 132 members celebrated Holy Communion.

September 24 Our guests left this morning. My wife and I and the children Katharina, Diedrich, and Heinrich left for Kronsgarten and arrived at my brother Johann's place at nightfall. Three ministers from the Molochna, the aged Elder Peter Wedel and the ministers Schröder and Riedger, who were also in Kronsgarten, held a service in church on Wednesday. Riedger and Elder Wedel preached in the morning, the former delivering the introductory sermon and the latter reading the text and giving the exegesis. Schröder spoke in the afternoon. All three preached by heart.[14] Riedger, however, often got stuck, his sentences did not hang together, and at times he simply resorted to reciting Bible and song verses. The other two were better, indeed one can even say that they preached well.

Thursday my brother Johann and I drove to the annual fair in Ekaterinoslav where he had some business to do at the post office, and I bought cabbages and other provisions. In Kronsgarten we visited several friends and acquaintances. Sunday was Thanksgiving, and I preached the sermon in their house of prayer, based on Jeremiah 5: 24–5. We took our leave in the afternoon, first driving to my cousin Johann Thiessen's place in Ekaterinoslav, where his sister, my aunt, is staying.

October 1 Monday we visited the Heinrich Heeses, who were just butchering two of their pigs. Since there was an exhibition of agricultural products at the Potemkin Palace, we went there in the afternoon, but arrived late. Peter Lepp from Khortitsa was exhibiting a chaff-cutter and had won a medal.[15]

October 2 We left Thiessen's place this morning, meeting my cousin Peter Thiessen at the inn in Engelbrod and spending the night at the Chernoglas inn. With a cold drizzle and driving rain, the journey was quite unpleasant.

October 3 We started out at 3:30 Monday morning, stopped to feed our horses on the Kudashev khutor and arrived home safely at 4:30 in the afternoon. A heavy snowfall from the north covered the ground, and the weather was unpleasant.

October 7 Sunday. A Ministerial Committee meeting at our house considered the sheep-butchering incident (see September 20). Present were Abraham Unger, Franz Dyck, and Heinrich Penner and the witnesses Isaac Friesen and Peter Teichröw. The latter informed us that Unger had finally confessed his wrongdoing, was genuinely repentant, and had asked forgiveness. Unger confirmed the report, and requested pardon, which we granted. I explained to him the nature of his failing and the seriousness of his habitual drinking, and he promised to reform.

Brotherhood Meeting. The episode involving Unger, including his request for forgiveness, was presented to the congregation. He appeared before the brethren, confessed his guilt, and asked for forgiveness. May the Lord Jesus help him to keep his promise.

Because the church is without a stove, I informed the brethren that we would not hold services there during the winter, but [in homes] in the villages, as we did before.

October 12 Friday. Diedrich Thiessen's wife Katarina (née Nikkel) was buried in Novopodolsk, having died in childbirth after delivering a stillborn child with the aid of the renowned doctor from Grushevka. Thirty-six years old, she had been married 16½ years and given birth to 8 children. Three had died and three sons and two daughters are still alive. Her stillborn child was placed in a small coffin next to hers and buried in the same grave. I delivered the funeral sermon.

October 25 Thursday. We could not attend today's celebration of the engagement of Jacob Pätkau and Helena Epp (my brother Diedrich's daughter) because of family illness. My wife has been in bed all week, and our infant Heinrich has sore eyes. From our family only Joh. Andres, Katharina, and David were present.

October 30 Tuesday. Our son-in-law Joh. Andres left for Khortitsa with our daughter Katharina, who has not been well since spring. Until she is better, she will be staying with the colony's doctor, brother-in-law B. Schellenberg. May the guardian angel protect them. My wife and little one are improving.

November 18 In Luke 17:10, the Lord Jesus says, 'So likewise ye, when ye shall have done all these things which are commanded you, say, We are unprofitable servants: we have done that which was our duty to do.' But what will those say who have done nothing, who have not produced a single thing honouring to God? And what of those ministers who have served with unregenerate hearts? How can they proclaim the Gospel to the unrepentant, saying that forgiveness is to be found in Christ's blood? Lord, why have I been chosen for this office? I am corrupted and there is only vanity in me. What is the fate of the indolent servant? Lord Jesus, thou powerful warrior and Saviour, almighty Lord and God, thou canst accomplish anything. Help me in my desolation. Let the sunshine of thy grace, dear Saviour, warm my frigid heart and illumine my darkened understanding.

November 23 Friday. In a clear dream last night, I had terrible chest pains and thought I was dying. I feared I was lost because of my sins, and out of the depths of my heart I cried out to Christ for grace, pity, and help. Then the pain subsided, and I awoke. The Lord is knocking at the door of my heart. Open it thyself, dear Lord, with thy almighty power.

November 24 Saturday we left for Khortitsa, spending the night on the Kudashev khutor and arriving on Sunday. In the evening my brother-in-law Pätkau drove us to see our daughter Katharina who is staying with my brother-in-law B. Schellenberg in Rosenthal.

November 27 Abr. Hiebert, Katharina and I left for home, taking with us a cow from my brother-in-law Corn. Hildebrand, which I will repay with four chetvert of barley when times are better.

November 28 During my absence, the doctor from Grushevka talked to my sick wife for about an hour and promised to send medicine.

December 25 Tuesday, Christmas Day, the first holiday. In our intercessory prayer at today's service, we mentioned Mrs Klas Heide, who has been ill for a year. May the Lord give her strength to bear her sufferings patiently and may they work to her salvation. Precious Saviour, remember also my marriage partner, who has been bedridden for ten weeks. Comfort her with thy presence and grant her the joy of faith. Reveal thyself to her that she may find strength and forgiveness in thee. Amen.

December 31 This has been for me a year of tribulation. In His wisdom our Lord God has decided to burden my soul with many temptations. Yet I praise and thank him for his merciful love which we have experienced through the wounds of Jesus in forgiveness of sins and in spiritual strength. Our external life has had its share of strains and grief. We suffered a crop failure and a cattle plague. We reaped virtually nothing, and of the three head of cattle we acquired since the last plague two heifers have died and only the calf is left. There was also much illness in our family. Katharina and Heinrich were sick for some time, but the most serious case is that of my dear wife. She has not recovered from her illness since spring, and has been going downhill since our return from Kronsgarten. Although she has been bedridden for 11 weeks, we still hope for a recovery.

Changes in our community [of the Jewish colonies]:

Births	25 males	21 females	46 total
Deaths	13 males	14 females	27 total
Increase	12 males	7 females	19 total
Couples married	7 total		

1863

January 1 New Year's Day. Before today's service, Isaac Friesen asked me to write out an invitation for the funeral of Mrs Abraham Unger (née Thiessen), who died suddenly at night after haemorrhaging in childbirth and suffering for 21 hours. Only last Sunday she was at the service in good health, and now she was a corpse. I took the occasion to call for repentance. Life can end without warning, and we must do what is necessary to find peace. Grant us repentance and faith, Lord Jesus.

January 4 Today my wife's illness reached a critical stage, and we had Mrs Peter v Kampen repeatedly attach the life awakener to her back.

January 5 The Isaac Friesens were here today, and Mrs Friesen, who is a midwife, told my wife she was pregnant. Dear Lord, now this burden has been added to her suffering.

January 6 Day of Epiphany. Lord Jesus, faithful redeemer, helper in need, Saviour from sins, have mercy on me. Illumine my anxious spirit, and reveal thyself to my troubled heart. I am afraid, Lord, that my sins are so great that I cannot find favour with thee. I have knowingly committed many sinful deeds. Cleanse me in thy blood, faithful High Priest. Thou wast sacrificed on the cross for the sins of the world. Wipe out my debts. Be gracious to me, grant me a clean heart and a joyful spirit, and remember not the sins of my youth. Eternal love, grant me the strength to continue in true repentance, that I may I find peace through thy blood of atonement. Amen.

January 11 Tonight, Klas Heide and Diet. Thiessen delivered a funeral letter from my brother Heinrich informing us that his wife Anna (née Siemens) had died of the measles after an illness of only 10 days. She was barely 31 years old. What a shock. The funeral is on Sunday. She is survived by one son David,[16] the other children having died when they were young.

January 12 This morning my cousin D. Klassen and I drove to Kamianka to talk to his mother (Johann Wieler's widow) and the widow of Jacob Wiebe. We had heard that a prominent member of the new sect, Pet. Berg, and Aron Lepp had spoken to them about joining the new sect.[17] I explained that salvation could be found only in the name of Jesus Christ and that no sect could help them in this regard. I urged them to seize hold of the Lord Jesus strongly in faith and not let themselves be led astray by individuals. I said other things in this vein, as well as I could, and they replied that they wanted to stay in our church.

January 17 This evening I accompanied Dietr. Thiessen on a visit to

[Isaac] Wiebe, who had asked to see me. Wiebe confessed that he had defiled himself with cattle in his youth and now asked the church to punish him. I replied that peace could only be found in the sacrifice of Jesus Christ, and not in the discipline of the church. The man thinks that he is dying, and these [unconfessed] sins have made him very fearful. I spoke to him about God's great love in Jesus Christ for repentant sinners, and urged him to plead with the Lord, who would certainly answer his prayers. It is difficult to wage the battle for atonement in the last hours of one's life, and the longer we put off our conversion and a change of heart, the harder it gets. I therefore urge you, my dear children, to save your souls before perdition overtakes you. Do not put off your repentance to the last hour, but be reconciled while there is still time. Jesus, thou son of David, be merciful to me as well. Free me of the love of sin, and clothe me in the mantle of thy righteousness that I might come before thee naked.

January 18 Towards evening, D. Klassen and I went to see Isaac Wiebe again and found his condition much worse than yesterday. I asked him if he had found comfort in the wounds of Jesus, and he replied that he had strong rumbling noises in his head.

January 20 My brother Diedrich brought along from Khortitsa the figures regarding [population] changes. Of those [members of the Khortitsa Church] born during the last century, 5 males and 10 females died and 114 males and 103, or a total of 217, are living. Of those born in this century, and added to the church through Holy Baptism, 17 and 26 women died, and 1874 men and 1903 women are still living. In summary, 58 church members died and 3994 are still living.

Figures for the [Khortitsa] community:

Births	295 males	242 females	537 total
Deaths	107 males	92 females	199 total
Increase	188 males	150 females	338 total
Confirmed in marriage		107 couples	

January 22 Today at noon I learned that Isaac Wiebe had died around midnight last night. There are great problems in my household, with shortages everywhere. We continue to make debts, and this worries me. Wait always on the Lord, and he will care for you. These words are a great comfort for poor people.

January 25 The body of the late Isaac Wiebe was buried in Novopodolsk this afternoon, and I delivered the sermon. He was 42 years old, had been married 16 years and a few months, had fathered 6 children, 5 sons and 1 daughter. His daughter had predeceased him.
January 28 We have heard of an incident that fills us with dread and horror. A servant in the inn at Chernoglas on the post road recently went to fetch water from the well and found a corpse in it. It was a deep well, and there had been problems with the water, which no one could explain. The body was that of a male dressed in a shift with a sack bound tightly around his head. The man was bearded, but I have not heard of any other identifying marks. It is not known whether he had been choked to death or thrown in alive. In any case, the water had been used in the meantime. As the body has been buried, it can be assumed that the authorities have investigated the case. Horrors of this kind are committed in secret, but God will bring everything to light.
January 29 Gerhard Thiessen and Peter Mantler lodged a complaint against the bachelor David Penner of Izluchistaia for causing a terrible row one evening at the Thiessens. He had beaten up Mantler's sons (who are still minors) and threatened to kill everyone present. Someone had called the Thiessens, who were visiting sick Mr Isaac Wiebe, and they rushed home to find their children weeping and David Penner and Johann Hildebrand running away. The Mantler children told their parents about the incident, and they went to discuss it with the Johann Hildebrands (whose son is mentioned above). David Penner had also been there, and he had given the Mantlers a tongue-lashing. Mrs Hildebrand had egged them on, saying, 'Boys, this is my house, and you can say what you like to the Mantlers. You have my permission.' I ordered the church members involved in the incident to appear before the Ministerial Committee next Thursday.
January 31 Thursday. All those mentioned above (entry for Jan. 29) appeared before the Ministerial Committee (in the home of my cousin and colleague David Klassen): David Penner, Mrs Hildebrand, her son Johann, and the Peter Mantlers. Gerhard Thiessen and Klas Heide of Novopodolsk were the summoners and witnesses, while Gerhard Andres and Peter Peters of Izluchistaia appeared on behalf of young Penner. Penner admitted striking the others and that

he had been in the wrong, but said he had been provoked. He showed little remorse and refused to apologize. The matter is very much as described above. Heide reported that Penner had also offended him with a stream of filth and abuse because his stepdaughter had rejected Penner [as a suitor]. Penner admitted this. The matter was held over until later. Young Johann Hildebrand, who had also been summoned, waited outside, and when we invited him to come in, he said, 'You can just as easily come out here.' I spoke to him earnestly, and only then did he finally ask forgiveness for all that he had done and was allowed to leave in peace. The Mantlers and Mrs Hildebrand, too, were reconciled and left in peace.

February 1 David Penner of Izluchistaia, the father of the David named above, came by to defend his son, saying it was unfair of us to demand that his son apologize to Gerhard Thiessen and Klas Heide and that the Mantlers should meet him half-way. He was full of anger and said that if his son was to be punished he and his wife would share in it. Lord, thou knowest my failings, forgive me and strengthen me in my calling.

February 4 I drove to Khortitsa in my brother Diedrich's enclosed wagon to bring back his wife, who had been there since the funeral of my brother Heinrich's wife Anna, and spent the night with Heinrich, who is still very sad. He lent me a sack of flour. May the Lord reward him.

February 10 Before today's service, David Penner appeared before the Ministerial Committee to apologize, and his attitude was now completely different. We asked him why he had not done so earlier, and he replied that he had wanted to, *but his father would not let him*. He also made his peace with the Mantlers, Gerh. Thiessen, and Klas Heide. *Brotherhood Meeting*. I presented the matter to the brethren, and it was resolved peacefully.

February 11 *School visitation*. Monday, my three colleagues and I visited the school in Novovitebsk, which is taught by my neighbour Heinrich Olfert in his house. Subjects: Bible stories (the Old Testament), reading, writing, arithmetic, and cipher singing. There was much to be pleased with. In the afternoon we visited the school in Novopodolsk, which is taught by Franz Nikkel, a student from the Zentralschule [in Khortitsa]. Subjects: Bible stories, reading, writing, mental and blackboard arithmetic, grammar, penmanship, geography and cipher singing. The school is very well run.

February 12 Today the schools in Izluchistaia and Kamianka were visited, but I stayed home with my sick wife. There is no school this winter in Novozhitomir and Novokovno.

February 15 Diedr. Thiessen of Novopodolsk and Jacob Wiebe of the Island of Khortitsa were here, the latter as a trustee for Mrs Isaac Wiebe in connection with the division of her late husband's estate. They also brought me medicine [for my wife] from my brother Diedrich.

February 19 Today was the engagement of widow Mrs Isaac Wiebe and widower Abraham Unger, but I was home with my sick wife.

February 23 This morning my cousin D. Klassen and brother Diedrich left for Khortitsa to fetch Bernhard Schellenberg, the doctor (and my brother-in-law), whom my wife has anxiously wanted to see for some time.

February 24 My wife was so ill this morning that we feared for her life. She has a strong desire to die and to be with Christ. She seemed a little better later on in the day.

February 25 Doctor Schellenberg arrived towards evening. He was driven to the Kudashev khutor by colony wagon and from there to the Ssolonne River by Germans from the [Kudashev] khutor. Then Isaac Wieler's widow had driven him by carriage to the Loshkarovka Inn on the steppe where Bernhard Bärgen had picked him up, driven him to Novopodolsk, and from there he had been brought to our place by Isaac Siemens. My wife was waiting impatiently for his arrival, and he is now finally here. May the Lord bless his healing ministry.

February 26 My son-in-law Joh. Andres drove Schellenberg to Novopodolsk, where he stayed for several hours. He has not been able to help my wife very much, telling me that she has consumption and is dying. Lord, I can find no words to express my misery.

February 27 This morning at 3:30, I asked Andres to drive my wagon to Loshkarovka, feed the horses there until Schellenberg arrived, and then take him to the Kudashev khutor. Schellenberg left three hours later.

February 28 Andres returned this evening at 9:30 after spending the night at Loshkarovka because of the rain. My wife's condition is worsening, but she had some restful hours today. In the midst of her suffering, she now also has terrible doubts about her salvation, and we prayed earnestly about this. Help her, Lord Jesus.

March 1 Last night and this morning my dear wife had terrible pains in her abdomen, and we thought it might be a premature birth. By evening, however, they had disappeared, and she was able to sleep peacefully for short periods. She feels a little better now. Thank thee, Lord Jesus.

March 2 My brother Diedrich, his wife, and my sister-in-law Mrs Abr. Epp, were here Wednesday afternoon. The sickness progresses. Labour pains began towards evening, and my cousin D. Klassen drove to fetch the midwife, Mrs Isaac Friesen of Novokovno. But before their return, my wife thought she was dying and called for the children, admonishing each one individually to lead good lives and, in particular, to love and obey me, their father. The children cried pitiably, and I thought my heart would break. Such a leave-taking is heart-rending. My dear children, if you should page through this diary in future and read these words, remember your mother in love. She took leave of you with the most tender kisses and touching words. Walk the narrow way of the cross, which leads to heaven, and accomplish your salvation in fear and trembling. This is all that you need.

March 3 Sunday evening. Last night my dear sick wife again experienced birth pangs, but they were not too severe. They became stronger in the morning, and at nine o'clock the waters burst. Then the labour stopped, and this is the present situation. This is a time of hard testing.

March 4 At 4:40 this morning, my wife, with God's help, gave birth to an infant daughter, whom we have named Margaretha. She suffered the greatest birth pangs for an hour and three-quarters, and human help was of little avail. But the Lord was present, and we praise and honour him. Our infant daughter lived only two hours. My dear wife feels great relief, except for some weakness and exhaustion, and for a brief moment I even had hopes for her recovery. If only the Lord would preserve her. Our dear daughter did not have to cry for long in this vale of tears, but passed quickly into the loving arms of Jesus Christ, the children's friend, who has redeemed these little lambs with his blood, and will pasture them to his glory.

March 5 I sent the midwife home by wagon this morning.

March 6 Morning. From 10:45 until 12 midnight, my wife had an attack of colic that almost took her life. Yet the Saviour helped in her suffering. The severe cramps let up a little, and she was able to sleep peacefully through the rest of the night.

March 7 Our infant daughter Margaretha was buried this afternoon, at a small service conducted by my cousin, the Reverend David Klassen.

March 9 It is three in the morning. Another night will soon be over, which I have spent watching over (truthfully, suffering over) my dear wife, who slept peacefully. Our neighbour Mrs Wilhelm Martens stayed with her until one o'clock, when it was my turn. While changing the bedding last night, as I helped her on to the bench, she insisted on falling to her knees (which was very difficult for her), where she prayed fervently for patience in her suffering, for strength to endure without complaining, and for an early and blessed death. She had another attack of colic, but it was less severe than the one several days ago. Lord, be her comfort and strength, renew her with thy heavenly peace.

March 10 Sunday. Her illness was critical today, and in the afternoon we thought she would die. But towards evening things got a little better.

March 11 Monday. Most of my neighbours have begun seeding, but the weather remains cold and raw.

March 12 My beloved, invalid wife told me today that she had seen the Lord Jesus (but whether while waking or in a dream she was not sure), and he had looked down upon her in a kindly way. A little later she told me the story of how she had lost her knife as a child while tending the sheep, and how this had made her very sad. She had then prayed that the dear Lord would show her the knife, and this he had done literally. The next day, while driving out the sheep, she had sat down and discovered the lost knife at that very place. She said, 'Even as God answered that prayer he will also answer my prayer now and forgive me my sins, for the sake of the blood of Jesus Christ.'

March 15 Friday morning. My dear sick wife continues to suffer and is becoming weaker and weaker. She has a fervent desire to die and to be with Christ. Last night she slept on and off, something she had not been able to do the night before. At sunrise, she told me she would die today, and when I asked her how she could know this, she replied that she had seen how she had been placed in a coffin. Our son David came in a little later, and she said that he too had told her that she would be seeing eternity this very day.

I laid her down again on the freshly made bed and thought she was sleeping, but then I heard her saying quietly, 'Should I continue to be a servant to sin now that my Saviour has appeared. Why should I, since I am now going to my father and the pathway is clear (she probably meant to heaven). I can go now. Yes, dear Saviour, I am coming.' Her poor spirit is tested so hard and for so long. She now has two bedsores as well, and they give her much pain. A bad case of diarrhea means that her bed clothes have to be changed often. She was a bit more alert around Vesper-time.

March 16 Sunday. This morning at nine o'clock, death freed my dearly beloved Maria from her suffering. Her death struggle continued for an hour, and the last words of hers that I recognized were, 'Jesus, Jesus, only Jesus.' Her bed of suffering lasted 21 weeks and 4 days, and she has achieved her most ardent wish, to enter into the peace of Jesus Christ. She lived 40 years, 6 months, and 18 days and was my faithful partner 21 years, 3 months, and 27 days. She bore five sons and five daughters, of whom two daughters preceded her in death. Lord, grant me in my time an equally blessed death. Then we will be reunited in thy kingdom.

March 17 I have a heavy heart and feel no Sunday today. Grant that we might meet in heaven again, Lord. Today was the first service of the year in the church, which my cousin Klassen conducted. My family and I did not attend.

March 19 Tuesday. Today was the funeral service for my beloved wife. My cousin David Klassen gave the funeral sermon. The cold rainy weather made the service difficult. Rest in peace, you mortal remains of my dearly beloved, rest in peace, until the great Easter morning. You have borne your sufferings to the end.

March 24 Palm Sunday. I preached a sermon in church on Luke 23:26–31. Lord Jesus, faithful Saviour, come into my heart and be with me in my sorrow and affliction.

April 1 I preached a sermon in the home of Klas Heide in Novopodolsk. At the close of the service I said a word of comfort for the wife of the house, who is suffering from gout. I visited my brother Diedrich with my children Maria, Diedrich, and Heinrich and my neighbour H. Olfert. My heart feels lonely and forsaken.

April 8 Last night I had a sweet and pleasant dream. It was past midnight when I dreamt that my dear, dear wife was standing at my side in a very familiar dress and saying to me that I should accompany her through all of this life. I was so happy. We walked hand in hand together towards our house, but we had to pass through deep water that reached up to our chins. We came to a hill, and I looked about and realized we had come from Kronsgarten and that the water was the Kritshe [Stream]. Then it seemed to me that we were coming from Abraham Hiebert's place and that there was water in our Sheltaia Stream as well. I took my dearly beloved Maria in my arms and carried her through the water, and on reaching home we sat down together in heartfelt love, just the two of us, and with a passionate kiss sealed our reunion forever. Then I awoke, and the sweet image was gone. My heart is still heavy from the separation, and I feel lonely and forsaken. Lord, renew me with thy comfort, lead me onto the path of salvation. Let all things work to the benefit of my soul.

April 29 Monday. Peter v Kampen, the local overseer, and the guardians of my children, Abraham Hiebert of Einlage and Reverend Peter Löwen of Novozhitomir, made an inventory of my assets which come to 530 silver R. and 60 C. My debts total more than 200 silver R. We therefore agreed on the following inheritance contract [regarding the distribution of my wife's assets among the children]: (1) each child will receive 20 silver R. on May 1, 1865; (2) each daughter will receive a chest and each son 10 R., also payable in 1865; (3) each child will receive a bible, a song-book and a catechism; (4) each child will receive a cow and five sheep; and (5), each child, when it comes of age, will receive a festive dress and bedding consisting of a comforter, two pillows, and a sheet.

May 6 Tuesday morning I asked our young people to answer the questions from the first half of the catechism, but I took no pleasure in it. I had asked the Lord for his help, but he did not answer. Yet I know, Lord, that thou canst breathe life into the dead words I have spoken.

May 7 Before the service, Martin Harder Jr appeared before the Ministerial Committee. A Jewish barmaid had accused him of stealing 3 silver R. from her, which he denied. Although he drinks a lot we nevertheless believed him, but also warned him about this sin. He promised betterment, and was allowed to go in peace. In the afternoon, we saw my brother Diedrich, who returned yesterday from Ekaterinoslav with a pot of lard for me from my niece, Mrs Heese, and an anonymous envelope with 11 silver R. in it, which was probably from Mrs Heese as well. The faithful Lord is looking after me in my poverty, guiding the hearts of my wealthy relatives to help at the appropriate time.

This afternoon our children Johann and Helena Andres moved their cattle and belongings out of our place to Izluchistaia.

[At this point six pages of the original diaries are missing. They cover the ten-week period from May 12 to July 21, 1863, during which Jacob Epp courted and married his second wife Judith Dyck, from the Old Colony village of Neuosterwick.]

July 2 Tuesday afternoon. My wife [Judith] and I attended the funeral for Abraham Günther's infant son Abraham who died at the age of 11 weeks and 2 days.
July 7 Our children the Johann Andres came to harvest their grain, staying for the night, and I drove them back with a wagon-load of fuel dung in the morning.
August 4 We had very dear guests this afternoon, my beloved wife [Judith's] relatives from the Khortitsa colonies, who visited us for the first time: her niece, the widow Fr. Rempel, and her married children, Franz Rempel of Rosengart and Johann Rempel from here.
August 10 Sunday. My dear brothers and sisters were here for the night: Jacob Pätkau and his wife, Heinrich Epp, and Johann Epp, and his wife.
August 11 We attended service together, and my brother-in-law Pätkau preached. This afternoon we had the funeral in our home for the daughter of my nephew Heinrich Rempel. The Diedrich Epps were also here.
August 13 Early this morning, my wife and I and the children Maria, Diedrich, and Heinrich left for the Khortitsa colonies. We caught up to the Pätkaus in Loshkarovka and drove together to Tomakovka, from where they continued on to Khortitsa and we turned off to Neuosterwick. But dear God, what a frightful sight greeted us there. Much of the village had been burned to the ground, and the smoking ruins spoke of a terrible conflagration. The fire had started Thursday morning at Johann Teichröw's place and then engulfed D. Klassen's outbuildings. The severe drought together with a raging wind, which whipped up great clouds of dust, spread the fire so rapidly that the devastation was complete within two

hours. Destroyed were some 70 buildings, including two storehouses, the new school, 58 dwellings (one our mother-in-law's cottage), and fodder and grain stores. Almost nothing was saved.[18] Another fire in Nieder Khortitsa burned down Johann Töws's buildings.

August 17 Thursday. We and my wife's brothers and sisters met at the home of my wife's parents to sell their property, which I purchased for 2500 silver R. Her parents are to build themselves a cottage on the yard and receive free fuel, a cow, and the necessary pasture.

August 24 On Friday I had the bad luck of losing my best horse, a gelding, and I hope the saying is true that a bad start will lead to a good end.

August 29 I sold my property [in Novovitebsk] to Reverend Peter Löwen for 550 silver R. My brother-in-law Abraham Hiebert of Einlage came in the afternoon to pick up a load of our belongings. He wanted to haul the fattened pigs at night, but decided that the great heat made that too risky.

September 10 Tuesday morning. The Brotherhood Meeting discussed several matters.

(1) I told the brethren about the deal I had concluded in Neuosterwick and asked them to approve our departure. They did not say exactly 'yes' nor did they say exactly 'no.' From some I had the feeling they would gladly see us leave. Most said they would very much regret our departure, but would also not oppose it. We will therefore move as planned. I promised the congregation to remember them and visit them, together with the Elder, if that should be necessary. Lord, be with me.

(2) Aron Neusteter and his stepdaughter Anna Peters were placed in the ban for committing fornication, which resulted in the birth of a child. Lord Jesus, our merciful Saviour, grant them genuine remorse to everlasting life. Amen.

(3) I asked communicants to pay their church dues to the ministers Dav. Klassen and Pet. Löwen: 15 C. per male and 8 C. per female.

Later in the afternoon. I have had no peace since the Brotherhood Meeting and feel a heavy burden. Many brethren expressed fears that our flock would now become scattered, and I have therefore begun to waver. As I was loading my wagon this morning for the trip to

Neuosterwick, P[eter] v Kampen dropped by and added to my misery. Since my wife and I think that these obstacles have arisen through God's will, we have decided to remain here. May his will be done. However obscure God's ways may seem, they are good and lead to eternal bliss.

September 15 The following appeared before the Ministerial Committee in the ministers' room: Bern. Giesbrecht, the Kamianka teacher, the maiden Sara Andres of Novovitebsk, her guardians Gerhard Andres and Corn. Krause, and four men who had summoned them. Sara had reportedly told her brother-in-law Giesbrecht that one morning last year while working for Franz Redekopp in Novokovno he had uncovered her as she slept above the cellar in front of the door and looked at her private parts. The Giesbrechts confirmed the story. Sara, however, denied it, yet seemed also to contradict herself a little, and it appeared to me she was playing with the truth. The matter was held over until next Sunday, when Redekopp is also to appear.

Aron Neusteter and his stepdaughter Anna Peters, who had been placed in the ban, asked to be readmitted to the church. *Brotherhood [Meeting]*. Aron Neusteter and Anna Peters were received back into the church.

My dear wife and I drove to visit our children the Johann Andreses. This morning at 3 a.m. our daughter, with God's help, gave birth to an infant daughter Maria. May the Lord of grace bless the child.

September 16 We drove to Neuendorf, where I did some business with Is. Bärgmann, head of the Orphans' Administration. We visited our brothers and sisters and also dropped in on Elder Gerh. Dyck.

September 17 We visited our brothers and sisters in Khortitsa and saw our parents in Neuosterwick, who have almost finished building their cottage. My wife's brother Diedr. Dyck is buying the parental Wirtschaft.

September 22 Johann Hiebert, Sara Andres's aged grandfather, apologized to me for having belittled the ministers, especially me, and I was happy to forgive him.

October 2 We reached Heinrich Heese's place in Ekaterinoslav towards evening.[19] His Imperial Majesty and heir to the throne, Tsarevich Nicholas Alexandrovich [1843–65], had arrived there in the afternoon, and in the evening we saw his quarters, where a huge crowd had gathered that repeatedly broke into shouts of 'hurra.' At 9 p.m. His Imperial Majesty proceeded to a ball, arranged by the nobility, in the Count Potemkin palace. Along the route taken by His Majesty, Bengal lanterns had been set aflame, and the entire city was illuminated. Many palaces had been decorated with the initial 'N' and several had both initials, 'N' and 'A,' topped by burning torches. The triumphal arch erected for His Imperial Majesty seemed all ablaze.

October 3 At night the entire city was again brilliantly lit.

October 4 At 8:30 Friday morning, His Imperial Majesty left Ekaterinoslav to shouts of 'hurrah' from an assembled crowd. We had a wonderful close-up view of the heir in his carriage as he took his leave. On Thursday morning we accompanied Mrs Heese to see the monument of Empress Catherine II and the Potemkin palace, with its magnificent ornamentation. We spent the night at Johann Thiessen's place, left the following morning, and arrived home safely Saturday afternoon.

October 6 Dear Lord, so few people were present at today's service. On this day it is our duty to gather in thy house and to give thanks, and yet we enjoy the gift without thanking the giver. Have mercy on thy church, O Lord, and awaken in us an active spiritual life, arousing the dead to true faith, and grant me, the least of thy servants, strength for my difficult calling. Fill me with thy Holy Spirit that I might do and teach only what is pleasing to thee. Amen.

October 12 Today, after a long drought, our loving God blessed us with a gentle drizzle.

October 15 Tuesday. On this cold and damp day, we left for the Khortitsa colonies, spent the night on the Kudashev khutor, and arrived in Neuosterwick the following day. Thursday the Orphans' Administration sold our parents' belongings at public auction.

October 19 We left for home on Saturday. My sister-in-law, Mrs Diedr. Dyck (who is also my wife's niece), invited us to their landed estate of 'Hoffnungsfeld,'[20] which is not far from the road, to conduct the marriage of their son. We drove there for the night.

October 20 In the morning I preached and in the afternoon united their son Diedrich in marriage with Katarina Wiebe.

October 24 Last night, after my wife woke up from a sharp pain in her finger, we applied a buttermilk poultice, which helped a little. But the pain and swelling got worse, and she became feverish and started to tremble. I finally sent for my brother Diedrich who prescribed a bread poultice (which we applied) and creeping beet [tea] (which helped very little).

October 25 Friday. My wife is much better today. The swelling is down and she is about again, for which we thank the Lord.

November 26 David Klassen and I met our colleagues Klassen and Löwen in Kamianka where, at my request, Jacob Hamm, the Herdsman Elder,[21] had assembled the villagers to discuss a letter of complaint from their former teacher Peter Klassen (see Sept. 20, 1862) addressed to the Elder G. Dyck. Klassen wrote that the community had failed to pay him what they owed, and had even refused to discuss the matter with him. At the Elder's request we now intervened, calling the villagers to account, and they agreed to pay up *as soon as they could*. This was satisfactory to [Peter] Klassen, and we consider the matter closed.

Evening. My wife's eyes are sore and painful, especially the right one. Mrs Peter v Kampen applied the life awakener to her neck and behind her ears and placed some cold fresh earth in a cloth on her eye. She also has a splitting headache from constipation, for which she took tablespoon doses of Glauber's salts. This began to work towards evening, and she soon felt a little better. When I awoke this morning, she was already up and about and doing as much housework as she could manage with her bandaged eyes.

December 8 Second Advent. My wife and I have had sore eyes all week, and could not attend today's service. Mine have improved a little, and I can see enough to write.

December 14 My wife and I and our young son Heinrich left for Khortitsa this morning, reaching the Kudashev khutor by nightfall where we took our lodgings with the Gerh. Giesbrechts. A dense fog under way inflamed my eyes, and they are now much worse. Racking pains and a burning sensation in my right eye gave me a sleepless night.

December 15 I had less pain in the morning and was able to conduct the service, with God's help. We resumed our trip at 11 a.m. in a thick fog, denser than yesterday's. To protect the sore eye from the dampness, I borrowed a pair of glasses from Giesbrecht. We reached our parents' place in Neuosterwick by evening, but by nightfall the pain was back with such force that I could not sleep.

December 16 The pain was worse, so at daybreak Diet. Dyck took me to my brother-in-law Doctor Schellenberg. He applied the screws [of the life awakener] to my right shoulder, with noteworthy results, for the pain abated. He asked me to take a nap after dinner, and I slept for three hours. When I awoke he continued the treatment, completing it with eye drops. Lord, thou hast created the medicine, and thanks is due to thee alone.

December 31 Review of the past year. When I think back over the sad events of the past year, I am overcome with feelings of melancholy and distress. Yet thou art great, Lord, a comfort for afflicted spirits, turning things to our benefit. Thou didst take my beloved wife, my bosom friend, from me, but thou didst also give me a devoted and faithful wife who has become a mother to my poor children. Lord, thy ways are marvellous.

The situation in my household is very hard. The harvest was poor and I have had problems with my cattle. But our Lord has sufficient mercies. I will bow before his will, for the path to the kingdom of God leads through cross and tribulation. I look back over my past life in shame, recognizing that many days I have failed to serve the Lord Jesus earnestly and in love. Cover over my failures, and be thou the Lord and guide throughout my future life. Grant that my humble work in the church might be blessed, to thy honour, Lord and Saviour. Amen.

1864

January 1 Wednesday, New Year's Day. At the service in Novopodolsk, I preached about the circumcision of the heart and the nurturing of the new life.

[Births and deaths in the Jewish colonies in 1863:]

Births	19 males	27 females	46 total
Deaths	6 males	16 females	22 total
Increase	13 males	11 females	24 total
Couples married	11		

In 1863, of [Khortitsa] church members born during the last century, who are therefore 64 years of age or older, 6 men and 5 women died and 107 men and 97 women are living, a total of 204. Of those born this century, and joined to the church through Holy Baptism, 16 males and 22 females died and 1945 males and 1980 females are still living. A total of 49 church members died and 4129 are living.

Figures for the whole community:

Births	280 males	239 females	519 total
Deaths	158 males	130 females	288 total
Increase	122 males	109 females	231 total
Couples married	91		

January 8 Since I was short of fuel and money, I asked Franz Redekopp of Novopodolsk to give me dung fuel on credit, which he agreed to do out of love. The winter is cold and fuel is dear.
January 21 At five this morning my son David (and Andres) left with a load of oats for a village on the other side of Voronzovka, where Cossacks are quartered. The cartage is for a Jew in Petrovka at 35 silver C. per chetvert.
January 23 I officiated at the wedding of Agatha Görzen and Isaac Fast of the Molochna colony of Wernersdorf. When we arrived at home David was already back from his trip, which had gone well. For this we are thankful.
January 26 This morning I served as young Gerhard Wiebe's go-between to ask for the hand of Reverend Peter Löwen's daughter Helena. She gave permission for him to drop by on Tuesday.
February 13 Under way we met the Andres and told them of the opportunity to have their child vaccinated. In the afternoon, our infant granddaughter Maria and our daughter Maria (whose previous vaccination had not taken) were vaccinated against smallpox at the Heinrich Olferts.
February 16 In Novopodolsk I preached a sermon on the dangers of spiritual indolence. Text, the story of the tares on the field: Matthew 13:24–30.
March 1 On our way home from Novokovno, we surveyed our winter rye, which looks promising.
March 3 Tuesday. At an auction where the estate of the late Gerhard

Thiessen of Novopodolsk was sold, I represented the Orphans' Administration. The farmstead was bought for 765 silver R. by Died. Epp's son-in-law, Jacob Pätkau, and the total proceeds came to 1276 R. 3 C.

March 17 This afternoon, my wife, daughter Maria, cousin David Klassen, and I drove to Izluchistaia to attend the funeral of our infant granddaughter Maria Andres, who died Saturday morning after a two-day illness. She was 25 weeks and 6 days old. What took place, however, was a double funeral, for the previous day, a son of my daughter's parents-in-law, Isaac Andres, had died at the age of 11 months. Our granddaughter and her infant uncle were therefore buried in separate coffins but in a single grave. My cousin David Klassen gave the funeral sermon.

March 27 I was awakened from my sleep last night by a loud crash. I heard sniffing sounds, lit a lamp, and found a large white dog in the porch. The doors were tightly closed, the trapdoor over the cellar in its usual place, so we assumed the dog had crept in last evening and hidden himself. I tried to lure him out the back door, but he obviously liked our place. He looked up at me in a friendly way and refused to move. Finally I gave him a sharp blow. He ran out howling, and we lay down again to sleep. In the morning we discovered that the dog had entered through the coal chute into the cellar, gotten into the butter and meat, and then forced open the trapdoor. Then I realized that the loud crash I had heard had been the trapdoor falling shut. Today we sealed all of the openings into the cellar.

March 29 After today's service, my wife and I and son Peter had dinner and Vesper with our married children in Izluchistaia. David Penner came by to talk about the sect. He told me that Aron Lepp [overseer in the villages of Kamianka and Izluchistaia] had convinced him from the [New] Testament that the [sect members] were correct. I replied as best I could that he should be converted to God and not to people, for salvation could only be found in Jesus Christ. After a long discussion, he admitted harbouring ill-feelings towards me since the earlier incident, and that only since Andres's funeral had he felt differently toward me. May the Lord himself care for his flock.

April 5 Today's congregation was small. I wonder why so few come to the service. Lord, we bring thee our troubles, asking thee to kindle fire in thy church, that it might warm and enliven our dead hearts. Have mercy upon us for our indifference. Amen.

This afternoon, my dear wife and I went to look at our crops and to enjoy the spring weather. The grain looks promising, and we have high hopes for a good harvest.

April 14 Tuesday. After breakfast, my wife and I and the children Jacob, Diedrich, and Heinrich left for the Khortitsa colonies with our guests the Diedr. Dycks and Peter Friesen. We spent the night in Hoffnungsfeld and arrived in Neuosterwick for dinner, where our parents now have a small house in the yard.

On Good Friday I preached a sermon in the Khortitsa church. Saturday was the funeral in Pätkau's home for our beloved mother Helena (née Thiessen). After a long illness, she died at the Schellenbergs on Tuesday at 5:30 p.m., at the age of 66 years, 8 months, and 10 days. She was married twice. Her first marriage lasted several weeks and was childless. She was married to our father (who died 21 years ago) for 27 years, 4 months, and 8 days and bore him 7 sons and 3 daughters, of whom 4 sons and 3 daughters are still alive. She became grandmother to 50 children, of whom 30 are living, and great grandmother to 2, of whom 1 has died. She was buried in the same grave as our father in the Khortitsa graveyard. The funeral sermon was given by Elder Gerhard Dyck. Rest in peace, dear mother.

April 21 Easter Tuesday. I attended a large Brotherhood Meeting in the Khortitsa church.

(1) Election of a minister. First my brother Heinrich was elected deacon with 125 votes. (Others who received votes: Peter Penner 17, Cornelius Giesbrecht 16, Heinrich Penner 14, Gerhard Dyck 13, and several others with 2 votes each.) A minister was then chosen from among the deacons, and my brother Heinrich was elected with 179 votes. (Other deacons receiving votes: Gerhard Löwen 27, Carl Grunau 7, and Jacob Klassen 1.) Since my brother was not present, two ministers went to fetch him. Then, in the presence of the brethren, he was formally installed as minister. May the Lord Jesus grant him the spiritual strength needed to labour in his vineyard.

(2) The meeting discussed the cases of the church members Johann Kirsch, who had married a Russian woman, and Johann Dyck, who had married a Lutheran woman. It was decided that such persons should not be placed in the ban but released from their church

membership in a way that would allow them to maintain relations with church members in the civil sphere.
(3) The congregation then considered what to do with persons who sought readmission to the church after withdrawing and being rebaptized. This was the case with Jacob Peters and Mrs Gerhard Rempel of Borosenko, who now desired close ties with the church. It was decided to wait and observe the genuineness of their remorse.
(4) Peter Peters of Schönwiese was placed in the ban because of adultery and fornication.
(5) The brethren were admonished not to tolerate sinful merry-making and pleasures at banquets and village and district civic functions. It was decided to prohibit store-openings on Sundays.
(6) A system of church dues was discussed and approved.
(7) Finally, people were encouraged to support missions through voluntary contributions.

I felt the presence of the Lord Jesus at this Brotherhood Meeting, which met in an atmosphere of peace and unity.

In the afternoon, we brothers and sisters gathered at the B. Schellenbergs to divide up our late mother's estate.

May 1 On the day before Easter our neighbour Heinrich Olfert and his wife left for the Khortitsa colonies. At Cornelius Heinrichs's estate,[22] where they stopped to visit his brother-in-law Peter Siemens (he works there as an administrator), Olfert came down with typhoid fever. His father-in-law Peter Breil told us about Olfert's grave illness, and we immediately took steps to have his children visit him. This morning my neighbour Abraham Günther left with the Olfert children for Heinrichs's estate, while my family and I will look after Olfert's affairs here.

May 3 There were large congregations in attendance at church this morning and afternoon. At the afternoon service, my brother-in-law Gerhard Dyck preached a touching sermon based on Matthew 1:21.

May 7 My neighbour Cornelius Krause and I drove to Heinrichs's estate to visit our sick neighbour Heinrich Olfert (see entry for May 1). We found him weak, but dressed and on his feet, and on the way to recovery.

May 9 There was considerable frost again today, and nature suffers. The potatoes were frozen for the second time, the onions devastated, the mulberries brown, the grain droops, and the leaves of the ash trees are frozen. Yet it is a trifle for the Lord to give us his blessing again, if that is his will.

Brotherhood Meeting.

(1) The two male and two female baptismal candidates were introduced for the first time.

(2) I informed our congregation of the decisions of the Khortitsa church at its Easter meeting (see April 21) in regard to: those who have withdrawn; banquets, weddings, and drunkenness in general; and keeping the Sabbath holy. I encouraged members to give generous support to the work of converting the heathen.

(3) I reminded the brethren to pay their arrears in church dues.

(4) It was decided to fetch our dear Elder for baptism and communion again, as we did last year.

May 13 With my brother Diedrich's enclosed springed carriage, we picked up our neighbour Heinrich Olfert and his wife from Heinrichs's khutor. Olfert is still weak, but better than when last I saw him.

May 20 Appearing before the Ministerial Committee were Jacob Redekopp and the teacher Bernhard Giesbrecht, both of Kamianka. Redekopp had complained that the teacher had been too rough in punishing his child, even rupturing his skin. Hermann Peters and Julius Janzen, who summoned the teacher and had examined the child, reported that they had found no such rupture and very little else. The two were reconciled and allowed to go in peace.

May 22 My brother-in-law Elias and I surveyed the grain fields. The wheat looks promising, but when I saw the rye on the hay steppe I thought my heart would break, for hail had almost completely destroyed the crop. The Lord has given, the Lord has taken away, blessed be the name of the Lord.

June 5 Friday evening, with three horses, we and a Jew drove out to the Izluchistaia fields to help kill the little grasshoppers. Saturday, David and Jacob drove over with a wagon and three horses to trample and crush them.

July 17 Last night I left the children David, Katharina, and Jacob out on the field for the first time, and during the night there was a terrific downpour with thunder and lightning. I could not sleep a wink for worry, and so at the break of dawn I drove out to fetch them. I found them soaked, sleepless, but otherwise in good spirits. In my heart, I thanked the Lord for protecting them, but also promised that I would never do that again.

August 12 An accident at my neighbour Heinrich Olfert's place seriously injured his son-in-law Heinrich Harder. Harder had been working on the threshing floor when he stepped on the tooth of a rake, which penetrated his foot and broke off. The tip could be seen just beneath the skin of the foot. Olfert cut through the skin and exposed about half an inch of it. The rake tooth could not be pulled backwards, however, and so v Kampen took a pair of pliers and seizing hold of it pulled it out from the top with all his might. Harder let out a terrible scream. The wound was washed with cold water and bandaged, and the pain gradually subsided.

October 17 Saturday morning, my son David and I and the neighbours Heinrich Olfert and Abraham Günther carted grain to Nikopol, where we took our quarters with Jews. On Sunday I preached in Nikopol at David Bärgen's. The drive home was cold and rainy so we stopped at Shiskin's Inn on the Ssolonne [River], spending the night under the Sarai (shed), out of the rain.

December 13 The Peter Mantlers appeared before the Ministerial Committee. Elder Gerhard Dyck had informed us that Mrs Mantler had committed adultery with old Jacob Dyck in Nieder Khortitsa. She confessed her transgression to the Brotherhood Meeting and was placed in the ban.

1865

January 1

[Births and deaths in the Jewish colonies in 1864:]

Births	16 males	20 females	36 total
Deaths	8 males	9 females	17 total
Increase	8 males	11 females	19 total
Couples married	5		

In 1864, of [Khortitsa church] people born during the last century, who are therefore 65 years of age or older, 3 men and 13 women died and 104 men and 84 women are living. Of those born this century, and joined to the church through Holy Baptism, 13 males and 21 females died, and 2015 males and 2042 females are still living. A total of 50 church members died and 4245 are living.

Figures for the whole [Old Colony] community [including the Judenplan]:

Births	248 males	234 females	482 total
Deaths	83 males	84 females	167 total
Increase	315 total		
Couples married	81		

January 19 This afternoon, Peter v Kampen, my brother Diedrich and I worked on the accounts of our church building.
February 6 After breakfast, my brother-in-law Schellenberg and I were taken to Novopodolsk where we expected to pick up a ride to Borosenko.[23] The people from there had already left, however, and seem, in any case, not to have been counting on a service. I therefore had more time for our guests.
February 9 *School visitation*. In the morning my cousin [David] Klassen and I visited the school in Izluchistaia with our colleagues Isaac Klassen and Peter Löwen. The school, taught by Abraham Andres, is still on a low level: reading is fair, writing not much better, arithmetic still in its infancy, and there is virtually no teaching of the life and sufferings of Christ. In the afternoon, together with the Herdsman Elder Johann Schellenberg, teacher Andres, and my son-in-law Johann Andres, we visited the Kamianka school, taught by Bernhard Giesbrecht. Beginners here were at least able to do a little arithmetic. As we left the school, Johann Bärgen asked me to accompany him on a visit to the miller Johann Hiebert, who is ill and had expressed a desire to see me. But I had difficulty making out what Hiebert really wanted. He kept going back and forth over events involving his mill and various humiliations he had suffered. There were also the same old feelings, especially his anger against Peter v Kampen. He wants very much to attend communion, but said he would not do so as long as v Kampen was present. I urged him to seek reconciliation and peace in the blood of Christ. Then he mentioned

that Satan was loose in his house, and when I encouraged him to pray to the Lord who could drive him out, he complained bitterly about his wife, who torments him. I could not speak to his wife privately, however, since several Jews were present, and promised to come back soon.

February 13 Sunday. Towards evening our children Johann and Helena Andres dropped off a wheelbarrow, which he had built.

February 16 I delivered the sermon at the funeral for Bernhard Wiebe's infant daughter Sara, who died at the age of 1 year, 4 months, and 10 days. As the coffin was lowered into the grave, it slipped and fell on its head, and this caused the grieving mother great anguish.

February 28 Peter Neufeld, the Herdsman Elder in Novozhitomir, told of a dispute in his village over hiring a teacher and complained about [the actions] of Reverend Peter Löwen. I suggested transferring responsibility for hiring to their overseer D. Epp. If the matter was then still unresolved, I would come over.

March 7 Sunday. The life awakener was applied for a painful toothache I have had for several days, and although it caused only slight inflammation, the pain let up a bit. This afternoon the Wilhelm Martens dropped by, and she asked me to read her a sermon, if my toothache allowed. I read the Good Friday sermon based on John 19:1–3, then we prayed silently on our knees and concluded by singing the last six stanzas of hymn number 61, 'Jesus Joy of My Desire.'

March 20 In the morning the ground was still frozen, but this afternoon the landholders gathered on the hay steppe with a plough and two wagons to cut boundary furrows between our fields. These, which we had marked off two days ago, allotted each landowner eight desiatinas of land.[24] Spring is slow and it is very wet.

March 22 It is still very wet, but I started ploughing anyway. Lord, bless the seed, that it might germinate and become our daily bread, under thy watchful eye.

March 31 We attended a double funeral at the home of Bernh. Wiebe. In fact, three people had been ill, but Wiebe was recovering. His wife Elisabeth had died on Sunday at the age of 39 years less 9 days, and yesterday her sister Katarina Siemens (née Thiessen) also passed away, at the age of 37 years and a few months. The Heinrich Siemens had been living with the Wiebes. The sisters were placed in separate coffins and buried in a single grave.

April 2 The Good Friday service was the first one held in our church this year, and the congregation was quite large.
April 5 Easter Tuesday. A Heinr. Janzen from the Molochna, who moved to the Grossfürstlich settlement, borrowed 10 merka of potatoes at 20 C. per merka, payable in fall.

This afternoon Reverend Isaac Klassen and his wife visited us. After yesterday's service in Kamianka, Bernh. Wiebe confessed that he had defiled himself with cattle in his youth and that after becoming a widower a second time he had slept with his fiancée [who had died before they could marry]. Dear Jesus, grant him genuine repentance, teach him the fear of thy bitter suffering and death, and lead him to eternal life. Amen.
April 7 Towards evening, David Klassen and I visited Bernhard Wiebe, who is still bedridden and anxious about his salvation, and talked to him about the Lamb of God who bears the sins of the world. He is truly repentant and fervently seeks God's grace.
April 9 We received a funeral letter from Rosengart announcing the passing of Maria Elias, who died Easter Tuesday at the age of 57 years, 7 months, and 26 days. She had been married 34 years, 2 months, and 2 days and given birth to 15 children, of whom 4 sons and 4 daughters are living. She had become grandmother to 15 children, of whom 10 are alive. Dear and noble soul, thou hast run thy life's course and followed the Lord Jesus faithfully. God gave her rich and wonderful gifts. Knowing that he had called her to a life of service as a midwife, she made the most of her opportunities, helping many in a true spirit of charity. Now she will have heard the voice of our Saviour say, 'Go in to the joy of thy Lord.'
April 11 I presented the articles of our Christian faith to a small congregation. It is seed-time, yet there is an indifference to God's Word. Later in the afternoon, I watched as a neighbour brought his ploughshare to the blacksmith Martin Harder, who hammered and forged as though this was any weekday. The brethren at the Brotherhood Meeting had acknowledged the need to keep the Sabbath holy, and my soul bled. The day was again being desecrated, and it was a mockery to the Jews. I therefore admonished the blacksmith, who stood there red-faced trying to shift the blame to his neighbours Rempel and Krause, who had brought him the work. But he stopped his smithing.

April 19 We finished seeding at noon. We have 8 desiatinas of wheat, 4 of barley, and 4 of oats, for a total of 16 desiatinas. God, give us again our daily bread this year.
April 21 Yesterday and today I ploughed and harrowed potato patches for several Jews, earning 4 silver R. 42 C.
April 22 David Klassen and I drove to Novozhitomir in regard to a letter from Isaac Klassen alleging that our colleague Peter Löwen was furious over an incident involving their teacher. [The letter reported] that the landowners [in Novozhitomir] had started negotiations with their former teacher Franz Klassen, but before these could be concluded, the Herdsman Elder Peter Neufeld and Reverend Isaac Klassen had hired Johann Banmann on their own and at a higher salary than what had been authorized. One party objected to having Banmann as teacher and another was dissatisfied that Klassen had not first consulted Löwen. Löwen was reported to have objected as well. We talked to Löwen, who remained calm throughout, and we realized he was innocent of the charge. We then proceeded to Reverend Klassen's place, who now made light of his letter. At Peter Neufeld's place there was a lot of idle chatter back and forth. I finally asked Neufeld to call the villagers together for a meeting tomorrow morning.
April 23 The landowners met at Neufeld's home this morning. There was much bickering, and the issue is still pending. But Reverend Peter Löwen and the Peter Neufelds were reconciled.
April 24 I carted 3 chetvert of wheat to Abraham Unger's mill and sold it to his associate, the Jew Stuppel, for 50 silver C. per pud. Last week Unger was involved in a collision with another wagon, seriously injuring himself and killing a horse. Drink was again the cause. Unger appeared genuinely contrite and asked to be spared [having to appear before the Ministerial Committee and the Brotherhood]. I said that I would be mindful of his behaviour in future.
April 25. *Brotherhood Meeting.* I presented the accounts from our church construction, and since 67 silver R. 57 C. is needed to discharge our debt, we decided to collect a further 1½ silver R. from each landowner and 50 silver C. from each [landless] cottager.
April 30 Aron Lepp came by on business this morning, and I asked him to stay for dinner, but he declined my invitation. He returned in the afternoon, however, staying until 2:30 p.m., and we argued about

his and his associates' withdrawal [from our church]. He still calls our church a harlot and maintains that he and his wife are on the right path. In the impending exile he would be able to look after himself, he said.[25] Dear Lord Jesus, turn this matter to our benefit, and lead these souls to a knowledge of thy truth.

May 6 At sunrise, my son David, son-in-law Johann Andres, and Peter Siemens left with wagon-loads of grain. There were 5½ chetvert on each wagon, and cartage is 75 silver C. per chetvert.

May 7 Friday. Peter v Kampen and I had dinner with Peter Janzen in Novozhitomir and reached the Krivoi Rog market-place late in the afternoon. We spent the night with a pedlar acquaintance named Peter Kornelovich Bogdanov, who received us in a friendly manner. We sold the butter for 3 silver R. a pud, but the next day it was selling for 6 silver R. and more.

May 9 *Brotherhood Meeting*. We decided to insure our church for ten units (Huben) with the Fire Insurance Administration [in Khortitsa].

May 17 A mounted messenger from Novopodolsk (he was Jacob Pätkau's Russian servant) brought us the news at sundown that Elder Gerhard Dyck and my brother-in-law Pätkau had arrived at my brother Diedrich's place and would be by in the morning.

May 18 We accompanied our dear visitors to church, where the beloved Elder baptized our young people. Lord, baptize them also with fire and thy Spirit.

At a general Brotherhood Meeting in the afternoon, the Elder discussed the dispute between the ministers Löwen and Klassen, which was a sorrowful experience. Isaac Klassen admitted that the matter regarding Löwen was not as stated in his letter, and the issue was settled peacefully. The two had already made their peace, so Reverend Klassen asked the brethren for forgiveness.

May 19 *Brotherhood Meeting*. The Elder presented the episode involving Bernh. Wiebe (see April 5 and 7, 1865) to the congregation, and it was decided that since he had shown genuine remorse, the matter should be considered closed. We celebrated communion in the afternoon with 121 participants.

May 23 Pentecost, the first holiday. I preached a sermon in the Neuosterwick church. My brother-in-law Reverend Ger. Dyck, his wife, and my wife and I visited my brother Heinrich in Khortitsa. On the second holiday, Heinrich and I were present for the baptism in church.

After the service, in the ministers' room, my brother-in-law Jacob Pätkau questioned Elder Gerhard Dyck about the [treatment of] the church members who had withdrawn [to join the new sect]. The Village [mayors'] offices had received copies of a report from the District Office to the Guardianship Committee in Odessa stating that it wished to have these people banished from our midst. Pätkau suggested that this sentiment was not in keeping with God's Word, and that these people should be left alone. The Elder grew very angry and two times told Pätkau, 'You do as you please, and I will do as I please.' He then shook hands all around and left without uttering another word. You children of the Almighty, love here is in a very bad way. I support the view of my brother-in-law. Since we have released these people [from their church membership], let them continue to live among us, as the Catholics and Jews do. This was also the sense of the Brotherhood Meeting (see entry for April 21, 1864).

June 2 Wednesday. We dropped in on Heinrich Dyck in Kamianka, where the heirs of his late wife and their guardians were meeting. Earlier, Overseer [Aron] Lepp had drawn up an inventory of the estate and submitted it to the Orphans' Administration. Dyck now handed this list to me and asked me to organize the division of the inheritance. There was some greed and avarice evident among the heirs, but the issues were resolved and the inheritance contract signed.

I talked to Bernhard Wiebe, the widower, after hearing of his intention to marry his stepdaughter (the daughter of his deceased wife), who is only a child of 16. He admitted having discussed this possibility with her, but said he had realized that it was unlikely to work. What a delusion! Heinrich Olfert and I discussed the case in the evening. He has agreed to bring it to the attention of the child's guardians in the Khortitsa colonies and will also give them my view that the child should be separated from her stepfather and hired out [in the Khortitsa District].

June 4 The local guardian [of the girl] in the above case came by, and I urged him to act jointly with the [second] guardian in Schönhorst to separate the girl from her [step]father, and the sooner this could be done the better.

June 5 Martin Harder complains that his son Martin is drinking heavily and not following his wishes. I instructed Wilh. Martens to summon young Martin before the Ministerial Committee for tomorrow. But in the evening, young Martin came by shamefacedly to ask that we pardon him for his drinking. I reminded him that he should look to God, whom he had offended deeply. He begged me to excuse him from tomorrow's scheduled meeting, and promised reform, and I finally agreed. Freeing oneself from the bonds of sin is a difficult thing.

June 6 At 2:30 a.m., my daughter Helena was, with God's help, delivered of an infant son Gerhard. She is well and in good spirits, and we praise God.

June 9 Since Abraham Unger has been drinking heavily again, I visited him and appealed to his conscience. He denied drinking to excess and seemed to make light of the matter, but as we talked his wife came in and then the real story emerged. He stood there red-faced. Lord Jesus, have mercy on him.

June 12 Saturday. My brother Heinrich and his son [David] were here for the night.

June 13 My brother preached a sermon based on 1 Corinthians 3:11: 'For other foundation can no man lay than that is laid, which is Jesus Christ.' We had announced the speaker in advance, and the church was full.

June 21 I left for Khortitsa Sunday morning with 5 chetvert of millet, which my brother Heinrich bought locally. A ring on the wagon came loose in Loshkarovka, and I had difficulty reaching the Kudashev khutor. There the blacksmith Jacob Lehn repaired it. The poor horses had a hard time making headway on the post road through the plough-lands, where it had rained heavily. Fortunately I met Peter Löwen and his brother Daniel from Neuhorst, who took four sacks onto their wagon until we reached the post station.

June 22 Thursday. I stopped on business at the Orphans' Administration in Neuendorf, where I met the teacher Cornelius Enz, who offered to deliver four sack-loads [of the millet] to my brother. I stopped briefly on the yard of my brother-in-law Jacob Pätkau, had dinner and coffee with Heinrich Epp, visited Corn. Hildebrand, loaded one and a half chetvert of hard coal in Rosenthal (which I carted for Martin Harder and Heinrich Rempel), and dropped by to see my brother-in-law Gerh. Dyck and Elder Gerhard Dyck, who was ill. I spent the night in Neuosterwick with my parents-in-law.

July 1 We left this afternoon on a visit to Khortitsa.

July 3 In the lumber yard in Rosenthal, my brother-in-law Diedr. Dyck and I bought wagon hoops for his wagon and threshing stones for me.

July 12 Isaac Klassen again mentioned the incident recorded earlier (see entry for May 18, 1865), but now affirmed his innocence and said the story was true as he had described it in his letter.

August 17 At 6 a.m. Klas Heide's wife Helena (née Rempel) died after many years of anguish, having sat largely motionless on one spot for five years. She had suffered greatly during the last eight days. She was 56 years and 6 months old. Her first marriage of 12 years, 6 months, and 6 days produced 3 sons and 3 daughters, of whom one son and one daughter had died. Her second marriage lasted 25 years, 5 months, and 9 days and produced a son and 2 daughters. She was grandmother to six children, of whom one had died.

August 19 David and I left for Nikopol with 5 chetvert of oats, which we sold for 2 silver R. 5 C. per chetvert. We spent the night at the home of my niece, Mrs Abraham Friesen.

August 21 We finished our business in Nikopol in the morning and then drove to visit our brethren in the Borosenko settlement.

August 22 Sunday. I preached in Borosenko, loaded bricks for my stove, and drove home in the afternoon.

August 27 I brought home a load of sand from Sofievka.

August 28 Jacob, Heinrich, and I carted bricks for the stove from Borosenko, which cost 1 silver R.

September 11 Elder Gerhard Dyck, Reverend Johann Dyck and Deacon Jacob Klassen went to the Grossfürstlich settlement to conduct a communion service and an election of ministers.

September 21 Tuesday. A big fire broke out at 1 a.m. in the Novopodolsk treadmill belonging to Unger and Stuppel. At first, the miller had mistaken the crackling flames for wind. When he saw flames shooting through the roof, he ran to the end of the mill, untied the horses in the stall, and woke people up in the house. He then dashed back into the mill to save the horses, but it was too late. The housing of the mill hammer had burned through, and all he could hear were the terrified screams of the doomed horses. An operating mill on fire is a terrifying sight. Klas Heide's buildings also caught fire from the mill and burned to the ground. Most of the furniture was saved, but Heide lost two barn horses. One was found under the ruins of the barn and the other stretched out on the stove in the kitchen. Heide's two pigs escaped the fire and were later recovered with scorched hides. News of the fire and a call to help in the clean-up arrived while we were out ploughing. The children helped clean the fire site in the afternoon while my wife and I visited my brother Diedrich. The cause of the fire is unknown, but God sees all.

September 23 Our neighbour Johann Rempel died yesterday at 8 p.m. at the age of 37 years, 10 months, and 8 days after an illness lasting 23 days. At 10:30 p.m., after we had washed and placed his body on the board, we sang a song. Then I went home to compose two funeral letters, which will be sent to the Khortitsa colonies tomorrow morning. I did not get to bed until 1:30 a.m.

September 29 We made an inventory of the estate of the late Johann Rempel, which totals 877 silver R. 50 C., with the property assessed at 400 R. The widow chose me and neighbour Cornelius Krause as her trustees and brother-in-law Reverend Gerhard Dyck of Rosenthal and neighbour Abr. Günther as her children's guardians.

October 1 The sheep managed to get out of Peter v Kampen's barn at night, and what a grim sight greeted us at dawn. Dead sheep lay scattered over the hillside opposite the churchyard, and others were running about in panic. Several sheep, including some badly injured ones, had taken refuge with the Jews. The bloodthirsty wolf had used the break-out for a great slaughter. Sixteen sheep were dead, only three of the seriously injured sheep could be butchered, and one is still missing. No sheep of mine were killed or injured. 'The wolf catcheth them, and scattereth the sheep,' our Lord Jesus says in John 10. Our faithful Saviour and shepherd gave his life for his sheep to save them from the devil's claws. For even as the wolf caught our sheep, the devil pursues men's souls and seeks to devour them. Woe to him who leaves his shepherd, for he will fall prey to the destroyer of souls. Thou faithful shepherd, do not abandon me in the desolation of this world. Let me be near thee, and number me among the sheep redeemed at great cost. Grant me blessedness under the protection of thy gentle staff. Amen.

October 6 Klas Heide owed more to his brother-in-law Cornelius

Rempel (in addition to monies owing the Orphans' Administration and others) than the value of his estate. Rempel had Heide's land, homestead, and other possessions sold at public auction. Proceeds will first pay the Orphans' Administration, and Rempel will have to make do with what remains. I kept the books at the sale. My brother-in-law bought the homestead for his son-in-law Peter Martens for 240 silver R. 25 C.

October 7 The Ministerial Committee met with Daniel Löwen and Isaac Müller of Schönhorst, guardians of Franz Giesbrecht's stepson Martin Penner. The latter had committed fornication with Maria Giesbrecht (his stepfather's daughter), and she is pregnant by him. We asked the parents to be present and impressed upon them their responsibility for what had occurred, which they acknowledged. The guardians agreed to hire out their charge, Maria Giesbrecht [in the Khortitsa colonies]. We exhorted her to genuine repentance, and she showed great remorse.

October 9 At a communal meeting in the home of the Fire Insurance Elder Bernh. Bärgen there was much controversy surrounding the question of obligatory cartage for Abraham Unger's burned-out mill.[26] Charity is often a scarce thing, and it was absent here. [After the meeting] Diedrich Epp, Isbrand Friesen, and Bernhard Bärgen discussed the issue with me. Although people at the meeting had agreed that owners of burned-out houses were entitled to communal cartage, there had been a great to-do regarding Unger's mill. Half the mill belongs to the Jew Stuppel, and for this reason the Novovitebsk villagers wanted to provide only half the cartage called for [in the insurance provisions]. The mill had been registered with the insurance office at 20 units (Huben), which entitled the owners to 50 loads [of cartage], but they wanted to provide only thirty. Although no one had called a formal meeting, the villagers gathered [later] at my house and finally agreed to cart fifty loads. I think that half this number would be fairer, but I persuaded them to accept the higher figure in order to preserve the peace.

October 11 My son Jacob and I left to haul material for Abraham Unger's mill in company with wagons belonging to Cornelius Krause and Johann Rempel's widow (driven by Franz Isaac and under our direction). We met several other wagons on the road.

October 12 First we loaded our wagon at the treadmill, which Unger has purchased in Burwalde, and then stopped in at my cousin Johann Thiessen's place next door to pay him 10 silver R. on behalf of my neighbour Abr. Günther. We also settled accounts with the teacher Johann Teichröw in Neuhorst (from whom the late Rempel had borrowed money), and fed the horses. Rempel had been unable to make his interest payments for four years, and Teichröw had compounded the payments at 6 per cent. We told Teichröw that this approach was not acceptable, and that only capital and simple interest would be repaid. He did not object to this, but his wife had little to say that was edifying.

October 19 Tuesday morning I dismantled my [old] stove and started constructing the new one, using the white bricks I had bought for 4 silver R. at Borosenko, and finished the job in 37 hours.

October 21 David and several others left for the Kudashev khutor to cart timber for Abr. Unger's mill.

November 3 We slaughtered our three fatted pigs with the help of our children, the Johann Andreses.

December 3 My neighbour Cornelius Krause and I carted a load of wheat (some four chetvert) to Unger's mill for the widow Rempel.

There was a communal meeting regarding the obligatory cartage for Unger's mill, which was held in the presence of the overseer, Diedrich Epp, and of the Fire Insurance Elder, Bernh. Bärgen. The dispute was over the fact that [Mennonites in] all of the villages had agreed to the required cartage except Novovitebsk and Novokovno, which refused to cart more than 30 loads. My Lord Jesus, it is no small matter to be keeper of a flock that is guided by spite, self-seeking, and malice. If I am to continue in this difficult calling, grant me strength and patience.

December 5 After the service, at his request, I visited Cornelius Thiessen. He complained to me that Gerhard Braun, Braun's wife, and son Jacob (for whom his daughter Susanna works) were talking behind his daughter's back, saying she had stolen provisions from the Brauns and taken them home. Thiessen also accused Braun of hiring his children to work for him and then refusing to pay them anything, etc., etc. I asked Gerh. Andres to discuss the matter with Braun, and if the accusations were true to work out a reconciliation.

December 8 The parties to the above dispute were unwilling to be reconciled, and I therefore directed them to meet tomorrow in Gerhard Andres's house.

December 9 Thursday. The ministers met in Gerhard Andres's home where Andres and Johann Schellenberg had summoned the following to appear: Cornelius Thiessen, the Gerhard Brauns, and their son Jacob. The Brauns, however, praised their maidservant and denied spreading hurtful rumours about her. On our urging all finally made their peace. But when I suggested that Mrs Braun shake Thiessen's hand as a sign of their reconciliation she declined saying that she did not want to risk losing her hand. I was stern with her, saying 'This is not the place to be light-hearted or foolish.' My words caught her off-guard, and she left without uttering another sound.

David Penner Jr then accused Gerhard Braun of stealing his leather [horse-]lead. Braun produced his lead, which Penner claimed as his own, but the latter could not identify a flaw in it, and Braun therefore kept it. After Braun and his family had left, Penner's mother burst into the room, insisting the lead was indeed her son's, and so we called Braun and Penner back in. Braun was [now] accused of petty thievery, which others had seen and to which he admitted, but no one could prove that the lead was Penner's. A reconciliation finally took place and they were allowed to go in peace.

December 10 Friday morning, while feeding the cattle, David climbed on to the loft, stumbled, fell, and seriously injured his shoulder, which is very painful. Peter v Kampen failed to reset it and we made arrangements for David to seek medical help in the colonies. At 10 a.m. we drove him to the crossroads near the edge of the Jewish land where he caught a ride with my brother Diedrich, who was happy to take him to see Doctor Schellenberg.

December 11 I received the startling news of the death of my dear friend Isaac Bärgmann [head of the Orphans' Administration]. As recently as November 18 and 19 he and I had discussed many issues in a spirit of genuine love. May his soul have found peace in the blood of the Lamb.

December 18 Before the start of today's engagement festivities for the widow Rempel and Peter v Niessen, I asked v Niessen, Bernh. Bärgen, and Corn. Krause to appear before me in the presence of my colleague Dav. Klassen to discuss a letter from a Prussian Diedrich Romanowsky. The latter had committed fornication with v Niessen's maid (the daughter of a Catholic Prussian), and gotten her pregnant, and now wrote bitterly that Abr. Günther, Peter Teichröw, and Peter Thiessen were spreading false rumours that his bride had also had relations with v Niessen. She was prepared to swear that she had carried on only with him, Rom., etc., he wrote. We appealed to v Niessen's conscience to say truthfully whether he was chaste and unencumbered respecting the woman. He assured us before God that he was, and was allowed to go in peace. We attended the engagement celebrations in the afternoon. May the Lord, who has established the institution of marriage, bless this couple.

December 19 Before today's service the Ministerial Committee met. Teichröw admitted spreading baseless stories, and I emphasized the wickedness of scandalmongering and the pain it caused. The Brotherhood discussed the matter regarding Peter v Niessen, and I asked if there was anything more to be said. The story was recognized as pure gossip, and I admonished those present to refrain from spreading hurtful stories of any kind. The Apostle exhorts us not to backbite, and the ninth commandment says, 'Thou shalt not bear false witness against thy neighbour.'

Diedrich Epp's children returned with David whose shoulder had been reset and treated by Dr Schellenberg [his uncle].

December 20 Thursday afternoon, Cornelius Krause and I (as trustees for the widow Rempel), and Abraham Günther and v Kampen, the overseer (as guardians of her children), carried out the division of Johann Rempel's estate. The six children are each to receive: (1) 14 silver R. 70 C., for a total of 88 silver R. 20 C.; (2) the two children of the first marriage, who had earlier been promised something extra as a dowry, will together receive 60 silver R.; (3) each of her four children will receive a cow or a horse or 20 R., 10 lambs (at 1 R. apiece), a quilt and a pillow (at 10 R.) and a songbook (at 1½ R. apiece), as well as material. The two children of the first marriage will receive 10 silver R. together. The money is to be deposited with the Orphans' Administration by May 1, 1866. The newly engaged couple were our guests in the evening.

December 27 This afternoon I joined in marriage Peter v Niessen and the widow Johann Rempel.

December 28 Following the breakfast after-wedding festivities, we went home. As we left we could hear drinking songs echoing through the house where the Lord's name had been spoken in song and prayer only yesterday. How can this be acceptable to Christ? We are guilty of such hypocrisy. Redeem thy straying flock, faithful shepherd, and have mercy on us.

Births and deaths in our community [of the Jewish colonies]:

Births	21 males	23 females	44 total
Deaths	7 males	11 females	18 total
Increase	26 total		
Couples married	8		

We had a good harvest last year, but it is sparse again this year. Through good crops and bad crops the Lord seeks to turn us from the path of sin. My harvest: rye nothing; wheat 11½ chetvert; barley 12 chetvert; oats 13 chetvert 2 merka; lentils 1¼ merka; and potatoes 5 chetvert. There was little hay or feed straw, but I hope to manage with the old straw. Spring and summer were very dry, and fall, especially late fall, was rainy and wet. The [winter] rye looks promising, and we pray that God may bless it. Winter has been mild and almost snowless. We have usually had light frosts and overcast skies, but there are also strong and cold winds. Grain prices are high: rye 3 to 4 R. and barley 3 R. per chetvert. Melon fields in our area did very poorly.

1866

January 6 The Epiphany of Christ. My wife stayed home from the service with a boil under her right arm, which my neighbour Olfert lanced in the evening.
January 8 Diedrich Dyck and his wife, my wife's brothers, and Reverend Gerhard Dyck arrived in the evening.
January 10 There has been little snow generally, and now the thaw gives us worries. To help our guests on their way, I offered to shoe my horses and load their sled-box on to my wagon.
January 11 This morning the ground was frozen hard and there was a thick fog. Our guests hitched their horses to my wagon, [with their sled-box on it], and I hitched my horses to their sled runners. When we reached Loshkarovka, where the snow was somewhat deeper, we

remounted the box on the runners, and after feeding the horses, our visitors left and we came home.

January 12 My brother Diedrich delivered the figures regarding births and deaths. Of persons born during the last century, 12 males and 7 females died, and 92 males and 79 females are living. Of those born this century, and joined to the church through Holy Baptism, 16 males and 25 females died and 2099 males and 2095 females are living. In sum, 60 church members died and 4365 are living.

Figures for the [Khortitsa] community:

Births	238 males	226 females	464 total
Deaths	100 males	71 females	171 total
Increase	138 males	155 females	293 total
Couples married	108		

January 21 Friday. A young Prussian named Joseph Kröger complained that Peter v Niessen, for whom he had worked, was holding back wages on the grounds that his (Kröger's) stepfather owed Niessen some wheat and wool (the latter for spinning). His understanding was that he was not personally responsible for the wheat. I called in my cousin, Klassen, and he summoned v Niessen to join us. We failed, however, to reach an agreement, and it seemed to me that Kröger was more truthful than v Niessen. I urged the latter to pay the full sum, but he refused, and the matter was therefore deferred. Jos. Kröger stayed for dinner. 'Thou shalt not withhold a servant nor the poor and needy his hire, etc.' Deuteronomy 24:14–15.

February 10 We have miserable weather today, a sharp frost and deep snow. The overseer, v Kampen, told me that a Jew from Novokovno on his way home from market had gotten lost and spent the night in the neighbouring village of Kudashev, where they had thawed out his frozen feet and brought him to Novovitebsk. Another wagon with Jews had lost its way, ending up half-frozen at the Petrova khutor, close to Biela. From there people had brought them to the village of Petrovka by ox-cart, but robbed them of their purchases under way. I also heard that two Russians had frozen to death on the road to Poiurka.

February 13 My cousin Klassen and the overseer Peter v Kampen asked me to confront Martin Harder Jr, who is becoming quite muddled from his heavy drinking. I therefore summoned Martin Jr (with his father), and reminded him of his promise to stop drinking, which he again repeated. Have mercy on him, Lord Jesus.

February 19 [We continued our school visitations] in Novokovno. The school meets in a hut, a zemlianka, dug into the ground, with rafters and a straw roof, and is poorly lit.

February 27 Although it was my turn to preach today, I was unable to do so because my lower right leg was swollen (and I could not get my boot on[27]) and the water in the Kamianka [stream] was too deep to ford. Isaac Klassen therefore did the preaching. A lot of snow melted this week, but the run-off is slow and the roads are muddy. Thank God spring is here, for we are almost out of fodder as well as fuel for heating and cooking.

March 5 Around noon we heard that wolves had again gotten in with the sheep. We rushed over and found 12 dogs among Jankel Kodak's flock. Four sheep were dead and four seriously injured. One dog was shot on the spot, and horsemen, including Cornelius Krause and Heinrich Sawatzki, followed the other dogs in order to identify their owner. He turned out to be the nobleman Kudashev who had, in the meantime, sent his administrator to assess the damage. A count of our flock revealed that one of Abr. Günther's sheep was dead and two from our flock were missing and had probably escaped. It would only be fair if the nobleman paid compensation. The Jew demanded compensation and received 5 silver R. for each of the dead sheep.

March 9 I sold two chetvert of wheat to Mishnik and Smelling for 80 silver C. per pud – a total of 16 silver R. 60 C.

March 10 Thursday. We drove to market in Sofievka today over muddy roads and in springlike weather. Yesterday we started spading up the garden and putting in vegetables. The herdsman has driven out the cattle, and Olfert has closed school for the year.

March 14 We started to plough and to seed this morning, but a heavy downpour forced a stop after only three hours.

March 15 It is still very wet, but several villagers began ploughing today. Father, we thank thee for the beautiful spring weather, for blessing our vanishing reserves of fodder, food, and fuel, and for helping us to survive the winter. Bless the seed we have sown, and give us our daily bread once more. Amen, yes Amen!

March 18 This afternoon we went to Abraham Günthers where several children, including our son Gerhard and grandson Gerhard, were vaccinated against smallpox.
March 20 Palm Sunday. I preached a sermon about Jesus' entry into Jerusalem and his suffering and death. Text Isaiah 53:4–7. This was the first service this year in church, but since this was announced only yesterday, the congregation was only from our locality. But there were many children, and perhaps the presence of the children prompted the precentor, teacher Olfert, to announce a cipher melody at the close of the service (number 62, starting with stanza 5). The children sang with ringing voices. This is the first cipher melody sung in this church, although such melodies have been sung in house services in Novopodolsk and Novovitebsk several times this winter. There has been cipher singing in the Khortitsa church since last fall.
March 25 Good Friday. We visited my brother Diedrich this afternoon, who gave me money that my brother Heinrich and brother-in-law Schellenberg had sent as a gift.
April 3 Sunday. When I saw Peter v Niessen harrowing his potato patch this afternoon, I was offended and reproached him. He admitted his error and promised not to work on Sunday again.
April 14 My neighbour Olfert and I ploughed the half-desiatina of old plough-land that we have leased from the Jew Moshsarska for a half silver R. We will use it as a melon patch.
April 24 I informed the congregation of the new printing of our song-book and requested that orders be in to me by next Sunday.[28]
May 1 Last week the Jew David Mishnik complained that Mrs Abraham Günther had screamed and sworn at him as he walked past her yard. v Kampen confirmed the episode, saying she should be called to account, and I ordered that she be summoned to appear [before the Ministerial Committee] next Sunday. But last night her husband dropped by and gave vent to his anger. May the Lord forgive him. The incident gave me a sleepless night and drove me into earnest prayer, which the Lord graciously heard. Early this morning Mrs Günther came by and, in a more subdued mood, admitted her failing, promised to avoid further quarrels with the Jews, and was dismissed in peace. Strengthen me, dear God, and grant me the power to do thy will.
May 10 Tuesday morning Reverend Elder Gerhard Dyck baptized

our young people, including my daughter Katharina. Before the service the ministers tried to achieve a peaceful resolution of the dispute between my neighbour Olfert and the Reverend Is. Klassen (see entries for May 18 and July 12, 1865), and this was partly successful. I was not present.

May 11 Wednesday morning, my neighbour Abr. Günther told me Corn. Harms was bitter because the matter involving Reverend Isaac Klassen had been settled only superficially. I therefore decided to raise the matter with the Elder, who was at the v Kampen's, and met him on his way to see me. The Elder advised Klassen not to take Holy Communion, which he accepted. Present at the Lamb's table were 121 people. After the service Reverend Isaac Klassen appeared in the ministers' room, where the Elder took him to task for the controversy in which he was embroiled and told him he would not be permitted to administer his office until he had straightened things out with the congregation. He would have to do this on his own, but could in the meantime take his place with the other ministers [at the front of the church].

Brotherhood Meeting (in the afternoon following the service). The beloved Elder informed the brethren about the matter involving Reverend Isaac Klassen and exhorted them to peace and harmony. He urged them not to make I.K.'s reconciliation with the congregation too difficult. The controversy was an intrusion on an otherwise beautiful service. Lord Jesus, grant us thy peace.

May 21 This afternoon, a Russian girl drowned while trying to wash her feet at the watering place. May God have mercy on her poor soul, and protect us from all danger.

May 23 We started sheep-shearing today, a total of 72 sheep and lambs. Thirty-two sheep and 29 lambs are ours and 2 sheep and 2 lambs belong to Abr. Hiebert.

May 31 We left for the Khortitsa colonies early Tuesday morning, reaching Neuendorf by 6 p.m., where I paid the Orphans' Administration the annual interest of 12 silver R. on my debt.

June 1 Wednesday. I paid down 2 silver R. on my account at the store in Schönhorst, where I still owe 14 silver R. ([Marginal note:] I sent these 14 R. with my neighbour Heh. Olfert a little later.) We drove to Neuosterwick to see my brother-in-law Died. Dyck and our parents. There we sold our butter to the storekeeper Jacob Klassen in

Rosenthal, whom I still owed 23 silver R. 44 C. He was not overly friendly, and this made me dejected all day. Dear Jesus, only thy peace, which we need, can make us happy. Klassen paid 12 silver C. per funt of butter, 1 silver C. less than the other storekeeper. We delivered 2 puds 13 funt, for a total of 11 silver R. 16 C., leaving a debt of 12 silver R. 28 C. Help me to pay off this sum, Lord, for thou art generous and hast bountiful resources. ([Marginal note:] Thank God, this was fully paid off one year later by brother-in-law D. Dyck.)

June 2 According to Elder Gerhard Dyck, Reverend Isaac Klassen had asked permission to serve as minister again, but his situation remains unchanged, as it was.

June 21 At 2:30 this morning, my cousin [David] Klassen asked me to visit v Kampen, who had come down with the cholera.[29] As I hurried over, I met v Kampen's son Johann running to see me with the same urgent plea. I found v Kampen gravely ill in bed, no longer vomiting but still with diarrhea and cramps. Each time we buckled on the life awakener the cramps let up a little. Brother Diedrich was here at daybreak. The attacks resumed around 7 a.m. The Feldsher Israelsohn, who arrived around 10 a.m., tried various treatments including rubbing the body with alcohol, warming it with bottles, and bleeding the patient. At first the blood ran freely and then slowed to a drip. As v Kampen slowly grew weaker, the cramps subsided somewhat. His death struggle started at 10:30 and ended at 12:05 noon. After his death, the widow and children wept and wailed pitifully. May God have mercy on them. After serving in office for 15 years, our dear friend and overseer, Peter v Kampen, has thus finished his course. We immediately made arrangements to have the coffin and grave prepared. Since the moon was not yet up, we worked by the light of many lanterns. At night, around 11 o'clock, his neighbours and we carried his body to the cemetery, placing the coffin in the grave, covering the grave with boards and shovelling dirt over the boards. Because of the intense heat, the body had already started to decompose. We returned to the house, sang a hymn together, and left for home.

June 22 Peter v Kampen reached the age of 53 years, 5 months, and 21 days and was married to his wife for 29 years, 7 months, and 24 days. He was father to 14 children, 9 sons and 5 daughters, of whom 7 sons and 2 daughters are living. The widow is grief-stricken. May the

Lord be her comforter. When I visited her again at nine in the evening, I found her sitting on the bench weeping, distraught and anxious about her salvation and earnestly exhorting her children to walk in the fear of the Lord. We talked together for a little while. She now has diarrhea as well and expects to die. I returned home, and to bed, at 11 o'clock.

June 23 Thursday. I was called to the bedside of the ailing widow v Kampen at midnight, who now has the cholera as well. In addition to diarrhea she has cramps and is vomiting. The sorrow in the family is intense. Lord have mercy. I stayed at her side throughout the ordeal. The guests for [her husband's] funeral arrived in the afternoon, but there were only a few. Silently, in my absence, the grave was filled in, and then, after lunch, we gathered in the overseer's office to sing a hymn about death. I spent the night at her bedside.

June 24 I was called to the home of my cousin David Klassen at 1 a.m. and found him stricken with the disease. After only 14 hours, his struggle ended at 11 this morning, and he was a corpse. At 12 noon, the just-widowed Justina v Kampen (née Dyck) expired as well, her critical illness having lasted 36 hours. And at three in the afternoon their young son Peter v Kampen died. I sent to Novokovno and Novopodolsk for coffin-makers and grave-diggers, and we buried the bodies late at night. First we buried my cousin, David Klassen, and then the other two, all by lantern-light. I concluded the burial with a prayer, after which my wife and I stayed at the v Kampen's place for the night. In the meantime, Martin v Kampen's wife, Mrs Johann Klassen, and Margaretha v Kampen have come down with serious cases of cholera, and both Abr. Günther and his wife are ill with the disease.

June 25 Mrs Martin v Kampen seems to be recovering, but Mrs Johann Klassen and the Abr. Günthers are still very ill. Lord, have mercy on me and on all those who are ill.

June 26 Sunday morning. Mrs Abraham Günther's condition has gotten worse, but the patients at v Kampen's place seem to be getting better. When I returned from my round of visits I found my wife ill in bed. Lord, let this end well. Our children, the Johann Andreses, were our guests. I attended service and preached a sermon to a large congregation based on Romans 13, 11–12. God helped me to deliver the sermon, and to him be honour and praise. A Jewish doctor by the name of Kursohn arrived with my brother in the afternoon and said my wife had typhoid fever. The Lord blessed his treatment, and my wife is on the way to recovery.

June 27 My colleague David Klassen's wife Anna (née Penner) departed this life at seven this morning. She followed quickly in her husband's footsteps, her acute suffering lasting only ten hours. Abr. Günther's Russian servant died at sundown, and many others have also been stricken.

June 28 Martin v Kampen's daughter Justina died at midnight on Tuesday. Our sister-in-law, Abraham Epp's widow, died this morning. Corn. Krause and I buried the infant Justina in the afternoon and sent a wagon to fetch the doctor from Grushevka. In Izluchistaia, Gerhard Braun's wife died of the cholera this afternoon. In the evening I was called to the home of Jacob Pätkau in Novopodolsk, whose wife is gravely ill and in need of comfort. Be thou her helper and comforter, Jesus my Saviour. Gerhard Andres's children helped us cut rye. May God reward them.

June 29 This morning, the landowner Abr. Günther and Martin v Kampen's daughter Anna died. God, have mercy on us. Sheath thy sword. Be gracious to us. After noon I was called to the bedside of Mrs Heinrich Rempel in Novopodolsk, who is seriously ill and troubled about her salvation. The Martin Harders Sr became ill this afternoon. This evening a wagon fetched me again to visit the Rempels in Novopodolsk, where I spent the night.

June 30 Thursday. Although Mrs Rempel is still gravely ill, she calmed down a little after I arrived. I visited several other sick people in the morning and then drove home. Mrs Pätkau, who is also ill, was successfully delivered of a still-born daughter. The wife of Johann Hildebrand Jr is also seriously ill. I arrived home at sunrise with my Jewish driver. My wife was very ill last night, but felt slightly better during the day (also the cholera).

July 1 My dear wife is still weak. But she is out of bed and starting to work around the house, and I think she will be better soon. I thank thee Lord Jesus for preserving her life.

July 2 Saturday. At the time of his death, my cousin David Klassen was 44 years, 9 months, and 15 days old. His wife died at the age of 44 years, 5 months, and 19 days. They had been married 24 years, 9 months, and 15 days. The deceased had served as minister for 3 years,

9 months, and 3 days. He had preached the word of God 135 times, delivered 18 funeral sermons, and officiated at 5 marriages. The couple had 10 children, 6 sons and 4 daughters, all of whom are still living. In the afternoon I visited the sick in Novopodolsk, where Martin Friesen and Mrs Heinr. Rempel are deathly ill. Mrs Johann Hildebrand and Mrs Pätkau were also quite sick (the latter is improving), and brother Diedrich is down with a bad case of diarrhea.

July 3 At church I learned that Mrs Heinrich Rempel had departed this life at 10 p.m. yesterday and Martin Friesen at 12 midnight. Lord Jesus, receive into thy kingdom those whom thou hast purchased with thy blood. As a memorial to our deceased colleague David Klassen and his wife Anna (née Penner), I preached a sermon to a large congregation on Hebrews 13:17 ('Remember your teachers ...').

July 4 While visiting the widower Heinrich Rempel and his infant son Heinrich this morning, the building of a Jew next door to the Jewish school and two large haystacks went up in flames. A few days ago we had a similar accident when a Jewish dwelling and two haystacks burned to the ground. Protect us from fire during this drought, dear Lord. In the afternoon we looked in on the sick at Diedrich Epp's place.

July 7 Diedrich Thiessen's wife Maria died this morning, and several others have become sick.

July 8 Friday morning, my neighbours Wilhelm Martens and Heinrich Olfert and I made the rounds of the sick in Novopodolsk. The aged Johann Hildebrand's wife Maria and David Friesen's daughter Aganetha died at night. There seems to be no end in sight. By the Almighty's command, death continues its harvest. Dear Lord, thou has tormented us so long. Have mercy. Turn thy countenance towards us and show us thy kindly face again. Sustain us, and be at our side during this time of dreadful trial and suffering.

July 9 This afternoon our children (except for the two youngest who stayed home) drove to pick cherries at my brother Diedrich's. There have been no deaths in Novopodolsk since yesterday, but the numbers of the sick continue to grow. Take pity on us, Lord, remove this scourge. Have mercy on us.

July 10 There was a large congregation, and I preached a sermon on the frailty of life (Psalm 90). In the evening, I received an urgent call to visit my neighbour H. Olfert, whose daughter Katarina had violent cramps. We massaged her vigorously, warmed her as best we could, and gave her hot lilac tea to drink. God blessed our efforts, and after an hour and a half the cramps subsided and there were no other symptoms.

July 12 Tuesday morning. I drove to Novopodolsk with Jacob v Kampen to visit the sick. The two grown sons of the foreigner Cornelius Douvensee, Johann and Jacob, died today. David Friesen and the schoolteacher Abraham Andres were gravely ill. A Jewish doctor sent here by the government worked to save him, soaking a linen sheet in fresh cold water, wrapping him in it naked, and covering him with blankets. God blessed the treatment. Even though there continue to be new cases, I believe the sick are on the road to recovery.

July 14 Thursday. Last night, Heinr. Sawatzki, Wilhelm Martens and I made the rounds in Novopodolsk. Sawatzki spent the night with the Diedr. Thiessens, Martens with the Abr. Andreses and I with the David Friesens. Diedr. Friesen arrived with the Jewish doctor from Novokovno, and I took him to see the Diedr. Epps. All the sick seemed somewhat better. We drove home this morning. I was called to the home of the v Kampens where Margaretha (Mrs Johann Klassen) was having an attack of cramps, which lasted an hour and a half. By vigorous rubbing and warming, the attack passed. She and Mrs Martin v Kampen are still bedridden, but the Mart. Harders are better. I preached a funeral sermon in church based on James 4:4. The congregation was again large.

July 17 Yesterday, Saturday, my son David had another accident, breaking his left arm when he fell from his horse while driving the horses to the corral. We were in a fix. It is in the midst of harvesting, I could not miss the service and David needed to be taken to the doctor. Finally, my neighbour Heinrich Sawatzki offered his services and left with my wagon in the evening. This is David's second accident (see entry for Dec. 10, 1865).

July 18 Sawatzki arrived back Wednesday at noon after delivering David to Hoffnungsfeld. There Diedrich Dyck set his arm, which was broken in two places. Dyck wanted David to stay on a little longer [for observation].

July 23 Saturday afternoon, I helped the trustees and guardians make an inventory of Abr. Günther's estate. The house was evaluated at 250 silver R. and the belongings at 685 silver R. 95 C. Michael Ham and Cornelius Krause are the trustees and Peter Löwen and Anton Günther the guardians.
July 24 This afternoon, my neighbours Wilhelm Martens and Heh. Olfert and I and our wives visited the Diedrich Epps. After coffee, we men made an inventory of Heinrich Rempel's estate.
July 25 Jacob v Kampen and I left for the Khortitsa District, spending the night in Schönhorst with the Head of the Orphans' Administration.
July 26 From the Orphans' Administration, we gave Gerhard Penner of Blumengart his confirmation as guardian of the Klassen children. My co-guardian and I found places for the Klassen children: Gerhard has been hired out for one year at Jacob Dyck's treadmill in Khortitsa for 75 silver R.; David has been hired out to his cousin Johann Klassen for 40 silver R.; Martin has been placed with the Peter Elias family in Neuosterwick to be educated; and Maria will stay with the Jacob v Kampens for now. The remaining youngsters have been placed in various homes as foster children: Katarina with Bern. Schellenberg in Rosenthal; Peter at the David Penners; Bernhard with the Gerhard Penners in Blumengart; and Helena with Anton Bärgmann in Neuendorf.
August 21 I preached a sermon in church on the subject of our lukewarm Christianity. Text, Revelations 3:14–16.
August 22 We left this morning for the Khortitsa colonies, stopping in Neuendorf to see Peter Dyck, head of the Orphans' Administration. I also spoke to District Mayor Hamm about carting the deceased's belongings. Friday morning, my brother-in-law Diedr. Dyck and I organized the disposal of the belongings of the late David Klassen and arranged the accounts at Reverend Peter Harm's place.
August 31 Wednesday. Auction sales were held of the estates of the David Klassens and the Peter v Kampens. Heinrich Krause, a young bachelor, bought Klassen's windmill and dwelling for 1600 silver R.
September 2 Martin v Kampen's wife Judith, who has been in bed since the cholera outbreak, is near death. I asked her about the state of her soul, and she prayed in a loud voice, earlier having told me about her great longing for her dead children.

September 3 Sunday morning at 3:45, Mrs Martin v Kampen passed away, and her death was a peaceful one. She had been bedridden ten weeks and two days.

September 12 Wednesday morning, Gerhard Penner, my co-guardian of Klassen's children, Johann Klassen, and I transferred the late David Klassen's debt on the mill, which was owing Julius Janzen, to Heinrich Krause, the new owner.

September 15 Thursday. The [remaining] belongings of the late David Klassen and Peter v Kampen were carted by communal transportation to Aron Thiessen's place in Neuendorf and sold at public auction. The sale did not finish today. I spent the night with Peter Dyck, head of the Orphans' Administration.

September 25 Brotherhood Meeting following the service. The Elder presented the matter regarding our colleague Isaac Klassen to the brethren (see entry for May 11, 1866). In the following vote 11 brethren supported Klassen's continuance in office and 24 voted for his dismissal. None of the ministers and deacons voted. In the afternoon a new minister was chosen. In the first election, for deacon, Jacob Pätkau received 34 votes and the others were as follows: Diet. Thiessen 7, Johann Schellenberg 3, Bernh. Bärgen 2, Abr. Andres 1, Johann Penner 1, and Is. Friesen 1. Forty-nine ballots were cast in all, including those of the ministers. In the second election, for minister, Jacob Pätkau was chosen with 42 votes.

September 26 Monday morning our visiting ministers left for Borosenko. My neighbours Heinrich Sawatzki and Heinrich Olfert and I accompanied them. In the afternoon they conducted a service in the manor house in Nicolaithal [Borosenko settlement]. *Brotherhood meeting*. The Elder asked the Borosenko congregation if they wished to chose a minister. Twenty-three voted 'yes' and two 'no.'

September 27 Tuesday. Brotherhood Meeting [in Nicolaithal] to elect a minister. Gerhard Enz was chosen by majority vote.

September 29 As I entered the church at the funeral of the aged Franz Klassen of Novozhitomir, Mrs Isaac Klassen hurried out to avoid meeting me. Her husband, Reverend Isaac Klassen, and his brother Gerhard Klassen were already in the churchyard, where I met them, and their bitterness towards me simply exploded. Grant them thy peace, Lord Jesus.

October 7 Friday. We sold what remained of the estates of the Peter v Kampen and David Klassen families, which had been wiped out by the cholera. The day was bitterly cold, with a thin layer of snow on the ground.

My brother Heinrich wrote me about Abraham Hiebert's tragic death. Hiebert had needed sand to cover or repair his roof. He went down into the pit, which was about 50 paces from his house and not very deep, shortly before dinner. But as he stepped down, the side of the pit collapsed, burying him. A herdsman and some potato-diggers working nearby rushed over to dig him out, but it was too late. People in Khortitsa and Einlage, hearing of the tragedy, came to help wash and place the body on the board. The family is grief-stricken, and the widow and children broke down and cried lamentably at the funeral.

October 10 A real winter's day, with lots of snow, cold and a strong east wind. We kept the cattle indoors and brought in the sheep, where they remained without fodder all day.

October 11 Tuesday. We sorted the sheep. We have a total of 29.

October 18 Tuesday at 8 a.m., Jacob and I carted a load of rye to the Khortitsa colonies, returning what we had borrowed earlier from the emergency granary [in Khortitsa].[30]

October 24 Monday afternoon we gathered at the home of the v Kampens to resolve a dispute between v Kampen's children and their uncle and guardian Wilhelm Martens.

November 31 This evening I received a long letter from Reverend Isaac Klassen in which he tries to justify his conduct. He blames others for the controversy, and especially me, and states that *he will preach in his house* and wherever else he is invited to preach. Comfort him with thy peace, Lord, and grant him rest.

December 1 This morning I went to Novopodolsk by sled to show Isaac Klassen's letter to my colleagues. They and my brother Diedrich are planning a trip to Khortitsa for tomorrow.

December 2 Friday. I delivered a sermon at the funeral of Johann Wieler's servant Franz Penner, who died at the age of 15. The lad was a foreigner whose father had come from Prussia, abandoned him here eight years ago, and has not bothered about him since. I preached to the congregation on the words of the Psalmist, 'Mother and father have abandoned me but the Lord has received me.'

December 15 Thursday morning, David and I drove to the bazaar in Sofievka where we bought coffee and plum tea.

December 16 A dear visitor, our colleague Johann Wiebe from Olgafeld in the Grossfürstlich settlement, stopped by today for dinner and coffee.

My wife's labour started in the evening. At 11 o'clock I sent David and Johann Klassen to fetch Mrs Isaac Friesen, the midwife, who arrived after one and a quarter hours. By morning the contractions had stopped.

December 19 At three o'clock Monday morning, my wife, with God's help, was delivered of a healthy daughter, Elisabeth. Her birth pangs started at ten last night, and the period of greatest anxiety lasted about two hours. The midwife stayed here two days and three nights. After the delivery, at daybreak today, David and Jacob drove her home, returning by way of Izluchistaia to tell the Johann Andreses about their new sister.

December 31 We are a year closer to eternity again, and God knows whether I will live to see the end of another year. Our dear Lord has put us to a hard test this year, sending first the cholera and then a cattle plague. The cattle plague raged in Novopodolsk and Kamianka and continues on in Izluchistaia and Novovitebsk, but not one head belonging to a German has died thus far. The cholera, however, devastated us, tearing huge gaps in our ranks. My colleague and cousin David Klassen and our overseer P. v Kampen fell victim to the cholera, along with their wives and many others. My senior colleague, Isaac Klassen, was dismissed from office, but rejects his ouster and is causing great division in the church. Faithful Lord and Saviour, grant that the interests of the church might prevail. A young colleague, my brother Diedrich's son-in-law, Jacob Pätkau, was elected in Isaac Klassen's place, and he enjoys the love and respect of the congregation.

Births and deaths in our community [of the Jewish colonies]:

Births	19 males	15 females	34 total
Deaths	17 males	20 females	37 total
Couples married	5		

There were thus three more deaths than births.

The crops were good in places and quite poor in others, but here there was no shortage of fodder. My crop yields were as follows:

wheat, oats and barley, a total of 16 chetvert. My stock of cattle and horses remained constant. The lambing was successful and we were richly blessed. Our 29 sheep gave birth to 32 lambs, 29 of whom survived. Our family increased by one, a daughter Elisabeth. We thank the Lord for his goodness over the past year, and pray that his grace may go with us again into the new year. Grant, Lord, that the afflictions visited upon us might awaken new spiritual life within the church. There is much that is still lacking among us. The love of the world is strong and Christianity is weak. Lord, spare thy church. Grant us the contrition and strength needed for true repentance.

BOOK III, 1867–1870

Contending with Change

'The great dispute over land ... will not
be a blessing for the community.'

December 31, 1867

'Everything in this world changes and passes away,
save alone the Word of God, which is eternal.'

October 1, 1868

'In the middle of Odessa one can fill a container
by simply turning a tap.'

June 14, 1870

1867

January 4 Around noon, the Jewish Desiatnik made his rounds, summoning the Germans to a meeting at the communal office. He invited me also, but I did not go. Later my German neighbours told me that the Jewish community wanted to limit our freedoms. They had claimed that I did not own any land but simply occupied a Jewish homestead. I am convinced, however, that my homestead was confirmed as conclusively by the Guardianship Committee as have been those of the other Germans. I would be happy to move if my duty to the church did not keep me here.
January 6 I was finally able to announce the changes [regarding births and deaths in the Khortisa church], which my brother- in-law Gerhard Dyck had delivered. In 1866, of those born during the last century, 8 males and 16 females died and 84 males and 74 females are living. Of those born this century, and joined to the church through Holy Baptism, 32 males and 30 females died and 2167 males and 2165 females are living.

Figures for the entire [Khortitsa] community:

Births	272 males	211 females	483 total
Deaths	156 males	141 females	297 total
Increase	116 males	70 females	186 total
Couples married	101		

January 15 There was heavy drifting this morning and then a thaw. Before today's service, we met at Reverend J. Pätkau's house where Elisabeth Wiebe, the unwed daughter of the late Martin Wiebe of Neuosterwick, had been summoned to appear [before the Ministerial Committee] by the brethren Isaac Siemens and Bernh. Bärgen. She had given birth to an infant shortly before Christmas. She confessed to having committed fornication with Heinrich Lepp, son of Peter Lepp of the Grossfürstlich settlement. *Brotherhood Meeting*. The congre-

gation placed Elisabeth Wiebe in the ban. Grant her the strength to repent, Lord. I wrote a letter to the beloved Elder informing him of the incident.

January 26 On their way to our place, my brother Diedrich and his son almost had an accident when the shaft on their sled, which was too short, caused the horses to bolt. For the trip home, my brother borrowed the longer shaft from my wagon, which will keep the sled at a safe distance from the horses.

January 29 *Brotherhood Meeting*. Elisabeth Wiebe was received back into the church (see entry for Jan. 15, 1867). Jesus forgives sinners.

January 30 My brother drove over by Jewish post [horse] this afternoon, and we worked on the estate accounts of the late v Kampen and Klassen until late at night.

February 10 I kept the books at an auction sale of the estate of the late Johann Hildebrand of Novopodolsk. The crowd was large and the prices high, with the proceeds coming to 1100 silver R. Earlier, the Wirtschaft had been sold to the son, Peter Hildebrand, for 760 silver R.

February 11 The Hildebrand heirs today divided the remaining possessions among themselves.

February 13 *School visitation*. On two sleds, my brother Diedrich, Jacob Pätkau, H. Olfert, and I drove to Novokovno, where we visited the school with several villagers. The teacher, Cornelius Penner, conducts classes in his home, a half- zemlianka (half dugout). In the afternoon, we visited our school in Novovitebsk, which is conducted in his home by my neighbour H. Olfert. The teachers Abr. Andres and Corn. Penner were present, as well as many observers. Bible stories were from the Old Testament, and the children had learned their lessons well.

February 14 Tuesday morning we visited the Novopodolsk school, taught by Abraham Andres. Bible stories were from the New Testament. In addition to the teaching of reading, writing, and arithmetic, there was also some geography, and the singing was exceptional. We visited the Izluchistaia school in the afternoon, taught by Gerhard Redekopp. It is on a very low level.

In the evening, in the presence of his widow and the guardians and trustees, my brother made an inventory of the estate of the late Franz Klassen.

February 15 Wednesday morning. The ground was snow-covered this morning, but by noon it had melted in the sun. The Novozhitomir school is in deplorable shape, except for the singing. Later at the home of the widower Peter Neufeld, my brother made an inventory and divided [the late wife's estate]. I kept the accounts. After dinner at Reverend Löwen's place, we visited the Kamianka school. It was first slushy and then froze, but the sledding was good. Jacob Andres teaches here, and his school was superior to the others. Mental arithmetic was especially noteworthy. Cipher music is taught in all of the schools, except Izluchistaia, where singing is still by ear. Bible stories are taught only in Novovitebsk and Novopodolsk. Sledding was excellent on the way home. There was a strong north wind, it was sharply cold, and I noticed that the windows on the north side of the house were frost-covered.
February 18 Towards evening, David and I drove to Novopodolsk to see my brother Diedrich about our fodder shortage. Winter has turned bitterly cold and my supplies are dangerously low. We are right out of straw and chaff and there is little hay left in the barn. My brother gladly helped us out. May God reward him.
February 20 My son and I went for the first load of fodder on our large sled this morning. David and Jacob will fetch what remains, carting two loads a day.
February 22 Today we had a wonderful opportunity to witness a ring-shaped eclipse of the sun. The day began overcast and with moderate frost. Then the clouds cleared in time for the eclipse. The room became dark and we could see only a thin sliver of light around the sun's disc. The eclipse's mid-point was around 12:30 a.m., two hours later than announced in the *Odessaer Kalender*.[1] In the evening there was a *meeting of [Mennonite] villagers* in the home of the Herdsman Elder, Heinr. Sawatzki. My neighbour Heinrich Olfert was appointed teacher for another year at a salary of 30 silver R. (10 R. less than last year), and dung fuel from the community sheep-fold, which will be cut [into briquettes] and delivered to his yard. He is obliged to keep school also between seeding and harvest times. We further decided to keep watch at night in pairs of two. This is much after the fact, since two horses have again been stolen from the Neusteters. Where the owner does not watch over his house, the watchman stands guard in vain.

March 2 I went to speak to Mrs Abr. Günther on behalf of Rempel, as his go-between. She agreed that he could come and visit her and then rejected his proposal.
March 3 At the Communal Office, my brother Diedrich, my neighbour, and I straightened out the accounts between the Jews and the deceased v Kampen and David Klassen.
March 6 Monday. For 5 silver R. I bought a straw pile for fodder and fuel from my neighbour Peter v Niessen.
March 7 There was heavy drifting yesterday afternoon, followed by a storm with a howling north wind. The snow had seeped through the cracks by morning, and the windows were frost-covered. It was bitterly cold under clear skies all day. May God protect all travellers under way. Since the teacher too was short of fuel, the children stayed home from school. There was a magnificent mock sun in the sky this morning.
March 9 This is the first day of spring, but it is like mid- winter, with ice-covered window panes, a strong southeast wind and heavy drifting.
March 11 A thaw this morning with fog and rain, and it seemed that spring was finally on its way. Then, however, as the fog lifted there was a strong north wind and bitter cold. When fodder is low, one longs for spring. When there is lots of everything, one naturally feels otherwise.
March 12 A north wind, bright sunshine, thawing, and a run-off in the valleys.
March 22 We seeded lettuce, cabbages, and turnips this afternoon.
March 23 I bought half a sazhen of hay from the Jew Josel Mishnik for 4 silver R. 50 C., and carted it home.
March 28 Tuesday. We started ploughing and seeding barley this afternoon.
April 1 Saturday. [Mennonite] landowners were gathered at H. Sawatzki's place before breakfast this morning, when my neighbour Wilh. Martens received a call to hurry home. There was a strong wind, and we found his chimney stack smouldering in several places and sparks shooting into the air. The straw roof was fortunately still wet from the night's rain, and so we succeeded in dousing the blaze. It was all the result of carelessness in lighting the stove. We thank the Lord, our preserver and shield, for his gracious protection.
April 3 Some time ago, the Jewish Village Office and the Germans

together hired the herdsman Sokolov. Then the Jews backed out of the deal, appointing Sokolov to herd only their cattle. This wilfulness compelled us to keep our cattle indoors. Yesterday, the Germans hired their own Russian herdsman, and today we were able to drive our cattle out to pasture.

April 9 Palm Sunday. My wife and I and the children attended service, meeting in our church for the first time this year. Despite beautiful spring weather, only 21 people were present, and the only children were from our village.

April 10 We ploughed on the Izluchistaia steppe, staying overnight with the children to finish the job.

April 11 In the morning I drove home, returning later.

April 12 I returned home from the field again in the morning. Then I drove to the market in Sofievka for some plums and soap. After seeding five desiatinas to wheat, our ploughers returned home at three this afternoon.

April 15 A welcome drizzle this morning. We ploughed and planted a potato patch in the afternoon.

April 16 There was rain again this morning. Then around 9 a.m. the sky cleared, and we drove to the Izluchistaia steppe to plough. Before we could finish, the rain returned and continued all day.

April 18 Easter Sunday. Martin v Kampen called for my son Peter, to help out with his ploughing until next Sunday.

[Some time ago,] the Jews submitted a communal resolution to the Lord Overseer asking that the ninth model farmstead in Novovitebsk, which is mine, be eliminated. My brother Diedrich tells me the Novovitebsk Village Office has received a reply formally confirming my farmstead and instructing the Office to affirm having received this notice. Lord, we praise thee.

April 21 At noon Friday we seeded the last oats, finishing the sowing for the year.

April 22 Saturday morning, we planted the melon patch.

April 24 At 7:30 a.m. we left for the Khortitsa colonies.

April 29 We spent the night with my brother Johann, who has worked as assistant secretary [of the District Office] for a month, living in the 'Charter of Privileges' building.[2] This afternoon, my brother Heinrich, Elder Gerh. Dyck, his wife, Reverend Jacob Regier, and I examined the Charter of Privileges.

May 2 Tuesday. While on a pleasure trip with my brother-in-law Gerh. Dyck on the Dnieper, we were caught by a thunder-shower.
May 7 Brother Diedrich and his wife were here after Vesper. He returned from seeing the Lord Overseer today, and is discouraged about our situation in regard to the Jews, believing we may be abandoned to their mercies. Later the Germans [of Novovitebsk] met and decided to send a delegation to Khortitsa to arrange for a petition on this subject addressed to his Excellency Lord Lisander [an official of the Guardianship Committee]. Jacob Dyck and Heinrich Sawatzki volunteered to make the trip, although I think it is quite wrong to sign a petition on behalf of all model settlers without their prior agreement.
May 12 Cornelius Krause and I consulted brother Diedrich about the matter, and after a long discussion decided to call a general Brotherhood Meeting in the church on Saturday. We made the necessary arrangements.
May 13 Saturday. *Brotherhood Meeting*. I reviewed our dispute with the Jews. The meeting asked me to go to Khortitsa, and I agreed on the condition that two other representatives be selected to accompany me, which was agreed to. The two chosen by majority vote are Cornelius Krause (26 votes) and Diedr. Thiessen (24 votes). The 32 landowners present cast 2 ballots each. It was decided to leave tomorrow, after the service. May the Lord crown this undertaking with success.
May 14 On the basis of yesterday's decision, Corn. Krause, Diedr. Thiessen, and I set out for Khortitsa, spending the night on the Kudashev khutor.
May 15 Monday. We stopped off at the Orphans' Administration to deposit money in the Orphans' Account and for other business. At noon we reached the home of my brother Heinrich, who drafted a petition from us to the Guardianship Committee. We then submitted the petition to the District Office, but the District mayor Hamm and assistant District mayor Töws refused to help, saying that 'We might receive a reprimand' [for this initiative]. Since the stamped [eagle] paper [on which the petition must be written] could not be found in the District Office, we had to send for it. This I finally managed with the help of a dear friend, Isaac Driedger from the Island [of Khortitsa], who undertook to fetch it from Alexandrovsk for 80 C.,

returning with it at sundown. He drove me to the ferry from where I crossed in the dark and spent the night with my brother Heinrich.

May 17 We reached home in one day. Bless our petition, Lord.

May 20 Saturday. My wife and I toured our grain fields on the steppe. God willing, the crop could be very good. Only the rye and the hay-land looks poor.

May 21 Before the service, we met in the ministers' room to consider an incident in which Mrs Heinrich Siemens had called Mr Gerhard Redekopp a rumour-monger. The Redekopps wanted a reconciliation, but the Siemenses refused, and self-righteousness prevented a settlement. Finally I accepted Mrs Siemens' suggestion that the matter be turned over to the Elder. *Brotherhood Meeting.* A copy of the petition dated May 16 was read to the brethren.

May 25 Day of Ascension. After a short sermon, I continued to catechize our young people. Three youths and a young woman were again unable to answer the questions, but the others responded satisfactorily. The colporteur, Riegel, spent the night with us.

May 30 Tuesday morning, the beloved Elder Gerhard Dyck baptized our young people. The dispute of May 21 was resolved before the service and the parties dismissed in peace. In the evening, Abraham Letkemann brought us the sad news of the passing of our beloved father Gerhard Dyck, who is to be buried on Friday.

May 31 Communion service in church this morning with 153 in attendance. Before the service, the beloved Elder asked the former minister Isaac Klassen to appear before him. Klassen had complained to the Elder in a letter that his case had been handled unfairly, and laid the main blame on me. He also accused Janzen and Harms of hating him without cause, etc., etc. I discussed the matter with Klassen before the Elder arrived, making it absolutely clear that I had not intervened in the dispute and had nothing to do with it in any way. All would be well, Klassen said, if only he were again *allowed to exercise his office*, which had been the main purpose of his letter. The Elder, however, rejected the suggestion. Janzen and Harms, for their part, denied that they had anything personal against Klassen and only wanted him to stop making trouble. Both took Holy Communion.

June 2 Friday. Our beloved father-in-law was buried today. The funeral was in D. Dyck's home, with Elder Gerhard Dyck delivering the funeral sermon. Our father died at six o'clock Tuesday morning.

Sickly for some time, he had been bedridden for only 24 hours and reached the age of 78 years, 4 months, and 22 days. He was married twice. A son and a daughter were born of his first marriage (both are dead), which lasted five years. He was married to our beloved mother for 50 years, 8 months, and 1 day, and they had 7 children, of whom 2 sons and 2 daughters are living. He became grandfather to 35 children, of whom 15 died and 20 are living. In sum, he had 72 children and grandchildren, of whom 33 died and 39 are living.

June 5 Tuesday. We returned to Neuosterwick where, in the afternoon, the Village Mayor's Office made an inventory [of my father-in-law's] estate in the presence of our dear mother and the heirs. There followed the division [of the estate]. I had urged that it not be too strict, given the heavy burden [of mental illness] mother is forced to bear. Several grandchildren (especially one), however, were flatly opposed [to any special consideration for mother]. As a result, almost half the assets were divided, with my wife's share coming to 191 silver R. 66 C. 'Greed is the root of all evil.'

June 9 There was an incident today involving Germans and Jews that may have unhappy consequences. It was my neighbour Olfert's turn to provide the herdsman, and his son Hermann permitted the cattle to wander on to the wheat fields of the Jews. There was a row and compensation will have to be made. We should avoid such disputes with the Jews. Often I wish that I had sold my place some time ago when that seemed possible, but God had other ideas and his will is sacred for me. Yet I would like nothing better than to move away, and the sooner the better. God, bless our petition. I wish that duty did not bind me so closely to the community, but thou, God, wilt see that matters turn out for the best. I commit my body and life to thee, as well as my soul.

June 11 At the close of today's sermon I gave a prayer of thanksgiving for God's protection of our beloved emperor and lord in Paris, the French capital, on May 25.[3] An assassin tried to shoot the emperor, but the treachery failed, by God's will, and we praise and thank him. My colleague delivered a second prayer of thanks in church, and the same was done in all of the churches of the Khortitsa fellowship.

This evening we Germans sold our unwashed sheep's wool to David Mishnik, a local Jew, for 7 silver R. 95 C. a pud. He advanced us 100 silver R., 10 R. of which is mine. We also reached an agreement with the Jewish community to use their shepherd to herd our sheep, at a cost of 1 silver R. per sheep. We had no choice unless we were prepared to risk a repetition of the uproar of the 9th. If the government does not offer us its protection, we will suffer ruin and have to leave this place.

June 12 I delivered 6 puds of wool to David Mishnik for 47 silver R. 70 C. My brother Diedrich came to our Village Office today about a case of deception. Heinrich Krause had sold some sheep to a Jew, confirmed the deal in writing, and accepted an advance. He had then sold the same sheep to someone else for cash, without returning either the agreement or the money. To avoid a lawsuit, Krause paid the Jew 10 silver R. [recompense], a high price for thoughtless behaviour.

June 16 Several matters were resolved today by the Village Office. As compensation for the damage caused by the cattle, Olfert is to cut and gather three desiatinas of wheat and one desiatina of hay [for the Jews]. In the meantime, the grain field in question is said to have grown back completely during the recent spell of good weather. Moreover, because my neighbour Martens' sons had gone at the mowing somewhat roughly (that was wrong and therefore sinful), Martens was made to pay 4 silver R. in damages.

June 17 Saturday. Our dear Lord is not withholding his blessing entirely. We had rain again recently, which comes too late for the hay but may help the grain.

June 18 I preached in church today about Jesus' great love for sinners. Later our children Johann and Helena Andres, his brothers, and sisters and the Johann Klassens were our guests. I was not home, but was told the Klassens and Andreses had gotten entangled in a hard-to-settle quarrel over the gooseberries in the garden. In the evening, David and Jacob accompanied the Andreses to their home. They will help the Andreses cut hay on the Repetten steppe-land leased from the Jews. Andres has undertaken the work for a one-third share.

July 1 Saturday. Our Khortitsa visitors, Bernhard Schellenberg and my brother Heinrich, dropped by on their way to Novopodolsk to extract my brother Diedrich's infected tooth.

July 2 This morning my brother Heinrich preached a lovely sermon based on Luke 15:1–9.

July 19 This evening, the [Mennonite] landowners gathered at Peter v Niessen's place, where we engaged an old Russian as watchman for our potato field for 4 silver R. per month. Finally, we also reached an agreement to sow wheat for the Jew Kakin as compensation for the damage caused by Olfert's careless cattle herding (see June 9, 1867). There was little evidence in the proceedings, however, of Christian love for one's neighbour. Some wanted to avoid any personal responsibility by insisting that Olfert till the three desiatinas (which had been agreed to as compensation) himself. Ultimately, each landowner agreed to till one-quarter desiatina, except W. Martens. He begged off, arguing that he had already paid a fine of 4 silver R. for some grass cut by his children on the field of a Jew. He and I exchanged heated words over this matter, and that caused me anguish. There seems to be only a glimmer of Christianity left among us.

July 20 Three neighbours and I tilled one-quarter desiatina of the wheat field each. Lord Jesus, grant us unfeigned brotherly love. There was more rain again today, and work in the grain fields is also difficult because of the [resulting] weeds.

August 3 We finished cutting the grain today and are grateful to the Lord. A Prussian by the name of Gag has agreed to mow two desiatinas of wheat for me for a quarter-share.

August 8 A wheel on the wagon broke while the children were carting a load of barley. David rode home on horseback and exchanged the broken wheel for a wheel from a wagon borrowed from our neighbour Martens. The broken wheel was repaired for 1 silver R. 80 C. by Martin Harder Sr.

August 11 This morning I carted a load of barley to Herman Peters's groats mill.

August 23 Last summer, many cattle in Novovitebsk died of the plague, all but one belonging to the Jews. The plague has returned this summer, but now the cattle of both Jews and Germans are dying. Today we lost a milk cow. This is a scourge of God. Prior to this outbreak, many horned cattle had come down with foot-and-mouth disease. Even sheep have sore hoofs.

August 28 This morning, the Jewish Village mayor Abraham Bresniak, the Jew Chaim Volbe Shlibakov, my neighour Heinrich Sawatzki, and I assessed the damage to the grain on the hay steppe caused by the merchant Babushkin's flock at 10 silver R.

September 1 Friday. We finished harvesting today.

September 19 I ploughed and sowed two desiatinas to rye on the hay steppe.
September 20 We harrowed three-quarters of a desiatina of rye.
September 21 Thursday. At the market in Sofievka we sold 16½ funt of butter for 16 silver C. per funt.
October 1 Sunday, Thanksgiving. My brother-in-law Died. Dyck accompanied me to Blumengart [Old Colony], where I preached a thanksgiving sermon. My main interest in going, however, was to see how the children of my late cousin David Klassen were getting along in Blumengart, where most of them live.[4]
October 4 Typhoid fever is rampant in the area. This afternoon my wife made the rounds of the ill in Novopodolsk. Diedrich's children Diedrich and Katharina are very sick, Abraham Wiebe and Mrs Isaac Klassen are near death, and the latter is also anxious about her salvation. May Jesus, the friend of contrite sinners, hear the lamentations of her heart. Diedrich Thiessen is sickly, and his wife, who gave birth to an infant daughter two weeks ago, is seriously ill, as are her daughter, Jacob Neufeld's wife, Isaac Siemens' wife, and their son Diedrich. This outbreak reminds me of last year's cholera epidemic. God stands at the door of our hearts and knocks.
October 8 Today's congregation in Novopodolsk was quite large. Before the service, Mrs Herman Peters appeared in my brother Diedrich's office (my two colleagues were not present). She had committed fornication with her brother-in-law Johann Peters before and after her marriage. Recently, before his death in the Grossfürstlich settlement, he had confessed the matter. Amidst a flood of tears, she admitted her guilt. Abraham Breil of Novozhitomir appeared also, Mrs Jacob Reimer having confessed to committing fornication with him in her youth, at the time of the catechism instruction. He would admit only to having touched her private parts, denying the rest. I urged him to be honest, but he stuck to his story. Even the unchaste deed merits severe censure.

Brotherhood Meeting after the service. Mrs Hermann Peters was placed in the ban. Lord, grant her true repentance. Abraham Breil, however, persisted in his story. I exhorted him to repentance. His case has been held over for now and rests on his conscience. The Lord will bring to light what has been concealed and reveal the secrets of the heart. I informed the brethren that the Guardianship Committee had postponed a decision on our petition, but confirmed the communal resolution of the Jews insisting that German landowners would be allowed free pasture for [only] five head of cattle and would have to pay [a fee] for pasturing additional head. This confirmation applies specifically to Novovitebsk. The document goes on to say that if [we] Germans reject the decision, our pasture land of 12 desiatinas per landowner will be sectioned off. It is clear that the [Guardianship] Committee has taken only eight farmsteads [in Novovitebsk] into account. What has happened to the ninth, my own, which the Guardianship Committee had previously confirmed? The brethren agreed to submit another petition to the government in this regard. May the dear Lord bless the undertaking. My brother Diedrich's children are still very sick. Anna is suffering such excruciating pains that she often wails. There were two deaths yesterday, Peter Harms's daughter and Isaac Klassen's wife.

October 14 When I got home last night, I found Bernhard Giesbrecht and Julius Janzen of Kamianka waiting for me. On behalf of Mrs Hermann Peters, they requested her readmission to the church tomorrow.

October 15 Sunday morning. With tear-filled eyes, Mrs Peters begged to be readmitted to the church. Janzen, Giesbrecht and I therefore drove to Novozhitomir, where the service was being held. *Brotherhood Meeting*. Hermann Peters's wife was received back into the church. May the Lord Jesus grant her the grace needed to keep her vow. My brother Diedrich's children are still ill: Diedrich and Katharina seemed somewhat better, but Anna, who has stabbing pains in her limbs and cries out in pain and alarm, seemed much worse. Yesterday my brother sent his son Peter to Khortitsa to fetch Doctor Schellenberg.

October 20 This morning, Gerhard Andres, his wife, two children and I left for the Grossfürstlich settlement, which I had long wanted to see.[5] We spent the night in Nikopol with a Russian, next door to the pharmacy and across the street from the church, resuming our journey next morning in beautiful clear and sunny weather. We were delayed for an hour at the Dnieper crossing while a log boom floated by and the bridge was put back in place. We drove through a truly magnificent area, reaching Michaelsburg at noon. After dinner at the Jacob Hoeppners, we accompanied them on a visit to Reverend Abraham Wiebe in Olgafeld.

October 22 Sunday. I attended service in the [Olgafeld] village school where I delivered the sermon. Since the congregation was small, I spoke about poor church attendance and its results. After the service I had dinner at Reverend Franz Bükkert's home in Georgsthal, where I met Reverend Abr. Wiebe, the teacher Abraham Andres, and their wives. In the evening, I visited the deacon Johann Enz, who suffers from a badly swollen hand, and the teacher Abr. Andres. I spent the night at Peter Lepp's place.

October 23 Monday morning, Lepp hitched up his horses and drove me to the Rosenbach and Alexanderthal colonies, which are next to one another and close to Georgsthal and Olgafeld. In the afternoon, Bükkert and his wife drove me to Michaelsburg, which is about 12 verstas from the other colonies. Here I visited acquaintances and friends, including Diedrich Wiebe and Peter Dyck, the local overseer, whose wife was buried on Friday.

October 24 In response to several requests, a service was held Tuesday morning in the Michaelsburg schoolhouse. The congregation was somewhat larger than the one in Olgafeld, and I preached a sermon on 2 Peter 3:9. May the Lord give to our church his spirit of peace. This settlement is solidly established and prosperous, with many fine and expensively built houses. The harvest this year was excellent, but much fodder and grain was still on the fields. The village of Michaelsburg is noteworthy in that it is set off from the surrounding flat landscape [by hills]. Yet the spirit of discord is present here too and causes great harm. A thousand pities, Lord, that people refuse to reckon the costs of achieving peace. We set out for home in the afternoon, but a long line-up at the Dnieper crossing and a drizzle delayed us considerably, and we reached Nikopol only at sundown. Andres again took his lodgings next to the pharmacy. I spent the night with the Abraham Friesens, where I met acquaintances and friends attending the annual fair.

October 25 After breakfast, we drove up the hill to the marketplace, shopped, and departed late in the afternoon, safely reaching Schöndorf by sundown and home by ten o'clock.

October 30 At two this morning our daughter Helena was, with God's help, delivered of an infant son Jacob. We visited her in the afternoon. She is weak and exhausted and thinks the child was born 11 weeks prematurely.

October 31 Tuesday morning, David and Jacob, who took chicken broth to our dear daughter Helena in Izluchistaia, were relieved to find her feeling a little better. My brother [Diedrich] begged me to talk to his son Peter, who is in great distress about his salvation. May the Lord Jesus be his comfort.

November 1 Wednesday. This afternoon my wife and I attended the funeral for Andres's new-born son Jacob in Izluchistaia, where I delivered the funeral sermon. In the evening, I visited Isbrand Friesen's sick daughter Elisabeth, who was in need of consolation. My brother Diedrich's son Peter, who is gravely ill, wanted comfort and has a strong desire to depart this life and be with Christ. I spent the night moving back and forth between the two sick beds in Novopodolsk.

November 2 At five this morning, Peter died, after being bedridden for a week. I had visited the other sick people, and then my brother Diedrich drove me home. In the evening we had several visitors: Diedrich Friesen and his son from the Molochna colony of Altonau, who have bought a landed estate on the Basavluk River, and Bernh. Rempel and Aron Rempel from the Borosenko colony of Schöndorf, who were on their way to Sofievka to buy rye.

November 4 We drove to Novopodolsk where I made the rounds of the sick, while my dear wife helped the Diedrich Epps prepare for the funeral [of their son Peter]. The children came along to see my brother, who gave them some medicine. Our little Elisabeth has a sore eye, and both of Gerhard's eyes are swollen and painful. It was a restless night.

November 5 We buried Peter Epp, my brother [Diedrich's] son. He was 21 years, 3 months, and 5 days old.

November 7 Johann and Helena Andres helped slaughter pigs today.

November 8 Today was icy, so we separated out the sheep. I have 63 head, including three belonging to Hiebert.

November 17 I borrowed Diedrich's large touring carriage for tomorrow's trip to the Khortitsa colonies.

November 20 My brother Heinrich drafted a petition from the model landowners [in the Jewish colonies] to His Excellency the Minister of State Domains. He encountered the same problems, however, as there was no stamped [eagle] paper available [on which to write our petition] and the ice on the Dnieper River above Einlage was a great jumble. Since it was also impossible to cross over from the Island of Khortitsa, we hired a certain Braun, who made the trip to Alexandrovsk for 2 silver R. In the meantime, my brother drafted the petition.

November 21 Tuesday. The messenger arrived from Alexandrovsk with the stamped paper, but it was the wrong kind and so we sent him back again, doubling our costs. While awaiting his return, I visited my brothers and sisters.

November 27 At a general meeting in Novopodolsk, the [German] landowners signed the petition to His Excellency [the Minister of State Domains]. Thiessen and Krause will mail it tomorrow.

November 28 Tuesday. I apprenticed David to Jacob de Veer of Izluchistaia to learn the wheelwright trade.

December 1 Gerhard Giesbrecht of the Kudashev khutor was here for the night. The Khortitsa District Office had authorized him to negotiate the purchase of the [leased] land on which they live, but he had come too late. Several days ago Kudashev had sold the land to a certain Babushkin from Ekaterinoslav.

December 3 My sore eyes gave me a restless night. Today my right eye was so painful that I thought I could not preach. Yet somehow, with God's help, I managed. After the service, I joined in marriage Heinrich Sawatzki and Aganeta Sawatzki. During the night and all of the following day, the intense pain made me frightened and drove me into prayer, which the Saviour graciously answered. I sent a messenger to fetch some medicine from my brother Diedrich, and this helped a little.

December 15 Friday. This morning, my wife, infant daughter Elisabeth, and I drove to visit my colleague Peter Löwen in Novozhitomir. He has been ill for some time and bedridden now for three weeks. He had stabbing pains in his arms, a swollen face, and difficulty in breathing, even when sitting up. His condition deteriorated in the afternoon (when we sent for his children), entering a critical stage around 3:30. When we went to light the tapers we could find no pulse. His eyes broke around 6 p.m., and when his daughter Mrs Gerhard Wiebe arrived at 7:45 his breathing had stopped. [Earlier,] in answer to my question about the state of his soul, he said he was confident that his sins had been forgiven through Christ's blood. Farewell my brother, thou hast the grace of dying in Jesus Christ. The poor widow and children cried and grieved. I washed the body and with the help of neighbours laid it on the board. After singing, 'Thou Hast Fought the Good Fight,' we went to Peter Janzen's home for the night.

December 16 I wrote a funeral letter for the widow Löwen. My son-in-law Johann Andres took it to Neuhorst for 3 silver R.

December 18 We drove to visit our children the Johann Andreses in Izluchistaia, where I was supposed to deliver a sermon in their parents' home, but encountered great problems. I could barely make out my written sermon and agonized over the matter until the text had been read, when I could see nothing at all. Realizing my dilemma, and sweat pouring from my face, I thought to myself, 'Risk it, in God's name.' So I took off my glasses, placed them on the table, and preached what the Spirit prompted me to say. My Lord and my God, I am grateful to thee for loosening my tongue, for putting words in my mouth and for helping me out of this serious situation. A sobbing in the congregation told me the Lord was standing loyally to his word. I had chosen a text I knew well, Isaiah 40:3–5.

December 20 Wednesday morning we drove to the funeral for the Reverend Peter Löwen where Pätkau preached first and I then spoke extemporaneously about his passing, his age, children, etc. The Lord gave me the needed strength.

December 24 The fourth Advent. A service was held in the home of Jacob Dyck, where I preached a sermon based on Psalm 3:20, again speaking freely because of my difficulty in reading. When I got stuck in the introduction, I called on the congregation to pray. After the prayer and the reading of the text, matters moved along more smoothly, and I thank the dear Lord for this.

December 25 Christmas Day. My eyes are still sore, but I take comfort from the knowledge that our true Helper was born and will save us from our sins. Lord Jesus, help me also with this physical problem. I again spoke freely. My text was Luke 2:6–7.

December 31 The crops were very good. I was able to harvest 38 chetvert of wheat, 22 chetvert of barley, 22 chetvert 2 merka of oats, 7 chetvert 1 merka of rye, and 9 chetvert 4 merka of potatoes. Our wheat measured 10 puds to the chetvert and sold locally for 9 to 10 R. per chetvert. In Nikopol wheat sold for 10 to 11 R. a chetvert, rye 5 to

7 R., barley 4 to 5 R., and oats 3½ to 4 R. a chetvert. This year we again suffered from the cattle plague, which killed two of my four cows. Wool sold locally for 7 R. 95 C. a pud and we sold 6 pud. But our dispute with the Jews remains unresolved. We anxiously await the response of our beloved government to the petition that our entire community sent to His Excellency the Lord Minister. The Khortitsa community is embroiled in a great dispute over land, involving landowners, cottagers, and officials at the District level. This will not be a blessing for the community. Our local congregation has suffered another loss in the death of our colleague, the deacon Peter Löwen. An extraordinary number of people have died and many of the sick are still bedridden. Our faithful Lord continues to bestow upon us heartaches and benefits, both of which are to lead us to repentance. Lord, help us, and be merciful to me, a poor sinner. Forgive me my sins for the sake of thy blood and thy great mercy and grant me peace. Be with me during the coming year, and let me walk with thee until that glorious and blessed eternity. In the evening, I again tried to get Martin Harder Jr to leave the path of drunkenness and depravity for that which leads to eternal life. Touch his angry heart, Lord Jesus, and give him the strength to repent and to mend his ways. Amen.

1868

January 1

Changes in our community [of the Jewish colonies]:

Births	18 males	23 females	41 total
Deaths	11 males	18 females	29 total
Increase	7 males	5 females	12 total

January 2 We took David back to his master de Veer, and when we returned home we found my wife very ill.

January 3 Yesterday my wife suffered from extreme shivering and fever, and today she is without appetite and has a terrible headache. Perhaps it is the 'Drepp.' In the evening I drove to Novopodolsk for an enema.
January 4 My wife is still in bed. In the evening I used Brauchscheidt's method on her sore breast.
January 5 My dear wife is getting better.
January 7 Yesterday I announced the births and deaths for 1867 [in the Khortitsa church]. Of those born during the last century, 8 males and 6 females died and 75 males and 69 females are living. Of those born this century, and joined to the church through Holy Baptism, 32 males and 25 females died and 2248 males and 2263 females are living. In summary, in our church 40 males and 31 females died and 2323 males and 2332 females are living, for a total number of 4655 living.

Births and deaths in the [Khortitsa] community:

Births	305 males	256 females	561 total
Deaths	150 males	99 females	249 total
Increase	155 males	157 females	312 total
Couples married	90 total		

January 14 Sunday. My dear wife is still ill in bed. I again preached freely at today's service.
January 20 This afternoon my neighbour Olfert let blood from my wife's sore breast, and there was less pain.
January 22 Yesterday, our daughter Katharina accepted a marriage proposal from the widower Jacob Neufeld. But when I came home today, after scheduling the engagement for next Tuesday and sending out invitations to Izluchistaia and Novozhitomir, I received a letter from Neufeld withdrawing his proposal. This is sheer folly. I will now have to send out another letter calling the whole thing off. Lord, we entrust this matter to thee.
January 23 I took the sled to Izluchistaia to look after the above matter, and Gerhard Andres kindly sent his son on horseback to let the widow Löwen know that the engagement celebration had been cancelled.
February 5 *School visitation.* We made a start Monday morning.

February 7 Comments regarding the various schools. Only the Kamianka school met my expectations. Bible stories are taught better there, as is arithmetic, which is done badly in the other schools. Singing, which is taught well almost everywhere, is done by ear only in Izluchistaia. That school, however, suffers from general neglect, having opened only recently because of illness in the family of the teacher, Gerhard Redekopp.

February 8 Thursday. This morning, my dear wife, Gerhard, Heinrich Olfert, and I attended a large service in Novopodolsk where our guest, the colporteur Riegel, preached a beautiful sermon based on Luke 1:41–6. I esteem this man more highly now than ever before and ask the Lord to bless his efforts.

February 11 The cold weather kept me from attending any services, which suited me fine. I therefore edified myself by reading Bunyan's *The Holy War*. Stand by me Lord Jesus, and grant me the strength to wage the battle against sin earnestly and to triumph completely through thee, Emmanuel.

February 15 Thursday. I sent a round letter to our villages announcing a collection of seed grain for Peter Löwen's widow.

February 20 The German landowners met at the home of the village mayor v Niessen to discuss whether to accept free pasturage for five head of cattle each or to create a separate pasture land for ourselves. We failed to reach a final decision. The mediation of my brother Diedrich established the principle that each German landowner is entitled to free pasture for ten head of cattle and would need to pay 1 silver R. for each additional head.

February 29 Wednesday morning. Since bad weather again forced us to postpone our trip to Khortitsa, I helped my brother organize his papers. Bernhard Bärgen of [Novopodolsk] is moving on to his own land, so my brother Diedrich purchased his homestead, well, and fences for me for 25 silver R. Bärgen's house will be dismantled and mine erected in its place. This should be one bone of contention fewer between Germans and Jews in Novovitebsk. Late in the evening, Heinrich Krause came to tell me that his wife intended to leave him because he had sold his mill privately to Diedr. Thiessen, rather than at public auction. I talked to the Krauses, and succeeded, with God's help, in restoring a little matrimonial harmony, or so it seemed. Grant them thy peace, Lord Jesus.

March 2 Saturday. We started our move to Novopodolsk by carting four chetvert of wheat and carrying it up on to my brother Diedrich's attic. This afternoon, Heinrich Krause (see entry for Feb. 29) told me that Thiessen refused to nullify the mill sale, and his wife was now determined to leave him. I dropped by again to remind her of her responsibilities, but she only screamed at me. Lord, have mercy on her and on her husband.

March 4 Monday. Today we moved to Novopodolsk, settling temporarily in my brother Diedrich's small carpentry shed. May thy grace go with us, Lord Jesus. I have lived in Novovitebsk for 16 years and have experienced much grief there as well as some joy in good times. Glory to the Holy Spirit.

March 9 I bought Bernhard Bärgen's implement shed for 200 silver R., payable at the end of May.

March 15 My wife, Katharina, Jacob, and Gerhard drove to Novovitebsk to dig out parsnips and flowers for planting.

March 22 Friday morning. We have had to stop ploughing for today, and maybe for longer because it is snowing hard, with a fierce north wind and heavy drifting, such as we have not seen this winter. This storm reminds me of the one that caught me in April 1852. In the middle of that difficult journey, I was forced to spend a day at Abraham Wiebe's place on the Kudashev khutor, far from my worried family in Novovitebsk. I am now at home, well supplied with fuel and fodder, and can watch winter's return without much concern.

March 23 The storm continued until noon yesterday, with a strong north wind. Today the sky is clear, there is a moderate north wind and six degrees of frost. Will the potatoes planted earlier this week freeze? David and Jacob carted our chaff-cutter home from Novovitebsk. This evening we had our daughter Elisabeth vaccinated for the second time at Jacob v Kampen's place.

March 25 Thank God, spring is back again. There is snow still in places, but it is warm with a west wind. The herdsman again drove out the cattle, and the sheep are on pasture. This morning I did a little ploughing in the yard and planted lentils. Later I resumed ploughing on the steppe and seeded some wheat.

March 28 Maundy Thursday. A bright, sunny, and quiet day with two and a half degrees of frost. I walked to Novovitebsk to arrange the start of church services and stopped in to see the Wilhelm

Martens. He was working on the field, but his wife, who is deeply troubled about her salvation, was happy to see me. Comfort her, thou Lamb of God, who didst tremble in the Garden of Gethsemane in order that thy disciples might be filled with courage.

March 31 Easter. I preached a sermon based on Matthew 16:1–7. Thou risen Prince of Peace, rise in my heart and strengthen my faith, for it is weak. This weakness caused me to read a written sermon today. My heart is barren.

April 1 Easter Monday. We had a cold rain at night and better weather later. My wife and I attended service in Novokovno, where I preached an extemporaneous sermon based on Matthew 28:1-10. I read only the text. Thank thee for thy help, Lord Jesus.

April 7 We sang hymn number 108, 'Christ the Lord Spoke Manifestly,' to a cipher tune at the close of today's service. At the second verse, Jacob de Veer walked out in a huff and stayed in the cloakroom until the singing was finished. Peter Peters, who followed him, slammed the door so hard that it sprang open again. De Veer also failed to attend the Brotherhood Meeting, and Gerhard Andres had to present de Veer's daughter for baptism in his place. This causes me great anguish.

April 24 Towards evening Jacob de Veer dropped by and talked about everything under the sun until he finally got to the point of his visit. This was to tell me that he found the cipher music repugnant, and would not attend services as long as it was sung. I asked him to show me one place in God's word which said that music of this kind was harmful, for only that would be reason for prohibiting it. But he could not, of course. I do not like this situation either, quite frankly, because of the conflict it provokes. About 15 years ago, I told Elder Jacob Dyck that unless we prohibited cipher music in the schools we would soon have it in the churches too. The Elder replied that there would be no such ban, and I mentioned this to de Veer. Yet if a person persists in closing his ears there is little that can be done. De Veer finally asked me if we intended to reject his daughter for baptism if he did not present her to the congregation personally. This is not my intention, nor will I do this, if the congregation is of a similar mind. Grant us thy peace, Lord.

April 28 *Brotherhood Meeting.* Our baptismal candidates were introduced for the second time today, and two more young men and one young woman came forward. De Veer and Peters were absent, however, and some members demanded that they be called to account as disturbers of the peace. I suggested we put off doing anything until the Elder arrives, and this was agreed to. Some members were also of the view that children of fathers who refused to attend church next Sunday should not be accepted [for baptism].

April 29 We had an auction this morning of wood and shavings from the attic of our church. I stayed at home and sent David to bring down the wood from the attic. In the evening, we had a visitor from the Grossfürstlich land.

April 30 Tuesday. I sent David to fetch a load of lumber from the Molochna settlement of Heubuden on the Ssolonne [River], to repair Peter Harms's windmill. Maria, Peter, and I walked to Novovitebsk to remove the plate from our stove and to spread out the manure for drying.

May 5 Sunday. Before today's service Martin Harder appeared in the ministers' room to answer for his heavy drinking. He again promised to reform and was allowed to go in peace.

May 6 These days my heart feels burdened, and I am weak and miserable. Dear Lord, be my comfort and do not let me go astray. Grant me wisdom and understanding for my calling and help me to teach our young people. Prepare their tender hearts for true faith through contrition and repentance, that they might become thy disciples. Make them worthy and fit for Holy Baptism.

May 7 The Schellenbergs left for home early Tuesday morning. My dear wife, who has been ill for some time and bedridden for the past three weeks, thought perhaps that the pain and other symptoms indicated pregnancy, but Doctor Schellenberg concluded otherwise. He performed surgery to repair various tears and injuries to her abdomen and prescribed medicine. God is blessing the treatment. She is still weak, but feels much better today, and we are confident she will soon be well.

At church today, I was deeply troubled again about my incapacity and unworthiness for this important calling. Gracious Saviour, fill me with the power of the Holy Spirit. God was gracious to me today. I catechized the nine baptismal candidates, who all said the catechism beautifully and to my satisfaction. Grant that their inner souls might be equally well prepared.

May 14 Tuesday. Elder Gerhard Dyck baptized our young people.
May 15 We celebrated Holy Communion this morning with 100 in attendance, including my beloved wife, who continues to improve from her long-standing malady.
May 16 Yesterday we forgot to collect the money from the church books, and when I went to fetch it this morning Heinrich Olfert had already done so. I therefore [went to him and] collected the 3 silver R. 55 C. for missions and 1 silver R. 94 C. for our church account and delivered the money to my colleague Pätkau. The mission donations will be sent to my brother Heinrich, who will send them on, and the church monies will be used for administration.
May 17 A Jew by the name of Schilling from Novovitebsk was here this morning to buy my house. I asked 200 R., he offered 150 R., and we agreed to discuss the matter further this afternoon. Heinr. Harder, who is now living in the house, wants to buy it as well and offered me the same sum. I decided to put off a decision because I had hoped for a better price and first wanted to discuss the sale with my brother Diedrich.
May 18 Johann and Helena [Andres] and their infant Gerhard dropped in at sunrise after spending the night on the steppe pasturing their horses. They left for Khortitsa after breakfast.
May 20 Early this morning, young people in our village hunted down and killed a rabid dog.
May 21 I am often anxious and sick at heart and think that the hour of my death is perhaps near at hand. Forgive me my sins, Lord Jesus, and grant me peace. Amen. There was much rain during seed-time, but it has been dry since, and the crops are suffering.
May 22 Cornelius Krause and Peter v Niessen asked about submitting our petition to His Excellency the President of the Guardianship Committee when he passes through the area. They also asked about buying my house to use as a school, but since I had entrusted the matter to my brother Diedrich, I did not make a decision.
May 24 We left for the Khortitsa colonies this morning on a business and social trip.
May 25 At Franz Thiessen's store [in Khortitsa] we sold 16 funt of butter at 16 silver C. per funt and did other business with the Orphans' Administration.
May 26 Sunday. I preached the introductory sermon in the Khortit-

sa church. We had dinner and coffee with the Corn. Hildebrands and then drove to my brother Heinrich's for the night.

May 28 This morning I asked Cornelius Epp, head of the Fire Insurance Office, in Rosengart, to lower the insurance on my Novovitebsk cottage to three units (Huben).

May 29 As guardian of David Klassen's orphaned children, I was present at the division of the estate of the late Johann Klassen. The discussions got a little heated, but finally God guided matters to a peaceful resolution.

We spent the night in Neuosterwick where we stopped by to see the widow Elias, where mother is living. Mother was in bed in her usual troubled mental state, and I asked her how she felt and whether she was improving. Then I was again forced to listen to her long litany of complaints, which I will not [bother to] record. I tried to give her a little comfort by saying that our Saviour, the Lord Jesus, was stronger than all her enemies. 'Yes,' she replied, 'the Lord Jesus would have been able to help me if he had not been nailed to the cross.' May God, in his great mercy, be gracious to her.

May 31 Friday morning. We met at Diedr. Dyck's home to decide on how much board Mrs Elias should receive for looking after our mother. Present were my wife and I, the Gerhard Dycks, the widow Elias, her trustee Johann Funk, our mother's trustee Reverend Johann Dyck. Funk, on behalf of Mrs Elias, asked for 125 silver R. board [per year], which she seemed willing to accept. All of this we found quite shocking, and I exclaimed that a child's love was not something one could buy. Moreover, unless we were very careful mother's capital would soon be depleted. Reverend Joh. Dyck offered Mrs Elias a sum of 25 silver R., which was clearly too little, and so we agreed on 100 silver R. I mentioned that if mother were willing [to live with us], we would be happy to look after her for 50 silver R. 'Greed is the root of all evil.'

June 3 Monday morning. My wife, Heinrich, and I toured our grain fields on the Novovitebsk steppe and dug out tulip bulbs and imperial crowns from our garden [in Novovitebsk]. We began shearing our sheep in the afternoon (46 of ours and 3 of Hiebert's), finishing on Tuesday.

June 5 We started ploughing the summer fallow.

June 6 I sold my house in Novovitebsk to the Jew Schmilling

Kisselhof for 165 silver R. He made a down-payment of 65 silver R., with the remainder payable on May 1, 1869.

June 7 I sold my wool (8 puds 33 funt) to the widow Hildbuch and her partner Berka for 6 silver R. 60 C. a pud, making a total of 58 silver R. 25 C. Since we owed the partners 36 silver R. 62 C., we received cash of 10 silver R. and have 11 silver R. 63 C. still coming. Before loading the wool onto a Jewish wagon, we weighed it at Diedr. Thiessen's windmill. I also picked up the large hook from our [Novovitebsk] house. Our renter, Heinrich Harder, protested that I had been unfair in not selling the house to him. To this I replied that I had given him and the other Germans an opportunity to purchase the house by putting its sale off for so long. I do not think Harder has any right to speak in this way since he used our straw as fuel and we had an agreement that he could live there only until after seed-time. His wife was presumptuous enough to suggest that we should have put off the sale for a month to give them time to pick the cherries. The cherries were not theirs in the first place and they were only ours until the house had been sold. In any case, Harder had failed to live up to his part of the bargain, a promise that he would fill in the cracks, whitewash the house, and weed the garden as part of the rent. The orchard is now rank with weeds. Nor should one forget that I had purposely delayed the sale to give the Germans an opportunity to buy the house for use as a school. After all of this, Lord, grant us thy blessing.

June 8 Today we planted the imperial crowns and tulip bulbs in the garden, and the children ploughed the fallow field. We plan ahead in the things of this world. Grant that we might also keep God in mind as we go about our daily work.

June 9 After the service a large crowd gathered at Maevski's dam where a team of horses and a wagon belonging to a German colonist[6] had plunged down the embankment into the swamp. The occupants were safe on the dam, the wagon box floated on the surface, but the horses and carriage had disappeared. Later my son-in-law Andres told me the colonist was from Novozhitomir, the dead horses and front end of the wagon had been pulled out, but the back half of the wagon was still missing.

June 10 The children finished fallowing by noontime. I repaired a wagon to use for carting the sheep dung, which is now dry.

June 11 We started haying today, but the grass is sparse and the weather dry. We dropped off the children this morning at the Novovitebsk hay steppe to mow grass.
June 12 God blessed us with a rainfall, and there was thunder and lightning in the distance.
June 15 Brother Diedrich told me he had received the Guardianship Committee's confirmation of my present house-site in Novopodolsk. I am now formally a model agriculturalist and will not have to live further in a state of constant uncertainty. We lived in Novovitebsk for 16 years, where I experienced much sorrow and vexation and also some pleasant hours. Only God knows what the future holds for us in our new home. Lord, continue to guide me and grant me thy peace.
June 17 We extended our wagon to haul hay, drove the children out to the hayfield, and bought wool for stockings from Spits in Novokovno. On the way home we picked up a load of hay from the Novovitebsk steppe.
June 18 A heavy downpour woke us up at 1:30 at night. It continued raining all day so we had a day of rest.
June 19 Brother Diedrich tells me that the Jews in Kamianka and Novozhitomir have lodged two complaints against the Germans in their villages: for refusing to place their sheep in the common pasture; and for turning loose some calves belonging to Jews. The calves had gotten into the grain fields of the neighbouring nobleman Sharik, causing considerable damage. Both of these deeds were wrong, the former because it violated a government regulation and the latter because it is unchristian.
June 20 I drove the children out to mow grass. Then Maria, Heinrich, and I brought in the last load of hay from the Novovitebsk steppe.
June 22 Today we celebrate the fifth anniversary of our engagement. I thank thee Lord Jesus from the bottom of my heart for thy love and faithfulness. We finished mowing grass and are busy carting it home today. There are a total of only eight small wagon-loads, but we are grateful even for this.
June 23 Sunday. The Johann Andreses say that Isaac Klassen conducted a service and preached a sermon in Peter Peters's home in Izluchistaia this morning. Will this lead to a rupture in our church?

God forbid that it would. Klassen can preach if he likes. I will do nothing to stop him.

June 24 Bernhard Bärgen [the renter in our recently sold house] left today with two wagon-loads of grain, household belongings, and odds and ends, and we are happy to see the last of all of that. What is left is an attic full of his grain, which he promises to remove before harvest-time.

June 27 We are having rainy weather, which may help the late grain. The rye is ripe, but empty, and the barley ears, which we started harvesting today, are very small.

June 28 My heart vacillates between good and evil and is perverse, and my love for the Lord Jesus is lukewarm. Dear Lord, create in me a new heart and do not weary of me, a poor sinner. Grant that I might be able to extinguish all fleshly lusts and be cleansed of the leprosy of sin, through thee.

June 29 We started cutting rye today on the Novovitebsk steppe, along the Novokovno border. I had dinner with the Isaac Friesens in Novokovno, took a nap there, drank coffee, and then drove out to see the children on the field.

July 3 Our children Johann and Helena Andres picked cherries at my brother Diedrich's place.

July 4 We carted home four loads of barley from a two-desiatina field and threshed it by horse in the shed.[7] It was not really worth our while to prepare the threshing floor on the yard and use the threshing stone. The harvest will be poor, but we are grateful for what little there is.

July 5 The rye crop is also poor, probably yielding less than the seed.

July 6 The Village assembly met this afternoon at the home of Isaac Siemens, the Village mayor. Present were my brother Diedrich (the local overseer), Corn. Krause (the fire marshal), and Heinrich Olfert and Isbrand Friesen (the assessors). The fire-insurance system is being reformed. Instead of insuring property by Huben [a land measure] it will now be insured for a given monetary value, with premiums calculated at 1 per cent of that value. I have spent the last two days transposing the insurance books on to new forms provided by the [Khortitsa] District Office, but have not yet finished the job. I have insured my own assets for 950 silver R.

July 13 Today I completed the new fire-insurance books and related tasks, and dropped everything off at my brother Diedrich's place. The entire job got to be quite unpleasant, and I thank God that it is done.

July 17 It started drizzling yesterday afternoon, continuing until late at night, and the children soon came home from cutting oats. Because of the poor pasture, the horses have been trying to break out into the grain fields, and today we sent out horseback riders to help the herdsman keep control. We have usually kept the horses in the corral at night, but recently I have been taking mine in. This afternoon the children returned to the oat field. We are grateful for the rain, which will make it easier for the cattle.

July 24 Monday and Tuesday. My son Diedrich and I each carted home two loads of wheat and rye from the Novovitebsk land. The price for wheat is very high. Today I sold Abr. Unger 11 puds 37½ funt (at 1 silver R. 1 C. per pud), for a total of 13 silver R. 13 C. We have finished cutting the grain. At the start of a thunder and lightning storm late in the afternoon, the children returned from the fields. First there were clouds from the west and then a thunder-cloud from the east with hail. The storm caused severe damage, tearing rafters from Jacob v Kampen's barn, snapping in two rafters from Peter Peters's barn, and toppling and partly destroying sheds belonging to three Jews. The storm also tore open our front door, knocked over and smashed a dish in the front porch, and damaged the sheep-pen.

July 26 At noon today we started threshing wheat with the stone, which was still a little firm in the straw.

July 27 I was at Jacob Friesen's blacksmith shop at noon today when the Jew Mottke came in. He swore at Friesen and caused a terrible row. I gather that Friesen owes Mottke 25 R. and refuses to pay him. I asked Mottke, 'Are you allowed to quarrel and make such a scene on the Sabbath?' Mottke looked at me, muttered something about Friesen being a bad man, and stomped out, all the while still shouting insults. After he had left, I advised Friesen to borrow money from a German and pay off the Jew, which he promised to do.

July 28 My sermon was on the parable of the tares among the wheat. Matthew 13:24–30. Grant, Lord, that no weeds might be found among us.

August 5 This morning we cut the last of the millet (from one-quarter desiatina), and carted the barley home.

August 6 Carted home the last barley (all the grain except the millet is now at home). During the last few days the sun has been blood-red, which earnestly warns of the end of all creation.
August 7 Thunder and rain interrupted our barley cleaning.
August 8 We measured out 13 chetvert 1 merka barley, which, together with the 6 chetvert already harvested, comes to 19 chetvert 1 merka. We have started cleaning the wheat.
August 9 A few nights ago we noticed our potatoes were being stolen so we dug them up, but the crop is quite poor.
August 10 We brought home the last load of millet.
August 14 We cleaned the last of the wheat. Our harvest totals 40½ chetvert from 11½ desiatinas, or an average of 3½ chetvert per desiatina. Earlier we had expected a very poor crop, but our Father has blessed us with a good though not overly rich harvest. Much of Bärgen's grain is still in our attic, so I stored 16½ chetvert of our grain with my brother Diedrich.
August 15 We left today for the Grossfürstlich settlement east of the Dnieper [River].
August 20 The Grossfürstlich settlement's harvest was much like ours: about 3½ to 4 chetvert per desiatina in Michaelsburg and Alexanderthal, 1 to 1½ chetvert (in places up to 2) in Olgafeld and Georgsthal. Their melon patches were exceptional, their soil being better suited to this crop. The price of rye now equals that of wheat, but their rye crop is as poor as ours.
August 27 I left for the Khortitsa colonies, fed the horses on the Kudashev khutor, delivered money to Peter Dyck, head of the Orphans' Administration, and spent the night with the Johann Sawatzkis in Schönhorst.
August 28 I bought 100 white clay bricks for my stove.
September 1 Aged Peter Mantler's wife complained some time ago that Johann Hiebert and his family had given offence to her and her family. Yesterday morning Hiebert made a similar complaint against the Mantlers. The couples met in the home of my colleague Jacob Pätkau to iron out their differences, but only traded insults and nastiness. There seems little room in their benighted hearts for the Word of God. They finally made their peace, but I doubt that it will last.
September 2 David and Jacob drove to Konstantinovka for a load of sand.

September 3 I started building our stove.
September 7 I am anxious about the salvation of my soul, whether the Lord has pardoned my sins. Thou art gracious and merciful, Lord, and I will bow at they feet and seek refuge under thy cross until thou hast answered my prayers.
September 9 Monday afternoon, David and I carted 5 chetvert and 5 merka of wheat to Joseph Mishnik's treadmill in Novovitebsk. He has agreed to buy three loads from us at 10 R. per chetvert. I took [an advance] of 12 R. in cash. I also visited Heinrich Olfert, who sent along 40 R. for the Orphans' Administration.
September 10 We delivered the last two loads to Novovitebsk and have thus sold Mishnik a total of 170 puds of wheat. I received 70 R. cash. The remaining 100 R. are to be paid by Easter 1869.
September 11 Wednesday morning Anton Bärgmann, who travels about selling wares for Franz Thiessen of Neuendorf, asked permission for our Peter to help him out, which I said I would allow until Sunday. Today we carried 8 chetvert of oats on to the attic.

A colonist, who stopped to water his horses at my well, told me about a terrible disaster in the Molochna last week. One evening a fire had broken out in one of Halbstadt's neighbouring villages, and about 50 houses with stacks of grain and fodder had been destroyed. In Halbstadt itself 48 houses were burned to the ground and several women and children had died. May God spare us such a disaster, which is even worse than the one in Neuosterwick (see entry for Aug. 13, 1863).
September 13 I tried to plough this morning, but had to stop because the soil was so dry and hard.
September 16 The possessions of Heinrich Krause were sold at auction to pay off his debts. The prices were fortunately high, and Krause was able to net 1438 silver R. 73 C., more than the sum of his debts. Aron Harder bought his place for 613 R. The sale continued until late in the evening, and I spent the night with the Heinrich Olferts.
September 19 I took barley to Peters's groats mill to be ground.
September 20 There was an uproar on our street this afternoon when a band of gypsies on eight wagons stopped off at the tavern and announced their presence through shameless begging. A district police officer, who was just passing through, forced them to come to

the local station where he took their passports, tied up the leader of their band (who became very abusive), and threw him into jail. The women screamed, and there was general pandemonium. The Jews happened to be in the midst of celebrating the Feast of Tabernacles, and so I was asked to sign the papers [of complaint] in place of the Village mayor. In the afternoon, the gypsies were taken to Kherson as prisoners. I wish from the bottom of my heart that the light of Jesus might shine into their darkened souls.

September 23 The wet weather was short-lived. This afternoon a cold east wind turned into a raging storm, whipping up dust clouds that filled the air and covered our furniture and belongings.

September 25 The weather is cold and there is no snow. It is too dry to plough and we need rain. Today we marked spots in the upper garden where holes for the new trees are to be dug. There is a season for everything, Solomon says, including tree planting. When will my body be buried in the ground like a corruptible seed of grain? I want to belong wholly to the Lord Jesus. Yet my soul is full of terrible doubts, and my heart is disobedient and cold.

September 28 I used our entire rye harvest to sow two desiatinas to rye, which I ploughed in with my three-shared plough.

September 30 Last night three of Johann Klassen's horses, their harnesses, and Peter Mantler's wagon were stolen.[8]

This evening, Gerhard Klassen and Cornelius Mantler appeared at my home in the presence of my colleague Pätkau. Mantler had accused Klassen of digging up his potatoes on the steppe. We decided the two of them should take two neighbours along with them out to the steppe and resolve the matter on the spot.

October 1 Cornelius Mantler told me this morning that Gerhard Klassen had wilfully broken the front leg of his, Mantler's, cow! I decided Klassen should take the cow home with him for the time being, since a decision would have to await the return of the local overseer. Klassen does not deny the charge, but only God knows whether it was done out of hatred or for revenge.

My dear wife, Maria, Gerhard, Elisabeth, and I left for the second auction sale of the belongings of my beloved mother-in-law in Neuosterwick. We spent the night with Klas Heides on Jacob Dyck's estate. I felt at home here even though I could find no trace of the buildings I once knew. This was the place where my blessed father had had a khutor, where I had spent much time as a youth,[9] and where I had also lived for a year with my first wife. Yet everything in this world changes and passes away, save alone the Word of God, which is eternal. Heide had built a new home over the summer, but it was unheated and too cold for the children.

October 3 We bought various household effects at the auction.

October 15 At 5:30 Tuesday morning David left for Nikopol with 4 chetvert of wheat, which he sold for 9 silver R. 30 C. He was home again by 8:30 p.m. the following evening.

October 18 I could not find a good slaughter cow and so was pleased when my neighbour dropped by with the cattle merchant Tripolski and a herd of slaughter cattle. I chose a young Russian cow for 11 R. (if I return the hide), and 14 R.(if I do not).

October 19 Our children the Andreses helped us slaughter the cow, which has excellent meat.

October 24 Last night Martin Harder came by with a letter from Johann Giesbrecht of Neuendorf. It was addressed to the two of us as guardians of Agatha Giesbrecht, the surviving daughter of the late B. Giesbrecht, whom we had hired out locally to work for the Jacob Pätkaus. The letter returned the salary advance [we had sent] and a statement informing us that Agatha did not wish to work in the Judenplan. While loading bricks in Schöndorf last August, I had checked in on Agatha and discovered that her brothers and sisters wanted to see her leave. This fact had prompted us to hire her out in the Judenplan. I gather from the letter that her brothers and sisters are now responsible [for Agatha changing her mind]. The matter is very annoying, so this morning I wrote to the Orphans' Administration, asking them to resolve it. If Agatha persisted in her refusal to take up her position with the Pätkaus, I wrote, Harder and I would be unwilling to continue as her guardians. I forwarded the letter, the salary advance, and Johann Giesbrecht's letter with Abr. Wiebe of the Kudashev khutor. Let them decide what is just.

October 28 Our neighbour Heinrich Sawatzki told us about the terrible fire in the Molochna (see entry for Sept. 11), which he and his wife had witnessed. The fire had broken out at 11 a.m. in [the village of] Sparrau. A strong wind had spread the fire rapidly to Contenius-feld, and within a short time 48 houses had been reduced to ash. He knew nothing about anyone being killed, but said that many had been left homeless.

Since herding was becoming too difficult a thing, a number of us sorted out the sheep flock. We found 69 sheep and 3 rams of ours, but 3 are still missing. We let the rams in among the flock for the night.

October 30 My neighbour Isaac Friesen complained that Jacob v Kampen, the teacher, was being so negligent in his duties that the children were getting into mischief. The teacher, admitting his fault, said he had simply been overworked, and promised to try harder in future.

October 31 Thursday. We fetched plum trees [to plant in our garden] from Julius Janzen's place in Kamianka.

November 2 Cornelius Mantler and I left for Borosenko.

November 3 Sunday. The service in the Schöndorf schoolhouse [Borosenko settlement] was poorly attended because of a dispute between two neighbouring villages. I therefore decided to preach about neighbourly love, the peace of God, and Christ's final judgment. Text, 2 Peter 3:2–10.

There has been a tragic accident in Borosenko involving the Peter Dycks, who lived in the Schöndorf schoolhouse. The couple were loading their wagon with sand from the Ssolonne River, when Dyck left to give someone a hand with their harness. Instead of waiting for her husband to return, his wife went back into the pit for another pail of sand. The side of the pit suddenly caved in, burying the poor woman, who was soon to have given birth. Her horrified husband, after first clawing at the dirt, dumped his wagon and raced to Schöndorf for assistance. But when the neighbours arrived they could only help to dig out the body of the woman and bring it home. Following our customary funeral service, she was buried. Yesterday, however, officials arrived to investigate the accident, and there may be problems because it is illegal to remove a body from an accident scene so quickly. The poor widower is very downcast. A year ago a young woman in Konstantinovka died under similar circumstances, and two years ago my brother-in-law was likewise killed when the side of a sand-pit collapsed on him.

November 6 Tonight the [Novopodolsk] Village assembly, by majority vote, elected Peter Hildebrand as its new mayor for 1869. It also hired the Kamianka teacher Jacob Andres to teach school for the coming year.

November 9 Saturday morning. The overseer, brother Diedrich, assembled the seven model landowners in Izluchistaia (Pätkau and I were also present) to hear a complaint brought against Gerhard Andres for refusing to help repair the schoolhouse cellar. Such disharmony is very discouraging, for it shows that love of God and love of one's fellow man is still weakly developed. We reached an agreement, but it was probably not from the heart.

November 13 David went to Novokovno at 8:30 a.m. to fetch Mrs Isaac Friesen, the midwife, and was back around 9:30. [My wife's] contractions had started yesterday afternoon.

November 14 At 2:30 a.m., Johann Klassen asked the midwife to come quickly and deliver his wife, and brought her back at 5 p.m.

November 15 Since nothing seemed to be happening [with my wife], I took the midwife home this morning. It is ideal sledding weather, with just a little thaw. I brought Friesen's old mare home to board with me since he has little fodder left himself.

November 16 At a general communal meeting with the Fire Insurance Elder, we discussed the question of obligatory communal transports [for victims of fires]. People in Novokovno want to abandon them, but everyone else wants to keep them and signed accordingly. I remained at home, but authorized Isaac Siemens to sign for me. One wonders what has happened to genuine brotherly love, which should seek the welfare of one's fellow man.

November 27 Wednesday. This is a day of special thanksgiving for us. At 7:30 this morning, David went by wagon (it was raining) to fetch Mrs Friesen, the midwife. As we waited, my wife's pains became intense and there were anxious moments before they returned two hours later. With God's help an infant son Johann was born at 3:07 p.m. Accept our heartfelt thanks, and grant that our beloved might be what his name signifies, pardoned by the Lord.

December 7 Saturday. The following appeared before J. Pätkau, my brother Diedrich, and me: Martin Penner (who is a bridegroom), Franz Giesbrecht, and his daughter Maria (see entry for Oct. 7, 1865). Also present were the witnesses Jacob Penner, Gerhard Andres, Peter Janzen, and Cornelius Harms. Martin Penner wants to marry, but first must agree on terms [of child support] with his step-father [Franz Giesbrecht, Maria's father], and with Maria. This was a difficult matter. According to the agreement reached, Martin, on behalf of his and Maria's illegitimate child, is required to pay 45 silver R. to the Orphans' Administration on May 1, 1869. The agreement, signed by all present, was to be forwarded to the Orphans' Administration by my brother. But in the afternoon Giesbrecht returned and demanded that Martin be required to apologize to his mother (Giesbrecht's wife) before marrying. The man wants simply to cause trouble. I ordered [those involved] to resolve the issue by tomorrow.

December 23 While travelling through [the Judenplan], von Schulz, the recently appointed inspector for the Khortitsa colonies, Josephstal, Rubalsk, and Hamburg, stopped for the night at my brother Diedrich's place and left for Khortitsa in the morning.[10] He told Diedrich that His Excellency the President of the Guardianship Committee had made the following awards for meritorious service: 100 silver R. to my brother Heinrich Epp, teacher in the Zentralschule; 50 silver R. to Hiebert, the village schoolteacher in Schönwiese; 50 R. to Jacob Koop, teacher on the Island of Khortitsa; and 25 R. to Cornelius Enz, teacher in Kronsthal. By these means our beloved government is trying to further education among us and raise its level. Faithful Lord, we thank thee for giving us a government that is so favourably disposed towards us, caring for us as a father would care for his children. Bless its undertakings.

December 26 Second holiday. Today I preached a sermon to a large congregation in the home of my neighbour Isaac Siemens and celebrated my 48th birthday. Over the years I have committed many sins and have often been unfaithful. Peter Klassen, the young teacher in Schöndorf, was here overnight and a number of other unmarried people and children were our guests today.

December 30 There has been a grizzly incident in the Grossfürstlich settlement, on the east bank of the Dnieper, involving a certain Quiring and a Dyck (whose wives are sisters). The two men had gotten quite drunk in a Russian village and had quarrelled, but patched up their differences before reaching home. Quiring then decided to follow Dyck to his home to see if he would beat his wife. This Dyck in fact did. Thereupon Quiring, taking a knife, stabbed his brother-in-law in the thigh and between the ribs. Dyck is said to be in danger of his life. Johann Klassen heard this story in the Khortitsa District Office.

December 31 The old year brought important changes in our household. By God's will, I moved, as is noted in this diary, having lived and experienced much pain in Novovitebsk for 16 years. An infant son Johann was born to us. The harvest was reasonably good in Novopodolsk, but much poorer in the other Jewish colonies. Cipher singing caused great unrest among several of our members. Grant us a new spirit and new life in the New Year, O Lord.

1869

January 1 New Year's Day. Changes in 1868: of those in our [Khortitsa] church born during the last century, 10 males and 8 females died and 65 males and 62 females are still living. Of those born this century, and joined to the church through Holy Baptism, 25 males and 35 females died and 2320 males and 2355 females are living. A total of 78 church members died and 4782 are living.

Births and deaths in the [Khortitsa] community:

Births	288 males	297 females	585 total
Deaths	148 males	136 females	284 total
Increase	140 males	161 females	301 total
Married	147 couples		

January 11 After many signs, bad weather finally settled in, and we have 11 degrees of frost. The east wind is so fierce that I cannot see my brother Diedrich's home from my window. May God protect all travellers under way. I had planned to spend the night in Novozhitomir to conduct a service there in the morning, but this now seems impossible. After the storm died down a little, we attended the funeral for Reverend Jacob Pätkau's son Peter, but the coffin will have to be stored for the time being.

January 12 The storm piled up huge snow-drifts everywhere. After breakfast, the children hitched up the sleigh, and Peter and I set out in deep snow over a scarcely recognizable road. Large drifts [in Izluchistaia] made it impossible for us to enter any yard, so we drove down the side street, past Heinrich Siemens's bakeshop, to the Andres' place. After taking my horses out of the traces and hitching up old Gerhard Andres's team, we left for Novozhitomir. It was again difficult finding the road since the deep snow made travel almost impossible. The yards in Novozhitomir were likewise blocked, except for Cornelius Harms's place, where the service was to be held. We arrived there at 9:30 in the morning. Harms immediately announced the service, which was attended by 7 males and 11 females.

Reverend Isaac Klassen is reported to have written a long letter to the Elder complaining bitterly about me. The most serious charge is that the congregation would like Pätkau and me removed from office. The man is going to such great extremes to vex me, but even if what he said were true (with God's consent), I would not be deeply unhappy. Yet I know that the church does not wish me to leave. Conflict over the cipher music has won Klassen a few friends. May the Lord examine this matter and resolve it to our benefit.

January 13 Isaac Friesen told me that Isaac Klassen was spreading rumours that a fiddle had been played and there had been dancing at a wedding at brother Diedrich's place. I had supposedly defended these goings-on in a sermon. What lies!

January 19 While travelling to [the] Borosenko [settlement] with my neighbour Isbrand Friesen, he asked me why I was still preaching freely and not reading my sermons since he had assumed that I had done the former because of my sore eyes. Since these were now healed I should again read my sermons, as that 'was more fluent and therefore better.' What should I do, Lord? Reveal thy will to me and I will do it gladly, for I seek thy glory and not my own.

[In this whole matter of preaching,] I feel very much like the man who was ill, suffered dizzy spells, and could not walk alone. He therefore started getting around on a pair of crutches he had built for himself. Many who saw him go by applauded, and this filled him with pride and a desire to walk again on his own. But the thought of walking unaided made him feel even more dizzy, so he grasped his crutches more tightly than before, and even abandoned the idea of ever again walking alone. This made him even more anxious, and soon he felt ill from the top of his head to the soles of his feet and was filled with thoughts of his own unworthiness.

Yet the physician of all physicians graciously looked down upon this poor man in his desolation and sent him an illness that made his crutches quite useless. The man now realized he would have to manage on his own. But he had come to love his crutches and was petrified at taking a first step for fear of stumbling and falling. And when he was told to go forward, his heart was troubled. Then, however, he learned that the physician of physicians had strength for the weak and would teach him to walk again. He took a first hesitant step, and despite the occasional dizziness was surprised that he could walk with the help of his physician, who stayed at his side. From time to time he would again feel less sure of himself and stop and gasp for breath, but then he continued on his faltering way.

But now some people said that they really preferred that he walk on crutches because they were used to seeing him in this way. The more reasonable ones, however, agreed that it was only right for him to throw his crutches away since he could now walk alone. And in the innermost part of his soul the man felt the physician's approval, *who had helped him.*

January 25 Saturday. In a letter which I received this morning, my nephew Heinrich Rempel of Michaelsburg writes that Peter Hiebert of Novozhitomir had said that I no longer preached the Word of God since starting to speak extemporaneously. This had now become a matter of ridicule, etc., etc. What a painful and crushing experience. Even though my written and freely spoken sermons have the same content, I will have to go back to reading my sermons again. Lord, relieve me of my calling, if that is thy will. Strengthen my faith, if it is not. Wherever he goes, Reverend Isaac Klassen makes an issue of the cipher music, causing unrest. He is also said to have written a long letter to Elder Gerhard Dyck alleging that the congregation would like to dismiss me and my colleague Pätkau. We have not heard this officially. I would gladly retire, if that were God's will, but I am also prepared to continue preaching. Help me, Lord Jesus.

January 26 Sunday. I stayed home today while Reverend Pätkau preached in Novovitebsk. Where is my Jesus, whom I desire? Where is my beloved? Where has he gone, after whom my soul doth pant?

In the afternoon we attended the funeral for Abr. Unger's infant daughter Katharina who died at the age of 1 year, 3 months, and 27 days, and I delivered a written funeral sermon. Lord, thou knowest how this weighs on me and that if I were to die soon (yes, very soon) and end my life blessedly, my soul would praise thee.

February 2 I preached a sermon on the joy of faith, but it was again a written one. If this is adequate, God, grant me thy blessing, yet there is travail in my innermost being, and I feel unworthy and unfit for preaching. May the Lord reveal his will.
February 3 Monday. The weather continues mild, and if there were grass, we could have pastured our cattle right through the winter. Most of the huge snow-drifts from the January 11 storm have melted, except for a few that remain among the mulberry bushes.
February 9 I preached a sermon on God's call, 'Adam, where art thou?' Genesis 3:9. The opening and closing hymns were sung to cipher melodies, this being the first time that this has happened in Novokovno. All of this caused me great surprise, since only last summer people had walked out of church on this account. Unrest among us will only end when this issue finally subsides. God, give us thy help.
February 11 *School visitation* in Borosenko. At the request of my brother Heinrich and Elder Gerhard Dyck we visited the Schöndorf school. It is taught by Peter Klassen, a former stipend student [in the Khortitsa Zentralschule], whom we had agreed to take under our wing. Accompanying us were people from the [Village] Mayor's Office. Subjects taught: Bible stories from the Old Testament, reading, arithmetic, penmanship, and singing, which the children did well. But I had expected more from the teacher, so I took him aside and reminded him of his duties. (He is still young and a little inattentive.) He asked me if I would visit the school again before Pentecost to observe the examinations, and I promised I would try.
February 14 Desperately short of cash today, I tried again to collect the 110 silver R. from Joseph Mishnik for the wheat. He was out, so I borrowed 3 silver R. from Corn. Krause, who can collect it from Mishnik.
February 18 Tuesday. My brother returned today from the Khortitsa colonies with distressing news about Heinrich Penner of Khortitsa, the aged, 86-year-old patriarch who had been minister since 1812. Penner suffers from cancer of the cheek, which spread rapidly last fall. In his illness, Penner confessed to having committed fornication with his blind stepdaughter Agatha Bärg soon after becoming a widower more than 30 years ago. Human corruption and misery seems to know no bounds. Yet human tribulation can also help lead us to eternal life. Grant that I might walk the narrow path, dear

Saviour. Forgive me my sins, extinguish my evil deeds, cleanse me, and grant me thy peace.

February 22 Heinrich Olfert (who does this now) vaccinated Elisabeth and Johann against smallpox (from Heinr. Harder's child). We hope God will bless this fourth attempt with Lieschen [Elisabeth].

February 26 Wednesday. We have wonderful spring weather. I started ploughing with the one-shared plow, and it went well. We finally put the sheep out to pasture in the afternoon.

February 27 Mist and frost forced us to stop ploughing, but we sent out two people to work on the dam.

February 28 Fog this morning, a south wind, and temperatures of four degrees. We ploughed with our one-shared plough, planted plum trees, and sowed lettuce.

March 1 We put in the last trees in the upper garden, a total of 107 plum trees and 12 cherry trees.

March 3 We started spring seeding today. Grant us thy blessing, Lord Jesus.

March 4 Rain this morning. The herdsman drove out the cattle, including our two yearlings. Isaac Friesen of Novokovno came by to pick up a load of straw fodder from the Pätkaus and his mare, which we boarded in winter.

March 6 Thursday. At 11:30 last night we were awakened from our sleep by a knock at the window. There stood Wilh. Martens's son Wilhelm who asked us if we knew the whereabouts of Heh. Olfert's daughter Margaretha, who had not come home from herding sheep last night. We did not, and he continued on his way. Restless with worry, we entreated the Lord in prayer. After breakfast, the ploughers went out to the field and I walked to Novovitebsk, my heart trembling as I entered Olfert's house. What a rejoicing that was when I saw the lost child standing there. Germans from Novovitebsk had searched frantically for her all night, finding her at daybreak at David Friesen's place in Novokovno.

The story was as follows. Towards evening, the 13-year-old Margaretha's parents had sent her out to help bring in the sheep. An old ewe had not been able to keep up with the flock, however, so Margaretha had said to her brother that he should go on ahead without her. Then the ewe had collapsed, and was unable to get up again, so the girl had sat down beside it and started singing happily, fully expecting someone to come by soon. Suddenly she realized that a wolf was approaching from the valley and she started running in terror. (That a wolf had indeed been there was proved by the fact that when searchers came to that spot a little later they found no trace of the old ewe.)

Fleeing, Margaretha had lost her way. She came to a large pond, which she walked around, and finally met up with a Russian who was loading sacks and feeding his horse. The man had taken her by the hand, led her to the Chumak road, and told her, in broken German, that she was about 'eight verstas from Shimar.' Running in that direction, she had finally reached Novokovno where Jews had directed her to the Germans. Around 11 p.m. she had reached Abraham Friesen's home, where the search party had found her and taken her to her anxious parents. Our loving Father had sent his guardian angels to protect her from all harm and to lead her home.

Harder hired our son Jacob to plough at 10 silver C. per day.

March 11 It rained Tuesday morning and then cleared enough in the afternoon for me to plough and seed a half-desiatina of wheat. I borrowed Tupke the tailor's horse, and I will repay him by ploughing two desiatinas of land. My wife took little Johann to the old Mantlers for a second smallpox vaccination, after his first vaccination of February 22 had failed. Towards evening, we took out the storm-windows and carried them on to the attic.

March 16 Sunday. Today we rest from our work and from the problems of earning our daily bread. According to God's fourth commandment, it is also a day when our draught animals are to rest, gathering new strength for their work. It is the Day of the Lord, set aside for the inner man, when our minds and spirits are to rest fully in him. The day should be spent in song and prayer, strengthening our weary spirits so that we might walk the path of the cross until our day of death. Then we will have eternal and perfect peace through Christ's atonement.

March 23 We attended the funeral for teacher Gerhard Redekopp's son Jacob, who died accidentally at the age of 12 years, 7 months, and 25 days. The tragedy occurred last Friday morning, while the boy was helping the Johann Bärgens of Izluchistaia to seed. On the way to the field, the boy had apparently tried to sit down on the plough. But whatever the case, Bärgen, who was on the wagon, suddenly heard a terrifying cry, 'Whoa, Whoa!' He immediately brought the horses to a stop and found the boy lying in front of the plough wheel, bleeding profusely from a deep cut from the ploughshare. Doctor Israelsohn was called, but arrived too late to help. The boy was dead within an hour.

March 25 My brother Heinrich writes: 'You will have heard of Reverend Heinr. Penner and his confession. In his old age he has been barred from the ministry. This was not our original intention, since he was no longer in office. Blind Agatha has been placed in the ban. She confessed to committing fornication not only with Reverend Heinr. Penner but also with the late bachelor David Dörksen, with a man from the Bergthal colonies and with Peter Hildebrand of Khortitsa. The matter will likely come before the brethren tomorrow since the blind woman will undoubtedly ask to be readmitted [to the church], and Hildebrand will be placed in the ban. It is unspeakably sad how sin can rule over us. "Lord, lead us not into temptation."'

March 30 Our son Peter returned from helping the Harders seed. He earned 2 R., half of which he paid for a merka of lentils.

April 1 We worked up tailor Janke Tupke's melon patch. We have had dry frosts and cold winds this spring, a serious danger during the lambing season. If one does not take great care, the wet little lambs can die quickly. The pasture is growing slowly, and I have little fodder left.

April 7 Monday. This morning David again failed to collect the money from Joske [Mishnik]. I therefore borrowed 8 R. from Corn. Thiessen for a week. We left for the Khortitsa colonies this afternoon with three chetvert of wheat.

April 8 We reached Neuendorf by noon, where I had the wheat ground at Wilh. Redekopp's treadmill.

April 12 Saturday. The Lord finally sent us rain, and our hopes are again high for a good crop. For a poor landed peasant, rich harvests are a great blessing and crop failures a tragedy.

April 15 We ploughed in the morning, planted millet and onions, and harrowed in the afternoon. We also seeded onions in the yard.

April 17 We tried again to collect the money from Mishnik. I am desperately short of money this year and have serious problems.

April 19 Hoof-and-mouth disease is rampant in Novokovno, where fodder supplies are virtually gone. Cattle in Novopodolsk also suffer, but I still have a little fuel and fodder left. One values such blessings when one has suffered shortages oneself.

April 20 Easter. Thou risen Prince of Peace, let me rise to serve thee in the strength of thy suffering.

April 22 Corn. Krause paid me 10 silver R. for preparing the fire-insurance books last summer. This came at an opportune time when I was desperately in need of money.

April 23 I borrowed 20 silver R. from Peter v Niessen, who will collect it from Joske [Mishnik].

April 25 Friday. We harrowed the potato patches and helped dig the village well. The horse ponds are dry, and we badly need water for our cattle. Many cattle continue to suffer from hoof-and-mouth disease.

May 5 A young woman appeared before the Ministerial Committee to confess that she had defiled herself with an animal (a dog) and committed fornication with a young man before the time of her baptism. Her contrite attitude showed genuine repentance, and she was allowed to go in peace. A young man, who had started a fight during a wolf hunt, appeared also. He gave the appearance of being penitent, but his attitude was quite different from that of the young woman. Nevertheless, he asked the brotherhood for forgiveness and was allowed to go in peace.

May 11 *Brotherhood Meeting.* The articles of faith were presented for the last time and the baptismal candidates (13 young men and 4 young women) were presented to the congregation.

May 13 Tuesday. There was rain again last night, and we look forward to a good crop. My brother Diedrich and I were in Novovitebsk this morning to mediate several disputes. Wilhelm Martens assembled the Germans, and we successfully resolved a boundary dispute between Heinrich Olfert and Peter v Niessen. Our best efforts failed, however, to make peace between Jacob Dyck and Cornelius Krause. Four years ago these men had quarrelled over some sheep and they have been at serious loggerheads ever since. Neither was ready to make peace. We pleaded with them, and particularly with Jacob Dyck, but were rebuffed. Lord, thou didst forgive thy tormentors and murderers. Soften also this stony heart that it might find peace.

May 14 Wednesday afternoon we looked at the grain. Drought had earlier stunted growth, but recent rains give us renewed hope.

May 19 Hostile actions by the Jews in regard to pasture for our sheep prompted this evening's meeting of the German landowners. During our visit to the Khortitsa colonies, the Jews had locked the gate of the sheep-pen. My brother Diedrich had ordered that it be forced open and the sheep let out to pasture. After my brother and Unger had consulted the local supervisor, the Jews reduced their demands. They now insist only that the sheep belonging to the German leasehold farmers (not of the model farmers) be banned from the [common] pasture. This, too, is very cruel. I left the meeting and went home.

May 20 We separated the sheep (57 sheep and 23 lambs), and began shearing them in the afternoon.

May 23 Martens and Olfert accompanied me to collect the 50 silver R. 30 C. from Joske that he still owes me for the wheat. He still did not have the money, but signed a promissory note for it on stamped [eagle] paper, which I had along.

May 25 At 3:30 this morning a son was born to our children the Johann Andreses. In the afternoon, my wife, Heinrich, Gerhard, Johann, and I drove to visit them in Izluchistaia.

May 31 Early this morning, Pätkau and I left to observe the examinations being given in Peter Klassen's school in Schöndorf, Borosenko settlement. They were from 9 a.m. to 1 p.m. Since our last visit in winter (see entry for February 11), the school has much improved.

June 3 Before the service, the Elder failed to make peace between Jacob Dyck and Cornelius Krause, but the reconciliation took place the following day.

June 4 Holy Communion was celebrated in our church with 132 participants. In the afternoon, my wife and I accompanied our guests to Borosenko.

June 5 Thursday morning, the Elder celebrated Holy Communion with 67 members of the Borosenko congregation.

June 6 I sold our wool to David Mishnik for 5 silver R. per pud. He offered me an advance of 20 silver R., but had only 18 R. on hand. He promised to pay me the 2 R. in a few days.

June 7 Towards evening we toured our fields and are deeply grateful for the excellent prospects.

June 11 I delivered 7 puds and 22 funt of wool to Mishnik.

June 21 It rained steadily all evening and night. We received an invitation this morning to attend the engagement festivities for the widow P. Löwen and widower Abraham Penner. Peter carried the [round] letter on to Novovitebsk. With the steady rain, we borrowed my brother Diedrich's covered wagon, teamed up with the Johann Klassens, and managed to reach the Novozhitomir celebrations over muddy roads.

June 22 On their way home to Ebenfeld, the bridal couple had their marriage agreement witnessed by my brother Diedrich. Should he die first, the widow's assets are to go to her children, and she will receive one-sixth of his assets, excluding land. In the event that she predeceases him, this sixth part will also be inherited by her children.

June 23 Several of us sold our sheep this morning. Mine went for 20 silver R. a head, which is not high.

June 24 Tuesday. David, Jacob, and I drove to the annual fair in Sofievka. On the way home we passed through several Russian villages looking for slaughter pigs, but they were all too dear. At the fair I met Abraham Friesen, who had contracted to share-crop hay-cutting on the Kudashev steppe. He was happy to divide up the job, so I decided to devote the week to haymaking. In the afternoon I therefore left home with the hay-cutters, David, Jacob and Peter, and their tools and provisions. We had a long wait for Friesen in Novokovno. In the meantime people came by from the Kudashev khutor and took the children along to the hay-land. I returned home with Gerhard and Lieschen.

June 26 I drove Maria, Diedrich, and Heinrich to the Kudashev land to rake hay. The grass was so sparse, however, that we called it quits. The mowers put away their scythes, raked up what little there was, and we returned home with our belongings.

June 30 Monday. The start of the grain harvest. We began cutting barley.

July 2 It rained again. We went out looking for slaughter pigs, finding several in the villages of Budakov and Sharika, and bought a boar for 10½ silver R.

July 3 The barley was not ripe so we came home to prepare the threshing floor. I had two loads of barley carted home in the afternoon. Katharina, Maria, and Diedrich weeded the melon patch.

July 4 After bringing home another load of barley, we threshed the three loads. A thunderstorm stopped the threshing, so we got out the fanning mill and cleaned barley.

July 5 We began cutting oats.

July 6 Wet weather. We drove to church, where the congregation was only small.

July 7 Yesterday my wife came down with a blinding headache and today she was seriously ill. We fetched a vomitive from my brother Diedrich, which seems to have helped since she started working around the house again.

July 8 Tuesday. My wife's illness was back with force today. She first felt hot and then cold, and had a fierce headache all night. May our Saviour help. We cut the last of the barley and continued cutting the oats.

July 12 Saturday. I thought my wife was finally over the fever, but it came back this morning, though less seriously. This is very hard on her, on our infant Johann, whose mother's milk is limited, and for the rest of us in the harvest. We cut the last of the oats today.

July 20 Review of the past week. It has been very busy. All the grain ripened at about the same time, and much of it is still in the blade. We had 12 desiatinas of uncut wheat at the start of the week and 2½ desiatinas remains uncut now. At noon Monday, the Lord sent such a heavy shower, with thunder and lightning, that we had to return home. There was rain again on Tuesday, but we continued our field-work. When it stopped there was sweltering heat, which made tying sheaves a little easier. The intense heat continued all week. Yesterday we examined the melon patch. We then drove to pick up the children who were out stooking and had been caught in a drenching thunder-shower. We were overtaken by another shower on the way home. Our merciful Lord has cured my wife of her fever.

July 22 We finished cutting grain and started carting it home.

July 23 David, Jacob, Peter, and Diedrich helped Joh. Andres with his mowing while Maria and I carted oats home.

July 24 Thursday. We cut lentils, did some after-raking on the oats field, and carted grain home.

July 25 All of the oats is home, and we have started carting rye. We brought the onions in from the steppe this afternoon.

July 28 We started threshing wheat. In the late afternoon the children threshed the cut millet.

August 1 Friday. There was a heat wave for several days, but a strong north wind brought down the temperatures last night. We learned we could not use the nobleman's horses today (they had been promised to my neighbour), so we restacked the sheaves that had already been laid out for threshing in the morning. Luckily, we could use two of our horses in the barn to cart wheat.

August 2 Last night the children slept out in the yard but came in when it started to rain. The rain turned into a downpour by noon, with a strong northwest wind. The cattle hovered around the pen for protection and had to be driven back to the village. We even took in the horses from the pen, and the yearling, old mare, and colt from the field. It finally got so cold that we had to light the stove. I have never experienced such cold at this time of year, and I am afraid the grain may have been damaged. The watchman on the Russian melon field in Izluchistaia was so drenched and cold that he sought shelter in our house. The houses of the Jews are so cold that a Jew by the name of David from the Chortamlik inn stabled his horses in our barn and warmed himself at our stove. We drove the sheep into the pens, and they stood there all day without feed. The wind has even driven rain through the gables, and we have had difficulty in keeping the attic dry.

August 3 Sunday morning. It is still raining, but the wind has shifted to the southwest. Our Russian visitor said goodbye after breakfast and left for his home in Sofievka. Our heated room is comfortable, and my dear wife has asked me to record the rarity [for this time of year] that she brewed coffee for breakfast in the chimney and cooked lentils for dinner in the oven. The rain stopped at 9 a.m., and we let the sheep and cattle out in the afternoon. I wonder what the damage will be.

August 4 We started cleaning wheat in the shed and then drove to Sofievka for lumber. There the storm had damaged the market-place, forcing it to close early.

August 5 The rain has given us much extra work. The piles of wheat sheaves had been almost dry, and now we have had to take them apart and set them up again to dry. On the field we turned over the wheat sheaves and found that many had started to germinate. We measured $11\frac{1}{4}$ chetvert of [clean] wheat.

August 6 We worked hard until noon cleaning wheat and carrying it on to the attic. We have a total of 28 chetvert 5 merka. One bin alone contains 24 chetvert. In the afternoon, we started carting barely and threshing it and also put the wheat [sheaves] together again.

August 9 The barley is home and threshed.

August 12 Tuesday. We cleaned the barley and measured out 47 chetvert.

August 15 Because of the rainy weather, today's Russian Orthodox holiday turned into a holiday for everyone. An evening thunderstorm grew fiercer through the night. A violent thunderclap around 1 a.m. awakened us and we got up and lit a lamp. This morning water was running in torrents along the ground.

August 16 Saturday. We cleaned 8 chetvert and 1 merka of wheat and have harvested a total of 36 chetvert 6 merka.

August 19 We brought home the last of the wheat yesterday and the last of the millet and lentils today. This concludes the harvest. Lord, we thank thee for thy grace.

August 24 After receiving a complaint from his mother, I asked David Penner to appear before me (summoned by his brother Jacob). But his story was quite different from that of his mother. I urged the Penner brothers to be reconciled with their mother, but David said that the problem was his stepfather, Heinrich Siemens, who had pursued his sister Maria with evil intentions. And though the mother now made light of the matter, she had herself reported as much to the teacher Johann Banmann earlier. We called in the teacher, and he confirmed the story. I therefore ordered that Jacob Penner, Gerhard Andres, Heinrich Siemens, and his stepsons David and Johann Penner appear before the Ministerial Committee this coming Sunday. Maria, who is still a minor, is also to be questioned.

August 25 Mrs Heinrich Siemens told me she did not think her husband should have to come to Novovitebsk about such a trivial matter. She admitted, however, that he had harboured illicit intentions towards her daughter and had pursued her. This was obviously not a trivial matter and deserved a reprimand. It is hard to deal with questions on the basis of God's Word when people choose to follow their own minds. If only help would come from Zion and God redeem his sinful people.

August 31 The following were summoned by Gerhard Andres and Jacob Penner to appear before today's service in the ministers' room: Heinrich Siemens and his stepsons David and Johann Penner. The

Penner brothers were at odds with one another in regard to their mother, but agreed that their stepfather had tried to take advantage of their sister Maria, who had reported this to Johann Penner's wife. We asked the brothers to leave the room and called in Siemens. He denied the whole story regarding his stepdaughter and appealed [to the testimony of] his wife. She seemed to have an understanding with him to disavow the episode. Jacob Penner reported questioning Maria. She confirmed that Siemens, who had tried to take advantage of her in every conceivable way, had left her at a loss as to what to do. She is determined to leave her parental home. Siemens, who persisted in his denial, was asked to absent himself. The Penner brothers returned and were reconciled with one another. David promised to apologize to his mother and move out of his parental home, as his parents wished. The testimony of the brothers showed their mother was not quite blameless in the episode, nor scrupulous about the truth. The two were allowed to go in peace.

Brotherhood Meeting after the service. Siemens appeared and solemnly affirmed his innocence. Lord, the man is so hard. His wife admits it, his under-aged daughter testifies it is so, and he continues to ...! This is the second time he has been under suspicion. The charges remain and rest on his benumbed conscience. Dear Jesus, thou hast power enough that even the mighty and hardened sinners shall succumb to thee. Look down upon us in grace and arouse the indifferent to repentance that they might find salvation in thee.

September 1 I wrote to Elder Gerhard Dyck asking him to inform Joh. Wiebe of Neuhorst, [Maria Penner's] guardian, of the scandal involving Heinrich Siemens and his charge and of my recommendation that Maria be removed from her stepfather's home.

We finished threshing wheat today.

September 3 We cleaned wheat yesterday, there being much grain in the yard. As we saw a lightning storm approaching from the west we redoubled our efforts, working feverishly until 9 a.m. With the storm almost upon us, we carried the remaining wheat into the shed (it was still mixed with a lot of chaff) and covered up what was left [on the threshing floor]. We also carried five chetvert of wheat on to the attic. Today we continued cleaning and measuring wheat.

September 4 Thursday. This morning we continued cleaning wheat and measured out 39 chetvert 2 merka. There is still much wheat mixed with chaff, but I am out of storage space and will have to cart some grain to Nikopol.

September 5 Friday. We left for Nikopol with 5 chetvert of wheat, which we had sold by nightfall to the Jew Nochim Palakov for 9 silver R. per chetvert. Wheat prices are falling.

September 9 Tuesday. David and I bought 2 boars for 10 silver R. apiece in Sharikov. They are very expensive.

September 12 Friday. We measured out the last wheat, 12 chetvert 2 merka, for a total of 78 chetvert 2 merka. We have harvested 33 chetvert of potatoes.

September 14 I preached to a fairly small congregation in the home of the late P. Löwen in Novovitebsk. Most people were under way, carting grain to Nikopol.

September 16 Our son-in-law Joh. Andres carted wheat to Nikopol.

September 17 David left at 3 a.m. for Nikopol with wheat.

September 18 David returned this evening, having sold the wheat for 8 silver R. per chetvert.

September 19 We again failed to collect the money from Joske Mishnik. I forwarded 100 silver R. to the Orphans' Administration with the Wilhelm Funks of Rosenthal.

September 23 Tuesday. Gerhard and I delivered 1 chetvert of barley to Hermann Peters's groats mill in Kamianka.

September 29 We seeded two desiatinas to rye and ploughed and harrowed it in.

September 30 Yesterday I paid my debt of 9 silver R. 27 C. at the lumberyard in Sofievka. My brother-in-law Diedr. Dyck was along to hunt wild ducks. Taking a roundabout route home, we saw many wild fowl. My brother-in-law was able to get off four shots and hit a flock, but we could not find any of the ducks in the grass and weeds. He also shot ducks on the local village pond, but ran out of shells, and that ended the sport. I was happy that the hunt had given our visitors such great pleasure.

October 5 Thanksgiving. I preached a sermon today on the subject of harvest blessings and the thanks we owe to God. Acts 14:17. Lord, bless us as thou hast blessed our fields. Grant, too, that we might reap riches for eternal life.

October 8 We left at 6 a.m. on a visit to the Khortitsa colonies, going by way of the villages of Kudashev and Tripolski, where I dropped off some money that my brother Diedrich had sent along for the Diedrich Dycks.

October 12 I attended service with brother Heinrich in the Khortitsa church, preaching a sermon based on 2 Peter 3:9. This afternoon, the Baptist Elder Oncken from Hamburg[11] preached a missions sermon to a large congregation. I also saw Elder Gerhard Dyck, whom the Lord is putting to a hard test. After recovering from a serious illness himself, the Lord took away his wife.

October 13 Monday. We visited Uncle Jacob Hoeppner on the Island of Kh[ortitsa], where we met the Johann Friesens of the Molochna. We spent the night in Khortitsa with the Corn. Hildebrands.

October 14 We visited the Bernhard Schellenbergs and spent the night with the Jacob Pätkaus. The Schellenbergs had an accident affecting his sister, the widow Penner, who lives with them. On her way home from Blumengart her horse fell while coming down the hill into Rosenthal, broke a leg, and had to be shot.

October 22 At 5 a.m. David and I left for Nikopol with a load of wheat, which we sold to David Bärgen for 75 silver C. per pud. We spent the night at his place.

October 23 We had breakfast at the Abraham Friesens' in Nikopol, did our shopping, and were home by nightfall. Shortly before her delivery this morning, Mrs Wienz, the wife of the schoolteacher in Nikopol, died. Considering the hustle and bustle in Nikopol, one wonders how anyone here would find time to die. And yet ...

October 24 The road to Nikopol was a difficult one, but on the way home it was dry and smooth from the traffic streaming in to the fair from all directions.

October 28 Today my brother Diedrich and his wife helped slaughter the boar. The Johann Andreses arrived early in the afternoon and stayed for the night.

October 31 My wife and I helped the teacher Jacob Andres slaughter two pigs.

November 3 Snow covered the ground this morning, but was gone by noon. We kept the horses and cattle at home, put up the storm-windows, and cleaned and carried 9½ chetvert of oats on to the attic. Jacob Andres started teaching evening school tonight. Peter and Diedrich are attending, and tuition is 1½ silver R. per child, plus lighting oil for the teacher.

November 4 Tuesday. The snow on the ground this morning soon melted, and we drove out the cattle again. David and Jacob carted a load of 'Dreikant' and barley to the windmill in Novovitebsk to be ground into horsefeed. The road was muddy. I bought a pud of tallow for 4 silver R. and two front quarters of beef weighing 4 puds 25 funt for $1\frac{1}{2}$ R. per pud from the Jews Tripolski and Passermann. The total bill was 10 silver R. 94 C.

November 5 It was cold and damp today, but we drove out our cattle anyway. We helped Jacob Pätkau slaughter three pigs.

November 6 Thursday. Today we cleaned the last of the oats and carried it on to the attic (a total of 26 chetvert plus $9\frac{1}{2}$ chetvert for Schellenbergs). [Total harvest]: oats $35\frac{1}{2}$ chetvert; wheat $78\frac{1}{2}$ chetvert; potatoes $33\frac{3}{8}$ chetvert; millet $3\frac{3}{8}$ chetvert; lentils 1 chetvert; barley 47 chetvert; rye $3\frac{1}{2}$ chetvert. Total harvest 202 chetvert. Thy blessings make us rich, dear God. Who is thy equal?

At the urging of Elder Gerhard Dyck, Peter Wiebe and Johann Wiebe (with his son), guardians of the children of the late David Penner of Izluchistaia, arrived to take Maria Penner from her parents' home (the Heinrich Siemenses) and hire her out in the Khortitsa colonies. They asked me to help, but I declined, saying this was the guardians' responsibility. My brother Diedrich dropped by, and we decided to negotiate the matter in Izluchistaia tomorrow.

November 7 We set out with our three visitors after breakfast, stopping for dinner at Hermann Peters's place in Kamianka, and then drove to Gerhard Andres's home in Izluchistaia. There I encouraged the guardians to resolve the matter amicably in a visit to the Siemenses. But they failed in this effort, reporting that Mrs Siemens refused to allow her daughter to leave and had threatened to use force to resist any effort to take her away. My brother Diedrich accompanied the guardians in a second attempt, but it was equally futile. Mrs Siemens is determined personally to ask the Elder for permission to keep her daughter. The Siemenses had also complained about me.

November 10 We helped Heinrich Olfert separate the sheep, which were on half-shares from my brother-in-law Bernh. Schellenberg. We divided them into equal parts, drew lots, and Schellenberg's half came to 26 sheep. These we marked and put back in with Olfert's sheep where they will stay until we hear from Schellenberg. A thick fog rolled in during the morning, and by evening our old mare, her foal, and our brown yearling stallion were missing. A search in the evening failed to find them.

November 11 At daybreak David and Jacob rode out on horseback to look for the lost horses, but came back empty-handed by 10 a.m. David rode out again on his own, but before he got back others had already found the horses. We separated the sheep and have 64 head of our own.

November 13 I sold 13 sheep to the Jews M. and H. for 26 silver R. and have 51 head left.

November 26 In the morning Diedrich Friesen of Friesenthal[12] dropped by with my brother Diedrich and invited me to hold services in Friesenthal. The currently dry weather seemed ideal for a trip, so I agreed to go.

November 28 Friday morning, Jacob and I drove through the neighbouring villages of Koshirne, Koshirski, and Boshanov looking for winter pigs, which are scarce and dear. At night I was down with a fever that caused me to shiver and my limbs to burn. Will the fever come back? God's will be done.

November 29 Although I still feel faint and my good eye is sore, my wife, Johann, and I left this morning with my brother Diedrich, his wife, and David for Friesenthal on the Basavluk River.

November 30 I was asked to preach a sermon in the home of Diedr. Friesen. This made me very anxious for my eyes were still sore from yesterday and this morning I was unable to read even with my glasses. What a remarkable [coincidence]. This affliction began exactly two years ago at Advent and today is again the First Advent. I therefore wondered whether God perhaps wanted me to stop preaching completely. Why otherwise would the ailment have returned? I pleaded for mercy, and God gave me just enough eyesight to finish the service, to the honour of his name.

December 1 My eye is worse and very painful.

December 2 My eye has improved to the point where I can make this diary entry.

December 12 Friday. My sore eye got worse and I was unable to see anything for five days. I was supposed to preach last Sunday but had to stay home. Today my eyes are a little better, and I was able to shave.

December 15 We still enjoy the most beautiful spring weather and wonder when winter will come. The landowners again drove their sheep out to pasture.

December 18 The weather is changing. It is colder, even raw, with a north wind but without frost. Son-in-law Johann Andres left with others for their new settlement on the Nepluiev land.

December 19 Today we slaughtered our two fatted pigs.

December 24 Moderate frost. We separated the sheep a second time. Jacob and I tried to settle our account with Joseph Mishnik but got nowhere. I dropped off the money for the silk to Martin Harder Sr.

December 31 *End of Year.* Our loving Father has overwhelmed us with rich blessings. Oh, that his goodness might lead us to repentance. The harvest was excellent, but sheep rearing is in decline, with very low prices for both sheep and wool. Prices for sheep were a little better towards the end of the year. The spiritual situation in our little church is not very good, however. *True Christianity* is disappearing more and more, and there is a certain clinging to externals. The uproar over cipher melodies, or singing by numbers, has subsided, but singing by ear is still done in Kamianka and Izluchistaia. When will things in our church improve and genuine love, unfeigned brotherly love, and love of God awaken in us? The poet was right when he wrote,

> Things won't get better here on earth
> Until we ourselves improve our worth.

1870

January 1 At the start of the New Year we are still alive, by God's grace, and look into the future with confident hope. Will we reach the end of this year? Will I? God, thou knowest it. Grant me the grace to celebrate joyfully this New Year of eternity and to join in the new song of the Lamb with the great chorus of the redeemed. Lord, save me from eternal perdition, and grant me the strength for true repentance.

Changes in our community [of the Judenplan] in 1869:

Births	14 males	18 females	32 total
Deaths	6 males	8 females	14 total
Increase	8 males	10 females	18 total
Couples married	9		

January 3 This afternoon my son-in-law Johann Andres and I discussed their settlement on the Nepluiev land. We decided, weather permitting, that they would move out of their cottage and in with his parents on Monday. Their cottage would then be dismantled and moved. We would leave for the new settlement on Wednesday, following the Day of Epiphany, dig a hole for the house, raise the rafters, and build a roof for their new dwelling.

January 4 My colleague Pätkau preached a written sermon in my brother Diedrich's home. After opening prayer, I suddenly realized that I had forgotten my church coat at home. This had never happened to me before. I thought to myself, if only one day I could stand before God's holiness clothed in the mantle of righteousness.

Our married children [Andres] told us his father could not leave for Nepluiev until next Monday, and so we changed our plans accordingly. Later my wife and I visited our neighbours the Isaac Siemenses, who have two Jewish tailors working for them. We got into a heated dispute, Siemens insisting that all Mennonite women darned and knitted on Sunday. I replied that this would not happen at our place with my knowledge. A neighbour's woman agreed with Siemens, who insisted the practice was quite proper. God had not given us the commandments in jest, I said, and they would have to deal with this matter presently. This irritated my brother-in-law Siemens. I thought it was my duty to speak God's Word in season and out of season, as Paul wrote to Timothy. We have small regard for Sunday and pay little heed to God's Word.

January 6 This winter is the mildest in memory, but it could still turn cold. Tonight my brother Diedrich told me that the Guardianship Committee had written that they could not decide the matter raised by our petition, but would have to submit it to the minister. Will the imperial government decide in our favour or will we be forced to leave the Judenplan? Lord, thou canst direct the hearts of the mighty like a stream.

January 13 Early Tuesday morning, Peter and I carted a load of wheat and my son-in-law Andres a load of wheat and oats to Nikopol. We fed the horses in Ebenfeld.

January 16 I was up at four this morning checking on the weather. It was snowing by daybreak, and so instead of travelling to Nikopol we carted the wheat to Unger's treadmill where it will be ground. When I awoke from my noon nap, my wife gave me a funeral letter from Peter Janzen of Novozhitomir announcing the funeral of his infant daughter Anna for Sunday. The funeral for Peter Hildebrand's daughter Helena is already scheduled for then, a service has been set for the same day in Novozhitomir, and I have promised to visit the Borosenko settlement. Since my colleague Pätkau cannot manage everything here himself, we first thought of rescheduling Hildebrand's funeral. Hildebrand did not object to this in principle, except that the funeral announcement had already been sent out. I then suggested that perhaps my brother Diedrich or the teacher Andres could read the sermon at the Hildebrand funeral, freeing Pätkau to conduct the morning church service and to officiate at the Novozhitomir funeral in the afternoon. This Hildebrand accepted, and I have one worry fewer. We really need three [ministers]. Once the government decides our future here we should probably elect another one.

January 17 Saturday afternoon, David and I left for Borosenko on an excellent sledding track.

January 18 I preached in the schoolhouse in Schöndorf.

January 21 My brother Diedrich returned from Khortitsa with the figures [regarding births and deaths in the Khortitsa church]. In 1869, of people born during the last century, 4 men and 5 women died and 61 men and 57 women are living. Of those born in this century, and joined to the church through Holy Baptism, 18 males and 35 females died and 2415 males and 2422 females are living. A total of 62 church members died and 4955 are living.

[Births and deaths for the Khortitsa community]:

Births	299 males	307 females	606 total
Deaths	88 males	116 females	204 total
Increase	211 males	181 females	392 total
Couples married	152 total		

January 26 This morning we witnessed the magnificent natural

spectacle of two giant mock suns in the sky, on either side of the sun, larger and more glorious than any I can recall seeing, and they were clearly mirrored at many places on the horizon. High above the sun was a round rainbow-like ring. The whole scene was matchless. Perhaps it heralds stormy weather, but it is, in any case, a reminder of Christ's return, of the signs in the sky proclaiming this important event. Mankind will then exclaim.

January 28 Today we conducted the second auction sale for widow Giesbrecht of Kamianka, at which I kept the books. The real estate was bought by Klas Heide for 561 silver R., the other belongings selling for about 120 silver R. cash. There was a good crowd, despite the bitter cold of 26½ degrees of frost in the morning. It was also very pleasant, with a clear sky and no wind. On our way home we visited our children, the Johann Andreses, whose infant son is seriously ill. May the Saviour be his physician.

February 4 Gerh. Andres Jr told us our dear grandchild had severe cramps, was in great pain, and was unlikely to survive.

February 6 At noon, Johann Andres brought us the sad news that their infant had died at 8 last night after an illness of 15 days. He was 7 months, 10 days, and 16½ hours old. Our daughter Katharina went along to comfort her sister.

February 8 Sunday. This afternoon we conducted a funeral service for my infant grandson Jacob Andres at the home of Gerh. Andres in Izluchistaia. My colleague Pätkau delivered the funeral sermon. A cipher melody was sung for the first time [at a service in this village]. It was melodious and beautiful. No precentors were present in the congregation, and so I asked Jacob de Veer to begin the morning song. He did so without hesitation, seemingly indifferent to the fact that a cipher melody was to be sung later. Yet once the funeral guests were seated, he started to pace back and forth in the entrance hall, his cap on his head and his lit pipe in his mouth, watching to see how we would sing. Once the singing began he walked out of the house and straight home. His wife stayed back until after the coffee and then left quickly herself. This is quite amazing. I think the time is coming when the singing in our church will be uniform everywhere. May God grant that this is soon.

February 9 At a small after-funeral today, another song, 'We Are All Proceeding to Eternity,' was sung to a cipher melody.

February 11 *School visitation.* This morning we visited the Izluchistaia village school, taught by Johann Banmann. It is in deplorable condition. Only the reading was passable and the rest is scarcely worth mentioning. The most advanced pupil in arithmetic was not beyond simple multiplication, which he did poorly. To fill the time, the teacher had his students recite memory work. Towards the close, the children sang a cipher melody, which unquestionably marks the start of cipher music [in the Izluchistaia school]. In the afternoon we visited the Kamianka school. Except for the reading, it was better all around. Bible stories are taught, but since the teacher did not want to discuss them in our presence, I asked the pupils several questions, which they answered to my satisfaction. Arithmetic was well done, and as for music, he said that he did not wish to sing [with the children] because of the discord it caused. We encouraged him to sing, even cipher melodies.

February 12 There was frost at night and the roads were again passable. We visited the Novovitebsk school taught by Heinrich Olfert. The pupils here are young, but the school seems to be in quite good shape. In the afternoon we visited our local school in Novopodolsk, taught by Jacob Andres, which is the best of the lot. The singing was exceptional. In the evening we visited the night school, and were again completely satisfied.

February 17 We are still having the most agreeable spring weather, especially today. The ground is drying out, and Germans and Jews were out pasturing their sheep. Everything lives in anticipation of spring, and nature celebrates renewal. Yet my heart is numb with the frost of winter and I feel burdened. If only spring would come and the morning star rise in my heart. My soul is afflicted and grieved because I do not love the Lord Jesus as I would and because my faith is so small. I begged the Lord on my knees today to forgive me my trespasses and to strengthen my weak faith. Lord Jesus, thou Lamb of God, who wast sacrificed for me on the cross. Thy holy blood was spilled to wash away the burden of my sins. Look down upon me, a poor sinner, in grace, and redeem me from the fetters of the devil and of the world. Amen.

February 19 Our son-in-law Johann Andres and his brother Gerhard left this afternoon for [village] number three of the Nepluiev settlement, to dig a zemlianka as a temporary dwelling.[13] David went along to help.

February 20 With the continuing warm weather I decided to start pasturing the sheep today. In the afternoon the [church members] chopped down the oleaster hedge around the churchyard, divided up the wood, and carted it home.

February 23 Early Monday morning, Jacob, Gerhard, and I drove to our children's place in Izluchistaia with a ladder wagon and three horses. We loaded lumber, straw for fodder, and reed-thatch for roofing, returning in the afternoon. Driving remains difficult. In the evening Johann Andres, his brother, and father stayed for the night with two wagon-loads drawn by three horses each.

February 24 We had hoped to make an early start, but changed our plans because of the rain. The Andres unloaded one wagon at our place, left the other loaded wagon next to mine, and returned with their horses to Izluchistaia.

This afternoon, Johann Bärgen and Gerhard Andres asked permission for Bärgen's son Johann to court our daughter Katharina. He was told he could come back on Thursday.

February 25 A quite sharp frost of two and a half degrees at night dried out the road. I am a little concerned that the ice crust may be gone by noon, but am tempted to leave for Nepluiev if the Andreses get here in time.

February 26 Thursday morning. A big snowstorm blew in from the south, and young Bärgen, on horseback, had difficulty riding against the wind. But the storm had died down by noon, and he had an easier time getting home. Our daughter Katharina has given him permission to visit again. May the Lord be her counsel.

February 27 Today is my dear wife's fortieth birthday. May our gracious Lord give her long life and illumine us in all eternity.

At 1 p.m. our son-in-law Johann Andres and his brothers Gerhard and Jacob arrived with the horses. After hurried preparations and a quick coffee they left for the Nepluiev settlement at 2 p.m. David drove our loaded wagon with three horses. The road was frozen, with two degrees of frost in the morning and two at noon, and there was enough snow for sledding.

February 28 Saturday. At breakfast, my daughter Katharina asked me to send young Johann Bärgen a letter of refusal, stating she did not wish him to come again. I took the opportunity to drive to Kamianka, where we saw the Julius Janzens and visited at the Johann

Schellenbergs. Janzen's son-in-law carried the letter to the Bärgens. We went by sled on the best track we have had all winter. Young Bärgen nevertheless tried his luck again in the evening, but the answer was still 'no.'

David and the Andres brothers returned from their Nepluiev trip at ten this evening.

March 6 Friday. Yesterday we had a very dear guest, Reverend Gerhard Kliewer of [the village of] Nicolaithal, Grossfürstlich settlement, close to Voronzovka. We spent much time talking about the sect that has emerged out of our church and organized itself as a Baptist church.[14] He told me that several members of his congregation had joined this group. Through active proselytizing, they were causing him much heartache. Kliewer also asked me to supply him with suitable materials for instructing the youth. I promised to have them ready for him when he returned at Easter-time.

At noon, Johann Andres, their little Gerhard, and our son-in-law's brother Gerhard stopped in with a load of belongings on their way to the Nepluiev settlement. Our daughter Helena and Gerhard stayed with us while the two brothers continued their journey. David accompanied them with a team of horses to the boundary of the Koshinski land.

March 8 Sunday. David and I drove to the service in the schoolhouse in Izluchistaia, where I preached a sermon about the sufferings and death of our Saviour Jesus Christ. Text, Isaiah 53:4–7. Today's singing was poor. The precentors are reluctant to lead the singing unless it is cipher music. Several verses of ear music were sung before and after the sermon. I hope we will soon be of one mind in regard to music. The majority have become indifferent about it, no longer viewing cipher music as such a great evil.

March 14 Saturday. Spring is finally on its way. At my wife's urging, I removed the storm-windows to let in the warm spring sun and will put out the sheep to pasture in the afternoon. Lord Jesus, warm my poor heart with the sun of thy grace.

Young Johann Bärgen arrived unexpectedly in the evening, asking for permission to speak to our daughter Katharina again. She consented, and they have agreed to become engaged. May God grant his blessing.

March 17 Today we celebrated the engagement of our daughter

Katharina to young Johann Bärgen, son of Johann Bärgen of Izluchistaia. The weather was beautiful, with less mud than yesterday and only a little rain. We invited our close neighbours for the celebrations and the Andreses for dinner. The Jacob Dycks were also here, and so the house was full. The groom's parents and the others arrived at one in the afternoon. (Earlier mother had sent our David on horseback to deliver engagement zwieback to Isaac Friesen's sick wife in Novokovno.) As the newly engaged couple entered the room, there was singing, first 'Supreme Creator,' and then 'On This Important Occasion.' After coffee, we sang 'God, Source of All Blessings,' and 'Let My Soul Sing.' The young people continued with various Christian songs until 11 at night. Grant us thy blessing, Lord Jesus. Amen.

March 18 Our children the Johann Andreses stayed for the night, and our close neighbours were here for breakfast. The Andreses took the newly engaged couple home with them.

The herdsman drove the cattle out to pasture.

March 21 Katharina's bridegroom and I drove to church this morning to install new panes of glass in the broken windows. We also ploughed up [the garden] in the yard and planted potatoes. Franz Giesbrecht of Novozhitomir told me his daughter Maria had confessed to behaving unchastely and committing fornication with both their Russian man-servant and Franz Klassen.

March 22 Before today's service Franz Giesbrecht and his daughter Maria appeared before me. They had been summoned by Peter Janzen and Johann Klassen. Maria admitted the truth of her father's story. The matter was held over until next Sunday.

Our daughter Katharina and Johann Bärgen were married this afternoon in the Novovitebsk church before a large congregation by my colleague Jacob Pätkau. Bless their marriage, Lord Jesus. We drove to church in two wagons, my dear wife, Helena, Jacob, and I in one, and the bridal couple, David and Maria in the other. Later our son-in-law Johann Andres arrived home from Blumenfeld [in the Nepluiev settlement].

March 24 Tuesday morning the Johann Andreses and son Gerhard stopped by for half an hour on their way to Blumenfeld, their [lease-land] settlement on the nobleman Nepluiev's land [also called the Seifart land]. Five villages are being established of 40 households each. The households will each have 50 desiatinas of land and pay an annual rent of 2 R. [per desiatina]. The lease contract has been concluded for ten years. Peter went along to help plough. May God grant them a safe journey and bless the new settlement.

March 25 Wednesday. At 10:30 last night, our son-in-law Johann Bärgen and his brother Jacob returned with a load of lumber from the Iasikovo settlement.[15] A heavy snowfall allowed us to cart our son-in-law Bärgen's belongings from Izluchistaia. After breakfast, David helped him to move his work-bench, tools, etc.

March 29 Sunday. Before today's service, Franz Giesbrecht, his daughter Maria, Franz Klassen, and the two summoners (see entry for March 22) appeared before the Ministerial Committee. Franz Klassen denied committing fornication with Maria. The girl said he had run his hand over her private parts and similarly described her unchaste behaviour with the Russian [servant]. But she contradicted herself and finally admitted her complete guilt. The matter was deferred until the Brotherhood Meeting. *Brotherhood Meeting*. The matter regarding Maria Giesbrecht and Franz Klassen was presented to the brethren. Klassen was summoned and admitted to having uncovered and touched Maria's private parts several times. Both were placed in the ban. Lord Jesus, grant them strength for repentance.

March 30 Monday morning, my son-in-law Bärgen took me to see Mrs Gerhard Redekopp, who is ill and had asked to see me. I found her in bed, deeply troubled and full of remorse. She begged me to forgive her for offending me. Before her marriage she and the young man Heinrich Enz had appeared before our Ministerial Committee. She had accused Enz of promising to marry her and of giving her a silver ruble, which he had stubbornly denied. She now admitted that she had lied. Had Enz not promised to marry her? I asked. 'Yes, of course he did,' she said, 'but he had not given me a silver ruble. That had been a bare-faced lie.' I asked her where she had gotten the silver ruble. 'I stole it from my employers, who had carelessly left it lying around.' She broke down crying about her great guilt and pleaded for God's grace. I directed her to the Lamb of God, who bears the sins of the world. Lord, Lord, complete the good work which thou hast begun in her soul, to the honour and glory of thy holy name.

April 4 All of nature seems downcast. Perhaps our dear Father intends to punish us with a crop failure? May his will be done. We have had springtimes in the past that were promising and ended in crop failure, and bleak seed-times that the Lord nevertheless blessed, as he did in 1864. But I am most troubled about the salvation of my family, which is getting quite large. Will I and my faithful life's partner, the devoted mother, will my children, will all of us find salvation through the grace of the Lord Jesus Christ? Lord, we need thy grace. Do not let one of my children, whom thou hast entrusted to me, go lost. Watch over them, faithful Saviour, that they might not leave thee, nor become entangled in the things of this world and enslaved to the lusts of the flesh and of the world. How long will I live? How much time will I have with my family? Lord, thou knowest it. At Christmas I began my fiftieth year. I once thought that death was far away. Whether my time here is short or long, be gracious and lead me to salvation. And if I walk a path of thorns, my heart will sing thy praises, glorifying thee forever. Halleluia.

April 5 Palm Sunday. *Brotherhood Meeting.* With the agreement of the brethren, I today readmitted Franz Klassen to membership in the church. Our children, the Johann Bärgens, attended service in Izluchistaia, where a cipher melody was sung. They reported that Peter Peters and Mrs Heinrich Siemens had walked out of the service (regarding Peters see entry for April 7, 1868).

April 6 We ploughed, sowed to wheat, and harrowed a desiatina of land for the schoolteacher and continued seeding for ourselves. Since finishing our ploughing a while ago, we have worked Jewish land, seeding six desiatinas to wheat (four for ourselves and two for the owner, who will receive a quarter-share at harvest-time).

April 9 Maundy Thursday. Rain at night and a strong east wind with intermittent rain today. We started ploughing Leib's lease-land, belonging to the colony of Novovitebsk, and will sow about eight desiatinas to wheat. Leib will receive a quarter-share.

I came down with the flu Monday night and have not felt well since. I'm a little better today and expect to be fully recovered soon. The smallest illness makes me think of my death. While down with the flu last night, I thought that God would perhaps carry me away, but it was not yet my time.

April 11 The Bärgen brothers [Jacob and Cornelius] and our children ploughed two desiatinas of Leib's lease-land for our son-in-law [Bärgen].

April 14 Easter Tuesday. The Andreses and son Diedrich left for Blumenfeld with a loaded wagon.
April 18 We finished sowing today. Leaving the potato patch aside, we have ploughed 43 desiatinas with our horses and plough. My share comes to $19\frac{1}{2}$ desiatinas wheat, 4 oats, and 6 barley. The Bärgens have seeded for themselves (not counting the fourth part) 4 desiatinas of wheat and $2\frac{3}{4}$ desiatinas of barley and oats. Our share together comes to 36 desiatinas. The fourth part, which we must deliver at harvest-time, consists of a further 3 desiatinas. Thus the area for reaping, including 4 desiatinas of [winter] rye, totals 43 desiatinas.
April 22 At nine this morning, Jacob and I, with four horses and our ladder wagon, left for Blumenfeld, Nepluiev settlement, to help Andres plow. We arrived in time to start work on the yard.
April 26 The morning service [in Nepluiev] was held in Peter Neufeld's implement shed. In my introductory sermon to the settlers I read Paul's words to the Colossians, 'All that ye do in word and deed ... and thank God the Father through Him ...'
May 3 *Brotherhood Meeting.* Seventeen baptismal candidates were registered, including our daughter Maria. Maria Giesbrecht was readmitted to church membership.
May 14 We left for Nikopol this morning with a load of oats, stopping in Blumenfeld to drop off my wife and Johann and to pick up Jacob (who had helped Johann Andres plough). Jacob came with me to Nikopol. After selling the five chetvert of oats (at 2 R. 60 C. per chetvert), we shopped, returning to Blumenfeld for the night.
May 15 At Elder Ger. Dyck's request, Abraham Peters of village number one appeared in our children's zemlianka in the presence of the witnesses David Klassen and Janzen. Peters, who was accused of having committed fornication with a Russian woman, admitted his guilt contritely and shamefacedly.
May 16 Saturday afternoon, Johann Bärgen and I looked for a cow. After asking Isaac Friesen's advice, we examined the Novovitebsk herd with Cornelius Krause and bought a red cow from him for 28 silver R. We brought the cow home to the Bärgens.
May 17 *Brotherhood Meeting.* I asked the brethren to keep their children from running around and making a racket as they had recently done during the [catechism] instruction. I also called a Brotherhood Meeting to consider whether to send several brethren to

Odessa to discuss our future on the Judenplan with the Guardianship Committee. Jacob Dyck and Diedrich Thiessen argued against the initiative, but the meeting was scheduled.

I rushed the service today in order to keep our promises to the Nepluiev settlement. Jacob Pätkau and I arrived in Blumenfeld at 2:20, and the service started at 3 p.m. in Peter Schellenberg's [unfinished] house, consisting of the outer walls, floor, and rafters. The window openings were closed with boards, and we opened one for light. There was a large congregation. In his introduction, my colleague Pätkau spoke of [the problems] of a new settlement, admonishing the congregation to seek Jesus' counsel in all things. In the rush to finish their work, they should, above all, not forget the only thing that really mattered. *Brotherhood Meeting*. Abraham Peters was placed in the ban because of his unchaste conduct.

May 18 Monday. We arrived home to find that a severe night frost had caused serious damage. The potato tops were black, the buds destroyed, and the mullberry leaves are frozen. But I did not detect damage to the young grain shoots.

May 19 Tuesday morning. In keeping with the announcement made to the last Brotherhood Meeting, I asked the brethren what they thought about sending a delegation to [petition] the Guardianship Committee in Odessa. In the discussion pro and con, Jacob Dyck, Johann Bärgen sen., and Heinr. Olfert opposed the move but the others thought it necessary. We finally decided to elect a delegation of two model settlers, including one minister. We [ministers] proceeded into the ministers' room and the brethren walked through, casting two ballots each. Johann Bärgen Sr and I were chosen by majority vote. The trip is scheduled to take place after the holidays.

May 20 There was another severe frost last night, and the leaves of the young acacia trees along the ditch were frozen. There was a like experience in 1864, but the Lord gave us a good harvest that year.

May 27 Wednesday. We observed Holy Communion in church with 130 participants, including my wife, the Bärgens, David, and Maria.

May 28 Our beloved Elder baptized our 17 candidates.

May 29 The Elder officiated at the communion service [in the Nepluiev settlement], with 75 people in attendance.

May 31 Pentecost, the festival of grace. I preached a sermon on John 14:23–31, to a large congregation. Lord Jesus, bless this sermon, as thou didst bless the first Pentecost. Grant that many souls, or even one, might be won to thee. Thou art the source of life, blessing, growth, and prosperity. Pour out thy Spirit richly over our church that many might be awakened to eternal life.

June 1 *The Trip to Odessa.* At 10 a.m. this morning Johann Bärgen and his son Jacob called for me on their wagon, and we departed in God's name.

June 2 We spent the night with the Gerhard Koslowskis in Nikopol and boarded the steamboat 'Akkermann' on the Dnieper River early Tuesday morning. Our fare was 1 silver R. 80 C. per person, third-class passage. It was a cold day with a strong wind, which made travel unpleasant, and we stayed close to the steam boiler. There were four stops along the river, and we arrived in Kherson at seven in the evening. A droshky took us to the home of my cousin Jacob Thiessen, who received us warmly.

June 3 After breakfast we returned to the Dnieper by droshky, which had been hired by my cousin, and boarded the steamboat 'Iason' (third-class tickets were 1 R. per person). We left at 8 a.m., arriving in Odessa at 4 in the afternoon. Despite a fairly stiff breeze, the trip was quite pleasant. There were droshkys and wagons waiting for passengers in Odessa, and we hired one to take us to 'J. Kraft's Inn for Germans,' where we stayed until our departure. It was still quite early so we decided to look up the residence of Afanassi Markevich Stepanov, the surveyor. But that was more than we had really bargained for in such a large city. Finally, after we had almost worn out our shoes walking, we hired a droshky to take us to the building of the Guardianship Committee. There a servant or custodian gave us the surveyor's address on Haud Philipake, and another droshky brought us to his door. He was not in, however, and we told his mother we would be back to see him early in the morning.

June 4 Thursday morning at seven, we were back at the home of the surveyor Stepanov. Bärgen handed him a letter from my brother Diedrich, and he said we should meet him in the offices of the [Guardianship] Committee at 9:30 a.m.

Meanwhile we toured the sights of the city.[16] We saw the statues of Duke Richelieu and Count Vorontsov and the railroad. The engine-driver was kind enough to show us the locomotive and to let us ride back and forth on it. We also toured the Vorontsov gardens. Then, as time was getting short, we went to the offices of the Committee and were given an appointment to see His Excellency the Lord President at 10:30.[17]

The president accepted our petition in a friendly way and asked us a few questions, which we were able to answer. He assured us that we would not have to leave our place of residence and promised us a formal decision within an hour. We waited for about two hours while a number of colonists presented their petitions to the Lord President. Several Committee officials stopped by to tell us that the land we held in use belonged to us and not to the Jews. Finally the president returned and told us we had nothing to worry about. We could stay where we were forever. He would instruct the local offices through his chancery to inform the Jews accordingly, so that they would have no choice but to understand their limits. We should return home, in God's name, he said, and work diligently. The time was one in the afternoon.

We spent the rest of the day touring the city. I was overjoyed, thanking God in my innermost heart for arranging everything to our benefit and that of our community.

June 5 Friday at 8 a.m. we boarded the steamboat 'Taganrog' for the return voyage. There was a strong wind that developed into a storm. The Black Sea became quite turbulent, and the waves rose higher than I have ever seen them before. The ship began to toss violently back and forth, making a number of passengers very seasick. I was not well either, but a glass of juice settled my stomach. The waves died down as we entered the [Dnieper] estuary, although the wind kept blowing. At 7 p.m. we were back again in Kherson with my cousin Jacob Thiessen.

June 6 My dear cousin drove us around to see the sights of Kherson.

June 9 We reached Nikopol at 8:30 in the morning and hired a Russian for one-half silver R. to drive us home, arriving there safely at 11 in the evening.

June 10 Thus the trip is ended and we have completed the task entrusted to us by the Brotherhood Meeting on May 19.

June 13 *Comments regarding our trip to Odessa.* On our return trip we stopped at Kachovka for an hour while freight was being loaded and unloaded. This gave us a good opportunity to watch a nearby steam mill sawing planks and boards. The mill is located high up on the bank and connected to the river by a steep bridge or chute. We were fascinated to watch a log being hauled up from below and horrified at the accident that followed. As the log was about to enter the mill it somehow came loose, hurtled back down the chute, and hit the water with an enormous splash. A worker in the water who had secured the log tried to duck out of the way but disappeared into the Dnieper with the log. People rushed up to help. We watched as the poor man was pulled from the water and laid on the shore. Soon, however, two men took him under the arms and walked off with him. We therefore assumed that the man was not seriously injured. Before long the log had been hauled up again into the mill.

The steam that operates these machines is truly remarkable. This I already observed in L. Nitzsche's printery in Odessa, in my cousin Thiessen's steam mill in Kherson, and in the large machine factories of that city. I also admired the power of the steam-engines on the boats.

There was much on this trip that astonished me. There are the already mentioned factories and steamboats and the railroad and its machinery. At the waterworks in the middle of Odessa, one can fill a container simply by turning a tap. Another pipe fills a cattle-watering trough. The statues of Richelieu and Vorontsov in Odessa, of Potemkin in Kherson, and the fortress of Kherson all struck me as being remarkable.

June 14 Sunday. We had [various guests] this afternoon, including the Klas Heides of Kamianka. I had asked to see Klas Heide regarding his daughter Katharina, who works for Jacob Thiessen in Kherson. She had asked me to talk to her father about staying on with her present employer for another year. If he gave his permission I was to give him 10 R. from her earnings and 10 R. from Jacob Thiessen. Failing that I was to keep the money for her. Heide was, however, firm and unyielding. He said his daughter could hire herself out anywhere in the colonies, but he would not permit her to work in the city. I told him his daughter had a strong desire to stay on in Kherson, even if only for another year, and that the 20R. might come in very handy for him. But he said he did not need the money.[18] I therefore wrote to Thiessen today asking if I should send his money directly to him by mail, to his parents in Khortitsa, or to my brother Heinrich. I forwarded the letter to Khortitsa with my colleague Pätkau, where he will put it in the mail.

June 16 This morning my son-in-law Bärgen and I went out looking to buy pigs for him and geese for us. We found several pigs in Bridakov, but they were not to my liking, and the geese in Sharik at 40 C. apiece were too dear. After Vesper, which we had at Bärgen's parent's place in Izluchistaia, we drove to Bozhanov, where I bought a mother goose for 20 C. and 20 little goslings at 4 C. apiece. Larger ducks were also for sale, but they were on the pond and could not be caught.

June 18 Thursday morning Jacob and I went shopping at the market in Sofievka and resumed our hunt for pigs and geese. There were geese for sale in the village of Koplistovo, but the owner was away. We returned in the afternoon, but the proprietress was asking 45 C. apiece, which was too dear, and we had no luck in the village of Baratov. Finally we bought a boar for the Johann Bärgens for 7 silver R. in the village of Kudashev on the Kamianka, returning home late at night.

June 19 Early Friday morning David, Diedrich and I continued our search for geese and bought 10 at 35 C. apiece in the nobleman's village of Koshinski. At breakfast-time a Russian from Boshanov dropped by and sold us a mother duck (20 C.) and 16 ducklings (10 C. apiece). My dear wife, Diedrich, Gerhard, Elisabeth, and I then drove to Boshanov where we bought 4 mother geese (at 50 C. apiece) and 25 young geese (at 40 C. apiece), for a total of 12 silver R. I think we have finally finished buying pigs and geese for the year.

June 21 Last night a raging fire in Novovitebsk burned down Diedrich Thiessen's windmill. The mill was working yesterday, and so we assume it was criminally torched. Thiessen had inspected the mill at 10:30 last night, but by 1 a.m. it stood in flames.

June 22 Before noon today I carted a load of sheep manure and a load of cattle manure to school, put the rest of the fuel dung into winter storage, and plucked the geese. Sufficient unto the day is the evil thereof. My wife, several of our children, and I drove out to look at the grain and found it sparse and small. God can still bless us, however. We have heard that the grain in the Khortitsa District is quite magnificent. We thank thee Lord that there will not be a general crop failure at least.

June 26 The dry and arid weather continues. Last night a strong wind and a dense cloud cover promised rain, but the Lord withheld his blessing, and today it is warm again. I also feel drought in my heart and crave the dew drops of Jesus' grace. The human heart is such a perverse thing. Hear my sighings and lamentations, Lord Jesus, and revive me with thy grace.

June 27 Elisabeth and our married children Johann and Katharina Bärgen left for Blumenfeld to visit the Johann Andreses. Bärgen is also delivering a finished wagon box to Nicolaithal.

June 29 My dear wife has had much pain from a large swelling under her right arm. Today my brother Diedrich lanced it with a milliner's knife, which hurt. But it also helped, thank God, releasing much puss and reducing the pain.

July 1 As I walked to the street from Jacob Braun's house today, I saw a large cloud of smoke and a burning house. It was a Jewish building, occupied by Risselweis at one end (where the fire had started) and by the Mantlers at the other. We managed to save the belongings of both occupants.

July 2 Start of the grain harvest. We started cutting rye today, which is sparse. Many stalks lie broken on the ground.

July 3 Friday evening. It was very hot yesterday and today, but the sky looks like rain.

July 5 It was much cooler today. In the afternoon my wife and I visited my brother Diedrich where we met a certain Diehl, a teacher from the Zentralschule in Gross-Liebenthal, who had attended church with my brother in the morning. He was examining schooling in the colonies at the request of His Excellency the President of the Guardianship Committee, who had given him a letter of introduction instructing [colonists] to provide him with free transportation.

He and my brother had supper at our place, and we talked about many subjects. Since this was his first contact with Mennonites, he was curious about the articles of our faith, our church practices, and so on. He is frank and honest and loves the Word of God, and I liked him. As for baptism, our beliefs are very different, each according to his faith. I did, however, find it strange when he said that young baptized children are more open to positive influences in school than are others. I disputed this strongly, citing the Word of God. He was happy to hear that we value books such as Arndt's *True Christianity*, Hofacker, etc.[19] He plans to visit Khortitsa tomorrow and then travel to the Molochna. May the guardian angels accompany our dear visitor.

July 12 It rained all afternoon. We were drenched driving home, the first time this summer. A Jew we met under way said, 'What good is rain now. It should have come sooner.' Yet I believe God makes no mistakes.

July 14 *A Village Story.* An incident in our village from Thursday night to Friday morning could have serious consequences for those involved. The Jews elected an assistant [Village] mayor on Thursday. That night the two contending Jewish camps partied and drank at separate locations. One of the drinking parties was in the home of Jankel Lippen, the Village mayor. Around midnight a Desiatnik[20] (a retired soldier, but a Jew) belonging to the other camp tried to eavesdrop on what was said and planned by the group partying in Lippen's home. He was spotted, seized, and dragged into the room, where the light was doused and he was badly beaten. Luckily he was able to slip away, and around one o'clock came whining and crying to my brother, the local overseer.

Friday morning Cornelius Mantler took the Desiatnik to see the justice of the peace. Jankel Lippen, the Village mayor, chased after him and tried to talk him into a reconciliation, offering him 25 R. as compensation. The Desiatnik remained firm, however, and lodged his complaint. On the Sabbath the entire Jewish community tried to talk the Desiatnik into a settlement, which was finally agreed to Sunday evening. If he accepts the agreement, they are offering to pay him compensation of 150 silver R. in the presence of the justice of the peace. Yesterday they went to talk to the justice of the peace, but have not returned. The Desiatnik has, in the meantime, sold his cow and does not intend to return to Novopodolsk.

Evening. The Jews are back from seeing the justice of the peace. The document of agreement has been prepared and signed. It is significant that Jankel Lippen has been relieved of his office by his superior, the overseer.

July 25 In the afternoon, my dear wife, Gerhard, Johann, and I drove to village number three,[21] Neu-Hamburg, on the Nepluiev settlement. After coffee with the Johann Hoeppners, we went to Johann Andres's place in Blumenfeld (number two) for the night. I was here at the settlers' request to proclaim the Word of God. We had rain and muddy roads on the way home.

July 30 Thursday. Tonight the model settlers met at my brother

Diedrich's home. We were given the Guardianship Committee's response to our efforts [to have our status clarified] (see entry for June 4, 1870), which was quite satisfactory. We signed a document stating that we had been duly informed.

August 1 Saturday. The rain since last night has forced us to stop threshing. After Vesper-time Johann Bärgen saw old Isaac Friesen in Novokovno about renting a dwelling for our children, the Bärgens. The old couple are willing to rent out half of their house, but have yet to state a price.

August 6 The wet weather continues to delay the threshing. Yesterday afternoon the children and the [village] scribe drove to Leib's [lease-]land to divide up the wheat sheaves and cart home those of the Jew. The rain put a stop to their work.

August 7 The continuing rain has prevented us from making much headway with the harvest. I have therefore had a few days' time to read a book I had not heard about before, *The Prince of David's House*, a collection of 39 letters written by a Jewess Adine (who was present in Jerusalem during the three years of Jesus' apprenticeship and suffering) to her father in Alexandria.[22] The book is delightful and spoke to my heart. I value it highly, next to the New Testament. The concepts and habits of Jesus' contemporaries are made so clear that I can now understand many scripture passages that I had previously found obscure. When I can, I want to buy it. The book would be worth reading to the whole family.

August 9 I preached a message in our church to a small congregation on the subject of the lost son. Luke 15:11-24. I find little interest in our churches in God's Word and wonder whether the Lord will have to lead his church through the valley of desolation before we hear his voice? Our church has become worldly, our Christianity and preachers lukewarm, and the congregations small and seemingly indifferent. There are among us so few real guardians of the Word of God. Lord, have mercy.

August 14 Last night in Kamianka, in a major robbery, the landowner Julius Janzen had a new wagon, two stable horses, and their harness stolen. As Corn. Thiessen, Janzen's son-in-law, and the latter's boy drove home from B. Wiebe's windmill after midnight, they heard the sound of a wagon travelling away from Kamianka at great speed. Thiessen commented that someone would be getting to bed even later than they would. Arriving on Janzen's yard, he cried out, 'My wagon (which had been standing on the yard) has been stolen.' When he looked around he realized that it was not his wagon that was missing but the brand-new wagon belonging to his father-in-law Janzen. The thieves had pulled Janzen's wagon out of the shed, taken the seats and backs of the wagon, and dumped them on the ground nearby. They had then pulled Thiessen's wagon into the shed [where it still stood]. The bedding on Janzen's wagon, which had been used for sleeping at night, the wagon, two horses from the barn, and two sets of harnesses had been stolen. This is a great loss for Janzen. It is high time that we kept a better watch at night. Julius Janzen was here this morning, and the robbery is not quite as described above. In fact, Janzen had two wagons in his driving shed, an old one, closest to the door, which had been pulled out and put back, and the new one, which had been stolen.

August 17 We left this morning for the Khortitsa colonies on Pätkau's covered wagon. Around three in the afternoon a strong wind became a raging storm, threatening to tip over our wagon. The storm forced us to unhitch the horses near Pilipinka, where the entrenchment has been dug through.

August 18 Tuesday after breakfast we went to see the widow Elias where my poor mother-in-law continues her struggle and suffering. She was pleased at our (for her) unexpected visit.

August 21 This evening Elder Gerhard Dyck told me he planned an election of ministers in the Nepluiev settlement on Sunday and asked me to be present.

August 24 Monday. We returned home at eight tonight. Last Monday's storm damaged many roofs [in the Khortitsa colonies] and capsized the cottager Diedt. Klassen's implement shed. It also damaged numerous roofs in the Judenplan colonies and snapped the tall poplar in front of our window.

In [the village of] Burwalde the Elder and several colleagues have just resolved serious disputes arising from the introduction of the cipher music. Opposition to this singing by some members caused the precentors to withdraw their services, and now there was no end of bickering. Reverend Isaac de Veer was blamed for starting the row, but I did not question the Elder about the truth of this. Many think this kind of singing is an innovation and contrary to Christianity. In the past I was greatly troubled about this question as well, as can be seen from my diary entries for April 7, 21, and 24 of 1868. Thank God for finally giving us peace and harmony on this issue.

I also visited the District Office to put in a word on behalf of the landless families in our congregation in regard to land purchases for a new settlement. I hope it is not in vain.

The war between Prussia and France, [1870–1], has entered a frightening stage, with the Angel of Death reaping an abundant harvest. The victorious Germans, who invaded France, are close to the capital, the world city of Paris. This was the topic of conversation wherever we came, since everyone was eagerly following the most recent dispatches.[23] Lord, when will the end come? Watch and pray, for you do not know when that time has come.

While we were away the children harvested a bit of grass and threshed the last wheat. We harvested a total of 31 chetvert of wheat, [an average] of 1 chetvert 6 merka per desiatina.

August 25 Around two in the morning, my son-in-law Johann Bärgen, his father, and our son Peter left for Ekaterinoslav to buy two loads of lumber for Bärgen's wheelwright trade.

August 28 Since returning [from Khortitsa] my wife has been in severe pain from a boil at a very awkward spot. She was in bed all day yesterday. I knew lancing would help, but was afraid to try. Last night she begged me to do something. Calling on the Lord for help, and with a steady hand, I did the operation with a millinery knife.

August 29 Sunday afternoon, Maria, my colleague [Pätkau], and I drove to the Nepluiev settlement, where we stayed in Blumenfeld with our children the Andreses.

August 30 Sunday morning my colleague Pätkau preached in [village] number five, Gerhard Enz in [village] number three, Elder Gerhard Dyck in [village] number one, and Jacob Regier Sr in [village] number two. I attended the latter service in the home of Jacob Klassen, where we held the large Brotherhood Meeting to elect ministers. First, Peter Klassen and Gerhard Enz were elected as deacons. Then, two ministers were chosen from among the three deacons by majority vote: Anton Sudermann (with 75 votes) and Gerhard Enz (with 51 votes). Sudermann was immediately installed in office, but, since Enz was absent from the meeting, his installation had to be postponed until evening.

September 5 A night frost damaged the potato plants in the lower garden but spared the dahlias among the weeds. David and Gerhard Andres returned from the Nepluiev colony of Blumenfeld, where the Johann Andreses have a roof over their heads. The floors, doors, windows, inside walls, fire wall, chimney and oven, etc., are still lacking, and the nights are getting cold. The start of every new settlement is difficult for poor people, especially when God gives them a crop failure in their first year. Grant them thy blessing, Lord, that they might find food and clothing in their new settlement. May thy peace fill their hearts.

September 7 At six o'clock Monday morning Jacob (on my wagon), Johann Bärgen (on his), Reverend Jacob Pätkau, and several neighbours left for Ekaterinoslav. Bärgen wants the two loads of wheelwright lumber bought earlier carted home (August 25, 1870).

September 11 Late Friday afternoon my colleague Pätkau and I left for the Grossfürstlich settlement, east of the Dnieper.

September 13 A general Brotherhood Meeting took place at 1 p.m. in Peter Lepp's implement shed in Georgsthal. Lepp is District mayor of the settlement. The beloved Elder [Gerhard Dyck] was there to conduct the election of an elder from among the three ministers. Of our Khortitsa colleagues only Reverend David Wienz had come. Deacon Johann Enz and we ministers from outside of the settlement took our places in the room where the brethren passed through to vote. Elected to the important office of Elder by majority vote was Reverend Johann Wiebe with 55 votes.[24] Abraham Wiebe received 41 votes and Franz Bükkert 23. May the Lord endow the elected bishop with his Holy Spirit and grant him the gifts needed for this high calling.

September 14 The consecration of the new Elder took place this afternoon in Lepp's implement shed in the presence of a very large congregation. The ceremony began with the singing of nine verses of Hymn 142, 'A Joyous Heart.' In his introductory sermon the beloved Elder Gerhard Dyck commented on the purpose of the ceremony and prayed. The text was then read, and I preached a sermon on the duties of an elder and his congregation to one another. After the newly elected Elder had answered the two customary questions by saying 'yes' and the congregation had answered the questions put to it by remaining silent, we again prayed.

Wiebe then kneeled before Elder Ger. Dyck, who ordained him an Elder with the Word of God and through the laying on of hands. He then raised him to his feet and kissed him. Elder Dyck invited his ministerial colleagues to congratulate the newly ordained Elder, and as Reverend Dav. Wienz had already left, I was first. After kissing him, I said, 'Thus saith the Lord Zebaoth: If you will walk in my ways and wait on me you shall rule my house and protect my court. I will ensure that those who surround you will follow you. May the blessings of Jehovah be poured out in torrents over your head that you might have the strength to pasture His flock according to His will and to His satisfaction.'

The congratulations of the other colleagues varied, but in each case they kissed one another. The deacon Johann Enz read his blessing. The newly ordained Elder spoke some deeply moving words, and we sang Hymn 603, 'Abide in Thy Grace.' Elder Gerhard Dyck delivered a sermon. The congregation kneeled for prayer and the ceremony ended with the singing of five verses of Hymn 244, 'Jesus Our Sanctification.'

This is a brief description of the ordination of this Elder, included so that people in future might know how it was done.

September 16 While I was away the children finished ploughing and sowing two and a half desiatinas of rye.

September 18 Friday morning Margaretta Hildebrand appeared before the Ministerial Committee, summoned by Isaac Siemens and Jacob v Kampen. She had recently recovered from an illness whose symptoms suggested a miscarriage. We considered this likely since everyone knew of her love affair with the bachelor Jacob Bastian. Thinking it our duty to call her to account, I asked her about the suspicion that she had committed fornication with Bastian, which she denied. She was frank in admitting that she loved him deeply and was often in his company, but vehemently denied having sexual relations with him. Since I still thought she was concealing something, I warned her against continuing her association with Bastian or entering into a common-law relationship with him. [I said] that God could not approve of a mixed marriage (Bastian is Prussian and of the Lutheran confession). She continued to declare her great love for him, and how he could not live without her. She also described how in her youth she had wanted to marry a certain young man by the name of Johann Thiessen. This her mother had forbidden, saying that if she did so she would never again be allowed to cross her threshold. Later a widower from Einlage, a certain Heinrich Friesen, had made a fool of her, seeking her hand in marriage and, with her parents' consent, arranging the engagement festivities. Then he had pressed her to have sexual relations with him, which she had rejected. Finally, while she was preparing for the engagement he had gone ahead and become engaged to someone else in Einlage. When she compared all of this to the love of Bastian, who had never proposed such a thing to her, she could not be indifferent to him, etc., etc. We reminded her, among other things, of the words of the Lord Jesus, 'He who loves something more than me, is not worthy of me.' She was allowed to go in peace.

September 22 David and I left for Nikopol at 5:30 this morning with 5 chetvert of wheat, which we sold to Peter Friesen for 7½ R. per chetvert. Wheat prices are again rising, probably because of the war. I also bought lumber for the cellar and the corner room from Lappen Davidorski for 9 silver R. 90 C.

September 26 We started digging a cellar for the back room and carted the dirt into the cellar under the corner room.

September 29 I finished relocating the stove today. The children have been digging the cellar for the back room.

September 30 I helped the Johann Andres put glass into the window frames [for their new home in Blumenfeld].

October 2 I sold 11 sheep to the [Village] Mayor Jankel Lippen: 3 old wethers at 3 R. each, 5 young sheep at 2 R. 10 C. each, and 3 mother sheep at 2 R. 25 C. each.

October 3 Friday afternoon Diedr. Friesen's sons-in-law Töws and Warkentin asked me and my brother for permission to hire our son Peter as the teacher for their small children. I finally agreed to a trial period, to see if he was suited to the calling, and asked for a salary of 30 R. until May. If it does not work out he would come back home.

October 8 Last night we finished digging a cellar and building a room. This morning we drove to the Sofievka market and bought 60 head of cabbage at 2 C. each and other provisions.

October 9 Heinrich Olfert bled me this afternoon, which had a good effect on my body. For this I thank the Lord.

October 11 Sunday. Jacob Friesen, the smith from Friesenthal, called for our son Peter, who is to start his teaching career (see entry for Oct. 3, 1870).

October 14 Yesterday we butchered five fattened pigs for ourselves and for our children, the Bärgens. Butchering is early this year because we were running short of feed. The weather was lovely, the warm sunshine making it all very pleasant. Helping were the Diedrich Epps, the Jacob Pätkaus, Franz Klassen, Mrs Isaac Siemens, and the Heinrich Olferts.

A phenomenon in the sky is currently agitating many people. It was seen for the first time the evening before last when the whole northern horizon, from east to west, turned fire red. It was very high in the sky and continued until 11 at night. I told the children it was the northern lights. It was even larger last night, again in the north, but so high as to reach above the line of my buildings. The blood or fire-red colour reminds us of Jesus' words, that there 'will be signs in the heavens' before his return. I finally thought that it was perhaps not the northern lights. In any case, it is a warning of our Lord to remember our end and the [last] judgment. Trembling in the face of sin, let me see Jesus until I find the grace to endure. Amen.

Late at night. At three this afternoon I visited teacher Jacob Andres's ailing wife, who has been sick for some time and in bed for 12 days. She was sitting on a bench, but I could find no pulse and realized she was dying. My wife and I came back as quickly as we could, but at 5 p.m. she had passed away. Lord, teach me that I must die in order that my life have a purpose.

October 20 Tuesday. Widower Heinrich Bartel of Kronsgarten asked for help in seeking the hand of widow Jacob Hamm.

October 21 I accompanied Bartel to Kamianka to ask for the hand of the widow Hamm. They have agreed to become engaged and plan the engagement celebrations for Saturday.

October 24 I attended the engagement festivities of the widow Jacob Hamm and the widower Heinrich Bartel.

October 26 My brother Diedrich, Isaac Siemens, and I drove to Kamianka to organize the division of the widow Hamm's estate. But when we arrived there she told us she regretted her engagement, although she had not yet decided to call it off. We stayed for dinner. In the afternoon the two finally decided to end the engagement. The division [of the estate] did not take place, and we drove home.

October 27 Tuesday afternoon, while driving to Izluchistaia to officiate at the marriage of Peter Olfert and Maria Penner, we met Jacob Andres, the teacher, and his mother who told us the wedding had been called off. The bridegroom had backed out. What foolishness! We turned around and drove home.

October 28 Jacob and I drove to Friesenthal to see how our son Peter was managing as a teacher, whether they were happy with him, and to take him home with us if things were not working out. Töws, in whose home the school meets, said they were completely satisfied, and Peter, in turn, is very pleased with his position.

Towards evening Heinrich Siemens raised the question of Peter Olfert's conduct [in not appearing for his wedding] and the great annoyance this had caused (see entry for Oct. 27, 1870). Siemens finally left after I suggested he be patient for now. Olfert might well come to his senses, and if he did not he could still be called to account. Around 6 p.m. Peter Olfert appeared at our door with Heinrich Harder and Heinrich Olfert Jr, seeking advice. He wanted to get together again with his bride, but feared the anger of her parents. He had backed out of the wedding, he explained, because his bride's mother had insulted his relatives, etc. I recommended he present the matter to the Lord in prayer. He should then think through what he might do and come to a firm resolve. If it was his decision to get together again with his bride he should apologize to her parents. This was, in any case, the least that he should do. With this advice he left for home.

October 29 Thursday we participated in the engagement festivities of the widower Heinrich Bartel and the widow Cornelius Kröker at the home of the Johann Schellenbergs in Kamianka. The villagers reported that widow Hamm was now sorry that she had rejected her suitor (see entry for Oct. 26, 1870). She was behaving in an excitable manner that had them worried. This was all quite predictable. Last Monday I warned her that she would live to regret her decision. As for old Bartel, he had come to [the Judenplan] to woo widow Hamm. The Lord our God had directed matters otherwise, and he would now return home with the widow Kröker. God does wondrous things for those who trust him. Widow Kröker is a clean and tidy Christian housewife, sensible and intelligent. The opposite can be said for widow Hamm. Bartel now has reason to rejoice and can sing from the bottom of his heart, 'The Lord Leads Marvelously.'

November 1 Sunday. After the service I joined in marriage Peter

Olfert and Maria Penner. This afternoon I officiated at the wedding of widower Heinrich Bartel and widow Helene Kröker.

November 6 My brother Diedrich, who still suffers from hemorrhoids, left for Khortitsa today to seek treatment from our brother-in-law Schellenberg. This afternoon I installed glass in Peter Janzen's storm-windows.

November 7 Finished the work this afternoon, earning 1 silver R.

November 10 I went to ask for the hand of Diedrich Thiessen's daughter Susanna in marriage on behalf of our son David. The parents were out, so I talked to Susanna alone, who said David could drop by this evening. On my return, David left immediately on horseback, returning at 9 p.m. with permission to come again.

November 14 Last night, I dreamt that I was living suddenly in a new wooden house. When I awoke I wondered whether the dream was perhaps a portent of the coffin that would soon enclose me. Times goes and death comes.

November 17 David left for Nikopol with 3 chetvert of wheat, travelling with several other wagons. Last week wheat was rising in price, selling for as much as 8 R. 80 C. per chetvert, but tonight prices were falling and are said to be as low as 7 R. 60 C. Had I known this, I would have kept my wheat a little longer.

November 18 Brother Diedrich returned from Khortitsa this afternoon (see entry for Nov. 6). He is a little better, but still not well. He brought a distressing piece of news that everyone will in future have to perform military service, as in Prussia.[25] Is the Charter of Privileges, exempting us from military service for all time, of no value? Can it not protect us from the ordinances of the imperial government? God's judgment is drawing near, and I fear our church faces a difficult future.

November 19 At a meeting this evening in the home of the German [Village] mayor, we hired Jacob Andres as teacher for another year at a salary of 50 R., 5 chetvert grain, 8 desiatinas of land (of which the community will plough 4) and free pasture. He teaches night school for 1 R. 50 C. per child.

November 20 It is getting colder, and if we had snow, winter would be here. Today I paid off my debts to the Office of the [Village] Mayor: the still outstanding herding fee of 2 R. 92 C.; tuition fees for school of 1 R. 35 C. per child, for a total of 4 R. 5 C. for three children. I also paid the teacher directly 3 R. for the two children in night school.

November 22 I preached a sermon in Abraham Unger's home in Novopodolsk. I still have a strong urge to preach freely and would probably risk doing so were I not burdened with such feelings of unworthiness and sin. Lord, I seek thy honour, not mine. Show me thy will, and be merciful to me, a poor sinner.

November 23 This morning I met Johann Heese of Khortitsa, who spent the night at my brother Diedrich's place while waiting for his travelling companions Jacob Niebuhr, chairman of the Agricultural Commission, and Jacob Wiebe, of the Kudashev khutor (they had stopped off in Novovitebsk on their way back from inspecting the land at Hannovka). Heese related that on their way to Borosenko, after dark, he and old Abraham Pauls had a strange experience. In a valley Pauls had gotten off the wagon to look for the road when suddenly the wagon had started bobbing up and down. Frightened, Heese had jumped down. At the top of the hill, Pauls had stayed on the wagon while Heese had gotten off, and the bobbing had happened again.

November 26 The Gerhard Andreses returned from Blumenfeld. Monday at 2 p.m. our daughter Helena gave birth to a son, Jacob.

November 28 The Heinrich Olferts of Novovitebsk dropped by, probably because of a gathering at the home of my brother Diedrich of subscribers [to *Die Odessaer Zeitung*].

November 30 I sent Jacob on horseback to Novokovno with an envelope containing a letter and Christmas and New Year's cards for our son Peter in Friesenthal.

December 1 *A Visit to the Nepluiev Settlement.* My dear wife, Gerhard, Johann, and I left at 8:45 this morning by wagon. There was a light frost, frozen ground, and a bumpy road in places. At 2 p.m. we reached Nicolaithal, Borosenko [settlement], where I dropped off three sacks of wheat for milling at Abraham Harms's treadmill. After an hour feeding the horses and drinking a cup of coffee, we resumed the trip, reaching Johann Andreses place at sundown, where we saw their new-born son for the first time. Their house is very cold. Andres was busy carting fuel dung from Abr. Penner's place in Ebenfeld. He is also very short of feed.

December 3 We had a slow start on our return trip because little Johann insisted on sitting on my lap rather than on that of his mother.

At an inn, mother and the children warmed themselves while I fed the horses, after which our little darling sat quietly on my lap until we reached home.

December 8 Tuesday. Jacob v Kampen's wife went into labour yesterday. Today at 11 a.m. Pätkau and Peter Hildebrand drove to fetch a trained (Russian) midwife from Voronzovka, who has developed a reputation in our area from previous visits. Martin v Kampen and Jacob Neufeld left an hour later for Konstantinovka [where they waited to pick her up]. The midwife was immediately ready, arriving finally at 11 p.m. She prescribed an enema, which brought a little relief, and said that the delivery could well be delayed a week. We very much need trained midwives [of our own]. It is incredible how the most untrained and ignorant midwives (people whom I otherwise respect and value) often think they are the best. Such persons deceive themselves.

December 10 Last night I dropped in to see my brother Diedrich who had just returned from Kamianka with his Jewish driver. A little later his driver returned in an agitated state, reporting that he had encountered two wolves under way. His frightened horses had bolted, making an about-turn, and galloped back to Novopodolsk, the wolves in pursuit until my brother's garden. It suddenly got dark today, indicating an eclipse of the sun that we could not see because of clouds.

December 12 I was of two minds whether to leave for Khortitsa since there was ice, but no snow, on the ground. My brother Diedrich thought that all would go well if we could only shoe the horses, and he would gladly pay the costs. Since the horses already had shoes on their front hoofs, we had the rear ones shod. I provided the horses, my brother the sled, and Jacob drove. We left at noon, in God's name, and spent the night on the Kudashev khutor, where I conducted a service the next day. The meeting room was quite dark because of the dense fog, pouring rain, and a strong north wind outside. The rain changed to snow, and when the sun finally broke through at 2 p.m., we packed and left for Hoffnungsfeld, arriving there at three. I held an evening service and preached another sermon.

December 14 We left Monday at sunrise under clear skies, with ten degrees of frost, and made good headway on the ice-covered roads. We would have reached Neuosterwick by noon if the Tomakovka

Stream, which runs through the state peasant village of that name, had been passable. The creek water had first risen and then run off, leaving a jumble of mud and ice. We hoped to cross the creek at Mikhailovka, but a Russian who had come from there advised us to go via the Krassen Kut Inn on the post road and then cut across the fields to Schönhorst. We did difficulty crossing the ice-fields, especially through the many clefts and valleys of the area. Our brown mare lost the shoes on her right front and rear hoofs.

December 17 During my absence our daughter Katharina [Bärgen] gave birth to an infant son Jacob. Both are well. The midwife from Voronzovka (see entry for Dec. 8, 1870), who was awaiting the v Kampen birth, had delivered our daughter. My wife said her skills had been of great value. We thank the Lord. The midwife told me that during the complicated v Kampen delivery the woman had discharged a piece of flesh the size of an ox's heart, which she called a 'polyp.' Her survival was extraordinary, she said, and worth publicizing in the press. At home I took out my dictionary of foreign words and found a second definition for 'polyp,' a 'growth.'

December 22 Winter seems here to stay, and one cannot travel with unshod horses. Four weeks ago Cornelius Mantler, our local smith, left with two wagons to haul wares from Kremenchug for the local merchant Leib Mendelssohn. Leib returned two weeks ago. The loaded wagon could not get across the Dnieper, however, and Mantler's family worried about him. Last night he finally got home, but I am sure without making a profit. Carting is a difficult business in winter.

December 26 Today is my 50th birthday, and I have reached the years of which it is said, 'I will say they give me no pleasure.' I am grateful to thee, Lord, for the faithfulness that surrounds me, and for the love revealed in the sacrifice of thy precious life. How many days and years are left to me?

December 31 *Year's End.* We are at the close of one year and the start of another. Looking back over the past year, I find much reason to praise God's grace, which has sustained me and my family. We have had no major changes in our family. In spring, after burying their youngest son Jacob, our children the Johann Andreses moved to the Nepluiev colony of Blumenfeld where another son Jacob was born to them as a replacement. In March our daughter Katharina married Johann Bärgen. They lived with us through the summer and then in fall rented the back room of my nephew Diedr. Epp's house. An infant son was born to them two weeks ago.

The crops in our area have been quite middling. I reaped an average of $1\frac{5}{8}$ chetvert of wheat per desiatina. Our total yields are as follows: wheat 32 chetvert; barley 23; oats approximately 20; rye 25 merka; and potatoes 7 chetvert. I think we have enough feed and fuel to see us through the winter, particularly since we still have some left from last year.

The world's political situation reminds us strongly of Christ's words proclaiming the coming Day of Judgment. The great blood-letting of the Franco-Prussian war is a sign of these serious times. War clouds also gathered over our fatherland, the Russian Empire, threatening bolts of lightning. But our Lord again graciously turned the danger aside.

Our situation in the Hebrew colonies has become more secure. In spring most of our settlers became discouraged as the Jews confronted us with awkward dilemmas and persecution. A Brotherhood Meeting in church decided to send Johann Bärgen Sr and me to raise the matter with the Guardianship Committee in Odessa. God blessed this initiative. His Excellency, Ettinger, president of the Committee, responded positively to our petition. A few weeks later, we received from the Committee a written guarantee of our continued stay here. In fall an important official from St Petersburg who was passing through told my brother Diedrich that the imperial government regarded us as having the status of colonist settlers.

But one cloud of affliction and a threat to our faith has appeared. It relates to our freedom from the bearing of arms. The government has not yet told us anything relating to this issue. We undoubtedly deserve to be chastised since life in our communities could be called more worldly than Christian. Cipher music, which was introduced earlier and caused a terrible uproar, has finally been accepted everywhere. The resulting animosities and conflicts have finally ended. Only two church members in Izluchistaia still refuse to attend services because of it, and that mainly out of stubbornness.

Old Colony Flemish Mennonite mother church, Khortitsa village, where Jacob Epp, his father David, and brother Heinrich preached

Jacob D. Epp (1820–90) and his first wife, Maria,
née Klassen (1822–63)

Jacob Epp and his second wife, Judith,
née Dyck (1832–1906)

Jacob Epp's daughter Helena
(1844–1925)
and her husband Johann Andres
(1841–1915)

Jacob Epp's daughter Katharina
(1846–1932)
and her husband Johann Bärgen
(1845–1916)

OPPOSITE

Jacob Epp's sons David and Peter, circa 1891, in Russia

Jacob Epp's son David (1849–1933)
and his wife Margaretha, née Heide
(1847–1935)

Jacob Epp's son Peter (1855–1920)
and his wife Elisabeth, née Epp
(1853–1929)

Jacob Epp's son Diedrich
(1857–1940)
and his wife Susanna, née Peters
(1861–1913)

Jacob Epp's son Gerhard
(1864–1919)
and his wife Katharina, née Janzen
(1868–1944)

OPPOSITE

Jacob Epp's daughter Maria (1850–1917)
and her husband Wilhelm Martens (1848–1923)

Jacob Epp's son Jacob (1853–1912)
and his wife Helena, née Janzen (1857–1937)

Jacob Epp's daughter Elisabeth
(1866–1946)
and her husband Heinrich Wieler
(1865–1949)

Jacob Epp's son Johann
(1875–1948)
and his wife Margaretha, née Janzen
(1877–1945)

Jacob Epp's brother Heinrich (1827–96),
Zentralschule teacher and Old Colony Flemish Mennonite church elder

Jacob Epp's brother Diedrich
(1819–1900),
master cabinet-maker and
Judenplan administrator,
and his wife Katharina,
née Siemens

Jacob Epp's brother Johann
(1830–88),
Khortitsa District secretary
for two decades

Jacob Epp's sister Anna
(1833–1919)
and her husband Cornelius Hildebrand
(1833–1920),
Old Colony farm-implements
industrialist

Jacob Epp's sister Katharina
(1839–1915)
and her husband Bernhard Schellenberg
(1840–88),
the Mennonite Old Colony's first
medical 'doctor'

Views of the Old Colony village of Rosenthal on the Dnieper River

Views of the former Judenplan village of Novovitebsk,
where the Jacob Epp family lived for many years,
photographed in 1989

1838.— 48.

ABOVE AND OPPOSITE

Cornelius Hildebrand's water-colour paintings of Khortitsa Island scenes

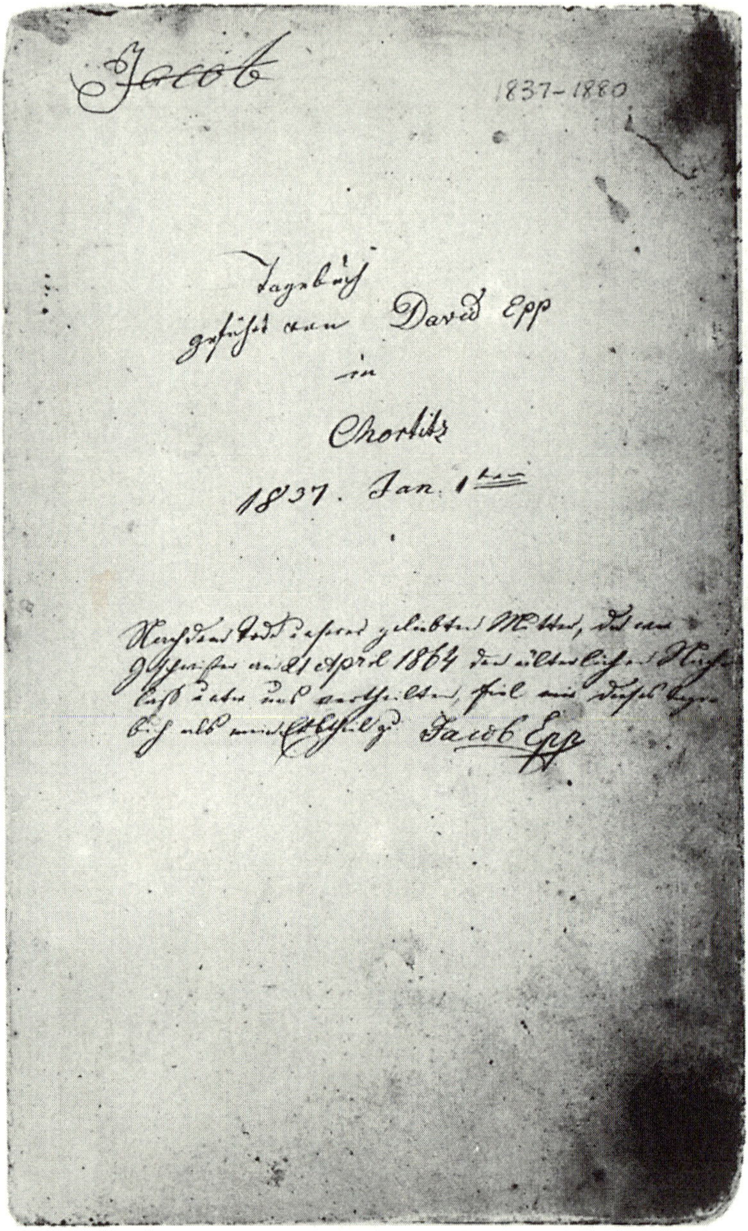

Title page of David D. Epp's diary for the years 1837–43
in which Jacob Epp also recorded a volume of his own diaries

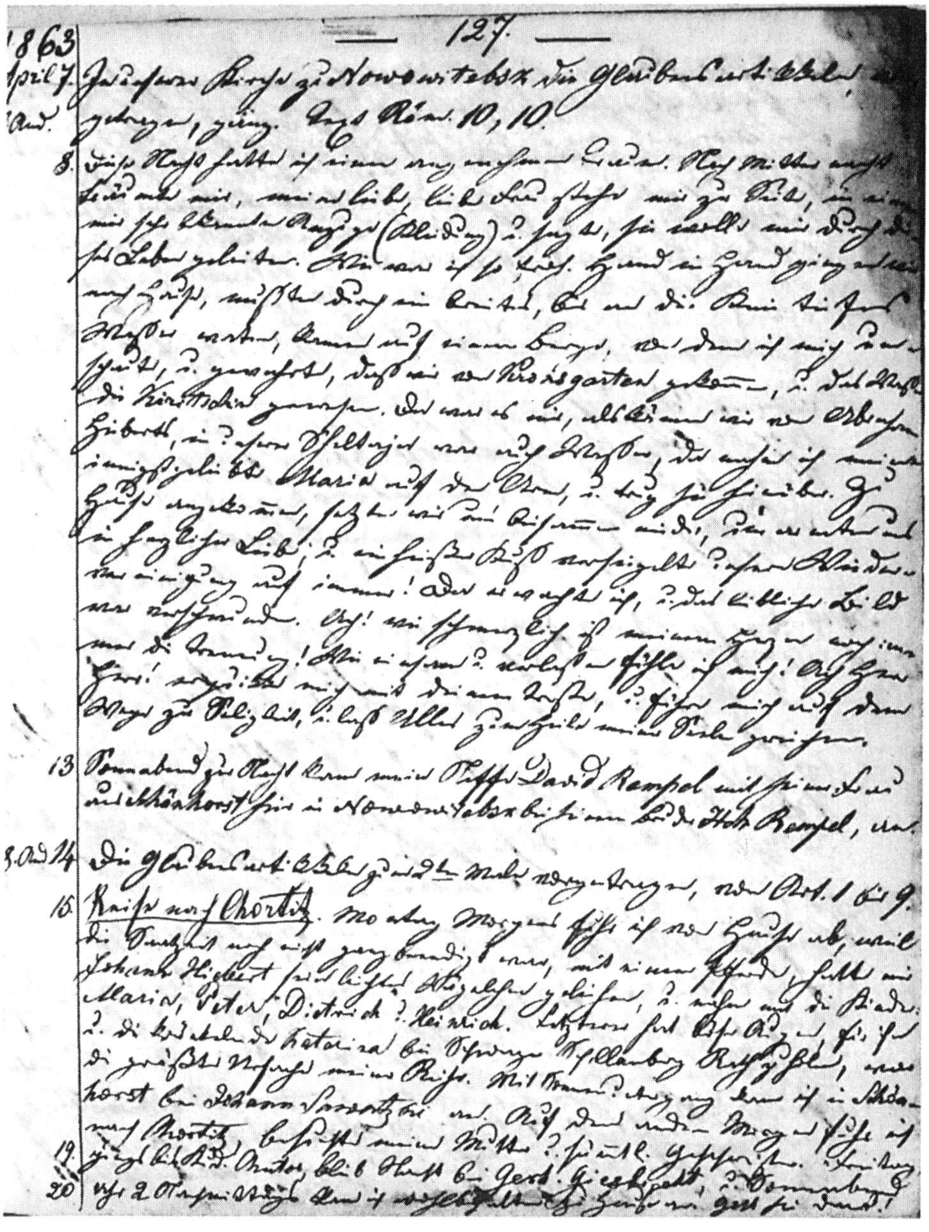

Diary entry, 8 April 1863,
in which Jacob Epp records dream of a reunion with
his recently deceased wife Maria

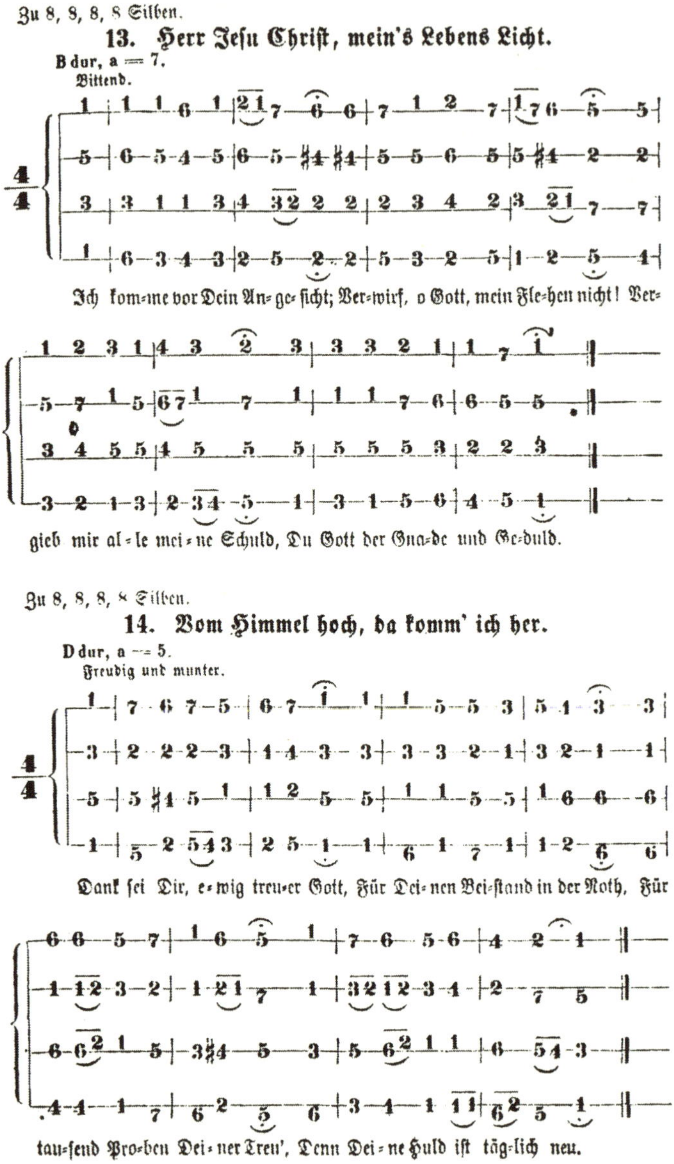

Four-part 'cipher music' in Heinrich Franz's *Choralbuch*, which helped spread knowledge of this form of music notation throughout the Russian Mennonite world

BOOK IV, 1871–1880

Balancing the Old and the New

'The heart of a husbandman ... is often like a pendulum, swinging back and forth between hope and despair.'

May 24, 1871

'Using the sword and launching law suits are really one and the same thing.'

December 6, 1873

'The remarkable temporal freedom enjoyed by our community for so long has come to an end.'

December 31, 1875

1871[1]

January 3 The Andreses and their father returned from the Khortitsa colonies with a letter from my brother Heinrich (among other documents and papers) containing a frightening story. After describing various of his sermons and trips and the collection for the building of [new] churches in Neuendorf and Neuosterwick, my brother writes: 'A terrible accident occurred in Kronsweide yesterday. One boy has killed another in a terrible and frivolous game. The dead boy is David Löwen, son of David Löwen of Kronsweide, and the perpetrator Cornelius Friesen, an apprentice watchmaker with our brother-in-law Hildebrand.

'The Friesen boy received a gun from his brother, which his master would not let him keep in the house. Yesterday afternoon, Cornelius was taking the gun away when he met several good friends who decided to go hunting together and tried first to shoot a magpie. The gun misfired, however, and after examining it the boys concluded that it lacked a tinder. Just then three other boys came by, good friends and about the same age (18), who had probably heard of the unsuccessful attempt to shoot the magpie. The friends teased the boys [with the gun], daring them to shoot them, and two of them, including the dead boy, even set up the [gun]sight themselves.

'Cornelius Friesen jokingly took the gun in hand and aimed. His friend Cornelius Krahn said, "You've got to cock the gun before you shoot," whereupon Friesen cocked the rifle, pulled the trigger, and the gun unexpectedly went off, striking Löwen in the chest. Seeing the gun aimed in their direction, the other two boys jumped. Löwen staggered and turned to his good friends. They caught him and asked if he had been hit. He simply answered "yes," and dropped to the ground dead. A terrible fear now seized all the boys, who ran for help to a nearby house. There was nothing, however, that they could do but to carry the body of the boy who had been killed so frivolously into the home of his grief-stricken parents. The perpetrator fled to his guardian, and out of the full anguish of his soul cried out, "Now they will shoot me too." The gun had been fired from about 30 paces.

'Last night our brother Johann [the Old Colony District Secretary] and the District Mayor drove to Kronsweide to record the facts of the case. The examining magistrate has been informed of the matter, and the body will not be buried until he arrives. Friesen has been taken into custody. Perhaps this terrible episode will make some people more careful. The victim's mother is my late wife's niece. Johann told me she had been shattered by the accident and could not utter a single word. This is easy to imagine, for a mother's heart experiences such grief especially deeply. May our dear Saviour comfort her.'

I heard another story today about a certain Goosen in the Molochna who had taken his life. I am not sure which village he is from, but they said that he had ridden to the home of his married daughter in Liebenau, taken a rope from the barn, and hanged himself from a tree in the corner of the wood-lot. Dear Lord, the devil and despair have such power over people. Lead us not into temptation and help us in temptation.

In Neuenburg a young, 24-year-old unmarried man by the name of Bernhard Krahn is obsessed by the idea that certain people dominate and rule him and that he must follow their wishes. Only he knows of their presence. Recently one such tormentor ordered him to jump into the well and bathe himself and promised to bring him out safely. He jumped. At present people are keeping watch over him, but it will be difficult to help him if the Lord does not cut through the dark veil enclosing his mind. Except for this idea and its consequences, however, he seems quite normal.

These are three remarkable cases. The first should be a lesson to all parents, guardians, and superiors to prohibit the use of all firearms, or at least their general use. The fate of poor Bernhard Krahn reminds us of the serious illness of our beloved mother in Neuosterwick, which has tormented her for years and has now become especially critical in her old age. Lord Jesus, if thou didst help her with thy power she would be truly helped.

January 17 Lord, empower me with thy grace as thou didst once empower Paul. If I am to preach thy Word, make me worthy of the task. Reveal thy will. Am I to preach thy Word freely, as before?

January 23 Elder Gerhard Dyck, my brother Heinrich, and several ministers from the Molochna Mennonite community left yesterday for St Petersburg where they are to present a petition to the imperial government or to His Majesty the Emperor regarding [the question] of our exemption from the bearing of arms. May the Lord Jesus crown their enterprise with success.[2]

January 25 We started weaning our little darling Johann several days ago, but he was quite difficult today. Finally his mother put peppermint drops on her breast, which he found bitter and unpleasant and turned up his nose at. Lord, let him grow up to thy honour, and grant salvation to all of our children.

February 11 Thursday. A conference of ministers of the Khortitsa and Kronsweide churches was scheduled for today in the Khortitsa church. We were therefore surprised to see many sleds rushing to the church. Apparently the brethren from Neuendorf, Schönhorst, and Neuhorst had been invited to the Brotherhood Meeting by mistake. Arrangements for a service had thus to be made on short notice, the church stove heated, and the singing arranged.

The purpose of the meeting of ministers, which I attended, was to discuss the forthcoming trip to St Petersburg, specifically the question of what we might do to end the threat of military service that hangs over us. Also, Elder Gerhard Dyck and my brother Heinrich, who had been elected from the Khortitsa and Kronsweide churches to visit St Petersburg, wished to take leave of their colleagues.

Elder G. Dyck had just returned from a conference in the Molochna at which the churches had elected Elder Leonhard Sudermann of Berdiansk, Reverend Peter Görzen of Rudnerweide, Reverend Franz Isaac of Ohrloff, and the District Secretary Peter Janzen [to represent them]. The conference had also decided to first seek the Guardianship Committee's permission to travel to St Petersburg and urged our representatives to do likewise. Representatives of the two groups would then meet at a certain lodging in Kharkhov.

We had therefore sent to Odessa Isaac Lehn, the assistant District mayor, and Jacob Hamm, the past District mayor, who had now telegraphed that the president [of the Guardianship Committee] had approved the plan and given [Heinrich Epp] permission to absent himself from his teaching duties to make the trip. The president had introduced the two to the governor-general [of New Russia] (who also planned to visit St Petersburg), to whom they had submitted a petition. They had submitted a further petition to the governor [of Ekaterinoslav Province] in Ekaterinoslav. Once these men returned from Odessa, Elder Dyck and my brother Heinrich planned to leave for the capital.

After singing several stanzas of a hymn we entered the church. Elder Dyck mounted the pulpit and explained the reason for the trip. This affliction from the Lord had come to pass because of our sins, he said, calling upon the church to return to God in Jesus Christ. Only if we did so in all seriousness could the Lord bless the trip. We should unitedly implore the Lord to dispose the heart of our gracious emperor to remove this threat from us. These words visibly moved the congregation. After saying a prayer, the Elder then invited my brother Heh. Epp to speak. His address, made without the use of any notes, was no less moving. Lord, grant them thy blessing.

My brother made special mention of the mothers, who had a deep interest in this subject. They were looking into a dark future and had anxious feelings about their young sons. He called on the brethren to implore the womenfolk to persevere in their prayers throughout the trip. Such pious prayers could accomplish more than could any deeds by members of the delegation. He promised that before retiring at night and upon rising in the morning he and the Elder would remember those at home in their prayers. The Elder led the congregation in a further prayer, the service concluding with the singing of a hymn. It was a beautiful and moving service. Lord, accompany them with thy blessing.

Various matters were then discussed in the ministers' room. Another service is to be held tomorrow morning in the Khortitsa church. It is to be announced in all of the villages (but not in Neuendorf, Schönhorst, and Neuhorst, who were here today). Elder Peter Klassen of the Kronsweide church was absent. Present were the ministers Heinr. Pauls, Cornelius Pauls, and Corn. Friesen. Tomorrow's service will presumably be very large.

February 16 Tuesday. Overcast skies, thawing, and water collecting in the valleys. My heart is burdened by an acute shortage of money. I am supposed to pay the poll tax for six people and do not have a single copeck. I had hoped to get a short-term loan from my neighbour Is. Friesen, but he is short of cash himself. Lord, help me out of this predicament, for thou hast rubles enough and art able to find a way out.

February 19 Friday. This afternoon, my wife and I drove to Novovitebsk to borrow money from the Jew Jericho Hillbauer, who would gladly have given me a loan, but was out of money himself. He promised to have some cash on Sunday, but I wonder if he will keep his word.

February 22 Towards evening, Jacob and I went to see Jericho Hillbauer about the money, but he had left for the synagogue. I therefore looked up Wilhelm Martens, who lent me 25 R. for an indefinite term. This helps me over the immediate crisis, but where will I get the money to pay off my debt?

February 26 While visiting the Nepluiev settlement I was witness to an unpleasant incident. On their way home to [the village] Steinau, Heinrich Giesbrecht and Jacob Wieler took a short cut that branched off from Schöndorf, along a road that is closed to traffic, but this they probably did not know. They were suddenly surrounded by three men on horseback, forced to return to the village, and treated like ordinary thieves who had been caught red-handed. I overheard them being rudely chided before finally being released.

February 27 Saturday. Andres returned from Khortitsa in the evening. A letter had arrived from my brother Heinrich in Kharkov reporting that their driver had capsized their sled close to Neuenburg. They had ended up together in a pile but were unhurt. The snow-drifts along the rail track had been almost as high as the coaches themselves.

February 28 Prior to the service in Steinau, Mrs Abraham Knelsen appeared before the ministers. The Grossfürstlich Elder Johann Wiebe had reported that she had committed fornication and adultery with Heinrich Friesen of the Nepluiev settlement, to which she confessed. She also admitted that during her first marriage she had done similar acts with Jacob Andres Sr in Einlage, with the teacher Peter Abrahams, and with Jacob Hiebert. I presented the matter to the Brotherhood Meeting. She was placed in the ban, in keeping with God's Word.

The poverty here [in the Nepluiev settlement] is very great, all of the settlers having suffered a great deal.

March 6 This afternoon I officiated at the wedding of the widow

Hamm and the widower Peter Peters. The troubles stemming from the cipher music are gradually coming to an end. Peters, who had not attended public services since April 21, 1868, has now ended his defiance. This morning he was with his bride at the service, where cipher melodies were sung. They were also sung this afternoon, and I saw him singing along. Only one stubborn hold-out remains, Jacob de Veer of Izluchistaia.

March 12 I bought a chetvert of barley for horse-feed from Leib Mendelssohn for 4 R.

March 13 The village community repaired the dam on the Sheltaia Stream so that it can again be used as a crossing. I removed the storm-windows.

March 18 The ground is again snow-covered and all the cattle are inside being fed. Fodder is scarce, and people have been buying it for some time. I hope to get by until after seed-time. To date I have only had to buy a little horse-feed, but will probably have to buy some flour.

March 23 I walked to Novovitebsk to repay Wilhelm Martens his 25 R. loan. As I was getting ready to leave, Peter v Niessen complained that his stepson Johann Rempel had run off to his guardian Krause. Neighbours and the runaway say that v Niessen had been overly strict with Johann from the very start, and had often mistreated him. This v Niessen denies. I urged v Niessen to discuss the matter with the boy's other guardian, Reverend Jacob Wienz in Kronsthal, but warned him that the boy was unlikely to return if he had really set his mind to leaving, etc., etc.

March 26 I sent a letter to my brother Heinrich asking for news about his St Petersburg trip.

March 27 Easter Sunday. The [Mennonite] landowners, who gathered at the home of Peter Hildebrand, decided to hire Diedrich Thiessen Jr as teacher. It was also proposed that we repair the dam to ensure that the pond would have enough water for the cattle over the summer. Isbrand Friesen and several others wanted the work done during the last day of [the Easter] holidays, to which my brother Diedrich objected. I supported him by saying, 'This would discredit us with the Jews, who are exceedingly strict in observing the Sabbath and other holidays.' I could not agree to the proposal and suggested that the manure or ashes be carted on to the dam on Wednesday.

Friesen continued to protest, however, arguing he had no time on Wednesday, when he planned to seed. His position struck me as being quite wrong so I got up, said 'goodnight,' and went home. There was in any case too much idle chatter for the great holiday.

March 30 Easter Tuesday. I received a letter from my brother Heinrich today, dated March 28, in which he writes: 'We are back from our trip to St Petersburg and are happy and well. The intercession of the brethren was important to the success of our trip. The angels of the Lord protected us and removed many of the obstacles standing in our way. What was done was done by the Lord, and we honour and praise him. I will not have time to write to you in detail now because I have to prepare a sermon for tomorrow. I hope you will understand and be satisfied with a general description for today.[3]

'We left on the morning of February 16, boarded the train on the 20th and reached St Petersburg safely on the 24th. The Molochna brethren were already there: Elder Leonhard Sudermann from Berdiansk, the two ministers Franz Isaac and Peter Görz, and the District secretary Herman Janzen. We were received by Selenoi, the minister of state domains,[4] on the 27th. He is somewhat stern but seems well-disposed towards us and promised to support our cause. But he could not give us definite assurances since the military [service] question is still being considered by the imperial government. Ettinger, president [of the Guardianship Committee], was also in St Petersburg (is probably still there), and he said we had made a good impression on the minister. This is also the result of God's grace.

'We had a further audience with Count Heyden, president of the Commission for the Drafting of the Military Law,[5] whom the two Elders had been to see earlier. The Commission is prepared to exempt Mennonites from military or armed service. They would demand, however, that Mennonites agree to being employed in caring for the sick. Count Heyden thought he could assure us that Mennonites born before the implementation of the military law would be fully exempt and that those born subsequently would have to be involved in medical service. Confirmation of such an arrangement might, however, take from one and a half to two years. This would mean that no one would be required to serve for a period of 24 or 25 years.

'We also talked to Senator Hahn,[6] but were unable to see Senator Gerngross, a member of the Commission, and Kotzebue, governor-general in Odessa, whom the two Elders had met. We had also planned to seek an audience with our Sovereign the Emperor and present our petition directly to him,[7] but let this idea fall when several people who genuinely are trying to help us suggested that such an initiative might alienate a number of important people who are sympathetic to our position. In response to several requests we drafted a short statement outlining the Mennonite position on non-resistance, which we submitted to Count Heyden, Senator Gerngross, and the Ministry of State Domains.[8] You can read copies of our submissions when you come here. Perhaps you will have an opportunity to do so earlier.

'Yet we did in fact meet the emperor [Alexander II] while he was on a promenade in the Summer Garden. Quite unexpectedly he even spoke to us, asking who we were and where we came from and what the purpose of our visit was. After we had answered his questions, he stepped into his carriage, saying "So that is it," and drove off. One would almost conclude from his questions that he knew we were Mennonites. We left St Petersburg on March 8, arriving home on the evening of the 17th. We were repeatedly delayed on the way home by flooding rivers. You must forgive me for breaking off at this point, etc.'

We thank the Lord our God for the success of the trip.

March 31 We resumed our seeding after the holidays, planting lentils and wheat on the steppe. We also planted 2 ash and 18 acacia trees in the upper garden.

April 2 Friday morning, we planted some mulberry bushes in hedges. Wilhelm Martens and Heinrich Martens dropped by for news of the St Petersburg trip, and I read my brother Heinrich's letter to them.

April 4 At the close of today's service, I read brother Heinrich's letter to the congregation.

April 13 Yesterday we ploughed two desiatinas for 7 R. for Tuchem, our Jewish neighbour, and continued tilling our own land today. The late spring means late seeding.

At my brother Diedrich's place, Asser Stuppel, the merchant, told me there had been a serious revolt of Greeks (and also Russians) against Jews in Odessa during the first Easter holidays and that the destruction was very serious. We have not yet heard any details, nor do we know why the police failed to step in immediately to stop the violence. I expect the Odessa newspapers will carry a full report.[9]

April 15 Yesterday several Germans, as a favour, ploughed three-quarters of a desiatina of land for Sewlewer, the secretary.

April 19 We harrowed the last two desiatinas of oats, prepared a quarter-desiatina melon patch and seeded one-half a desiatina to millet. We have seeded a total of 20 desiatinas to wheat, including 1 desiatina for David and 1 desiatina for Tupke (his part of the 4 desiatinas we are share-cropping). My own share is 18 desiatinas of wheat, 1 of summer rye, 6 of barley, 4 of oats, for a total of 29½ desiatinas (including the melon patch and the millet). With the Lord's blessing, we should again have a living.

April 20 The tailor Tupke pleaded with me to plough a further two desiatinas for him. The horses are bone-tired, but I agreed. He will work off the 6 R. by tailoring.

April 21 We ploughed three-quarters of a desiatina of land for Johann Hübert, making a total of 37 desiatinas ploughed.

April 22 Brother Diedrich's wife brought Mrs Wilhelm Martens to see me. She is physically and mentally ill and anxious about her salvation. I read words of comfort to her from the Bible, especially chapters 11 and 12 of Paul's letter to the Hebrews.

April 25 Sunday. Martin Harder Jr appeared before me this morning in regard to his drinking. He blamed his father, who is always angry with him, for his heavy drinking. Drinking to excess is not a serious sin, to his mind. He believes he could not do his tailoring without brandy. But once he saw that we meant business, he pleaded with us [not to take disciplinary action against him] and promised to reform. We decided to give him one more chance, but only for a short time, and allowed him to go in peace. I will seek the Elder's advice in this matter.

May 3 Today we suffered another blow with the death of a milk cow, our third in a short time. There is only one left. Our children the Johann Bärgens, who lived in the home of Diedr. Epp Jr, moved into rented quarters, a Jewish home with 13 desiatinas of land leased for 30 R.

May 7 Mrs Heinrich Siemens complained that her daughter had moved back in with them because of her husband Peter Olfert's brutal treatment of her. She related that her daughter and son-in-law had been living in Steinau with Olfert's brother-in-law Abraham Breil. The Breils had at first protected their daughter from her husband's abuse. Then, however, the Breils had taken to egging Breil on. Matters had now reached the stage where their daughter could endure no more and had left her husband. I promised to look into the matter and bring it to the Elder's attention.

God willing, I will continue my diary as volume v in the empty pages of my blessed father's diary.[10]

May 11 My blessed father was not allowed to fill all the pages of this volume when he was called home from the difficult course of his life in his 62nd year. Eleven years remain until I reach that age, and God knows whether I will live that long. I will continue my diary in the remaining pages of this volume [of my father's diaries],[11] but wonder whether I will be able to fill them all. God, thou knowest this. Grant me the grace that my children might find much in these diaries to make them think seriously about the only thing that really counts, to seek salvation in Christ Jesus through fear and trembling. Amen.

I built a brick-wide wall along the side of the house where we have the cupboard, to keep the house warmer in the winter and to keep the moisture out.

May 12 I awoke this morning, got myself dressed, but then felt ill and sleepy and lay down again on the bench to rest. I dozed off, slept for an hour and a half, and dreamt that someone had told me that I had no more than 11 years to live. This time would soon be over, I replied, and were I to die sooner I had resolved to have nothing further to do with the world of military service. I wanted to live only for the Lord Jesus. Then I awoke and was happy at having made this resolve. My deepest wish is to be found always in Christ Jesus. The dream about the 11 years probably relates to my thinking last night and my introduction to this volume. Yet I would also like to think of the dream as an admonition from God, with a purpose, speaking to my heart.

May 15 It is 28 years ago today since my beloved father passed to his final rest. In that time much in the world has changed and many things in our community have become different. Years ago, while still teaching on the Island of Khortitsa, several neighbours got together and talked about the value of our Charter of Privileges. Most everyone thought it had been given to us in perpetuity and that the promised freedoms were guaranteed for all time. But I suggested things could change rapidly if there were a major transformation in the country and in the central administration. The discussion became heated, one person saying that our charter was irrevocable as long as a descendant of blessed Emperor Paul I sat on the Russian throne.

I replied that nothing in this world would last forever, except the Word of God. It alone would endure in all eternity. The Charter of Privileges had been given to us and could as easily be taken away. Only the Charter of Privileges of the Lord Jesus, sealed with his blood and with the New Testament, was irrevocable and would remain valid through all upheavals. And though heaven and Earth would pass away, the Word of God would remain forever. As things turned out, the Charter of Privileges did indeed lose its validity within a short period of time.

For a long time we placed our trust in the charter, even as the Jews had placed theirs in the temple of the Lord (according to the prophet Jeremiah). It is because of our sins that the changes have now come. Emperor Paul personally signed the charter in 1800, his son Nicholas confirmed it, and now during the reign of Paul's grandson Emperor Alexander Nicholaevich it is losing its validity. Yet we are thankful that God has blessed the trip to St Petersburg (see entry for March 30). I can see from the entries in my brother Heinrich's diary that people of the highest rank are well disposed towards us. God will thus continue to help us.

My wife and children washed three sheep to render their wool easier for spinning after it is shorn.

May 16 We have heard that Johann Pätkau's wife recently hanged herself because of a serious temptation. In Burwalde, a carelessly guided carriage tipped over leaving the church. The frightened horses bolted, running over the widow Thiessen, who died three hours later. In another accident, the aged Abraham Wiebe, who had moved from the Kudashev khutor to the Iasikovo settlement, had, while hauling a load of thatch straw from Kudashev, fallen off the front of his wagon in among the horses' hoofs. The frightened horses had driven over Wiebe, killing him. Pending a judicial investigation, the body had not at first been moved, but yesterday it was finally brought to the khutor and buried. These cases remind us powerfully that we must die. Watch and pray, for you do not know when you may die.

May 19 I was called home from my brother Diedrich's place to talk to Jacob de Veer of Izluchistaia, who poured out his troubles to me. His daughter Katharina had committed fornication with the young man Jacob Bärgen and been delivered of a healthy son. Bärgen admitted his guilt, but refused to have anything to do with Katharina or the child. I told de Veer we would be able to work something out once Katharina was up and about and we could call her and her lover to account. Sin brings people to ruin.

May 20 The wet weather is ideal for growth. Should the Lord continue his blessings we could have a very good harvest. In the household there is an endless amount of work to do. The garden is rank with weeds from the moisture, the brick walls we erected need plastering, and the old mud walls need repairs. There is simply one thing after another.

May 21 Friday. Yesterday we divided the sheep manure from the communal sheep-pen [among the villagers], and today I had mine cut into bricks [for fuel] and carted home. I am spending my time weeding the garden and working on the church register, while mother and the children are busy in the garden.

May 22 Saturday. Hot weather and a south wind. We started ploughing the fallow today.

May 24 It is as dry now as it was wet before, and our fields need moisture. God knows best when to send rain. The heart of a husbandman who looks out over his fields is often like a pendulum, swinging back and forth between hope and despair. I am not yet ready to believe that we are in for a crop failure. This morning we had a few drops of rain and heard the sound of thunder in the distance. I expected a shower, but this afternoon the sun is beating down again and there is a strong south wind.

May 25 Tuesday. The Elder baptized 15 young people this morning, including 2 young men and 4 young women from Borosenko.

May 26 This evening the Elder conducted a Holy Communion service with 103 members in attendance.

May 27 Thursday morning [Elder] Gerh. Dyck celebrated Holy Communion in the Schöndorf schoolhouse, [Borosenko settlement,] with only 39 members present. In the afternoon, I accompanied the ministers Anton Sudermann and Gerhard Enz of the Nepluiev settlement to the village of Hamburg, where I helped Enz prepare a church register.

May 28 This morning we celebrated Holy Communion in a storage shed of the manor [in the Nepluiev settlement] in the presence of 186 members.

May 30 Before today's service, Jacob Bärgen and Katharina de Veer, who had committed fornication with one another, appeared in the ministers' room (see entry for May 19, 1871). They were summoned by the witnesses Gerh. Andres and Bernhard Wiebe. Her father, Jacob de Veer, was also present. They openly confessed their guilt. De Veer was permitted to take his daughter home. *Brotherhood Meeting* following the service. I presented the case to the brethren, and Jacob Bärgen and Katharina de Veer were placed in the ban. Lord, grant them strength to repent. But before my colleague Pätkau and I could leave the church, Johann Bärgen, the father, approached us and said that the time of Katharina's pregnancy proved that she must also have committed fornication with others. The Lord knows what is concealed.

May 31 Gerhard, Johann, and I left our wool on consignment with David Mishnik in Novovitebsk (a total of 5 pud 18 funt).

June 1 Yesterday afternoon and this morning, my children weeded the melon patch. We started haying this afternoon.

June 3 Last night God blessed us with a soaking rain that was accompanied by thunder and lightning. The chances for a good crop are now better, but it is all in God's hands.

Johann Bärgen Sr asked that his son be readmitted to the church.

Since all the villagers had sold their sheep I had no choice but to do likewise. Pet. Hildebrand, Reverend Jacob Pätkau, my brother Diedrich, and I sold ours to Orlanka, the ewes (including the lambs) selling for 2 R. 60 C. each and the yearlings for 2 R. I sold a total of 22 old sheep and 14 yearlings for 85 R. 20 C.

June 4 Johann Bärgen and Jacob de Veer, the fathers of the two members placed in the ban, asked me to help them reach a settlement in regard to the costs of raising the child born out of wedlock. Veer demanded 100 R. plus 25 R. support per year for 8 years, and Bärgen offered to pay no more that a total of 50 R. I suggested that the best solution would be for the two to marry. Bärgen replied that he had recommended this as well, but that his son was set against such a marriage. I then told them they would have to reach a settlement on the payment of [maintenance] costs before the children could be readmitted [to the church]. A multi-year settlement was also out of the question. They finally agreed that Bärgen would pay de Veer 60 R., half by Michaelmas and the rest by May 1, 1871. The two men shook hands and parted in peace.

June 6 *Brotherhood Meeting*. Jacob Bärgen and Katharina de Veer were readmitted to the church.

June 12 We helped our neighbour I. Friesen put up the rafters of his house. The walls are made of air-dried bricks.

June 13 On my instructions, Cornelius Krause and Peter v Niessen appeared before my colleague Pätkau and me in the ministers' room. They had been summoned by Heinrich Olfert and Martin Harder. My brother Diedrich was also present. Krause had written to me that v Niessen had accused him of making a lewd proposal to his wife, and so on. Mrs v Niessen was still in child-bed and could not be present, and so the matter was held over.

June 14 I had the rest of the fallow ploughed, making a total of three-quarters of a desiatina.

June 17 The present weather is ideal for the crops. It started to rain around noon and continued until around three o'clock. When it rains like this I regret that the roof on our implement shed is in such poor repair, but am also encouraged to think that a good rye crop (rye has failed for a number of years) will give us the thatch needed for repairs.

June 20 Sunday. We examined the matter raised last Sunday (see entry for June 13) and found it was merely gossip, tomfoolery, and loose talk: 'Avoid all appearance of evil.' [The background to the incident was] the quarrel between the Krauses and v Niessens regarding v Niessen's stepson Joh. Rempel, who had run off in spring to live with his guardian, Corn. Krause. In the meantime, the stepson had been hired out in Neuosterwick, and Krause had asked the v Niessens to provide the boy with clothing. The v Niessens were now trying to revenge themselves on Krause. [Today] Krause had been drinking and smelled of brandy. There was much idle talk. I exhorted the two couples to heed God's Word and to be reconciled, but it was in vain. The matter will come before the brethren.

June 27 Sunday. *Brotherhood Meeting*. Mrs v Niessen declared that

Krause had pursued her with illicit intentions. Krause stated, on his conscience, that he had not. As only God knows the truth, we let the matter rest on their consciences. But as we left the meeting there was an unexpected scene in which Krause and Heh. Olfert, supported by Martin Harder Sr, criticized me with great bitterness. Krause was angry that v Niessen had not had to appear before the brethren to apologize to him (the question regarding v N's stepson cannot be dealt with until it has been decided by the Orphans' Administration). Even Diedr. Thiessen Sr was somewhat sympathetic to my critics. Olfert said he would not attend church anymore. Lord, look down upon us in mercy and resolve this matter to our benefit.

June 29 Towards evening Corn. Krause and Heinrich Olfert of Novovitebsk apologized to me for their offensive behaviour on Sunday. I was delighted and thanked God from the bottom of my heart. May God grant that the dispute involving v Niessen can also be resolved peacefully. By arrangement with my brother Diedrich, the quarrelling parties are to meet at his place on Saturday.

July 3 Saturday. All of the model landowners in Novovitebsk (with the exception of Aron Harder), my colleague Pätkau, and I, met at my brother Diedrich's place to try to resolve the dispute between Krause and the v Niessens. It was all in vain. Lord, Lord, we pour out our troubles to thee. I have never seen v Niessen in such a state. Finally Krause accepted the proposal that, since his co-guardian [of v Niessen's stepson] lives in Kronsthal, the dispute involving the boy should be turned over to the Orphans' Administration. v Niessen stubbornly refused to make peace, speaking insultingly. My brother told him sharply that if this continued, 'You will have to leave Novovitebsk, and there will finally be peace.'

July 4 My brother Heinrich [Epp] gave a freely spoken sermon in the Novovitebsk church. The sermon gave me great pleasure.

July 9 After breakfast my brother Heinrich went to visit my brother Diedrich, and we started to thresh barley. Around 2 p.m. a storm suddenly threatened. We stopped working on the threshing floor, cleaned up the barley before the storm struck, and spread out a load brought in from the field. It was a fierce storm, raining torrents and snapping off a cherry tree in my brother Diedrich's garden. When it finally stopped, we could see a cloud of smoke rising over Novovitebsk where the lightning had struck Heinrich Sawatzki's house. The fire had spread from there to the Jewish house where we used to live, and to the homes of Wilhelm Martens and Heinrich Olfert. All of us from Novopodolsk drove over to help, including David, Jacob, and my son-in-law Johann Bärgen. The four houses and neighbouring buildings had gone up in flames. The victims were devastated. All of Martens's barley was already at home. When we drove home at night the barley and hay stacks were still smouldering and burning.

July 10 Saturday. The Germans from all six colonies helped to clean up the fire. My son Jacob drove with our wagon and stayed all day. My brothers Diedrich and Heinrich and I went to see the Fire Insurance Elder Corn. Krause, drew up a statement for the Khortitsa District Office, and were home by dinner.

July 11 Sunday. David, Maria, and Jacob were along to the service in Novovitebsk. My colleague Pätkau was to have preached in Novozhitomir, but cancelled that service. At the fire site yesterday, fellow believers from Novozhitomir expressed a wish to hear my brother preach in Novovitebsk. The service was quite large. My brother's sermon was based on the words, 'Come to me all ye that are weary and heavily laden ...' The message was deeply moving. How I wish that everyone there would take it to heart. It related entirely to the tragic fire in Novovitebsk. My brother identified the weary and the burdened, who had invited them, and the circumstances of the invitation.

July 13 Abr. Penner of Ebenfeld spent the night with us. He had been to Sofievka to hire workers, dropped off lumber for his carpentry at Mart. v Kampen's place, and delivered six sacks of flour and some lard for the victims of the fire. Let us do good, and not grow weary, and we will harvest without ceasing.

July 15 I carted the Ebenfeld donations to Novovitebsk, dropping them off at the home of the [Village] mayor, Martin Harder.

July 16 Late this afternoon I got a call to visit our children, the Johann Bärgens, whose infant son Jacob was deathly ill. Bärgen was working on the steppe. I first thought the boy might recover, but then recognized that the cramps were signs of approaching death. He took sick a week ago and had suffered a great deal. At 7 p.m. Jesus, the children's friend, called him home at the age of seven months and one day.

July 17 This afternoon my children dug a grave for the little one (this interrupted our wheat cutting).

July 18 The funeral service was held in the home of the Joh. Bärgens. Rest in peace, little darling, until the end of time.

July 19 Monday. There is a scorching heat and an east wind, and the wheat is ripening quickly. Our son Heinrich still suffers from fever every other day, so mother helped cart home three loads of winter rye.

July 24 At the time of our grandson's death, our son Heinrich had two attacks of the fever, which has since returned every second day. Heinrich now also has diarrhea, which has turned into bloody dysentery. Only God knows how this will end. I asked him yesterday if he wanted to die, and he answered, 'As God wills!' Lord Jesus, receive the suffering.

July 25 Last night Peter Thiessen's wife came by, crying and lamenting her fate. She had learned that her husband planned to join the Russian [Orthodox] church and wanted me to help find him. This I promised to do. Peter Thiessen has developed a bad reputation in his dealings with people. He has worked as a supervisor or foreman in the construction of various mills and has always ended up in some kind of trouble. On the last occasion, he had hired on for a year as a miller with a rich colonist, earning more than a master or supervisor of a mill. He had taken an advance of 70 R., and then about three weeks ago he had disappeared. Thiessen's wife and small children are staying with my brother Diedrich for now.

July 26 Monday. At four this afternoon, Cornelius Thiessen (he provided the wagon and a horse and Martin v Kampen provided the other horse), Peter Thiessen's wife and youngest child, and I left to search for Peter Thiessen. We stopped to feed our horses at an inn, waiting there for the moon to rise before continuing our journey.

July 27 We reached the home of Peter Siemens, administrator of the Heinrich's estate near Besborodka. He is an uncle of this Thiessen. Siemens told me that the secretary of his village had said that the Mikhailovka priest (close to Ekaterinoslav) had received a petition from Thiessen requesting his admission to the Russian church. After breakfast, Siemens ordered a carriage, and we accompanied him to see Abr. Wiebe (whose wife is Thiessen's aunt), on a nobleman's estate about eight verstas away. Peter Thiessen had spent some eight weeks there, hiring on as a miller with another nobleman and taking an advance of 10 R. The Wiebes had not heard of his disappearance. A Russian servant girl, who lives at a nearby inn, had kept company with Thiessen, but he was no longer with her. Siemens promised to try to find his nephew and send him home.

July 28 We started to thresh barley but stopped around noon when we heard that fire had broken out in the grain fields on the Novovitebsk steppe. We were asked to gather people together. I rushed over with the children and found fire burning on the pasture land close to the grain fields. Despite strong winds, there were enough of us to put out the fire before it could reach the grain.

August 1 Sunday. Today's congregation was small and there was no precentor. There were presumably more church members present at the fair in Sofievka, people who are little interested in [Christ's] invitation to the wedding.

August 7 Heinrich is much better today and we think he will soon be well, with God's help. Jacob has in the meantime come down with the fever, mother is also quite sick, and I do not feel well. This is most difficult, coming as it does in the midst of the harvest.

August 17 After being bedridden with bloody dysentery, I feel well enough today to catch up on my diary. The Lord is merciful to us. I was ashamed at my unfaithfulness, and he gave me the inner conviction this Sunday that all my sins were forgiven.

August 20 The Martin Harders came by last night with their son on their way to the Zentralschule in Khortitsa. I sent Peter along to Khortitsa, where he will attend the Zentralschule as a community stipend student, boarding with my brother-in-law Gerhard Dyck in Rosenthal. May the Lord bless his plans.

August 21 Saturday. We drove out in the evening to the melon patch and regret now that we did not hire a watchman.

September 6 Since we need straw for the roof, and rye for bread and for seed, we started threshing the rye.

September 9 I visited the Heinrich Siemens in Izluchistaia, whose stepdaughter, Mrs Peter Olfert of Steinau, is staying with them. She is sick in bed from a miscarriage, which they blame on her husband's cruelty. I was curious to see if they might be willing to take Olfert back in love if he returned as a repentant son and husband. But they hate him with such an intensity that I realized there was little hope of a reconciliation. The poor sick woman said very little herself.

September 10 I drove to the Nepluiev settlement, spending the night with my children in Blumenfeld.

September 11 Friday. This afternoon, Peter Olfert (see entry for Sept. 9), his brother-in-law Abraham Breil, and the witness Wilhelm Friesen appeared before the Ministerial Committee. I called Olfert to account for the sinful treatment of his wife. He first tried to deny everything, but his brother-in-law's testimony put a halt to that. As it turned out, his parents-in-law's behaviour had not been exemplary either. We exhorted him to try winning back the love of his wife, and deferred further consideration of the matter for now.

September 13 The rainy weather prompted us to start re-thatching the roof on our back building. I was able to hire Franz Klassen, David Wölk, and the teacher Thiessen, at 80 C. per person per day.

September 20 My sore eyes have improved to the point where I can keep my diary again. But I still cannot read the newspaper, even with glasses.

October 4 While we were away on a trip to Nikopol at the beginning of September, Diedrich caught a hamster and tied him to a rope. When we got home, mother objected to keeping the hamster, so I suggested to Diedrich that he leave him tied up until morning when we would decide what to do with him. That night the animal got away, crawled under the floor, and we have been looking for him every since. Today we dug up his passageway and found his storehouse full of potatoes and Turkish wheat, but he was nowhere in sight himself. I suppose he will continue to make his home with us. This should be a lesson to us to keep vermin of this ilk at a safe distance.

October 21 My brother Johann arrived unexpectedly early this morning, he and Johann Heese having spent the night at my brother Diedrich's. They were on their way home after taking possession of the recently purchased landed estate of Baratov, close to Sofievka. At my brother's urging, I too have applied for a hearthstead in the new settlement, although only God knows if I can manage it [financially]. Today Isaac Siemens and I went along with Jacob v Kampen to the market in Sofievka. On the way back we drove through Baratov to look at the building on the estate that Siemens wants to move into for the winter.[12]

November 1 Monday. Settlers for the newly purchased land [of Baratov] met in the District Office [in Khortitsa] to draw lots for the hearthsteads and to make down payments. I have been assigned a hearthstead in colony number one and paid down 50 R., which I borrowed from my brother Heinrich. A mayor was then elected for each village. We chose Jacob Wiebe of the Kudashev khutor by majority vote. Finally three men were elected to lay out the village site: my brother Diedrich, Jacob Redekopp, and I.

November 4 We arrived home Thursday afternoon accompanied by [Khortitsa District] Mayor Jacob Niebuhr, Assistant Mayor Lehn, a number of settlers for colony number one, and Peter Regier, the surveyor. All drove to the Baratov estate for the night.

The new Russian court system has been introduced in the [Khortitsa] colonies. The government's insistence on the use of the Russian language [in the keeping of administrative records and in correspondence with the Guardianship Committee] has upset many people. How I wish that these changes would lead the community to repentance, for only then would God continue to show us his grace.

November 5 Early this morning, Jacob and I drove to the new settlement, where a number of settlers had gathered to survey the land. It took quite a while to pick a site for village number one, which we did once the boundary between the two villages had been established. We reached an agreement only towards evening and then started to plough the boundary furrows. We and my brother Diedrich drove home for the night, but the others stayed.

November 6 We again drove out to the new settlement early Saturday morning. May God bless all of the settlers.

Late in the evening: the job is finished. The house-and-garden plots have been marked off by furrows and distributed. I drew lot number 18, my brother-in-law lot number 7, and my brother Diedrich lot number 17.

November 7 Peter Regier, the surveyor, was our guest today. Also here for the night were our married children the Johann Andres and their small family.

November 8 This morning David and the surveyor Peter Regier drove back to the newly acquired land.

November 11 I drove with my brothers-in-law Gerhard and Dietrich Dyck to examine our house-and-garden lots in the new settlement. I also provided a wagon and two workers [for the communal work], which is to be completed today.

November 12 Friday. The settlers for village number one met at our place this afternoon. Under the direction of [Village] Mayor Wiebe, we decided to accept cattle for pasturing this winter and made a record of the communal work already done.

November 15 Peter Blatz of Hochfeld repaired several pieces of our agricultural equipment, including a fanning mill, ploughs, harrows, etc. He is one of the settlers in village number two of the Marian estate [also known as Baratov]. He plans to move in the spring. He borrowed my wagon to drive to Novovitebsk to see Dietrich Thiessen, the recently elected mayor of his village. He was to be assigned a homestead site by lot and then planned to visit the place of settlement.

November 22 At eight o'clock last night, after the start of my wife's birth pangs, we fetched Mrs Peter Mantler, the midwife. But it was not until 6:37 this evening that a healthy daughter was born to us whom we have named Judith, after her mother.

November 27 My dear wife was hale and hearty for three days following her delivery. Our infant daughter, however, was very restless, a real squaller, and forced mother to sit up at night to nurse and to calm her. My wife became chilled and is now ill. Yesterday afternoon, after she experienced severe after-pains, we called the midwife, who applied heat. With God's help, she is much improved today, although she is still weak and in bed.

December 3 David returned from Khortitsa this afternoon, overjoyed that Margaretha Heide, Jacob Dyck's maidservant, had accepted his proposal [of marriage].

December 4 After our visitors left, David and I dropped in on the Klas Heides to make wedding arrangements.

December 22 Peter arrived home today [from the Zentralschule] with the Klas Heides, who had gone to fetch their daughter Margaretha (see entry for Dec. 3). In the meantime David had been to Kamianka to talk to the Heides and informed us that the engagement celebrations have been set for the second day of Christmas.

Johann Andres has sold his property in Blumenfeld and was here for the night.

December 26 The engagement festivities for our son David and Margaretha Heide were held this afternoon in the home of her parents in Kamianka. Today was also a special day for me, my 51st birthday, which Peter and Diedrich observed by singing a birthday song for me. This touched me deeply.

December 31 This year has brought many changes. The Charter of Privileges, which guaranteed the community's religious liberties, seems to have lost its force. At the beginning of the year, the Elder and my brother Heinrich together with the Molochna Elder and two Molochna ministers travelled to St Petersburg in this regard. The results are recorded elsewhere in this diary.

The administrative structure of the German colonies has taken on another form: the District Office is now a Volost Office and our superiors have been given new titles. Also, the Khortitsa District has purchased the Marian estate (also known as Baratov) for the landless (at 33 R. per desiatina) and has divided it into two villages: number one with 36 landowners and number two with 38. The villages have not yet been named. I have been assigned a hearthstead in village number one. If all goes as planned, it will be settled by my children. My son-in-law Johann Andres has sold his property in Blumenfeld for 700 R. (it has a nearly finished house), and will be moving to village number one of the new settlement. Johann Bärgen, who rented a Jewish property this year, will be moving to village number two.

During this year the Lord has also sent us much illness, but I have the sure hope that this will work to our betterment. Mother, Jacob, and Heinrich became ill late in summer, which caused problems in the threshing and the carting of the grain. Early in summer, nature turned lush from the plentiful rain, and we had hoped for a bumper crop. Then there was a heat wave and drought, which caused us worries. In the end, however, the Lord preserved our fields and we harvested a middling crop. The yields in Novopodolsk, Kamianka, and Izluchistaia were about three to four chetvert per desiatina, but in Novozhitomir, Novovitebsk and Novokovno they were only about one chetvert. I harvested a total of 53 chetvert wheat, 17 chetvert winter rye, 2 chetvert 2 merka summer rye, and 32 chetvert barley. We have threshed about half the oats, around 17 chetvert, and what remains could yield about as much again. Potatoes 32 chetvert.

1872

January 1 I preached a sermon in Kamianka. The schoolhouse was crowded, the sky overcast and dark, the room gloomy, and I had to strain my poor eyesight to read the sermon, which however went reasonably well. Should I preach by heart again? Let thy will be done, Lord, only reveal it to me.

January 2 After today's service, Reverend Pätkau joined our son David and Margaretha Heide in marriage. Our newly married children accompanied her parents home at night, where they will be living for the time being.

January 7 My son-in-law Johann Bärgen left for Khortitsa this morning with our son Peter and his schoolmate Peter Penner.

January 13 Peter Thiessen's wife came to see me this morning about her runaway husband (see entry for July 25, 1871), requesting that I collect money for her to buy a wagon that would allow her to hunt for him. She asked if I would initiate the collection at next Saturday's meeting of Judenplan model agriculturalists, at the home of my brother Diedrich (overseer of all Hebrew colonies of the 4th District of the Province of Kherson). The poor woman hopes she can win her husband back by speaking to him personally. May God give his blessing.

Johann Bärgen is back from Khortitsa. He told us that Elder Gerhard Dyck and Elder Peter Klassen had left to attend a general conference of elders and ministers in the Molochna called to discuss the military question.

January 15 Meeting of model agriculturalists in the home of the local overseer, my brother Diedrich Epp.

(1) The overseer asked us to discuss what might happen if model agriculturalists, who had acquired homesteads on the Marian land [Baratov settlement], settled there. He reminded us that we had petitioned the government repeatedly to guarantee our rights. Recently we had even sent a two-man delegation (Bärgen and myself)

to Odessa in this regard. Would this not disrupt our [Judenplan] community? He asked us to speak our minds frankly so that no one would later be blamed, etc. The unanimous view was that no one, including model agriculturalists who had acquired homesteads [in Baratov], should move to the new settlement.[13]

(2) It was decided to re-roof the church. The thatch was to be bought and a roofer hired. Heinr. Olfert was asked to take the matter in hand.

(3) The request of Thiessen's wife (see entry for Jan. 13) was presented to the meeting. It was decided that each village mayor should receive donations on her behalf.

(4) My brother reported that the model settlers in Novovitebsk had submitted a statement of claim against Diedrich Thiessen for refusing to pay his herdsman's fees. Thiessen was holding back monies in a dispute over the communal bull. He argued that cottagers [that is, Mennonite residents without land allotments] contributed as much to the purchase of breeding stock as did model settlers, yet received no compensation when they moved away. Since the hide of the recently deceased breeding bull had been sold, he demanded his share of the proceeds. The meeting decided that Thiessen was not entitled to any compensation. What may have prompted this dispute: selfishness, quarrelsomeness, or obstinacy? Lord, grant us thy peace.

January 20 Thursday morning my colleague Pätkau and I gathered to consider a dispute [in the Nepluiev settlement] between Abraham Breil and the deacon Peter Klassen. Breil had borrowed a fanning mill from Klassen. During a rainy period he had covered it with straw. Klassen had protested strongly, taken his fanning mill home, and said, 'That's what you get when you lend things out.' Later Breil had again borrowed the fanning mill, and the two men had gotten into a quarrel for which Klassen was mainly to blame. A reconciliation was difficult to achieve. It is strange that such a long trip was needed for such a trivial matter. I helped Peter Klassen organize the church register and urged him to keep it up to date.

January 22 This evening Klas Heide and our children the David Epps returned from Khortitsa with a cow and some chests. They told us that my brother Heinrich, Elder Peter Klassen of the Kronsweide church, and the ministers from the Molochna were leaving for St Petersburg on February 3 in regard to the military-service matter.

January 25 This morning we had 11 degrees of frost, a clear sky and a brisk north wind. Diedrich and I drove by sled to Novovitebsk where we dropped off the children's shoes for repairs at Diedr. Thiessen's place, bought 10 funt of tallow from Ziporovich, and were home within two hours.

January 30 I preached a sermon in Novokovno. In the afternoon we left to visit Mrs Isaac Friesen, who is ill, but our little Judith was not co-operative. She screamed at the top of her lungs, and we had to come back.

January 31 This afternoon mother and I left Judith at home and finally visited Mrs Friesen. Our neighbour, Mrs Diedrich Epp Jr, kindly looked after her at our place, promising to suckle her if that was necessary.

February 2 My brother Diedrich and colleague Pätkau left for Khortitsa to see my brother Heinrich before his departure tomorrow for St Petersburg.

February 4 At Pätkau's place this afternoon I vaccinated several children against smallpox. Mother and Judith were along, but our baby is still too young and had not fully recovered from her illness.

February 6 My brother Diedrich and Pätkau returned from Khortitsa yesterday. They told us that our beloved envoys, my brother Heinrich and the Kronsweide Elder Peter Klassen, together with my nephew Joh. Epp, had left for St Petersburg on February 3. May the Lord bless the trip.

In the afternoon, my brother Diedrich, Peter Siemens, Corn. Martens, Abraham Unger, and I gathered at my brother Diedrich's place to talk to Peter Thiessen. He was called in, made a complete confession, and asked for permission to live among us again. I asked him about the rumours that he had committed fornication, and he admitted that they were true. In reply to our question as to how far matters had gone regarding his [rumoured joining of the] Russian [Orthodox] church, he said that he had made only one inquiry in this regard and had not pursued the matter further because he knew it was wrong. The issue will be placed before the brethren on Sunday.

February 9 Last night a wolf made off with one of David Redekopp's pigs. It had done the same with Heh. Krause's pig the night before, and not long ago the wolf also killed one of Peter Martens's sheep.

February 10 We visited the school in Izluchistaia, taught by Johann Banmann. It has not improved since last year. The oldest pupil, a lad of 14 years, could not even write the number 40. May God have mercy on us and awaken among us a desire for good schools.
February 13 *Brotherhood Meeting.* I presented the matter involving Peter Thiessen. The brethren decided that since he had gone astray and committed many transgressions, including fornication, he should be placed in the ban. Friesen, Isaac Siemens, and I were instructed to inform him of our decision.
February 19 Saturday. I finally have some time to catch up on my diary. Our guests arrived Tuesday afternoon: brother-in-law Jacob Pätkau, brother-in-law Gerhard Dyck, Peter Priess Sr, and his son Jacob Priess. On Wednesday we attended the auction sale on the [Baratov] estate purchased by the Khortitsa community from Prince Repnin. There was a large crowd. The auction started with the farm buildings of the village of Marianovka (Baratov) on the Kamianka stream. My brother-in-law Dyck purchased part of a barn. In the afternoon we assembled in village number two where a Russian house, etc., was sold. The auction returned to village number one Thursday after breakfast and continued in Petervetski in the afternoon. Several leaders were present, including the [Old Colony] Volost Elder Jacob Braun [formerly called District mayor], the Assistant Volost Elder Jacob Andres, the Chairman of the [Agricultural] Commission Jacob Niebuhr, and the member of the [Agricultural] Commission Franz Janzen. My brother-in-law Dyck was also interested in visiting the market in Sofievka, and so we stopped there on the way home.
February 20 Sunday. A great and unexpected misfortune befell my son-in-law Johann Bärgen last night when his two horses (each worth more than 100 R.) were stolen. After we discovered the theft this morning, I ran from neighbour to neighbour asking for help. Most had excuses, however, saying their horses were not shod, etc., etc. But a few immediately volunteered. We shod our own gelding, got the wagon, and Jacob and Bärgen drove out to search.

Brotherhood Meeting. Peter Thiessen appeared before the brethren, asked their forgiveness, and was readmitted to church membership. Lord Jesus, forgive him, let him keep his renewed vow and walk in the fear of thee. Have mercy on thy flock. Do not let a single lamb go astray.

Peter Blatz and his wife, who will settle on the Marian land (Baratov) in spring and were looking for rented accommodation until that time, spent the night with us.

February 21. At three this afternoon, while Bärgen was still away searching for his horses, our daughter Katharina [Bärgen] gave birth to a daughter. The children had followed the tracks of the thieves to Novovoronzovka, where they had lost them. They had reported the robbery to the District police officer.

February 24 To be close to the new settlement [of Baratov] in spring, the Andreses have moved back to Izluchistaia.

March 8 The weather is cold and there is mud, yet spring seems around the corner and I have removed the storm-windows. The teacher, who will be moving to the Baratov settlement himself, closed school today.

March 11 Spring weather gives birth to new life. The settlers on the Marian land are beginning to move out. The Johann Bärgens, who have been living in the house of a Jew, moved in temporarily with us. Our daughter Katharina wants to stay here with the children until the seeding is done and then move directly into their own house.

March 17 Friday. Quite a large number of settlers from the Khortitsa District are passing through. Today one of our relatives, Heinrich Neufeld, stopped by for dinner on his way to the Marian land.

March 19 Luck was with us tonight. We finally managed to catch the hamster who has been creating havoc since last September (see entry for Oct. 4, 1871). Mother caught sight of our troublesome guest on top of the potatoes in the cellar, took up a position in front of its hole, and screamed. We all came running, made a quick search, and Johann Bärgen had the honour of dispatching our friend. Some time ago, Gerhard and Dietrich Dyck had unsuccessfully tried to smoke the rodent out of its hole. It was probably deep in its winter sleep. The hamster reappeared in spring and much to mother's annoyance resumed making trouble. We spotted it several times. One night, before going to bed, we had heard screaming while the cat tried to play with it. We had lit a lamp, but it was already gone. We are all quite pleased that the story has now ended.

March 22 When I see so many settlers with their belongings passing through, I am reminded of the hymn in our song-book, 'My life is a pilgrimage. I am bound for my Fatherland, that Jerusalem on high.'

Last night, Heinrich Vogt and his wife, their possessions piled high on two Jewish wagons, spent the night with us. He is moving to Iasoorsa as a miller.

April 4 Our ploughers came home for dinner after ploughing a desiatina of land for the teacher. Little Johann and I then drove them to the other field to plough, Johann begging me to let him stay with his brothers. That seemed to excite him. I managed to get him to come home with me, promising that mother would have refreshments for us. During our break he insisted we go back at once, saying 'It's time to get going.' I replied, 'Not so fast. We'll first have a nap and then be on our way.' Towards evening we were told that a small boy had been seen walking along the road alone. Only then did we miss him. Thank God we were able to find him quickly, Maria spotting him on the plough-land. As it turned out, Johann had thought I had left without him and set out to find his brothers on his own. We thank the Lord for his merciful protection.

April 6 We finished seeding our own land, and I now want to till several desiatinas for David on the Baratov land.

April 9 Palm Sunday. We returned yesterday from the Baratov settlement to find our mare having difficulty foaling. Mother had no luck in getting the neighbours' help. In the evening we finally took the foal by force, and this morning the mare is dead. Another mishap. Two cows are seriously ill and may not survive. May his will be done.

April 10 Today the cow we bought from my brother Diedrich a year ago died. As both fortune and misfortune come from the Lord, he can again give us cattle, if that is his will.

April 11 Early this morning, mother, Diedrich, Gerhard, Johann, Judith, and I drove to the Baratov settlement to plant the melon patch, which had been ploughed by the Russians, and only needed harrowing. We drove through the village of Marianovka, where the old manor house is located, to village number two, where we looked at the house-and-garden plots assigned to our children, the J. Andreses and the Bärgens. We also visited Isaac Siemens's place in [village] number one and stopped by to see Jacob Sawatzki Sr in the manor house 'Petervetski.' There we watered the horses, and I announced a service in the gornitsa [i.e., in the large room of the manor house] for Good Friday.

April 19 A sharp night frost severely damaged the cherries. Yet everything comes from our loving God – storms, frost, and rain as well as bumper crops and crop failures.

April 26 David bought a wagon for 50 R. from Died. Dyck in Neuosterwick. We brought it along from the Khortitsa colonies, and David fetched it from our place with his horse.

April 28 Around 5:30 p.m. my wife's brothers Gerhard and Diedrich Dyck stopped by, each with a loaded wagon. Gerh. Dyck is adding another building to his homestead in village number one. Our sons Jacob and Diedrich returned from Nikopol with two loads of lumber for Is. Friesen. They had sold 77 puds 38 funt of wheat to Peter Friesen's steam mill for 93½ C. per pud, a total of 72 R. 89 C.

April 30 Our married children, the David Epps, plan to work on my brother-in-law G. Dyck's new place and move into the house he is building in the [Baratov] settlement.

May 2 I arrived in Ekaterinoslav at two in the afternoon, and my cousin Johann Thiessen kindly took me on my round of errands in his carriage. Malzov's store had not yet received a shipment of glass, and their supplies were low. I bought only a half case of number two glass for 19 R. The boat with the fresh supplies is expected on May 14. I also purchased a diamond glass-cutter from the merchant Alekievka for 4 R. 50 C. I spent the night with the Heinrich Heeses, where my aunt is staying.

May 3 We left at noon after loading the glass and buying an iron pail for 60 C. and two pairs of shoes for 2 R. 50 C.

Saturday. His Excellency, Ettinger, president of the Guardianship Committee, spent the night at my brother Diedrich's place, and resumed his journey to Khortitsa in the morning. Mother, Heinrich, Gerhard, Elisabeth, Johann, Judith, and I left early for Baratov, stopping by to see the Johann Andreses and Johann Bärgens in village number two. In the afternoon, we visited my brother-in-law Gerhard Dyck and the David Epps in village number one. In fact, we met David on the road to the manor house, returning from Kamianka with a load for Gerhard Dyck. For the time being, the children will be living in the Dyck's house.

May 7 A man by the name of Bärgmann from Friedensfeld, who fed his horses at our place today, is on his way to the new land that the Molochna has bought at Zagradovka, [Kherson province].

May 10 Peter Penner, his wife and children from the Molochna colony of Gnadenheim, who are also settling in the [new] Zagradovka [settlement], had dinner with us. Members of our Mennonite community seem to be scattering to all corners of Russia. The Molochna community has bought 23,000 desiatinas of land from Prince Kochubei [at Zagradovka].[14]

May 13 We have been having a July-type heat wave, and it is hotter than I can ever remember it being at this time of year. It was oppressive yesterday, a little cooler after last night's thunderstorm, and terribly hot again today. Late in the afternoon we drove out to survey our grain fields on the steppe. The grain seeded first is not doing badly, but that planted last is spotty. The winter rye seems to have suffered most, many stalks having fallen over. It is hay time.

May 16 At Petervetski today, the manor house, out-buildings, machinery, and other things were auctioned off by Jacob Niebuhr, chairman of the Agricultural Commission, and my brother Johann, [secretary of the Khortitsa Volost]. I accompanied my brothers Johann and Diedrich. Village number one bought the manor houses. The two villages have been given names. Number one is Gnadenthal and number two Neu Khortitsa. Johann spent the night with us.

May 17 David Wölk's wife came by late at night in a very agitated state. Her mind is deranged and her speech incoherent. Everything was getting worse, she said. She wanted her David back, the horses had disappeared, etc. Finally she also lamented having committed fornication with a certain Janzen of Iasikovo, who had gone mad. Jacob and Maria accompanied her to her home to fetch bed clothes and brought her back to our place for night. She knelt down on the floor to pray and then went quietly to bed.

May 18 Mrs Wölk did not cause any commotion at night and left for home early in the morning. She wanted, as she said, 'to work.' Her mind is deranged. Dear Saviour, have mercy on her.

May 19 The mentally ill Mrs Wölk was here again for the night and seemed a little better.

We were told last night that my brother Diedrich had suddenly become very ill. I hurried over to see him. My sister-in-law had already sent her children to Novokovno to fetch Doctor Mendel. Diedrich had sharp stabbing pains in his abdomen and a great heaviness around the stomach. He thought he was dying, as we did too, but by the time Doctor Mendel arrived at ten o'clock, he was already feeling a little better. The medicine has now provided complete relief.

May 20 Saturday. At midnight David Wölk told me that his wife desperately wished to see me. He, Mrs Franz Klassen, and I went over together and found her sitting on a bench, holding a hymn-book and singing. She again lamented the sins she had committed with Janzen, but the rest of her speech was confused. I urged her to lie down to sleep, which she finally did, next to her husband.

May 26 Friday. We started haying today. Jacob and Diedrich drove out to mow, but the little hay there is does not look promising. The drought has gone on too long. Nevertheless, God lives and can grant us a good harvest. I also had a mishap today. The diamond glass-cutter I bought in Ekaterinoslav (see entry for May 2, 1872) cut beautifully. When I went to fetch more glass today, Gerhard and Lieschen picked up the cutter and the stone fell out. Fortunately, I found it again.

May 31 We observed Holy Communion in church with 115 people, including mother, Jacob, Maria, and the Johann Andreses.

June 5 I preached to a large congregation in the manor house in Neu Khortitsa, which is called Petervetski. While Diedrich rocked little Judith, my dear wife attended the service. Little Johann was also along. We were at the Andreses and Bärgens for dinner.

Jacob Sawatzki of Neu Khortitsa died last night, and his sons-in-law are busy building a coffin. We visited the David Epps, who have moved into Gerh. Dyck's house in Gnadenthal. Heinrich, who had stayed with the Bärgens, drove home with us.

June 7 Wednesday morning. A hamster got into the upper garden, damaging the onions and threatening to ruin the whole garden. This was not quite as bad as having the beast in the house, however. The children dug up his passageway, found his home (which was softly padded), but the lord himself was out. Then the children heard the dog barking madly and found him grappling with the hamster. The children dispatched the rodent on the spot and were enormously proud of their deed. It was a pregnant female.

This afternoon we attended the funeral for Jacob Sawatzki of Neu Khortitsa, who died at the age of 67 years, 2 months, and 18 days. The body was lowered into the grave already this morning, the first burial in this cemetery.

June 9 Friday. This morning my brother Diedrich and I made an inventory of the estate of the widower Isaac Friesen. His assets totalled 600 R. and his debts 700 R.

June 11 Peter returned home last night after taking the [Zentral-schule] examinations in Khortitsa on Friday.

June 12 We started cutting rye today, the earliest I can recall. Prospects are not bright since field mice caused much damage, which the extreme heat has simply compounded.

June 15 Thursday. Daniel Janzen of Neu Khortitsa appeared before the Ministerial Committee. While he and his wife were living with the Redekopps in the spring, he is said to have committed unchaste acts and fornication with Helena Kehler, their maidservant. These goings-on are supposed to have continued after her dismissal, on her trip back to the Khortitsa District. I had informed Elder Gerhard Dyck of these stories, who had called her to account. She admitted that this had happened also on the field and that Janzen had used force. Janzen confessed that the accusations were true, that he had committed fornication with her repeatedly, here as well as there and on her trip home, but he denied using force. I ordered him to appear before Elder Gerh. Dyck next Thursday, which he promised to do. He seemed relieved that the matter had finally been brought into the open.

In the afternoon, Heinrich Olfert of Novovitebsk begged me to talk to his brother-in-law Peter Siemens, who was ill and wanted to see me. Olfert had arrived on Siemens's springed carriage, and my wife, our little Johann, and I drove back with him. I found Siemens sick and anxious to confess his sins. He was especially tormented by his heavy drinking and the fornication he had committed. In his youth he had also defiled himself with cattle and committed fornication with a girl named Aganetha Schmidt (the daughter of Peter Schmidt of Kronsweide), whom he had seduced by promising to marry her. As a married man, he had had relations with Johann Siemens's wife (who had seduced him), and with eight Russian women. Dear God, sin has such power. Siemens was contrite. I am sure the Saviour will not reject him.

June 18 *Brotherhood Meeting*. I outlined Peter Siemens' transgressions, and he was placed in the ban. May the Lord grant him the strength to repent. It was also decided that if he asked to be readmitted, and could not do this personally [in church], it could be done at his bedside.

June 22 Peter, Gerhard, Johann, and I drove to market in Sofievka where I bought two sacks of rye flour for 80 C. each and some linen cloth. In the afternoon we dropped in to see the Johann Andreses in Neu Khortitsa. They were just putting up the rafters for their house. Bloody dysentery is rampant here.

June 23 Peter Siemens asked to be readmitted to the church. In keeping with church practice, I received him as a member in the presence of several church members, and we sang a hymn in closing. Siemens is very sick and close to death.

June 24 We had a scare this morning when our little daughter [Judith] suffered an epileptic attack, which lasted almost an hour. How we pitied our little one, and I prayed fervently to Jesus, the great children's friend. She was still very sick this afternoon. The attack may mark the start of an illness, perhaps teething fever.

June 27 Jacob and I left at 6 a.m. for Ekaterinoslav to buy glass, stopping in at Heinr. Olfert's place in Novovitebsk to see poor Siemens on his sick-bed. The latter kindly lent me 35 R., which got me out of a predicament. We reached Ekaterinoslav by daylight and met the Heinrich Heeses just leaving for an exhibition in Kronsgarten. We went along and witnessed a marvellous fireworks.

June 28 Jacob and I went to Malzov's store after breakfast and bought a half-case of clear glass, number one, for 23 R. and two half-cases of opaque glass for 14 R. each. I could only manage the 51 R. by borrowing 20 R. from my cousin Johann Thiessen.

July 7 We started cutting barley. Mice have destroyed much of the barley and wheat that was sowed early. The heat is stifling.

July 25 We finished cutting the grain today. We had no choice but simply not to bother with the desiatina of wheat and two desiatinas of barley destroyed by the field mice.

August 3 A series of storms and rainfalls have delayed the harvest work without soaking the ground. The flowers have withered, the dahlias grieve, and watering does not seem to help.

August 7 A story. Some time ago a person by the name of Eduard Puringer, who claimed to be a foreigner, appeared in our neighbourhood. He had spent a night at Diedrich Epp Jr's place last year, and Peter had met and talked to him at my brother-in-law Gerhard

Dyck's place. Recently the adventurer showed up at Abraham Unger's door and offered to transport and install a cylinder drum in Unger's mill for 80 R. The drum, he said, was on Jacob Dyck's estate, and he claimed to have built an identical drum for Dyck's mill. To complete the deception, he pretended to be a religious person and to abstain from strong drink. He also refused to take money for the work until it was finished, asking only for enough to transport the drum. Unger gave him an advance, and he hired a Jew. The wagon, however, returned without the drum, and Puringer blamed the heavy rain and asked for a covered wagon. The second wagon, likewise outfitted by Unger, also returned without the drum. I forget what excuse he gave now.

By now Puringer's drunkenness had become manifest. Yesterday, Unger finally drove to Dyck's estate and realized he had been swindled by a liar and a cheat. No one knew anything about a Puringer and there had never been a drum. Unger found his wagon covering at an inn and discovered the man had been drinking like a fish. After swindling Unger of 64 R., Puringer had disappeared without a trace. Today Unger drove to Eigengrund and discovered that Puringer was an assumed name and that the man was not a foreigner, but a [German] colonist from the east bank of the Dnieper. What does it profit a man to gain the whole world and to lose his own soul?

Tonight my brother Heinrich arrived with his wife and children.

August 8 We attended the funeral for Margaretha Wieler in Gnadenthal, who died at the age of 1 year, 5 months, and 13 days. I delivered the funeral sermon: 'Of such is the kingdom of God.' The Wielers, who buried one daughter today, had another daughter born to them.

August 12 Saturday. After breakfast our dear visitors [including my brother Heinrich and his family] observed a Jewish worship service in the synagogue.

August 13 Sunday. Our dear visitor, my brother Heinrich, preached a sermon this morning on the topic 'The Lord Sees.' Text, Psalm 33:13-14. May the Lord bless these precious words to the benefit of the congregation, which was large. The Lord has given my brother a great gift of speech, and what am I, miserable one, by comparison.

August 18 Mother, Heinrich, Gerhard, Elisabeth, Johann, Judith and I visited our children the David Epps in Gnadenthal. I brought along the threshing stone, and Heinrich stayed to help thresh. In the meantime, the children helped clean the oats, which measured 13 chetvert. We harvested most of this from two desiatinas. The mice had ruined the other two.

August 27 I had a lovely dream towards morning in which I saw the dear Saviour here on earth in human form, surrounded by a large crowd. I was in the midst of that throng as well, but not at his elbow, and rejoiced at seeing the Lord Jesus with my own eyes. I had often wished to be close to him, as his disciples had been, and this wish was now granted me. A voice said, 'Force your way through to the Lord, tell him your wishes and he will hear you.' And then I awoke and was glad of the dream that invited me to come to the Lord.

August 28 Peter, Gerhard, and I left for Ekaterinoslav at 5 a.m. to cart another load of glass.

August 29 This afternoon I purchased a half-case of clear glass, number one, for 23 R. and a half-case of semi-clear glass, number one, for 18 R. 50 C.

September 3 I have cancelled regular services in church because of the poor attendance.

September 4 We drove Peter back to the Khortitsa Zentralschule, which he will attend on a stipend, boarding with his teacher and uncle, Heinrich Epp.

September 8 Friday. We spent the day with the Cornelius Hildebrands who are leaving for Odessa tomorrow.

There was a meeting this afternoon in the Khortitsa church of village mayors (now called village elders), the ministers of the Khortitsa and Kronsweide churches, and their two elders. The Molochna ministers had already left for St Petersburg in regard to the military [service] question. We deliberated as to what we might do. If we decided to send a delegation who should go? Finally we decided to telegraph Pastor Hans[15] in St Petersburg asking his advice. Should representatives be sent and when? We will consult further. At the close of the meeting we sang the hymn, 'Be with Us in Grace.'

September 10 I preached a sermon in the Khortitsa church, after which Elder Dyck brought several matters before the Brotherhood Meeting. (1) The confession of sick Mr P[eter] S[iemens] (see entry for June 18, 1872) regarding the widow J. Siemens in Rosenthal, who categorically denies the accusation. It was decided to let the matter rest on her conscience. (2) Two young married couples who had given birth before their time (and hence had slept together before marriage) contritely asked forgiveness and were allowed to go in peace.

September 11 We visited several of our relatives on the Island of Khortitsa. A great fire has altered the appearance of the Island. Eight houses with their barns, storage and implement sheds have disappeared. Five families are rebuilding, and the other three are putting off construction until springtime.

September 12 Tuesday. This morning I attended a meeting of the directors of the Orphans' Administration in the Khortitsa Volost Office [formerly District Office]. They considered my request to re-establish a branch of the Orphans' Administration here [in the Judenplan], as it existed earlier. They finally decided to found an independent Orphans' Administration here, which I do not favour.

October 1 Thanksgiving. Lord, we thank thee for the gifts we receive from thy gentle hand. Thou hast given us a meagre harvest, but it is our daily bread. Thou hast clothed us and provided for our cattle. Why should we worry and complain?

Jacob and I drove to Novokovno, where I preached a thanksgiving sermon. The lectern was low, and the reflection of the sun created such a glare that I had a hard time seeing. With God's help, I managed to get through the sermon. Yet on the way home my heart was heavy at the thought that I had given up preaching freely. I wonder now whether it is not perhaps God's will that I should again speak extemporaneously in the services. Lord, reveal thy will to me and grant me the needed strength.

October 4 Johann and I drove to Gnadenthal. We had dinner at David's place, stopping in to see the Johann Andreses in Neu Khortitsa on our way back. We also dropped off several barrels for repairs at David Janzen's and bought a chetvert of millet as pig fattener from Is. Görzen.

October 8 A general Brotherhood Meeting to elect ministers was held today in the Novovitebsk church. Heinrich Neufeld was elected minister with 71 votes; Diedrich Epp Jr was elected minister with 58 votes; and Jacob v Kampen was elected deacon with 24 votes. The earlier election for deacon had the following results: Heinrich

Neufeld 67, Diedr. Epp 44, Joh. Wiebe 20, Gerh. Klassen 17, Joh. Klassen 9, Diedr. Thiessen 5, Heh. Neudorf 3, Heh. Klippenstein 2, and several others 1. Neufeld was not present, so the Elder authorized me to install him in office next Sunday.

The Brotherhood Meeting also decided to establish a local poor tax. The widow Sawatzki and her idiot son Bernhard in Neu Khortitsa *need* support. The following assessment was agreed to: 25 C. per household; and 15 C. each male and 8 C. each female church member.

Following the election, the Elder asked the newly chosen individuals these questions:
(1) If you agree with the church of God in regard to matters of faith as you affirmed and gave witness to in Holy Baptism, then answer 'yes.'
(2) If you accept this calling to the service of the Word [of the Lord], recognizing it as legitimate and from God, then answer 'yes.'
(3) If you are willing, as God has given you the ability, faithfully to discharge your service to the church through instruction and discipline, as the Word of God teaches, then answer 'yes.'

I welcome you into our midst. May God our heavenly Father, who has called you to his service, illumine you through his Holy Spirit, strengthen you with his mighty hand, and rule over you, that many may be encouraged and find salvation through you, to the honour of God and the Kingdom of Jesus Christ. Amen.

October 15 Sunday. Jacob, my brother-in-law Gerhard Dyck, and I drove to our children's home in Neu Khortitsa. There we met my colleague Pätkau. Heinrich Neufeld finally arrived and told us he was not willing to accept the office of minister. He is a man of great wilfulness, which I was not able to overcome. Since we were not making any progress we decided to go to the service. *Brotherhood Meeting*. I again asked Neufeld if he would accept his calling. He said that his answer for the present was 'no,' but he suggested that the matter might resolve itself later on. We have decided to let the matter rest for now.

October 19 Thursday. This afternoon, Jacob Pätkau, Diedrich Epp, Peter Hildebrand, and I were summoned to the communal office, where the cattle herdsman was tried. In spring he had poked out the eye of one of Motke's horses and ridden Peter Mantler's horse [so hard], and tied it up for several nights in a row, that its hoofs were raw. We decided the herdsman should pay Motke 10 R. and Mantler 2 R., and signed a statement confirming the decision.

October 21 Saturday. Around noon I had an attack of rheumatic pain that was so acute that I was barely able to make it home. I asked Pätkau to take tomorrow's service. Around 3 p.m. my wife strapped the life awakener to my back. God blessed the treatment. The pain is now bearable, and I am able to write these lines.

Brother Diedrich brought news from Khortitsa that Elder Gerh. Dyck and brother Heinrich had left for Yalta, in the Crimea, to petition His Majesty the Emperor to exempt us from military service and to preserve our religious freedoms.[16] May the Lord bless the journey.

October 24 Tuesday. We slaughtered five fatted pigs. Although each pig received only two chetvert of fattener (we having to buy the feed), they were nevertheless very good.

October 26 Thursday afternoon. I united in marriage Isaac Dyck and Katharina Veer, the daughter of Jacob Veer of Izluchistaia.

October 28 Saturday afternoon we buried the late administrator [of the Heinrichs estate] Peter Siemens, and I delivered the funeral sermon. The service was held in the manor house in the presence of many Russians. He was 53 years, 11 months, and 25 days old.

November 6 My eye flared up again on my way home from the funeral, but I can see enough today to catch up on my diary. On Tuesday, October 31, I sent Jacob to Nikopol with 2 chetvert of wheat, which he sold for 10 R. 10 C. per chetvert. He returned with several new lamps, including one for us, and the petroleum for the lamp. This kind of lighting, which we have not had before, is said to be cheaper than the tallow candles. Everything is changing except the Word of God, with its unchanging power through all eternity. Since I was unable to preach yesterday, Pätkau took my place.

November 13 Monday. Several Khortitsa officials dropped by briefly this morning: the District mayor Jacob Braun, Jacob Niebuhr, chairman of the [Khortitsa Agricultural] Commission, and their coachman Johann Klassen of Neuosterwick. They were looking for more land [for the landless families of the Khortitsa Volost].[17] They reported that the two new settlement villages of Gnadenthal and Neu Khortitsa [Baratov settlement] are to be incorporated [administratively] into a neighbouring Russian volost. According to them, the situation in the Khortitsa community [in regard to the landless dispute] is critical, and God only knows how it will end.

November 22 Yesterday I thought my wife would soon be over her illness, but she is down again today with a splitting headache and violent retching. It is also our youngest daughter Judith's first birthday. A great deal has changed over the past year. May our Lord preserve my wife's life and restore her to health.

November 25 Maria, Jacob, and I attended the engagement festivities of my charge Maria Klassen and Jacob Wiebe.

November 26 This morning, Heinrich Olfert and his daughter Margaretha came to ask for the hand of our daughter Maria for his son Peter. They also sought my brother Diedrich's advice. This afternoon Peter dropped by himself, but without luck. One wonders about the purpose of all this.

December 6 While living in Friesenthal, Jacob Friesen borrowed large sums from a nobleman, which he could not repay on time. He then hired a Jewish lawyer and started a lawsuit against the nobleman. The Jew, who encouraged him to think he could easily win the case, charged him a pretty penny. But now Friesen has lost the suit, must repay his debt, and has been sentenced to two months in jail. Yesterday he was taken away to Verchnedneprovsk on foot as a common criminal. This is what quarrelsomeness and lawsuits lead to. Our community has so degenerated that church members have grown distant from Christianity and quarrel and launch suits in defiance of the teaching of our Saviour. Using the sword and undertaking lawsuits are really one and the same thing. As I look into the future I am filled with deep misgivings. Lord have mercy on us.

December 12 Last night Abraham Penner and his son Bernhard of Ebenfeld and Diedrich Penner of Schöndorf came to see me about Jacob Friesen's problems (see entry for Dec. 6, 1872). Friesen's wife is their niece. I went with them to talk to the Jew Motke, who had appeared before the justice of the peace at the same time and knew the details of Friesen's case. Motke told us that Friesen had also taken some hay and refused to return all of it. The court had seized the hay and placed Friesen in detention. If Friesen personally, or someone on his behalf, were prepared to put up a security of 350 R., he would be able to continue with his appeal. But he would have to do his time for the hay in any case. Our guests returned home this morning.

December 13 This morning, Jacob and I delivered a letter to Vasilii Ivanovich Vornov from his son, a student in the Khortitsa Zentralschule.[18] We also made arrangements for the Christmas holidays. Vornov will bring the students home for the holidays and we will drive them back later.

December 26 Tuesday. Second Christmas holiday. This morning Peter and Diedrich sang a birthday song for me and gave me a birthday card. May God grant that their wishes come true. At home, I read Hofacker's second Christmas sermon to my wife and children, and we sang a Christmas song together.

This year, the teacher Peter Klassen prepared a Christmas tree for the holidays. On Christmas eve the children gathered around the tree in school in the presence of people from most of the villages. My dear wife was also there with all of our children, except Judith, who stayed home with me. Last night the teacher sent a note inviting me to attend as well, so I went over while my wife baby-sat our little one. The children went back to school this morning and came home with presents of various sweets. This was a true celebration for children.

December 28 Thursday. There appeared today before the Ministerial Committee Peter Neufeld, Gerh. Andres Sr, Johann Schellenberg, and his mother-in-law the widow Bartel. Peter Neufeld is said to have spoken badly of Elder Gerhard Dyck and was egged on by Schellenberg. Neufeld, who seems to be a defiant sort, was let off with a warning that he should guard himself against such outbursts in future. Do not backbite amongst yourselves, dear brethren, and pray for the servants of the Word.

December 31 We have reached the end of another year. When I look back, I am filled with fear and misgivings. The sword of God's wrath hangs over us. Dark thunder-clouds gather, lightning can be seen flashing on the horizon and thunder sounds in the distance. Our freedom of religion is in danger, and all of the efforts of our representatives to petition our sovereign have thus far failed. Several years ago, our neighbours, the Mennonites [Hutterites] in Hutterthal, bought land close to Sofievka and settled there.[19] But they have now sold their land, are preparing to emigrate to Canada in America, and will be sending a deputation to America after the New Year.

There are also stirrings among us in favour of emigration as a means of preserving our religious freedom. I have a letter from my brother-in-law Bernh. Warkentin of Altonau, whose son is in America now. The English government would very much like to have us as settlers, and the land there is supposed to be very fertile. May the Lord reveal his will to us.[20]

The crops were quite poor, on average 1½ chetvert of wheat per desiatina. But we thank and praise the Lord for even this little. A cattle plague ravaged the area, and was especially rampant in Rosenthal, Khortitsa, and Neuosterwick. Many of the horned cattle belonging to the Jews in Novovitebsk died. The Germans took their cattle indoors, and only H. Olfert lost 12 head. In Novopodolsk we were spared this judgment. The Lord took only our cow, a calf, and a mare (while foaling).

1873

January 2 I spoke to Isaac Friesen about a complaint that his under-aged foster son Isaac Friesen (whose guardian I am) had been keeping company with his housekeeper, a Russian woman, and had probably committed fornication with her. Friesen insisted the rumours were groundless. But since he is often away and could not really know, I suggested that his foster son go and live with his wife (whom he had recently married), until she had moved in with him. He agreed.

January 4 I accompanied my neighbour Isbrand Friesen to Neuhutterthal (Liubimovka), where we arrived in the late evening. We took our quarters with Lorenz Tschetter, who received us with great friendliness. We had heard the Hutterian Brethren had obtained a copy of the new military law, and wanted to read it. After coffee we met their preacher Wipf and several others.

The community has sold its land to the nobleman Lappen Danilevsky for 50 R. per desiatina, including buildings, cattle and agricultural implements (but not the two windmills). The Hutterians still own their furniture, chickens, and pigs. Only a certain Hofer and his sons has not sold his 200 desiatinas of land. Their second preacher and several others had gone to the Molochna colony of Alexanderwohl. A delegation is to leave from there for Canada in America to arrange the emigration.[21]

We were told that these men had taken the above-mentioned law with them. We should believe them when they said that the law was explicit in stating that once it entered into force, people living on private lands would be subject to personal military service. People on crown lands would be required to render medical service. I had taken along a letter from my brother-in-law Berh. Warkentin, in which his son Bernhard [who had been in America] reports on the great advantages of emigration to America. I read the letter several times, and they heard it with rejoicing.

Our meeting [with the Hutterians] tends to confirm the fears I have been expressing for some time about the threat to our religious liberty. We have gone our way securely, knowing we had a Charter of Privileges from our beloved sovereign, and were thankful and happy. But now!!

January 5 We reached home around noon and found Dietrich Friesen of Friesenthal waiting to see me. He is alarmed about the danger [that the military-service law] represents to our faith and is considering selling his landed estate [and emigrating].

January 8 Maria, Peter, and I left for Khortitsa in Pätkau's covered wagon.

January 10 We buried my sister Helena Pätkau this morning, Elder Gerhard Dyck delivering the funeral sermon. She had been sickly for some time and bedridden for six weeks and five days. She was 47 years, 5 months, and 7 days old. A son and two daughters were born of her first marriage, which lasted seven years and six days. The daughter died and the son Martin Dyck is alive. In her second marriage, to Pätkau, lasting 15 years, 3 months, and 25 days, she gave birth to two sons and two daughters, all of whom are still alive. Rest in peace in your portion, my sister, until the day of resurrection.

January 11 A raging storm at night continued until daybreak, tearing the rafters from Thiessen's roof in Neuosterwick, destroying a house in Burwalde, and burning Herman Bükkert's windmill in Schöneberg to the ground.

January 16 There is great uneasiness throughout the Khortitsa colonies in anticipation of the new military law. It arouses widespread fear about the future of our religious liberty. The mood is generally in favour of emigrating to America, where we have been given the prospects of complete religious freedom. May the Lord guide everything to our benefit.

January 18 Today we left for the Molochna in the Province of Taurida. Jacob drove me to Friesenthal.

January 19 Friday. This morning Diedrich Friesen, his son Julius, and I left [from Friesenthal] in his springed carriage, drawn by four horses and driven by a Russian coachman. Jacob returned home with a chetvert of rye, which Friesen let me have. The road was quite smooth from traffic, and only a strong cold east wind made travel a little uncomfortable. A covered carriage is better and warmer than an open wagon in any case.

We reached Nikopol at 2 p.m. We had planned to cross the Dnieper, but Peter Friesen, at whose place we stopped, noticed that one of our wagon hoops was broken and had a large piece missing. We therefore waited patently while the repairs were made. Finally we drove to the crossing, but had to return. We took our quarters with the Peter Friesens, where we met travellers from the Fürstenland [settlement].

January 20 To the ferry dock this morning and a difficult crossing because of the drift ice. Our fare was 2 R., the crossing took 1½ hours, and we reached the east bank at 11:30. Despite the delay at the Dnieper, we nevertheless travelled 90 verstas today. We spent the night with Diedr. Friesen Jr.

January 21 Sunday. We attended service today in the schoolhouse in Neutroch. The Johann Martenses and David Schroeders visited with the Friesens in the afternoon. They are simple and honest folk, and I liked them. I did, however, get into an argument with Martens about the military-service question. He thinks military service is quite acceptable and ridicules the thought of emigration.[22] One can only conclude that true Christianity in our communities has disappeared to that degree that the question of leaving [Russia] or remaining here is treated superficially. We still fail to acknowledge our own sinfulness and the need for repentance. That alone can lead us to the Saviour.

January 22 We resumed our journey Monday morning, travelling via Fedrovka and Tirpinge, where we had coffee at the Bernhard Warkentins (she is my niece). Brother-in-law Warkentin was not at home. I spent the night with my cousin Diedrich Hiebert in Altonau. Warkentin visited us there in the evening, bringing along letters from his son Bernhard in America. These letters suggest that many advantages await immigrants [to America].

January 23 This afternoon Hiebert drove with me through [the Molochna settlement villages of] Ohrloff, Tiege, Blumenort, Rosenort, Tiegerweide, Rückenau, Fürstenwerder, Alexanderwohl, Gnadenheim, Friedensdorf, Landskrone and Hierschau to Waldheim,[23] where we spent the night with my cousin Jacob Hiebert.

January 24 This morning, Jacob Hiebert harnessed his horses and took me through Gnadenfeld to Pordenau, where the conference and Brotherhood Meeting took place in the church. It was conducted by Elder Isaac Peters. The subject was the prospective emigration and the question of sending a deputation to America. About 2000 R. had been allocated for this purpose and a further 1000 was collected. Elder Leonhard Sudermann of Berdiansk was chosen as one of the deputies by majority vote, the others having been elected earlier. Present from Bergthal were the deputies Reverend Heinrich Wiebe and District Mayor Peters. The deputation is scheduled to leave towards the end of February.

My nephews Bernhard, Heinrich, and David [Friesen], children of my late sister Maria, recognized me in the congregation and invited me to their place in Alexanderthal.[24] I spent the night at Heinrich Friesen's place. The Cornelius Dörksens, his in-laws, are very old, and the aged grandfather impressed me as a true disciple of Jesus.

January 25 Thursday morning I accompanied the two Friesens on a drive through Elisabetthal, Steinbach, Steinfeld, Traktir am Wege, Prangenau, and Neukirch. I also stopped in to see the Hermann Epps and thanked Katharina, his wife, for looking after me with such devotion when I had come down with the measles [as a youth on a previous trip with my father]. We continued through Lichtfelde (the so-called three roses) and the estate of Iushanlee to the home of cousin Jacob Thiessen in Schönau. Abraham Wölk, whose wife is my cousin, lives on his yard. It was past midnight when I finally got to bed.

At four in the morning I was awakened by my cousin Thiessen who said that Wölk had suddenly taken ill and was deeply troubled about the state of his soul. Both of us hurried over. I hope we succeeded, with God's grace, in guiding him to the arms of our propitiator, Jesus. He soon calmed down, in any case.

We had breakfast with the Thiessens. Thiessen read the appropriate passage for the day from Gossen's *Schätzkästchen* in the presence of the workers from the dye plant.[25] Thiessen's son Heinrich then drove me through the villages of Fischau, Lindenau, Lichtenau, Blumstein, and Münsterberg to Altonau. In the afternoon, I was able to have a word with Jacob Dyck of Brodsky and his son Peter, who had recently returned from America.

January 27 Saturday afternoon we left for home, stopping over for the night at the home of Peter Penner in Bielseska. Penner has joined the Baptists.[26] In the evening, two other brethren [of this group], who were visiting him, conducted a devotional hour, elevated by song and prayer.

January 30 We reached home this afternoon. It should be mentioned that another issue is causing much rumbling in the Molochna [settlement], the question of land. A certain Abr. Thiessen, who has launched a court action with the imperial government, has now sent a manuscript to press that supposedly reveals all the injustices perpetrated in this regard.[27] I assume it also contains many falsehoods. Where is this likely to lead? May the Lord have mercy on us and cure the ills of his church.

January 31 Wednesday. The following Khortitsa officials passed through on their way home from the recently purchased estate of Shlakhtin on the Ssaksagan Stream: [Old Colony] District Mayor Jacob Braun and Assistant District Mayor Andres. They had dinner with my brother Diedrich and then left for home via the Nepluiev settlement. The threatening thunder-cloud hovering over us is being variously assessed. In our Khortitsa community most people do not think it is particularly serious.

I have been variously accused of arousing our community [of the Judenplan] out of its sweet indolence. Still, I fully agree with the author of a new song, who writes, 'Hasten now to Golgatha, and not first to America.' I pray that, in these earnest times, we might remember the only place where peace can truly be found and kneel before the Lord in sincere contrition. Surely he would then direct the lightning away from us.

February 5 *School visitation.* Monday morning my colleagues Pätkau and Epp and I went by sled to Gnadenthal, called for the Village mayor Jacob Wiebe and assistant Village mayor Jacob Redekopp, and proceeded to the school. It is held in the home of my brother-in-law Gerh. Dyck, where our children, the David Epps, live. Our son David is the teacher. Given the brief time that the school has existed, it is run quite well. Subjects taught: Bible stories, reading, writing, and arithmetic. Several songs were sung in closing. The school in Neu Khortitsa was markedly inferior.

February 6 We were pleased with the school in Novopodolsk, taught by Peter Klassen.

Our dinner guests told us that a letter had been received from Pastor Hans in St Petersburg inviting our Mennonite leaders to come to the capital to discuss the question of our freedom from military service. The Molochna delegation had postponed its departure until the Khortitsa community had made its decision in this regard. An election was therefore quickly conducted throughout the entire District and my brother Heinrich chosen as delegate. They did not know the name of the other delegate.

In the afternoon we visited the school in Novovitebsk, taught by Heinrich Olfert, which is distinguished by its penmanship.

February 7 The Izluchistaia school, taught by Wilhelm Janzen, is better than it was a year ago. I was, however, bothered by the ink blots everywhere. School is not being held this year in Kamianka, Novozhitomir, and Novokovno.

February 21 Wednesday. Khortitsa District officials arrived yesterday: Commission Chairman Jacob Niebuhr and my brother Johann, the District secretary. I took the opportunity to travel to the Nepluiev settlement in my brother's carriage. First I went to Heubuden to see David Klassen, who had been chosen to visit America as a deputy of the Kleine Gemeinde.[28] He had been present with me at the Pordenau conference, where it was decided that the delegation would leave on February 20. But in the meantime the trip had been postponed until the end of April. He now intends to leave next week for America with the Hutterthaler.

I then drove to [the village of] Hamburg, the object of my trip, where my colleague Gerhard Enz and I looked in on Heinrich Friesen, who is sick in bed. The latter confessed that he had sinned grievously in his youth, before his baptism, by defiling himself with cattle, a sin that had now brought him to the edge of despair. I urged him to look to the Lamb of God, who had borne our sins. He replied that he had lain at Jesus' feet and believed him to be his Saviour and redeemer.

February 22 Enz told me that Abraham Klassen, the teacher in Steinau, had punished one of Gerhard Dyck's children, and the two were now at loggerheads. We asked them to appear before us. We concluded that the parents were more to blame for the dispute than the teacher. Dyck, however, rejected our advice to make his peace and said he had launched a suit against Klassen in the Khortitsa Volost Court, where the matter would be resolved.[29]

March 1 Wednesday. My dear wife and I, who wanted to sell butter in Sofievka market, could not because of the Lenten fast.

March 5 Our little boy Johann is very ill today with an inflamed throat, which has turned into a cold.

March 6 Our darling's illness is becoming grave, and we fear the worst. Wilt thou take him from us, Lord Jesus? Thou knowest how my heart would bleed. He is our jewel. Yet I know that thou wilt do what is to the child's benefit, and to ours. Let thy will, and not mine, be done.

Late at night. The ways of the Lord are not our ways, and his thoughts are not our thoughts. Our darling son Johann has died, and his early death is unspeakably painful. Yet it is thy will, O God, and so let the pain of our separation be a blessing for us. He died at 5:30 p.m., after an illness of only two days. At least he did not have to choke to death, as I had feared he might. I had prayed about this to the Lord, and his death was a gentle falling asleep. Lord, we entrust his soul to thee. Our beloved son reached the age of 4 years, 3 months, 7 days, and 23 minutes. His life on earth was brief, but God will give him a better life in heaven.

March 8 Thursday. My dear wife frets and grieves over our darling boy, and I, too, am in danger of being overwhelmed by sorrow. Yet I have found comfort and peace in the Lord Jesus. The grieving mother is also gradually being consoled by the positive belief that it is God's will. The Lord has given and the Lord has taken away, praised be the name of the Lord.

March 9 Friday. The funeral day of our beloved son Johann. Our married children, the David Epps, Johann Andreses, and Johann Bärgens, arrived in the morning. David has a fever and his wife also is not well. The Gerhard Andreses Sr and the Johann Bärgens from Izluchistaia came for dinner. It rained at night, and the day was wet and muddy.

The service began at 1:45, my colleague J. Pätkau delivering the funeral sermon. We sang hymn no. 545, 'Parents Cease Your Crying,' before the sermon and no. 704, 'Victory, Victory, My Struggle Is Ended,' when it was finished. As the coffin was closed, the congregation sang 'Let us set Forth on the Final Journey,' and as it was lowered into the ground and the grave closed, 'No, No, There Is No Death.' After coffee we first sang two stanzas of the hymn of praise, no. 39, 'Grace Sufficient and Marvellous,' and then no. 658, 'Let Us Pass Through the Valley of Time.' So rest in peace, treasure of our hearts, joy of our entire family. May the Lord reunite all of us one day.

March 10 Saturday. Most of the invited guests were here for breakfast, after which we sang two songs, no. 386, 'Praise the Lord Always,' and no 294, 'What God Does Is Done Well.' Andres came down with a fever yesterday, but was feeling better today. David, however, is worse.

March 19 Monday. The Franz Giesbrechts, who had been to the Khortitsa District, told me that our deputies, Elder Gerhard Dyck, my brother Heinrich Epp, and Heinrich Heese of Ekaterinoslav, had returned from St Petersburg last Wednesday. They had not seen the emperor, but had spoken to the grand duke, and expect a decision around Eastertime.

March 24 We visited our children in Neu Khortitsa and Gnadenthal this afternoon. Thank God we found them well. We spent the night with the David Epps. I had barely dozed off when I was awakened by my wife, whose body was trembling all over. She had been gripped by a terrible fear that an accident had befallen our son Gerhard at home. It was a contagious fear, and my sleep was gone like fog in the sun. There was nothing to do but entrust our children to the Saviour.

March 25 When we found our children safe and sound at home, we thanked God from the bottom of our hearts.
March 28 We saw a magnificent sunrise today.

God keeps us in remembrance,
For see what he has done.
He painted the rainbow,
With the blood of his son.

May the visible signs of thy grace remind us of thy mercy.
March 29 Thursday. We finished seeding today, harrowing in the last of the wheat in the morning and planting potatoes in the lower garden in the afternoon. Not counting the potatoes, we have ploughed a total of 24 desiatinas this year. One was for the teacher, leaving us 23: wheat 15½, barley 4¼, and oats 3¼. We seeded a further 4 desiatinas to winter rye, making a total of 27 desiatinas to harvest.
March 30 We rolled the fields, which is the first time we have followed this procedure.
April 1 Palm Sunday. Jacob and Maria attended the service in Novovitebsk, where Died. Epp Jr delivered the sermon. He also read a report from my brother regarding the trip to St Petersburg and a copy of the petition presented to the grand duke Constantine Nikolaevich, which I received yesterday.
April 4 Wednesday. I teamed up with my brother Diedrich for the trip to Khortitsa, he providing the carriage and a horse and I the other two horses. There were seven of us in all: he and his wife, I and my wife, and our children Gerhard, Elisabeth, and Judith. We spent the night with my brother Heinrich.
April 13 We arrived home safely this evening. The situation in the [Khortitsa] community is very sad because of the unchristian activities of its landless members. This illness, which threatens to destroy the Molochna communities, is raging in the Khortitsa community as well.[30] The cottagers (but not all of them) demand land and are petitioning the imperial government to divide up the landowners' land [equally among all families].

It seems that the danger to our community arising from the loss of our privileges no longer alarms many, and interest in emigrating to

America has declined accordingly. People nevertheless anxiously await the decision from St Petersburg. We pray that God may guide the hearts of the powerful in such a way that we might continue to live our faith here [in Russia].

Abraham Thiessen, who caused such an uproar in the Molochna, St Petersburg, and Odessa, is said to have lost his *scandalous* court action and to have been banished from the country.[31] But will this end the matter? Corn. Janzen of Berdiansk, who has been actively promoting emigration to America among our fellow believers, has also been expelled!![32]

[Postscript]: Thiessen is said to have lost his case but not to have been banished.

April 16 We used two horses to plough the patch in our yard for onions and melons and we used one horse in the orchard.

At the request of Elder Gerhard Dyck, I met with him and Reverend Gerhard Enz in Schöndorf, Borosenko [settlement]. Abr. Bärgen, who had attempted suicide, was summoned to appear before us. Also present were the [Borosenko] District mayor Gerhard Rempel and the [Schöndorf] Village mayor David Penner. Bärgen, who is addicted to drink and lives in discord with his wife, showed not the slightest remorse, refusing even to admit that he was a drunkard until the District and Village officials proved otherwise. He was allowed to leave until tomorrow.

April 17 At Elder G[erhard] D[yck's] suggestion, G. Rempel and I spoke to Abr. Bärgen early this morning, trying to impress upon him the sinfulness of his hatred of [his wife]. We had hoped he would recognize the wretchedness of his condition and be moved to genuine contrition. I did what I could, but, O God, it made almost no impression on Bärgen. His wife wept bitter tears. They did, however, agree to come to G. Enz's place in Schöndorf, where we exhorted him further to a genuine change of heart.

A service followed in the school. There was then a Brotherhood Meeting at which Elder Dyck reviewed Bärgen's transgressions. Bärgen appeared, asked forgiveness of the brethren, and was dismissed in peace. Lord, Lord, soften his hardened heart to repentance. Lead this lost sheep on to the path of eternal salvation.

April 19 All the Germans [in Novopodolsk] have leased land for a melon patch from the Jews at 1 R. per desiatina. The weather promises a good crop.

April 20 Friday. This morning Julius Friesen of Friesenthal invited me to their place where his father, Diedr. Friesen, wanted my help in dividing up his wife's estate among the children. I accepted. Of the children, only Mrs Braun was absent. After long discussion an agreement was reached providing for the distribution of 900 desiatinas of his 1385 desiatina estate among his nine adult children, that is, 100 desiatinas for each child. The heirs will receive the land this fall, assuming all related obligations. I made a clean copy of the inheritance contract.[33]

April 21 Saturday. When the time came to sign the agreement today, the children expressed reservations. The inventory of the estate showed that half of the assets were not being divided [as Mennonite inheritance practices required]. The children wanted significantly more [than their father was willing to give]. This grieved the aged father who asked me to follow him into an adjoining room where he sought my advice. He was reluctant to distribute more of his property, but also did not want to be unfair. His children feared he might remarry, I pointed out to him, and that his assets would then pass into the hands of strangers. He had no intention of ever remarrying, he replied, and were he to change his mind he would first distribute a part of his assets to his children, ensuring that they received their rightful share. This undertaking was acceptable to all of the children, who now willingly signed the agreement. Then the witnesses signed: Isaac Zacharias and Gerhard Braun of Neuhausen, Jacob Friesen Sr of Friesenthal, and I. Finally, the deceased mother's clothes were distributed among the children by lot or sold at auction to the highest bidder.

April 23 Monday morning I drove to Friesenthal to install glass in Julius Friesen's windows.

April 24 For the work [with the glass] and my help with the inheritance, old Friesen gave me 12 chetvert of rye and the chetvert of grain that I had borrowed in January.

April 26 I had a difficult day today. My brother [Diedrich] had called the Novokovno Mennonites together to resolve various disagreements, but my colleagues Pätkau and Epp could not be present. Peter Peters criticized me harshly because his mother-in-law, the widow J. Friesen, had given her son a plough at her auction sale, where I had kept the books. How absurd. Can a mother not dispose of her belongings as she likes? There was much idle talk, but we finally made peace in my brother's office, except for a dispute between Peters and Isaac Friesen. As Village mayor, the latter had hired some Jews to dig a well and build some troughs. This angered Peters, who demanded 1 R. 40 C. as his share of the earnings. I told him that I would gladly have paid the sum myself if that could have ended the quarrel. As we left, my brother gave Friesen 1 R. 20 C., urging him to give it to Peters. Friesen, who was moved by this gesture, promised to seek a reconciliation and to repay the sum as soon as possible. Look down upon us poor sinners in thy mercy, Lord, and break these hardened hearts to contrition and repentance.

Among the many business people at our place today was Jacob Friesen of Friesenthal. Last night a certain Peter Gräber and his two children Maria and Jacob also appeared. Gräber is a Mennonite brother from the community of Kutuzov in Volynia (Poland),[34] who has leased a dairy farm in Hannovka, about 50 verstas west of here. He gave me a formal certificate [of church membership] from Elder Jacob Stukki and asked that his daughter be permitted to join our church through baptism. When Mrs Gräber raised the matter with me last summer, I advised her to discuss it with the Elder. I then spoke to him myself, sensing that he had no reservations about us proceeding in this way if the congregation agreed. I therefore agreed to the request on the condition that it was accepted by the Elder and the congregation.

April 28 Saturday. This morning we arranged the division of the Abraham Unger inheritance at the home of his widow. Without making an appraisal or formal evaluation, Mrs Unger distributed 1500 R. among her husband's children as his heirs. This came to 300 R. each, payable to the Orphans' Administration on May 1, 1874. Present with my brother Diedrich and me were her trustees and the children's guardians. The proceedings took place in an atmosphere of peace and harmony, for which we thank God.

April 29 Martin Harder Jr appeared before the Ministerial Committee in connection with his heavy drinking. As before, he showed little contrition, a fear of punishment alone prompting him to promise reform. We were again gentle in our treatment, and he was allowed to go in peace. *Brotherhood Meeting.* After reading Maria Gräber's certificate and her father's attestation, the brethren agreed to register her name for baptism.

May 1 Tuesday. Bernhard Bärgen asked me this morning about repaying my debt of 300 R., which I still owe him for the house, barn, and shed. Recently he had discussed the matter with the Orphans' Administration, which was willing to pay him his share and to assume the debt. I wrote to Abr. Klassen, head of the Orphans' Administration in Neuendorf, accepting the proposal. The arrangement, if it works out, is extraordinarily helpful. It is the Lord's doing, who has lifted this burden from me.

May 12 Saturday. Around nine this morning Abraham Letkemann of Neuosterwick informed us of the death of my dear wife's sister, Elisabeth Teichröw. After an illness of two weeks, the angel of death took her from her world of suffering. About 25 or 26 years ago (or was it 27?) she entered into an unhappy marriage and fell into serious temptation. Her husband abused her and slowly, bit by bit, she grew weaker until she finally lost her mind completely. Her possessions were sold, her children placed with various families, and she herself was boarded out.

Ten years ago, when my dear Judith and I were married, she had been living with her brother Diedr. Dyck. Once her own assets had been used up, my blessed father-in-law paid her expenses. At the time of the sale of our parents' belongings, she was boarded out by her guardian to a certain widow Janzen in Kronsthal, and it was there that she had died. In addition to the inheritance left her by her father, she had been supported by the community. She reached the age of 54 years, 4 months, and 21 days and had two sons (both already married). A married daughter died some ten months ago.

The funeral is tomorrow afternoon in the home of my brother-in-law Dietrich Dyck. Poor suffering one, your affliction is at an end. Perfection is with the Lord Jesus. There your mind will again be made clear and well and you will enjoy his eternal love and mercy. My dear wife wanted very much to attend the funeral. As the catechism instruction prevented me from going, I borrowed Pätkau's covered wagon and had Jacob drive her and our little Judith to the funeral. Lord, I entrust my loved ones to thy care.

May 15 I have waited anxiously these days for the return of my dear wife and children. I am confident they will return safely, but still am terribly lonely. Yesterday my neighbour told me she had heard that they had reached Neuosterwick safe and well. At 5:15 my loved ones arrived home.

[My sister-in-law] had given birth to four children, of whom two sons are still living. She became grandmother to four children, of whom one died and three are still living.

May 22 Elder Gerhard Dyck baptized our young candidates, including Maria Gräber, whose mother was present.

May 23 The Elder conducted Holy Communion this morning in the presence of 156 members. Mrs Gräber and her children left in the afternoon. Since I had refused to take board for her daughter while she lived with us, she put 5 R. in my pocket and drove off.

Yesterday afternoon, Heinrich Neufeld, who had earlier rejected his election as minister (see entries for Oct. 8 and 15, 1872), appeared in the ministers' room at the joint invitation of the Elder and myself. Since his first refusal, I had raised the issue [with him] twice. The second time he had simply replied, 'I do not accept the calling.' The Elder had no greater success in changing his mind, the old wilfulness again being evident. The Elder has deferred further discussion for now. May the Lord help Neufeld to do the right thing.

May 28 Jacob Klassen of Schöndorf and Heinrich Löwen of Nicolaithal, appearing on behalf of Mrs Abraham Bärgen, requested her readmission to the church. The Elder had placed her in the ban last Thursday because of the discord in her marriage. Her husband (see entries for April 16 and 17, 1873) has been under arrest in Khortitsa for some time. I promised to visit [the Borosenko settlement].

May 30 To keep my promise, Heinrich and I drove to Borosenko where I consulted a number of church members about Mrs Bärgen's readmission to the church. She appeared, but showed little contrition, and we decided to leave matters as they were. Since her husband is still under arrest in Khortitsa, it seemed best that she and her trustees appear before Gerh. Dyck in Rosenthal on Sunday. Her husband would also be asked to appear, and the two could be reconciled. She could then be readmitted to church membership on Sunday, in the Neuendorf church. Indeed, this is what happened.

June 25 The condition of my son Diedrich, who has smallpox, is getting worse. The pox are close together, covering his entire body, and have caused his face to swell. Dear Saviour, be thou his physician and help.

June 28 Abraham Andres, the Georgsthal [Grossfürstlich settlement] teacher, his son, and a young man had dinner here. Settlers in the Grossfürstlich settlement, who are suffering close to a total crop failure, have been feeding their cattle for some time.[35] Andres brought back horses of theirs to pasture on the lands of the new Shlakhtin settlement.

July 6 Diedrich left his sick-bed for the first time today and ventured out on to the porch. The pocks have left scars, but Diedrich complains only about his feet.

July 12 Thursday. 'The field is ripe for harvest, but there are few workers.' This is currently the situation with our grain, which ripened this week. Diedrich is well enough to help around the house, but not to do field-work. Jacob became ill Saturday evening, and I have been running around looking for workers ever since. We finally took matters into our own hands on Monday. While Peter and I mowed, Maria and Heinrich tied sheaves. Jacob, who was not quite up to it yet, came along to help in the afternoon. We stopped mowing around noon yesterday. I hope we can hire some workers for tomorrow. At the Kamianka market last week, mowers were fetching 50 to 60 C. per day, but by Sunday they were being hired to mow two desiatinas of grain, and gather it together in small piles, for 1 R. 50 C. to 1 R. 80 C. If they look after their own board, they receive 5 R. 50 C. for the same work. Towards evening I hired Russian workers without board to cut two desiatinas of grain and put it in small piles for 5 R. and showed them the field.

July 28 We have worked non-stop all week, carting wheat home and threshing it with the stone. God willing, and there is no rain, we should easily finish by the end of the week. Klas Heide told us last night that our children David and Maria had come down with the smallpox. We therefore stopped work a little early and drove to Gnadenthal to see them.

July 29 Sunday. We reached Gnadenthal late at night. The last stretch was difficult going because our brown mare, who had been overfed on grain, had a bad case of diarrhea. We found David and his wife in bed with the smallpox. This comes at a bad time, in the midst of harvesting.

After preaching a sermon in Jacob Schellenberg's house, I urged the Gnadenthaler not to leave our sick children at home alone. Fearing contagion, people had virtually ignored them. The villagers promised they would visit our children and help them bring in their harvest.

David's parents-in-law, the Klas Heides, dropped by at noon. Heide bled the front leg of my sick mare, which seemed to help a little, but she still refused to eat and was stiff in all fours. The trip home was at less than a slow walk.

August 2 My nephew Heinrich Rempel arrived from Michaelsburg Thursday morning and spent the night with my brother Diedrich. After harvesting a total of only 5 chetvert of wheat and 7 chetvert of barley, he had come in search of food [for his family] and winter quarters for his cattle.

August 7 Our dear guests the Johann Epps arrived yesterday morning, leaving after breakfast today for the Baratov and Shlakhtin settlements. We had several guests for dinner, Reverend Abr. Wiebe, Johann Bartsch, and a certain Neufeld, all from the Grossfürstlich settlement. They were going to Steinfeld to arrange pasture for their cattle.

August 14 Wheat prices are very high. Today I sold a load of wheat to Peter Friesen in Nikopol for 11 R. 80 C. a chetvert. Later wheat prices rose to 12 R. 25 C. per chetvert.

August 15 [On the way home from Nikopol] I visited David Klassen in Heubuden who, as a deputy of his community, had been to America. He had returned a week ago. Very briefly he told me a great deal. They have decided to settle in Manitoba. What will the other communities do now? Will they sleep-walk their way into the coming danger? Lord, help me to see thy will in this matter.

August 21 At five this morning, Jacob and Peter left for Khortitsa. Peter is returning to the Zentralschule on a stipend and will be boarding again with his uncle Heinrich Epp.

August 24 Our first night frost after the harvest. Jacob is back from Khortitsa and reports considerable uneasiness around the question of emigration to America. Lord, what will happen? Reveal thy will to me.

August 28 For some years, contrary to God's Word, Peter v

Niessen has been involved in lawsuits against Jews, most of them of a highly questionable nature. [In one] case he sold sheep to a Jew named Mark, taking back a promissory note at high interest rates. A few years ago he asked me to calculate what Mark still owed him. I computed that v Niessen already had more than his capital, but that because of the high interest more than 200 R. was still owing. As he had already received more than his fair share, I urged him to let matters be. But he insisted on the full sum, arguing that he, too, had to pay interest.

[Some time ago] v Niessen told my brother Diedrich that the Jew had asked to pay off his debt in instalments. Instead, a year ago, v Niessen had launched a lawsuit against him in Kherson, which v Niessen had now lost. In fact, the court had rejected interest rates of more than 6 per cent and ordered v Niessen to repay Mark more than 60 R. This he had in the meantime failed to do. When Mark appeared today with a court official, and v Niessen again refused to make restitution (the sum had now grown to 83 R. 73 C.), the official ordered that a team of v Niessen's horses be seized. After five days, if v Niessen persists in his refusal, the horses will be sold at public auction.

Faced with this dilemma, v Niessen today appeared at my brother's home with his neighbour Heinr. Olfert and threatened to shoot himself. But in the evening he left to pay off his debt and get back his horses. Saviour, grant that this experience might shock v Niessen out of his passion to litigate and to quarrel. God's staff is being broken over our community because it has fallen so deeply.

September 7 Yesterday several unexpected visitors from the Molochna colonies passed through on their way to the new Molochna settlement of Alexanderfeld (Zagradovka).

September 10 Mother, Gerhard, Elisabeth, Judith, and I left for Khortitsa this afternoon.

September 16 This evening I met Elder Gerhard Wiebe of the Bergthaler church and Elder Johann Wiebe of the Grossfürstlich settlement.[36] Our conversation revolved solely around the subject of the impending emigration to America. Elder Gerhard Wiebe and the Bergthal District mayor Peters had been to see the governor in Ekaterinoslav about the sale of their land. Although the imperial government had given the Bergthal landowners title to their land a year ago, its sale was to be prohibited for a period of three years from then. The governor had now advised them to submit a petition [to him] in this regard. He would then make a suitable proposal to the [imperial] State Council.

September 22 On the way home I paid a visit to the Borosenko settlement.

September 24 I stopped in for dinner today at the home of Reverend Gerhard Enz to tell him that I had decided against emigrating this coming spring. That would have to wait for another year.

September 29 On a visit to our children the Andreses, my wife and I found them in deep mourning for their son Jacob, who had died this morning after an illness of six days. It was the same illness that killed our beloved son Johann.

October 1 At four this morning, with the help of God, our daughter Katharina Bärgen was delivered of an infant son, Johann.

I arrived at home to find an urgent message asking me to come immediately to visit Abraham Friesen in Novokovno. Jacob got fresh horses from the pen, and I left at once. Friesen had difficulty speaking and seemed mainly concerned about his tangled financial affairs. As for his salvation, he said he had prayed fervently and been reconciled to his heavenly father. Lord, save him from a false sense of security. Grant that thy blood might work his salvation.

October 4 My neighbour Isbrand Friesen and his brother-in-law Johann Hildebrand asked my permission to hire young Isaac Friesen, whose guardian I am. I had asked the widow Unger on two occasions whether she wanted to keep young Friesen on for a further period of service and received an inconclusive answer. I had advised him to stay on with her if she offered him the pay I had recommended and to keep me posted. But since nothing had happened in the meantime, I called Isaac Friesen over and hired him out [to Isbrand Friesen] for a year for 50 R., two shirts, foot coverings and 1 R. earnest money.

October 8 Gerhard Andres Sr and I left for Khortitsa early this morning.

October 9 This morning a large Brotherhood Meeting was held in the Khortitsa church regarding the question of emigration. It was decided to wait out the winter until the publication of the military law and then have another meeting in the spring of 1874. The issue was discussed in a peaceful atmosphere with only Johann Hiebert Jr of Einlage pressing for an early decision to emigrate. But he, too, had little specific information [about the government's plans] other than what he had heard. The church was crowded. Present, in addition to the Khortitsa and Kronsweide elders, were more than 30 ministers and deacons.

October 11 On arriving in Khortitsa, I heard about an incident involving our son Peter that made me very unhappy. Peter, who had met several boys carrying a loaded rifle, took the rifle into his hands just as five Russians asking for directions had walked by. The high-spirited boys had played and fooled around. In the meantime the Russians had complained to the Village mayor that Peter had pointed the gun at them. Peter, who admitted raising the gun but denied aiming it in their direction, was nevertheless fined 8 R. 40 C. (paid by my brother Heinrich) – the results of culpable light-mindedness.

October 14 Sunday. I preached in Neu Khortitsa. There appeared before me Johann Sawatzki, the precentor, and Johann Dyck. They had reportedly imbibed brandy on the premises of the merchant Andrei Mironovich and embraced a Russian woman. The folly had been witnessed by Jacob Hildebrand. Joh. Dyck twisted and turned, trying to deny the story, but Sawatzki ended the pretence with a frank and open confession. I tried to impress upon them the sinfulness of their behaviour, which God blessed. When I asked them if they would shun such deeds in future, as God gave them strength, both answered 'yes.' They were allowed to go in peace.

October 23 My wife has an inflamed and painful eye, which drops from my brother Diedrich relieved a little. Our youngsters, Gerhard, Elisabeth, and Judith, have also had very sore eyes.

October 29 My nephew David Rempel of Hoffnungsort brought three of his brother Heinrich Rempel's horses here for the winter. Pätkau, Rev. D. Epp, and I will each board one.

October 30 I was called to Abraham Friesen's bedside, who admitted lying to me and asked my forgiveness (see entry for Oct. 1, 1873). He confessed to committing fornication with numerous Russian women and defiling himself with animals, etc. Since seeking the face of God he had come to realize, he said, that he would not find peace until he had confessed his sins to the church. He showed great remorse. May the dear Saviour lead him along the path of repentance and have mercy on him.

November 4 *Brotherhood Meeting*. Abraham Friesen was placed in the ban for his transgressions.

November 12 Monday morning, Abraham Friesen, excluded from the church because of his carnal sins, was readmitted to membership. In reply to my question whether there was any obstacle to his readmission, he replied 'no.' We then sang the hymn 'Jesus Accepts Sinners.' Walking home Peter Peters stopped me to say that Abraham Friesen should not have been readmitted until he had settled matters regarding the [horse-]leads. I did not know anything about this matter, I said, and it should in any case have been raised earlier. He grumbled a little and left for home. Jacob Friesen told me the two men had been reconciled over this issue at my brother's place. May the Lord turn reprimands into blessings.

November 21 Johann Andres brought over window frames he had built for David to be fitted with glass.

Jacob rode back this afternoon from Hamburg [Nepluiev settlement], where he had proposed marriage and where things had developed as he had hoped.

November 30 At noon today, Jacob returned from Johann Hoeppner's having been told that Hoeppner's daughter, who accepted his proposal of marriage a week ago Wednesday, would celebrate her engagement to someone else tomorrow. I have entrusted the matter to God's guidance, and it is my understanding that this is his will.

Around 8:30 tonight, our neighbour Mrs Klassen rushed over and fearfully told us that two of her horses had been stolen. We sounded the alarm, then went out to search. Fortunately Jacob and my neighbour Reverend Diedr. Epp found one of the horses not far from the barn, but the thieves had made their escape with the mare. The search continued for a long time on horseback and on foot. Jacob, Franz Klassen and Hildebrand's manservant went as far as the so-called corner tavern, but returned empty-handed at one in the morning.

December 7 The widow Unger, who had been to Novokovno, told me that Abraham Friesen, who is still sick, was anxious to see me. Jacob drove me over. As I entered his darkened room he repeatedly broke into a loud lament, saying he had not told me the whole truth (see entry for Oct. 30, 1873). He had also committed fornication with his maidservant (a Prussian girl of the Catholic confession). Sin is so powerful a thing that it is hard to free oneself entirely of guilt and to lay one's burden completely at Jesus' feet. I spoke to him about the Lamb of God, who bears the sins of the world, and quoted the words of 1 John 1:7, 'The blood of Jesus Christ, the son of God, cleanseth us of all sin.' Johann Friesen, his brother, and the Johann Heides kept the sick man company at night.

December 15 A hemorrhage brought a sudden end to Abraham Friesen's sufferings, and he was buried in Novokovno yesterday afternoon.

December 17 At two last night we were aroused from our sleep by a knock at the window. It was Franz Klassen's wife telling us that she and her husband had been awakened by their dog barking. Looking out, her husband had seen a thief at the barn door and another coming around the corner to steal the Klassens' only remaining horse. Klassen had knocked at the windowpane and the robbers had run away. Since the last theft, when the thieves had removed the lock and cramp from the barn door, the door had been fastened with only a piece of rotten cloth. Jacob and Diedrich went out again to help look for the thieves.

December 31 This past year God created a great void in our family through the sudden, premature death of our beloved son Johann. We will long cherish his memory. Yet when one thinks of the tribulations gathering along the distant horizon like a dark thunder-cloud (and which could inundate our community at any time) we may take comfort from the fact that we have lost Johann according to God's wisdom and will. We do not lose little children when they die. They are heaven's heirs, for the death of Christ has reconciled them to God.

This past year our beloved Elder Gerhard Dyck, my brother Heinrich, and others, twice visited St Petersburg in defence of our religious liberties. They are said to have arrived home on the evening of the second day of Christmas, but we have had no more definite news. Many of our fellow believers from here in Borosenko on the Ssolonne and Basavluk [streams] are getting ready to emigrate to America. Show me thy will in this matter, O Lord, and let my decision be pleasing to thee.

This year's harvest was good in places and poor elsewhere. An epidemic among horned cattle in the area is raging among cattle belonging to the Jews in Novopodolsk. This is God's punishment. The grain prices were high, from 11 to 12 R. per 10 pud chetvert in Nikopol. Lord Jesus, we thank thee for thy love and faithfulness and honour and praise thee.

1874

February 13 Trip to Khortitsa. Three of us, my young colleague and nephew Diedrich Epp, Johann Bärgen Sr and I, left at noon today for Khortitsa to attend a Brotherhood Meeting called by Elder Gerhard Dyck.

February 15 A general Brotherhood Meeting was held in the Khortitsa church. This was in keeping with the decision of the meeting of October 9, 1873, to consult amongst ourselves again once the military law had been made public. The authorities have now reached a decision stating that we will either have to serve in the medical services or to emigrate during six free years granted us by the imperial government.

After much discussion, Elder Gerhard Dyck proposed that we send a deputation to America this coming summer. After many objections had been voiced the proposal was finally agreed to. Whether this plan will be realized only God knows. Reveal thy will to us clearly in these difficult days. Many are not in favour of emigration, but dark foreboding has gripped many a heart. Numerous ministers were present at the meeting as well as Elder Peter Klassen of the Kronsweide church and Reverend Abraham Wiebe of Fürstenland.

March 1 Towards evening I received a letter from Elder Gerhard Dyck asking me to consult our local congregation about the costs of sending a deputation to America. I am asked to report these views to another meeting in the Khortitsa church on the 8th.

March 5 Tuesday morning Brotherhood Meeting in the home of my son-in-law Johann Andres in Neu Khortitsa. Following introductory words and prayer, I asked the brethren for their views. After lengthy discussion, we agreed unanimously that the costs of sending a deputation to America should be distributed on the same basis as the costs of our fire-insurance system. But the brethren did not want to pay before September, if possible, because of the serious shortage of money.

March 8 At the conference this morning in the Khortitsa church, Elder Gerhard Dyck again stressed the importance of sending a deputation to America. He then asked the [village] mayors present for the views they had reached in this regard since our last Brotherhood Meeting of February 15. Those from Khortitsa, Einlage, Kronsweide, and Neuhochfeld reported they were not in favour of sending a deputation and had no wish to participate in the undertaking. The others strongly supported the initiative, however, and were willing to help pay the costs. But they were not of one mind on the question of approach. Finally the decision was made to seek voluntary contributions in the villages as soon as possible. These are to be authorized by the Village mayors. Once lists of donations had been sent to the Elder we could decide whether the project was feasible. It now seems unlikely that the government will allow us the promised free years [during which we can emigrate], but God can direct this matter.

March 14 Franz Dyck of Izluchistaia gave me a list of the donations for the sending of a deputation to America. There has been another development, however, which causes me anxiety and distress. A mounted messenger just delivered an express communication from the Khortitsa Volost Office (following orders of the Marshal of the Nobility and the District police officer), instructing me to prepare an induction list from the church register of men born in 1853. It is to be submitted by the 22nd. What has happened to the six years for unhindered emigration, promised by His Imperial Majesty? Lord, take this burden from me. Help us in our hour of need.

March 17 When we arrived home from today's service three young men from Friesenthal, Bernhard, Jacob, and Julius Friesen, were waiting to see me. They too had been told to submit a list of men born in 1853. By providing them with birth certificates, I was to confirm that there was no one of that age in Friesenthal.

April 6 Heinrich Siemens of Izluchistaia, who has been suffering from sore eyes for many years, told me that Doctor Schellenberg had advised him to seek help for his condition in Kharkov. I agreed to organize a collection for this purpose.

April 16 After breakfast we accompanied the Gerh. Dycks to the Island of Khortitsa to visit Uncle Jacob Hoeppner. We also looked in on the Jacob Wiebes and David Penners. Our friend Wiebe, who is crippled and presents a truly pitiable sight, was someone whose opinion was always respected. As long-time Village mayor and a member and chairman of the Agricultural Commission he had exerted a strong and positive influence on the entire village community. Now he is reduced to this. Faithful Saviour, be thou his rod and staff and a comfort for his soul.

April 17 On orders of the imperial government, all ministers have left for Halbstadt. His Imperial Majesty has sent His Excellency General von Todleben to negotiate with the Mennonites. What positive results are likely to come from this initiative? The imperial government, which does not want us to leave the country, may change the law, bringing it into conformity with our confession of faith. May God grant this.

April 21 *Brotherhood Meeting*. We registered 20 baptismal candidates. Lord Jesus, record their names in the book of eternal life. I also informed the brethren that Heh. Siemens (see entry for April 6, 1874) had requested contributions to help finance his trip to Kharkov. I encouraged them to contribute their pittances.

April 22 An express messenger (Johann Klassen's stepson Johann Funk) arrived today from the Nicolaithal Volost[37] with a notice of a general Brotherhood Meeting to be held in Khortitsa on the 24th. All church members, and ministers in particular, have been invited to attend. The latter are to give His Imperial Excellency Adjutant-General von Todleben the community's decision regarding emigration. An enclosed letter explains that His Excellency, on behalf of our Gracious Emperor, will offer the Mennonites important concessions freeing them of the obligation to join the [military] medical services. Instead, they will be permitted to discharge their compulsory service by planting forests, in artisanal work, and so on. Those serving will also be permitted to remain among their own (and not serve with others). I took the letter to my brother Diedrich who immediately sent around a notice to all the [Judenplan] colonies announcing the Brotherhood Meeting. Johann Bärgen offered to drive me to Khortitsa.

April 23 My brother Diedrich and I left this morning for Khortitsa with our driver Johann Bärgen.

April 24 Wednesday. A general Brotherhood Meeting in the Khortitsa church. Present, in addition to the elders Gerhard Dyck, Peter Klassen, and Johann Wiebe, were more than 30 ministers and deacons. Elder Gerhard Dyck addressed the brethren, and following a prayer outlined the purpose of our gathering. At the express command of His Excellency, Adjutant-General von Todleben,[38] all of the elders and ministers had been present in Halbstadt. The Elder reported that His Excellency, in the name of His Most Gracious Emperor, was now prepared to allow us to render service outside of the military realm, as follows: (1) in civilian hospitals; (2) on the railroads; (3) in city fire departments; and (4) in the forestry service. Those in service would remain under our own spiritual supervision. Those choosing not to serve on these terms would be free to emigrate without hindrance during a period of six years. A vote was then taken. Out of a total of 560 brethren casting their ballots, 528 voted resolutely in favour of remaining here and 32 voted to emigrate.

April 25 Thursday around four in the afternoon, the Adjutant-General von Todleben, in the company of the governor of Ekaterinoslav Province and other persons of high rank, appeared at the home of Hermann Niebuhr in Khortitsa. Next to the platform, a triumphal arch had been erected with an inscription from Psalm 134:3, 'The Lord bless thee out of Zion.' My brother Heinrich gathered with his students in front of the arch and welcomed His Excellency by singing the national anthem, 'God Save the Tsar.' At the request of our honoured guest, they also sang a German song. The courtyard was packed with people.

The adjutant-general had expressed the wish to speak to the ministerial group and the Village elders, and the church had been set aside for this purpose. But the entire crowd streamed in that direction, pushing its way into the church. The adjutant-general was driven to the church, entered, took his place below the pulpit, and gave a speech in which he outlined the favours the monarch was prepared to offer. But the noise and tumult of the crowd as they pushed and shoved their way into the church seems to have made a bad impression on our distinguished guest, for the tone of his speech was grave and firm.

At the close of the adjutant-general's speech, Elder Gerhard Dyck walked over to our guest, thanked him, and announced that the community wished to render service and had decided on service in the workshops. The adjutant-general's answer, delivered in the same harsh tone, was that we could not negotiate with the sovereign on these matters, but had simply to accept what was being offered us through his grace. These words created a serious and discordant note and aroused ill-feeling in the congregation, which was heightened by the sense of injury felt by the Elder.

I spent the night at the home of my brother-in-law Gerhard Dyck in Rosenthal. He and the Reverend Isaac Veer had returned from the Molochna a few days ago with that community's decisions.

April 26 Friday morning the congregation and ministerial group gathered inside and outside the [Khortitsa] church and then proceeded to Niebuhr's courtyard. Here the adjutant-general greeted us with friendly words in regard to our duties and privileges and the emperor's good will. In the District [Volost] Office we signed a document addressed to His Excellency, which he intends to submit to His Imperial Majesty, outlining our understanding, namely that: (1) if the [military service] law violated our confession of faith we would be free to emigrate without hindrance; (2) we would continue to enjoy full freedom within our churches, and our schools would remain under our supervision; and (3) the placement of our young men would be in closed groups that would remain under our spiritual superintendence. The document had been prepared by the Molochna brethren, and since it was fully in agreement with our own views, we signed it as well.

Our Molochna brethren had also submitted a letter of thanks to His Imperial Majesty. My brother Heinrich had drafted a letter on our behalf that the two elders, as well as several ministers including me, signed. May our dear, faithful Saviour accompany these missals with his blessing and pour out his blessing over our beloved sovereign and the entire imperial house.

I spent the night with my brother Johann [secretary of the Volost Office]. My cousin Jacob Thiessen of Kherson, who had navigated his recently purchased steamer 'Anna' through the [Dnieper] rapids, organized an excursion on the Dnieper this afternoon. It was joined by my brother Diedrich and son-in-law Joh. Bärgen, but I was unable to participate.

April 28 *Brotherhood Meeting*. The [baptismal] youth were introduced for the second time. Four more had come forward, making a total of 17 young men and 7 young women. Two young men, Heinrich Klippenstein and Bernd Janzen of Neu Khortitsa, had gotten into mischief at Christmastime (mentioned at Sunday's Brotherhood Meeting). At my home last night they were remorseful and begged for pardon (especially the former). Their apologies were accepted, and the brethren allowed their names to stand [as baptismal candidates]. Before the service, I also talked to Susanna Janzen about reports that she had lain in bed with her father-in-law Löwen, although she had been fully clothed. Gerh. Wiebe of Gnadenthal (who witnessed the story and reported it), as well as Susanna, her stepfather Isaac Friesen, and her brother-in-law Peter Löwen, made light of the incident, explaining it away as something quite innocent. Avoid all appearance of evil. The matter was held over.

May 3 Friday. Our teacher, Cornelius Giesbrecht, arrived last night and started keeping school this morning.

May 8 Wednesday. A cold rain this morning. This afternoon Mrs Heinrich Siemens of Izluchistaia, whose husband had left for Odessa to have his eyes treated, asked for help in her poverty. I gave her the 6 R. I had collected. She told me also about the goings-on of our church members in her village and of the hostility [of some of them] towards me. I felt in my heart that this humiliation was to my benefit. May our true Saviour lead me through all tribulations to salvation. Lord Jesus, draw my adversaries to thee through thy great love that they might share in thy heavenly salvation. Our community has become deeply sunk in ignorance and coarse secret desires. Our teaching and preaching is of little consequence.

May 13 Monday. Peter Gräber and his daughter Maria got here at Vesper-time. Elder Gerhard Dyck arrived at 8:30 p.m. The Elder's driver, Johann Klassen of Rosenthal, and his infant foster-child Jacob Siemens spent the night at Rev. Jacob Pätkau's place.

May 14 Tuesday morning. After we had hitched my three horses to the wagon on which our guests arrived, the Elder, our friend Gräber, his daughter, my children Jacob and Maria, and I drove to church in Novovitebsk. My sons Diedrich and Heinrich walked. The holy ordinance of Christian baptism was administered by the Elder. Lord Jesus, baptize our beloved young people with thy spirit and with fire. May their conduct show that they have been baptized into thy death.

This afternoon's preparatory sermon by my young colleague and nephew [Diet. Epp] was based on Revelations 3:20.

May 15 Wednesday afternoon Elder Dyck held communion service in the presence of 161 guests, including my dear wife, the children Jacob and Maria, our three pairs of married children, and me, unworthy as I am. Following the service, the Elder, Diedrich Epp, Jacob Kampen, and I dropped in to see the widow Abr. Unger. Her daughter-in-law, Mrs Jacob Wiebe, was sick in bed, and the Elder gave her communion at her request. The Johann Bärgens, who arrived in the morning, left their child at our place and later visited with us until evening. Peter Gräber and his daughter Maria departed in the afternoon. Following coffee, around three o'clock, the Elder left for home via the Borosenko and Nepluiev settlements. May the Lord send his angels to watch over you.

May 17 Friday. The rain continued until late last night, and there was still a cold drizzle this morning. The cattle were driven out to pasture earlier in the day. But with a heavy rain around noon, the children rode out to drive the herd back into the village. Everyone was glad to have their cattle home in the barn. Now at Vesper-time, as I write these lines, I can hear rain falling outside. I have heard that some 200 recently shorn sheep froze to death last night on the nearby khutor of a Jew. My dear wife was sick in bed today. She was bled this morning by my brother Diedrich, who also gave her drops. Bless them, Lord Jesus. She is just out of bed and getting dressed, and I hope she will be well soon. Evening. My wife crawled back into bed almost immediately. By 5:15 the rain had let up enough to allow us to pasture the cattle and horses in the yard.

May 18 Saturday. I met Jacob Friesen of Novokovno on the street, coming from my brother Diedrich Epp's place where he had sought advice for his sick neighbour Peter Hiebert. He told me that Thursday's storm had overturned and smashed Hiebert's barn and torn off the house rafters from the end of the barn to the chimney. Hiebert's cattle, which had been kept indoors because of the bad weather, had been buried in the rubble and one horse had been killed. This had given bedridden Hiebert such a fright that his condition had become much worse. May the Lord help him in his troubles and lead him to eternal life, through Jesus Christ our Lord. Amen.

May 22 Wednesday. My son Diedrich and I left for Ekaterinoslav this morning to buy glass. We went via Khortitsa, where I had business to do, and arrived at my brother Heinrich's place at nightfall.

May 23 Thursday. To obtain an allotment of land in the [new] village of Grünfeld [Shlakhtin daughter settlement], I waited all day to see the District mayor Braun, who was supposed to come in. I finally left. My brother Heinrich has offered to lend me the needed 200 R. plus interest and to deposit the money with the [Old Colony District] Office. He also lent me 50 R. to purchase glass. At 6 p.m. I resumed my journey, spending the night with my nephew Martin Dyck in Franzfeld.

May 24 We started out for Ekaterinoslav at six in the morning. We bought a half-case of number-one clear glass for 22½ R., a half-case of number-one opaque glass for 15 R. 50 C., and after several other purchases from the merchant Alekeievna, we left for home. We spent the night in Simporovich.

June 4 Thursday. At noon today Isaac Friesen of Novokovno rode over on horseback to tell me about the discord in his family. He asked me to mediate between his wife and himself, whose marriage has always been stormy. Now the decision to marry of his stepson Jacob Janzen had given rise to a new dispute. Friesen refused to permit Jacob and his wife to live with them after their wedding. Dear God, grant them thy peace. While Friesen was still a widower I had urged him not to enter into a second marriage without a lot of thought. He should weigh matters carefully and pray in order that his choice might be in accordance with God's will. I wonder if Friesen did this? May this trial lead him to salvation, and, Lord, give his deluded wife an opportunity to repent.

June 13 Jacob, Heinrich, and I drove to Grünfeld to rake the cut hay on our house-and-garden plot. The strong wind was a problem, but we nevertheless managed to make four trips.

June 14 Friday. I spent the night with sick Jacob Hiebert. When I got to my children's place they were already at the [hay]stack with another load. Then a drizzle interrupted our work, and we still have a load of hay to cart from the field as well as the hay that the settlers had divided among themselves. On our way home we stepped at David's place in Gnadenthal to pick up my brother-in-law Gerh. Dyck's cow, which we will look after until he arrives. Jacob stayed there to do some work as a day-labourer.

June 23 I preached a sermon in Grünfeld to a fairly large congregation on the subject of the two paths and their ends. But many were also at the Sofievaka fair, cutting themselves off from the Word of God. Lord, arouse in us a thirst for thy Word.

My dear wife and I and our children Gerhard, Elisabeth and Judith left home yesterday after Vesper, spending the night with our children the Johann Andreses in Neu Khortitsa. After a heavy downpour, water was still standing in puddles and the road was muddy. This morning my son-in-law Andres teamed up a horse with mine and came along to Grünfeld. There had been less rain in Gnadenthal and more again on the Grünfeld land. We had dinner with the Johann Bärgens in Neu Khortitsa, where the David Epps arrived in the afternoon from Gnadenthal. We left for home after coffee. Just as we arrived home, we were deluged by a heavy downpour with thunder and lightning. The rain on the fields was heavier than in the village. We thank the Lord for his blessings.

June 24 After breakfast I went along with my neighbour Franz Klassen to Chomenko's khutor on the Koshinski steppe, where I bought four pigs for 30 R. Our son Heinrich and Klassen's son Franz drove the pigs to our place, but one kept trying to run back home and became quite a nusiance. I made a down payment of 10 R. and gave a promissory note for the remaining 20 R., payable on August 1. Lord, help me to keep this promise. This morning Jacob and Peter helped with the communal work in Grünfeld of improving the roads and dams. They are due home on Thursday.

July 5 Friday. On their way back from Nikopol, the Heh. Peters stopped in for dinner and told us that the emigration fever is again on the rise in [the] Borosenko and Nepluiev [settlements]. My brother Diedrich returned from Khortitsa today and reports that there are restless spirits there as well.

July 10 We brought home the rye, raking together what was still loose, and had a yield of 10 merka. After Vesper we drove out to the steppe to inspect the grain. It is time to harvest, but much of the grain is still not ready. Some barley ears are ripe, but others are still green, and it could be very busy later on.

July 24 Wednesday. Since we had run short of feed for the pigs and horses, Gerhard and I stone-threshed three loads of oats, and mother naturally helped. Today we cleaned the barley, which yielded 5 chetvert 3 merka. It is hot, the grain is suddenly ripe everywhere, and mowers have become very dear. This week a mower was fetching 3 R.!! That means that for 2 desiatinas of grain the costs of cutting and tying in sheaves will be from 12 to 15 R. That is a good part of the harvest profit.

July 28 Towards evening our son David Epp came looking for workers, which he desperately needs to harvest his crop. He has 10 desiatinas of wheat still standing in the field and cannot find any workers close at hand. We therefore hitched my horses to his wagon and he and Jacob went out searching into the neighbouring villages. They finally found several workers from Konstantinovka in our own village, and hired three men, two to mow and one to rake for 5 R. a day. Since the men had their own cart and oxen, they left immediately for Gnadenthal, which could be an exhausting trip. Workers this year are very scarce and dear.

August 7 Wednesday. This year I used improved seed to sow six desiatinas of land to wheat. Today we cleaned the grain from half of this land, which came to 17 chetvert 6 merka, or almost 6 chetvert per desiatina. In the lower garden, my wife started digging the potatoes, which needed to be done because of the pilfering at night.

August 15 Thursday. Monday evening's drizzle continued into the night, and although the weather was better on Tuesday morning it was still too damp to cart or to thresh with the stone. We have therefore been cleaning the wheat already in the barn, a total of 24 chetvert 6 merka. We expect to get back to carting and threshing today, even though it is not as dry as it was. We praise God for the rich harvest he has graciously given us. May he also grant us eternal salvation, for Jesus' sake.

August 16 This afternoon, Peter caught a ride to Khortitsa with the teacher C. Giesbrecht where he will be attending the Zentralschule for another year. May the Lord protect them on their way and keep Peter from straying.

August 18 I preached a sermon in Peter Harder's home in Novozhitomir. My dear wife, Elisabeth, and I stayed with the Joh. Klassens and visited the Pet. Janzens in the afternoon. There is great unrest in the community since many have been gripped by the emigration fever. Lord, reveal thy will to me.
August 30 Friday. We carted the last oats today, which means that all of the grain is home now and threshed, except for the rye, which we will harvest with flails.
September 4 Wednesday. Our neighbour Isbrand Friesen is convinced that a mare that ran on to his yard last Sunday is the one that was stolen from him last fall. Joh. Heide and several other neighbours confirmed that it was his, only the teeth suggesting that it might be somewhat younger. Friesen told me about his good fortune, especially that the features of the horse proved that it was his black mare. I suggested he report the incident to my brother, the local overseer, which he did. But yesterday, in a state of great agitation, [Village] Mayor Leib Mendelsohn told Friesen that the mare was his. It had vanished after workers had let it go last Sunday, and he had been looking for it ever since. He claimed to have bought it a month ago in Kamianka from the Jew Chertok. Friesen refused simply to hand over the horse in this way.

This morning the [Village] Office awarded the horse to the mayor as his own. Friesen's witnesses testified that the colour of the horse and its other features were identical to those of the mare he had lost, and that only the teeth indicated that it might be a little younger. Chertok, for his part, attested to having purchased the horse at a fair in May, while Friesen's horse disappeared only in fall. When the [Mayor's] Office freed the mare it made a bee-line for its place in Friesen's barn. A Jew went after it with a bridle and brought it back.
September 6 Jacob and Heinrich returned from Nikopol, having sold the wheat for 7 R. 70 C. per chetvert. A tin containing a pud of petroleum broke on the way home, spilling the liquid. Our other purchases were also ruined and only a little oil remained. Another misfortune.
September 13 Last Tuesday at 5 p.m., Jacob, Diedrich, and I loaded the stone on the wagon and left for Grünfeld to thresh our grain. It was late by the time we reached Gnadenthal, so we spent the night with the David Epps. Our daughter-in-law suffers from sore breasts.

Be thou her physician, Lord Jesus. The next day, we left at sunrise and reached our place in Grünfeld at breakfast-time. Since our Russian workers had not yet brought home our millet, we drove out to the field to plough (we also had the plough along) and seeded two desiatinas to grain. Once this job was done by noon Thursday we prepared the threshing floor and started to thresh, the Russians in the meantime having unloaded the millet. This morning the children stayed behind with a team of horses to continue threshing while I drove home through Gnadenthal and Neu Khortitsa. I picked up the plough wheel we had lost on the way down, which had been found near Novopodolsk by Joh. Bärgen.

On Monday, September 4, there was a huge fire in Neuhorst that destroyed the entire village including its bumper crop. Only six homesteads and a cottager's house were spared. The fire started in a straw pile at two in the afternoon. Within two hours the destruction was complete. What a terrible conflagration. May the Lord have mercy on the poor victims.

September 21 Jacob and Maria returned from Nikopol on Saturday. They were forced to sell the wheat for 6 R. 80 C. per chetvert. The low level of the Dnieper [River] is chiefly responsible for the depressed wheat prices.

September 24 Tuesday. The Peter Gräbers of Hanovka arrived last night and left again this morning after breakfast. They had come in regard to the emigration question. Since the residence period mentioned in their emigration agreement will end on December 24, they are in a perplexing situation. Some of their brothers and sisters are already in America, but they would prefer to stay here and to join the Khortitsa church. We had a refreshing rain today after a very long drought. God be praised.

October 1 Tuesday. Jacob and Diedrich left for Nikopol yesterday at daybreak with a load of wheat and returned today before sundown. The prices have fallen even further. They now sold the wheat for 6 R. 20 C. per chetvert. On the way home they stopped in to see Franz Isaac and bought an easy chair for 12 R.

October 5 We ministers gathered this morning at the home of Diedrich Epp where the Isaac Friesens and Mrs Peter Hiebert of Novokovno appeared. They live in a state of perpetual conflict. Recently Mrs Friesen had appeared at widow Hiebert's home in a rage and sworn at her. She had returned later with a stick and smashed in a window, and so on. The two were finally reconciled and allowed to go in peace. We seldom ask about God's ways.

October 18 Friday. We left for Khortitsa last week Wednesday, the 9th. My brother Diedrich's son Heinrich was along to attend the Zentralschule. I visited my colleague Gerh. Pätkau, who plans to emigrate to Canada in spring. On Tuesday we looked in on my uncle Jacob Dyck and the Reverend Jacob Regier, had dinner with the Johann Sawatzkis in Schönhorst, and stopped in at Franz Thiessen's store in Neuendorf in the afternoon. While my wife shopped, I attended to my business with the Orphans' Administration. By 8 p.m. we were in Neuosterwick, at Diet. Dyck's place. We stayed to visit with Uncle Jacob Hoeppner, his wife, and their children, the Peter Hoeppners from Michaelsburg, who also plan to move to Canada.

Emigration fever among our Mennonites both in the Khortitsa District and on the Molochna continues to be very strong, and only God knows what the end result of this will be. Elder Isaac Peters, whose preaching is said to have included abuse of the government, has received formal notice from the imperial authorities that he must leave Russia within a short period of time. Farms are selling for next to nothing. Those earlier priced from 5000 to 6000 R. are now selling for 2000 R. or, at most, 3000 R. Other possessions are similarly cheap.[39]

November 12 Tuesday. We butchered our four pigs with the help of the D. Epps, Jacob Pätkau, Cornel. Mantler, and Franz Klassen.

December 26 Thursday. The second holiday. Our children from Neu Khortitsa, Johann and Helena Andres, and their sons Gerhard and Johann were here this afternoon. Before Christmas, Cornelius Töws of Friesenthal (Erikovich) came to fetch his children for the holidays (they attend village school and board with my brother Diedrich), and told me the following story. In Nikopol three Mennonites had struck a deal with a Jew, Alter, each promising to deliver 100 chetvert of wheat (a total of 300 chetvert). They had received a down payment of 600 R., falsely claiming to be members of the Friedensfeld [Village] administration, and signed an agreement with the Jew. Alter had planned to accompany the men to Friedensfeld, but when he arrived at their quarters with the Koslowskis [in Nikopol] the following morning, they had vanished.

This story turns out to be exactly as related. These three deeply fallen individuals are Johann Dyck and Gerhard and Klas Thiessen of Neu Khortitsa. The Jew Alter had already been to Neu Khortitsa before these men arrived home. Koslowski is said to have given him their names for 25 R. The offenders arrived home with 450 R. after spending the rest. In the meantime the [Neu Khortitsa] Village administration has reached an understanding with the Jew to give him several hundred rubles more than the sum he had advanced. The three are to be turned over to the District Office in Khortitsa. This story attests to the decay of our community.

December 31 Tuesday at 10:30 a.m., with God's gracious help, a son was born to us, whom we have named Johann.[40] Grant us thy help, dear Lord, that our beloved newborn might grow up to honour and glorify thee.

1875

January 14 Tuesday. Winter set in during the night from Saturday to Sunday, with five degrees of frost, but this morning it is warm with a strong south wind and the snow has disappeared. My brother Diedrich returned from Khortitsa with a letter from Elder Gerhard Dyck informing me that a Brotherhood Meeting in the Khortitsa church on January 6 had placed Gerhard and Klas Thiessen and Johann Dyck in the ban because of their Nikopol swindle. I am to inform their families and the Neu Khortitsa Village assembly accordingly to ensure that they are treated as separated persons. I forwarded the letter to the Village Elder [of Neu Khortitsa], Dietrich Braun. Heinrich Harder of Gnadenthal, who had been in Khortitsa on business, brought the wrongdoers (together with a formal report from the Khortitsa Volost) home on the 11th.

January 17 Friday. Reverend Pätkau tells me that the three men in question had yesterday been turned over to the District police officer in Sofievka. Lord, grant them the strength to repent.

January 20 Trip to Nepluievka. Monday evening Heinrich Harder and Isaac Friesen of Steinau delivered a letter from Reverend Anton Sudermann requesting that I accompany the two men to Nepluievka to help out with a church matter.

January 23 Thursday. We met in the home of the deacon Peter Klassen in Steinau. Mrs Johann Enz had confessed that before her marriage she had committed fornication with Cornelius Fast of Rosenthal, but was blameless in that Fast had used force. Our questioning revealed, however, that it had happened with her consent. Not wishing to be punished, she withdrew in a fit of anger.

As for the brawl [which was also the reason for my trip], it appeared that there was equal blame on all sides. Also, the story had become much exaggerated in the telling. At the evening engagement festivities for Heinrich Harder and the widow Neufeld, brandy had been consumed. Herman Olfert had objected when Peter Janzen and others had kissed his wife. Janzen confirmed this part of the story (the others did not), but insisted that it had been nothing more than a prank. Then Johann Olfert had beaten up his brother Hermann for talking about the matter. Johann Löwen testified that the story was as I have related it. Hermann Olfert, however, said that Löwen had also been drunk at the party and that the quarrel had been provoked by Peter Harder. It seemed to me that the other wedding quests were also to blame, and so I urged a general reconciliation. Herman Olfert was coarse and shameless at first, but finally peace was made all around and they were dismissed in peace.

A public worship service was held in the building in Steinau, and I preached a sermon about Revelations 3:14–16. At the Brotherhood Meeting that followed the brethren unanimously placed Mrs Johann Enz in the ban for having committed fornication. I then spoke to them about the sinful goings-on at their celebrations, holidays, and weddings and earnestly appealed to them to celebrate their festivities in a Christian manner.

January 24 There is a great controversy in the Nepluiev settlement between those emigrating and those remaining here. A coarse and slanderous denunciation of the [Village] Mayor's Office was found on the street in Blumenfeld and has caused quite a commotion.

Dietrich Braun, the mayor of Neu Khortitsa, and Jacob Neufeld came to talk to me on behalf of the three men placed in the ban, requesting their readmission to the church on Sunday, that is, tomorrow. Johann Dyck and Klas Thiessen dropped by to make a similar plea personally. Finally, I met with my colleagues Pätkau and Epp to discuss the possibility of our going [to Neu Khortitsa] tomorrow.

January 26 I preached a sermon in Johann Veer's home in Neu Khortitsa on the words of Jesus, 'That the son of man is come to seek and to save sinners.' *Brotherhood Meeting*. The brethren consented to the readmission of Johann Dyck and the brothers Klas and Gerhard Thiessen to the church. Lord Jesus, accept their remorse and wipe away their guilt. Their case has not yet been decided by the courts, however.

January 27 Monday. Auction sale of agricultural implements and cattle at Cornelius Krause's place in Kamianka. I kept the books. The sales totalled 453 R. I bought a pair of harvest ladders. My brother and I travelled there by sled on a wonderful track.

February 3 The unrest continues within the Nepluiev settlement, arising from the plans of those wishing to emigrate to America. The emigrants would like to be able to sell their properties to people of other confessions, while those remaining here are prepared to permit such sales only on the condition that no more than one or two villages are sold in this way. People in such [designated] villages, who are staying, would then purchase properties in other villages, making it possible for Mennonites to remain together [in villages] on their own. In Blumenfeld, however, villagers remaining [in Russia] refuse to allow any sales to outsiders. *That is causing bad blood!* For reasons of faith the quarrelsome want to emigrate, yet Christian church members try to prevent this, thereby disadvantaging their neighbours.

February 27 Thursday. A strong cold east wind, and 14 degrees of frost. My brother Diedrich and I made a deal last night to trade properties, exchanging mine here in Novopodolsk for his in Gnadenthal. I will dismantle the implement shed in Novopodolsk and move it to Gnadenthal. Today I went to discuss this matter with Johann Schellenberg, the mayor of Gnadenthal, and then visited my son David [also in Gnadenthal].

March 1 Saturday. It is almost mild today with a snowfall from the west. We have had a lot of snow this winter and there could be a heavy runoff. As overseer for the building of the [Grünfeld] school, Jacob

Hiebert was here today to conclude an agreement with the master carpenter Konshorovski.

March 4 Tuesday. Jacob and Diedrich left this morning with a load of lumber to build a shelter for our cattle in Gnadenthal.

March 8 Saturday. *Gnadenthal* is now our home. Our children returned from Gnadenthal on Wednesday, and Friday the wagons arrived to move us. Earlier, Jacob, Diedrich, Heinrich, and Gerhard had driven our cattle to Gnadenthal. They now loaded our wagon, which was pulled by three horses. The children Maria, Elisabeth, and Judith accompanied their brother David while my dear wife and I and our infant [Johann] left in the afternoon on the small sled. Then the child started to scream, and we had to turn back, breaking a shaft on the sleigh. Johann soon calmed down and went to sleep, and we started out again. The trip went smoothly until we reached the last Russian village, where we sought out a warm room to quieten the child. That did not help much, however, and he continued to cry until we reached our destination. As our house is small and very cold, mother and I and the little one stayed at David's place. We were busy moving in until this afternoon. There were 11 degrees of frost yesterday, but it was pleasant during the day. Today it is again cold and windy. Faithful Saviour, give us thy blessing in this new settlement.

March 9 This morning there was frost, a southeast wind, and fog lasting an hour, a warmer afternoon, then snow from the southeast, a mixture of snow and rain from the south, and finally rain from the west. The sun shone after Vesper.

March 10 Monday. Jacob and Diedrich went to Novopodolsk by sleigh, taking along two extra horses to bring back our wagon, which was still there. Heavy frost in the morning, a thaw in the afternoon, and frost again at night.

March 25 Tuesday. Heinrich went to work for Heh. Neufeld, our neighbour, until after seed-time. Towards the end of today's meeting of the Village assembly, after finishing the discussion of village affairs, I mentioned the conflict between former Mayor Jacob Wiebe and Wilhelm Martens (at the latter's request). In the second year of the existence of this settlement the two men had bought some wheat together and were now not agreed on the accounts. Martens insists that he had received only 50 R. [of wheat], while Wiebe had an account showing 100 R. I suggested that Martens pay the difference of 50 R., and tried to show from the Scriptures that this was God's will. It was thus resolved. Lord Jesus, grant them thy peace.

March 30 Ground frost prevented us from drawing the boundary furrow between our home-and-garden plot and that of our neighbour Wilhelm Mantler. Our infant Johann became ill last night. May the loving Saviour be his physician and helper.

April 2 A heavy rain at night and snow and a strong north wind this morning again prevented us from going out with the plough. We also could not put the cattle out to pasture.

April 3 This afternoon the Wilh. Martenses suggested that our son Johann had dislocated his left arm. At Mrs Martens's urging, I sent Jacob to Grünfeld to fetch a certain Prussian worker by the name of Lemki, who has some medical skills. Lemki confirmed that Johann's left shoulder was out of joint and set it right. When I asked what we owed, he said, 10 C. When I protested that that was too little, he asked for a ruble, which I paid.

April 4 Friday. A night frost. We ploughed the boundary furrow between Mantler's place and our place. Then David, Jacob, and I drove out to start ploughing, but the fields were still too wet.

April 9 Wednesday. At 9:30 this morning I sent the children out to the field to plough. Soon thereafter the shepherd boy told us that our cow had been found in the watering pond and needed help. By the time we and several neighbours arrived, the cow, though still alive, was already out in the middle of the pond among the reeds and out of reach. David rushed back to the village for a trough and extra men. Taking ropes, Isaac Siemens's son Dietrich and W. Martens's son Peter climbed into the trough, laboriously paddled out against a strong southwest wind, and fastened the rope to the cow. But the cow was dead and the rope too short, so David drove back to the village for more rope. This time Abr. Dyck Jr paddled out on the trough and brought the dead cow back to shore. Another misfortune. But thou art still the wise Lord, full of grace and with abundant blessings, which thou wilt bestow on us as we have need of them.

April 16 Wednesday. We ploughed and planted a half-desiatina potato patch in our yard.

April 17 Thursday. Today we began ploughing our Grünfeld land and seeded barley.

April 22 Tuesday. I sent the children out to plough yesterday morning but a drizzle brought them back home. They tried again in the afternoon, but a heavy downpour intervened. This, however, had its advantages because our plough, which Corn. Mantler had repaired, was working badly, so we took it to the local blacksmith Franz Rempel and asked him to try his wizardry on it. The children are out ploughing again today, but in the meantime we have lost a day and a half.

April 24 This morning brother-in-law Gerhard Dyck arrived in Gnadenthal with a load of his belongings. He has sold his house in Rosenthal, but is moving his implement shed to Gnadenthal.

April 29 We had a cold drizzle and northwest wind from early morning until noon. In the afternoon brother-in-law Gerh. Dyck left with a team to plough two desiatinas of my Grünfeld land.

On my way home I stopped in to see Wilh. Martens, who had been to yesterday's funeral for Jacob Dyck's daughter in Novovitebsk. The girl had become feeble-minded from epileptic seizures, had often wandered away and caused her parents, who had to search for her, great anguish. Last Friday, around Vesper-time, she had disappeared again, and her parents and neighbours had fruitlessly searched for her until late at night. Finally, Saturday morning, she was found in the waters of the Sheltaia [Stream], presumably having fallen in from the stream's high bank. In her 21st year, her pitiable life thus came to a violent end. But in thy presence, Lord Jesus, her spirit will be well again, her mind bright, and she will praise thee for redeeming her with thy blood. May she rest in peace.

May 3 Saturday, a rainy day. My dear wife and I planted 12 plum and 2 cherry trees and 10 gooseberry bushes. I wonder whether they will take so late in the spring.

May 8 Thursday. I accompanied my brother-in-law Gerh. Dyck to the market in Sofievka, he providing the horses and I the wagon. Peter Isaac was along. On the way back we stopped in at the old manor house at Marianovka, which the community owns, to pick up his [threshing] stones. He had bought the stones with the shed, but the stones had disappeared.

May 10 Seed-time is ended, but it is very late. The year we settled in Novovitebsk 23 years ago, seeding continued until well into May, but it has never been later than this. We seeded the last wheat on

Monday, the last oats and barley on Thursday, and two desiatinas of millet yesterday. Total area seeded: 24½ des. wheat, plus an additional desiatina for our son Jacob, making 25½ desiatinas; barley, 8½ desiatinas; oats, 3½ des.; millet, 2 des.; potatoes, melons, and corn, 1 desiatina. We have ploughed a total of 40½ desiatinas. Lord, we entrust our seed to thee. Bless it according to thy will. This afternoon, Gerhard and I went to Izluchistaia to hire Gerhard Andres Sr to dismantle and rebuild our implement shed.

May 12 Monday, my children Jacob, Diedrich and I drove to Novopodolsk to pick up a load of wood, fuel dung, and grain.

May 13 Tuesday, Jacob and Diedrich each carted a wagonload of our wheat from Novopodolsk to Nikopol.

May 16 Friday we went to Novopodolsk to dismantle our back building. Jacob and Diedrich drove there via Neu Khortitsa to pick up our son-in-law Joh. Andres, and I went via Izluchistaia to call for the building overseer Gerhard Andres and his sons Gerhard and Jacob. We finished the job by evening and drove home for night, dropping off the carpenters in Izluchistaia.

May 17 Saturday. Friends in Novopodolsk carted loads of lumber from my back building, and friends in Neu Khortitsa delivered stones from Petervetzki.

May 19 Monday. We started rebuilding my back building. Here for the night was Franz Klassen, the carpenter. This morning Gerhard and Jacob picked up the master carpenter Gerhard Andres, his sons Gerhard and Jacob, and Heinrich Siemens. After breakfast, Heinrich and I went to buy brandy for the carpenters from Meier Hillbuch. Our children, the Johann Andreses, arrived from Neu Khortitsa in the meantime, and in the afternoon he and Jacob hauled a load of lumber from Terny.

May 22 Visiting us this afternoon were the Jacob Hiebert of Grünfeld and the Franz Janzens of Ivanenko. Janzen bought my property in Grünfeld, assuming full responsibility for the property and its liabilities, including the loan from my brother Heinrich Epp. He has also agreed to discharge all related communal obligations and will receive, for his part, the appropriate share from each desiatina of grain and hay, while I retain ownership of all the seeded grain, including the two desiatinas sown by my brother-in-law G. Dyck.

May 27 Early Tuesday we left for Ekaterinoslav with two wagons.

We arrived at my cousin Johann Thiessen's place the following morning, loaded lumber, two half-cases of opaque glass, and two puds of nails, and were back home by Friday afternoon.

June 2 Pentecost Monday. There appeared before the Ministerial Committee Johann Dyck and Klas Thiessen. Dyck, who was appearing for the third time, was defiant, demanding to know who had complained about him. This was a matter for the police, he said, and of no concern to us. We permitted him to leave. While tippling together in Sofievka, Thiessen and Dyck had become embroiled in a dispute with a tar merchant and assaulted him. Thiessen earnestly asked our forgiveness. The service, held in the home of Jacob Hiebert in Grünfeld, was followed by a *Brotherhood Meeting*. The brethren were told of Dyck's disobedience, and unanimously decided to place him in the ban. Thiessen asked the congregation's forgiveness, promising to seek a reconciliation with the Russians, and was dismissed in peace.

June 11 Our children, the Andreses, dropped by today. He had been hired by Gerhard Dyck to cart a load of lumber from Rosenthal.

June 14 We finished laying the roof on the back building.

June 16 Monday afternoon. We erected the back building at my brother-in-law Gerhard Dyck's place.

June 17 Gerhard Dyck left with Heinrich to cart a load of lumber from Rosenthal. After Vesper, Jacob and Diedrich left with two wagons to load grain in Novopodolsk and to cart it to Nikopol.

June 22 As I stood in the yard this afternoon, I noticed a great cloud of smoke rising in the east. Others saw it as well, hitched up their horses, and drove to Neu Khortitsa. The children report that the fire, which started at Peter Kasper's place, also burned down Johann Wieler's buildings. Kasper is said to have come home drunk from the bazaar and had been heard shooting, presumably at pigeons on the roof, for that is where the fire started. Wieler's furniture and possessions were saved. But the Kaspers were burned out completely, losing their pigs and a horse, and Mrs Kasper, who tried to rescue the horse, was seriously burned and is not likely to survive. Lord Jesus, be thou her physician and saviour.

June 23 Mrs Kasper died this morning from her injuries.

June 25 Katharina Kasper, née Siemens, was buried today. She was 63 years old, had been married for 31 years and 2 days and given birth to 6 children, 2 sons and 4 daughters. One son and two daughters are still living. I gave the funeral sermon in the home of the Peter Blocks.

June 30 Monday. This morning Jacob left to pick up a load of lumber in Verchnedneprovsk. He travelled via Neu Khortitsa in order to keep company with Johann Andres and others.

July 4 Gerhard and I drove to Zelene Kut to pick up 250 bricks at 20 C. Jacob was back from Nikopol in the evening, having sold the wheat for 10 R. 25 C. a chetvert.

July 7 The harvest, which we started today, will be very light. In the morning Jacob carted 250 bricks home from Zelene Kut, and in the afternoon he, Diedrich, Heinrich, and Gerhard started cutting barley and rye on our Grünfeld property.

July 8 The bricklayers finished their work at noon. Cost 15 R.

July 12 In Grünfeld on Saturday, we celebrated the engagement of our son Jacob to Helena Janzen. Our visitors, my brother Heinrich and his wife, their children David, Heinrich, and Diedrich, and Katharina Thiessen, arrived in the afternoon. My brother embellished the afternoon's proceedings with a homily. My brother Johann, his wife, and youngest child Heinrich arrived yesterday and stopped by briefly today.

July 19 Saturday. We had a drenching rain with thunder and lightning yesterday afternoon. It delayed the barley threshing but may put a little life into our crops. The rain, which came first from the north, then from the east, and continued until late at night, forced the landowners to take in their cattle. This morning the water in our valley is running almost as strongly as it does in spring. We drove our engaged couple to her parents' home and used the occasion to survey our Grünfeld grain fields and then, after coffee, the Gnadenthal fields. It will be a meagre crop all around.

July 24 Tuesday. We started cutting wheat a week ago. In places it is so sparse that we had the horse rake simply follow the scythe without first gathering the grain in stacks. Yesterday I drove the children and two Russians (whom I had hired to cut grain at 50 C. a day) to the wheat fields behind Grünfeld.

August 7 Today his Excellency Durnovo, the Lord Governor of the Province of Ekaterinoslav, passed through Grünfeld where he was welcomed by the German Village mayors and three of the oldest inhabitants. He assured them of the emperor's good will and promised they would not have to bear arms in violation of our Confession. May the Lord God grant that this is so.

August 16 Saturday. The wheat (only 25 loads), is home.

August 18 A man named Schink, I believe, from Hannovka and a smith by trade, dropped in to see me with his daughter. He reports that while working for the Gerhard Hieberts, she had been unchastely treated by their son Abraham. Furthermore, the matter had not been satisfactorily resolved. I therefore gave the man a letter addressed to the Grünfeld mayor asking him to conciliate. In some households of our community the disciplining of children is lamentable!!! Lord, have mercy.

August 24 When I arrived on the yard of Johann Klassen in Novozhitomir, where the service was to be held, I learned that the Corn. Harms family refused to attend any service in the Klassen's home because of a recent quarrel between the two families. I therefore dropped in on the Harms to see what might be accomplished in love. As it turned out, the Harms wanted the service held in their home, and that was done, and the Klassens, at my urging, participated. Twelve people were present. What a pity when the devil sows seeds of bitterness among neighbours.

August 31 Our five pairs of married children were home today.

September 1 Three degrees of frost this morning, the first frost of the year. Our children the Peter Epps left for Nepluievka in the morning, and a little later Heinrich and Gerhard drove our children Jacob and Helena Epp to their home in Grünfeld. May the Lord bless all of you, my dear children, granting you eternal salvation through his grace.

September 10 I carted home another 250 bricks at 25 C. each. We had a thick fog this morning, then rain, and finally sunshine.

September 11 Thursday. We hauled another 250 bricks, and my brother-in-law Gerhard Dyck sent his hired man Kirill to haul an equal number. I drove through Sofievka to visit the bazaar.

September 12 We cleaned the wheat. Our crop totals 21 chetvert 3 merka. For this, too, we thank thee, Lord and Saviour.

September 15 Jacob, Diedrich, Heinrich, and Maria left for Novopodolsk to pick up manure.

September 17 We sold the last wheat in the attic of our former home in [Novopodolsk] to Bleiweisz and Leib Mendelsohn for 9 R. a chetvert. Since it was hard to get to and I had not been able to clean it, we agreed that I would discount the weight by 1 funt per pud. I took an advance of 50 R. It is their responsibility to remove it from the attic and weigh it. My brother Diedrich offered to supply a hired man. I then drove to Novovitebsk, where I bought 75 C. worth of tar and 2 R. 25 C. worth of petroleum from Gedalia Krugel, who is to deliver it. I had dinner with the Gerhard Andreses Jr in Kamianka, bought some white sand, and drove home via Neu Khortitsa, where I did some business. Isbrand Friesen of Novopodolsk returned from America last Sunday completely cured of his emigration fever.

September 20 Jacob Hübert of Grünfeld, who bought my Grünfeld property, paid down 50 R. on his debt and gave me a note for the remaining 170 R. He is to repay the full sum by October 1, 1875.

September 21 This morning we celebrated Holy Communion in the Grünfeld schoolhouse [Shlakhtin Settlement] (82 people), and this afternoon in the home of Jacob Redekopp in Gnadenthal [Baratov settlement] (123 people). My dear wife attended the service in our village and I attended both services.

September 22 Monday. This morning the dear Elder Dyck left for home via the Borosenko and Nepluiev settlements. Since I have now moved farther away, the Elder and I reached an agreement that I would no longer be obligated to serve Borosenko and Nepluiev, which had become a burden for me.

December 30 Tuesday. This afternoon we visited the Jacob Janzens in Grünfeld, with whom our children the Jacob Epps are living.

December 31 Wednesday. This has been a busy year and many things have changed. We moved from Novopodolsk to Gnadenthal, where we live in a small house built by my brother Diedrich. We dismantled the driving shed (Scheune) of our place in Novopodolsk and have rebuilt it here. We had a poor harvest. There was considerable rain in spring. Then it turned hot unusually early and we finally had a lot of rain again half-way through the harvest, spoiling part of what little was left. The potatoes started slowly but the melons were splendid, especially at our place and that of my brother-in-law Gerhard Dyck. We had a first night-frost on September 1, then rain, usually from the east, and we have had winter weather now for some time. Our dear Lord has also given us our share of illness. My wife was down with a fever for some time, and she was then sickly, as were also our daughter Judith and our infant Johann. All of us are now well, by God's grace. Jacob and Peter were married. The former lives in Grünfeld with his parents-in-law and the latter teaches school in Neu Kronsweide.

The great uneasiness in our community, which disturbs many people, has led to the emigration to America. This past May and June some three to four hundred families from the Khortitsa churches left Russia. Thereafter the promises of His Excellency von Todleben apparently had a calming effect. Now, however, the [government's] rejection of the guarantee of free emigration for the future promised to my brother Heinrich, Elder Jacob Wiebe from the Crimea, the deacon Andreas Voth, and the Molochna District Mayor Abr. Wiebe during their visit to St Petersburg has again increased apprehensions. Thirty-three families in the Grossfürstlich settlement and more than 300 in the Khortitsa colonies are said to be preparing to emigrate this coming spring. God only knows how this will end. The remarkable, temporal freedom enjoyed by our community for so long has come to an end. I earnestly hope that this time of tribulation might lead us into the loving arms of our Lord and saviour Jesus Christ. Let our help come from Zion in order that God might redeem his captive people. We thank thee, our faithful saviour, for thy guidance during the past year. I commit the guardianship of thy church, which thou hast entrusted to me, to thy care. May it grow and flourish in the fear of thee. Amen.

1876

Luke 13:7–9. 'Then said he to the dresser of his vineyard. "Behold, these three years I come seeking fruit on this fig tree, and find none: cut it down; why cumbereth it the ground?" And he answering said unto him, "Lord, let it alone this year also, till I shall dig about it, and dung it: And if it bear fruit, *well*: and if not, *then* after that thou shalt cut it down." '

January 1 On Thursday I delivered a sermon in the schoolhouse in Gnadenthal on Jeremiah 4:3–4.

January 12 Monday. Yesterday we returned from our one-week trip to Khortitsa. We left last Monday, travelling via Sofievka and Nikolaievka, and stopped for the night at the home of Isaac Zacharias, where I conducted a service the next day. At the close of the service I asked for missions donations. Is. Zacharias gave me a ruble, which I passed on later to my brother Heinrich. We were in Kronsthal in the afternoon where there is a strong movement in favour of emigration to America. Johann Klassen told me that as many as a hundred families (including those from the Grossfürstlich settlement) were preparing to leave this spring. Lord, direct matters favourably and to the honour of thy name. We saw Elder Gerhard Dyck Wednesday afternoon and spent the night with my brother Heinrich. Thursday afternoon we drove to Neu Kronsweide where our son Peter teaches school. In the evening we visited his parents-in-law, the Heh. Dycks, and Thursday afternoon my brother-in-law Jacob Pätkau. We spent the night with the Hildebrands. On our way home we stopped in Neuendorf to do some business with the Orphans' Administration (Waisenamt), but found no one in. Our son Jacob loaded his new wagon on to our sleigh in Neuhorst.

Today my colleague Jacob Pätkau, Jacob v Kampen and their wives discussed our community's petition to the Khortitsa [District] administration requesting a remission of the interest payments on our land debt for the past year. The crop failure has left most people without money. We agreed that the ministers should present the matter to the village assemblies [of the Baratov-Shlakhtin settlement.][41]

January 13 Tuesday. I travelled to Steinfeld by communal transport where, at my request, the Village assembly met in the home of the Village mayor to consider the previously prepared petition requesting the remission of interest payments on our land debt for 1875. The Steinfeld landowners signed the petition [in the morning] and those of Grünfeld in the afternoon. May God bless the undertaking.

January 17 My son-in-law Johann Bärgen had procured the smallpox vaccine from my brother-in-law [Doctor] Schellenberg, which I used to vaccinate our son Johann and our granddaughter Maria Bärgen.

January 25 Since the vaccination of our granddaughter Maria had taken but that of our son Johann had not, my wife and I drove to the

Bärgens' in Neu Khortitsa where Johann and several other children were vaccinated.

February 1 I went along to Sofievka with my brother-in-law Gerhard Dyck to exchange a chetvert of potatoes for a bottle of petroleum. But as the merchant Israelsohn was willing to pay me only 3 R. for the potatoes and demanded 4 R. 25 C. for the oil, we returned home without making a deal. Isaac Lehn, the Khortitsa District mayor, and Johann Hildebrand, the assistant District mayor, visited the local [Gnadenthal] Village mayor's office to sort out a dispute and were also in the other villages. We passed the Jacob Pätkaus (not the minister) on the road to Sofievka, and have since heard that they found their infant daughter Anna dead at her mother's breast on reaching Gnadenthal. The mother is grief-stricken. Be thou her comfort and support, Lord Jesus.

February 9 Monday. Since the Jews [Bleiweisz and Mendelsohn] had not yet picked up any of my wheat, I drove to Novopodolsk. Bleiweisz said he had no money but finally gave me 5 R. at my urgent request.

February 25 Franz Harder appeared before the Ministerial Committee, which met in my home. Mrs Harder had asked the guardians of her still under-age daughter to place her in a foster home after her grandfather, who had been raising her, had died. Harder refused to give up the child, however, and so we asked the Orphans' Administration to make a decision in the matter.

March 7 A year ago we moved from Novopodolsk to Gnadenthal, and we are a year closer to eternity, the goal of my earthly journey. As a desert traveller craves cool waters for his thirst does my soul yearn for that promised place where God's people will find peace. Saviour, guide me on this troubled journey and keep me from losing my way. What is my calling, Lord? I know my duty well and feel it deeply, but I am so imperfect, and pitifully few fruits of the spirit flourish in our community. My unworthiness, my weakness, my failings and sins cause me such deep anguish. But thou canst help where all seems lost, for in thee is power and strength, and to thee be honour and glory and praise. Amen.

March 28 Palm Sunday. I preached a sermon in the home of Corn. Froese in Steinfeld on Isaiah 53. In the afternoon I gave the funeral sermon in Grünfeld in the home of Peter Klassen for his elderly father Peter Klassen who died at the age of 77 years, 6 months, and 18 days.

April 6 Easter Tuesday. There was a conference in my home this morning of the local ministers, village elders, and my brother Diedrich Epp, the local overseer. We decided that (1) instruction of our baptismal candidates would take place in my driving shed (Scheune); (2) divine services would be held in each village every third Sunday; and (3) the Ministerial Committee would continue to supervise the schools (a school committee will not be elected).
April 14 Wednesday. Monday we sowed the last of the millet and harrowed it in. Yesterday we ploughed the fallow with the Schraz-plough and seeded onions. In total we have ploughed and seeded 23 desiatinas: 16 desiatinas to wheat, 4 to barley, 1 to oats, and 2 to millet. In addition we have two desiatinas in fallow, a desiatina of potatoes, and a quarter-desiatina as a melon field. In fall we seeded two desiatinas to rye.
May 5 There was a tragic incident in the Nepluiev settlement where Johann Bärgen, a miller, had bought a rifle to hunt wolves. His 15-year-old son Johann picked up the gun, thinking it was not loaded, and threatened to shoot his one-and-half-year older sister. 'Go ahead,' she said. The thoughtless boy pulled the trigger and the gun went off, striking the girl in the chest. She was dead within the hour. Thus does God permit carelessness to punish itself. The legal ramifications of this tragic incident may now complicate matters for the parents and children, who had been ready to leave for America. The situation among us Mennonites is really quite amazing. We work ourselves into an emigration sweat in order not to have to bear arms. Yet among us are many fanciers of guns and hunting. Lord, let us turn to thee in heartfelt penance and remorse.
May 31 Monday morning. Maria, Gerhard, and I went to Golitsin's store where we sold 22½ funt of butter for 15 C. per funt, taking in exchange a pair of shoes for Maria for 2½ R. and other small items. God protected me this afternoon on our way home from the field. As we turned the corner at Corn. Th.'s place, Heinrich, who had the horses trotting, relaxed the reins. The horses began running and the upended barrel on which I was sitting tipped over, throwing me and it from the wagon. Thank God that I was only painfully bruised, for I could easily have broken something or been accidentally killed.
June 10 Thursday. I went along to the bazaar in Sofievka with my brother-in-law Gerhard Dyck, who wanted to buy buckwheat. We

could not find any so we drove home via Kudashev where the administrator told us that it could be bought on the khutor.

June 11 A letter from our son Peter, who teaches school in Neu Kronsweide, informs us that his wife Anna successfully gave birth to a daughter, Aganetha, last Saturday, June 5, at 9:45 a.m.

June 18 Ploughed the fallow the second time with the Schraz-plough.

June 24 The following appeared before the Ministerial Committee in Neu Khortitsa: Mrs Isaac Friesen of Novokovno, the Isaac Wiebes of Novopodolsk, Bernhard Janzen and Franz Driedger, and their summoners. Gossip had led to a quarrel. Mrs Friesen had accused Janzen of grinding too little flour while Janzen and Driedger had told Mrs Friesen that people were saying her daughter was a harlot, etc. They were all finally reconciled and allowed to go in peace. Brethren, do not speak ill of one another, and further: people will know that you are my disciples when you love one another.

July 2 Friday. All of the rye is at home and we have started cutting the barley.

July 8 Thursday. Since the wheat was not ripe we prepared the threshing floor and started carting the barley and threshing it with the stone.

July 10 Saturday. Rain forced us to stop carting [sheaves of grain]. This afternoon our children and several neighbours helped sick Peter Isaac cut his grain. We had our own problems last week when my wife, our daughter Maria, and I were all quite ill. Mother and Maria are now much better and my sore eye has also improved.

July 23 After awakening this morning I dozed off again and had a dream in which an old, friendly man followed me. This made me quite uneasy so I redoubled my steps, climbing over high walls, but I could not shake him off. My fear mounted, and I was at a loss as to what to do next. Then I awoke and thought about the meaning of the dream. It became clear to me that my inseparable companion was the old man whom I was to crucify with all of his lusts and desires, but that I could not accomplish this without the help of the Lord Jesus. Lord Jesus, help me to put off the old man of sin more and more and, armed with thy grace, put on the new man of unfeigned purity and godliness, created in God's image.

July 26 Monday. My brother Diedrich and I went to seek a reconciliation between the Peter Kaspers in Novokovno. The guilt seems to be equally great on both sides. She is pregnant and he is determined to leave her. They have been married less than a year and already there is so much bickering. They were deaf to my admonitions regarding the sanctity of marriage and my appeal that they should seek peace in the blood of Jesus Christ. We left without having accomplished a thing. Lord Jesus, Prince of Peace, accomplish thy work of reconciliation between this deluded couple and grant them thy peace.

August 2 Monday. At two o'clock this morning our son Jacob knocked on our window. His wife's labour pains had started and he wanted mother to come over. We hurried over, and Jacob left to fetch the midwife, the widow Bartel, with our wagon. At 8:30 a.m. a son, Jacob, was born to them. Our other children, the Peter Epps, left for home with their infant daughter Aganetha an hour later. May the angels of the Lord accompany you my dear children.

August 4 Wednesday. An afternoon shower forced us to gather up the wheat [from the threshing floor]. We finished ploughing the fallow for the third time and completed threshing the above-mentioned wheat after Vesper. Maria and Diedrich left for another load, but were caught in a shower and returned home soaking wet.

August 7 Saturday. After measuring out 29 chetvert of wheat, Diedrich and Maria carted 2 chetvert to Joh. Janzen's treadmill in Grünfeld to be ground into flour.

August 14 We cleaned oats in the morning (6 chetvert 1 merka from ¾ desiatina) and carried it on to the attic. This afternoon my wife and I and the four youngest children visited the Andreses in Neu Khortitsa, to whom a son Jacob was born last Thursday.

August 17 Tuesday. The last of the rye is out of the straw, and we have finished the threshing.

August 19 Thursday. Last Tuesday I poked a rye stalk into my seeing eye. It became infected, causing me much pain, and even now I can barely see enough to write these lines.

August 24 Diedrich, Heinrich, and I left at sun-up for Nikopol with 9 chetvert (a little more), which we sold to Schwarz for 86 C. a pud. That came to 80 R. 84 C. for both wagon-loads. We returned via Nepluievka, reaching Blumenfeld just after Wilhelm Peters's building had gone up in flames.

August 28 Saturday. This morning the elders of the local villages met in the home of the Gnadenthal Village Elder (I was also invited) to discuss the promised creation of a volost office [for the four villages of Steinfeld, Grünfeld, Neu Khortitsa, and Gnadenthal of the Baratov-Shlakhtin settlement]. To facilitate this development it was decided that the village elders Schellenberg and v Niessen should consult with the Khortitsa District Office. If they were agreed, a petition in this regard should then be submitted to His Excellency the Lord Governor Durnovo. May God give his blessing.

August 30 Monday. We seeded rye and worked it in with the Schraz-plough, using two desiatinas of land I had rented again from the village community, the first desiatina for 3 R. and the second for 3 R. 15 C. A light drizzle did not last long. We have had little rain this summer.

September 3 Friday. Gerhard and I were picking up our flour from the treadmill in Grünfeld when the miller rushed in to tell us that he could clearly see from his mill a fire burning in Gnadenthal. We rushed home but there was no fire in the village, thank God. We presume that weeds had caught fire in the field.

September 5 The fire spotted from Grünfeld was not a weed fire, as I presumed, but a major conflagration in Novopodolsk. It started in the shed of the Jew Feltschinski, where two boys had been smoking. It spread from there to his buildings and the threshing floor and finally consumed the treadmill, buildings, and threshing floor (where much grain was stored) belonging to Bleiweisz. The damage is very great.

September 7 Tuesday. My dear wife and I and our children Heinrich, Judith, and Johann left at five this morning for the Khortitsa colonies. Accompanying us were our neighbours, the Heinrich Neudorfs.

September 10 We spent the night with our son Peter Epp, who teaches in the factory school in Khortitsa.[42] We were at my brother Heinrich Epp's for dinner, where we spent the night. My brother and I called on Elder Gerhard Dyck in the afternoon.

September 12 Sunday. We attended service in the Khortitsa church where I preached a sermon on the great damage caused by our spiritual lethargy. Matthew 13:24-30.

September 17 At an election of ministers in Nicolaifeld last Sunday, my nephew Martin Dyck was chosen as minister and my cousin Heinrich Rempel as deacon.

September 20 Rain in the morning, and we seeded a desiatina to rye in the afternoon.

September 22 Wednesday. Diedrich left to fetch a load of lumber from Verchnedneprovsk, travelling with several others.

September 25 Sunday. At 4:30 this morning Diedrich and the others returned from Verchnedneprovsk with loads of lumber.

September 26 At the invitation of the Steinfeld village community, I delivered a sermon at the dedication of their new village school. Text, 1 Corinthians 3:16. Lord Jesus, make evident your presence in this school.

October 4 Since the establishment of the Neu Khortitsa community [also known as Baratov-Shlakhtin], we have been seeking the establishment of a separate volost administration. This was also the wish of His Excellency, the Lord Governor Durnovo, as expressed to us during his visit last year. Well before our move to Gnadenthal, the Gnadenthal [village] community had chosen Jacob Wiebe and Jacob Redekopp to pursue the matter and Gnadenthal had been chosen as the location for the volost office. It was done only half-heartedly, however, and after hearing in summer that nothing would come of it I decided to do something myself. During our last visit to Khortitsa my brother Heinrich Epp drafted a petition to the Lord Governor on our behalf. After members of our community had signed it, the two above-named individuals had taken it to Ekaterinoslav [capital of Ekaterinoslav Province].

We then received a document informing us that a certain Mr Pototsky had been instructed to incorporate the villages of Gnadenthal and Neu Khortitsa into the Marian Volost. We met this gentleman, who graciously promised to desist from his action until after our two representatives had had an opportunity to petition the governor. On Sunday, Jacob Wiebe and Jacob Redekopp returned from Ekaterinoslav with the unhappy news that after reading our petition His Excellency had returned it with the comment that, although he favoured such an arrangement personally [that is, the establishment of a separate Mennonite volost], St Petersburg was opposed. Two of our villages are therefore to be incorporated into the Marian Volost and two into the Ternian Volost. If promises made by imperial officials count for so little, then we and our children face a very uncertain future.

October 10 *Brotherhood Meeting*. My colleagues Pätkau and v

Kampen were present. I reviewed the difficult situation regarding the volost office. There was much discussion, but a lot of it was beside the point. Of our representatives, only Jacob Redekopp was present, and he asked to be relieved of his post. We sent for Wiebe, who agreed to continue the work. Wilhelm v Niessen, the [Village Elder] of Steinfeld, was then elected as the second representative, but he declined, and I was chosen.

The brethren decided that the four village elders and Jacob Wiebe should first contact Mr Pototsky, seeking his support. Wiebe and I would then solicit Heinrich Heese's advice and help [with the negotiations] in Ekaterinoslav. Finally I reminded the brethren of the implications of our concern, expressed to the government, that [in a mixed volost] we might be forced to do [volost] business on Sundays.[43] It was sinful and damaged our cause when so many people desecrated the Sunday with their worldly work and professional and business dealings. I called on the community to lead lives pleasing to the Lord. Only then might he save us from all peril.

October 15 I drove to Neu Khortitsa by communal transport to have the petition requesting the creation of our own separate volost signed. Several were opposed, preferring to belong to a Russian volost, but I nevertheless got the necessary signatures.

October 18 All Grünfeld landowners gathered at the home of the Village Elder to sign the petition. In Steinfeld, the Village Elder Wilhelm v Niessen was present at the widow Abr. Neufeld's auction sale, where all village landowners signed the petition.

October 22 Jacob Wiebe and I left for Ekaterinoslav this morning. We stopped for the night at the Kumitzki Inn, where the owner, a Jew by the name of David Michel, received us warmly. May the Lord reward him. There was a heavy snowfall from the north on the afternoon of the second day, obscuring the road and making travel difficult for the horses. We reached Ekaterinoslav in the evening and took our quarters with the Pole Pikarsky (where my feet were icy). Worse, our door faced the samovar, whose coal smoke gave me a headache and kept me awake all night. Sunday, after having breakfast with my cousin Johann Thiessen, we sought Heinrich Heese's support for our initiative, but he wanted first to learn of Mr Pototsky's response.

October 25 This morning we made our purchases and then went to the Gubernskaia Zemskaia Uprava, where we walked the street for several hours waiting for Mr Pototsky to arrive. He finally informed us that the Lord Governor had said, 'I cannot help them, since I was on my own [that is, I had no support].' Mr Pototsky then added in a friendly manner that once this session of the Uprava was ended he would again seek support for our cause. We should in the meantime go back to our homes and if prospects improved he would write to us again. We could then start the process over again by making a written submission to Verkhnedneprovsk. That was the end of the matter.[44]

While Wiebe made preparations for our departure, I went to see Heese, telling him what Pototsky had said, and he promised to help. He would get in touch with the governor and others to find out the basic reasons for the denial of our request for a separate volost. He suggested we not undertake anything on our own until he had written. Then we might have to make a further submission to the prisudstva. Dear brother Heese, we thank you for your help. May the Lord our God bless and reward you.

After we had paid Pikarsky we loaded the half-case of number-one opaque glass, which we had purchased from the merchant Alekeievka for 14 R., and started for home. We did not reach the Engelhard Inn until late at night. There was little snow on the ground when we arrived, but it snowed heavily after midnight.

October 26 At four in the morning we left in a snowstorm, but travelling with the wind was pleasant. We reached Nicolaifeld at 8:30 a.m., stopping there for the day. In the afternoon, I had one of Giesbrecht's sons take me by sled (because of the deep snow) to Franzfeld where I visited my nephew Martin Dyck, who had recently delivered his inaugural sermon.

October 27 Wednesday. We resumed our burdensome journey after breakfast. Along the post road, where other travellers had broken through the snow, the going was tolerable, but it became very difficult for the horses in the deep snow away from the post road. Along the way, we met Jacob Görzen and his son Heinrich and stopped for the night at the Saizov Inn.

October 28 We reached home Thursday afternoon after a strenuous journey. The snow here is deep as well, and we thank our dear Saviour for his protection and care.

November 3 At midday we were ordered to appear at the Marian

Volost Office with all of our horses [for the selection of remounts for the army]. They were taken there by Diedrich, David, and Jacob. Yesterday our brown wagon stallion, whom we had used last Sunday, choked to death from the yellow croup. Our children returned in the evening. [The officials] had liked our black stallion, but it was lame, so they had not bought any of our horses. They did, however, take 5 horses from Gnadenthal and 11 from Neu Khortitsa.

November 7 For some time now I have been wrestling with the thought that it is perhaps God's will that I should preach freely again, as I did nine years ago when I felt the presence and help of the Lord. Today I therefore risked it again, preaching freely and trusting in the Lord's support, who did help. To him be honour and glory.

A government official came by today for more horses for the military. Our son Jacob was forced to give up his gelding, which he brought to Poiurovka, along with others. The Russo-Turkish conflict is getting very serious, and I only hope that it does not develop into a great world war.[45]

November 9 Ten degrees of frost today. Jacob returned from Poiurovka in the evening, where he had been paid 96 R. for his gelding.

November 10 Wednesday. On the way home from the market, Judith complained of a headache and became ill. She is often incoherent today. Be thou her physician, faithful Saviour.

Written later. At five this morning our dear sick child Judith became confused. Soon thereafter she started having epileptic convulsions and at 11:30 this evening our dearly beloved daughter expired. Receive thou her tender spirit, Lord Jesus.

November 15 Monday. The funeral day of our beloved daughter Judith. In the morning six degrees of frost and a cold east wind. Our dearly departed reached the age of 4 years, 11 months, and 18 days. My brother-in-law Gerhard Dyck delivered the funeral sermon, which touched all of our hearts.

November 17 Heinrich was called for today. He has been hired for 25 R. until seed-time to teach school in Izluchistaia.

November 29 While visiting the Steinfeld school, the [Village] mayor v Niessen informed me that the landowners Johann Olfert and Heinrich Schapansky had gotten into a quarrel over the hired man Cornelius Wölk. They had finally agreed to hire him out to someone else to resolve their dispute. v Niessen requested that I arrange this in our village. Schapansky brought Wölk over, but then wanted to take him home again. The Neufelds were willing to hire him on until Mrs Neufeld found a louse in his clothes. Finally, after I had informed David Schellenberg that a manservant could be hired at my place, he took him on until St Martin's Day, 1877 for 56 R., clothes, and board.

December 4 The Second Advent. I preached a sermon in Peter Harder's home in Novozhitomir on the topic of the signs of the last days as they relate to present occurrences. Luke 21:25–36. Diedrich and I had started on our journey yesterday. The road to Langova, where we arrived at nightfall, was badly drifted over. The horses managed to get into the sled track of a cross-road at Zhilnikov, which brought us to Beresena's khutor. From there an old Russian brought us to our destination for 15 C. This afternoon we attended the funeral of Peter Martens's son Wilhelm, who was almost four.

December 23 In Izluchistaia we picked up our son Heinrich, who is apprenticing there as a carpenter. Sledding was magnificent.

1877

January 1 Saturday, New Year's Day. Hitherto hath the Lord helped us! So we ask thee, Lord Jesus, help us further and grant us rich fruits of repentance and faith this New Year. I preached a sermon in the Steinfeld schoolhouse based on Luke 13:6–9.

Last year the following changes occurred in our [Judenplan] community.

Births	41 males	40 females	81 total
Deaths	19 males	15 females	34 total
Increase	22 males	25 females	47 total
Couples married	14 total		

January 19 I and my brother-in-law Gerhard Dyck drove to Novozhitomir. Dyck asked Mrs Franz Harder whether she would

permit Dyck to take on her illegitimate daughter Katharina as his foster child.[46] She discussed the offer with her husband, and declined.

February 14 *School visitation.* Monday. This morning we visited the Neu Khortitsa school, which is taught by David Redekopp. My brother-in-law G. Dyck and my colleagues Pätkau and Epp were also present. After dinner we visited the Gnadenthal school, taught by Corn. Giesbrecht, and found it to be quite satisfactory.

February 15 Tuesday. This morning we visited the Grünfeld school, which is taught by Peter Siemens. He and his pupils have all made good progress. Afternoon in Steinfeld, where the teacher is Peter Klassen. The school is only fair.

February 16 Our son-in-law Johann Bärgen, who has sold his Neu Khortitsa property and moved into the vacant Izluchistaia schoolhouse, arrived at night and left for home this morning.

March 7 Monday. After breakfast, I accompanied my brother-in-law Gerhard Dyck to Grünfeld where he hired on Susanna Friesen, daughter of my brother-in-law Heinrich Friesen, for a trial period of a month and until Christmas if things work out. We also visited the sick. There is much snow and a good sledding track, but there was heavy thawing this afternoon.

March 19 Saturday. Our young mare died this evening. Two of our horses and two head of cattle have died on this new settlement.

March 20 Our son Heinrich was home from Izluchistaia, where he is keeping school. Our children, the Johann Bärgens, who now live in the Izluchistaia schoolhouse, were also here for dinner.

March 22 Rain kept us from ploughing so we started to dig the well at the street.

April 6 Wednesday. This morning, the Khortitsa District elders Isaac Lehn, Johann Hildebrand, and Peter Dyck dropped in on their way from Steinfeld before continuing their trip to Khortitsa. They have reached an agreement in Steinfeld to relocate that entire village on to the hill in order to prevent another great water shortage. On their way to Steinfeld they dropped off a number of letters from Khortitsa friends.

April 11 This afternoon my brother-in-law Gerhard Dyck pulled out my infected tooth that had caused me great pain, but part of it broke off and this makes me more miserable than ever.

April 13 My toothache, which got worse overnight, gave me a sleepless night. I am truly at my wit's end. Be thou my physician, Lord Jesus. We have finished ploughing the softer soil and have only the potato patch and melon field left to do.

June 4 Because of my inflamed eye, there is a big gap in my diary, which I do not quite know how to fill since I do not remember everything that has happened. I was unable to attend either the Ascension Day service on May 5 or the Sunday service on the 8th, where my brother-in-law Gerhard Dyck continued to catechize our young baptismal candidates. Elder Gerhard Dyck arrived on the 19th and stayed at our place throughout his visit. He conducted the services of Holy Baptism on the morning of Tuesday, May 11, and Holy Communion on Wednesday morning. One hundred and fifty-four communicants were present, including my dear mother and I. With some help, I was able to attend the preparatory service, but we celebrated Ascension Day at home among ourselves.

On Ascension Tuesday, I accompanied our children, the Jacob Epps, to Khortitsa, where they were taking their infant son Jacob to be treated by Doctor Schellenberg. We stayed in Khortitsa with our children, the Peter Epps, and straightaway dropped in on the doctor, who took me into his care. God blessed the treatments.

The immigrants to America gathered in the Khortitsa church on Friday, May 20, to celebrate Holy Communion. They expect to depart within a week. I met a number of them at the home of my brother-in-law Schellenberg, where many a tear was shed. May the Lord go with you, my dear ones.

On Monday, my son Diedrich and I hauled a load of lumber from Terny, and on the way my sick eye became inflamed and more swollen than ever. Before we left for Khortitsa, my brother Diedrich provided an eye salve that worked wonders, but then I was somewhat careless and the problem recurred. Now my neck is also seriously swollen (as a result of the application of Spanish fly adhesive), and gives me great pain. In the meantime, however, God has helped me, and to him be praise. Our children, the Peter Epps, have moved to Neu Khortitsa, where he teaches school.

June 5 There has been a horrifying accident in Khortitsa involving the families of my brother and sister. My brother Heinrich writes that on the morning of June 5 their foster-son Gerhard Nachtigall died after eating Beluga fish that had been bought. Cornelius Hildebrand's daughter Katharina died in the afternoon and their daughter Helena is also deathly ill of the same cause.

June 22 My dear wife, Elisabeth, Johann, and I visited the Diedrich Epps in Novopodolsk. They had attended the funerals in Khortitsa of the three young people who had unexpectedly died.

September 11 I preached a sermon in the Neu Khortitsa schoolhouse. My wife, Gerhard, and Johann visited the Peter Epps (he teaches school there), to whom a son Peter was born at 2:45 this morning. Lord Jesus, grant that he might grow up to the honour of thy name and to the joy of his parents.

October 1 Saturday. Yesterday, Heinrich and I drove to Izluchistaia. Johann Bärgen Sr had planned to take Heinrich along to Eichenfeld, where I have hired him out as a teacher's helper for Peter Klassen for 25 R. Bärgen had put off the trip because of rain, however, and we returned home.

October 2 Thanksgiving. I gave a thanksgiving sermon based on Matthew 13:24–30. As the Lord gave me the power, I spoke of our earthly harvest, of the general harvest of death, and, finally, of the great world harvest [of judgment], towards which each one of us is moving with certainty. Lord, prepare us to endure [this great trial].

November 4 Friday. Following a complaint by the Wilhelm Mantlers, there appeared at our home the Bernhard Giesbrechts and Julius Janzen, who had been summoned by Jacob Redekopp and Wilhelm Martens Sr. Also present was my brother-in-law Gerhard Dyck. Mrs Giesbrecht had accused Mrs Mantler of stealing a new earthen pot from them and Mrs Janzen charged Mrs Mantler with stealing indigo from her. She steadfastly denied both charges. We allowed the matter to rest on her conscience. The Lord will reveal what is hidden and make evident the secrets of the heart.

December 5 *School visitation.* We visited the schools in Steinfeld, taught by Abraham Enz; in Grünfeld, taught by Peter Siemens; in Gnadenthal, taught by Cornelius Giesbrecht; and in Neu Khortitsa, taught by our son Peter Epp. The four schools are still in their infancy. This is especially true of the Steinfeld school. The Gnadenthal school is the best of them all. Attendance is very poor, principally because of the late harvest (caused by poor weather) but also because of the relocation of the village of Steinfeld. It would be surprising under such conditions if the schools had made any progress at all. I hope our second visit will show more positive results.

December 22 I had an unexpected visit from Peter Warkentin, Friesenthal, who told me he had been placed in the ban, but largely without cause. He claims that while walking past his Russian maidservant he placed his hand on her shoulder. At that moment the teacher entered the room. The latter had probably related what he had seen, and his own brothers and sisters had interpreted the story as meaning that he had committed fornication with the girl. Other prejudicial rumours had been spread among his siblings as well. Last spring the incident had nevertheless been fully aired and peacefully resolved. Then, four weeks ago, his cousin Enz, a minister from the Molochna, had arrived and, without first discussing the story with him in detail, had placed him in the ban. He asked my advice and pleaded for my help. I suggested he talk to his Elder, telling him of the unfair treatment, and bring his concerns to him who judges rightly. He was not in a position to undertake such a trip, he replied. I then advised him to write a letter to his Elder and I would do the same, if he wished.

1878

January 1 Monday. At 9:45 this morning our beloved granddaughter Margaretha, daughter of our son David, completed her pilgrimage at the age of 1 year, 7 months, and 10 days. For 12 days she suffered from the measles, which are rampant here.
January 4 Wednesday. Present at the meeting of the Ministerial Committee were the four ministers, the deacon, v Kampen, and my brother, Diedrich Epp, local overseer in the Hebrew colonies. Some time ago, Peter v Niessen of Steinfeld told me that he faced two days of imprisonment in connection with a dispute in which he had been involved in the Terny Volost. After discussing the matter, we decided to call a general Brotherhood Meeting in Gnadenthal on Friday, January 20, to consider the following issues:
(1) Should disputes between brethren not be judged by brethren and resolved on the basis of the Holy Scriptures?

(2) Members should be warned against drinking and drunkenness and reminded of their obligation to report such transgressions.
(3) Church members should be familiarized with our rules, namely: a. how to relate to members who have been separated from the church, [that is, placed in the ban]; b. how to behave during the period of the [Orthodox] fast; and c. how to conduct themselves peacefully at meetings of village assemblies.
January 6 Friday. The funeral for our late granddaughter Margaretha was held in the home of her parents, the David Epps. Her tiny body was then buried.
January 21 Friday morning. *Brotherhood Meeting* in the home of Heinrich Neudorf in Gnadenthal. I asked the brethren for their views in regard to the question of our practices (see entry for January 4, above). They were all of one mind. Only a few wanted to have [secular] judges established over us. We therefore agreed to reaffirm our church practices as laid down in 1 Corinthians 6:1–8. Abraham Isaac and Peter Peters of Neu Khortitsa, in particular, spoke out of turn. The latter even said that he would rather be judged by the Khokhols [that is, by Ukrainian peasants] than by the church. Reverend Pätkau had once told him, 'You are going straight to hell.'
January 23 Johann Friesen of Friesenthal invited me to their place to discuss the matter involving Warkentin (see entry for Dec. 22, 1877). I accompanied him, stopping off at the home of Jacob Friesen, where the rest of the family gathered later on. [It appears] that Warkentin had made rather too light of his guilt in speaking to me. Töws related that he had been to discuss the case with Elder Töws in the Molochna. The latter insisted that Warkentin appear personally in regard to the question of his readmission to the church. I thereupon advised Warkentin to travel to the Molochna, but he replied that he had already written to the Elder, and he asked me to do the same. He sugggested I enclose a document from people here stating that a reconciliation had taken place. Otherwise he refused to do anything more until he had received a reply. I advised him to meet with his brothers and sisters before the morning's service, which he did, but they too insisted that he visit the Molochna. This I strongly support.
January 24 Tuesday. In the morning I preached a sermon in the manor house where Jacob Friesen lives. In the afternoon Dietrich Friesen and I drove to talk the matter over with Warkentin, but failed to convince him that he should visit the Molochna. A letter from

Elder Töws made such a strong impression on the Warkentin couple, however, that Mrs Warkentin came to see me, crying and pleading with me to speak to her husband again. This I did on my way home. Warkentin agreed to make the trip if Cornelius Friesen went with him. Töws conveyed this promise to Friesen. I hope all will soon be well.

February 17 Friday. This morning Khortitsa District officials Peter Andres and Dietrich Löwen attended a meeting of the Village assembly to question each settler about how they planned to make payments on their land debt this spring.

February 19 My nephew Diedrich Epp and Reverend Jacob Pätkau plan to start visiting the local schools tomorrow. Epp told me that Khortitsa officials had appointed them as members of the schoolboard. This means that I am relieved of this burden, for which I thank God.

March 2 Katharina Klassen was here for the night. God willing, we will raise her as our foster-daughter. She was born on December 9, 1870. Her parents are Hermann Klassen and Katharina Klippenstein. The mother died in 1870.

April 2 I preached in Izluchistaia in the home of our son-in-law Johann Bärgen. He has bought and moved into the property of his parents, who plan to emigrate to America. Our daughter Katharina, who gave birth to a daughter, Judith, two weeks ago, suffers from painful breasts. May the Lord be her physician and helper.

April 6 Thursday. At 5 p.m. a daughter, Judith, was born to our children, the David Epps.

April 11 After ploughing the stubble field, we did some ploughing for Jacob, who cannot plough himself because of an accident with his horse. Neighbours also helped out. Our Father gives us our share of trials. We lost a cow after calving and now David had to cut their cow's throat after she was unable to calve.

June 6 Saturday. I caught a ride to Novopodolsk with my children, the David Epps, who were on their way to Borosenko. I wanted to consult my brother Diedrich about my eyes, which have been so sore since last Monday that I have been unable to see. Diedrich did what he could, and God is giving his blessing.

August 20 I preached in the Khortitsa church. Monday my brother Heinrich left for Tiflis with the Peter Lepps and Reverend Isaac Dyck, leaders of the Grossfürstlich settlement.

September 4 Monday. This afternoon my dear wife, Johann, and I visited our children, the Peter Epps, in Neu Khortitsa. Sunday at 2:30 p.m., our daughter-in-law had given birth to a son, Heinrich.

September 11 Monday. Gerhard, who will be a teacher's helper for his brother [Peter], left at noon on foot for Neu Khortitsa. He will also be studying on his own. In the evening our son Heinrich got a lift with Peter Peters to Izluchistaia, where I have hired him out as a teacher for the winter for 40 R.

September 14 Thursday. Jacob's wagon was stolen last night. May the Lord help him to find it.

September 22 Friday. We had visitors from the Khortitsa colonies last night, District Elder Peter Andres and Kröker, head of the Orphans' Administration. An Orphans' Administration is to be established here and they requested my help. I am to call a Brotherhood Meeting.

October 25 I accompanied [Gnadenthal] Village Mayor Jacob Janzen to Khortitsa. He was travelling in regard to the establishment of a [local] Orphans' Administration. Janzen also delivered the Steinfeld and Grünfeld village payments on the land.

November 7 *Brotherhood Meeting* in the home of Jacob Wiebe in Gnadenthal. It was decided to create an Orphans' Administration here. Reverend Pätkau read the rules governing his office as school inspector. Several other matters were also discussed.

November 26 I preached a sermon in Novopodolsk about the imminence of Christ's judgment. Matthew 25:13.

December 20 This afternoon a fire destroyed the home of our children, the Johann Bärgens, in Izluchistaia. I hear the children will be living for now with their neighbours, the Isaac Dycks.

1879

May 15 Tuesday. This morning Elder Gerhard Dyck baptized our young people, 15 young men and 14 young women, including our son Heinrich. In the afternoon my nephew Diedrich Epp gave the preparatory sermon [for the communion service]. There followed an election of ministers. My cousin Cornelius Rempel was elected minister with 43 votes. Lord, grant him thy Holy Spirit.

September 4 Monday at 1 a.m. our son David's wife gave birth to a son, whom they have named Jacob. A premature death soon called him to his true home.

December 13 I drove to Khortitsa to put in an order with my brother-in-law Cornelius Hildebrand for two ploughs, one for me and the other for my son Jacob.

1880

January 4 Friday morning a son was born to the Johann Bärgens in Izluchistaia. Our son Heinrich arrived at night with the Bärgen's horses and sled, on which he had taken the midwife, the widow Bartel, home. In the afternoon, we visited our children, the Peter Epps, in Neu Khortitsa. She will soon be giving birth as well and is ill.

January 25 There is a wretched quarrel going on among our church members on the Grossfürstlich settlement. In Snamenka we met my brother Heinrich Epp and Khortitsa District officials (District Mayor Peter Andres, and the Assistant District mayors D. Löwen and Peter Braun). May God help them to re-establish the peace.

January 28 Some two weeks ago a grisly incident was discovered in the Khortitsa colony of Schöneberg, where the Andreas Schmidt couple were found dead. The woman was in the porch and the man in the implement shed with his throat slit and a rope around his neck. The children were still asleep in their beds. What a terrible suicide. The reason for this gruesome deed is still not known. May God have mercy on these poor misguided souls.

February 2 At 3:20 a.m. a son, Heinrich, was born to our children the Peter Epps in Neu Khortitsa.

February 20 Wednesday. After losing a mare in foal in January another one died on us last night. Matters in regard to the maintenance of our household economy thus again look somewhat bleak. Yet I know for a certainty that no sparrow or horse or other head of cattle dies without the Lord's will.
April 12 Saturday. My brother-in-law Gerhard Dyck sold his [Gnadenthal] property to Johann Klassen of Olgafeld for 2500 R.
April 22 Monday. Yesterday, God's grace saved us from a terrible tragedy. Towards evening our grandchild David, son of the David Epps, fell into the bottom of the canal and almost drowned. His father arrived just as the child came to the surface and was able to pull him out. The Lord rescued him.
September 7 An atmospheric phenomenon appeared between eight and nine o'clock last night and made a great impression on a number of people. On this moonlit night there suddenly appeared a bright beam of light that illuminated the entire room. There followed two mighty claps, one after the other, that shook the windows. This reminds us of the words of our Saviour that there will be many signs in the heavens shortly before his reappearance. Our son Johann was so frightened that we had to move his bed, and today he is ill and complains about a headache.
December 7 I preached a sermon in Neu Khortitsa on the signs of the Last Judgment. Luke 21:25–36.
December 9 Tuesday. Last Saturday I received two letters from my brother Heinrich Epp. He reports an invitation to me from Elder G. Dyck to accept a position as a preacher in one of the afforestation camps where our young men will be [doing their alternative] service. That gave me a sleepless night. On Sunday our son Peter suggested that I travel to Khortitsa between Christmas and New Year's. But as I thought more seriously about the matter I finally decided to ask the Village Elder, J. Wiebe, if transportation could be provided for me now. He called a meeting of the Village assembly which agreed to arrange a communal conveyance. Joh. Schellenberg will be the driver. Lord, reveal to us thy holy will and what is in the best interests of the church. Bless the trip. If it is thy will that I should accept this calling, then accompany me with thy grace and make me worthy of this important task.

Notes

Introduction and Analysis

1 'The Saskatchewan Valley News Visitors' Guide,' Supplement to *Saskatchewan Valley News*, 30 June 1988.
2 H.T. Klaassen, *Birth and Growth of Eigenheim Mennonite Church, 1892–1974* (Rosthern, Sask., n.d.).
3 To retain the flavour of the original, translated into English from German inscription.
4 See my 'Mennonite Community in an Age of Troubled Change: The Diaries of Jacob D. Epp, 1851–1880,' *Mennonite Historian* 14 (Dec. 1988), 1–3. The only other scholarly reference to the diaries is by John B. Toews, 'The Diary of Jacob Epp, 1860–1880,' *Journal of the American Society of Germans from Russia* 5 (1982), 1: 37–44, 2: 23–8.
5 The surviving volumes cover the following years: I (1851–3); IV (1859–71); V (1871–80). MSS Mennonite Heritage Centre Archives, Winnipeg, Man., vol. 1017. Hereafter cited as JDE, with the date.
6 Typescript of original, entitled 'Familien-Register,' made available by the late David G. Epp (Eigenheim, Sask.). Hereafter cited as JDER, with the page number of the original.
7 See H. Auerbach, *Die Besiedlung der Südukraine in den Jahren 1774–1787* (Wiesbaden, 1965); Roger H. Bartlett, *Human Capital: The Settlement of Foreigners in Russia, 1762–1804* (Cambridge, Eng., 1979); E.I. Druzhinina, *Severnoe prichornomore v 1775–1800 gg.* (Moscow, 1959), *Iuzhnaia Ukraina v 1800–1825* (Moscow, 1970), and *Iuzhnaia Ukraina v period krizisa feodalizma 1825–1860 gg.* (Moscow, 1980); and V.M. Kabuzan, *Zaselenie Novorossii (Ekaterinoslavskoi i Khersonskoi gubernii) v xviii–pervoi polovine xix veka (1719–1858 gg)* (Moscow, 1976) and 'Zahl und Siedlungsgebiete der Deutschen im Russischen Reich (1796–1917),' *Zeitschrift für Geschichtswissenschaft* 32 (1984), 866–74.
8 For the background of their Vistula lowlands homeland see Peter Klassen, *A Homeland for Strangers: An Introduction to Mennonites in Poland and Prussia* (Fresno, CA, 1989); Horst Penner, *Die ost- und westpreussischen Mennoniten in ihrem religiösen und sozialen Leben in ihrem kulturellen und wirtschaftlichen Leistungen*, vol. 1, 1526–1772 (Weierhof, Germany, 1963), vol. 2, 1772 to the present (Kirchheimbolanden, Germany, 1987); and John Friesen, 'Mennonites in Poland: An Expanded Historical View,' *Journal of Mennonite Studies* 4 (1986), 94–108.
9 David G. Rempel, 'From Danzig to Russia: The First Mennonite Migration,' *Mennonite Life* 24 (Jan. 1969), 8–28, and Lawrence Klippenstein, 'The Mennonite Migration to Russia, 1786–1806,' in John Friesen, ed., *Mennonites in Russia: Essays in Honour of Gerhard Lohrenz* (Winnipeg, Man., 1989),

13–42. See also Adolf Ehrt, *Das Mennonitentum in Russland von seiner Einwanderung bis zur Gegenwart* (Berlin, 1932), 21–8.

10 See Franz Isaac, *Die Molotschnaer Mennoniten: Ein Beitrag zur Geschichte derselben* (Halbstadt, Russia, 1908) and G.G. Pisarevskii, *Pereselenie prusskikh mennonitov v Rossii pri Aleksandre I* (Rostov-on-Don, 1917).

11 The best known of these, based on travels in the early 1840s and appearing in numerous European languages, was by the noted German conservative social scientist August von Haxthausen. In its most recent abridgment, translation, and edition, it appears as *Studies on the Interior of Russia*, ed. S. Frederick Starr, trans. Eleanore L.M. Schmidt (Chicago, 1972), 160–75, 193–7. See, further, Alexander Petzholdt, *Reise im westlichen und südlichen europäischen Russland im Jahre 1855* (Leipzig, 1864).

12 Leonard G. Friesen, 'New Russia and the Fissuring of Rural Society, 1855–1905' (PhD diss., University of Toronto, 1988); Patricia Herlihy, *Odessa: A History, 1794–1914* (Cambridge, MA, 1986); I.P. Khlystov, *Don v epokhu kapitalizma* (Rostov-on-Don, 1962).

13 James Urry, 'The Closed and the Open: Social and Religious Change amongst Mennonites in Russia (1789–1889)' (PhD diss., Oxford University, 1978), 2–62. Since the completion of this study of the Epp diaries, Urry's revised thesis has been published as *None but Saints: The Transformation of Mennonite Life, 1789–1889* (Winnipeg, Man., 1989).

14 David D. Epp's diary ended on page 90. Jacob Epp introduced volume IV of his own diary (May 11, 1871) with these words: 'My beloved blessed father was not able to fill *all* of the pages of this book. He was called away from the difficult course of his life in his sixty-third year, and there are eleven years before I reach that age myself. Will I live long enough to fill these pages? God, thou knowest it.'

15 JDE, May 11, 1871.

16 The main in-group histories of the Khortitsa settlement are Peter Hildebrand, *Erste Auswanderung der Mennoniten aus dem Danziger Gebiet nach Südrussland* (Halbstadt, Russia, 1888); Heinrich Heese, 'Kurzgefasste geschichtliche Übersicht der Gründung und des Bestehens der Kolonien des Chortizer Mennonitenbezirkes,' *Unterhaltungsblatt für deutsche Ansiedler im südlichen Russland* (hereafter *Unterhaltungsblatt*), Aug, Sept., Oct., 1851, 57–60, 66–71, 73–7; and D.H. Epp, *Die Chortitzer Mennoniten: Versuch einer Darstellung des Entwickelungsganges derselben* (Odessa, 1889).

17 E.I. Druzhinina, *Iuzhnaia Ukraina v 1800–1825 gg.* (Moscow, 1978); A.A. Skalkovskii, *Opyt statisticheskogo opisaniia Novorossiiskogo kraia*, 2 vols (Odessa, 1850, 1853).

18 David G. Rempel, 'From Danzig to Russia: The First Mennonite Migration.' See also Marc Raeff, 'The Style of Russia's Imperial Policy and Prince G. A. Potemkin,' in G.N. Grob, ed., *Statesmen and Statecraft of the Modern West* (Barre, MA, 1967), 1–51.

19 Is. P. Klassen, *Die Insel Chortitza: Stimmungsbilder, Gedanken und Erinnerungen* (Winnipeg, Man., 1979).

20 Tsentraln'ii statisticheskii komitet, *Statistika pozemel'noi sobstvennosti i naselennykh mest Evropeiskoi Rossii*, vol. VIII: *Gubernii Novorossiiskoi gruppy* (St Petersburg, 1885).

21 J.N. Westwood, *A History of Russian Railroads* (London, 1964).

22 Epp, *Chortitzer Mennoniten*, 97–101.

23 H. Epp, *Heinrich Epp, Kirchenältester der Mennonitengemeinde zu Chortitza (Südrussland)* (Leipzig, 1897).
24 'Diary of David D. Epp, 1837–1843,' MSS Mennonite Heritage Centre Archives, vol. 1017 (hereafter DDE, and the date), May 17, 1837.
25 DDE, Oct. 6, 12, 1837.
26 DDE, Nov. 15, 1837.
27 DDE, Jan. 12, Feb. 2, 1839.
28 Isaak, *Die Molotschnaer Mennoniten*, and H. Görz, *Die Molotschnaer Ansiedlung: Entstehung, Entwicklung und Untergang* (Steinbach, Man., 1950).
29 D.H. Epp, *Johann Cornies: Züge aus seinem Leben und Wirken* (Berdiansk, Russia, 1909); and Harvey L. Dyck, 'Imperial Servitor and Mennonite Hero: Light and Shadow in Images of Johann Cornies,' *Journal of Mennonite Studies* 2 (1984), 9–28.
30 DDE, Feb. 2, 1839. Another entry of Sept. 20, 1838, described Cornies's approach to governance in the Molochna settlement as 'more desp[otical] than Christian.'
31 The existence of this latter office is based on the memories of the parents of David G. Rempel, transmitted by the latter to the editor/translator in a letter of May 1989.
32 DDE, May 15, 1839.
33 DDE, May 28, 1839.
34 DDE, Aug. 24, 1839.
35 DDE, Sept. 4, 5, 1840.
36 DDE, Oct. 1, 5, 1840.
37 The 'Frisians' and 'Flemish' were two Netherlands Mennonite groups that had arisen in the sixteenth century out of conflict rooted chiefly in cultural and theological differences. The division, which had largely disappeared in the Netherlands by the end of the seventeenth century, lingered on in the Vistula lowlands and was carried to the Old Colony by the first settlers. There the Flemish majority organized into the Khortitsa Mennonite church and Frisians became the Kronsweide (later Schönwiese) Mennonite church (after the village locations of their main churches). Their practices varied somewhat. The Flemish minister, seated, read his sermon while his Frisian counterpart spoke freely while standing at the pulpit. In popular parlance, from their mode of baptism, the Flemish were known as 'pitcher pourers' and the Frisians as 'hand sprinklers.' See C. Neff and N. van der Zijpp, 'Flemish Mennonites,' in *Mennonite Encyclopedia* (Scottdale, PA, 1955–9) and D.H. Epp, *Handbuch zum Gebrauch bei gottesdienstlichen Handlungen zunächst für die Ältesten und Prediger der Mennoniten-Gemeinden in Russland* (Berdiansk, Russia, 1911).
38 DDE, Aug. 24, 1841.
39 DDE, Nov. 2, 18, 1841.
40 Copy preserved by the late David G. Epp, of Eigenheim, Sask.
41 DDE, Aug. 6, 1841.
42 N.M. Druzhinin, *Gosudarstvennye krestiane i reforma P.D. Kiseleva*, 2 vols (Moscow, 1946, 1958). The David G. Rempel Collection, Conrad Grebel College Archives (Waterloo, Ont.), contains extensive documentation from the Ministry of State Domains in regard to Kiselev's interest in the Mennonite settlements.
43 David Hausknecht, a trained teacher from Switzerland in the Pestalozzian method, was a highly successful progressive private tutor in the Old Colony village of Einlage in the 1830s and 1840s (P.M. Friesen, *The*

Mennonite Brotherhood in Russia, 1789–1910, trans. J.B. Toews et al. [Fresno, CA, 1978], 777–8).

44 DDE, Oct. 2, 1841.

45 DDE, May 27, June 21, 22, 23, 28, July 7, Oct. 2, 1841. The history of the school is surveyed by A. Neufeld, *Die Chortitzer Zentralschule, 1842–1892* (Berdiansk, Russia, 1893).

46 DDE, Feb. 1, 9, July 9, Aug. 6, 1841; Mar. 7, July 22, Dec. 31, 1842. Among numerous other guests, David Epp, on July 22, was host to John Melville, a well-known agent of the British Bible Society and prominent evangelical. Several days later the latter preached a sermon in the Khortitsa church and then joined the Epps for dinner. See, further, James Urry, 'John Melville and the Mennonites: A British Evangelist in South Russia, 1837–ca. 1875,' *Mennonite Quarterly Review* 54 (1980), 305–22.

47 For introductions to pietist history and ideas see Erich Beyreuther, *Geschichte des Pietismus* (Stuttgart, 1978); F. Ernst Stoeffler, *The Rise of Evangelical Pietism* (Leiden, 1971); and Martin Schmidt, *Der Pietismus als theologische Erscheinung* (Göttingen, 1984).

48 This summary is based on an analysis of all cases mentioned in the DDE diary (1837–43).

49 DDE, Sept. 8, 1840.

50 On June 29, 1841, David Epp wrote: 'Lord have mercy on us – since the arrival of the Mennonites in Russia, this is the first case of the murder of a child.'

51 On March 6, 1838, David Epp records cases of ten persons placed in the ban, including one for 'sodomy.' This is the one case of homosexual behaviour recorded in either the D.D. Epp or Jacob D. Epp diaries.

52 In one case, the unwed daughter of a certain Claas Krann of the village of Schönthal, after becoming pregnant by a 'Russian,' quietly moved to the nearby state peasant village of Tomakovka. There, after her delivery, she had the local priest baptize her infant child into the Orthodox church. Questioned personally by D.D. Epp, whom the Ministerial Committee sent to Tomakovka expressly for this purpose, she affirmed her own intention of joining the Orthodox church. DDE, Nov. 15, 1841.

53 JDE, 'Background.'

54 JDE, ibid.

55 Epp, *Heinrich Epp*, 1–2.

56 DDE, Sept. 20, 1838; Feb. 2, 1839; Nov. 3, 1842; Mar. 27, 1843.

57 DDE, Nov. 3, 1842.

58 DDE, Dec. 31, 1839, and Dec. 31, 1841.

59 JDE, 'Background.'

60 D.H. Epp, 'Aus der Kindheitsgeschichte der deutschen Industrie in den Kolonieen Süd-Russlands,' *Botschafter*, July 1–Aug. 2, 1911.

61 Cornelius Hildebrand, 'Unsere Lebensbeschreibung, 1891' (photocopy of MSS, made available by Hildebrand's granddaughter, Anna Dyck, Leamington, Ont.).

62 JDE, Sept. 26, 1851.

63 Hildebrand, 'Lebensbeschreibung,' and Klassen, *Insel Chortitza*, 1–4, 25–6, 96–106.

64 Hildebrand, 'Lebensbeschreibung.'

65 See note no. 37.
66 JDE, Mar. 28, 1851.
67 JDE, Book I, passim.
68 W. Bruce Lincoln, *Nicholas I: Emperor and Autocrat of All the Russias* (Bloomington, IN, 1978), and Nicholas Riasanovsky, *Nicholas I and Official Nationality in Russia* (Berkeley, CA, 1959).
69 David G. Rempel, 'The Mennonite Colonies in New Russia: A Study of Their Settlement and Economic Development from 1789 to 1914' (PhD diss., Stanford University, 1933), 113–22.
70 D.G. Rempel, 'The Mennonite Commonwealth in Russia: A Sketch of Its Founding and Endurance, 1789–1914,' *Mennonite Quarterly Review*, part 2, 48 (Jan. 1974), 8–15.
71 Rempel, 'Mennonite Colonies,' 147–78.
72 Urry, 'Closed and Open,' 257–61.
73 Pointed out in a letter of May 1989 by the anthropologist/historian Herman Konrad, University of Calgary.
74 For the background and early history of Jewish agrarian settlements in Russia, see F. Zakharievich, 'Istoriko-statisticheskoe opisanie Evreiskikh kolonii Novorossieskogo kraia,' *Novorossiiskii kalendar na 1853* (1852), 396–416; M. Stanislawski, *Tsar Nicholas I and the Jews: The Transformation of Jewish Society in Russia* (Philadelphia, 1983); Julius Elk, *Die jüdischen Kolonien in Russland* (Frankfurt a. M., 1886). For background see also John D. Klier, *The Origins of the 'Jewish Question' in Russia, 1772–1825* (Dekalb, IL, 1986).
75 David H. Epp, 'Judenplan,' in *Mennonite Encyclopedia.*
76 Stanislawski, *Tsar Nicholas I and the Jews.*
77 Elk, *Jüdische Kolonien in Russland*, 204.
78 Epp, *Johann Cornies*, 101, and Harvey L. Dyck, ed. and trans., 'Agronomist Gavel's Biography of Johann Cornies (1789–1848),' *Journal of Mennonite Studies* 2 (1984), 29–41.
79 'Die Hebräer-Kolonieen in Süd-Russland' and 'Aufforderung an deutsche Kolonisten, sich als Musterwirte, Schmiede und Wagner in den Juden-Kolonieen niederzulassen,' *Unterhaltungsblatt*, Mar. 1848, 20–1.
80 The landless question among Russian Mennonites, as P. M. Friesen already wrote in 1911, 'has still to be written' (*The Mennonite Brotherhood in Russia, 1789–1910*, trans. J.B. Toews et al. [Fresno, CA, 1978], 123). Existing studies deal with the topic almost exclusively in terms of the Molochna settlement and from a moralistic angle. For an introduction see Rempel, 'Mennonite Colonies,' 179–211.
81 Based on scattered statistical and other references in the *Unterhaltungsblatt* for the years 1846–57.
82 Heinrich Heese, 'Geschichtliche Übersicht,' *Unterhaltungsblatt*, Sept. 1851.
83 *Unterhaltungsblatt*, Mar. 1848, 20–1. The Epps visited the Judenplan twice before settling there. JDE, Apr. 27, July 2, 1851.
84 JDE, Mar. 10, 25, 1851. Diedrich Epp had a long and distinguished career in various supervisory posts in the Jewish agricultural settlements from 1851 to 1900. In 1861, he received a letter of commendation for distinguished service from the minister of state domains (*Unterhaltungsblatt* May 1861, 36). His death in 1900 was the occasion for tributes from Jewish friends and admirers (Epp, 'Judenplan,' *Mennonite Encyclopedia*).

85 JDE, Apr. 27, July 2, 1851.
86 The Mennonite population is an estimate derived from annual birth data included in Jacob Epp's diary. It assumes that the Judenplan Mennonite birth rate was similar to that in the Old Colony at the time, that is, between 4 and 5 per cent annually, and that the Judenplan Mennonite family was also about the same average size, that is, between 5 and 5.5 persons per family. The total Judenplan population in 1858, according to the Tenth Revision, was 3110. In 1898–9, according to a study by the Jewish Colonisation Society, it was 3317 (Leo Bramsohn, 'Statistische Untersuchungen über die Lage der Juden in Russland,' in Verein für jüdische Statistik, *Jüdische Statistik* [Berlin, 1903], 184).
87 JDE, Mar. 23–7, 1852.
88 Dave Stobbe, 'Novovitebsk: A Jewish and Mennonite Village in Russia and Its Pattern of Life' (student paper, Canadian Mennonite Bible College, 1975), Mennonite Heritage Centre Archives, Winnipeg, Man. This informative term paper is based on interviews of Stobbe with his grandfather, a Mennonite resident in the Judenplan until the mid-1920s.
89 JDE, Apr. 6 to July 1, 1852.
90 Epp, *Die Chortitzer Mennoniten*, 143–5. D.H. Epp, a nephew of Jacob Epp, often visited the Judenplan with his father, Heinrich Epp, who had himself briefly served as overseer in one of the Jewish agricultural settlements in the mid-1850s.
91 JDE, Oct. 18–19, 1852.
92 JDE, Apr. 11, 1865.
93 JDE, May 19 to June 13, 1870.
94 Epp, *Chortitzer Mennoniten*, 145.
95 JDE, Feb. 29, Mar. 4, 1868.
96 JDE, Feb. 14, Mar. 4, 1852.
97 JDE, Feb. 2, Mar. 5, 9, 1860.
98 JDE, Aug. 7, 29, Sept. 10, 1852.
99 JDE, Dec. 31, 1872, Jan. 4, 31, Sept. 24, 1873.
100 JDE, June 3, 1871.
101 Postnikov, *Iuzhno-russkoe khoziaistvo*, 1–33; Rempel, 'Mennonite Colonies,' 212–89.
102 JDE, Apr. 28, 1852.
103 Increases in the area tilled by the Epp family are derived from a comparison of the following entries in JDE: Apr. 28, 1863; Apr. 19, 1865; Apr. 18, 1870; Apr. 19, 1871; Mar. 23, 1873; May 10, 1875; and Apr. 14, 1876.
104 D.H. Epp, 'Aus der Kindheitsgeschichte der deutschen Industrie,' *Botschafter*, Sept. 30, 1911.
105 This reconstruction of a typical year is based on JDE, passim, and on Postnikov, *Iuzno-russkoe khoziaistvo*, 222–55.
106 Epp family memories recounted by the late Mr and Mrs David G. Epp, Eigenheim, Sask.
107 D.D. Epp, comp., *Familien Stammbaum* [of the David Epp (1750–1802) Family] (Winkler, Man., 1958), 1.
108 Ibid., 7.
109 JDE, Feb. 23 to May 7, 1863.
110 Copy of letter made available by Otto Andres, Toronto, Ont.
111 JDE, Aug. 17, 29, Sept. 10, 1863.

112 Computed on basis of JDEJ, passim.
113 Computed on basis of JDE, passim.
114 Computed on basis of JDEJ, passim.
115 Christine D. Worobec, 'Family, Community, and Land in Peasant Russia, 1860–1905' (PhD diss., University of Toronto, 1984), 269.
116 For approaches to the social history of the Russian peasant family see Peter Czap, Jr, 'Marriage and the Peasant Joint Family in the Era of Serfdom,' in David L. Ransel, ed., *The Family in Imperial Russia: New Lines of Historical Research* (Urbana, IL, 1978), 103–23. For views on the role of inheritance systems in family history see Jack Goody, 'Strategies of Heirship,' *Comparative Studies in Society and History* 15 (1973), 3–16.
117 JDE, June 11, 1876.
118 Epp, *Familien Stammbaum*, 2.
119 JDEJ, 15–59, 86–91.
120 JDE, June 2 to July 14, 1866.
121 The fundamental linkage between family structures and land-tenure systems among Russian peasants is systematically explored in Worobec, 'Family, Community, and Land in Peasant Russia, 1890–1905.'
122 JDE in late 1860s and first half of 1870s, passim.
123 See, for example, JDE, Aug. 20, 1871; Dec. 31, 1875; Sept. 11, 1878.
124 This was especially true of the family started by Epp's eldest daughter Helena and her husband Johann Andres, whose building activities are evocatively reflected in photographs, sketches, and genealogical entries in Otto Andres, comp., *Pioneer Builders: The Story of the Andres Family* (Toronto, 1989).
125 For instance, JDE, Aug. 1, Sept. 5, 1870; May 1, 1871.
126 Overview provided in Epp, *Chortitzer Mennoniten*, 143–9, and Friesen, *Mennonite Brotherhood*, 843–65.
127 Cornelius Krahn, 'Nepluyevka' and 'Nepluyevka Mennonite Church,' and J. J. Toews, 'Nepluyevka Mennonite Brethren Church,' in *Mennonite Encyclopedia*.
128 Jacob Redekopp, *Es war die Heimat ... Baratow-Schlachtjin* (Filadelfia, Paraguay, 1966), 5–37, and copy of typescript manuscript, 'Ansiedlung Schlachtin im Jekaterinoslawischen,' n.a., Conrad Grebel College Archives, David G. Rempel Collection.
129 Gerhard Lohrenz, *Sagradowka: Die Geschichte einer mennonitschen Ansiedlung im Süden Russlands* (Rosthern, Sask., 1947).
130 JDE, Mar. 22, 1872.
131 J.S. Curtiss, *Russia's Crimean War* (Durham, NC, 1979); Daniel Field, *The End of Serfdom* (Cambridge, MA, 1976); S. Frederick Starr, *Decentralization and Self-Government in Russia, 1830–1870* (Princeton, 1972); A.J. Rieber, ed., *The Politics of Autocracy: Letters of Alexander II to Prince Briatinskii, 1857–1864* (Paris, 1966); Hugh Seton-Watson, *The Russian Empire, 1801–1917* (Oxford, 1967); and P.A. Zaionchkovskii, *Otmena krepostnogo prava v Rossii* (Moscow, 1960).
132 W. Bruce Lincoln, *In the Vanguard of Reform: Russia's Enlightened Bureaucrats, 1825–1861* (DeKalb, IL, 1982).
133 The term appears typically in Aleksandr Nikitenko, *The Diary of a Russian Censor*, ed. and trans. Helen Saltz Jacobson (Amherst, MA, 1975), 185, 192.

134 Starr, *Decentralization and Self-Government*, 51–109.
135 Well-reflected in the documentary complications and commentaries of Isaac, *Molotschnaer Mennoniten*, and Friesen, *Mennonite Brotherhood.*
136 Urry, 'Closed and Open,' 460–586.
137 Friesen, *Mennonite Brotherhood*, 201–311; Jacob P. Bekker, *Origin of the Mennonite Brethren Church*, trans. D.E. Pauls and A.E. Janzen (Hillsboro, KS, 1973); John A. Toews, *A History of the Mennonite Brethren Church: Pilgrims and Pioneers* (Fresno, CA, 1975), 38–50.
138 Isaac, *Molotschnaer Mennoniten*, 207–66; H. Sawatzky, *Templer Mennonitischer Herkunft* (Winnipeg, Man., 1955); Urry, 'Closed and Open,' 587–608; and Victor G. Doerksen, 'Mennonite Templars in Russia,' *Journal of Mennonite Studies* 3 (1985), 28–31.
139 See note 137.
140 Bekker, *Origin of the Mennonite Brethren Church*, 43–7.
141 Friesen, *Mennonite Brotherhood*, 280–325.
142 Ibid, 230–79.
143 JDE, May 12, 1862, and May 23, 1865.
144 Friesen, *Mennonite Brotherhood*, 547.
145 Ibid, 283–4, 290, 463–4.
146 JDE, Apr. 15, 1862, and Apr. 30, 1865.
147 I am grateful to Peter P. Klassen, author and editor of the Paraguayan Mennonite bi-weekly newspaper *Mennoblatt*, for drawing this aspect of Epp's piety to my attention. The role played by various modes of Mennonite and Russian Mennonite piety in Paraguayan Russian Mennonite settlements is discussed in Klassen's *Die Mennoniten in Paraguay: Reich Gottes und Reich dieser Welt* (Bolanden-Weierhof, West Germany, 1988), 232–365.
148 The land crisis is surveyed in Rempel, 'Mennonite Colonies,' 179–211, and Urry, 'Closed and Open,' 609–47. From the early 1860s to the 1890s, the *Odessaer Zeitung* carried numerous detailed letters from Mennonite settlements and informative, often polemical, articles by Mennonites and outsiders regarding the landless question in the Molochna and Old Colony settlements. The D.G. Rempel Collection, Conrad Grebel College Archives, contains microfilm copies of significant files of the Ministry of State Domains dealing with the issues of landlessness and pasture rights in the Mennonite settlements. No existing studies deal adequately with the emergence, resolution, and long-term results of this controversy.
149 Isaac, *Molotschnaer Mennoniten*, 27–86, contains a rich source of contemporary government and in-group documents for the 1870s that captures the temper of the time. The continuing controversy over pasture rights for the remaining landless and small holders after the great reform has not been explored in the literature. The *Odessaer Zeitung*, the D.G. Rempel Collection at Conrad Grebel College, and the writings of Abraham Thiessen contain the main sources for this subject.
150 Socially radical ideas among Mennonites at the time are played down in the Isaac and Friesen studies. Such viewpoints are, however, reflected in letters and articles in the *Odessaer Zeitung* and in various writings by Abraham Thiessen, especially *Ein Brief nur für die Mennoniten im berdjanschen Kreise* (Odessa, 1872) and *Die Agrarwirren bei den Mennoniten in Südrussland* (Berlin, 1887).

151 Isaac, *Molotschnaer Mennoniten*, 66–70. A.A. Klaus, a German-speaking official in the Ministry of State Domains, was intimately familiar with the landless dispute. His study, published in Russia in 1869, analyses the impact of land tenure and inheritance practices on Mennonite social relations and agricultural productivity: *Studien und Materialien zur Geschichte und Statistik der ausländischen Kolonisation in Russland*, trans. J. Töws (Odessa, 1887), 228–335. Postnikov based his informative study of agricultural development in the southern Ukraine on Klaus's highly promising approach. No modern scholarly study of Mennonite farming has, however, developed it further.

152 Traditional Russian Mennonite historiography, based on D.H. Epp's sanitized centennial anniversary history of the Old Colony, has suggested an almost tension-free resolution of the landless issue in the Old Colony. This view is contradicted by copies of records of the Ministry of State Domains contained in the David G. Rempel Collection and by numerous contemporary letters and articles from the 1860s to 1890s in the *Odessaer Zeitung*.

153 *Odessaer Zeitung*, Dec. 3, 11, 1881.

154 Postnikov, *Iuzhno-russkoe khoziaistvo*, 10–13, 38, 298ff.

155 Land purchases for daughter settlements followed Russia's gradually receding steppe frontier. In the first stage, from the 1860s to 1880s, the main daughter settlements were established in New Russia, including the Crimean peninsula. See, for example, the in-group histories of the Iasikovo, Baratov-Shlakhtin, Zagradovka, Memrik, and Crimean settlements: Julius Löwen, *Jasykowo. Siedlungsschicksal am Dnjepr* (Winnipeg, Man., 1967); Redekopp, *Baratow-Schlachtjin*; Lohrenz, *Sagradowka*; D.H. Epp, *Die Memriker Ansiedlung: Zum 25-jährigen Bestehen derselben im Herbst 1910* (Berdiansk, 1910); H. Görz, *Die mennonitischen Siedlungen der Krim* (Winnipeg, Man., 1957); and Martin Dürksen, *Die Krim war unsere Heimat* (Winnipeg, Man. 1977).

During a second stage, starting in the 1890s and continuing until 1914, rising population coupled with economic development in New Russia drove up land prices dramatically. New daughter settlements were henceforward founded in remoter areas north of the Caucasus Mountains, east of the Volga River, and in western Siberia: J.H. Brucks and H. Hooge, eds, *Neu-Samara am Tock* (Clearbrook, BC, 1964); N.J. Neufeld, Mrs H.F. Klassen, and Peter H. Mierau, eds, *Ufa: The Mennonite Settlements (Colonies), 1894–1938* (Steinbach, Man., 1977); *Die Kubaner Ansiedlung* (Winnipeg, Man., 1953); C.P. Töws, *Die Tereker Ansiedlung, Mennonitsche Kolonie im Vorderkaukasus: Entstehung, Entwicklung und Untergang, 1901–1918/25* (Steinbach, Man., 1945); and J.J. Hildebrand, *Sibirien: Allgemeine übersicht über Sibirien und der Gründung der Mennonitensiedlungen in Sibirien* (Winnipeg, Man., 1952).

156 The chief publicist of this view was A.A. Velitsyn (pseudonym of A.A. Paltov), *Nemtsy v Rossii* (St Petersburg, 1893); English translation of excerpts in Harvey L. Dyck, ed. and trans., 'The German Conquest of Southern Russia,' *Mennonite Quarterly Review* 56 (1982), 318–41. See also Harvey L. Dyck, 'Russian Mennonitism and the Challenge of Russian Nationalism,' *Mennonite Quarterly Review* 56 (1982), 307–18, and David G. Rempel, 'The Expropriation of the German Colonists in South Russia during the Great War,' *Journal of Modern History* (1932), 49–67.

157 D.G. Rempel, 'Russian Mennonite Commonwealth,' *Mennonite Quarterly Review* 48 (Jan. 1974), 33–4; Urry, 'Closed and Open,' 647–56.

158 F.A. Miller, *Dmitri Miliutin and the Reform Era in Russia* (Nashville, 1968), and John H.L. Keep, *Soldiers of the Tsar: Army and Society in Russia, 1462–1874* (Oxford, 1985), 351–81.
159 Lawrence Klippenstein, 'Mennonite Pacifism and State Service in Russia: A Case Study in Church-State Relations, 1789–1936' (PhD diss., University of Minnesota, 1984) and Jacob Sudermann, 'The Origin of Mennonite State Service in Russia, 1870–1880,' *Mennonite Quarterly Review* 27 (Jan. 1943), 23–46.
160 Cornelius Hildebrand, 'Meine Lebensbeschreibung, 1891'; 'Stambuch für die Familie Jakob Hildebrandt hier auf Insel Chortitz 1860,' photocopy of MSS, David Rempel Collection, Conrad Grebel College Archives; D.H. Epp, 'Aus der Kindheitsgeschichte der deutschen Industrie,' *Botschafter*, July 29, 1911; and N.J. Kroeker, *First Mennonite Villlages in Russia, 1789–1943: Khortitsa-Rosental* (Vancouver, BC, 1981), 91–7.
161 D.H. Epp, 'Aus der Kindheitsgeschichte der deutschen Industrie,' *Botschafter*, Feb. 22, 1911, and Kroeker, *First Mennonite Villages in Russia*, 130–6.
162 Johann Epp is mentioned in passing in studies of the Old Colony and in greater detail in articles in the *Odessaer Zeitung* in the 1870s documenting the development of various Old Colony daughter settlements.
163 A. Braun, 'Heinrich Epp,' in *Mennonite Encyclopedia*; H. Epp, *Heinrich Epp. Kirchenältester der Mennonitengemeinde zu Chortitza* (Leipzig, 1897); and Heinrich H. Epp, 'Mein Vater,' copy of typescript made available by Mary Heinrichs, Toronto.
164 Based on conversations with members of the Heinrich Epp family in Canada.
165 JDE, Nov. 6, 1872.
166 JDE, June 1–14, 1870.
167 JDE, passim.
168 Peter Letkemann, 'The Hymnology and Choral Music of Mennonites in Russia, 1789–1915' (PhD diss., University of Toronto, 1985), 152–5, 167–93, and JDE, passim. See, further, James Urry, 'The Snares of Reason – Changing Mennonite Attitudes to "Knowledge" in Nineteenth-Century Russia,' *Comparative Studies in Society and History* 25 (1983), 306–22; and J.B. Toews, 'Harmony and Disharmony: A Diary Portrait of Mennonite Singing during the 1860s,' *Mennonite Life* 40 (1985), 4–7. For an overview of a related area see W. Berg, 'The Development of Choral Singing among Mennonites in Russia to 1895,' *Mennonite Quarterly Review* 55, (1981) 131–42.
169 JDE, Aug 9, 1870.
170 JDE, in 1870s, passim.
171 JDE, May 28, Dec. 31, 1871.
172 JDE, Dec. 23, 1868.
173 JDEJ, 61–3.
174 JDE, Feb. 19, 1878.
175 JDE, Dec. 9, 1880.
176 Descriptions by the late Mrs David G. Epp, Eigenheim, Sask., based on family stories and perhaps on her reading of a diary volume for the 1880s, which has since been lost.
177 JDEJ, 60–1, 63, 68–9.
178 JDEJ, 74.

179 JDEJ, 54.
180 JDEJ, 14.
181 JDEJ, 101, 140–1.
182 Memoirs of Jacob Epp's son-in-law Heinrich Wieler, dated Sept. 12, 1913, and made available by his grandson, W.H. Roth.
183 Gerhard Epp diaries, Nov. 5, 8, 1890; lent by W.H. Roth.
184 Heinrich Wieler Memoirs.
185 G.B. Robbins, *Famine in Russia, 1891–1892: The Imperial Government Responds to a Crisis* (New York, 1975).
186 Heinrich Wieler Memoirs.

BOOK I

1 The division of the diary into 'books' is by the translator-editor. Diary dates are given according to the Julian calendar, which lagged behind the Gregorian calendar by twelve days in the nineteenth century.
2 For details see 'Genealogy of the Jacob D. Epp Family' following the Notes in this volume.
3 The five-village Mariupol Mennonite settlement, also known as the Bergthal settlement, some two hundred kilometres southeast of the Old Colony near the port of Mariupol on the Sea of Azov, was established in 1836 on crown land as the first daughter settlement of the Old Colony. Quite isolated from modernizing developments in the Old Colony and Molochna settlements, it remained staunchly conservative, fearful of the changes under way in much of the Mennonite world in the 1860s and 1870s. In the 1870s virtually the entire Bergthal population of some three thousand persons emigrated to Manitoba, Canada. The settlement, then sold to German colonists, thus disappears from Mennonite history. See William Schroeder, *The Bergthal Colony*, rev. ed. (Winnipeg, Man., 1986).
4 Little is known about the obviously important role played at this time by the District Office in leasing land for its landless households and administering such leases.
5 Heinrich Franz (1812–89), a pioneer of the Russian Mennonite secondary school system, headmaster of the Khortitsa Zentralschule from 1846 to 1858; his influence penetrated Old Colony life through graduates of the school who took up positions as village schoolteachers. Through his *Choralbuch: Zunächst zum Gebrauch in den mennonitischen Schulen Südrusslands* (Leipzig, 1860), the number notation ('cipher music') form of four-part singing entered Russian Mennonite school and church life, gradually supplanting the traditional chant-like unison singing of the 'old way.' Peter Letkemann, 'The Hymnody and Choral Music of Mennonites in Russia, 1789–1915' (PhD diss., University of Toronto, 1986).
6 The evolution of schooling among Russian Mennonites is surveyed by Leonard Froese, 'Das pädagogische Kultursystem der mennonitischen Siedlungsgruppe in Russland' (PhD diss., University of Göttingen, 1949).
7 This entry is the only surviving eyewitness account of the activities of a small, informal Old Colony reading and discussion circle, a cultural-intellectual proto-élite, whose beginnings likely date to the late 1830s or early 1840s. D.H. Epp describes it as a 'society without statutes,' consisting originally of Jacob's father David Epp, the master cabinet-maker Christian Hamm, the master gardener Carl Jäger, and others: 'They read together, discussed

what they had read, and took up questions of contemporary and local importance. However different they were in occupation and age, they shared a love of knowledge and of the good, and strove for truth and genuine understanding.' A decade later, the group, as described by Jacob Epp, had been joined by the secondary school teacher Heinrich Franz and Jacob Epp's younger brother, the talented young administrator-teacher Heinrich Epp (1827–96). 'Aus der Kindheitsgeschichte der deutschen Industrie in den Kolonien Süd-Russlands,' *Botschafter*, March 2, 4, 1911.

8 For the role of the agricultural commissions in Russian Mennonite life, see 'Introduction and Analysis.'

9 Johann Siemens (n.d.–1855) became chairman of the Old Colony Agricultural Commission following Johann Cornies's death in 1848. Continuing its work much in the latter's spirit, he was pitted against Jakob Bartsch, District mayor from 1841 to 1854.

10 Jakob Hildebrand (1795–1867), long-time Elder of the Kronsweide (Frisian) Mennonite church, lived on the Island of Khortitsa. He was the father of Cornelius Hildebrand, Jacob Epp's pupil, later brother-in-law, and farm-implements industrialist.

11 Jacob Dyck (1779–1854), Elder of the Khortitsa (Flemish) Mennonite church, was known for his devoutness and warm evangelical sensibility.

12 Johann Wall. Parts of the letter appear also in P.M. Friesen, *The Mennonite Brotherhood in Russia, 1789–1910* (Fresno, CA, 1978), 153–6.

13 Petr Andreevich Kleinmichel (1793–1869), Russian minister and statesman.

14 Father of Elder Jakob Hildebrand (see note 10), Peter Hildebrand (1754–1849), of Lutheran background, Mennonite deputy Jacob Hoeppner's servant at the time of the original Old Colony settlement in 1789, later married Hoeppner's daughter and was elected a minister in the Kronsweide Frisian Mennonite church. He wrote the first memoir-history of the Mennonite Old Colony, entitled *Erste Auswanderung der Mennoniten aus dem Danziger Gebiet nach Südrussland* (Halbstadt, Russia, 1888); repub. in V. Peters, ed., *Zwei Dokumente: Quellen zum Geschichtsstudium der Mennoniten in Russland* (Winnipeg, Man., 1965). See 'Stambuch für die Familie Jacob Hildebrandt,' David G. Rempel Collection, Conrad Grebel College, Waterloo, Ont.

15 Baron F.F. von Rosen (1808–54), president of the Guardian's Committee, 1849–53.

16 In 1849 a large Russian army supporting the Habsburg Monarchy crushed the Hungarian revolution and independence movement.

17 Johann Cornies (1789–1848), lifetime chairman of the Molochna Agricultural Commission since 1830, was appointed chairman of its Old Colony counterpart in 1846.

18 In ultra-conservative Russian Mennonite circles at the time a self-composed prayer or sermon was regarded as a mark of pride.

19 The *Waisenamt* (Orphans' Administration) was a highly developed church-run mutual-aid organization of great importance in Russian Mennonite religious and civil life. It seems to have emerged out of the needs of a pre-modern society and the Anabaptist and Mennonite martyr past, which produced large numbers of widows and orphans. Its responsibilities were threefold: one, to ensure that inheritances were divided among heirs on the

basis of the principles of a community of property between spouses and an equal division of inheritances among sons and daughters; two, to protect the interests of widows and orphans by overseeing the appointment of two trustees for the former and two guardians for the latter; and, three, to serve as a trust-institution, investing and managing the inheritances of bereaved underaged children and, as a near-bank, lending out money in its care to dependable borrowers. Its administrative officers, appointed by the church, operated with a detailed set of rules. These were periodically revised and had the force of law, according to the Charter of Privileges of 1800. The shaping role of inheritance practices and administration on Mennonite society awaits detailed scholarly study.

20 The conflict over authority in the Old Colony between the District Office and the Agricultural Commission (described and analysed in the 'Introduction and Analysis') was especially hard-fought in regard to village schooling.

21 'Colony' was normally used as a synonym for 'village' under the jurisdiction of the Guardianship Committee.

22 This is JE's first mention of the millenarian 'end times,' a subject of concern to his father and of continuing interest to JE throughout his adult life. His interest in the apocalypse peaks in the mid-1870s to the early 1880s. See also 'Introduction and Analysis.'

23 I have been unable to trace this term.

24 In 1789, copies of this volume accompanied the first Mennonite immigrants to the Old Colony. Sermons from it were routinely read at services where ordained ministers were not present. The author, Isaac Kröker, was a former Elder and minister of the Königsberg Mennonite church: *Zwanzig Predigten über verschiedene Texte der heiligen Schrift* (Königsberg, 1788).

BOOK II

1 The decade-long controversy over the mode of singing in the churches and village schools of the Old Colony was a highly symbolic confrontation over modernity. The conservatives clung to singing 'by ear' and in 'the old fashion,' as done traditionally in their communities. They objected to 'newfangled' ways, based on external models, as an assault on the integrity of their Christian community. Innovators, in contrast, influenced by singing practices originating in Prussia and introduced through the Khortitsa Zentralschule and its head teacher Heinrich Franz (1812–89), championed singing by 'notes,' in the 'new style,' using a form of number notation – hence the term, 'cipher singing.' Peter Letkemann, 'The Hymnody and Choral Music of Mennonites in Russia, 1789–1915' (PhD diss., University of Toronto, 1985), 152–5, 167–93; and J. B. Toews, 'Harmony and Disharmony: A Diary Portrait of Mennonite Singing during the 1860s,' *Mennonite Life* 40 (1985), 4–7.

2 The salutation 'Ohm,' in the West Prussian Low German spoken by Russian Mennonites, signified 'Minister' or 'Reverend,' and was spoken with great respect.

3 Friedrich Starck (1680–1756) authored one of the most popular Pietist prayer books used for generations in the German-speaking world.

4 Gerhard Dyck (1809–87) was Elder of the Khortitsa [Flemish] Mennonite church from 1855 to 1885.

5 Abraham D. Epp, 1836–60.

6 Jacob Epp's son Heinrich J. Epp did not emigrate to Canada with the rest of his family in the 1890s, and we know nothing of his life beyond that date. According to his father's journal, he was baptized on May 15, 1879, and married on August 28, 1888, to Anna Pauls, his junior by seven years.

7 Karl Brauchscheidt's 'life awakener' was a novel medical instrument from Germany that came to be used often in the Epp family and throughout Russian Mennonite society. Bernhard H. Pauls (1877–1963), who grew up in the Old Colony village of Rosenthal, and later married Jacob Epp's niece, describes its use during his childhood: 'In cases of illness there was a cure-all: lilac tea. It was good for colds and stomach aches. If lilac tea did not work, there was always the "Life Awakener."

'This was an apparatus suitable perhaps for curing horses. When I saw father bringing it out, I wanted only to be well. It was a well-constructed thing, about ten inches long. Made of dark wood, and tubular in form, it had a spiral spring running down its hollow centre. At the bottom of the tube was a stopper. This stopper was covered thickly with sharp needles, so that it looked almost like a brush. At the top of the tube a handle was affixed. When the handle was pulled upward and released the needle-studded stopper struck the spot where the Life Awakener had been attached. The spring could be pulled more tightly or less tightly, depending on one's wishes and needs.

'When the back or chest had been worked over in this way, the skin was quite red. This was good against colds and anything else. To achieve the maximum effect, the treated spots needed then to be rubbed with oil – I think it was called Baumschedt [Brauchscheidt?] oil. The area was finally covered with cotton wool and the body kept warm. Small, puss-filled blisters were thus formed, and in this way the illness was drawn out.

'I remember the time when my back and throat had been worked over so thoroughly that I had to miss school for some time. Father used the Life Awakener regularly. When he was tired, he worked over the calves of his legs, but dry, without using oil. He was particularly tired during seed-time, when he walked over the ploughed land all day long, casting the seed by hand.' From unpublished manuscript made available to me by the author's son, Bernard Pauls (Leamington, Ont.).

8 The diaries make no further mention of this possibility although the decision to build a new church indicates that it was rejected.

9 This opposition may have arisen from Aron Lepp's early adherence to the Brethren movement. See 'Introduction and Analysis.'

10 This presumably refers to entries in the missing diary volumes for the years 1853 to 1859.

11 The village of Einlage, Old Colony, lay on the Dnieper River and was the leading centre of the Mennonite Brethren church in the Old Colony. In 1872, out of a total membership of 600 Mennonite Brethren in Russia, 188 members belonged to the Einlage church. P.M. Friesen, *The Mennonite Brotherhood in Russia, 1789–1910* (Fresno, CA, 1978), 280–324.

12 Gerhard Wieler (1833–1911), one-time employee of the Guardianship Committee in Odessa and sometime village schoolteacher, was an early Mennonite Brethren leader in the Einlage Mennonite Brethren church. He was a proponent of the 'exuberance' movement and of a policy of missionizing

among Russians and Ukrainians. Friesen, *Mennonite Brethren*, 274–5, 289–90, 317–18, and 325–6. On his equally influential brother in the religious turmoils of the time, see Lawrence Klippenstein, 'Johann Wieler (1839–1888) among Russia Mennonites: A Source of Mennonites[?] and Evangelicalism in Imperial Russia,' *Journal of Mennonite Studies* (1987), 44–60.

13 The Brotherhood Meeting, an assemblage of all male members of the congregation, elected their ministers from a pool of previously elected deacons.

14 Conservative ministers in the Russian Mennonite Flemish church either read or spoke memorized sermons from several favourite sermon volumes.

15 Peter H. Lepp (1817–71), who had been trained as a watchmaker in West Prussia, was a leading and widely recognized pioneer of the farm-implements industry in New Russia in the 1850s and 1860s. Lepp's widow, his second wife, became Heinrich D. Epp's second wife. D.H. Epp, 'Peter Lepp, der Vater der deutschen Fabrikindustrie in unsern Kolonien,' in 'Aus der Kindheitsgeschichte der deutschen Industrie in den Kolonien Süd-Russlands,' *Botschafter*, Jan. 14–Apr. 8, 1911.

16 Jacob Epp's nephew, David H. Epp (1861–1934), teacher, minister, historian, and editor of the *Botschafter* during imperial times and minister and church elder during Soviet times, became one of Russian Mennonitism's most prominent leaders and publicists. His historical publications, including invaluable studies on the Old Colony, Johann Cornies, the Memrik settlement, and Russian Mennonite industry, are cited often in this volume. See David G. Rempel, 'An Introduction to Russian Mennonite Historiography,' *Mennonite Quarterly Review* 48 (1974), 409–46.

17 Aron Lepp (n.d.), an early leader of the Mennonite Brethren church in the Old Colony. In the mid-1860s the Guardianship Committee dismissed him from his post as Village overseer in two Judenplan villages, presumably for his missionizing activities. Elder of the Einlage Mennonite Brethren church from 1876 to 1903, he is remembered as a staunch opponent of moves to merge the Brethren with the Baptist church. Friesen, *Mennonite Brotherhood*, 283, 290, 463–4, 562–6, and 919.

18 With attached barns and sheds, thatched roofs, and wooden smoke flues, houses catching fire were a recurring experience among Russian Mennonites until the late nineteenth century. Repeated large-scale conflagrations, noted in the Epp diaries, account for the increasingly stringent rules of the Khortitsa Mutual Fire Insurance Office (Brandordnung), one of the most important mutual-aid institutions of the Old Colony. These required fire walls between dwellings and barns and ready access to fire ladders, hooks, pails, water, and so on. Participants in the Brandordnung were required to help put out fires, appearing with the appropriate equipment. They then assisted in the clean-up of the fire site, contributed money for the purchase of materials needed for reconstruction (in proportion to their coverage), and carted materials.

The 1863 Neuosterwick fire described by JE was long remembered as the 'great fire.' It broke out over the noon hour on August 8, just as an extraordinarly strong east wind blew through the area: 'At the east end of the village lived the Johann Teichröbs. To cook dinner, Mrs Teichröb had placed the frying pan with lard on the stove, and as she went to the attic to fetch flour, the overheated pan caught fire. In a moment the house stood in flames. The great storm did the rest, flinging pieces of burning thatch and other debris over the entire village. Soon flames were everywhere, with much calling and screaming. Nothing could be saved, only the cattle could be let loose and driven out ... And the cause of the calamity, poor Mrs Teichröb? How did she bear the responsibility. She went insane. For several decades more she lived driven by a constant agitation to move from village to village with her husband.' D.H. Rempel and David H. Epp, 'Zur Jahrhundertfeier der Kolonie Neu-Osterwick, Jetzt Pawlowka, Anno 1912,' in J.J. Neudorf and others, eds, *Osterwick, 1812–1943* (Clearbrook, BC, n.d.), 14–16.

19 Heinrich Heese (1846–1903), wealthy miller, businessman, and public figure in the provincial capital of Ekaterinoslav, was the grandson of the educator Heinrich Heese (1787–1869). C. Krahn, 'Heinrich Heese,' in *Mennonite Encyclopedia*.

20 The 1860s and 1870s, decades of explosive growth of plough-land agriculture in New Russia, witnessed a rapid expansion of Mennonite estate agriculture. Individual families or several related families or friends would purchase a large, undeveloped or run-down gentry estate close to a Mennonite settlement and establish a private estate or small hamlet. Changing fashions in naming such estates reflect growing forces of individualization at work in Mennonite life. Earlier Mennonite estates tended to be named after geographic features of the surrounding landscape such as a stream (Cornies's Iushanlee Estate), or express a theologically rooted aspiration or hope, as in the example of Hoffnungsfeld. Then in the 1860s and 1870s many new estate owners took to naming their properties after themselves, as in the examples of Friesenthal and Zachariasfeld.

21 The Herdsman Elder seems to have had a function among Judenplan village Mennonites akin to that of Village mayor.

22 An old, large, and very wealthy Mennonite estate first called Heinrichsfeld and later, during the period of Russification, changed to Kornievka, after the first name of the founder of the family's vast landholding, Kornelius Heinrichs (1782–1828). M. Janzen et al., eds, *Kornelius Heinrichs and His Descendants, 1782–1979* (Altona, Man., 1980).

23 Originally, Borosenko was a multi-village daughter settlement established by Molochna Kleine Gemeinde Mennonites in 1865–6 to the southeast of the Judenplan and about 30 kilometres northwest of Nikopol. Several villages of Old Colony Mennonites were established nearby. Virtually all Kleine Gemeinde adherents emigrated to North America in the mid-1870s. Vacated properties were sold both to German colonists and to Old Colony Mennonites. Delbert F. Plett, *Storm and Triumph: The Mennonite Kleine Gemeinde (1850–1875)* (Steinbach, Man., 1986), 191–4.

24 This conversion of hay-land into plough-land shows the manner in which grain cultivation was being rapidly expanded at this time. An increase of eight desiatinas per landholder was a quantum jump in land tillage and the labour required to work it.

25 By 'impending exile,' Lepp seems to refer to the prospect of Brethren being expelled from the Mennonite settlements en masse, as was still threatened by Mennonite church and District officials, or voluntarily moving (as some Brethren had already done since 1862), to crown lands in the Kuban River area. See *Die Kubaner Ansiedlung* (Winnipeg, Man., 1953).

26 Fire insurance with the Khortitsa Mutual Fire Insurance Office (Brandordnung) obligated the insured to provide labour, cartage, and payments in goods and money to the victim of a fire in one's area.

27 Ministers in the Khortitsa (Flemish) and Kronsweide (Frisian) Old Colony churches were traditionally garbed in long black coats and shod in high black boots. The latter tradition was based on a reading of Ephesians 6:15: 'And your feet shod with the preparation of the gospel of peace.'

28 The hymnary used by traditional Russian Mennonite churches consisted of 150 psalms and 505 spiritual songs and was without notes: *Geistreiches Gesangbuch* (Königsberg, 1767). There were numerous Prussian editions and seven Russian Mennonite editions, the first in Odessa in 1844. Peter Letkemann, 'The Hymnody and Choral Music of Mennonites in Russia, 1789–1915,' 842–5.

29 Cholera first appeared in Russia in the 1820s. See R.E. McGrew, *Russia and the Cholera, 1828–1832* (Madison and Milwaukee, 1965). The epidemic of 1866, as the *Odessaer Zeitung* reported, was widespread in New Russia, including the port of Odessa.

30 Mennonite settlements maintained emergency granaries that were kept stocked by the landowners. It was expected that grain borrowed in time of need would be replaced by the recipient at the earliest opportunity.

BOOK III

1 Supplement to the *Odessaer Zeitung*.

2 A building of the Old Colony District Administration where the historic 'Mennonite Charter' of 1800 was kept.

3 The first of many attempted assassinations of Alexander II by social revolutionaries, culminating in his violent death in 1881. Their effect was to dampen the government's reform wing and strengthen its conservative and reactionary tendencies.

4 When one or both parents died, two guardians were appointed to represent the interests of the child or children, including their financial interests. Where a family had numerous orphaned children, the guardians' duties were correspondingly onerous.

5 Also known as Fürstenland, this six-village leaseland settlement lay east of the Dnieper River in the Province of Taurida. Established by poor Old Colony landless families in the mid and late 1860s, it was named after its owner, Grand Duke Michael Nikolaevich. The insecurity of their landholding and their conservatism drove most Fürstenlanders, a total of about 1000, to emigrate to Manitoba in the 1870s. D.H. Epp, *Chortitzer Mennoniten* (Odessa, 1889), 96–7, and C. Krahn, 'Fürstenland,' in *Mennonite Encyclopedia*.

6 All settlers of foreign origin on state lands and under the authority of the Guardianship Committee were legally designated as 'colonists.' The practice of state officials, the press, and settlers, however, was to call Mennonites 'Mennonites' and all others 'colonists.'

7 That is, the grain was trodden out with horses' hoofs, a more time-consuming method than with the horse-drawn threshing-stone.

8 The incidence of horse-stealing apparently increased markedly as the expansion of plough-land agriculture drove up the price of heavy draught animals.

9 This was the sheep-land leased by JE's late father in the 1830s and early 1840s from the estate owner Kromida. Here JE had lived with his wife for a year early in their marriage. See Book I, 'Background.'

10 The large Old Colony and nearby separate German colonist villages came under the administrative supervision of a Guardianship Committee Inspectorate located in Josephstal.

11 Johann Gerhard Oncken (1800–84), a Hamburg Baptist who founded the European Continental Baptist movement in 1834. In 1869, he visited a number of Mennonite Brethren congregations, where he helped several to organize, even ordaining a number of Brethren ministers. He also visited other Mennonite congregations, including the Old Colony Flemish mother church in Khortitsa.

12 Named after its owner, Friesenthal was a Mennonite-owned estate on the Basavluk River, close to the Judenplan.

13 A zemlianka was a temporary abode for a settler family in a new colony, consisting of a dug-out with a roof or a dwelling of low sod walls and a roof.

14 After a lengthy debate, the Einlage Brethren church rejected the idea of joining the Baptist church on both prudential and theological grounds. Yet the undeniably close ties between the Einlage Brethren and Baptist groups explains JE's identification of the two.

15 Following the government-arbitrated land reform in the Mennonite and colonist settlements in 1866 and 1867, the Iasikovo settlement, also known as the Nikolaifeld settlement, was the first daughter settlement established by the Old Colony administration on purchased land. Favourably situated on good soils about 25 kilometres north of the Old Colony, it prospered. See J. Löwen, *Jasykowo*. Iasikovo is also the setting for Arnold Dyck's evocative Bildungsroman, *Verloren in der Steppe*, *Collected Works*, vol. 3, ed. Victor G. Doerksen and Harry Loewen (Steinbach, Man., 1985).

16 With a population approaching 200,000 at the time, Odessa was emerging as Russia's premier Black Sea port and one of the empire's most vital urban centres. Patricia Herlihy, *Odessa: A History, 1794–1914* (Cambridge, MA, 1986).

17 Until its abolition in 1871 (when its functions passed to provincial and county levels of adminstration), the Guardianship Committee administered German, Mennonite, Bulgarian, and other New Russian agricultural settlements of foreign origin as well as state-sponsored Jewish settlements in the region. Operating under the authority of the Ministry of State domains, the committee had a president, a staff in Odessa, and several local inspectorates. The latter oversaw a settlement or group of settlements.

18 Later JE's son David married Katharina Heide's sister.

19 Staples of the pietist bookshelf, the works of Johann Arndt (1555–1621), a man of practical piety, and Ludwig Hofacker (1798–1828), a Swabian revivalist preacher, were widely disseminated among Mennonites in Russia where they became important sources of pietist influence.

20 A Desiatnik, or 'tenth man,' was an elected village official with the functions and authority of a peace-officer or constable.

21 The Old Colony practice was to assign both a name and a number to daughter-colony villages, the latter in the sequence of their founding. To the present day, surviving Old Colony Mennonite daughter-settlement villages in the Trans-Volgan and Western Siberian regions are still familiarly known by their original number.

22 J.H. Ingraham, *Der Fürst aus Davids Haus order Drei Jahre in der heiligen Stadt* (Constanz, n.d.).

23 JE, with seemingly no sympathy for either side in the war, sees the conflict as a herald of the divine apocalypse. Germany's unification did, however, help trigger a powerful Russian nationalist upsurge that, within two decades, stereotyped Mennonites and other German-speaking colonists as agents of German imperialism and pressed the government to abridge their right to buy land. For an introduction see Harvey L. Dyck, 'Russian Mennonitism and the Challenge of Russian Nationalism,' *Mennonite Quarterly Review* (Oct. 1982), 307–41.

24 Elected Elder of the Fürstenland affiliate of the Khortitsa (Flemish) Mennonite church, Johann Wiebe (1837–1906) soon became an active proponent of emigration to Manitoba, persuading the bulk of his parishioners to follow him. In Manitoba he pursued a staunchly conservative church policy, successfully spearheading a reversion of church music to singing 'by ear' and in the 'Old Way.' C. Krahn, 'Johann Wiebe,' in *Mennonite Encyclopedia*.

25 This first mention of a military reform began more than three years of uncertainty and soul-searching among Russian Mennonites. It culminated in the establishment in Russia of the Forstei as an alternative-service institution and the emigration to Canada and the United States of a quarter to a third of all Russian Mennonites.

BOOK IV

1 With this year the birth/death data abruptly, and without explanation, disappear from the diary, reappearing, in brief, only in 1877.

2 This was the first of several Mennonite delegations in the years 1871 to 1874 to petition the imperial government for an exemption of Mennonites from military service under the planned universal conscription system.

3 These experiences and those of subsequent delegations to St Petersburg are described by Heinrich Epp's son, David H. Epp, often from entries in his father's no longer extant diary: *Chortitzer Mennoniten* (Odessa, 1889), 100–14. Also extensively reported in P.M. Friesen, *The Mennonite Brotherhood in Russia, 1789–1910* (Fresno, CA, 1978) and Franz Isaac, *Die Molotschnaer Mennoniten* (Halbstadt, Russia, 1908).

4 Aleksandr A. Zelenoi (1819–80), minister of state domains from 1862 to 1872. *Russkii biograficheskii slovar'*, vol. 7, 338–40.

5 Count F.L. Heyden (1821–81).

6 As first a member and then, from 1845 to 1849, reforming president of the Guardianship Committee, Eugen von Hahn (1807–74) had worked closely with Johann Cornies in introducing reforms in the Molochna and Old Colony settlements. For an overview of the central administration of the colonist settlements, see Erik Amburger, *Geschichte der Behördenorganisation Russlands von Peter dem Grossen bis 1917* (Leiden, 1966), 250–2.

7 Alexander II Nikolaevich (1818–81), emperor, 1855–81.

8 Reproduced in Epp, *Chortitzer Mennoniten*, 103–5.

9 The Odessa pogrom of 1871 was the first of a series of violent anti-Jewish pogroms in post-reform Russia. Among the most violent were those in 1881, after the assassination of Alexander II. The pogroms triggered a mass emigration of Russian Jews to North America. Patricia Herlihy, *Odessa: A History, 1794–1914* (Cambridge, MA, 1986), 299–304. JE was able to follow these events in the *Odessaer Zeitung*.

10 This entry concludes volume IV of JE's diaries.

11 See 'Introduction and Analysis,' 11.

12 The two-village Baratov Mennonite settlement, some 15 kilometres north of the Judenplan, was established in 1871. This was the second such Old Colony-sponsored daughter settlement founded in these years, the first being Iasikovo.

13 In practice, this prohibition against Judenplan Mennonites settling in the recently established Old Colony daughter settlements of Baratov and Shlakhtin was largely ignored.

14 After the land reform of 1866–7, the Molochna settlement founded Zagradovka as its first daughter settlement on community-purchased land. Located in Kherson guberniia, at a considerable distance from the Molochna, it eventually consisted of 16 villages. The Molochna Mennonites went so far afield for land because there were few gentry estates located in their immediate environs. The Old Colony, in contrast, had many large gentry estates closer by, and hence had less difficulty in accommodating its landless population in new settlements.

15 Theodor Hans, pastor of the Moravian Church in St Petersburg from 1862 to 1880, assisted the Mennonites as adviser and intermediary in their negotiations with the government regarding the question of military service.

16 This Mennonite delegation visited Yalta at the suggestion of the governor-general of New Russia, who was ill at the time of their arrival and could not arrange an audience with the emperor. But he did receive them on the veranda of his villa and promised to transmit their concerns personally to the monarch. D.H. Epp, *Chortitzer Mennoniten*, 107.

17 This land search culminated in the establishment of the two-village Shlakhtin settlement, which abutted directly on the recently founded Baratov settlement. Epp family members would take up properties in both settlements.

18 The Khortitsa Zentralschule developed an excellent academic reputation, and over the years sons of a number of gentry from the area matriculated from it. A. Neufeld, *Die Chortitzer Zentralschule, 1842–1892: Zum fünfzigsten Jahrestag der Schule* (Berdiansk, 1893).

19 The Neu-Hutterthal settlement, composed of Hutterites from the villages of Hutterthal and Johannesruh in the Molochna area, was established in 1866 and dissolved in 1875 when most Hutterites in Russia emigrated to the United States.

20 The various emigration and settlement initiatives of Russian Mennonites in Canada and the United States are surveyed in C. Henry Smith, *The Coming of the Russian Mennonites* (Berne, IN, 1927).

21 For an introduction to Hutterian history see Robert Friedmann, 'Hutterian Brethren,' in *Mennonite Encyclopedia*.

22 The division of opinion among Russian Mennonites in regard to military service is confirmed by other observers, including General Eduard Todleben, who travelled widely in the Mennonite settlements in 1874 as the personal envoy of Alexander II. In a report to the minister of the interior he analysed the range of in-group views, which is reproduced in A.A. Velitsyn, *Nemtsy v Rossii: Ocherki istoricheskago razvitiia i nastoiaschchago polozheniia nemetskikh kolonii na iuge i vostoke Rossii* (St Petersburg, 1893), 163–71.

23 These, too, are villages of the large Molochna settlement.

24 His late half-sister Maria (1815–46) had married Bernhard Friesen (1810–66)

from the Molochna settlement. Such marriages between persons from the two mother settlements were not common. D.D. Epp, *Familien Stammbaum* (Winkler, Man., 1958).

25 Gossen's *Schatzkästchen* contained daily devotional readings in a pietist spirit, based on scripture passages. The religiously Orthodox Ukrainian dye-plant workers present were thus being exposed to a missionizing outreach by a member of the young Brethren church. This was prohibited by law.

26 These were probably members of the Mennonite Brethren group, whom JE identified as Baptists because of the close links existing between the Old Colony Einlage Brethren church and the Baptists. JE's participation in the devotion suggests a gradual lessening of the bitterness in relations between devout members of the established churches and the Mennonite Brethren church.

27 As a young landless Mennonite in the 1860s, Abraham Thiessen became one of the leaders of the landless movement. In the final land distribution of 1870 (which established the class of smallholders) he was himself denied land. Accusing Molochna landholders and members of the District administration of having conspired with officials of the Guardianship Committee and its inspectorate to foil the government's plan for a more generous land distribution, he was arrested in 1874 and sent into an internal Russian exile. From here he escaped, settled in Nebraska, became an American citizen, and in the early 1880s returned to Russia, including the Molochna settlement. There, in a brief flurry of activity, he both publicly took up his old cause and defended the interests of smallholder and landless Mennonites in regard to their pasture rights. Within a short time, however, he was expelled from Russia.

28 The Kleine Gemeinde was a small, strongly traditionalist and puritanical Mennonite denomination in the Molochna settlement. Almost its entire membership emigrated to Canada and the United States in the 1870s. In the 1860s a high proportion of Kleine Gemeinde families moved to the new settlement of Borosenko, quite close to the Judenplan, where JE was often in touch with them. For a richly documented, in-group history, see Delbert F. Plett, *History and Events: Writings and Maps pertaining to the History of the Mennonite Kleine Gemeinde from 1866 to 1876* (Steinbach, Man., 1982), *The Golden Years: The Mennonite Kleine Gemeinde in Russia (1812–1849)* (Steinbach, Man., 1985), and *Storm and Triumph: The Mennonite Kleine Gemeinde (1850–1875)* (Steinbach, Man., 1986).

29 The Khortitsa Volost Court, a court of first instance for minor offences, was run by local elected members. A new institution, it was a product of the Great Reforms and reflected the secularizing trend of assimilating colonist practices to broader imperial patterns. JE was sharply critical of Mennonites who brought cases of dispute to the Volost Court rather than having them resolved in the traditional manner by the Ministerial Committee and Brotherhood Meeting on the basis of biblical injunctions and church rules.

30 The bitter conflict in the Old Colony over the implementation of the land reform program of 1866–7 increased pressure on Mennonite Volost (District) officials to establish new daughter colonies as quickly as possible. These included the twin settlements of Baratov and Shlakhtin close to the Judenplan.

31 JE is mistaken. Abraham Thiessen was sent into internal exile in Russia, from where he escaped abroad.

32 Told in detail by Gustav E. Reimer and G.R. Gaeddert, *Exiled by the Czar: Cornelius Jansen and the Great Mennonite Migration, 1874* (Newton, KS, 1956).

33 Mennonite villagers and estate owners were equally bound by the Mennonite inheritance system, which provided for a community of property between husband and wife and the equal division of inheritances among all children. Imperial regulations that forbade the fragmentation of family allotments in Mennonite and colonist villages did not apply to estates, however, where fragmentation was the rule, as in this case.

34 This was a small community of Mennonites of Swiss and south German background, who migrated to the United States in 1874. See Solomon Stucky, *The Heritage of the Swiss Volhynian Mennonites* (Waterloo, Ont., 1981), 1–134.

35 This crop failure may have been a significant spur for Fürstenland Mennonites to emigrate to Canada.

36 The elders of these two Old Colony daughter settlements were cousins. In the 1870s both became strong advocates of emigration to Manitoba, where, subsequently, they continued as influential leaders of their pioneering communities.

37 Also known as Iasikovo settlement.

38 In 1874, on behalf of the imperial government, General Count Eduard Ivanovich Todleben (1818–84), Russian hero of the Crimean War, tried to dissuade Russian Mennonites from emigrating to North America in protest over the new compulsory military-service law. Among the concessions offered were alternative-service afforestation camps for Mennonite enlisted men.

39 Since the sale of properties in the Mennonite settlements was legally restricted to Mennonites and colonists, the emigration, in thc 1870s, of from one-quarter to one-third of all Russian Mennonites resulted in a short-term precipitous drop in Mennonite land and property prices. The glut of cheap properties eased the landless problem for at least a decade. Not until the mid-1880s did the founding of new daughter settlements resume.

40 When a child died, the Russian Mennonite practice was to name the next child born of the same sex after the deceased.

41 The obligation of the Baratov and Shlakhtin settlements to repay their land debt troubled their relations with Old Colony administration until the mid-1880s. At that time, JE's brother Johann, secretary of the Old Colony administration, played a key role in resolving the issue amicably. The dispute was the subject of frequent readers' letters to the *Odessaer Zeitung* in the 1870s and early 1880s.

42 The Khortitsa village factory school was a private institution collaboratively financed and run by several farm-implement factories for the children of their non-Mennonite employees.

43 As Russian nationalism took wing in the 1870s and 1880s, there was a growing tendency to incorporate Mennonite and colonist daughter-settlement villages into Ukrainian volosts. The separate Ukrainian volosts (townships) into which the Baratov and Shlakhtin Mennonite settlements were administratively integrated apparently conducted business on Sundays.

44 The Baratov and Shlakhtin settlements failed in this and were integrated into separate Ukrainian peasant volosts. The regime's reluctance to accommodate

their wishes also reflected a rising anti-German Russian nationalist tide within the bureaucracy. In Mennonite society Russian nationalist pressures enhanced in-group solidarity and helped to overcome some of the strains surviving from the disputes over religion and land.

45 The purchase of remounts for the army was prompted by the Balkan crisis of 1875–8, which did indeed culminate in a major Russo-Turkish war. See M.S. Anderson, *The Eastern Question, 1774–1923: A Study in International Relations* (London, 1966), 178–219.

46 Presumably in order to work in the house.

Glossary

Anwohner A landless 'cottager' in a village with a house on a half-desiatina garden-and-orchard plot.

chetverik Dry measure also called *merka* in diaries, equal to one-eighth of a *chetvert.*

chetvert Dry measure equal to 2.099 hectolitres or 5.95 bushels.

desiatina Land measure equal to 1.092 hectares or 2.7 acres.

Einwohner A landless 'renter,' often young and recently married, who occupied rented rooms in a village.

funt Weight equal to 0.41 kilograms or 0.9 pound.

guberniia Major administrative division, a province, of the Russian Empire.

khutor An owned or leased individual farm or group of farms outside of a village.

pud Weight equal to 40 funt, 16.38 kilograms, or 36 pounds.

Reaumur Temperature scale used in nineteenth-century Russia, with freezing point at zero and boiling point at eighty degrees.

ruble Monetary unit, equal to 100 copecks. In 1839 the value of one silver ruble was fixed at 3.6 paper rubles.

sazhen Length equal to 2.134 metres or 7 feet.

Sommerstube 'Summer room' at the rear of a Mennonite home, often occupied by recently married children or 'Einwohner.'

versta Length equal to 1.065 kilometres or 0.633 miles.

volost Administrative subdivision of the peasantry comprising a number of villages; the equivalent of a Mennonite District before 1871.

Waisenamt Mennonite 'Orphans' Administration' with executive authority to enforce Mennonite inheritance practices.

Wirtschaft Mennonite family farm, normally with 65 destiatinas of land, consisting of house and farm buildings on a 1½ desiatina home-and-garden plot in a village, and plough, hay, and pasture lands in common fields around the village.

DAVID EPP — ANNA BERGMAN
1750–1802 1762–96

(1) MARIA WIENS — DAVID EPP —
1779–1815 1781–1843

BARBARA
1810–91
(1) P. Rempel
(2) J. Sawatzky

DAVID
1812–55

MARIA
1815–46
B. Friesen

Six Infants
Died

DIEDRICH
1810–1900
K. Siemens

JACOB
1820–90

HELENA
1825–73
(1) M. Dyck
(2) J. Pätkau

HEINRICH
1827–96
(1) A. Siemens
(2) E. Lepp
(née Perk)

(1) **MARIA KLASSEN** —
1822–63

HELENA
1844–1925
J. Andres

KATHARINA
1846–1932
J. Bärgen

MARIA
1848

DAVID
1849–1933
M. Heide

MARIA
1850–1917
W. Martens

JACOB
1853–1912
H. Janzen

PETER
1855–1920
(1) **A. Dyck**
(2) **S. Dyck**
(3) **E. Epp**

GENEALOGY OF THE JACOB D. EPP FAMILY

(2) HELENA MARTENS
(née Thiessen) 1797–1864

JOHANN	ANNA	ABRAHAM	KATHARINA	Two Infants
1830–88	1833–1919	1836–60	1839–1915	Died
H. Siemens	C. Hildebrand	A. Friesen	B. Schellenberg	

(2) **JUDITH DYCK**
1832–1906

DIEDRICH	**HEINRICH**	**MARGARETHA**
1857–1940	1860–?	1863
S. Peters	**A. Pauls**	

GERHARD	**ELISABETH**	**JOHANN**	**JUDITH**	**JOHANN**
1864–1919	1866–1946	1868–73	1871–6	1874–1948
K. Janzen	**H. Wieler**			**M. Janzen**

Index